Also by Michael Paul Rogin

The Intellectuals and McCarthy: The Radical Specter   (1967)

Political Change in California:
Critical Elections and Social Movements, 1890–1966
(with John L. Shrover)   (1970)

FATHERS
AND CHILDREN

FATHERS
AND
CHILDREN

*ANDREW JACKSON AND
THE SUBJUGATION OF
THE AMERICAN INDIAN*

MICHAEL PAUL
ROGIN

*ALFRED A. KNOPF
NEW YORK
1975*

Portions of this book appeared, in an earlier form, in *Politics and Society*, I (May 1971). I am grateful for permission to use that material again here. The lines from Allen Ginsberg's "America" on page 113 are reprinted from *Howl and Other Poems* (San Francisco, Calif., 1956), by permission of City Lights Press.

Library of Congress Cataloging in Publication Data

Rogin, Michael Paul. / Fathers and Children.

Includes index. / 1. Indians of North America—Government relations—1789–1869. 2. Jackson, Andrew, Pres. U.S., 1767–1845. 3. Indians of North America—Land transfers. I. Title. E93.R8 / 970.5 / 74–21310 / ISBN 0–394–48204–2

Manufactured in the United States of America
First Edition

AUTHOR
Rogin, Michael Paul

TITLE
Fathers and children: Andrew Jackson and
the subjugation of the American Indian

Edition or Series

Place

Recommended by
Fairbanks

Choice 075 p1068

Volumes

Publisher
Knopf 645

Year
1975

Fund Charged
History

Cost

Thou just Spirit of Equality, which hast spread one royal mantle of humanity over all my kind! Bear me out in it, thou great democratic God! . . . Thou who didst pick up Andrew Jackson from the pebbles; who didst hurl him upon a war-horse; who didst thunder him higher than a throne! Thou who, in all Thy mighty, earthly marchings, ever cullest Thy selectest champions from the kingly commons; bear me out in it, O God!

—Herman Melville, *Moby Dick*

CONTENTS

ILLUSTRATIONS

(following page 202)

Andrew Jackson, Asher B. Durand, 1835. Courtesy of the New-York Historical Society.

The Death Struggle, Charles Deas, 1846. Courtesy of Shelburne Museum, Inc., Shelburne, Vermont.

Colonel Guy Johnson, Benjamin West. Courtesy of the National Gallery of Art, Washington, D.C.

The able Doctor, or America Swallowing the Bitter Draught, Paul Revere. *The Royal American Magazine*, June 1774.

The Downfall of Mother Bank, lithograph, 1833. Courtesy of the New-York Historical Society.

American Progress, chromolithograph, after a John Gast painting, 1872. Issued by George Croffut's *Western World*, 1873, courtesy of The Library of Congress.

Death of Jane McCrea, John Vanderlyn, 1804. Courtesy of the Wadsworth Atheneum, Hartford, Connecticut.

Andrew Jackson, John Vanderlyn, 1819. Courtesy of the City of New York.

Andrew Jackson, Lafosse lithograph, c.1856, after a Mathew Brady daguerreotype. Courtesy of The Library of Congress.

ACKNOWLEDGMENTS

Norman Jacobson, Louis Hartz, and Leslie Fiedler provided models for my understanding of American politics and culture. I have also received an invaluable education from the students at Berkeley; among the many to whom I am indebted, Greil Marcus, Pat O'Donnell, Bruce Parker, and Margaret Samuelson each decisively influenced interpretations made here. Dr. Jules Weiss' seminar at the San Francisco Psychoanalytic Institute helped me understand psychoanalytic biography. Richard Busacca, James C. Curtis, Frederick Crews, J. David Greenstone, Hanna Fenichel Pitkin, Paul Roazen, Charles G. Sellers, Jr., Michael N. Shute, Henry Nash Smith, Ronald T. Takaki, and Mary E. Young made helpful comments on varying versions of the manuscript. Mary Young's encouragement at an early stage was particularly important. I am also grateful to Ashbel Green at Knopf for his good judgment and care.

Mark Gross, Mark Morris, and Joel Schwartz helped me on different occasions with special research tasks. The Committee on Research at the University of California at Berkeley paid for their time, and for other substantial research expenses. The staffs at the National Archives and the Tennessee State Library and Archives directed me to important documents. A fellowship from the John Simon Guggenheim Memorial Foundation provided a year free to write. Francesca Archer contributed a superb job of typing.

My wife, Deborah Donohue Rogin, played an indispensable role in the development of this book. Her insights have had fundamental impact on my work.

THE JOHN DONELSON
FAMILY TREE

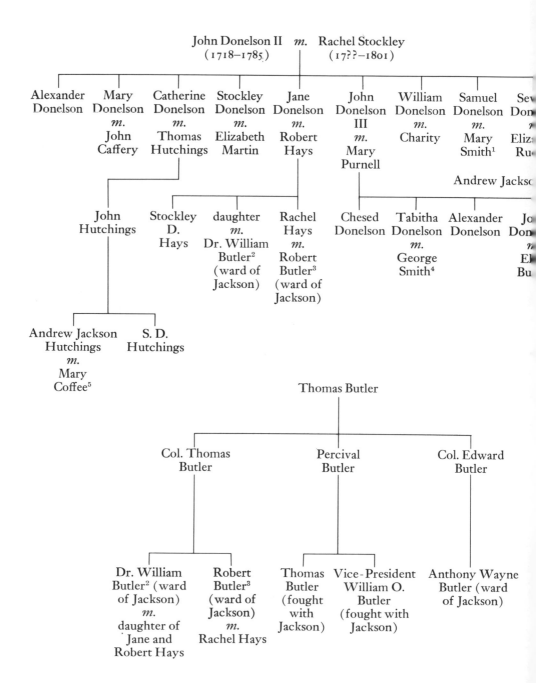

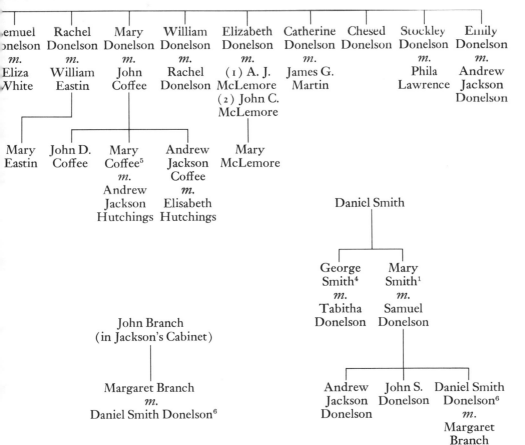

Rachel Leven
Donelson Donelson
m.
Andrew
Jackson

Sarah Yorke

| Lemuel Donelson | Rachel Donelson | Mary Donelson | William Donelson | Elizabeth Donelson | Catherine Donelson | Chesed Donelson | Stockley Donelson | Emily Donelson |
| Eliza White | William Eastin | John Coffee | Rachel Donelson | (1) A. J. McLemore (2) John C. McLemore | James G. Martin | | Phila Lawrence | Andrew Jackson Donelson |

Mary   John D.   Mary   Andrew   Mary
Eastin Coffee   Coffee[5]   Jackson   McLemore
                 m.   Coffee
                 Andrew   m.
                 Jackson   Elisabeth
                 Hutchings   Hutchings

Daniel Smith

George   Mary
Smith[4]   Smith[1]
m.   m.
Tabitha   Samuel
Donelson   Donelson

John Branch
(in Jackson's Cabinet)

Margaret Branch   Andrew   John S.   Daniel Smith
m.   Jackson   Donelson   Donelson[6]
Daniel Smith Donelson[6] Donelson   m.
                                                  Margaret
                                                  Branch

The Donelson family tree is complete only for the second generation. Corresponding superscript numbers indicate intermarriages.

FATHERS
AND CHILDREN

INTRODUCTION

LIBERAL SOCIETY AND THE INDIAN QUESTION

Our conduct toward these people is deeply interesting to our national character.

—Andrew Jackson, First Annual Message to Congress, December 1829

"In the beginning," John Locke wrote, "all the world was America."[1] Then men relinquished the state of nature, freely contracted together, and entered civil society. That was not the way it began, in America. True, settlers came to escape the corruption and traditional restraints of Europe, to begin again, to return to the state of nature and contract together. They aimed, as Hamilton put it in the *Federalist Papers*, to build a state based on "reflection and choice" rather than "accident and force."[2] But while the origins of European countries were shrouded by "the chaos of impenetrable antiquity,"[3] America clearly began not with primal innocence and consent but with acts of force and fraud. Indians were here first, and it was their land upon which Americans contracted, squabbled, and reasoned with one another. Stripping away history did not permit beginning without sin; it simply exposed the sin at the beginning of it all. The dispossession of the Indians, moreover, did not happen once and for all in the beginning. America was continually beginning again on the frontier, and as it expanded across the continent, it killed, removed, and drove into extinction one tribe after another.

The years spanned by Andrew Jackson's life were the great years of American expansion. Born on the frontier, Jackson joined the movement west as a young man. In the years of his maturity and old age, from Jefferson's Presidency to the Mexican War, expansion across the continent was the central fact of American politics. Two-thirds of the American population of 3.9 million lived within fifty miles of the ocean in 1790. In the next half-century 4.5 million Americans crossed the

Appalachians, one of the great migrations in world history. The western states contained less than three percent of the U.S. population in 1790, twenty-eight percent in 1830. In two decades the west would become the most populous region of the country.[4]

Indians inhabited in 1790 almost all the territory west of the original thirteen states. If America were to expand and take possession of the continent, they would have to be dispossessed. Indians had not mattered so much, in the history of Europeans in the English new world, since the colonial settlements. They would never matter so much again. Indian removal was Andrew Jackson's major policy aim in the quarter-century before he became President. His Indian wars and treaties were principally responsible for dispossessing the southern Indians during those years. His presidential Indian removal finished the job. Martin Van Buren, Jackson's ally and successor, listed Indian removal as one of "the old Hero's" major achievements. During the years of Jacksonian Democracy, 1824–52, five of the ten major candidates for President had either won reputations as generals in Indian wars or served as Secretary of War, whose major responsibility in this period was relations with the Indians. Historians, however, have failed to place Indians at the center of Jackson's life. They have interpreted the Age of Jackson from every perspective but Indian destruction, the one from which it actually developed historically.[5]

125,000 Indians lived east of the Mississippi in 1820. Seventy-five percent of these came under government removal programs in the next two decades. By 1844 less than 30,000 Indians remained in the east, mainly in the undeveloped Lake Superior region. Most of the eastern tribes had been relocated west of the Mississippi; the total population of Indians indigenous to the east had declined by one-third.[6]

How reconcile the destruction of the Indians with the American self-image? This problem preoccupied statesmen of the period. "The great moral debt we owe to this unhappy race is universally felt and acknowledged," Secretary of War Lewis Cass reported in 1831. John Tipton, land speculator, Indian agent, and Indiana Senator, explained, "There is something painful in the reflection that these people were once numerous, and that by our approach they have been reduced to a few. It is natural that we should feel averse to the admission that the true causes of their decline are to be found among *us*." In our relations to the Indians, wrote Van Buren, "we are as a nation responsible *in foro conscientiae* to the opinions of the great family of nations, as it involves the course we have pursued and shall pursue towards a people comparatively weak, upon whom we were perhaps in the beginning unjustifiable aggressors, but of whom, in the progress of time and events, we have become the guardians, and, as we hope, the benefactors."[7]

Van Buren and the others felt the eyes of the world on America. They needed to demonstrate that our encounter with the Indians, "the most difficult of all our relations, foreign and domestic, has at last been justified to the world in its near approach to a happy and certain consummation."[8] They needed to justify—the Puritan word means save for God—a society built on Indian graves.

American rhetoric filled the white-Indian tie with intimate symbolic meaning. Indians were, every treaty talk insisted, our "friends and brothers." "Our red brethren" were the "voice of nature" in "the human family." "Members of the great American family," they were, like us, "descendants of Adam." "We take an interest in your fate," Secretary of War Calhoun told one tribe, "as you were the first proprietors of this happy country." But white Americans had displaced "this unhappy race—the original dwellers in our land."[9] In the words of Virginia Congressman Thomas Bouldin,

I think they are a noble, gallant, injured race. I think they have suffered nothing but wrong and injury from us, since the Anglo-Saxon race . . . first landed in this country. . . . Sir, a melancholy overcasts my mind whenever I think of this too probable issue in regard to the red man— his gradual but entire extinction. . . . Many of our first families and most distinguished patriots are descended from the Indian race. My heart compels me to feel for them for some of my nearest relations (not that I have myself any of their blood) are descended from the Indian race.[10]

Yet Bouldin insisted that whites must continue to dispossess their brothers. Norman O. Brown writes,

The comic wearing of the Indian mask, in the Boston Tea Party, or Tammany's Wigwam, is the lighter side of a game, a ritual, the darker side of which is fraternal genocide. Indians are our Indian brothers; one of the ten lost tribes of Israel; the lost sheep we came to find: now unappeased ghosts in the unconscious of the white man.[11]

The European psyche in the new world, D. H. Lawrence believed, contained the Indian brother as an inner double.[12] Early American painting often portrayed this theme. Benjamin West's serene, classical portrait of Colonel Guy Johnson reveals on closer inspection a dark, shadowy Indian half hidden behind him. An Indian horseman fights with a white in Charles Deas' turbulent painting; horses and human limbs inextricably intertwined, the two men are locked in *The Death Struggle*. (See Plates 2 and 3.)[13]

Indians could not remain "unappeased ghosts," however. The south, bound in slavery, was prey to visions of violent, immoral possession.

Southerners like Bouldin often rooted authority in unredeemed force and contaminated inheritance. Whites must take Indian land, Bouldin suggested, but the process was contaminated at the core. The fraternal conflict of Indians and whites contained no moral resolution. But neither the south nor the country as a whole could rest with such a birthright. Whites developed, as they took Indian land, a powerful, legitimating cultural myth. America's expansion across the continent, everyone agreed, reproduced the historical evolution of mankind. "The first proprietors of this happy country" were sometimes said to be the first people on earth. Early in time, they were also primitive in development. Human societies existed along a unilinear scale from savagery to civilization. As civilization advanced westward, it must inevitably displace savagery.[14]

"The unfortunate sons of nature," said the young John Quincy Adams, "had no cause of complaint" against the Plymouth founders.

> What is the right of a huntsman to the forest of a thousand miles, over which he has accidentally ranged in quest of prey? . . . Shall the exuberant bosom of the common mother, amply adequate to the nourishment of millions, be claimed exclusively by a few hundreds of her offspring? Shall the lordly savage not only disdain the virtues and enjoyments of civilization himself, but shall he controul the civilization of the world? . . . Shall the fields and valleys, which a beneficent God has formed to teem with the life of innumerable multitudes, be condemned to everlasting barrenness.[15]

The Indian was the brother with original title to the land. But, explained Hugh Henry Brackenridge, "there is no right of primogeniture in the laws of nature and of nations." Whites followed the biblical injunction to "subdue and replenish" the earth; "the lordly savage" did not. In sole possession of "the exuberant bosom of the common mother," he lived in a "state of nature," and gained "subsistence from spontaneous productions." Agricultural people represented a superior stage of development; they had the God-given right to dispossess hunters from their sovereignty over nature.[16]

The evolution of societies from savagery to civilization was identical to the evolution of individual men. The Indian was the elder brother, but he remained in the "childhood" of the human race. "Barbarism is to civilization," wrote Francis Parkman, "as childhood is to maturity." Indians were "children of nature." They were "part of the human family" as children, children who could not mature. Their replacement by whites symbolized America's growing up from childhood to maturity.[17] Winthrop Jordan writes,

The Indian became for Americans a symbol of their American experience; it was no mere luck of the toss that placed the profile of an American Indian rather than an American Negro on the famous old five-cent piece. Confronting the Indian in America was a testing experience, common to all the colonies. Conquering the Indian symbolized and personified the conquest of American difficulties, the surmounting of the wilderness. To push back the Indian was to prove the worth of one's own mission, to make straight in the desert a highway for civilization.[18]

Not the Indians alive, then, but their destruction symbolized the American experience. The conquest of the Indians made the country uniquely American. But this conquest was, in the language Americans used, a conquest of their own childhoods. Jordan is right: America identified at once with the conquered and the conquering. The Indians —that "much-injured race" who were once "the uncontrolled possessors of these vast regions"[19]—became a symbol of something lost, lost inevitably in the process of growing up.

America was born with the modern age, with discovery and expansion, Protestant reformation, and bourgeois development. Liberalism—to identify the modern impulse by its name in political thought—transformed European societies; it operated on a state of nature in America. Americans were, in Tocqueville's phrase, "born equal." There was "no right of primogeniture in the law of nature" (Brackenridge), and none took deep root in America. America had no feudal past. It lacked a hereditary nobility, a long-established church, a standing army, and a peasantry bound to the soil. Settlers lived by the covenants of God with man and men with each other. They reproduced in westward migration their self-imposed exile from mother country. The wilderness exposed them to the dangers of domination by nature. Fleeing European traditional ties, they set out self-consciously to conquer the wilderness, and to people the land with God-fearing, self-reliant families.

Liberalism encountered resistance in Europe, first from feudalism and then from revolutionary socialism. But the Europeans who settled America were confronted with no alternatives to liberal uniformity save the psychically charged presences of "the black race within our bosom . . . [and] the red on our borders." Subculture conflict and historical change mark white American history. Nevertheless, the country lacked the historical bases for political alternatives to liberalism, and radical historians who search for such alternatives mistake the American experience. Liberalism reached everywhere in white America; the resistance it encountered came from within.[20]

Modernism enforced, throughout the west, a monumental, systematic ordering of external and internal worlds. It separated men from the customary universe as they had historically experienced it, and from their own spontaneous emotional life. It generated anger at buried parts of the self and their images in the world. It also generated nostalgia. Underneath the "ambitious expansionism" of modern Western societies, writes Henry Baudet in *Paradise on Earth*, "with their economic savoir faire, their social ideology, and their organizational talents," lies "a psychological disposition out of all political reality. It exists independently of objective facts, which seem to have become irrelevant. It is a disposition that leads [its adherent] 'to die' rather than 'to do,' and forces him to repent of his wickedness, covetousness, pride and complacency." The worldly orientation, Baudet argues, points to history and practical consequences, the inner disposition to a primitiveness beyond history. The first is expansive, the second regressive. The regressive inner disposition, Baudet believes, has fastened on images of the noble savage, the garden of Eden, and paradise on earth.[21] In America "aggressive expansionism" encountered the regressive impulse as a "political reality." That is the precise meaning ante-bellum Americans gave to their destruction of the Indians, and it is the meaning we shall give to it here.

At the outset the contrast between expansionist, liberal America's self-conception and its image of the Indians seems clear enough. Liberalism insisted on the independence of men, each from the other, and from cultural, traditional, and communal attachments. Indians were perceived as connected to their past, their superstitions, and their land. Liberalism insisted upon work, instinctual repression, and acquisitive behavior; men had to conquer and separate themselves from nature. Indians were seen as playful, violent, improvident, wild, and in harmony with nature. Private property underlay liberal society; Indians held land in common. Liberal relations were based, contractually, on keeping promises and on personal responsibility. Indians, in the liberal view, were anarchic and irresponsible. Americans believed that peaceful competitiveness kept them in touch with one another and provided social cement. They thought that Indians, lacking social order, were devoted to war.

Disastrously for the liberal self-conception, however, its distance from primitive man was not secure. At the heart of ambitious expansionism lay the regressive impulse itself. Indians were in harmony with nature; lonely, independent liberal men were separated from it, and their culture lacked the richness, diversity, and traditional attachments necessary to sustain their independence. Liberalism generated a forbidden nostalgia for childhood—for the nurturing, blissful, primitively violent connection to nature that white Americans had to leave behind.

They did not have to leave it behind forever. The west healed the division between Indian childhood and adult white maturity. America did not create its history in closed space. It returned to childhood on the frontier. There Americans, as they understood their history, began again; there they regenerated themselves and their society in heroic Indian combat.[22] There they created a uniquely American identity, emancipated from old-world forms and wilderness savagery. They then took upon themselves, to recall Van Buren's words, the obligations of "benefactors" and "guardians." In paternal benevolence toward their "red children," white fathers redeemed the debt to the childhood they replaced. What meaning can be given to a policy of death and dispossession, centrally important to American development, which is justified by the paternal benevolence of a father for his children?

Indian dispossession, as experienced by the whites who justified it and carried it out, belongs to the pathology of human development. Indians remained, in the white fantasy, in the earliest period of childhood, unseparated from "the exuberant bosom of the common mother." They were at once symbols of a lost childhood bliss and, as bad children, repositories of murderous, negative fantasies. Psychoanalytic theory suggests that the infant at the breast and the small child experience world-destroying rage at separation from the mother, dependence upon her, and fear of her loss. Culture affects the resolution of separation anxiety, and liberal culture lacked libidinal ties to replace those forsaken in childhood. Suspicious of the pleasure principle, it inhibited the mature enjoyments which sustain loving interdependence and quiet primitive rage. Liberalism accentuated regressive pressures on the mature, isolated ego. The encounter with Indians and the virgin land returned America to the natural world. Projecting primitive rage onto Indians, independent adult whites revenged themselves for their own early loss. The Indian's tie with nature was broken, literally by uprooting him, figuratively by civilizing him, finally by killing him.

Replacing Indians upon the land, whites reunited themselves with nature. The rhetoric of Manifest Destiny pictured America as a "young and growing country"; it expanded through "swallowing territory," "just as an animal eats to grow." Savagery would inevitably "be swallowed by" civilization.[23] Whites imaginatively regressed, as they described expansion, to fantasies of infant omnipotence. They entertained the most primitive form of object relations, the annihilation of the object through oral introjection.

Expansion, whites agreed, inevitably devoured Indians; only paternal governmental supervision could save the tribes from extinction. Paternalism, however, met white needs better than Indian ones. The new American world undermined the authority provided by history, tradition, family connection, and the other ties of old European existence. Political

ism. We may respect modern historians who insist that the meeting of red man and white was a "culture conflict" not to be judged by standards outside the cultures. But white culture was deeply riven within. White men encountered not merely another culture in Indians, but their own fantasies, longings, and fears. Self-proclaimed liberal values cracked under this pressure. The culture conflict overwhelmed liberal values of individual responsibility, "reflection and choice" (Hamilton). Modern social science defends historical actors against retrospective moral condemnation; the actors themselves, in flight from responsibility for their actions, often described their own behavior in the detached, objective language of social science. Whites experienced their own activities and desires as alien, external forces. Petrification of the self closed them to the Indians' fate. This is evidence of disassociation within the victorious culture, not of scientific objectivity. Would the apostles of social science or pragmatic common sense prefer that whites had left no evidence of disturbance behind?[30]

If our concern is with the experience of historical actors, however, surely the Freudian categories and the talk of madness are gratuitous intrusions upon the language actually employed. The problem is this: Americans uniformly employed familial language in speaking of Indians; most historians and political scientists have been systematically deaf to it. Lacking a theory which sensitized them to such a vocabulary and helped them interpret it, they could not hear what was being said. Let us, to begin with, take seriously the words of those who made our Indian policy.

Pragmatism, behaviorism, and materialism are theories; they violate the perceptions of the men who mattered in Indian policy. Freudian theory is closer to the language of these men, but it is a theory too. It is not simply a restatement of actors' perceptions, but an interpretation of them. I am concerned with a partly conscious and partly unconscious set of symbols, its historical power, its sources in human personality and liberal culture, and its consequences for red and white Americans.

It is a peculiarly split view of human existence in which symbolizations of meaning operate in a closed universe of their own, divorced from the "real" facts of historical causation. Men make history; they develop complex inner worlds because they do not make it in circumstances of their own choosing. These inner worlds, projected outward, become part of the continuing history men do make. Objective forces act only through men; men transform external causes into internal principles of action.[31]

Liberal America was not a static social system, and the transformation it underwent during Jackson's lifetime found the Indians at center stage. Indian dispossession is part of the history of American capitalism. Jackson and other political figures, freeing Indian land for the commodity economy, initiated a market revolution. They cleared the obstacles to free market relations, politically and by force, before the market could act on its own. The state and private instruments of violence massively assaulted tribal structures. They acquired the resources under Indian control for capitalist development. Force and fraud characterize American-Indian relations throughout our history, but their scope and timing give the Age of Jackson its significance. Indian destruction defines for America the stage of primitive capitalist accumulation.

In Europe stages of development succeeded each other in time; in America they were juxtaposed in space. American history exemplifies Trotsky's law of combined development, not from feudalism to socialism, but from nature to capitalist civilization. The symbiosis between developed east and virgin west not only fueled American economic development; it also created the psychology and ideology which sanctified capitalist hegemony. Wilderness expansion established a heroic American identity transcending the petty transactions of market self-interest. Indian destruction generated a powerful nationalism. Jackson developed in Indian relations the major formulas of Jacksonian Democracy.[32]

The economic motives of ordinary men feed the market once it has established its sway. Such motives were unequal to primitive accumulation, and they fail to define Jackson's life. Primitive accumulation is the heroic stage of capitalism, and it found its hero in Jackson. He was the single figure most responsible for Indian destruction in pre-Civil War America. He won battles, signed treaties, and forced removal not simply over Indian resistance, but often over the recalcitrance of his own troops and the timidity of settlers and civilian politicians. Indian elimination was not the smooth by-product of mass westward expansion. Jackson's monomania powered westward expansion; his psychology had large historical significance. The history of westward expansion and psychic regression, of regeneration through violence and flawed maturity, is the biography of Jackson.

The study of an individual life roots cultural myth in concrete personal experience. It brings floating symbols down to earth. Disembodied cultural myths do not act; individual men living out myths do. But Jackson was only one man, even if he played a crucial historical role. His significance differentiates him from the American mass, and from ordinary politicians as well. Jackson's very specialness, however, enhances the cultural significance of his life.

A great man embodies in extreme form the central cultural tensions of his time. Often his subculture, like Jackson's slaveholding southwest, poses special problems for assimilation to the dominant culture. Ordinary men rely on cultural myths, but their entire personalities are not at stake in them. The leader, by contrast, experiences widely shared social tensions as personal trauma. What is ideology for the mass of men is psychology for him. He breaks through cultural defenses, illuminating material better-defended men keep buried. The hero is distinctive not merely for what he suffers but for what he achieves. He transforms his problems into national political solutions. He defeats those demons which, in bad moments, overwhelm ordinary men. His life offers special historical enlightenment.[33]

No such claim for any man is convincing in the abstract. It requires locating the hero in history; its persuasiveness depends upon the story the historian tells. To pick Jackson to represent ante-bellum America, however, is to make the same choice as his contemporaries. Jackson was no ordinary President. He captured the American imagination as no figure had since Washington. His life became, as John William Ward has demonstrated, a symbol for his age. The men of the Age of Jackson made archetypical American biography from "the old Hero's" personal history.[34]

My analysis of Jackson's life begins with his childhood. It derives not merely from the circumstances of a particular childhood, however, but from the primitive forces originating in childhood and at work in all adults. Infantile sexuality and prolonged infant dependence shape the human personality. These forces do not finish their work in childhood. Crises in the life cycle return the ego to its early roots. Adult traumas—war, depression, death of a parent—do so as well. Crises open fissures in the ego, making it particularly vulnerable to disorienting contemporary experience, and bringing childhood longings into play. Primitive forces also take decisive shape from the culture into which the individual matures. How does the culture address sexuality? How does it value public life? What role does it give the family? Culture forms the unconscious throughout life, not simply in child-rearing patterns.[35]

Two dominant cultural symbols formed Jackson's life. Indians, embodying a lost childhood world, inhabited one-half of the split in the white psyche; revolutionary fathers dominated the other. The revolutionary fathers, as idealized by their sons, had heroically established American independence. But they bequeathed an ambiguous heritage to the post-revolutionary generation. The sons lived in the shadow, in Jackson's words, "of the illustrious actions of their fathers in the war of the revolution." They had to prove they were not "a degenerate race . . . unworthy of the blessings which the blood of so many thousand heroes has purchased for them."[36] The sons contrasted their own materialism unfavor-

ably with the public spirit of the fathers. They longed for paternal authority to control acquisitive behavior. They feared for the decline of that
republican virtue which distinguished America from the old world.

These fears were not imaginary. Liberal America transformed itself
while Jackson lived from a family-based, eighteenth-century, household
order to the market society of the Age of Jackson. Family ties, unmediated
by traditional social institutions, played a greater role in eighteenth-
century America than in Europe; and the family-based order provided
revolutionaries with a model of American virtue. But the household order
could not sustain itself, in bourgeois society, against internecine conflict
and market expansion. The rise of market society threatened the achievement of the fathers—an independent, virtuous American identity—as it
destroyed family-based society.

The revolutionary world contained, in Marxist terms, the capitalist
seeds of its own destruction. Revolutionary thought, sensing the fragility
of the world which gave it birth, sought to contain the tensions between
American virtue and old-world domination. Andrew Jackson inherited the
traditions of revolutionary thought, the disintegrating eighteenth-century
world, and the constitutional system created when revolutionary hopes
gave way to revolutionary fears. We must examine Jackson's patrimony,
if we are to comprehend his achievement.

Revolutionary fathers, blaming monstrous parental England, obscured
internal forces at war with republican virtue. Committed to the market as
well as the household, they helped advance commodity capitalism. The
disintegrating family order liberated achieving individuals. But it also intensified loneliness, vengeful disappointment, and separation anxiety. Jackson's own family life—father dead at birth, mother in adolescence, traumatic
early speech difficulty—prefigured in exaggerated form the problems of
Jacksonian society. Returning to childhood, in Indian war, Indian treaties,
and Indian removal, Jackson mastered its regressive appeal. He infused
American politics with regenerated paternal authority. His model was not
the actual household order or any actual family, however. These had
proved too vulnerable, and they bore the unacknowledged weight of
Jackson's own ubiquitous rage. Jackson constructed instead a familial politics purified of the temptations to conflict, dependence, and vice, purified
of the power of women. We begin with the fathers.

PART I

WHITES

CHAPTER 1

REVOLUTIONARY FATHERS

The people of America had been educated in an habitual affection for England as their mother country; and while they thought her a kind and tender parent (erroneously enough, however, for she never was such a mother) no affection could be more secure. But when they found her a cruel Beldam, willing like Lady Macbeth to "dash their brains out," it is no wonder that filial affections ceased and were changed to indignation and horror.

—*John Adams to Hezekiah Niles, February 13, 1818*

I

Freudian theory places the family at the center of personal experience. It may seem to divert our eyes from actual politics and intrude the family upon actors' understandings of their own political life. This is not the case for early America. Statesmen not only universally employed familial language about Indians; family was also "the very *lingua franca* of the Revolution,"[1] and influenced men's conceptions of all their political relations. Family was the single integrating institution in eighteenth-century liberal America. It linked individual psychology to political action in historical reality, not simply in psychoanalytic theory.

Eighteenth-century America was organized around families. In European societies other long-established institutions—church, state, standing army—stood alongside the household and shared social functions with it. Massive disruptions of local household patterns, as in the English enclosure movement, shattered families and created large classes of dependents and vagabonds; poorhouses and prisons, rather than families, were created to deal with them. American society, lacking deep historic roots and developed social institutions, made the family supreme. Tradition, culture, and technique were transmitted almost solely through the family. Family and society were not split from one another; family was the center from which radiated out other social institutions.[2]

The colonial household was the economic unit. Subsistence farming, household manufacture, and barter relations of exchange supported the majority of Americans. Money and commodities played a small role in their lives. Small cash-crop farmers existed, particularly in the tobacco-growing regions of Maryland and Virginia, but they remained primarily within a household world; there was little purely commercial agriculture in the colonies. Shopkeepers, innkeepers, artisans, ministers, teachers, and doctors participated in a primitive market economy. They exchanged goods and services in a local, limited market, but they produced them in the home; home and workplace were one.[3]

Lawyers, landed gentry, and merchants at the top of colonial society did depend upon extended market relations. But family supplied the economic context for their lives. Mercantile houses were family businesses. Personal friendship and family connection dominated mobility within merchant houses and influenced the relations among them. Firms lacked rationalized recruitment and business accounting procedures. They did not operate on long-term credit. Large farmers sold cash crops and, like other members of the colonial elite, speculated in land. But they also lived in a setting emphasizing family connection. The plantation, with its planter-"Patriarch," subsistence-producing slave "family," and its slave artisans, was a household world of its own.[4]

Family was the central caretaking institution for orphans, delinquents, servants, paupers, and the insane. It performed the police and welfare functions for society. Many social dependents lived with actual members of their extended families. Towns also paid families to take in dependents. The occasional almshouse looked and was run like an ordinary dwelling. It resembled a farmhouse in architecture, its residents wore no uniforms, they ate with the keeper and his family, and they were subject to no organized discipline. David Rothman writes, "It was an alms*house*, not an asylum. The residents were a *family*, not inmates."[5]

The structure of the colonial family reflected its central social role. The family was not an isolated conjugal unit. Extended-family members lived near one another, and often moved together to the frontier. Orphans boarded with grandparents, uncles, or aunts; widows and their children often lived with parents or siblings. Apprentices and servants "in filial discipline" inhabited the wealthier homes. Most families had memory or expectation of a household containing more than the nuclear family.[6]

The extended American family was not a patriarchy. Fathers ruled their households, but not with the power they enjoyed in the seventeenth century. The extraordinary authority of English fathers over their grown sons, reproduced to some extent in the new world, was giving way to a Lockean "natural family." Seventeenth-century American fathers, controlling the disposition of land, kept grown sons under the paternal roof.

By the beginning of the eighteenth century sons were marrying younger and settling on their own homesteads. The supply of land and the absence of a deeply rooted, aristocratic family undermined absolute paternal power. Women performed economic tasks, some of which gave them a measure of independence. Father, mother, and children enjoyed mutual rights and obligations in the natural family.[7]

Locke's *Thoughts on Education* gained growing popularity in the colonies. Locke favored mutual contractual obligations between father and son, rather than brute exercise of the paternal will. Reason and manipulation should replace "Force and Blows," and grown men should enjoy a measure of independence from their fathers. Neither Locke nor the colonists intended to overthrow "natural" paternal authority. Paternal rule should rest, like all authority structures, on "reason and experience," rather than arbitrary force and will. Locke's belief that children had a natural right to protest parental misconduct squared with contractual doctrine and with everyday American experience. A grown man, wrote Locke, should not obey his father if his father should "treat him still as a boy."[8]

The natural-family model meshed with the structure of the colonial political order. Leading families dominated colonial politics. The great bulk of colonists did not expect to rule directly; they paid deference to the leading families. Liberal America provided no basis for explicit leading-family claims to paternal rule over the mass of free whites. Nevertheless, colonial society promoted "natural" deferential authority.

The advantages of birth, John Adams explained, were greater in America than in despotisms. A despot chose his advisers and underlings from every rank; he destroyed established families, whose independence challenged his absolute power. In America, wrote Adams, "the children of illustrious families" were fairly well assured of future political preeminence. They had advantages of education, political experience, and "habitual national veneration for their names." The family-based structure of colonial political authority gave substance to the hopes Adams shared with Jefferson for a "natural aristocracy." Adams distinguished the natural advantages of birth and wealth from "artificial inequalities of conditions, such as hereditary dignities, titles, magistracies, or legal distinctions." Jefferson wanted lower-class children of talent annually "raked from the rubbish" in the early school grades; he placed talent above birth in theory, but in practice found most men of talent among the members of the old leading families. Ties of marriage and kinship united these families. They had long political experience in relative colonial self-government.[9]

Leading families ruled, but their authority derived in large part from the people. White men who owned land or taxable property—the majority—could vote; some women property-owners could vote as well. Yeomen and artisans held minor local offices and some served in colonial assemblies. Mob action for limited purposes, to redress specific grievances, was a recognized, legitimate, oft-practiced form of political participation. Mobs did not aim to shatter the colonial social order, and were not generally perceived as doing so. "*A certain degree of equality* is essential to human bliss," Thomas Shippen wrote back to his father during a visit to London. "Happy above all Countries is our Country, where *that equality* is found without destroying the necessary subordination." Only in hereditary monarchies, wrote Paine, could the government "be possessed by a minor at any age."[10]

Family also underlay traditional English political authority, and the English tradition enhanced familial authority in the new world. Anglican thought derived political authority from family connections and organic personal relations. Political authority was "as a general family or household wherein good governors do put on the same carefull affection to the advancement of their subjects, which wise and dear fathers use to their entirely beloved children." The Anglican view had roots in feudal society, and in the origins of political power from kinship bonds. It also expressed, however, the rise of centralized royal power at the expense of actual ties of clan and blood. Seventeenth-century divine-rights theorists, like King James I and Sir Robert Filmer, defended royal patriarchal power against traditional family loyalties; they used familial language against the actual family. The king's patriarchal power was based not on blood ties nor on mutual feudal obligations of lords and vassals, but on the absolute, arbitrary, patriarchal will. Divine-rights theory read royal patriarchal power back into the family, transforming family relations as well as political authority. "For as kingly power is by the law of God," wrote Filmer, "so it hath no inferior law to admit it. The father of a family governs by no other law than by his own will, not by the laws or wills of his sons or servants."[11]

Absolute patriarchal claims lost out in England after the Glorious Revolution. Charles Leslie cited the story of Abraham and Isaac as evidence that children had no natural rights against paternal demands, but such arguments no longer commanded wide respect. Images of the Lockean family, Burrows and Wallace suggest, were replacing patriarchal justifications of political authority. Eighteenth-century political men did not draw merely on the political Locke. They supplemented Locke's contractual derivation of political authority with metaphors drawn from his writing on education and the family. Englishmen and colonists alike accepted the king's paternal authority over the new world. The rhetoric of colonial relations also attached new-world migrants to mother England. "The colonists are yet but Babes that cannot subsist but on the Breasts, and thro' the Protection of their Mother Country," wrote an American in 1741.[12]

There was, however, a crucial divergence in familial political authority in the old world and the new. This divergence set leading colonial families against the crown, and influenced the future course of American politics. The crown, thanks to its feudal and absolutist roots, exercised power in England for which there was no equivalent in the new world. King and court, dominating Treasury, Judges, and Commons, integrated English social and political authority at the top. The aristocracy performed the same role in the countryside. In the colonies the unified lines of political and social authority diverged at the top. The royal governors and their cliques, separated from the leading colonial families, exercised local political authority. Behind them lay the foreign power of the crown. The leading colonial families were not self-governing. They experienced power at a distance, unintegrated into social life. Bernard Bailyn, describing colonial Virginia, writes,

> To a Virginia planter of the early eighteenth century the highest public authority was no longer merely one expression of a general social authority. It had become something abstract, external to his life and society, an ultimate power whose purposes were obscure, whose direction could neither be consistently influenced nor accurately plotted, and whose human embodiments were alien and antagonistic.[13]

Tories and loyalists continued to insist on the familial bonds uniting England and America. But royal power was "external" in the new world, and colonists began to attack its character in England as well. Revolutionaries argued that the centralization of crown power in the eighteenth century departed from the Glorious Revolution and resurrected patriarchy. "The monarchy has poisoned the Republic, the crown has engrossed the commons," wrote Paine.

> The corrupt influence of the crown, by having all the places in its disposal, hath so effectively swallowed up the power, and eaten out the virtue of the House of Commons (the republican part of the constitution) that the government of England is nearly as monarchical as that of France or Spain.

George III, wrote Patrick Henry, "from being the father of his people degenerated into a tyrant, and forfeits all rights to his subject's obedience." The king was a "wretch," in Paine's words, "with the pretended title of FATHER OF HIS PEOPLE."[14]

The king and his governors had real power in the colonies; revolutionary fears of patriarchy were plausible. The colonists reserved their most intense wrath for mother England, however. Mother England, they charged, was reducing them from children to slaves. Sam Adams protested, "Slavery, my dear mother, we cannot think of; we detest it. If this be a crime, remember, we suck'd it with your milk." "*Great Britain adieu!*" wrote John Cleaveland in 1775. "No longer shall we know you as our mother; you are become cruel; you have not so much bowels as the sea monsters toward their young ones."[15]

Republican fears of parental usurpation derived from a psychology of power, as well as from considerations of political structure. Revolutionaries, writes Bailyn, divided society

> into distinct, contrasting, and innately antagonistic spheres: the sphere of power and the sphere of liberty or right. The one was brutal, ceaselessly active, and heedless; the other was delicate, passive and sensitive. The one must be resisted, the other defended, and the two must never be confused.

Power was naturally aggressive; it trespassed beyond legitimate boundaries. "The love of power is natural; it is insatiable; it is whetted, not cloyed, by possession." Liberty, naturally weak, passive, and innocent, was "hunted and persecuted in all countries by cruel power."[16]

Republicans gave liberty the feminine persona and identified her with America. Paul Revere titled his cartoon against the tea tax *The able Doctor, or America Swallowing the Bitter Draught*. He pictured reclining, bare-breasted maid America surrounded by foppish British gentlemen. One forces a liquid down her throat; another, as if to illustrate the "grasping" "hand of power," lifts up her skirts and peers under them. (See Plate 4.)[17] Tom Paine's fable "Cupid and Hymen" imagines a feudal lord, Gothic, insisting on marriage to the maid Ruralinda. In the marriage procession, "The Lord of the manor looked like the father of his village, and the business he was on gave a foolish awkwardness to his age and dignity." Cupid intervenes, convinces Gothic to relinquish Ruralinda, and restores her to her shepherd lover. There was no Cupid peacefully to free America from England. "As well can the lover forgive the ravisher of his mistress," wrote Paine in *Common Sense*, "as the continent forgive the murders of Britain."[18]

Images of lustful paternal power did not exhaust the revolutionary imagination. Revolutionary metaphors associated patriarchal "trespass" with maternal seduction and violence. England, "from being the nursery of heroes, became the residence of musicians, pimps, panders, and catamites." She was declining, like the republics of antiquity, because of a "dull . . . animal enjoyment" which left "minds stupefied, and bodies enervated, by wallowing forever in one continual puddle of voluptuousness." "Dear mother, sweet mother, honored mother country," pleaded James Otis. "I am her most devoted son, and humble servant! But . . . Every inhabitant in America maintains at least two lazy fellows in ease, idleness, or luxury, in mother Britain's lap."[19]

Revolutionaries insisted that slavery to the passions created political slavery. In the words of one pamphleteer, "Before a nation is completely deprived of freedom, she must be fitted for slavery by her vices." "Vanities, levities, and fopperies," wrote John Adams, "are real antidotes to all great, manly, and warlike virtues." Forsaking the temptations to pleasure in "mother Britain's lap," her American offspring faced murderous maternal revenge.[20] "We have been told," wrote the young John Adams,

> "that Britain is the mother and we are the children, that a filial duty and submission is due from us to her." . . . admitting we are children, have not children a right to complain when their parents are attempting to break their limbs, to administer poison, or to sell them to enemies for slaves. Let me entreat you to consider, will the mother be pleased when you represent her as deaf to the cries of her children—when you compare her to the infamous miscreant who lately stood on the gallows for starving her child— when you resemble her to Lady Macbeth in Shakespeare (I cannot think of it without horror), who had given suck, and knew How tender 't was to love the babe that milked her, but yet who could even while 't was smiling in her face, Have plucked the nipple from the boneless gums, and dashed the brains out.[21]

Revolutionary pamphlets pictured the colonists as innocent victims of murderous, sexual, parental assault. The mother England who "plucked the nipple from the boneless gums," like the "puddle of voluptuousness" at the English court, threatened to obliterate the child. Crown conspiracies, the colonists believed, gave substance to these fears. There was an important conspiratorial strain in republican thought, and it transcended literary metaphor. "A licentious ministry," republicans charged, held secret meetings and hatched secret plots. England had laid, Jefferson believed, "a deliberate and systematical plan of reducing us to slavery." "The system of slavery fabricated against America," wrote Hamilton, "is the offspring of mature deliberation." Revolutionaries believed they had discovered "profoundly secret, dark, and deep" crown secrets. Men had, wrote John Adams, the "right to that most dreaded and envied kind of knowledge— I mean of the character and conduct of their rulers."[22]

Political power was patriarchal in the early modern world. Revolutionary language reflected the efforts of a colonial middle class, which did not derive its power directly from royal favoritism, to claim authority against monarchic and feudal privilege. Such efforts, and the literature which expressed them, appeared in the old world as well as the new. Only Americans, however, could claim that king and lord had no legitimate place on their soil. History spared America, John Adams wrote, "the canon and feudal law." Our ancestors "had an utter contempt for all that dark ribaldry of hereditary, indefeasible right." The colonists thought they could make a political revolution without overturning society from top to bottom.[23]

Eighteenth-century liberal thought distinguished state from society. Society was, left to itself, orderly and harmonious. Coercion derived from the state alone. Such a view operated with particular force in America. Revolutionaries distinguished colonial society from English state power. They blamed the English court for the corruption of English and American life. They counterposed a virtuous native population to a lustful, self-aggrandizing English court. Expel the royal presence, and republican virtue would reign at home. The American republic would be small in size and relatively homogeneous in population. Its government would concern itself solely with "the public good." It would base itself on a virtuous people, frugal, temperate, and industrious, living a simple life. The republic would not permit license but true liberty, "natural liberty restricted in such a manner as to render society one great family; where every one must consult his neighbor's happiness as well as his own."[24]

Republican dreams, utopian as they sound, had a solid basis in American realities; that was the promise of liberalism. America lacked deeply rooted, legal, hereditary feudal distinctions. It did not contain the traditional European social divisions or (among whites) European extremes of wealth and poverty. Nothing in provincial America compared to the urban squalor or court luxury of the European capitals. Crown representatives in the new world benefited from royal preferment, but they were (Bailyn) "external to [colonial] life and society."

Republican psychology also made a certain sense. There was reason to fear corrupt English court life, and to identify political domination with moral decay. Republicans feared, in psychoanalytic language, regression in the service of the superego; their analysis foreshadows Marcuse's description of repressive desublimation.[25] They feared Americans would become the helpless tools of the symbolic parents who stimulated and satisfied their passions. They believed that crown influence corrupted Americans, set them against one another, and perpetuated royal domination. These fears early gained substance from the behavior of crown favorites in America; crown efforts to rationalize and centralize colonial rule after the French and Indian War and to extract a greater surplus from the colonies seemed further evidence for the republican view.

The revolutionaries blamed crown power for contaminating American life. Bailyn suggests, however, that the crown was too weak to bring political order to America, not so strong that it accounted for all American ills. Royal governors had greater formal powers than the executive enjoyed in England, but they lacked the social weight to rule. They had none of the informal mechanisms of crown power in England. They had no power over the Treasurer, and no money to create an executive party in the assembly. The crown manipulated rotten boroughs and the tiny English franchise to control Parliament; royal governors had no comparable advantages. They faced, as the crown in England did not, an independent judiciary. Indeed, the governors' ties to the crown itself were weak; their decisions were not final, and once in America they were cut off from the sources of patronage necessary to maintain their influence. The governors had competitors at home, and the colonists' commercial and Anglican church contacts gave them access to court.[26]

Revolutionaries understood that royal political power was unintegrated into colonial social life. But they attributed to the parent country powers which it did not have. "An inordinate love of money" may have been, as Sam Adams thought, "the root of all evil,"[27] but royal governors did not plant it. Factions characterized colonial politics; royal governors contributed to colonial factiousness, but they were also too weak to control it. First the revolutionary fathers, then the founding fathers, and then Jackson successively inherited this weakness.

Republican rhetoric rightly pointed to a reality of English domination. But it also reflected the existence of repressed internal threats to the colonial household order. "The innocent Children" (John Adams)[28] were all too fascinated by lust, sadistic power, and conspiracy. They loaded upon parental England a weight of grievance it could not bear. They conjured up monstrous parents to preserve American innocence.

The colonists, wrote Paine, "fled not from the tender embraces of the mother, but from the cruelty of the monster." They escaped, wrote Adams, the canon and feudal law. But they brought slaves and they encountered Indians. These people of color were not born equal, and their presence inspired republican nightmares. Paine imagined England as "that barbarous and hellish power which hath stirred up the Indians and the Negroes to destroy us." Refusing to acknowledge that their own settlements and land speculations provoked Indian war, revolutionaries blamed George III. The Declaration of Independence charged, "He endeavored to bring on the inhabitants of our frontiers, the merciless Indian savages, whose known rule of warfare is an undistinguished destruction of all ages, sexes, and conditions."[29]

Americans guilt-ridden about slavery feared English-inspired slave insurrections. Jefferson, ignoring southern slaveholders and the New England slave-trading merchants, imagined England imposing slavery on the colonies. George III, he concluded,

> is now exciting these very people to rise in arms among us, and to purchase that liberty of which he has deprived them, by murdering the people on whom he also obtruded them; thus paying off former crimes committed against the liberties of one people, with crimes which he urges them to commit against the lives of another.[30]

The colonies, which enslaved one-fifth of their inhabitants, charged England with enslaving them. "That barbarous and hellish power" lay deeply embedded within America. Jefferson owned slaves and pushed westward expansion; he deplored the effects of slavery and mourned Indian extinction. He and other republican leaders were imprisoned in racial patterns to which they did not want to consent but which their revolution would not alter.

The American social order also generated disharmony among whites. Revolutionaries blamed monarchical feudalism, hardly an American danger, for social inequality, love of money, and political domination. They averted their eyes from the internecine, personalized factional conflict endemic to the colonies, and from the commodity capitalism beginning to sprout from household soil.

"Natural" family authority offered no lasting alternative to feudalistic patriarchy on the one hand, free marketplace and acquisitive individualism on the other. The natural family was a bourgeois family. It maintained private, individual property, insisted on formal equality, and defined legal relations in contractual terms. Republicans rejoiced at the absence of a native feudal aristocracy. "These young agrarian states, where no such being as a Lord exists," lacked a class with state-sanctioned, ancient legal privileges. Instead every man was "lord of his soil." Feudalism would have centralized fraternal structures within the leading extended families; but it would also have provided cohesion. The colonial upper class, not based on inherited legal status, was based on property instead. It was bourgeois to the core.[31]

European aristocracy centered on the family estate, inherited unbroken by the eldest son. He dominated the entire, extended, collateral family; he was patriarch over brothers and cousins as well as his own sons. America not only lacked a feudal past; it lacked the material basis for feudalism as well. Available land diminished the value of the original paternal estate. Subdivided by inheritance, it lost importance as the children acquired new land. No single paternal inheritor, controlling economic resources and the ancient estate, dominated the entire extended family. Soil exhaustion, moreover, diminished the economic significance of the original estate *vis-à-vis* virgin soil. To entail slaves to the original plantation, attempted in the south, merely diminished their value. Entailed slaves could neither be sold nor work new and more valuable land.[32]

Primogeniture and entail inhibited economic exploitation of the land. Rarely used in America, they met opposition from the natural aristocracy. The leading families lived on landed estates. But they were also bourgeois farmers living off the land; they wanted freely to buy and sell it. Most had made their fortunes in land speculation. In North Carolina a state legislature dominated by speculators abolished primogeniture and entail after the Revolution.[33]

Colonial politics could not base itself on deep, inherited, familial social cohesion. It was dominated instead by personal competition among family-based factions. Eighteenth-century factions were held together by personal ties to particular men of influence. Revolutionaries deplored the factionalized, personalized character of colonial politics; they blamed crown influence. In fact colonial social relations were intrinsically far more competitive than republicans wanted to believe.[34]

The personal character of eighteenth-century politics, as Gordon Wood suggests, fed conspiratorial thinking; eighteenth-century men found conscious design everywhere.[35] Conspiratorial images are striking, however, not merely for their attributions of consciousness, but for their unconscious content. The problems which the Revolution failed to solve —problems of power, sexuality, family authority, and worldly materialism—reveal themselves in the materials of fantasy. These were the problems, shaped by the Revolution and revolutionary language, which returned to face Andrew Jackson.

Protestant household psychology generated both the monstrous parental imagos who tyrannized the American imagination and the commodity capitalism beginning to dominate its life in the world. Middle-class Protestants settled the colonies. Their faith redirected attention from the created world to individual, personal salvation; it devolved into Protestant capitalism in America. Protestantism, in Weber's classic analysis, subjected inner life to "systematic self-control." Taking an "entirely negative attitude . . . to all sensuous and emotional elements in culture and religion," it subjected believers to an "unprecedented inner loneliness." Protestantism sought a disciplined relation to God, unmediated by maternal forgiveness and love. Grace was scarce in the Protestant psychological economy, not bountiful and freely available to all. A sinner could not rely on maternal love; instead, aided by his minister, he prepared himself to receive God's grace. Protestants asserted individual autonomy against maternal power. They feared the revenge of the papal "whore of Babylon"; they feared, in secular, revolutionary metaphors, the monster mother England.[36]

Protestant asceticism condemned worldly activity practiced for its own sake; it drove men to disciplined, sanctified worldly success. Disciplined life reduced the threat posed by inner self-doubt and worldly temptation. It provided "outward and visible signs of inner and spiritual grace." But ascetic Protestantism set in motion a dynamic which undermined both individual religious intensity and communal religious bonds. Men began to take satisfaction from worldliness itself; they liberated commercial intercourse from inner and communal religious authority.

At the same time, worldliness troubled the Protestant conscience. American ministers preached jeremiads from early in the settlement of the new world, warning their flocks that worldly concerns antagonized a jealous, angry God. Revolutionary pamphlets, recalling America to virtue, were kinds of jeremiads. There was a fundamental difference, however, between Puritan and revolutionary pamphlets. The angry God now appeared as George III, and the colonists sat in judgment upon him. Destroying royal statues in the cities, Winthrop Jordan shows, the "sons of liberty" carried out a symbolic killing of the king. The revolution itself, loyalists insisted, was the act of a "PARRICIDE."[37]

Just as early Protestantism resurrected the angry God, so it allied itself with patriarchy. It shattered feudal, local, traditional, communal bonds. It opposed women's power in religion and society, and sought to confine them in the home. At the same time, by substituting private judgment for social coercion, Protestantism undermined patriarchy. It rooted marriage in free individual choice—conscience and romance—rather than in family alliance. Protestantism gave marriage a contractual basis, and may also have improved the legal position of women.[38] The disciplined Protestant conscience ultimately substituted internal restraints for patriarchal control. Was there fear that love would turn to lust in the new family, that the decline of patriarchy offered temptations to mothers and sons, and that the Protestant conscience was insufficiently strong to resist them? Was the monstrous mother a scapegoat for renewed temptations of the flesh? Revolutionary rhetoric suggests this possibility. But revolutionary solutions failed to meet revolutionary fears. Both the constitutional founders and Jackson retreated to a purified paternal authority "external to [household] life and society." The struggle to create a reified paternalism, to rescue sons from maternal power, informs Jackson's life. The revolutionary attacks on corrupt parental England mixed envy with horror. And Jackson's internal colonialism exercised over Indians the patriarchal domination, purified of lust but not of sadism, that the colonists, with some justice, accused England of imposing on them.

Worldly materialism reconnected Protestants to the physical universe. They were not liberated freely to enjoy sensuous life, however, and the American innocent spoke a language of sexual anger. For the world returned loaded with the effort at systematic domination imposed by the Protestant ethic. The world, it seemed, sought actively to control the self. This fear was not simply a return of repressed fantasies operating within the psyche. The Protestant ethic materialized itself in a market which did control the lives of men linked to it by work or acquisitive desire. The family order was giving way to possessive individualism, structured by the power of the market. Had the autonomous Protestant emancipated himself from the virgin to succumb to the market? Revolutionaries, their metaphors suggest, experienced material luxury as maternal revenge. The revolutionary fathers failed to establish frugality among their sons. Jackson, responding to this failure, progressed from domination of Indian "children of nature" to war on "the mother bank."

Fraternal rivalry and paternal usurpation undermined American confidence in all personal authority. Republicans, in the course of pre-revolutionary struggle, identified certain abstract principles of legitimacy—liberty, equality, natural right, rule of law. They did not intend that these principles of natural authority corrode the natural family order. Revolutionary principles, however, furthered a process by which impersonal, secondary, social institutions—market, factory, party, state, asylum—replaced the family. The Protestant household order, thanks to its bourgeois rationalizing thrust, generated these institutions and was particularly vulnerable to them.

The market was primary. Leading families made a revolution to protect household autonomy. They themselves were deeply enmeshed in the market, however, and their revolution ultimately aided market expansion. It did not subordinate the market to American family control.

Leading families derived their position from acquisitive market behavior. Staple-crop agriculture and the debt structure that supported it; shipbuilding and ocean commerce; land speculation; and the western fur trade provided important market involvements for the colonial elite. A few English radicals critical of imperial policy wanted to substitute the freedom of the international marketplace for imperial political domination. Adam Smith, for example, rejected the parental colonial metaphor for the formal equality of free trade. American spokesmen also favored trade. They did not want to sacrifice family-derived political relationships to market expansion, however. They wanted to utilize the market without surrendering political control over it. They imagined a society governed by family and social loyalty rather than pure commodity exchange. Eighteenth-century social structure gave substance to what Daniel Calhoun calls "a community-oriented style, accepting gracefully the use of authority to promote group interests."[39]

Commodity capitalism, however, was undermining the "isolated, closely-knit, largely subsistence society of self-governing and self-supporting communes." Market interests and economic opportunities worked within, intensified, and began to explode family-based lines of cleavage. Capitalism provided the spoils in the factional struggle, configured its character, and undermined the household order which brought it forth.

> "Family interests," like the Livingstons and De Lanceys in New York, observed Ambrose Serle in 1776, "have long been in gradual Decay; and perhaps a new arrangement of political affairs may leave them wholly extinct." Yet by freezing factional politics . . . around the issue of British authority, the controversy with the mother country at first tended to obscure these developments and to drown out the quarrel Americans had among themselves.[40]

The leading families wanted more than republican virtue. They wanted freedom to pursue their market interests. The British proclamation line of 1763, for example, sought to restrict settlement west of the Appalachians and avoid the expense of future Indian wars. The proclamation line antagonized land speculators such as George Washington, who favored westward expansion to increase the value of their lands. Washington urged a friend, in violation of British regulations, to enter land claims for him in Indian territory. British efforts to regulate the fur trade also provoked western resentment.[41]

Leading colonial families may actually have experienced a long-term deterioration in their position *vis-à-vis* British capitalism. British capital and decisions, Ernst and Egnal suggest, increasingly dominated the colonial economy in the decades before the Revolution. British domination reduced the profits and the autonomy of the colonial elite. Tidewater tobacco planters had once enjoyed intimate relations with their English consignment merchants; now large Scottish banking houses held their debts. Coastal merchants suffered from the extension of British trade. British houses flooded the colonial market, bypassing the established merchant families. They sold goods in auction sales or through upstart provincial subordinates. Established merchants lost money in the worst years; they feared for their survival as an autonomous class.[42]

"I would have you not bee to forward in pushing goods upon people," a Philadelphia importer complained to a London house. The aggressive role of British capital fed republican ideology; threats to household autonomy lay in the "inordinate [British] love of money," not at home. Revolutionaries similarly attacked crown representatives for distributing political privileges over the native economy. The dominant provincial elite in mid-eighteenth-century North Carolina, for example, struggled with British-based speculator Henry McCulloh for colonial wealth. The provincial elite, called "the family" because of its extended family relations in trade and speculation, lacked McCulloh's ties to the royal governor and his influence at court. Foreigners like McCulloh, whose English connections gave them advantages in the race to engross American wealth, added bitterness to increasing English restrictions on colonial freedom.[43]

The state did play a crucial role in distributing colonial economic resources. It acted because of the nature of the colonial economy, not because of alien feudal values. The undeveloped economy provided the government with previously unappropriated largesse; colonists participated wholeheartedly in the struggle for land and development privileges. Royal favoritism made it seem that government, not society, generated acquisitiveness in America. This obscured desires for preferment within colonial society. "Political offices and emoluments were the major source of social distinction and financial security" because they made property available, not because, as in England, they offered hereditary privilege, "empty ornament and unmeaning grandeur." The Revolution might return power to local, legitimate families; it would not thereby end competitiveness among them, or prevent challengers from contesting their position.[44]

Competitive struggles for economic advantage characterized the colonial governing class, and those aspiring to membership in it. These struggles undermined the household order. Significant numbers of new men gained entry into the economic elite in the years before the Revolution, creating anxieties among the established families. Growing economic opportunities at the top and diminishing ones at the bottom widened the gap between wealthy and poor. Market expansion created an impoverished urban class of sailors and day laborers; vagabonds and landless agricultural workers increasingly appeared in the countryside. Family did not integrate these urban and rural dependents into a communal order. Beginning to transform household society, market expansion was introducing not merely factional conflicts among families and small groups over economic privilege, but deeper social and class conflict as well.[45]

American maturity justified the Revolution, the colonists believed. In the words of one pamphleteer, "A parent has a natural right to govern his children during their minority and continuance in his family, but he has no such authority over them as they arrive at full age." Dependence on Great Britain was proper, wrote Richard Wells, when the colonies were infant states. Now "the day of independent manhood is at hand." As Paine put it, "To know whether it be the interest of the continent to be independent, we need only ask this easy, simple question: Is it the interest of a man to be a boy all his life?"[46]

Revolution liberated America from English, parental domination; it failed to preserve the family order at home. Elimination of the parents did not preserve American innocence and, in the symbolism of the founders, the parents returned. They returned with the distinctive meanings implied by the special revolutionary horror of monstrous mother England: mother returned as menace, father as authority. The Revolution, argued the founders, failed to protect America from the temptations of the flesh. The constitution-makers turned from a discredited republican virtue to a strengthened paternal rule.

Maturity, republicans came to believe, simply made America vulnerable to European corruption. "There is no special providence for Americans," John Adams now said; conflict, envy, and the thirst for privilege were endemic to American society. Revolutionaries expelled the British; leading families were challenged, in turn, by men "*whose fathers they would have disdained to have sat with the dogs of their flocks.*" Popular despotism, fraternal strife, and the rise of men from obscure families all undermined social deference. "LUXURY, LUXURY, the great source of dissolution and distress, has here taken up her dismal abode," republicans complained, destroying "that simplicity of manners, native manliness of soul, and equality of station, which is the spring and peculiar excellence of free government." The disappointment of republican dreams, Gordon Wood has shown, produced a series of constitutional crises in the states, a revolution in political thought, and the new national Constitution.[47]

The natural aristocracy dreamed of connecting the lines of authority at the top. Instead the Revolution further split political power from social position. The leading families had greater social standing than the royal cliques, but it was insufficient to permit them to govern. Threatened by social conflict and the rise of new men, the leading families tried to reestablish their political rule through the Constitution. They erected a constitutional machine above society, and sought to protect, with constitutional mechanisms, organic, deferential, political authority. The Constitution set up a national authority, far from the work and daily lives of most Americans, to compensate for the experienced social weakness of the leading families. The natural aristocracy supported the Constitution "to defend the worthy against the licentious." It fell back upon that fatherhood, supported by state instead of society, which characterized colonial rule. "The tyranny of Philadelphia may be like the tyranny of George III," charged the Anti-Federalists.[48]

The revolutionaries counterposed liberty to power, a virtuous society to a self-aggrandizing state. But in America, wrote Madison, liberty granted the charter of power; republican America had less reason than Europe to fear strong government. The founders identified the people as the source of republican political authority; but in a republic, they argued, the people did not need to exercise direct power. The founders made the claim, unprecedented in republican thought, that officeholders represented the people simply because they had been elected. The founders resisted populist tendencies recurrent in eighteenth-century society and intensified by revolution. They opposed annual elections, efforts to bind representatives, and other democratic reforms which enjoyed widespread currency in the states. They argued that popular rebellion and mob action, necessary in monarchies, had no place in America.[49]

Factions destroyed republican virtue, the revolutionaries believed. The founders abandoned hope that the mass of Americans was capable of republican virtue, and they feared a majority faction. They encouraged competition among private interests and among the branches of government. Classic republican thought envisioned a small, homogeneous republic; factional competition, the founders believed, would destroy it. Democratic despotism would more likely triumph in a simple, household republic than in a large, economically complex state. Citizens in a large state, argued Madison, would be more likely to choose members of the natural aristocracy to represent them. A large, expanding nation increased the number of factions and decreased communication among the members of a potential majority faction. The west provided, in addition, enormous potential wealth. Expansion turned men outward; it substituted for economic conflict and social control of wealth at home.[50]

Republican thought reflected the roots of the leading families in the household order; the Constitution established their commitment to market expansion. The founders solved the problems avoided in revolutionary thought in terms congenial to the development of a market, commodity economy. A new constitution was needed, said Hamilton, to fit government to "the commercial character of America." The Constitution created a strong national government to protect property and control social disorder. It made possible a federal army to suppress lower-class uprisings, put down slave insurrections, and defeat Indians and safeguard westward expansion. Ratification was supported in commercial areas and among classes dependent on the market. Subsistence farmers opposed ratification, except in frontier regions where settlers and speculators wanted federal protection against Indians. Hamilton's economic policies established a sound American credit basis, and financed "speculative enterprises in lands, industry, and finance." His funding of the debt, "drained originally from the small-propertied classes and met by taxes paid by the masses," allied the economic interests of a wealthy, paper-holding class to the success of the new nation.[51]

The Constitution failed to protect the natural aristocracy against its political decline. Federalist efforts to establish centralized political rule lacked sufficient grounding in social deference. Hamilton's economic policies, moreover, and Federalist allegiances in European politics antagonized the Tidewater planters. Jackson and other aspirants to national power who had supported ratification of the Constitution rebelled in the 1790s against the Federalist political fathers. Jefferson lamented the rise of "an Anglican monarchical aristocratical party" composed of men who were "Samsons in the field and Solomons in the council, but have had their heads shorn by the harlot England." Jefferson defeated the Federalists, but he called upon their ghosts. His Presidency—fostering westward expansion, economic development, and a strong executive—sanctified the founding; it raised the Constitution and the founders above reproach.[52]

Authority derives from foundings, writes Arendt. Alternative to the egalitarian relations of persuasion among living men, it is traditional, paternal, and hierarchical in character. American republicans tried to create a politics in which brothers, supported by social deference, could act together. Fearful of human speech and action, the founders erected a constitutional machine to control behavior.[53] Leading families embedded in ongoing social relationships were losing political authority as the nineteenth century opened. They were being replaced by the traditional authority of the mythic revolutionary and founding fathers, and by the impersonal authority of the constitutional structure itself. Beneath these authority structures, however, the problems of a faction-ridden, acquisitive society, which had plagued the revolutionary generation, continued to trouble its sons. The revolutionaries rebelled against England to purify America; the Constitution offered their sons nothing but obedience to the law. Parson Weems' immensely popular *Life of Washington*, first published in 1800, reminded Americans of the father of their country's Farewell Address. Weems hoped

> that they will read it with the feelings of children reading the last letter of a once-loved father now in his grave. And who knows but it may check for a while that fatal flame of discord which has destroyed all the once GLORIOUS REPUBLICS OF ANTIQUITY, and here now at length in the United States has caught upon the last republic that is left on the face of the earth.[54]

The American genius, for the founders as for Weems, resided in the achievements of the fathers. Imprisoned by the paternal machine, the sons could not be trusted to create their own identities. The colonies won their independence; but articulate Americans in the decades that followed strove to define the special character of the new nation. Had the post-revolutionary generation to choose, as loyalists insisted to their revolutionary fathers, either to "fan the fatal flames of discord," or else to remain "children" forever?[55] Andrew Jackson, westward expansion, and Indian removal offered another alternative.

II

"Our age is retrospective," began Ralph Waldo Emerson's *Nature*. "It builds the sepulchres of the fathers."

> The foregoing generations beheld God and nature face to face; we through their eyes. Why should not we also enjoy an original relation to the Universe? . . . Embosomed for a season in nature, whose floods of life stream around and through us, . . . why should we grope among the dry bones of the past?[56]

Andrew Jackson sought an original relation to the universe, and he sought it in nature. He emancipated himself from the fathers, but he carried their sepulchers into the woods.

> In the woods, too, a man casts off his years, as the snake his slough, and at what period soever of his life, is always a child. In the woods is perpetual youth. . . .
>
> The sun illuminates only the eye of the man, but shines into the eye and the heart of the child. The lover of nature is he whose inward and outward senses are still truly adjusted to each other; who has retained the spirit of infancy even into the era of manhood.[57]

Jackson returned to childhood in nature, not as a lover of nature, but to sanctify possessions and dominate childhood. The American Indians, wrote Thoreau, burned their possessions in a yearly ritual of purification. Jackson's life was purifying too; as his friend Judge John Catron eulogized him, he burned everything before him like a prairie fire.[58] The spirit of infancy he retained into manhood was the spirit of infantile rage.

CHAPTER 2

ANDREW JACKSON: THE FAMILY ROMANCE

"I reckon you know one of the new twins gave your nephew a kicking last night, Judge? . . . But Tom beat the twin on the trial." . . .

"The trial? What trial?"

"Why, Tom had him up before Judge Robinson for assault and battery."

The old man shrank suddenly together like one who has received a death stroke. . . .

"You cur! You scum! You vermin! Do you mean to tell me that blood of my race has suffered a blow and crawled to a court of law about it? Answer me!"

Tom's head dropped, and he answered with an eloquent silence. . . .

"You have challenged him?"

"N-no," hesitated Tom, turning pale.

"You will challenge him to-night. Howard will carry it."

Tom began to turn sick, and to show it. . . . "Oh, please don't ask me to do it, uncle! He is a murderous devil—I never could—I'm afraid of him!"

Old Driscoll's mouth opened and closed three times before he could get it to perform its office. Then he stormed out:

"A coward in my family! A Driscoll a coward! Oh, what have I done to deserve this infamy!" He tottered to his secretary in the corner repeating that lament again and again in heartbreaking tones, and got out of a drawer a paper, which he slowly tore to bits. . . . "There it is, shreds and fragments once more—my will. Once more you have forced me to disinherit you, you base son of a most noble father!"

—*Mark Twain*, Pudd'nhead Wilson

I

Andrew Jackson was born March 15, 1767, in a backcountry Carolina settlement. His parents, Andrew and Elizabeth Jackson, had recently traveled to America with relatives from the north of Ireland. In the new world they joined the Scotch-Irish migration south from Pennsylvania to the outlying southern frontier. Jackson's parents brought one son of two and another of five months from Ireland. Andrew, the youngest son, was the only child born in America. His father died two months before his birth. Elizabeth Jackson went to live with her sister, married to James Crawford and the mother of a large family. Andrew's aunt was an invalid; his mother took charge of the Crawford household. Andrew and his brother Robert lived there with her; she sent her eldest son, Hugh, to the neighboring home of James' brother Robert Crawford. Robert Crawford, also called Uncle by the Jackson children, was the leading citizen of the backcountry Waxhaws settlement.

The Revolutionary War reached the Carolina frontier when Andrew was twelve. Tory raids ravaged the backcountry, and there was virtual civil war between loyalists and revolutionaries among the settlers. These battles often divided families; frontier Tories, one patriot wrote, "imbrued their hands in the blood of their brethren." There is no record, however, that any of the Crawford clan sided with the British. Uncle Robert was an officer in the revolutionary militia. Jackson's oldest brother served under him, and died of a fever after his first engagement.

British victories disrupted homes in the Waxhaws region; as families dispersed and fled, many households, including James Crawford's, broke up. Andrew and his remaining brother, Robert, were captured by the British in 1781. They were kept prisoner for several months, and both were badly wounded by a British officer when they refused to black his boots. The boys caught smallpox and suffered from high fevers; Robert died. Andrew, back under his mother's care, was hardly out of danger when she left him to nurse two of his cousins aboard a British prisoner-of-war ship in Charles Town harbor. She saved one cousin, but caught cholera herself on board ship and died. At fourteen, Andrew was an orphan.[1]

Jackson's early years became legendary during his lifetime. Deprived of father at birth, of mother and brothers in adolescence, refusing as a youth to bow to British authority, Jackson embodied the proud independence of the new nation. Born on the farthest frontier, lacking the advantages of birth and family connection, he seemed entirely responsible for his own life. In the west, an early biographer wrote in 1820, "each individual may almost be said to make a province by himself." So it was with Jackson. "Without any extrinsic advantage to promote his advancement, he had to rely solely upon intrinsic worth and decisiveness of character, to enable him to rise rapidly with a rapidly rising people." In the words of a eulogist a generation later, "He seems to have been an orphan from the plow to the Presidency. He must, therefore, be regarded as the architect of his own fortunes."[2]

Jackson symbolized, in the years of his ascendancy, the free American, dependent on and subservient to no one. America was engaged, Harriet Martineau reported, in "the process of world-making." Pioneers were creating new societies along the frontier and in utopian communities. The Jacksonian period was a time when human choice and action seemed to make a genuine difference. Ideas of independence and self-help had begun to enter the household as well. European observers saw an erosion of paternal discipline. "Almost from the cradle," children were inspired to get ahead, to make themselves.[3]

The adult Jackson shared the prevailing view of his own childhood. He often said, although it was not true, that he had no living blood relatives in America. He was surrogate parent to many young men, and told Richard Call, "At the Hermitage you will always find a father's dwelling." But when Call failed to receive a post for which Jackson had recommended him, Jackson wrote,

> My dear Call I have been Tossed upon the waves of fortune from youthhood, I have experienced prosperity and adversity. It was this that gave me knowledge of human nature, it was this that forced into action, all the energies of my mind, and ultimately caused me to progress through life as I have done—hence this neglect of the Government may be of service to you. It has and will bring forth, from necessity, the best energies of your mind, and with your application and industry, you will, nay, you must succeed.[4]

Jackson's youth appeared the perfect preparation for the new century. Simply to read Jacksonian ideals back into Jackson's childhood is to make an important mistake, however. Young Jackson lived in the eighteenth-century household pattern. The Waxhaws was a region of subsistence agriculture, with small farms and few slaves. Blacks formed only ten to fifteen percent of the frontier Carolina population; Jackson's uncles both owned slaves, but probably no more than a few. The journey which brought the Jacksons to the Waxhaws was far longer than typical, but they traveled with other clan members to a region which friends and relations had already settled. Elizabeth Jackson had several married sisters on the Carolina frontier, in addition to the extensive Craw-ford connection. Clan ties protected the fatherless family.[5]

Clan connections dominated southwestern frontier life. Secondary social institutions—churches, schools, newspapers, towns—came late to the frontier. Clans did not enforce stable, collective loyalties, however. Often the trip to Carolina followed the death of a family patriarch. As else-where in colonial America, but in more intense fashion, the southwestern frontier experienced competition within and among lineages. Rivalry took the form of litigation over property, debt, trespass, land title, and defa-mation of character; boasting, gambling, and displays of individual prow-ess; and feuds, duels, brawls, and other forms of personal violence. Young Jackson participated in these conflicts; they ended with the destruction of his inherited clan ties.[6]

An embattled life, close to nature and uninhibited by traditional so-cial restraints, produced humorous claims to violent omnipotence. Asked to identify himself by a supporter of John Quincy Adams, Davy Crock-ett is said to have replied,

> I'm that same David Crockett, fresh from the backwoods, half-horse, half-alligator, a little touched with the snapping turtle; can wade the Mis-sissippi, leap the Ohio, ride upon a streak of lightning, and slip without a scratch down a honey locust; can whip my weight in wildcats, . . . hug a bear too close for comfort, and eat any man opposed to Jackson.[7]

Jackson himself was as famous for his violence as for his independ-ence. His displays of temper were extreme even by southwestern stand-ards; and they lacked the mitigating humor of the legendary backwoods-men. Rage fed Jackson's self-reliance. His anger expressed itself in recur-rent symbols; let us begin with one example of his language.

Jackson flew into a rage in 1812 because the Choctaw Indian agent required whites to carry proof they owned the slaves traveling with them through Indian country on the Nashville-Natchez road. When his sister-in-law was detained at the Indian agency with ten slaves, Jackson wrote an enraged letter to a Tennessee Congressman. It reads in part:

> Can the Secretary of war for one moment retain the idea, that we will permit this petty Tyrant to sport with our rights secured to us by treaty and which by the law of nature we do possess, and sport with our feel-ings by publishing his *lawless tyranny exercised over a helpless and un-protected female*—if he does he thinks too meanly of our Patriotism and galantry—were we base enough to surrender our independent rights se-cured to us by the bravery and blood of our fore fathers, we are un-worthy of the name of *freemen*, and we view all rights secured to us

by Solem treaty, under the constituted authority, *rights* secured to us by the blood of our fathers and which we will never yield but with our lives. . . . the right of nature occurs, and if redress is not afforded, I would despise the wretch that would slumber in qu[i]et one night before he cutt up by the roots the invader of his Solem rights. . . . This may be thought strong language, but it is the language that freemen when they are only claiming a fulfilment of their rights ought to use. It is a language that they ought to be taught to lisp from their cradles, and never when the[y] are claiming rights from any nation ever to abandon.[8]

"Our rights," in Jackson's words, come directly from "nature"; *"free-men"* had the "right of nature" violently to enforce them. The natural-rights theorists Locke and Hobbes gave men in nature the right to defend themselves. Jackson drew, more directly, on a self-assertive frontier tradition of appeals to nature. His language suggests that natural right was the right to violence.

Even the most innocent natural man, in Herman Melville's representation, was given to violence. Billy Budd, a seaman on the *Rights-of-Man*, was an orphan, like Jackson, of unknown lineage, natural authority, and commanding personal presence. He had, however, a flaw. "Under sudden provocation of strong heart-feeling, his voice . . . was apt to develop an organic hesitancy, in fact more or less of a stutter or even worse." Unable to defend himself verbally, Billy struck and killed his accuser.[9]

Melville did not invent Billy's flaw; he found it on the frontier. Back-woodsmen flew into rages so fierce, said Davy Crockett, that they stammered in anger or grew entirely dumb. Unable to speak coherently, they fought instead. Jefferson is alleged to have made the identical comment about Jackson. "His passions are terrible," are the words ascribed to Jefferson. "When I was president of the senate, he was a senator, and he could never speak on account of the rashness of his feelings. I have seen him attempt it repeatedly, and as often choke with rage."[10]

Jefferson may never have spoken these words about the mature Jackson, but they accurately describe his childhood. Billy Budd stammered; Jackson drooled. He slobbered when excited and had difficulty speaking. Ridiculed for this defect by older boys, Jackson literally choked with rage. He could not defend himself verbally, and attacked his tormenters instead.[11] *"Freemen,"* insisted the grown Jackson, "ought to be taught to lisp from their cradles" a violent defense of their rights.

Natural goodness, in Hannah Arendt's interpretation of *Billy Budd*, is dumb. It is not sufficiently separated from nature to develop coherent speech. It shares with natural depravity, therefore, resort to violence. Frontier conflict, in Jackson's language and Crockett's observation, also seems to connect nature, violence, and difficulties with speech.[12] Closeness to nature, however, is not a simple cause of human violence. Human relations derive from human cultures, from the intimate relations among men. Parents transmit ways of being to their children, on the frontier as in developed societies. Clan conflict and nature itself had their impact on Protestant frontier culture, to which this chapter and the one following will return. To understand Jackson, however, we must examine unique personal history as well as shared cultural characteristics. Jackson's personal history exaggerated tensions present in the southwest and in American society more generally. Resolving his personal tensions, Jackson raised himself above the ordinary. Showing his society it could triumph over the difficulties it faced, he achieved heroic stature. He made himself, in Emerson's phrase, a "representative man."

The boy Andrew grew up in a society characterized by fighting, boasting, and short tempers. He was remembered, an early biographer wrote, as "self-willed, somewhat overbearing, easily offended, *very* irascible, and upon the whole 'difficult to get along with.'" Mothers, in Jackson's phrase, teach infants to "lisp from their cradles," and the reminiscences of Jackson and those who knew him derived his violence from his mother. If the "half-alligator" backwoodsman was insufficiently separated from nature, Jackson himself had to struggle against a powerful maternal bond. Captain Vere's words, "so fatherly in tone," had made Billy's stammer worse and caused him to strike Claggart. Jackson's relationship to his mother may well have precipitated his slobbering and his violence.[13]

Sarah Childress Polk, wife of Jackson's protégé James Knox Polk, once speculated on the sources of Jackson's temper. That Jackson was a "fighting man," she thought, was not altogether his own fault.

> A favorite figure in all history is the "Spartan mother." Such was Aunt Betty Jackson, who brought forth the General. He used to relate to his intimate friends that when he was not more than five years old, Aunt Betty saw him crying one day. "Stop that Andrew," she commanded. "Don't let me see you cry again! Girls were made to cry, not boys!"
>
> "Well, then, mother, what are boys made for?"
>
> "To fight!" she told him.[14]

Mrs. Polk was an old woman when she shared this memory, but other evidence also suggests that Jackson associated his mother with his violent self-reliance. Jackson often quoted his mother's last words to him, in more than one version, and not all reports are equally reliable. There are two basic variants, those which Jackson wrote or authorized, and those which he did not see in print. Consider the latter first:

I have nothing to give you but a mother's advice. Never tell a lie, nor take what is not your own, nor sue anybody for slander or assault and battery. Always *settle them cases yourself!*[15]

Jackson's own version omits the maternal injunction to fight, only to have it return in a disguised form:

One of the last injunctions given me by her, was never to institute a suit for assault and battery, or for defamation; never to wound the feelings of others, nor suffer my own to be outraged; these were her words of admonition to me; I remember them well, and have never failed to respect them; my settled course throughout life has been, to bear them in mind and never to insult or wantonly to assail the feelings of any one; and yet many conceive me to be a most ferocious animal, insensitive to moral duty, and regardless of the laws both of God and man.[16]

His mother's words, Jackson insists in this variant, will refute those who find him "a most ferocious animal." Is Jackson's "ferocious animal" a return of the repressed content of his mother's last words? What have ferocious animals to do with the mother-child bond?

The infant at his mother's breast, psychoanalytic theory suggests, experiences pain and rage as well as bliss. He suffers from the mysterious pains of infancy, like teething; attributing omniscience to his mother, he assumes, in Erikson's words, "that she should have prevented the table from hitting him, or at any rate from being hard and sharp; or that she should be able to hold him firmly and to let him go freely at the same time." Prolonged dependence fills the baby with fear of loss; he responds to pain and separation with vengeful fantasies. The infant attacks the breast in these fantasies, and devours the mother's bodily contents. Devouring rages express anxiety over separation from the mother, and longings to return to a blissful "dual-unity" state in which child and mother are one. Vengeful fantasies blame the all-powerful mother for the pains and separations of infancy. The child also blames his own anger for driving his mother away, and he cannot tolerate the imagined retaliation. He fantasizes a bad mother alongside the good, and creates ferocious monsters upon whom he projects his own infantile rage.

Gradually the child learns that pain will go away and mother will return. He integrates images of the good and bad mother into a single person, separate and distinct from himself. He learns that his own anger is not world-destroying; he can make reparation for his rage, restoring his mother and his inner feelings of self-love. The child applies these lessons to other significant objects in his environment. He learns that he need not incorporate and control everything he desires to prevent it from going away; he has overcome separation anxiety.[17]

Feelings of loss and vengeful resentment never disappear, however. In Robert Lifton's words, "the imagery of helplessness and abandonment experienced by the very young child when separated from its mother can be unconsciously revived with every subsequent act of individuation."[18] All children experience separation anxiety and primitive rage; these feelings can be mobilized in all adults. Shocks in adolescent or adult relations can throw a person back into the grip of early fears. Those with early tensions in the maternal tie, later traumas, or culturally created anxieties about nurturing relationships are particularly sensitive to primitive feelings of anger and loss. Aggression is often the servant of desire, instrumental to attain a love object. But a man in the grip of primitive rage wants vengeance for wounds to the core of the self. Sources of rage deriving from separation anxiety are intense, fantasy-ridden, and ego-destructive. They devour the self, and express fears of being devoured. The self experiences primitive rages as ego- and world-destroying; such rages are often called maddened. They characterized Jackson, and he gained his mature political power from his ability to sublimate them.

We have, of course, no clinical evidence to root Jackson's rages in early childhood experience. Certain facts are suggestive, however. Jackson was a posthumous child; did his father's death affect his mother during his infancy? Problems in infancy, involving feeding, weaning, or holding the child, often intensify infantile rage and accentuate later difficulties in the struggle of the child to break securely free of the mother. Jackson's slobbering suggests early problems with speech, mouth, and aggression. Speech difficulties often indicate a problematic oral relationship. Jackson wrote repetitive, incoherent, vengeful letters as an adult, and often expressed himself in metaphors of devouring violence.

Disturbances in the parasympathetic nervous system, like slobbering, commonly derive from tensions in the early maternal tie. Jackson was plagued throughout his life with other disturbances of the parasympathetic system. He suffered recurrently from dysentery and constipation. He had a bad chronic cough, and worried that spitting up phlegm drained his body of a valuable substance. His illnesses may not have been psychosomatic at all. Nevertheless, combined with recurrent fevers, rheumatism, and hemorrhaging, they contributed, in the words of one doctor, to Jackson's "frantic bellicosity." Rage against and triumph over his body, as we shall see, fed Jackson's public performance.[19]

Finally, Jackson had moods of manic omnipotence, paranoid rage, and occasional deep depression. Such moods are common in personalities which remain dominated by the early maternal relationship. They reach back into childhood feelings of dual-unity with the mother, in which the child seems sometimes in command of the whole world and sometimes to have lost it entirely. Adults in manic or paranoid states confuse wish with reality. They have an insecure sense of where ego leaves off and world begins. Their insecure ego boundaries promote fantasies of invasion on the one hand, omnipotent control on the other.

Jackson had such fantasies, but they rarely overwhelmed his sense of self; they did not drive him mad. He successfully externalized inner enemies, and battled them in the world. His triumphs resonated widely in a society which combined fears of invasion with assertive, successful expansion. Liberal culture undermined traditional, bounded senses of self; it promoted, amid shifting roles and boundaries, what Quentin Anderson calls "the imperial self."[20] The imperial self draws identity from incorporation, possession, and power. Describing "the paranoid style in American politics," Richard Hofstadter writes, "The difficulty many Americans have in understanding that their power in the world is not unlimited—a difficulty shared by no other people—was created by a long history that encouraged our belief that we have an almost magical capacity to have our way in the world."[21] Madmen fantasize omnipotence. The American hero had the power to make dreams come true—"ride upon a streak of lightning, . . . and eat any man opposed to Jackson."[22]

Infant separation anxiety did not overwhelm young Andrew. Rather he emerged aggressively self-assertive into childhood, and continued to fight his battle for independence. Elizabeth Jackson seems to have been a powerful woman who dominated her fatherless family. She insisted that her youngest son fight and take care of himself. Manifestly she pushed him to masculine independence, but she may actually have impeded his struggle to break free. To be independent meant not to act for himself or to follow masculine models, but to obey his mother's orders. A man was supposed to protect the honor of helpless women; it must have been hard to cast Elizabeth Jackson in that role. Did her influence leave her son in doubt about whether his manhood was securely achieved?

Our picture of Elizabeth Jackson is refracted through her son's eyes. All children long at times for protection, and Elizabeth Jackson may well have supplied it. The adult Jackson could not experience "helplessness and abandonment," however; in his memory such feelings caused maternal rejection. His mother's last remembered push to independence came when she left her sick son to care for his cousins. A child prematurely denied maternal protection may seek it all his life. Alternatively, he may develop an assertive self, mistrustful of dependence and suspicious of the world. Jackson took the second path. His childhood and adolescence, I believe, produced buried rage against his mother for at once dominating him, abandoning him, and denying him nurture.

American culture idealized mothers; it was not permissible to express anger against them. Jackson imported into rage at men who oppressed women forbidden anger which actually derived from the maternal bond. He would, in the language of his attack on the Choctaw Indian agent, "cutt up by the roots" the *"lawless tyranny exercised over a helpless and unprotected female."* Since his anger went back beyond masculine rivalry, however, it could not find satisfaction in contests with ordinary men. Indians were different. They "butchered" women, and left "the cradle stained with the blood of innocence." "Wild sons of the forest," Indians carried out forbidden infantile assaults against the mother and the baby at the breast. As Jackson put it, "When we figure to ourselves our beloved wives and little, prattling infants, butchered, mangled, murdered, and torn to pieces by savage bloodhounds and wallowing in their gore, you can judge of our feelings." Identifying with Indian "cannibals" and triumphing over them, Jackson integrated primitive violence into mature political authority.[23]

A fatherless boy may fear both maternal domination and the forbidden fulfillment of dangerous nurturing and sensual desires. He may fantasize losing bodily control to sensual, dominating women. This terror had cultural roots in America; it characterized, as we have seen, revolutionary thought. Jackson's mature politics idealized and defended women while raging against institutions which dominated and devoured men.

Normally a child loosens his tie to his mother as he develops trust in stable, satisfying object relations in the world. Conversely, he transfers early mistrust from family to world; apparent self-reliance may reflect not emancipation from the mother, but internalization of her. "The general state of trust," Erikson writes,

> implies not only that one has learned to rely on the sameness and continuity of the outer providers, but also that one may trust oneself and the capacity of one's own organs to cope with urges; and that one is able to consider oneself trustworthy enough so that the providers will not need to be on guard lest they be nipped.[24]

Basic trust develops from the oral relationship; the infant gains confidence in the world through being fed and touched by his mother, and experiencing her available presence.

> But even under the most favorable circumstances, this stage seems to introduce into psychic life (and become prototypical for) a sense of inner division and universal nostalgia for a paradise forfeited. It is against this powerful combination of a sense of having been deprived, of having been divided, and of having been abandoned that basic trust must maintain itself throughout life.[25]

Jackson does not appear to have taken confident feelings of trust from the oral stage. He expressed "a sense of inner division and . . . nostalgia" in his public life. His adult inner world was intrigue- and conspiracy-ridden. Advising self-reliance to Richard Call in the letter quoted above, Jackson continued,

> Long experience has made me well acquainted with human nature. . . . You will find many, professedly, friends, who by, and from their openness of conduct, and specious professions, the inexperienced youth, at once places the utmost reliece [reliance]—when in many Instances these professions are made with a view to obtain your confidence that it may be betrayed. . . . guard against such impositions.[26]

One friend's betrayal, Jackson complained, "displays another viper I have cherished in my bosom." Warnings against the "snares [that] will be laid for the inexperienced youth to draw him into dissipation, vice, and folly" filled his avuncular letters to wards and nephews, his reproaches to erstwhile friends, and his laments to family intimates. He warned his ward Andrew Jackson Donelson

> against that vile hypocricy, and deceipt, that often lurks beneath a fair exterior which is cloathed with power. and my young friend let me now tell you, that in our republican Government—(where it ought not to exist, and nothing but integrity and virtue in our officers be found) you will find, hypocrisy, duplicity, and the lowest kind of intrigue. . . .[27]

Jackson's suspiciousness was not the product of his unique childhood alone. It found confirmation in the social experience he shared with other Americans. Clan conflict on the Tennessee frontier reinforced Jackson's mistrust of the world. So did intrigue, acquisitiveness, and social mobility in American society as a whole. There was a growing loss of trust in the environment, and in the motives of the men one had to deal with there. This suspiciousness was deeply personal in Jackson; personal experience fitted him to embody generalized American fears.

Jackson was not simply the innocent victim of social intrigue. Like his compatriots, he participated in the contentious existence he deplored. Projecting "dissipation, vice, and folly" onto others, Jackson took up the task of purifying the republic.

Personal history made Jackson mistrust dependent relations; he imagined domination and submission only, not mutuality. He wrote Andrew Jackson Donelson,

> Independance of mind and action, is the noblest attribute of man. he that possesses it, and practices upon it, may be said to possess the real curage of his creator. without it, man becomes the real tool in the hands of others,

and is wielded, like a mere attamaton, sometimes, without knowing it, to the worst of purposes.[28]

Family ties provided the major social bonds of the eighteenth century, standing in the path of equality and "independance." These ties did not disappear in Jacksonian America, but they withdrew from center stage. In a society "born equal" (Tocqueville), lacking feudalism and the deeply rooted, aristocratic patriarchy, family could not stand against mobility and market capitalism. Jackson's childhood prefigured, in traumatic form, the social changes of Jacksonian society.

Social developments in nineteenth-century America removed the father from the home and the family from the center of society. Mothers played a greater role in raising their children. Fathers did not lose authority to mothers in the world, and their word was still law at home. But fathers were often away, particularly in the urban middle-class homes where mothers read the new child-rearing literature. New opportunities in trade, business, or the west thrust sons into environments where the fathers' skills were less relevant. As fathers lost the ability to teach work, mothers were to inculcate a state of mind. With the growing disjunction between family on the one hand, work and worldly relations on the other, greater attention was lavished on the conjugal family and the sentimental tie between mother and child. The child-rearing literature substituted maternal love for paternal discipline. Separated from work and worldly intrigue, the home became in Jacksonian America an isolated repository of virtue; mother was its symbol.[29]

Jacksonian culture glorified mothers; it also expressed fears of maternal domination. Jackson's tie to his mother acquired ambivalent force from traumatic personal experience—drooling, bowel complaints, family disruption, mother's death. Jackson expressed in intensified form ambivalence toward nurturing mothers widespread in Jacksonian society. Child-rearing volumes warned against infant gratification: "men are made monsters in life by indulgence in infancy." Children given free rein of the candy shop by their mothers would go from "those houses of pollution, *directly* to the grog shop, the gambling house or the brothel." Children, it was said, imbibed a mother's bad temper with her milk. Oral indulgence, in this language, made children dependent on their mothers and victims of pleasure. Denied easy gratification, they would learn to resist temptation and care for themselves.[30]

Jacksonian political rhetoric taught the same lessons. Isaac Hill, the New Hampshire Jacksonian, was pictured as a self-made man, not one of "those sons of fortune who have been from their very cradle nursed in the lap of luxury, who have never known what it is to grapple with adversity, who have found every wish anticipated and every want supplied almost before it was experienced." Jackson himself, as one eulogy put it, "was not dandled into consequence by lying in the cradle of state, but inured from infancy to the storms and tempests of life."[31]

Society proclaimed the special role of mothers at the very time it told them not to indulge their children. Sons should not depend on mothers, but mothers played a larger role in raising sons. Mothers must not, with their new power, weaken their sons' characters. Growing worldly temptations necessitated self-conscious attention to character-building at home. The child must be prepared for a hostile world. At the same time, much child-rearing literature emphasized the dangerous willfulness of the child. A willful son would pursue worldly gratification and find himself trapped in a stagnant, profligate existence. He could go safely into the world only once his parents had disciplined his will. The need for control implicitly contradicted the emphasis on self-reliance; the child had to be prepared by his mother for independence.[32]

In words which recall Elizabeth Jackson's, Sam Houston's mother told her son, "While the door of my cabin is open to brave men, it is eternally shut against cowards."[33] Mrs. Houston and Mrs. Jackson made men of their sons; but they were hardly the models for the new child-rearing literature. Its concerns postdated Jackson's childhood. Books and magazines pictured soft, delicate, maternal qualities foreign to the "Spartan" Elizabeth Jackson. Genteel urban mothers trained their sons for self-advancement in business or the professions, not for physical combat. The frontier symbolically perpetuated heroic patterns, however; these met needs in settled society. Jackson's life had appeal precisely because it partially fitted the new patterns and was partially disjunctive from them. Jackson always praised his mother's influence. Reverence had not, however, inhibited his martial independence. Jackson's life gratified a softer generation living prosaic lives. Sons, his childhood seemed to promise, could emancipate themselves from powerful maternal bonds.

The extended family had guided maturing children into the adult working world; by the Jacksonian period it was losing this role. Childhood merged gradually with youth in colonial America. Children were dressed like adults, and stepped easily into performing adult tasks; no extended, disjunctive adolescence intervened between childhood and maturity. Biography and autobiography ignored childhood, except insofar as it revealed embryonic traits of the adult. Beginning early in the nineteenth century, childhood replaced family antecedents as the introduction to a subject's life. The two earliest biographies of Jackson, published in 1817 and 1820, exemplify this change, as does William Wirt's *Sketches of the Life and Character of Patrick Henry* (1817), published under the shadow of Jack-

son's early triumphs. Works like these celebrated childhood and the natural man over birth, breeding, and family connection.[34]

Jackson's history prefigured declining family support not as gradual
social change but as intense personal trauma. His independence exploded
from mother and brothers dead in adolescence, and from the shattering of
extended family ties. He experienced a radical break between childhood
and adolescence not from prevailing social norms but from revolutionary
upheaval. Jackson's adolescent losses reinforced his independence, his mistrust of the world, and his vengeful self-reliance.

Were Jackson's brothers among, or unconsciously associated with,
the older boys who had teased him as a young child? Fraternal rivalry is,
specific incidents aside, normal in any family; it is not normally truncated
by the death of one's brothers. Jackson's brothers died, moreover, during
his puberty, a time of reawakening sexual desire. It must have been an imposing moment to have his mother to himself.

New sexual feelings may bewilder and overwhelm an adolescent; he
longs for an earlier time of innocent childhood protection, or for freedom
from imprisoning physical longings. A world of adult identities before
him, the adolescent may also both desire the maternal security of childhood
and resent its regressive appeal.[35]

Jackson's mother, as he remembered her, had always discouraged dependence. Briefly now she nursed him; then she left him forever. Did her
desertion and death help teach Jackson it was dangerous to become dependent on anyone? Certainly he had difficulty sustaining close relationships without fear of betrayal. To lose a mother during puberty, moreover,
may promote belief in the destructive effects of one's desires. The son may
identify love and death in his mind. He may interpret his loss to signify
that libido is dangerous and destructive and will drive the loved object
away. Mother's death may reactivate separation anxiety and undermine
basic trust in the world.

A mourner, wrote Freud, reproaches himself for the aggressive feelings
which have, in fantasy, caused his parent's death. He rages against the
deceased for deserting him; setting her up inside his ego, he seeks at once
to preserve her within him, and to direct against the self reproaches not
permissible against the dead. Gradually the son relinquishes to the reality
principle his claims on the dead parent; he emerges from melancholia.[36]

Far from renouncing pleasure after his mother's death, Jackson
plunged into a profligate life. He squandered the inheritance left by an
Irish grandfather on horse-racing, cockfighting, and good living among
the young gentry of Charles Town, South Carolina.[37] This behavior may
seem far removed from Freud's classic pattern; it is not. As Jackson remembered it, while still ill with a fever which had brought him close to

death, his mother told him he had to rely on himself. Then she left him and died. He boasted of her push to independence; did he suppress underlying feelings of abandonment and grief? Did he gamble in self-destructive expiation, in the city where his mother had died, acting out reproaches over her death?

One of Jackson's memories suggests this possibility. He attributed his desire to fight, at the outset of the 1812 War, to his experiences during the Revolution. "Brought up under the tyrany of Britain," he wrote, "altho young embarked in the struggle for our liberties, in which I lost every thing that was dear to me, *my brothers and my fortune.* . . ."[38] Jackson's memory replaced his mother by the fortune he himself had squandered. He forgot his mother's death and, confusing her loss with that of his inheritance, by blaming the British for the one, he blamed himself unconsciously for the other.

Jackson destroyed with his inheritance his last remaining family tie. Family had betrayed him; he would begin a new life totally alone. As an early admirer summarized Jackson's revolutionary experience, "The attachment to *home,* which may be said to constitute a part of our nature, must have been alienated from the bosom of Jackson." Jackson left Charles Town penniless; he returned briefly to the Waxhaws, and then left his boyhood home for good. He went to read law in the frontier town of Salisbury, North Carolina.[39]

Jackson's Charles Town adventures imitated the upper-class southern life-style. "Andrew Jackson was the most roaring, rollicking, game-cocking, horse-racing, card-playing, mischievous fellow that ever lived in Salisbury," an old resident remembered. One of his pranks went beyond contemporary standards of propriety, and suggests elements of sexual anger in Jackson's sporting adolescent life. Jackson had gone to "the gambling house"; now he went to "the brothel." He invited the only two white prostitutes in town, a mother and daughter, to the annual society ball. Those in attendance were shocked; Jackson apologized to the respectable ladies, and asked his guests to leave.[40]

Jackson was admitted to the North Carolina bar in 1787. After desultory efforts to practice near Salisbury, he determined to go farther west. John McNairy, a wealthy friend with influential connections, was appointed Judge of the Western District of North Carolina. This region, soon to become west Tennessee, was the farthest settled outpost of the American frontier. McNairy took Jackson with him to fill the unsalaried post of prosecuting attorney. Jackson argued some cases in east Tennessee, and challenged an opposing lawyer to a duel. In the autumn of 1788 he purchased a Negro girl and took her with him across the Cumberland Mountains to Nashville. He was twenty-one years old.[41]

II

A self-made man, in the cultural stereotype, not only matured without maternal indulgence; he also did not depend on paternal aid. He was free of the weight of the paternal inheritance. Men knew their fathers in traditional society, R. W. B. Lewis writes. The heroes of ante-bellum American letters were orphans, alone in space, who created themselves. Jackson, a posthumous child, was the perfect representation of the new American.[42]

Fathers played, however, an intimate and obsessive role in Jackson's imagination and in Jacksonian culture as well. Jackson threatened, in his attack on the Choctaw agent, "to cutt up by the roots the invader of his Solem rights." He promised to defend "*rights* secured to us by the blood of our fathers and which we will never yield but with our lives." Filial cowardice, in Jackson's language, must neither betray the deaths of admired fathers nor permit a "petty tyrant" to establish his authority. When Jackson appealed to the "blood of our fathers," he spoke metaphorically. His own father had died before the Revolution and secured no rights for him. The Jackson who came to Nashville was, like Lewis' orphans, searching for a legitimate father.

Imaginary fathers may exert a more powerful influence over sons than real ones. Absent from the child's experience, a missing father is bigger than life, and split into heroic and villainous parts. "The normal impact of reality on this fantasy object," Annie Reich writes of one case, "to reduce to normal size the figure of the father that was seen in such supernatural dimensions, was absent." Maternal approval does not suffice in a male-dominated society. The child may long for the approbation of a man who symbolizes the absent father. The imagined father may, in childish fantasy, rescue the son from the dangers of maternal domination. Because children inevitably feel wronged and neglected, they often substitute mythical or famous heroes for their own fathers; an orphan may be particularly likely to do so. His idealized hero is a model; but the image, presenting an ego ideal impossible of attainment, may oppress the child. "Intangibly good fathers are the worst," says Erikson.[43]

What right, moreover, does the son have to enjoy benefits which belong to the dead father, or claim rights the father did not secure for him? Here the bad father enters the imagination, to punish the child for forbidden wishes. Parental images embody fears of punishment for all children, but a fatherless boy may experience these fears with particular severity. The sense of dangerous restrictive power may well be greater than where an actual father is present. The child may fantasize a dangerous triumph of forbidden impulses; projecting these outward, he transforms them into imminent retaliation. The strength of the impulses—and Jackson's were powerful indeed—feeds the strength of the terror. A child anticipates punishment for aggressive wishes as well as desires, and the death of Jackson's mother and brothers may well have confirmed fears of paternal wrath. The bad father, filled with the child's own projections, is a monster who must be killed.

Missing is an actual father, combining restraint with love, presenting an ego ideal the child can concretely experience and learn from. Unembodied in an actual father, the superego appears as generalized rage. It fails to offer a specific sense of agency, competence, and limits, specific targets for anger, and specific models to emulate. Lacking a secure birthright inherited from the father, the son has more difficulty sustaining adult independence. He cannot draw strength from the paternal inheritance, and must demonstrate his authority alone. When enemies challenged Jackson's reputation, they spoke the language of his inner accusers.

Fantasized fathers do not dominate all fatherless boys. American cultural patterns, however, promoted mistrust of paternal pretenders, and made the search for legitimate paternity a widely shared one. Colonial experience, revolutionary thought, and nineteenth-century social changes all called fatherhood into question. Paranoid images of paternal oppression in revolutionary thought derived in part from the absence of integrated political fatherhood in the new world. Colonial society liberated desires, but revolutionaries blamed colonial passions on the royal presence. They eliminated the king and opened society all the more. Revolution and rising capitalism weakened the authority of the leading families; ordinary fathers also faced a world in which their households were less central. Desiring advancement and enmeshed with the market, men did not feel as free as their doctrines told them they were. It was as if the ghosts of the royal governors had entered family and society. Americans experienced a mysterious and punitive paternal authority. They turned for help not to living fathers but to the founders. They idealized the dying generation of revolutionary fathers, who had, in Jackson's words, secured rights for their children by their "bravery and blood."[44]

Substitutes replace absent fathers in traditional society, as James and Robert Crawford must have done for Jackson. But a boy may also dream of his authentic father, and American culture encouraged sons to suspect usurpers of the father's place. The Crawford clan disappeared from Jackson's life after the Revolution, and he did not in subsequent reminiscences refer to its members. Young Jackson left Carolina without family or birthright. Liberated externally, he carried with him an internal world dominated by paternal figures. His early politics and personal relations expressed powerful grievances against fathers on the one hand, and a powerful need, on the other, to live up to their ideals.

Jackson established himself, within a few years of his arrival in Nashville, as one of the leading citizens on the Cumberland frontier. His success was a tribute to his personal qualities, and to fluid frontier social conditions. It reflected as well his marriage into a leading Cumberland clan, his attachment to the wealthiest pioneer families, and his membership in the Blount faction which controlled Tennessee politics. Jackson's first clients were wealthy creditors suing men who, taking advantage of the undeveloped state of western law, refused to pay their debts. He also represented defendants and plaintiffs in suits, common in early America, for defamation of character. In 1793 alone, Jackson appeared in 206 of the 435 suits of record at Nashville.[45]

Currency was scarce on the frontier, but land was plentiful. Jackson often took his legal fees in land. Like the rest of the frontier elite, he speculated in land, and soon acquired immense holdings. He began a mercantile establishment and bought a plantation, following, as land speculator, merchant, and gentleman farmer, the traditional southern path to wealth. He built an expensive frame house on his plantation while most wealthy Tennesseeans still lived in log houses, and spent large sums on whiskey, horses, and expensive home furnishings imported from Europe. He soon acquired over 100 slaves, placing him among the largest Tennessee planters.[46]

Clan connections dominated west Tennessee politics and social life, and Jackson benefited from them. He married one of the daughters of Colonel John Donelson, founder of Nashville. Donelson, a leading frontier speculator, had lost a fortune in an ironworks speculation before moving to the Cumberland. Still, he was the wealthiest of the original settlers. Among his sons, John Donelson III became one of the richest men in Tennessee, and Stockley Donelson was a leading speculator and frontier politician in the 1780s and 1790s. Other Donelson children married into wealthy families, like the Hayses and the McLemores. (Elizabeth Donelson married a second McLemore brother when the first died.) One of Jackson's business partners, John Hutchings, was Donelson's grandson; the other, John Coffee, married a Donelson granddaughter. Jackson's political mentor, Daniel Smith, was related by marriage to the Donelsons; one daughter married a Donelson son, and a son married a Donelson granddaughter. Smith was the first Tennessee Secretary of State, and later succeeded Jackson in the U.S. Senate. (For the Donelson clan relationships, see page xv.)[47]

Smith, Jackson, and the other members of the Donelson clan belonged to the family-based Blount political faction. William Blount, leading North Carolina speculator and the first Governor of the Territory South of the Ohio, ran Tennessee politics in the 1790s. Blount appointed Jackson's brothers-in-law Stockley Donelson and Robert Hays to territorial office. Hugh L. White and John Overton, leading Blount subordinates in east and west Tennessee respectively, were brothers-in-law. Blount's half-brother Wylie Blount served as Tennessee Governor early in the nineteenth century. W. B. Lewis, John H. Eaton, and Alfred Balch, prominent Cumberland settlers and future members of the Nashville junto (which ran Jackson's first presidential campaigns), all married daughters of the wealthy landowner W. T. Lewis. W. C. C. Claiborne, member of the Blount faction and future Governor of the Louisiana Territory, also married into the Lewis family. This was the world in which Jackson moved.[48]

Jackson's marriage connections, political activities, legal practice, and gentry status re-created the extended-family personal relations of his boyhood. These relations were particularly fragile, competitive, and violence-prone, however. Jackson gained not a stable, ordered life, but one of intense conflict and endangered personal ties. His environment stimulated both a desire for personal authority and a mistrust of personal relationships. Jackson sought to demonstrate, in this milieu, his right to command obedience.

Jackson's life as a young lawyer involved him in the intimate, violent patterns of the Tennessee bar. Tennessee lawyers in the early years rode circuit together with the sitting judge. They drank, bet, ate, and often roomed together. Often the same lawyers opposed each other in a series of cases; courtroom and betting rivalries produced numerous duels. Fee payments in horses or land rather than money reinforced their shared, personal, concrete existence. So did the premium placed on courtroom forensics rather than legal expertise. Unlike eighteenth-century communal life, however, the traveling legal community was limited to professionals, and lacked stable, continuing roots in the surrounding countryside. It was vulnerable, moreover, to increased legal rationalization, and to the replacement of local land and character disputes by the concerns of large economic interests. These pressures killed the traveling bar within two decades of Jackson's appearance in Nashville. A commodity economy undermined communal relations which had emerged from the household pattern.[49]

Plantation life provided more stable personal relations than those in the itinerant bar. Governing a plantation was one way southern leaders exercised authority. Unlike liberal contractualism, slavery acknowledged personal interdependence. Southerners compared the impersonal exploitation of the northern "white hireling" to the "easy . . . company" of master and slave. Slaves were members of the planter's "family," a relationship recognized in Tennessee law; they could not be appropriated in payment of debts, for example. The south developed, by the end of the Jacksonian period, a full-blown paternal defense of slavery. C. C. Meminger wrote, "The Slave Institution of the South increases the tendency to dignify the family. Each planter in fact is a Patriarch—his position compels him to be a ruler in his household. . . . The fifth commandment becomes the foundation of Society."[50]

Familial rhetoric stressed the planter's concern for his slave family. Jackson worried in later life about mistreatment of his slaves, although he never developed the personal intimacy with slave favorites that characterized some slave-owners. Even kindly paternalism, however, required total power from the owner, total submission from the slave. There was genuine human feeling in the master-slave relationship, but the master's feelings often included pleasure in the exercise of sadistic domination. Jackson advertised in 1804 for a runaway slave carrying forged certificates of freedom. He offered a fifty-dollar reward "and ten dollars extra for every hundred lashes any person will give to the amount of three hundred."[51]

Slaves were property as well as people, and Jackson also conspicuously exercised his property-owning rights. He traded slaves in his first Tennessee decades, and wagered them on horse races. Ownership of slaves, like violence against them, placed domination at the center of southern society.[52]

Jackson gained authority as a member of the planter aristocracy; slave society generated hierarchy among whites, as well as in the relations of white over black. The master-slave relationship, however, intensified anxieties about personal liberty among whites. Liberal men, as Tocqueville saw, feared the loss of individual power in human interdependence; slavery intensified that fear. Urging war with Spain in 1820, Jackson condemned the "state of disguised vasalage" in which he found the country. "I would be free and independent or the acknowledged slave," he wrote. Men who exercised the power of masters feared that other men wanted to dominate them. Fears of slave uprisings and doubts over the legitimacy of slavery fed fears of being enslaved, and increased preoccupation with intrigue and conspiracy. Northern commercial relations forced formally equal men into instrumental interdependence; men joined together to solve common problems. These "free institutions," said Tocqueville, counteracted liberal isolation; they were largely absent in the south. The "manly independence" (Jackson) of some southerners developed from the domination of others. Liberalism wiped away traditional status relations; it left only slavery. Slavery in return offered liberal society a paternal model which did not support political authority among free men.[53]

Neither bar nor plantation provided secure authority in the southwest. Jackson also sought out duels. He issued his first challenge at the age of twenty-one, as he was leaving forever the country of his youth. Jackson had unsuccessfully sought to read law with Waightstill Avery, a leading North Carolina revolutionary and the first Attorney General of the independent state. On his way to serve as western North Carolina's first Attorney General, Jackson argued several cases in what is now east Tennessee. These cases were among the first he tried, and Avery was often his courtroom opponent. Avery, twenty-two years Jackson's senior, ridiculed his abilities. "My young friend on the other side seems to think he can make up in noise what he lacks in knowledge," the older man is reported to have said. As one biographer put it, "So far as concerned legal acumen, learning or forensic power, Jackson was a baby in his hands."[54]

Jackson responded with a duel challenge. His note reads, "My charector you have injured; and further you have Insulted me in the presence of a court and a larg audianc . . . and I hope you can do without dinner untill the business done." Jackson and Avery met on the field of honor, but friends intervened and both men fired in the air.[55]

Jackson issued several more duel challenges during his first decade in Nashville. He broke with John McNairy, who had gotten him his job, and challenged him to a duel. "My friendship," Jackson complained to McNairy, "was attached to a Jealous reed not to be Dependend on." Jackson challenged William Cocke, who was first his counterpart as Attorney General in east Tennessee and then achieved Senate election before him. He challenged Governor John Sevier, a prominent revolutionary like Avery and the most popular figure in the state. Always, however, the intervention of friends or the reticence of opponents aborted an actual duel. Jackson did not fight his first formal consummated duel until 1806. He killed his man.[56]

Dueling was common in early America. In the south, and among lawyers and military men, it enjoyed special popularity. Dueling enforced a code of honor which held men accountable for their conduct in the absence of stable, routinized standards of professional behavior. It reflected preoccupation with family, reputation, and honor under circumstances in which personal and clan loyalties were intense but fragile. Jackson, entering Tennessee as a man without a past, was particularly sensitive about his reputation. "My reputation is dearer to me than life," he wrote Cocke. "The opprobrium that has been attached to my character upon false evidence must be publickly washed away." Jackson's rush to duel was precipitate even by southwestern frontier standards. Jackson had become a lawyer, choosing a source of mobility important in early America; most lawyers were among the nation's elite. But the law was also looked on with suspicion, and there was mistrust of lawyers who used the fine points of land litigation to acquire acreage for themselves. Elizabeth Jackson shared this disdain for the law. "The law affords no remedy that can satisfy the feelings of a true man," she told her son. Yet Jackson represented clients in suits for defamation of character, the sort his mother had warned him against. All the more reason,

when his own personal honor was at stake, to "settle them cases yourself."[57]

Jackson learned as a young man to mistrust those, "professedly,
friends, who by, and from their openness of conduct, and specious professions, the inexperienced youth, at once places the utmost relience."[58]
A youth, Jackson warned, must not accept aid from seductive older men,
or bow to the threats of vengeful ones. Men illegitimately assumed paternal authority, as did the British officer who ordered Andrew to black
his boots. Young Jackson challenged fraternal rivals and demonstrated
his independence of paternal pretenders.

Late in life Jackson praised dueling as the only way to defend a
slandered reputation. The slanderer, he wrote, is worse than the murderer. "The murderer only takes the life of the parent and leaves his
character as a goodly heritage to his children, whilst the slanderer takes
away his good reputation and leaves him a living monument to his children's disgrace."[59] Inheritance from fathers to sons, Jackson feared, was
easily contaminated; children could not assume that their fathers were
without sin. Calvinism, capitalism, liberalism, and mobility shattered secure links between the generations. It was not easy to be a father; fatherhood itself was called into question. Freeing sons from fathers liberated
sons; but sons grew up and found their own paternal authority undermined. Fathers had to demonstrate they had not acquired their positions
illegitimately, or their sons would inherit their sins. Fatherhood had to
withstand the scrutiny young Jackson had visited upon it.

Mistreatment of women was the worst sort of duel-provoking of-
fense. A "petty tyrant" like the Choctaw Indian agent oppressed "helpless and unprotected female[s]." Slanders against a man's wife or sister
were often explicitly sexual, as Jackson knew from personal experience.
He had married his wife in dubious circumstances, and most of his
quarrels led inexorably to insults against her honor.

Jackson boarded at the residence of Rachel Stockley Donelson when
he arrived in Nashville. Her husband, John Donelson, had been killed
in 1785 by Indians or white outlaws, and the widow took in boarders
to protect her isolated dwelling against Indian attacks. Jackson and John
Overton shared a cabin, and became lifelong friends. Several of her
grown children also lived with Mrs. Donelson; among them was a married daughter, Rachel Robards, estranged from her husband.[60]

Historians have accepted Jackson's account of the relationship among
Rachel, Lewis Robards, and himself which Overton presented during the
1828 presidential campaign. Shortly after Jackson began living at the
Donelsons', according to Overton, Robards traveled to Nashville from
his Kentucky home and reconciled with his wife. He went back to Ken-

tucky to fetch the household belongings; returning to Nashville, he accused Jackson of paying unseemly attention to Rachel. Jackson indignantly denied the charge. Robards' jealousy had caused his wife to leave him once; Jackson now warned that if Robards ever linked Jackson's name to Rachel's, he would clip Robards' ears. Jackson left the Donelsons to protect Rachel's reputation and found quarters elsewhere.

Rachel accompanied her husband to Kentucky, but they soon quarreled again. The Donelson family, Overton explained, sent Jackson to Kentucky to bring Rachel back home. Rachel returned to Nashville; then, fearing Robards would follow her, she joined a small party of traders making the thousand-mile trip through Indian country to Natchez. The traders were unwilling to take an unescorted woman on such a dangerous journey, wrote Overton. Jackson, reproaching himself for "having innocently and unintentionally been the cause of . . . [her] loss of peace and happiness," accompanied her. He would protect her against the threat of Indian attack. Jackson left Rachel in Natchez and returned to Nashville. There he heard that the Virginia legislature had granted Robards a divorce while Kentucky was still part of that state. He went back to Natchez and married Rachel in August 1791.

The Virginia legislature, however, had not granted Robards a divorce but only, as was customary, the right to sue for one. Robards obtained the divorce in 1793; his grounds were adultery, since Jackson and Rachel had been living together for two years. The couple, learning to their dismay of Robards' suit, married again in January 1794.[61]

Jackson and Rachel suffered for thirty years from this series of events. The history of insults against them culminated in the 1828 election campaign. Charges against Rachel's virtue were a major campaign issue; one pamphlet asked, "Ought a convicted adulteress and her paramour husband to be placed in the highest offices of this free and christian land?"[62] These slanders helped bring on Rachel's death shortly after the election.

Jackson did not confine his outrage against charges of adultery to those who vilified Rachel. When Washington society ladies ostracized Margaret Eaton, wife of Jackson's Secretary of War, they broke up Jackson's first Cabinet and helped deepen the breach with Calhoun. Jackson confused Rachel with the recently widowed and remarried Mrs. Eaton, with whom his friend John Eaton had been keeping company for years. Much earlier, in 1802, Jackson demonstrated his antagonism toward husbands who accused their wives of adultery. Russell Bean, the first white man born in Tennessee, had clipped the ears of his wife's infant, claiming the child had been fathered by another man. Jackson, then a Tennessee Supreme Court Judge, took unprecedented personal charge of Bean's arrest.[63]

Jackson always insisted his relationship with Rachel was perfectly innocent before their first marriage; he did not court or marry her, Overton explained, until he thought she was divorced. There is evidence against this claim. On January 10, 1791, Robards wrote the Donelson family asking for a fair share in the division of the Donelson estate. This letter, written after Jackson had taken Rachel from Kentucky, must have been part of planned divorce proceedings. On January 28 the Donelson estate was evaluated for purposes of division, and Rachel was listed as Rachel Jackson. This was seven months before her marriage to Jackson in Natchez (of which no record has been found). Jackson and Rachel left for Natchez sometime between January 20 and April 12, 1791. Overton, explaining the trip as a flight from Robards, wrote that they left before knowing of his divorce plans. If that is the case, the use of the name Rachel Jackson is particularly striking.[64]

Marriage customs on the frontier were casual in the late eighteenth century; this was particularly true in the southwest, where formal divorces required legislative action and were hard to obtain. The newspaper reports that reached Jackson stated only that the Virginia legislature had granted Robards the right to sue for divorce. This procedure was standard, and Jackson's failure to discover it, if he was in ignorance, indicates a casual attitude toward the legal formalities of marriage.[65] Possibly Jackson and Rachel began to live together before a formal ceremony. Certainly, it is now clear, they intended to marry when they traveled together to Natchez. Jackson did not make the trip selflessly to defend Rachel against violent Indians and a vengeful husband; their journey had a later-denied sexual significance.

These facts do not make Jackson "guilty"; historians preoccupied with the actual circumstances of his marriage have oddly missed the point. They share this mistake with Jackson, who sought during his entire life to prove his innocence of various charges with depositions, affidavits, and facts. Feelings of guilt stem from desires, fulfilled or unfulfilled. Jackson's marriage, given the charges which plagued Rachel all her life, implicated the two of them in the secret sin of desire. Ultimately, retribution for desire killed Rachel; it was a lifelong lesson in the destructive effects of physical love.

Jackson led a wild life before his marriage; he was surely no innocent when he met Rachel. Southern gentry, however, radically distinguished pure women from those who were the objects of masculine sexual adventures. Rachel clearly belonged to the former class. She needed protection from a jealous, tyrannical, violent husband, and Jackson entered the lists as her defender. Protecting her from violence provided the form in which their romance developed. It permitted the repression and redirection of powerful sexual feelings. Jackson's protection of a married woman against her husband charged the triangle with Oedipal significance; but Robards, not Jackson, was guilty of selfish passion.

The false divorce reports and the subsequent history of slander deprived Jackson's victory of the purity it could otherwise have claimed. His precipitate marriage turned Jackson's triumph into a guilty one, and confused the idealized with the sexual woman. Guilty in fact or not, Jackson felt implicated in the charges against his wife; this contributed to the force of his rage against her accusers. Circumstances defeated Jackson's attempt to bring together in marriage the sexual with the ideal woman. The trauma of marriage reinforced the lessons of Elizabeth Jackson's death. Women and the world did not go together. Wife, like mother, undermined trust in secure worldly relations.

Wealth may give a man worldly well-being and replace mother-love. The money he controls substitutes for the mother who has gone away. At the same time, sadistic feelings of control over money and other possessions express buried resentment against the abandoning mother;[66] loss of wealth may seem her revenge. Jackson had confused his mother with his fortune after her death, and gambled it away. Ten years later he gambled in land; he speculated with tens of thousands of acres, taking personal notes in payment. Shortly after his remarriage to Rachel, the failure of a man whose notes he held threatened Jackson with financial disaster. Perhaps Jackson lost his first fortune to free himself of his mother after her death. Did he experience the threat to his second as punishment for his precipitate marriage?[67]

It would not be surprising had Jackson's marriage, like his mother's death, undermined the security of his attachment to women. The marriage reads, in Overton's version, like an eighteenth-century political allegory. Like a revolutionary hero, Jackson protected feminine virtue against debased masculine oppression. The journey to Natchez, with its threat of Indian attack, lent elements of chivalric adventure at a time when, art just beginning to imitate life, most Americans failed to discover the dramatic utility of native materials and were turning to medieval settings instead. A Nashville newspaper, for example, serialized a European tale of adventure several years after Jackson's marriage. The wicked father in this story sent his daughter to a convent to keep her from a poor but virtuous suitor; aided by the abbot, the lovers were finally united. Within a few years Cooper's tales transposed such stories into the American wilderness; the Jackson-Rachel romance, in Overton's version, could have been one of them.[68]

The charges against Rachel and Jackson, however, exposed the undercurrent of desire beneath the story of Indian danger, tyrannical husband, and innocent love. The courtship now seemed to fit a rather different pattern in the sentimental novel. Here the suitor, an independent, glamorous man with an unknown past, entered a respectable family. Often one parent, usually the father, had recently died. The weakened family could not protect its daughter, and the villain seduced her. Gothic versions of this pattern added a series of harrowing adventures, and shifted the center of energy from the virtuous maiden to the debased protagonist. His courtship cast Jackson as the Faustian hero of a gothic tale.[69]

Coming to Nashville without family connections or traditional ties, Jackson quickly acquired wealth and power. He was taken into a highly respected local family where the father had recently died. Accompanying a married daughter through Indian wilderness, he took her from her husband. This story came straight from the novel of seduction.[70] The Jacksonian period would glorify Jackson's self-advancement, but it had first to strip it of elements which the family-centered perspective of eighteenth-century America found sinister. Jackson's courtship, moreover, may have derived from an eighteenth-century relative sexual worldliness. Spurred locally by a Great Awakening on the frontier, this tolerance was giving way to a nineteenth-century religious emphasis on moral purity. The gothic hero stood rebelliously and illegitimately against the new morality. Eighteenth-century chivalric adventure had turned for Rachel and Jackson into gothic nightmare.

A self-image rooted in corrupt desire was hardly one Jackson could accept. The eighteenth century had combined natural virtue with family social order. The nineteenth-century natural man—Jackson was the prototype—stood against a corrupt social order.[71] But he did not stand forbidding and alone. He built with his home a defense against worldly slander and strife. The Hermitage offered an early model for the nineteenth-century sentimental, conjugal family.

III

A split had opened between family and society by the Jacksonian period. The family lost functions to other institutions—schools, workplaces, asylums, markets. Schools grew to supplement or replace informal education in the home; other social institutions—hospitals, prisons, factories, poorhouses—also carried out functions and cared for people once accommodated within the household. Goods used in the home were increasingly made or grown outside it. For increasing numbers of families, workplace was separate from home. Even for farmers, domestic fortunes depended less on work in the farm home and more on price, market, and transportation. These developments undermined not only the household economic and social order, but also the political authority of the leading families. J. R. Pole writes, "It was this which collapsed in ruins in the upheaval of Jacksonian democracy. And that, perhaps, is why the election of so ambiguous a leader was accompanied by such an amazing uproar." The extended, historically rooted family of eighteenth-century America—the Adamses—was giving way to the conjugal, sentimental family of the market epoch—Andrew and Rachel Jackson.[72]

As the family lost functions to society, it became the reserve of natural feelings. Tocqueville observed, "The natural bond is drawn closer in proportion as the social bond is loosened." Emotion was withdrawn from social ties, bolstered by extended family connections, and concentrated within the conjugal unit. So long as communal religious values, embodied in a social elite, influenced economic and political life, the external world was not consigned to the realm of immorality. By the Jacksonian period, as Barbara Welter puts it, men seemed to have turned society into a vast countinghouse; but they left behind in the home a hostage to the moral values of their forebears. Women and children around the domestic hearth now embodied morality. No intrinsic pleasure was to be found in public pursuits, and those who enjoyed them were almost surely corrupt. But to protect and enhance the home, men justified social action immoral on its own terms.

John Demos has summarized these developments:

> The family became a kind of shrine for upholding and exemplifying all the softer virtues—love, generosity, tenderness, altruism, harmony, repose. The world at large presents a much more sinister aspect. Impersonal, chaotic, unpredictable, often characterized by strife and sometimes by outright malignity, it requires of a man that he be constantly "on his guard." It goads and challenges him at every point, and occasionally provokes responses of a truly creative sort, but it also exhausts him. So it is that he must retreat periodically within the family circle, in order to rest and marshal his energies for still another round. In this instance the family is important not so much as the foundation for an ideal social order, but as the foil to an actual state of social disorder. It forms a bulwark against the outside world; destroy it, and anarchy reigns everywhere. It forms, too, a bulwark against anxieties of the deepest and most personal kind.[73]

Jackson longed from early in his career to "retreat . . . within the family circle." Here again personal experience fitted him to express pervasive social doctrine. Financial straits, he complained in 1801, forced him to remain in public life. "My real wish would be, would my circumstances permit, to retire from the busy scenes of the world, and entirely domesticate myself, but I am got a little involved and untill I extricate myself must give up that Idea." He moved to a new plantation in 1804; he named it the Hermitage, signifying withdrawal "from the stage of public life" and "return to domestic ease." But his hopes proved illusory. Two decades later, while the 1824 election was still in doubt, Jackson wrote his old friend John Coffee,

> My happiness and choice would be to return to the Hermitage, enjoy the sweets of domestic quiett, but the Lords will be done. How much your situation are to be envied and how prudent you have been to keep yourself free of political life, surrounded as you are by your lovely children, and amiable wife, you ought not to abandon it for anything on earth.
>
> Here there is a bustle continually; the man in office greeted with smiles and apparent friendship, his confidence often sought to be betrayed; surrounded thus, where a man must be always guarded, happiness cannot exist.[74]

"Surrounded" in the conjugal family, "by . . . lovely children and amicable wife," a man enjoyed "the sweets of domestic quiett." "The conjugal bed," Michel Chevalier wrote after a visit to Jacksonian America, was the single stable center in an agitated, ever changing society.

> Here all is circulation, motion and boiling agitation. Experiment follows experiment; enterprise follows enterprise. Riches and poverty follow on each other's traces and each in turn occupies the place of the other. Fortunes last for a season; reputations for the twinkling of an eye. An irresistible current sweeps everything away, grinds everything to powder and deposits it again under new forms. Men change their houses, their climate, their trade, their condition, their party, their sect; the states change their laws, their officers, their constitutions. The soil itself, or at least the houses, partake in the universal instability. One is tempted to think that such a society, formed of heterogeneous elements, brought together by chance, and following its own orbit according to the impulse of its own caprice or interest—one would think that after rising for one moment to the heavens, like a waterspout, such a society would inevitably fall flat in ruins the next; such is not, however, its destiny. Amid this general change there is one fixed point. It is the domestic fireside, or to speak more clearly, the conjugal bed.[75]

"The cult of true womanhood" in the ladies' magazines of the Jacksonian period elaborated the conjugal-family ideal. Women were required to be chaste before marriage and pure thereafter, to make the home a center of religious life, to love and morally educate their children, to submit to their husbands, and to provide in the home a refuge from the continuous bustle of the world. These ideals were addressed to genteel urban women, who no longer functioned in the work worlds of their husbands. Their situation was rather different from Rachel Jackson's. She helped manage a frontier plantation, was barely literate, smoked a pipe, and was neither fashionable nor genteel. Nevertheless, the plantation lady shared certain traits with her northern class counterpart, and Jackson's home prefigured the sentimental-family ideal. It did so, however, as troubled aspiration rather than consummated reality. The Hermitage originated in personal trauma. It served, in an intensified form, as (Demos) "a bulwark against anxieties of the deepest and most personal kind."[76]

Changes in Rachel cast the Hermitage in the sentimental-family pattern. Gay, flirtatious, and independent before her marriage, she grew pious, submissive, and domestic thereafter. This fitted the conjugal ideal. Tocqueville observed that American girls were free and forward until they married, and submissive to their husbands thereafter. But Rachel's independent relationship with the bachelor Jackson occurred after she married; it had not, so the accusations went, been innocent. A European maiden who acted like an American girl, Tocqueville wrote, would be suspected of sexual license. Innocence protected the American girl; it had not protected Rachel. Her domestic retirement had an element of expiation, and gave a melancholy cast to the Jackson conjugal family.[77]

The wife, according to the sentimental ideal, made the home a moral refuge from worldly turmoil. In the words of one writer, "The domestic fireside is the great guardian against the excesses of human passions." Rachel's marriage was contaminated from the beginning by the invasion of human passion into the home. In ladies'-magazine fiction, women were punished by madness or death for the premarital loss of their purity. "Death preferable to Loss of Innocence," one writer proclaimed.[78] Rachel suffered periodic fits of melancholy, before succumbing to a death she had long awaited.

The cult of true womanhood directed itself to wives whose husbands were often away from home. Land speculation, politics, military affairs, and Indian treaties took Jackson frequently from Rachel. He spent half his time traveling in the first years of their marriage.[79] Later he left her for long periods in Indian country and in Washington. These frequent absences from home were the major cause of Rachel's melancholy. She could not tolerate separation from him. Jackson's letters from the years following their second marriage until Rachel's death are filled with concern for her health and state of mind. In 1797 he wrote his brother-in-law Robert Hays,

> I must now beg of you to try to amuse Mrs. Jackson and prevent her from fretting. The situation in which I left her—(Bathed in Tears) fills me with

woe. Indeed Sir, It has given me more pain than any event in my life, but I trust She will not remain long in her dolefull mood, but will again be cheerfull.

In 1804 when Jackson had ended his extended absences from home and planned to retire from public life, Rachel was in good health. When the absences began again, in 1812, so did her melancholy. Learning of the death of a nephew in the Creek War, she wrote Jackson,

> My Dear pray Let me Conjur you by every Tie of Love of friend ship to Let me see you before you go againe. I have borne it untill now it has thrown me Into feavours. I am very unwell . . . how Long o Lord will I remain so unhappy. no rest no Ease I cannot sleepe. . . . you have served your Country Long Enough.[80]

Jackson left Rachel for the U.S. Senate in 1823 "more disconsolate than I ever knew her before." She remained ill during his entire absence. John Donelson wrote his son-in-law John Coffee, "Sister Jackson is making a great fuss about him for when ever she is alone she goes to crying tho he writes to her almost every week." Did Rachel feel, as punishment for their ambiguous courtship, that she would lose him?[81]

The cult of true womanhood provided women with childbearing functions to occupy them during their husbands' absences. Rachel, to her sorrow, bore no babies of her own. Nevertheless, the Hermitage was filled with children. She and Jackson raised a dozen, mostly sons of Rachel's deceased relatives. They adopted one nephew in infancy, naming him Andrew Jackson, Jr. Andrew Jackson Donelson and Andrew Jackson Hutchings, a nephew and a great-nephew, entered the Jackson family as children and were raised as sons.[82]

Men were not expected to attend church regularly. Women had to make the home, in the conjugal ideal, a center of religious values. Jackson belonged to no church while Rachel was alive, but she sought consolation in religion. Occasionally her piety brought her into the world. Accompanying Jackson to Florida, for example, she forced the Sunday closing of all Pensacola stores and amusement places. A letter to Nashville described the scene:

> The Sabbath profanely kept; a great deal of noise and swearing in the streets; shops kept open; trade going on, I think, more than on any other day. They were so boisterous on that day I sent Major Stanton to say to them that the approaching Sunday would be differently kept. . . . Yesterday I had the happiness of witnessing the truth of what I had said.[83]

For the most part, however, Rachel's religion was inward, private, intensely otherworldly, and preoccupied with death. She did not want Jackson to run for President, and told a friend, "I assure you I had rather be a doorkeeper in the house of God than to live in that palace at Washington." She was said to have repeated these words on her deathbed. Women too pure for the world commonly died in ladies'-magazine fiction. Jackson buried Rachel shortly before leaving Nashville for his first inauguration.[84]

Rachel and Jackson, in letters exchanged while they were apart, beautifully expressed the love between them. It was, however, a love tied to death. Death was the ultimate refuge from worldly cares and separations. It offered happiness "clear of the bustle of this world," as John Coffee wrote his wife on the death of her brother. Worried over Rachel's melancholy as his presidential aspirations took him from the Hermitage, Jackson wrote Overton, "I have no doubt but that providence will protect her and myself as well absent and present, we are travelling our journey through life, when our time is fullfilled below we will *rest*. . . ." Only death, Rachel wrote Jackson, could permanently unite husband and wife. In her words of 1813, this is beautifully conveyed:

> my blessed redeemer is making intersession with the father for us to meet again restore you to my bosom what Every vein Every pulse beats high for your helth your safety all your wishes Crownd, Do not My beloved Husband let the love of Country fame honour make you forget you have me Without you I would think them all empty shadows You will say this is not the Language of a patriot but it is the language of a faithfull Wife . . . My time passes heavily not in good health but I hope to see you once more on this globe & after this frail life Ends be with you in happyer Climes where I shall Experience no more painfull separation & then I'll be at rest. . . . our little Andrew is well the most affectionate little Darling on Earth often does he ask me in bed not to cry. Sweet pappa will Come home to you again. . . . I wish I was with you, vain wish praying Dear write to me often its a cordial balm to my mind lonesome hours I treasure them up as miser does his gold.[85]

Life, Rachel believed, brought separation and loss; only death offered permanent union. These sentiments were not unique to Rachel. Just as the adventure serialized in the 1801 Nashville newspaper exemplified Jackson's courtship, so the poems printed ten years later characterized his marriage. In the earlier decade the paper had published poems glorifying simple rural life, on the eighteenth-century pattern. Ten years later these verses, like the gothic adventure serial, had disappeared. They were replaced by a number of sentimental, morbid poems glorifying death. In "The Dead Twins," for example, the poet describes

> . . . a sight which made me grieve
> And yet the sight was fair.
> Within a little coffin lay
> Two lifeless babes, as sweet as May.
>
> Like waxen dolls, that infants dress,
> Their little babies were;
> A look of placid happiness,
> Did on each cheek appear, . . .
> Their mother, as a lily pale,
> Sat by them on a bed—
> And bending o'er them told her tale
> And many a tear she shed:
> Yet oft she cried amidst her pain,
> My babes and I shall meet again![86]

The similarities between this poem and Rachel's letter to Jackson a year later are striking. By 1821 the morbid verses had disappeared from the Nashville paper, replaced by glorifications of women closer to conventional Jacksonian images of the plantation lady and the genteel woman.[87] Jackson's marriage, like "The Dead Twins," suggests the sentimental family had roots in traumatic disengagement from the world, in the breakup of sustaining worldly connections, and in the association of family serenity with death.

The isolated southwestern frontier in the early decades of the nineteenth century had a particular fascination with violence, death, and "graveyard poetry." Images of catastrophe were not restricted to the southwest, however, and seemed to strike chords across America.[88] If Rachel expressed frontier religious values, her own personal history also contributed to her morbidity. In addition, the sentimental family provided a receptive structure for idealizations of the home resembling wishes for death.

The split between conjugal family and society suggests a bifurcation of the feelings associated with death and aggression rather than with libidinal ties. Aggression was directed outward in the service of militantly competitive social relations. Propelled by the desire to advance family interests, men struggled in the world to achieve final peace. As Tocqueville observed, "At every moment they think they are about to grasp it; it escapes at every moment from their hold. They are near enough to see its charms, but too far off to enjoy them; and before they have fully tasted its delights, they die."[89]

Men fled to the crowd, Tocqueville believed, to escape pressures on their lonely, competitive egos; they fled to the home as well.[90] If serenity was always beyond reach in the world, the home provided refuge from conflict and aggression. Separated from the world, the home was the locus of regressive fantasies; entwined with social life, it could not so easily serve that function. Idealizations of the home were all the more powerful since one's own ambition and desire for independence took one away. In theory, men combined life in the world with rest at home; Jackson and Rachel could not sustain this balance, and their failure was symptomatic. In the words of a European traveler, "Domestic ties, the affections of home and hearth, are powerless over the immense majority. Action carries them away, and they change with wonderful facility spots, abodes, regions, and states." Nostalgia and idealization grow in proportion to the self-inflicted injuries they must obscure. Ante-bellum painting too, Lilian Miller concludes, pictured only idealized women and idyllic communities, as if to shut out the chaos underneath.[91] And the removal of Indians from their homes characterized the Age of Jackson.

Idealization of wife and mother also expressed hidden violence against her. Husbands set up in the home, as wife to minister to their needs, the mother they had left to enter the world. But their desire for nurturing endangered the very independence which had called it forth. Indeed, the sentimental family activated fears of domination by women. Some women, it was said, were happy only when they could nurse their sick husbands, "thus gratifying their medical vanity and their love of power by making him more dependent upon them."[92]

Men met the danger of infantile regression by infantilizing their wives instead. The sentimental ideal insisted on feminine submission. Wives were to submit, as Rachel did, to their husbands' will, to reverses in family fortune, and to worldly masculine ambitions. Jackson was surely the patriarch at home. Once a wife began to "feel and act for herself," a writer explained, "the golden bowl of affection is broken."[93] Perhaps the requirement of feminine dependence was revenge against the early power of mothers over children and the experience of separation anxiety. Perhaps Jackson created a dependent wife to replace his independent and powerful mother. American culture failed to provide a "second womb" symbolically to reproduce maternal care in a manner suitable for adults. Perhaps American men revenged themselves against their women for this absence; wives must depend on husbands, as Rachel required Jackson.[94]

Men governed the conjugal family, but they did not relinquish their demands for support. A man buffeted in the world was at least king in his own castle. Threatened by unstable social relations, he re-established authority at home; there he gained the succor fitting him to return to battle. As Tocqueville described the pioneer, "Even his feelings for his family have become merged in a vast egotism, and one cannot be sure whether he regards his wife and children as anything more than a detached part of himself." Conversely, should women leave the home and seek social power, they would deprive their husbands of the security of "the conjugal bed." In the years following the adoption of the Constitution, state after state deprived women of their political rights. With the rise of the professions in the early nineteenth century, men took over tasks women had often informally performed. If women sought a political voice, one ladies' writer predicted in an image suggesting madness, "society shall break up and become a chaos of disjointed and unsightly elements."[95]

Women sacrificed worldly lust and power for spiritual purity; they governed "an empire of softness." The spiritual ideal deprived women of their bodies. They could no more make sexual demands on their husbands than they could demand power at home or in the world. Here too masculine idealization masked aggression against women. The sexual, potent woman, Géza Róheim writes, reminds men of infant dependence and pain. *"From this point of view the double standard or the ideal of chastity is the infant's revenge for oral frustration."* American ideals infantilized women. Did Americans fear a return of the repressed, a persecutory bad mother who would take revenge for being deserted by her children at independence, and for being infantilized by her husband in the home? The medical belief that pregnant women were mentally unstable suggests such fears, as does the story in two popular books on women's physiology of a pregnant wife who killed her husband and ate him. Fears of devouring women reversed the actual situation: they were fears of what women would do if they got free. Jacksonian symbolism, particularly in the Bank War, suggests the hold of devouring, imprisoning maternity on the American political imagination.[96]

The sentimental ideal of women, then, expressed terror of feminine physical authority. It longed for the serenity of infantile bliss—that "universal nostalgia for a paradise forfeited" (Erikson). It revenged itself against the all-powerful mother imagined in infant frustration. The conjugal ideal contained forbidden temptation permanently (Demos) to "retreat . . . within the family circle." Both in what it feared and what it desired, it threatened to destroy the individuated ego.

A final twist completed the diabolical interlock of home and society. Women were not to enter the world, but the demands of wife and children required men to return to its battles. Women wanted worldly goods and children required a start in life. Family drove the husband into the world; it did not protect him from it. Men desiring refuge from "the human passions" felt trapped by the home. There was a tradition of escape, in literature and in life, to the freedom of Indian existence. Sam Houston left his home twice to live among Indians, once in adolescence and a second time just after he married. It fell to Jackson to demonstrate that a family man could be a free man too.[97]

IV

Jackson entered politics in the pursuit of private interests, to which the next chapter will turn. The political realm was more than a marketplace, however. Jackson cast his early political involvement in familial terms; his politics was a struggle not simply for goods but for authority.

The Blount faction supported ratification of the federal Constitution; a strong national government would increase the value of land speculations and protect the frontier against Indian attacks. Washington appointed Blount Governor of the Territory South of the Ohio in 1790, and Blount chose Jackson as Attorney General for the Cumberland district. In 1793, along with the other leading men on the southwestern frontier, Blount joined the Republicans. Jackson followed him, and rapidly gained a prominent position in Tennessee politics. He was elected to the Tennessee constitutional convention in 1796, was chosen the new state's first Congressman, and then served briefly in the Senate. In 1798 he returned to Nashville as a Judge of the Tennessee Superior Court.[98]

Jackson stood in Tennessee with the established forces of law and social order. He represented creditors against debtors, benefited from Blount's sponsorship and Rachel's family connections, and belonged to the slave-owning, land-speculating gentry. He stood high among the second generation of Tennessee leaders. He lacked, however, the stature of a man like James Robertson, whom Blount called "the political father" of "this infant country." Jackson longed to match the achievements of Robertson and the other Tennessee founders. His efforts would bring him, by the end of the century, into conflict with some of them. First, however, Jackson joined Blount, Robertson, and Sevier in challenging Federalist power. The frontier gentry sought to displace the leading national families who governed "the American nation yet in its infancy." Jackson embraced this rebellious role. He defended the purity of "the infant republick" against aggrandizing, constricting Federalist designs. A politician, he believed, "must be a *Republican, and in politics like Caesar's wife,* not only chaste but unsuspected." Jackson accused the Federalists of imitating George III and using executive power to corrupt republican virtue. He attacked John Adams' efforts to "strengthen the executive patronage." It aided the Tories, and was an "insolent attack [on] those who fought the battles" of the Revolutionary War. Adams, he believed, had formed a plan "to remove from office every man who professes republican principles, and fill those offices with men who will bend to the nod of the Executive. . . . This is sweet reward for seven years servitude to obtain freedom."[99]

Jackson supported Jefferson for President, but insisted he would become the tool of no man. He hoped to be appointed Governor of Louisiana Territory, but would not pay "the call of a courteor" on Jefferson. "Of all charecters on earth," he wrote, "my feelings despises a man capable of cringing to power for a benefit or office."[100]

"Aristocratic neebobs" denied frontiersmen what was theirs "by nature"—western lands, protection against the Indians, and free navigation of the Mississippi. Jackson called for the impeachment of Washington in 1795, when Jay's treaty seemed to sacrifice the Mississippi to British and Spanish interests. He asked,

> Will it End in a Civil warr; or will our Country be relieved from its present ignominy . . . [and] the insulting Cringing and ignominious Child of aristocratic Secracy; removed erased and obliterated from the archives of the Grand republick of the united States.[101]

Jackson feared civil war and the dissolution of the "infant republick"; like other frontier leaders, he also threatened it. He contemplated dividing the Union and attaching the southwest to Spain, unless the central government provided protection against Indian attacks. If the frontier could not rely on the father of the country, it would have to look out for itself. Jackson was one of twelve Congressmen to vote against a resolution of gratitude to Washington in response to the Farewell Address.[102]

Jackson's hero in European politics was Napoleon, who had risen from obscurity to govern an empire. He admired "the emperor's energy"; his library contained five books on Napoleon. Should Napoleon invade England, he wrote in 1798, "Tyranny will be Humbled, a throne crushed, and a republic will spring from the wreck, and millions of distressed people restored to the rights of man by the conquering arm of Bonaparte." Other republicans supported France against England; by trading with England, Senator Henry Tazewell wrote Jackson, "we are feeding a power whose interest it is to devour our political tenets." Other republicans, however, did not share Jackson's enthusiasm for Bonaparte. They admired republics, not the emperors who overthrew them. Jackson rarely alluded, unlike the founders, to classic republican experience. When he did, he invariably indicated sympathy with Caesar. It was a special sort of republican who chose Napoleon and Caesar for models.[103]

Forty years after he voted against Washington's Farewell Address, Jackson delivered a Farewell Address of his own; no President in the intervening years had done so. The "paternal counsels" of "the Father of his country in his Farewell Address," said Jackson, were prophetic, "warning us of the evil to come." The country had successfully fought a foreign war in 1812, "with our Constitution yet in its infancy." But now land speculation and sectional jealousies—the very activities which defined the young Jackson—were generating "new vices which are, I fear, undermining the purity and complicating the simplicity of our virtuous government as left us by our fathers." With the death of the revolutionary fathers, Jackson implied, there was nothing to protect the young country from material temptations. President Jackson had shown a paternal regard for republican virtue. Now, like Washington, he was leaving office. The only secure barrier to selfishness and internal dissension (the "Civil warr" of Jackson's youth) lay in the "fraternal attachment which the citizens of the several States bear to one another as members of one political family."[104]

Jackson well knew the nature of the evils he warned against; they summarized his early activities. He had rejected paternal political control, and early engaged in a life of material indulgence and sectional strife. By what process could he now stand as the paternal embodiment of the national will, who would return the country to the ways of its fathers?

CHAPTER 3

NATURE, PROPERTY, AND TITLE

Richard, Duke of York:
Edward the Third, my lords, had seven sons:
The first, Edward the Black Prince, Prince of Wales;
The second, William of Hatfield; and the third,
Lionel Duke of Clarence; next to whom
Was John of Gaunt, the Duke of Lancaster; . . .
Edward the Black Prince died before his father;
And left behind him Richard, his only son,
Who, after Edward the Third's death, reign'd as king,
Till Henry Bolingbroke, Duke of Lancaster,
The eldest son and heir of John of Gaunt,
Crown'd by the name of Henry the Fourth,
Seiz'd on the realm, depos'd the rightful king. . . .

Earl of Warwick:
Thus got the house of Lancaster the crown.

York:
Which now they hold by force, and not by right;
For Richard, the first son's heir, being dead,
The issue of the next son should have reign'd.

Earl of Salisbury:
But William of Hatfield died without an heir.

York:
The third son, Duke of Clarence,—from whose line
I claim the crown,—had issue, Philippe, a daughter,
Who married Edmund Mortimer, Earl of March;
Edmund had issue, Roger Earl of March;
Roger had issue, Edmund, Anne, and Eleanor. . . .
                                        Anne,
My mother, being heir unto the crown,
Married Richard Earl of Cambridge; who was son
To Edmund Langley, Edward the Third's fifth son.
By her I claim the kingdom: she was heir
To Roger Earl of March; who was the son

Of Edmund Mortimer; who married Philippe,
Sole daughter unto Lionel Duke of Clarence;
So, if the issue of the elder son
Succeed before the younger, I am king.

Warwick:
What plain proceeding is more plain than this?

—*William Shakespeare*, Henry VI, Part 2, *Act 2, Scene 2*

I

Andrew Jackson, his admirers said, was "educated in Nature's school." "His infancy sported in the ancient forests, and his mind was nursed to freedom by their influence." One of "nature's noblemen," "he grew as the forest trees grow"; "he was the noblest tree in the forest." By Jackson's death, a century and a half of American identification with nature had culminated around his figure.[1]

Nature was a powerful source of value in eighteenth- and nineteenth-century Europe, but it underwent a transformation, Henry Nash Smith and Perry Miller have shown, in America. Americans alone tied the identity of their entire nation to nature. Nature made America an organic whole, compared, in John Quincy Adams' words, to the "fragments of territory" in Europe. Only Americans could locate nature in actual, physically available, virgin land. "There, in that great sloven continent," wrote Emerson, "still sleeps and murmurs and hides the great mother, long since driven away from the trim hedge rows and over-cultivated gardens of England." The words of *philosophes* and romantics were made flesh in the new world.[2]

Ninety percent of the American population farmed the land in 1790. Only a minority of the rest lived in the cities of Boston, New York, Philadelphia, Baltimore, and Charles Town.[3] Nature in the eighteenth-century imagination was static and ordered, but it contained romantic elements as well. "This hunger after land," a New York colonist complained, "seems very early to have taken rise in this Province, and is become now a kind of epidemical madness." In Europe, wrote Hector St. John Crèvecoeur,

all the objects of contemplation, all the reveries of the traveller, must have reference to ancient generations and to very distant periods, clouded with the mist of ages. Here, on the contrary, everything is modern, peaceful, and benign . . . ; we are strangers to those feudal institutions which have enslaved so many. Here nature opens her broad lap to receive the perpetual accession of newcomers and to supply them with food.[4]

Beginning with the Kentucky migration, the first substantial westward movement after the Revolution, nature increasingly acquired associations of fantasy and primitive bliss. The pioneer, wrote Frederick Jackson Turner, "dreamed dreams and beheld visions." Identification with the land was not located on specific historical estates or villages rich with tradition and family history. For a population seeking to improve itself, the virgin land undermined actual attachments. Do you think, asked a Kentucky pioneer in 1787, "to prevent the emigration from a barren country loaded with taxes and impoverished with debts, to the most luxurious soil in the world? You may as well endeavor to prevent the fishes from gathering on a bank in the sea which affords them plenty of nourishment." John Breckenridge, prominent Kentucky pioneer and author of the Kentucky Resolutions, called Kentucky "the Eden of America." James Robertson, who founded Nashville in 1780, located his "infant settlement" in "the promised land." Andrew Jackson, imagining victory over Creek Indians a generation later and possession of their territory, wrote he "would soon reach the promised land that flows with milk and honey."[5]

Daniel Boone personified the theme of "communion with nature," as Henry Nash Smith has called it, "the static ideas of virtue and happiness and peace drawn from the bosom of the virgin wilderness—the ideas symbolized in Charles W. Webber's Peaceful Valley." Boone's explorations opened Kentucky to American settlement. To one prominent Kentucky pioneer, he was a "second Adam, entering a second Paradise." In Webber's words, "He only felt yearnings—ungovernably strong—the meaning of which he could not know—but which led him, deeper and deeper, with yet more restless strength, into the cool profound of the all-nourishing bosom of his primeval mother." Kentucky, one historian has summarized, symbolized a world of plenty "which satisfied desires of every fundamental kind."[6]

The dream of paradise was Columbus' first. The earth, he wrote in 1498, "is not round . . . but of the form of a pear, which is very round except where the stalk grows . . . ; or like a round ball, upon one part of which is a prominence like a woman's nipple, the protrusion being the highest and nearest the sky." Columbus located this spot in the Caribbean beyond the Gulf of Paria. There, he wrote, "I believe in my soul that the earthly paradise is situated."[7]

Pioneers did not simply dream of plenty, passively permitting nature to nourish and sustain them. At first, in Frederick Jackson Turner's famous words,

> The wilderness masters the colonist. It finds him a European in dress, industries, tools, modes of travel, and thought. It takes him from the railroad car and puts him in the birch canoe. It strips off the garments

of civilization and arrays him in the hunting shirt and moccasin. It puts him in the log cabin of the Cherokee and Iroquois and runs an Indian palisade around him. Before long he has gone to planting Indian corn and plowing with a sharp stick; he shouts the war cry and takes the scalp in orthodox Indian fashion. In short, at the frontier the environment is at first too strong for the man.[8]

The Protestants who settled America, however, had not fled the Virgin Mary to succumb to the virgin land.[9] Nature's appeal lay less in its power over helpless men than in its untarnished availability. Unconquered, the land would overwhelm men; it was not, in Erikson's language, a source of "basic trust." But men could conquer the virgin wilderness and put it to their purposes. They would not encounter on American soil the feudal structures and historical traditions of Europe. A new, natural man would arise in the west, uncontaminated by history.[10]

"The sons of men," in Turner's words, had "escaped the bondage of the past." Freed from a historic relation to the land, they were at once more in danger of domination by nature, and peculiarly able to assert their own power.

> The very fact of the wilderness appealed to men as a fair, blank page on which to write a new chapter in the story of man's struggle for a higher type of society. The western wilds, from the Alleghenies to the Pacific, constituted the richest gift that was ever spread out before civilized man. . . . the West offered an exit into a free life and greater well-being among the bounties of nature, into the midst of resources that demanded manly exertion. . . . "To each she offered gifts after his will." Never again can such an opportunity come to the sons of men.[11]

American literary romanticism celebrated a nature uncontaminated by man's presence. American romanticism in practice celebrated nature for "the gifts" she "spread out before" "the sons of her loins." "The right of nature," in Jackson's language, was the right to work one's will on nature, unhindered by other men. "The Americans arrived but as yesterday on the territory which they inhabit," wrote Tocqueville, "and they have already changed the whole order of nature for their own advantage." Americans possessed nature; they turned it into property.[12]

Men established ownership in the Lockean state of nature by mixing their labor with the land. History and law did not connect them to nature. Traditions of use had not established customary, cooperative rights and obligations. Instead each man, working the land, appropriated it to himself. Lockean theory mythologized the origins of property, in the new world as in the old, but it had powerful appeal in America. It tied ownership to individualism, work, and self-control. Yeomen working their farms, thought Jefferson, learned discipline, responsibility, and government of the self. An owned portion of nature could neither overwhelm men nor escape from their control. The virgin land gave America its identity; ownership gave Americans the land.[13]

Appropriating the virgin land, however, men transformed it into its opposite. Land in America was not only a symbol of national identity, but also—in a more thoroughgoing fashion than anywhere else in the world—a commodity. Malcolm Rohrbough writes, "Land was the nation's most sought after commodity in the first half-century of the republic, and the effort of men to acquire it was one of the dominant forces of the period."[14] Land had not only symbolic value and use value, but exchange value as well. It was at once sustainer of American uniqueness and uniquely available to be exploited, bought, and sold. At bottom the two meanings of the land shared common roots. They were joined, first, by primitiveness. The land lacked, or had been stripped of, specific historical memories; it provided space to act out fantasies of total sustenance, great fortune, and omnipotent control. Second, the economic importance of the land sustained its spiritual meaning. Glorification of the virgin land did not float in an empyrean realm, irrelevant to daily American business. Nature gave higher meaning to dreams of future fortune; it sanctified the frenetic quest for wealth, and offered promise of bliss at the end of the road.

Nevertheless, nature and the commodities created from her stood in dialectical tension. We shall first elaborate the concrete importance of the land in early America, and then explore title conflicts over land ownership. Jackson's land business will provide the major illustrations. Finally, we will suggest how the transformation of land from nature to product troubled America's inner world and influenced Jacksonian politics.

Land was the major economic resource, the major determiner of social status, and the major source of political power in early America. It created most American fortunes in the eighteenth and early nineteenth centuries, provided the basis for American economic development, and fueled public and private business transactions.

Land was, to begin, a medium of exchange. It served as money, particularly on the frontier, where currency was scarce. Lawyers like Jackson took land titles in payment for services. Land paid gambling debts, and was directly bartered for merchandise and slaves. Land was, second, the major source of public money in early America. Money from land sales provided the new American government with the revenue without which it could not have survived. Sale of public lands continued to contribute importantly to the federal treasury, providing, with the tariff, the largest proportion of public funds before the Civil War. Disposition of the public lands and other land issues occupied fully one-fourth of all congressional debating time in the several decades after ratification of the Constitution.[15]

Western lands were the most important single source of American economic development from 1815 to 1845, the decades during which market capitalism transformed America. We shall subsequently explore the role of land in American economic development.[16] Land also dominated the eighteenth-century economy. Most colonial fortunes were founded on land. Most yeomen owned their own land, but outside New England most land was owned by relatively few men. Landed gentry were at the top of society except perhaps for New England, where the seaboard commercial elite had prospered in trade. A Philadelphian wrote in 1768, "It is almost a proverb in this neighborhood that 'Every great fortune made here within these fifty years has been made by land.' "[17]

Those who made fortunes in land did not, contrary to Locke, make them by work and agriculture. Ultimately land gained its value from the use to which it would be put—crops, towns, roads, and canals. But actual use did not determine the value of western land. Men made their fortunes by speculating with the land, not working upon it. Land derived its value from the hope of future settlement; this dream, this speculation that land would rise in value, gave land its commodity importance. "Were I to characterize the United States," an observer wrote in 1796, "it would be by the appelation of the land of speculators."[18] Whether as paradise or commodity, land gained its importance in America from the future.

The method chosen to build the nation's capital symbolized the importance of land speculation in the new republic. Seeking a location free from the history and partial perspectives of any existing city, the founders located the capital on a marshy stretch of land between Maryland and Virginia. This land had neither use value nor historic value, but the founders reasoned that, as capital of the republic, it would surely have exchange value. They secretly bought up land along the Potomac before announcing the site of Washington. They planned to finance construction of the city by selling this land after knowledge of the capital's location appreciated its value.[19]

The founders badly overestimated the appeal of the new capital, and Washington failed as a land speculation. The principle was sound, however. George Washington and the others who planned the capital knew from personal experience that fortunes made on the land in eighteenth-century America derived not from the products of cultivated soil, but from speculation in largely virgin land. The fortunes of the Tidewater planters, for example, did not come from tobacco. As tobacco farmers they participated, with thousands of yeomen, in a barely profitable activity. A family gained wealth because one or more of its members had engaged in mercantile activity, the extension of credit, or, most typically, land speculation. Most eighteenth-century American fortunes derived from grants or purchases of enormous tracts of land, held or sold for speculative purchases. Land was the major investment opportunity in early America.[20]

Land speculation also played a central role in early American politics. Most of the leading families outside New England, and many there as well, acquired by speculation the fortunes and landed estates that were a prerequisite to political leadership. Land speculators played a major role in westward expansion; without the settlement of the west their land would not increase in value. English efforts to contain the settlement line east of the Appalachians endangered the value of speculative holdings. The settlement proclamation antagonized leading speculators in western lands, like George Washington and Patrick Henry, and helped bring on the Revolution. Speculators led or sponsored pioneer colonies, and were responsible for early settlement of Kentucky, Tennessee, and Ohio. Their influence often lay behind democratic western constitutions (written to attract settlers), western demands for greater representation in state and national legislatures, and "democratic" pressures for cheap purchase of western lands. Speculative purchases and settlements often thinned the frontier and pushed it west more rapidly than yeoman pressure alone would have done. For these reasons, and in their desire to safeguard expansion, speculators involved the frontier in Indian wars.[21]

Speculator influence was nowhere greater than in the old southwest. Twenty-one speculators in 1800 claimed one-fourth of Kentucky. The Marshall family alone (including Supreme Court Justice John Marshall) held 400,000 acres.[22] Speculators aggrandized Tennessee lands too. Speculation, as it had for the founding fathers before him, established Andrew Jackson among the American elite.

II

Virginia speculator Richard Henderson purchased an enormous tract of land from the Cherokees in 1775. His purchase included most of the present state of Kentucky and a large portion of Tennessee. John Donelson and James Robertson led the first settlers in west Tennessee to Henderson's land on the Cumberland. Private speculators, however, lacked authority to purchase Indian land. Virginia and North Carolina, in whose territory the purchase lay, repudiated it. Both states generously compensated Henderson in land, but many actual Cumberland settlers were not so fortunate. In 1783 North Carolina opened all its land west of the Appalachians, except for a Cherokee reserve in the southeast, to purchase and settlement. Most of this land belonged to the Cherokees and Chickasaws. The only relevant treaty, which John Donelson held with the Chickasaws that same year, guaranteed that tribe title to much of the land involved. North Carolina, ignoring Indian treaty rights, reserved the Cumberland valley to holders of military warrants. Henderson received 200,000 acres in what is now east Tennessee, and the remainder of the land was open to general purchase.[23]

The Chickasaws fought with the colonists in the Revolution, only to see their land offered to white American soldiers. Soldiers, however, benefited from the North Carolina statute no more than Indians did. North Carolina acted under the pressure of wealthy speculators, led by William Blount. The Creeks, understanding Blount's appetite for western Indian land, called him the "dirt king." He and his associates had bought up most of the military warrants; only speculators, not most actual and potential settlers, had facilities to survey and enter the lands. The land office was open just six months, long enough for the speculators to enter claims, but too short a time for the Cumberland pioneers to hear of the law and make the trip over the mountains and back. The politicians and speculators who promoted the North Carolina law entered two-thirds of the six million available acres, including the best land in west Tennessee.[24]

North Carolina and private companies of land speculators hired surveyors to survey and enter land; these men reaped a personal bonanza. John Donelson, a surveyor and land speculator, had represented western Virginia in the House of Burgesses. Associated with Henderson's speculating ventures, he had led one of the original settling parties to the Cumberland, but Indian attacks had driven Donelson and his family back to Kentucky. Now he returned as North Carolina surveyor for west Tennessee, and he and his numerous children became large landowners there. They obtained much of the best land in the Cumberland valley, often at the expense of original settlers who lacked the means to file for the land they were on. Stockley Donelson, one of John Donelson's sons, was named state surveyor for the land district east of the Cumberland Mountains. He entered 20,000 acres for himself near the present site of Chattanooga, as well as other land, and made himself at a young age one of the largest landholders in east Tennessee.[25]

North Carolina finally ceded its western lands to the United States, with the proviso that the federal government guarantee all North Carolina land grants whether or not they violated Indian treaties. This proviso satisfied the speculators. They acted precipitously in 1783 because they feared imminent transfer of the western lands to the Union. The United States would be more respectful than North Carolina of Indian treaty rights, and less amenable to large speculative purchases. Their interests protected, speculators took the lead in organizing the new territory. Blount, appointed territorial Governor by Washington, believed the post "of great importance to our Western Specs." Tennessee was born from a giant land grab.[26]

Blount and Donelson triumphed in the Cumberland valley; they failed in their other major regional venture. There was valuable land at Muscle Shoals, in the Big Bend of the Tennessee River just over the present Tennessee border in Alabama. Donelson had led his party to the Cumberland in 1780 with plans to continue on by water to the Shoals, "so as to include, for me and my heirs, as rich land *there* as Colonel Henderson and his heirs will obtain on the Kentucky." Indeed, he was more interested in land at the Shoals than in the Cumberland region, but his scheme proved too ambitious. Blount formed a land company three years later. He convinced Georgia, which claimed the Shoals, to permit settlement there. Georgia appointed members of Blount's company, including Donelson, as surveyors. They were joined by surveyors actually from Georgia, who agreed to make enormous grants of land to Blount's surveyors for their services in opening the territory to settlement. Blount, in turn, rewarded the Georgia surveyors. "They all appear to have a great thirst for Tennessee lands," he explained. The Georgia surveyors and those from Blount's company entered large tracts for Blount and for each other.[27]

Muscle Shoals was too far from other frontier settlements, however; pioneers could not protect themselves against Cherokees resisting invasion of their land. Donelson was killed on his way back to Nashville, after failing to open a land office at the Shoals. But his "heirs" retained an interest there. The Yazoo companies of land speculators, through wholesale bribery of the Georgia legislature, gained title to lands Georgia claimed west to the Mississippi. Lands on the Tennessee River were among those acquired, but the Shoals was still Indian country, where settlement was forbidden by law. In 1797 John Cox of Georgia, leader of one of the Yazoo companies, sought to promote a settlement of the Shoals. Cox made lavish grants of land to secure the friendship of prominent politicians. He gave 50,000 acres to Tennessee Governor John Sevier. Senator Andrew Jackson received 1,000 acres. This Yazoo settlement also failed, and Blount's conspiracy, which aimed to open the Shoals to white settlement, failed too. The Cherokees did not cede the land north of the Shoals until ten years later. Jackson conquered the land south of the Shoals in the Creek War of 1813–14, and he and his friends made large purchases there.[28]

The Yazoo speculators failed to settle the Shoals, but they did further the course of southwestern expansion. Georgia, in return for federal settlement of the Yazoo claims, ceded its western lands to the Union in 1802. The government promised, in return, to "extinguish" Indian title to Georgia's remaining lands "as early as the same can be peaceably obtained, on reasonable terms." U.S. failure to fulfill this compact, Georgia claimed in the 1820s, justified its seizure of Indian land. The original Blount-Donelson speculation also bore fruit. Georgia, upon the failure of Blount's scheme, granted each surveyor 5,000 acres for his services. The acreage was to be located in Georgia's unclaimed western lands. These lands passed to the United States in 1802; in 1816 the commissioners or their heirs put forth their claims for 5,000 acres. The House Committee on Private Land Claims rejected these claims in 1820. In 1824 Congress granted the claims, permitting each commissioner or his heirs to locate 5,000 acres in Alabama or Mississippi. Andrew Jackson was lawyer for his wife and the other Donelson heirs.[29]

Jackson arrived on the Cumberland three years after John Donelson died; his career followed that of his father-in-law. He took his law fees in land titles, and acquired enough land in fees, he later said, to make a country. Jackson also bought land. He settled after his marriage on a large, desirable tract in the bend of the Cumberland. Most of the rest of his land was unimproved acreage, and much of it lay in Indian territory. By 1795 he had made twenty-two trips between Nashville and Jonesborough in east Tennessee, a total distance of 4,400 miles, on legal business and land jobbing. He often speculated in alliance with his friend and fellow lawyer John Overton. The two men quickly acquired immense holdings. Records covering Jackson's first twenty-five years in Nashville show his constant involvement in buying and selling land.[30]

He acquired with Overton, for example, 5,000 acres at the Chickasaw bluffs on the Mississippi. Speculators had long coveted this land, and Overton later located the city of Memphis there. Overton bought the land first, and Jackson acquired a half-interest from him in 1796. He paid Overton $100, and immediately sold half his interest for $312. He sold half this remaining interest in 1818 for $5,000, after the Chickasaw treaty he negotiated that year opened the area to white settlement.[31]

Jackson learned in Washington in 1798 that the government had ordered a treaty with the Cherokees. He wrote his brother-in-law Robert Hays, "Therefore lands on Duck river, should the Tennessee become the line will be valluable. This is as much as to say to you keep all you have and get what you can." In 1805 he sought and failed to obtain 44,000 acres in west Tennessee, anticipating a Cherokee treaty ceding that land to the United States. He made unsuccessful efforts early the following year to exploit confidential information that the treaty had been signed. For the next several years Jackson continued to respond to inquiries from prospective settlers and speculators and to buy and sell land.[32]

Early in his career Jackson established a pattern for his speculating activities. He bought large tracts of Tennessee land, sold them in Philadelphia, bought Philadelphia goods to sell in Tennessee, and used the proceeds from the sale of merchandise to buy more land. He established a series of stores near Nashville to sell his merchandise, taking as partners friends and relatives like John Hutchings and John Coffee. Jackson also won and lost land in horse races, mixed slave trading with land deals, and was plagued like other speculators by problems of tax liens, imperfect title, Indian claims, and bankruptcy.[33]

Other speculators lived with these problems and sought to resolve them pragmatically. They had turned virgin land into money; they remained in the material realm in the conflicts that resulted. Jackson, however, did not. His personality and the threat to his fortune forced him to return to the nature of things. Worldly success failed to rescue Jackson from separation anxiety and establish his authority in the world. He returned to instinctual sources, in nature and in his maternal bond, to rebuild his authority on a firm foundation. Plagued by title conflicts and insecure possession, he went back to the Indians, at the beginning of it all.

III

As Europe turned its back on New England, Perry Miller writes, the power of the land took over. The Puritans had undertaken an errand to the new world for the redemption of the old. Religious purpose united them in the midst of a savage wilderness. Within two generations, however, the English Puritans had triumphed at home, and forgotten New England orthodoxy. Civil War and Restoration brought religious fragmentation across the ocean. America was plagued by conflicts among innumerable warring sects whose genealogical origins, Miller remarks, were "as labyrinthine as the genealogies of York and Lancaster." Americans turned gratefully from political and religious strife to "the enduring, the consoling, the uncontentious, verities of nature."[34]

Nature offered promise of consolation, but did not fulfill it. Title to the land was as confusing as title to the English throne had ever been. Conflicts over land title dominated early America, from Puritan New England in the seventeenth century to the southwestern frontier two hundred years later. Men lacked (Madison) "that domination which one man claims and exercises over the external things of the world, in exclusion of every other individual."[35] Land-title disputes, challenging their ownership, threatened to reverse the process by which they had appropriated the land to themselves, and return them to a contentious, unconsoling state of nature.

Problems of title and state of nature originated not in private American disputes over land title, but in public English conflicts over political authority. Disputed claims to the throne among related feudal lineages unleashed fraternal anarchy on England. The centralized Tudor monarchy promised secure, inherited, family authority. When it blew up in the English civil war, royalists like Sir Robert Filmer again proposed patriarchy as the answer to political disorder. Filmer derived the king's authority from the power of a father over his children.

The Glorious Revolution rejected absolutist claims like Filmer's. Norman O. Brown writes,

> Freud seems to project into prehistoric times the constitutional crisis of seventeenth-century England. The primal father is *absolute monarch* of the horde; the females are his *property*. The sons form a *conspiracy* to overthrow the despot, and in the end substitute a *social contract* with *equal rights* for all.[36]

Contract and patriarchy competed for authority in seventeenth-century England. Locke rejected patriarchy. Cannibalism of sons by fathers, he wrote, was the consequence of unrestrained paternal authority. In opposition to Filmer, Locke derived political legitimacy from contractual relations among free men. Brown continues,

> Liberty means equality among the brothers (sons). Locke rejects Filmer's rule of primogeniture, which transmits the full power of father Adam to one of his sons, and makes one brother the father of his brethren. . . . "Brother," he says, "is the name of friendship and equality, and not of jurisdiction and authority." Locke has father Adam's property divided equally among all his sons. Liberty, equality: it is all a dispute over the inheritance of the paternal estate.[37]

Political authority in feudal Europe was tied to the land. When the eldest son inherited "the paternal estate," he inherited political power as well. The king's authority originally derived from ownership too; the extension of royal power beyond the royal estate began a separation of property rights from political authority. Defenders of royal patriarchal authority had now to argue metaphorically, not from an actual, inherited, paternal estate. This change in the basis of royal power transformed and weakened feudalism, and laid the basis for the triumph of contractual, liberal authority.

Englishmen brought the tension between patriarchy and contract with them to the new world. If in England contract struggled against a historic feudalism and never completely replaced it, in America patriarchy had no such formidable roots. Puritan Massachusetts organized itself on the patriarchal model, but the first Puritans signed the Mayflower Compact before landing on American soil. "In the beginning all the world was America," wrote Locke; lacking a common judge, men contracted together and entered civil society. They established political authority, and gained protection for their property. The Mayflower Compact, said John Quincy Adams, "is perhaps the only instance, in human history, of that positive, original social compact, which speculative philosophers have imagined as the only legitimate source of government." Locke's description, however, only partially fitted the Mayflower Compact. Its aims were communal, not individual, and it confirmed power on the leaders of a preexisting, hierarchical community.[38]

By the late eighteenth century, patriarchy had declined and a purer state of nature existed in the American wilderness. Western migrants entered into social contracts to protect their individual property rights in the land. Such contracts were often written by the leader of a land company; they did not arise spontaneously from the state of nature. No land-company leader, however, claimed fatherhood over his colony. Wilderness compacts indicate the source of contentiousness on the frontier, and the method taken to meet it.

Watauga settlers in east Tennessee signed the first Lockean social contract in America in 1772. They had settled beyond the Indian treaty line, and wanted to justify their own authority over the land. The 250 original male settlers in the Cumberland valley, John Donelson and his sons among them, also signed a "Compact of Government" on May 13, 1780. It reads in part:

> That as this settlement is in its infancy, unknown to government, and not included within any county within North Carolina, the State to which it belongs, . . . we find ourselves constrained from necessity to adopt this temporary method of restraining the licentious, and supplying, by unanimous consent, the blessings flowing from just and equitable government. . . . So we think it our duty to associate, and hereby form ourselves into one society for the benefit of present and future settlers.[39]

"Unanimous consent," Locke's criterion, established this compact. Those refusing to join, the contract stated, were free to settle elsewhere. ("Let them plant in some inland vacant places of America," said Locke.) The Nashborough Compact, like the *Second Treatise*, established elections, a common judge, and civil society.[40]

The major source of disputes in the state of nature, wrote Locke, was property. On the frontier, property meant land; most of the provisions in the lengthy Nashborough Compact established rules to validate land title. The paragraph on political elections, for example, provides that

The free men of this country over the age [of twenty] one years shall immediately, or as soon as may [be convenient] proceed to elect or choose twelve conscientious and [deserving] persons from or out of the different stations, that is to say: from Nashborough, three; Gasper's, two; Bledsoe's, one; Asher's, one; Stone's River, one; Freeland's, one; Eaton's, two; Fort Union, one; Which said persons, or a majority of them, . . . having due regard to the regulations of the Land Office herein established, shall be competent judges of the matter, and . . . hearing the allegations of both parties . . . shall have [power] to decide the controversies, and determine who is of right entitled to an entry for such land so in dispute, when said determination or decision shall be forever binding and conclusive.[41]

"Every man has a 'property' in his own 'person,'" wrote Locke, and civil society protected him against personal violence. The Cumberland political order had binding power over capital crimes. In addition, the elected officers of each station were to call out and command the militia in the event of Indian attack. Since Indians fought the settlers over possession of the Cumberland valley, this provision too sought to establish secure title to the land.[42]

The Nashborough Compact gave no man paternal authority over his brothers. Instead fraternal contractual obligations resolved title disputes and provided each settler with a share of the land. The contracts, however, failed to be "forever binding and conclusive."[43] They did not establish secure title to the land. The Lockean solution, far from resolving conflicts over title in America, transferred them from kings, nobles, and pretenders disputing title to the throne to farmers, speculators, and land companies disputing title to the soil.

Lockean liberalism shifted conflict from the public to the private realm. Contractual authority sought to protect private property from political interference. It depoliticized society. Men withdrew both from the complex network of communal rights and responsibilities which governed feudal property relations, and from claims to paternal political power over an entire society. They gained in return "despotic dominion" (Blackstone) over their own estates. "A man's home is his castle," James Otis insisted, "and whilst he is quiet is as well guarded as a prince in his castle."[44] There were no kings in republican America, but men exercised over their own land the absolute power sought by the Tudors and Stuarts over an entire society.

Colonial social structure protected the political authority of the leading families against contractual theory. No revolutionary, nevertheless, postulated a natural right to inherit political power. Jefferson, indeed, wondered "whether one generation of men has a right to bind another." In the private realm the claims of inheritance were asserted more strongly.

Few Americans objected to the inheritance of property from father to son. They objected rather to feudal restrictions on the right of the father to dispose of his estate as he wished. Primogeniture required the father to leave his entire estate to his eldest son. Just as kings in the new nation-states objected to feudal restrictions, so American liberal doctrine freed private fathers. Under the law of primogeniture, a Georgia colonist complained to Governor Oglethorpe,

> Their younger children, however numerous, are left to be fed by Him who feeds the ravens; and if they have no children, their labor and substance descends to strangers. How, sir, could you, or indeed any freeborn spirit, brook such a tenor? Are not our younger children and daughters equally entitled to our bowels and affection?

Abolishing primogeniture, the colonist insisted, would increase paternal authority and filial dependence, since it would deprive the eldest son of his "interest independent of the parents."[45]

The appeal to a "freeborn spirit" suggests the pitfalls in this argument. Given the availability of virgin land, the sons were born free of paternal authority. Contractual theory ultimately freed not the father but the sons. It was difficult to deny paternal authority in the public world and enforce it in the private. Why should children be dependent on the "bowels and affection" of their parents; why should they not control their own? Radical Lockeans—Thomas Skidmore and Orestes Brownson in the Jacksonian period—argued that the father should not be permitted to control his inheritance after he died. If a man could "by *natural right*," wrote Jefferson, oblige his successor to pay his debts, "he might, during his own life, eat up the usufruct of the lands for several generations to come." Jackson, too, feared burdening his son with debt after his death.[46]

Proposals to abolish inheritance did not get far; but the west, as Jefferson sensed, served a similar function. Fathers in early New England restricted their sons' access to land, but they could not do so for long. Clans migrated from the middle colonies to the southwestern frontier after the family patriarch had died. Freed of inherited sins and possessions, western men established title themselves, contractually, "peaceably congregating and mingling together on virgin soil." But the western pioneers, however much they had overthrown external paternal restraints, were not innocent. "The sons of men" (Turner) brought the problems of paternal inheritance—ownership, property, and title—to the virgin land. This meeting provided the dynamic for frontier land conflict. Liberalism privatized title disputes; private land conflict returned to plague public authority.[47]

IV

Americans occupied themselves with land-title conflicts from the first settlements in the new world. The Waxhaws community where Jackson was born lay on land disputed between North and South Carolina. Some settlers had their title from one state, some from the other. Adherents of the two colonies fought sporadically over the territory between 1764 and 1772, and armed settler conflicts broke out during Jackson's childhood. Robert Crawford, leader of the Crawford clan, was a North Carolina partisan. The compromise boundary line finally drawn placed his home in South Carolina, invalidating his North Carolina grant. He traveled to Charles Town and acquired South Carolina title to replace it.[48]

Land-title conflicts were most complex, caused most trouble, and created greatest insecurities in the old southwest. Title confusions of every possible kind plagued Kentucky and Tennessee. Virginia and North Carolina, the mother states, had issued enormous land grants and sold large tracts. The acreage they disposed of far exceeded the actual land. Their grants lay, for the most part, in Indian territory. Particularly before 1789, these states and others issued warrants for lands disputed among them, and lands to which their claims were dubious indeed. States issued military warrants in unlocated and unsurveyed lands to soldiers in the French and Indian and Revolutionary wars. Speculators traded in military warrants and other claims to unspecified and disputed land. Claim-trading enormously proliferated land titles, varying greatly in legitimacy and monetary value.[49]

Most land surveyors were inexperienced and only loosely bound by moral standards. Their major aim was to acquire large tracts for themselves and their associates. They marked lines carelessly, and followed natural boundaries like ridges, rivers, and trees which were ambiguous and shifting. The land was poorly marked; much surveyed land remained unoccupied for years while the markings disappeared. The public-land states required rectangular surveys of contiguous blocks of land. No such requirements inhibited surveyors in the old southwest. There land was claimed in odd patches, along rivers, to take advantage of variations in soil quality, and to include springs and salt licks.

Claiming original title was not a simple matter. Typically, a claimant had first to enter his land at a land office, often hundreds of miles from the actual property. Then he had to survey the land and enter the boundaries. Fees were required at both stages. Failure to complete the process invalidated the title. Faulty claim-filing resulted in imperfect and conflicting titles. Often no one discovered filing errors for years; often the actual title history could not be reconstructed. Land-office records were poorly kept. Imperfect records, added to the distance from land to office, created great discrepancies between land-office record books and actual frontier transactions.

To make matters worse, frauds were extensively practiced in surveying, filing for, and claiming land. Forged grants and false swearing at land offices not only affected original title, but returned to plague subsequent holders who had made their own transactions in good faith. Legal proceedings moved slowly, and suits often dragged on for years while the original parties died or sold their claims.

Squatters claimed occupancy rights; often recognized in court, squatter rights conflicted with other, legally established claims. Many squatters sold their claims to new settlers or to claims speculators. These squatter claims offered yet another source for litigation. Settlers and speculators also derived land rights from private agreements with Indian villages or with a scattering of local chiefs.

One source of conflict spared the old southwest permeated politics and society in every state south of Tennessee, from Florida to Missouri. France, England, and Spain issued private grants in territory they held or claimed. These grants produced prolonged litigation; important Jacksonians like Thomas Hart Benton and Richard K. Call made political careers and sought personal fortunes from representing private land claimants; some were claimants themselves. Most private grants involved enormous tracts of valuable land, vaguely bounded and poorly surveyed. Conditions of the grant, such as actual settlement, had often not been fulfilled while the land was in foreign hands. The private claims were often fraudulent; speculators scrambled to acquire them by forgery and bribery as territory passed under American control. Ultimately government and the courts were generous to the claimants, but litigation dragged on for years, and cast a shadow over title to some of the best southern lands.[50]

Transfer of imperfect title multiplied the uncertainties of ownership. Imperfectly foreclosed mortgages, conflicts among relatives or creditors over inheritance, land sold for failure to pay taxes, and tax and other liens (particularly on unimproved acreage) all created conflicting claims to the same land. So did sales of portions of an original claim, particularly where speculators sold subdivisions of poorly surveyed, large grants originally made years before in Indian territory.

A French traveler to Kentucky in 1802 "declared that the occupant of every house at which he stopped expressed doubts as to the soundness of his neighbor's title." Humphrey Marshall, a large Kentucky landowner whose title litigations involved 12,000 acres or more, complained:

> The face of Kentucky was covered, and disfigured by a complication of adverse claims to land. . . . The face of the earth was covered, again—and again—and again; with locations of the one or the other description. . . . [This] retarded her population—obstructed her improvement—distracted her people—impaired her morals—and depreciated the value of her rich soil, throughout the country.

Ignorant land-locaters, spurred by greedy employers, "strewed the locations over the face of the country, as autumn distributes its falling leaves."[51]

"Brother is the name of friendship and equality," wrote Locke. Had the dissolution of paternal authority simply freed the brothers to squabble among themselves? The absence of stable, hierarchical order did promote efforts at fraternal cooperation. Fraternal loyalties operated within families as clan members cooperated in buying and selling land. Men also tried to extend fraternity beyond relations of blood and marriage. They wanted to stabilize and act collectively in an uncertain, wildly competitive social order. The local associations which Tocqueville found ubiquitous formed themselves for these purposes.[52] Some had limited, specific goals, but others sought to create a more primordial loyalty.

Jackson and some friends organized a lodge of the Masonic fraternal order in Greenville, Tennessee, in 1801. This secret society provided an organization for mutual aid, and often dominated economic life on the frontier. The economic power of the Masons helps explain the rise of local Anti-Masonic parties in the late 1820s. (Strongest along the frontier, the Anti-Masons opposed Jackson for President.) The Masons, as their opponents knew, did more than simply share interests. Secrecy and elaborate ritual bound "brother Masons" together, protecting them from anarchic, contentious social life. Economic interests alone would not have united the "brothers"; ritually pledged loyalty created fraternal cohesion. Most of Jackson's friends were Masons; Overton was "Worshipful Master" of the Cumberland lodge.[53]

Jackson spoke before his "friends and brothers" when he addressed a Masonic lodge; this was also the form of salutation he used to communicate with Indian tribes. "Brothers" corresponded confidentially with one another; in 1802, for example, Mississippi Governor W. C. C. Claiborne, a member of Jackson's lodge, asked Jackson to solicit the advice of the *"brothers"* on his contemplated resignation. Jackson's "Brothers" helped arbitrate his duel challenges, but were expected to stick by him in the event of an actual duel. One Mason would never betray another, Jackson insisted. John Eaton and John Timberlake were brother Masons, and Eaton married Timberlake's wife as soon as Timberlake died. Resisting rumors that Eaton had long been intimate with Margaret Timberlake, Jackson explained that a Mason "could not have criminal intercourse with another mason's wife, without being one of the most abandoned of men." Slanders against a brother Mason, since they violated ritually sworn loyalty, were unforgivable. A Mason who would slander a "brother," Jackson wrote fellow Mason W. B. Lewis, would be guilty of any crime. Since his letter contained references to the secret society, Jackson instructed Lewis to burn it.[54]

The fluid social conditions which called forth Masonic bonds also made them fragile. Masonic loyalty no more prevented conflict among brother Masons than family connections prevented conflict within a clan. Instead, strife within the order acquired the significance of betrayed fraternal bonds. Land hunger and title conflict set friend against friend, brother against brother. Disputes over property recurred within the Donelson clan. Thus Jackson's great-nephew and ward, Andrew Jackson Hutchings, married to Jackson's great-niece, fought a land litigation with his wife's grandfather, Jackson's brother-in-law John Donelson. The suit followed the death of Hutchings' father-in-law, John Coffee.[55] Two land disputes, in particular, played a major role in Jackson's life. The first, at the outset of Jackson's career, brought him into conflict with his brother-in-law Stockley Donelson. The second created a rift between Jackson and his friend and brother Mason John Overton.

Stockley Donelson inherited most completely his father's career as surveyor and land speculator. A leading Tennessee landowner in the 1790s, Stockley played an important role in frontier affairs. Blount made him a member of the Tennessee territorial legislative council in 1794. Stockley and Jackson bought land together during this period, and Stockley kept Jackson informed of his ventures. Jackson's land agent James Grant reported in November 1795 that he was traveling with Stockley in Virginia and North Carolina "on some speculations of his." Stockley alleged that he was buying up military warrants from soldiers and speculators who could not wait for the land to be cleared of Indian title. He urged Jackson to send him all the military survey plats he could lay his hands on, promising he would be well rewarded for his labors.[56]

Jackson learned two years later of an enormous land fraud involving four million acres, something over one-sixth of Tennessee. There was evidence that Tennessee Governor John Sevier was involved. Sevier had earlier joined politically with Blount, but was now on the outs with the Blount faction. Nevertheless, and in spite of his personal antagonism toward Sevier, Jackson did not publicize the fraud. One reason for his silence was that Stockley was heavily implicated. In 1794 Stockley had written his own brother-in-law, North Carolina Secretary of State James

Glasgow, thanking him for keeping secret the "lucrative news that now presents us more capital in the Western Territory than any yet discovered," and offering him a share in the proceedings. Stockley's plan was to forge North Carolina military warrants, land titles, and surveys of Tennessee lands, and sell the forged titles in the east and in Europe. When Jackson initiated his inquiry, he wrote Overton, he had not known that Glasgow and "my friend Starkely" were involved. "But sir Even had I suspected this, my duty would have impelled me to have made the communication that I have done." Nevertheless, Jackson made no public disclosure of the fraud at this time.[57]

Jackson may have wanted to protect Stockley, but he was also urged to discretion from another source. Leading Tennessee speculators and politicians, including those on the outs with Sevier, did not want to publicize the fraud. They feared that Congress would pass a law invalidating all North Carolina grants of Tennessee land, from which they derived their own titles. They had passed a law to legitimize their land grab, but exposure of their activities would diminish the difference between their "legal" speculation and the Stockley-Sevier fraud. Overton warned Jackson not to make a disclosure. Jackson replied that people with legitimate titles had nothing to fear, but he remained silent for several years. He continued working with Stockley in land deals; the latter, evidently now in financial trouble, was grateful. "I've received brotherly treatment from you," he wrote Jackson when he feared arrest in a taxation suit. In 1802 Jackson acquired two sections of land granted by North Carolina to his brother-in-law.[58]

That same year, after Jackson and Sevier had quarreled again, and as part of his effort to defeat Sevier for governor, Jackson published the fraud. Sevier gained reelection, but Glasgow and Stockley, imprisoned in North Carolina, were ruined.[59] Jackson's blood brothers died for revolution, while Jackson survived. But Stockley was no martyr. His title claims were fraudulent, and Jackson virtuously brought him down. Those worried for their own titles urged caution; those with legitimate titles, said Jackson, had nothing to fear.

Jackson did not speak from a secure position, however. During these same years, his own fortunes suffered a reverse which called his right to his possessions into question. In 1795 Jackson and Overton decided to buy land in North Carolina and sell it in Philadelphia. They hoped to sell much of their own substantial holdings as well. James Grant, their agent, made a trip through the country and wrote back optimistic reports. He believed he could sell 130,000 acres in Tennessee belonging chiefly to Overton and Jackson, but he warned that congressional action had diminished the chances of Indian land cessions. This delayed settlement in Indian territory and would keep land prices down.[60]

Early in 1795 Jackson set out for the south. He could purchase no land, but received a large parcel from Joel Rice to sell on commission. He proceeded next to Philadelphia, his first visit to an American city since his ill-fated adolescent Charles Town adventures. Overton wrote him he should warn prospective purchasers that the lands in question lay in Indian territory, and offer to guarantee the title; upon reflection, however, he advised Jackson to raise as few obstacles to a sale as possible. He told Jackson to return to Nashville by way of the south and purchase slaves for Rice with the money from the sale of the land.[61]

"I have left you a rough sketch of our landed speculation," Jackson wrote Overton when he returned to Tennessee. The failure to purchase and resell southern lands made his trip disappointing. He sold the Rice land, plus 50,000 acres he and Overton owned, to David Allison of Philadelphia. Allison, a former Nashville lawyer, was associated with Blount in large speculations of dubious legality. Jackson received twenty-five cents an acre for land selling for ten cents in Tennessee, but he was forced to guarantee the title, and later lost money when part of Rice's title proved worthless.[62]

Jackson used Allison's notes to purchase merchandise and establish a store. Allison, however, had been on the verge of bankruptcy, and failed that fall. Jackson had endorsed Allison's notes, and was called upon to pay them as they came due. Although he protested that he had not meant, in signing his name, to stand surety for Allison, he well knew that under law he was liable. He sold his store and its stock for 33,000 acres of land, and sold the land to meet the first note. As succeeding notes came due, he was forced to relinquish more land. Jackson's landholdings and his fortune never recovered from Allison's failure. He continued to live the life of a wealthy planter, but, like so many others, he was plagued by debt troubles the rest of his life.[63]

Land speculators typically paid for their purchases with personal promissory notes. Profits from land resale, staple crops, trade, or other transactions paid these notes as they came due. Currency was scarce on the frontier, and there were no established forms of credit limiting personal liability. Personal notes were used as currency, and endorsed by each successive user. Failure of the original issuer made the signers liable for the debt. Jackson briefly sought to escape from this web of personal interdependence when Allison went bankrupt; he then paid, over many years, every penny of his obligation. He developed, from this experience, permanent hostility to paper note issues, and to those who sought to escape their debts.[64]

Allison's failure not only sensitized Jackson to money and debt; it also drove him back to the root of property ownership. Land speculation had first made Jackson's fortune and then threatened to ruin him. Now he turned to the issue of legitimate possession. Repercussions from Allison's failure thrust Jackson deeply into land-title disputes.

Allison mortgaged 85,000 acres on the Duck River to Norton Pryor in a futile effort to rescue himself from debt. Pryor hired Jackson to foreclose the mortgage, and Jackson and Overton filed a foreclosure suit in federal court in 1798. Jackson obtained title to 5,000 acres as his fee. He sold this land in parcels to settlers, warrantying himself to buy back the land at its current market value if his title proved unsound. Jackson discovered in 1811 that his title was in doubt, since the federal court had lacked jurisdiction in the foreclosure suit. If Allison's heirs could raise the $20,000 necessary to free the land of its original mortgage, they would acquire legal title. Jackson had sold this land when it lay in Indian territory. The Duck River valley was a prosperous agricultural region by 1811; were Jackson now forced to buy the land back, it would ruin him.

Allison's impoverished heirs, living in Georgia and ignorant of the law, were not likely to pose a threat to Jackson. He took no chances, however. He rode to Georgia and, for a small fee, obtained a relinquishment of their claim to the title in return for a relinquishment of his claim to the old mortgage. Jackson obtained from the Allison heirs the right to convey proper title to the purchasers not only of his 5,000 acres but of Pryor's and Overton's land as well, and to name his own fee for so doing.[65]

All the holders of this land reached agreement with Jackson but one. Andrew Erwin, a wealthy planter who held 20,000 acres of Allison land, believed his more than seven years of undisputed ownership and occupancy gave him color of title. Jackson had killed a member of the Erwin clan, Charles Dickinson, in a duel a few years earlier. Jackson's friend John Eaton fought a duel with Andrew Erwin during the Jackson-Erwin litigation. The Erwin clan opposed Jackson in Tennessee politics, and Andrew Erwin's son was married to Henry Clay's daughter. Jackson's protracted suit against Erwin clearly involved more than money. Jackson and his associates finally won in 1823. His allies got their money, but Jackson grandly relinquished his $5,000 to the tearful and now widowed Mrs. Erwin.[66]

Personal enmities commonly worked themselves out in land disputes, the law was a weapon of aggression. Jackson, however, transformed personal quarrels into matters of principle. He defended law and legitimate original title against actual residents whose long-standing possession was contaminated at the core.

Confusion over title undermined freeholder security; it made it difficult for states to sell their land and for settlers and speculators to buy it. Land laws were as harsh in their effects, said Kentucky Judge John Rowan, as "the infliction of savage warfare." Much of the trouble in Kentucky and Tennessee stemmed from old land grants made by Virginia and North Carolina when each "infant settlement" was still part of its "mother state." Overton negotiated a compromise with North Carolina in 1803 over the right of that state to dispose of Tennessee lands; Tennessee relinquished ownership of the western third of its territory to the United States, North Carolina warrants were recognized throughout Tennessee, and Tennessee obtained clear title to whatever land remained. Thanks to the Blount speculation of 1783, virtually all unsold land was subject to North Carolina warrants. Governor Sevier (who may have sanctioned land-grant forgeries to share the North Carolina wealth beyond the original Blount group) complained to the Tennessee legislature,

> Happy it would have been for the people of this Cntry after conquering the savages and supporting our Indep. without the aid of the parent (or any other State) . . . if we had maintained and supported our own justly acquired rights and converted the fruits of our labour to our own Emoluments.[67]

The Overton compromise facilitated sale of unclaimed land; it did not protect actual settlers. Settlers, from yeomen farmers to wealthy planters like Andrew Erwin, favored occupancy laws which protected settlers against absentee claimants with better formal legal title. Many established speculators, like Overton and Humphrey Marshall, also favored occupancy laws; such laws would protect their own holdings and ancient transactions against disturbance. Occupancy laws were, in the words of a Kentucky resident, a bulwark against the "exterminatory litigation of non-residents and aliens."[68]

Absentee and aspiring speculators, claims speculators, and land lawyers opposed occupancy laws. So did such purists over contractual rights as Supreme Court Chief Justice John Marshall and Andrew Jackson. These men had little support in the Kentucky and Tennessee legislatures; both states passed occupancy laws. The Supreme Court, however, twice struck down Kentucky's law. Complained one native, it "disposed of the rights of a half a million people with as little ceremony as a Frenchman eats a frog." "It disenfranchises Kentucky," another resident said, "and deprived her of her sovereign power over her own soil."[69]

The mother states, Virginia and North Carolina, were not sympathetic to occupancy laws; they did not want to relinquish rights stemming from their original land grants. In spite of a compact between the two states, Virginia refused to support Kentucky against the U.S. Supreme Court. The *Louisville Public Advertiser* complained,

> In this affair Virginia accurately personifies the waspish, hysterical mother who, while she is proclaiming us "bone of her bone and flesh of her flesh," rebukes us because we have dared to consult the prosperity and tranquility of our own household, in preference to sacrificing both, that we might retain the affection of the good old lady.

Ultimately Kentucky enforced its law over Virginia and Supreme Court objections until the court finally reversed itself in 1831.[70]

The Tennessee Supreme Court struck down that state's occupancy law. The legislature passed a new law in 1819, and added an additional member to the court to insure that the new law would not go the way of the old. Overton played a major role in these events. The leading codifier of Tennessee land law, he favored simplifying ownership in favor of settlers and speculators whose title had long gone unquestioned. This would free the courts from land litigation to address the problems of a growing commodity economy.[71]

Jackson, in the middle of his title dispute with Erwin, vehemently opposed a statute of limitations on land-title inquiries. He hardly favored the right of the "waspish, hysterical mother" state to control "our own justly acquired rights." But he was willing, as Humphrey Marshall put it, to strew land locations "over the face of the" state. He sacrificed illegitimate rights to "her rich soil" in the search for securely grounded ones. Jackson also wanted to sustain the personal, combative courtroom style, which flourished when land disputes were the major legal business, against an impersonal, routinized, economic legalism.[72]

Jackson returned from Florida in 1821, in the middle of the occupancy-law controversy. He allied himself in land litigation and politics with Patrick Darby and Jenkins Whiteside, and against his old friend Overton. Whiteside, a former Tennessee Senator, was an experienced land lawyer; Jackson had consulted him a decade earlier about his title to Allison's Duck River acres. Darby represented speculators who had bought up disputed titles, and also acquired titles of his own. Darby and Whiteside, threatening to overturn land titles everywhere in Tennessee, were opposed by Overton and most of the state's leading planters and speculators.[73]

How, Overton asked Jackson at the beginning of their quarrel, could there ever be a difference between us? Overton was Jackson's oldest friend. The two had boarded together at the Donelsons', where Overton introduced Jackson to Rachel. They were brother Masons, and partners in land speculation. After they reconciled, Overton played a leading role in the Nashville junto, which ran Jackson's presidential campaigns. When Overton died, in 1833, Jackson said he "could lament in the language and feelings of David for Absalam." Nevertheless, Jackson's fight with Overton separated the two men from 1821 through 1823.[74]

The quarrel originated in rights Jackson claimed to former Allison holdings, through his 1811 agreement with Allison's heirs. Jackson's claim conflicted with Overton's, who claimed title through the original foreclosure of Allison's mortgage in 1798. Soon Jackson's alliance with Darby went beyond the specific land dispute. He supported Darby and his running mate for the state legislature against Overton's candidates, Felix Grundy and William Lytle. Overton, charged Jackson, was involved in a "corrupt combination" to pack the Tennessee Supreme Court.[75]

Jackson insisted that men "high in society" who aspired to "honor and tryst" had to demonstrate to "rising generations" that they had acquired their title legitimately. The victorious Lytle, wrote Jackson, was guilty of "frauds, forgeries, and villainies." Overton, by supporting him, would lose his reputation for honesty.

> Men high in society who support men of villainy . . . by this act disgrace their country, & inflict a wound in the breast of every honest man in the country; and establish a precedent that strikes at the root of morality, religion, and virtue, by holding to the rising generations, that it matters not what crimes you commit, how you acquire property, prov[id]ed they do, and revel in their ill gotten wealth, they are the proper subjects for preferment to offices of honor & tryst. . . . The time will shortly arrive when men thus acting in support of villains will meet with the indignant frowns of every honest man.[76]

Jackson's break with Overton and the Nashville elite did not involve him in the defense of popular interests. He allied himself with claims speculators and land lawyers, not small farmers. He did not argue for redistributing the land. Tennessee leaders, including Jackson, speculated in lands to which they had dubious moral and legal title. Jackson thought it possible to purify this history. He wanted to demonstrate, by land litigation as by dueling, that his position could stand public scrutiny and did not derive from "crimes."

Overton thought it best not to look too deeply into the past. As one of Allison's creditors, he complained to Jackson, he had as much right to "scramble" after the estate as Jackson did; he would be satisfied, nevertheless, if he could simply get a release from the "explorers and rectifiers" of land titles. Overton had acquired and sold considerable Allison property after the bankruptcy; now, twenty-five years later, Jackson was forcing him to defend these ancient transactions. Overton well knew the danger of inquiring too deeply into title. Contaminated history is all too evident beneath a lengthy explanation of how he acquired a piece of Allison's Nashville property. Overton had as little secure confidence his title would stand as did Richard, Duke of York, in the title he claimed.

> As to the lot in Nashville I am in no way uneasy about it, for if any property on earth is free secure that must— The facts were simply these —after receiving Judgt against Allison heirs on one of the notes—Colo Wm Gage told me, that for $100 he would inform me where I could find a piece of property—then told me that he had a title from the Trustees of Nashville for lot no 40, but that he had *verbally* agreed with David Allison to convey it to him; that A. had never paid him, but he deemed himself bound to convey to Allison or his heirs—that if the court would decree, he would make no objection—I pd Colo Gage $100—had the lot sold under my Judgt. for $200 more, being the highest bidder myself—filed a bill in equity and obtained a decree against Colo Gage & the heirs of Allison—took possession sold it, and those to whom sold have been at least fifteen years in possession—At the time I purchased, two hundred dollars was thought the full value—besides this I gave Colo Gage $100 for his information—Allison owed me, as you know. I gave the value of the lot without cheating or defrauding any person—a court of Equity gave me a decree for the lot—and have been from 15 to 20 years in possession—If such matters as these are to be compromised, it would seem prudent to go further and give Darby and Whiteside one half of all my property both real and personal; for the liberty of enjoying my other half![77]

Title challenges, Overton imagined, could cost him half his property. "Explorers and rectifiers" were dangerous in America, because property was theft. Title derived from force and fraud against Indians, from speculation, and from manipulation of the law. The preoccupation with property rights, pursued in litigation, was an effort to build a firm foundation on quicksand. Overton, who had made a fortune as land speculator, land lawyer, and judge, sensed this; it was best not to inquire too deeply into original title. Overton would not, like the Duke of York, risk madness in a monomaniacal effort to establish a birthright legitimate to the core. Jackson was Ahab to Overton's Starbuck. His search for legitimate title had by 1821 sent him back to the Indians, not to return their land but to end all doubts about America's right to it.

The Nashville gentry had no quarrel with Jackson's Indian policy, and they apparently rallied behind his presidential ambitions. Overton and Jackson reconciled late in 1823. Jackson broke with Darby the next year, and Darby supported Adams for President. But Jackson's effort to ground tainted acquisitions in law and natural right, whatever the cost in social conflict and broken loyalties, distinguished him from his peers and set him on his individual political course. Overton, secretly using Jackson as a stalking horse for Clay, had sensed his unreliability by now. But Jackson had tapped chords in the country which overwhelmed Overton's intrigues.[78]

V

Land litigation flourished in the absence of respected, legitimate title. If from that point of view it makes perfect sense, from another it has a more mysterious aspect. Surrounded by plentiful vacant land, men fought as if there were not enough to go around. More was at stake than simply a good life on the land.

Unbounded nature, as John Demos points out, enhanced the danger to individual ego boundaries. Some men, rejecting the psychological economy of Protestant capitalism, went wild in the woods, or went to live among Indian tribes. Most resisted regression to so primitive a state. Offered, as Turner put it, "rebirth" in nature, Americans worked to individuate and separate themselves, and establish ownership of the land. A set of feelings rooted in the early stages of child development accompanied these efforts.[79]

Faced with the loss of maternal sustenance, children magically manipulate their own body products. Power over these replaces union with the mother. Now children will control their own "bowels and affection." In the language of land-title disputes, they have "converted the fruits of our labour to our own Emoluments," "without the aid of the parent (or any other State)." They have (Blackstone) "the right of property; or that sole and despotic dominion which one man claims and exercises over the external things of the world, to the total exclusion of the right of any other individual in the universe." "There is nothing which so generally strikes the imagination and engages the affection of mankind."[80]

Loss of property and title reversed the process by which men appropriated nature. It exposed them to "the waspish, hysterical mother," to contamination, invasion, and control. Fears of "the mother state" had a practical basis in land disputes, but they also suggest that psychological autonomy was insecurely achieved. Property served Americans, in the Puritan phrase, as the "outward and visible sign of inward and spiritual grace." Just as in Protestantism, however, so in the development of childhood independence the symbols of power were filled with ambivalence. Ownership partly expressed anger at bad internal objects and the need to control them.

The stage of autonomy, Erikson reminds us, is "a stage originating in the child's sensual experience in that fascinating part of his body which faces away from him, and which excretes that which he learns to consider dirty, smelly, and poisonous." The child's ambivalence toward his own body products marks the anal stage as the stage of shame and doubt. Autonomy "can and does mean independence, but does and can also mean defiance, stubbornness, self-insistence. . . . Defiance, obviously, is shame's opposite." Feelings of shame, doubt, and inner filth are feelings about the body. We have earlier noted Jackson's concern for reputation, and his demands that insults to his character be "publically washed away." Men fighting title conflicts similarly exposed the contaminated possessions of others, and demonstrated their own legitimate right to the land.[81]

Aggression characterizes the healthy child's struggle for autonomy. Child-rearing patterns and cultural values, however, can intensify "defiance," and form a character structure sensitive to invasion and insistent on establishing its rights.[82] Aggression directed outward fed the struggle to conquer American nature. "The still empty cradle of a great nation," as Tocqueville called the west, offered more than sustenance; it offered space for self-assertion as well.[83]

The virgin land, moreover, promised more than a modest competence; it promoted fantasies of enormous possession. Land speculation made some of these dreams come true. Men, it seemed, could regain Eden from a position of control instead of dependence. "The bounties of nature" (Turner) promised to satisfy an insatiable land hunger; competing claimants for the soil threatened to frustrate it.[84] Settled, small freeholders might have resolved land disputes fraternally or pragmatically, without spawning a mass of litigation. Speculators and land companies, engrossing vast acreage in the search for wealth, produced the bulk of land-title disputes in eighteenth-century America.

Dreams of riches spread throughout society in the decades after the Revolution. Speculation was democratized; the middle reaches followed the example of the wealthy. Many easterners, responding to rising land values brought by farm improvements and increased population, sold out and moved west. The declining value of eastern soils also spurred mobility among New England yeomen and southern planters alike. Establishing themselves on new land, Tocqueville believed, American farmers created not a home but a commodity.

> Almost all the farmers of the United States combine some trade with agriculture; most of them make agriculture itself a trade. It seldom happens that an American farmer settles for long upon the land which he

occupies; especially in the districts of the far west, he brings land into tillage in order to sell it again, and not to farm it; he builds a farmhouse on the speculation that, as the state of the country will soon be changed by the increase of population, a good price may be obtained for it. . . .

Thus Americans carry their business-like qualities into agriculture; and these trading passions are displayed in that, as in their other pursuits.[85]

Men did not rest once they had made farms from the wilderness. Some pioneers intended to stay where they were, but land hunger pulled them farther west. As one migrant put it, "When I got to Ohio my Ohio feever began to turn but I soon caught the Missouri feever which is very catchin and carried me off." A nineteenth-century English traveler reported,

There is as yet in New England and New York scarcely any such thing as local attachments—the love of a place because it is a man's own—because he has hewed it out of the wilderness, and made it what it is; or because his father did so, and he and his family have been born and brought up, and spent their happy youthful days upon it. Speaking generally, every farm from Eastport in Maine to Buffalo on Lake Erie, is for sale.[86]

Resolution of title, then, did not usher in an era of pastoral stability. Title disputes were part of a process by which men turned virgin land into revenue, and exchanged one abode for another. This process of change brought a powerful sense of loss into America. Feelings of nostalgia were in part personal. Men lost their farms, as Tocqueville suggested, to litigation, speculation, debt, and mobility. The sense of loss was social as well; it reflected evolutionary changes in American society.

Jackson promised his troops, after their victory in the Creek War,

The weapons of warefare will be exchanged for the utensils of husbandry; and the wilderness which now withers in sterility and seems to mourn the disolation which overspreads it, will blossom as the rose, and become the nursery of the arts.

The blossoming was only temporary, however. An 1849 series of engravings picturing the evolution of a New York valley begins with a leafless, tree-filled, sterile wilderness. Leafy trees and receptive nooks predominate in the first ten years of farming. Within half a century the area has entered commercial wheat production; the rectangular fields appear barren, and the few remaining trees lack leaves. Beyond agriculture, in the imagination of Thomas Cole, lay empire, decadence, decline, and fall. Cole's series of paintings depicting this transformation, *The Course of*

Empire, expressed widely shared fears. His paintings traveled the country to meet constant demands for exhibition.[87]

Economic developments in the Age of Jackson underlay concern for agrarian America. Western virgin lands sustained American economic growth from 1815 to 1845. They functioned, however, to transform America irrevocably away from household arcadia. The percentage of farmers in America declined steadily after 1790. By the 1840s manufacturing and industrialization were gaining in economic importance, and the relative importance of staple-crop agriculture had declined. Development of the virgin land never again dominated American growth. Shifts in the background of political leaders reflected the declining importance of nature. The men who filled the top appointive posts in Jackson's administrations were more likely to be the sons of farmers than their counterparts in the early national period. They themselves, however, were more likely to have made their money as lawyers or business promoters than in land; Adams and Jefferson appointees made theirs in land speculation.[88]

It was the task of American painting, a reviewer wrote, to preserve scenes of nature as the busy country destroyed them.

> The axe of civilization is busy with our old forests, and artisan ingenuity is fast sweeping away the relics of our national infancy. What were once the wild and picturesque haunts of the Red Man, and where the wild deer roamed in freedom, are becoming the abodes of commerce and the seats of manufactures. Our inland lakes, once sheltered and secluded in the midst of noble forests, are now laid bare and covered with busy craft; and even the primordial hills, once bristling with shaggy pine and hemlock, like old Titans as they were, are being shorn of their locks, and left to blister in cold nakedness in the sun. "The aged hemlocks, through whose branches have whistled the winds of a hundred winters," are losing their identity, and made to figure in the shape of deal boards and rafters for unsightly structures on bare commons, ornamented with a few peaked poplars, pointing like fingerposts to the sky.[89]

Had "our national infancy" replenished itself in nature by destroying the land's sustaining power? When they turned land into property, did Americans gain wealth, like Midas, by killing what they touched? Southern planters were known as "land-killers," and northern staple-crop agriculture also depleted the soil. "We can buy an acre of new land cheaper than we can manure an old one," Jefferson complained as Americans neglected centuries of European experience in soil conservation. Rushing to make nature serve their purposes, men girdled and burned trees and promiscuously killed fish and game. A writer surveying the transformed landscape exclaimed, "Nature has been penetrated in her wildest recesses and made to yield her hidden stores." Anxiety over the country's assault on nature gathered momentum during Jackson's lifetime.[90]

Land hunger, many men feared, was fast depleting the virgin wilderness. "Voracious speculators," it was said, "come like the locusts of Egypt" to "devour" the public lands. A Jacksonian registrar of public lands, with his own speculative interest in the public domain, wrote to the General Land Office, "A set of ravenous speculators are carrying everything before them. Already they have blown up the sales at Columbus, and after devouring that carcase, they have commenced here." John Quincy Adams believed there "was something akin to the thirst of the tiger for blood . . . in the rapacity with which the members of the new states fly at the public lands." Such fears were present from the beginning of the republic. An opponent of a 1781 plan to sell the public lands to the states wrote, "It would be like killing the goose that laid an egg every day in order to tear out at once all that was in her belly."[91]

"The infant," writes Donald Winnicott, "aims at breaking through into the mother to take out of her everything that is felt there to be good."[92] Did America's growth from "our national infancy" liberate fears that primitive, destructive, infantile fantasies had triumphed in the world? The burgeoning rural-cemetery movement of the Jacksonian period made reparation for the assault on nature. Its supporters expressed appreciation of natural beauty, and repugnance for the man-made landscape. The movement established cemeteries in idyllic rural settings. It rediscovered and celebrated Indian burial mounds. Even nomadic peoples, its promotional literature pointed out, built sanctuaries for the dead. Wilson Flagg explained that cemeteries in nature provided links to the past when paternal homes were changing all the time. The cemeteries sank permanent roots in American soil. Neil Harris summarizes,

> With nature offering history and mystery as well as beauty, Americans expiated their devastations against her—the jagged, man-made wounds into the benevolent land, the ditches, fences, railroads and highways. These were still new and ugly, and needed to be healed and disguised. Men wished a return to harmony with a once-hostile environment; having been mastered it could now be won more amiably. In covering up the dead with trees and flowers, in adorning their final homes in the soil, such a reconciliation had been begun. "Let us go to the resting-places of the dead, where the turfs lie in verduous heaps, and the flowers of the fields scatter their incense [wrote Flagg]. . . . Here will the gentle mother receive us, and when we can no longer be comforted by religion or philosophy, she lulls us to rest by the assurances of religion."[93]

When in the 1780s Colonel Robertson called the Cumberland valley "our promised land," his wife responded, "The promised land ought to insure rest to its inhabitants." Their neighbor Mrs. Jennings added, "Our rest will be in the grave: not here, but hereafter; not upon earth, but only in heaven." The cemetery movement half a century later finally offered rest upon earth, for the dead.[94]

Fears for the destruction of nature may seem a far cry from the ordinary concerns of nineteenth-century Americans. It would be wrong to exaggerate the articulate presence of such fears, but it would be equally wrong to think they were restricted to a genteel, nature-loving elite. The pastoral ideal, which flourished in Jacksonian America, arrested at the stage of rural idyll the changes wrought on the American landscape. It sought to create lasting national symbols from American love for the cultivated soil. It denied the European charge that Americans lacked "local attachments." As a Tennessee historian born early in the nineteenth century remembered the Carolina country of his (and Jackson's) boyhood,

> The primitive simplicity of the pastoral stage of society, with its calm, quiet, and security, its freedom from care, from avarice and the rivalries of the older communities, stamped the infant settlements with the impress of another Arcadia, pure, contented, free, enlightened, enterprising, and independent.[95]

This reminiscence is typical of pastoralism. It placed the ideal among "the infant settlements" of the past, powerless to resist the transformation of American society. Pastoralism celebrated the past, or a present slipping rapidly away. It derived its power from the fear of loss, was essentially nostalgic in character, and often sentimentalized self-inflicted wounds. Pastoralism flourished in an ideal realm, split from the acquisitive temptations which undermined arcadia. The pastoral dream expressed the fantasy life of a nation going about its business. Rural cemeteries were perhaps the most telling monuments to pastoralism. Jacksonian Democracy was its major political expression.[96]

Marvin Meyers has described Jacksonian Democracy as the "struggle to reconcile again the simple yeoman values with the free pursuit of economic interest, just as the two were splitting hopelessly apart."[97] For Jacksonian leaders, who had left their fathers' farms to enter the business and political world, this struggle was a personal one. It was yet more deeply personal for Jackson himself. Jackson secured "the wild and picturesque haunts of the Red Man" for white settlement. He was the single man most responsible for opening the development of the west. He sought as President, we shall argue in Part III, to save white Americans from the unintended consequences of the devastation he had wreaked on their red brothers.

V I

Anxiety for the loss of nature reached its height in the 1840s. This was also the decade of Manifest Destiny—Oregon, Texas, California. Agrarian nostalgia did not imprison men in history, helpless to resist the march of time; it fed the westward movement instead. "Land enough—land enough," Major Davezac, Jackson's aide-de-camp at New Orleans, told the New Jersey State Democratic convention.

> Make way, I say, for the young American Buffalo—he has not got land enough; he wants more land as his cool shelter in summer—he wants more land for his beautiful pasture grounds. I tell you, we will give him Oregon for his summer shade, and the region of Texas for his winter pasture. . . . He shall not stop his career until he slakes his thirst in the frozen ocean.[98]

The "great, powerful, enterprising and rapidly growing nation" (John Quincy Adams) never had finally to face the consequences of growing up. It could begin again on the frontier. In Turner's words, "Here was an opportunity for social development continually to begin over again, wherever society gave signs of breaking into classes. Here was a magic fountain of youth in which America continually bathed and was rejuvenated." At the age of twenty-one, Jackson had begun again on the frontier. Nostalgia for the land did not enter his politics until he had gained secure possession of nature in Indian war and watched it begin to slip away. Westward expansion, however, dominated his public life from the beginning.[99]

The founders themselves underlined the importance of expansion. Space, Madison argued in *Federalist* No. 10, diluted the violence of faction. Jefferson agreed. The people would remain virtuous, he wrote Madison in 1787, "while there remain vacant lands in any part of America. When we get piled together upon one another in large cities, as in Europe, we shall become corrupt as in Europe, and go to eating one another as they do there."[100]

The early national administrations, however, sacrificed southwestern expansion to other interests. This brought the frontier into conflict with national authority, and made southwestern expansion sectional and divisive. The major southwestern political aims in the 1790s—protection against Indian attacks, the free navigation of the Mississippi, and the rapid settlement of the southwest—shared an expansionist thrust. Chapter 5 will examine frontier Indian policy. Indians aside, the Mississippi question was the major issue of frontier politics from the close of the Revolution to the Louisiana Purchase. Frontier leaders demanded that the Mississippi River be opened to American commerce. The frontier would be strangled without the Mississippi, its leaders insisted; it could not market its crops and could not grow. Spain controlled the river, but smuggling and Spanish permission removed the barriers to existing trade. The problem, as frontier leaders saw it, lay in the future. The southwestern economy would remain primitive until planters were guaranteed permanent free access to the New Orleans harbor. Speculators in southwestern lands, who had put their money where their dreams were, pushed for a resolution of the Mississippi question.[101]

The Bill of Rights of the Tennessee constitution declared, "The free navigation of the Mississippi is one of the inherent rights of the citizens of this state. It cannot be, therefore, conceded to any prince, potentate, power, person or persons whatever." A frontier petition sent to Jackson in 1793 proclaimed, "Your remonstrants are entitled by Nature and by stipulation to the undisturbed Navigation of the river Mississippi." "The God of Nature," declared the Democratic-Republican Society of Frankfurt, Kentucky, gave America the right to the Mississippi. "If the General Government will not procure it us, we shall hold ourselves not responsible for any consequences that may result from our own procurement of it."[102]

Spain was a weak power; southwestern agitation increased markedly after France acquired New Orleans. Fears that France would become, in Jackson's words, "masters of the mouth of the Mississippi" and shut off commerce for good contributed heavily to Jefferson's Louisiana Purchase.[103]

The Louisiana Purchase, Jefferson believed, provided the "vacant lands" that would preserve agrarian virtue. Expansion of settlement was also a frontier aim. Frontier leaders sought to push back the Indians, and to assert American sovereignty over territory claimed and occupied by Spain. Spain had strong claims to all the land south of the 31st parallel, from western Georgia to the Mississippi River. This territory, frontiersmen insisted, belonged of right to the new nation.[104]

Federalist administrations, frontier leaders believed, opposed the growth of the west. Oppressed by the national government, the frontier pursued an independent course. "Attachments to governments," declared the Kentucky Democratic-Republicans, "cease to be natural when they cease to be mutual." Kentucky and Tennessee leaders contemplated independent military adventures in the southwest and actual secession and alliance with Spain. The Spanish intrigue was furthest advanced in Kentucky. James Wilkinson and other Kentucky politicians schemed for over a decade to detach Kentucky from the Union; Wilkinson remained a

Spanish pensioner long after he was appointed brigadier general in the American army. The Cumberland settlement also made overtures to Spain which involved Jackson in his first political intrigue. The year he arrived in Nashville he joined James Robertson and Daniel Smith in a proposition to Spain. America's failure to protect the Cumberland settlement from Indian attack, they wrote Spanish authorities, might lead the settlers to "seek a more attractive connection." Cumberland leaders named their region the Mero district in honor of the Spanish Governor of West Florida, Esteban Miró.[105]

The talk of secession was probably intended only to assuage Spanish fears of southwestern expansion. Robertson, Smith, and Jackson wanted Spanish help in establishing frontier trade with the Indians, as an alternative to Indian raids. Nevertheless, Jackson continued to threaten secession if the national government were not more solicitous of frontier interests. He wrote in 1794 that unless the government defended the settlers from Indian attacks, they would have to "seek a protection from some other Source than the present."[106]

As Spanish power in the southwest grew weaker, frontier leaders gradually shifted from placating Spain to planning filibusters against her territory. Some plans envisioned attaching the Spanish southwest to the United States after an unauthorized war of conquest. Others imagined an independent empire, from Kentucky south to Florida, allied with Britain or France. The western Democratic-Republican societies formed in 1793–94 did more than support the French Revolution. They planned to "revolutionize" Spanish possessions in the American south. French representative Edmund Genêt promoted this scheme; he was expelled by the Federalist government only after frontier invasion plans were well advanced.[107]

Pinckney's 1795 Spanish treaty gave America possession of the territory east of the Mississippi and north of the Floridas. It did not resolve navigation of the Mississippi. Tennessee Senator William Blount planned a filibuster against Spain's remaining southern possessions a year later. Blount, whose speculations covered millions of acres, suffered from a collapse in the price of western lands in 1796. David Allison's failure brought him close to ruin. Settlement of the western country, he wrote, particularly the region around Muscle Shoals, was essential if "my western lands" were to recover their value. Blount believed that only an invasion of Spanish territory, in alliance with England, could free the southwest from Indian attacks and permanently open the Mississippi. It is not altogether clear what his plans were. Presumably England would get Louisiana and the Floridas, the American frontier would gain an open Mississippi, and Blount and his supporters would acquire ownership of land in the conquered territory.

Blount raised troops and enlisted widespread frontier support. Exposed at the last moment, he fled the Senate to avoid arrest and found refuge in Tennessee. Jackson, Robertson, and other Tennessee leaders were probably ignorant of the Blount conspiracy, but they did not find it morally opprobrious. Expelled from the U.S. Senate, Blount was elected to preside over the Tennessee Senate. Jackson, still loyal to Blount, took his place in Washington.[108]

Frontier speculators like Blount and Jackson merged their personal economic interests in an aggressive sectional expansionism. They grounded their politics in appeals to nature. Expansionism in the 1790s, however, promoted sectional particularism at the expense of American nationalism. It had a divisive rather than a unifying thrust. Jackson, involving himself in Burr's southwestern conspiracy ten years later, remained for a time a sectional expansionist hostile to national power.[109] It was his genius that, early identified with frontier particularism, he ultimately harnessed expansion to American national solidarity. He owed this triumph to the Indians.

PART II

WHITES AND INDIANS

CHAPTER 4

CHILDREN OF NATURE

America you don't really want to go to war.
America it's them bad Russians.
Them Russians them Russians and them Chinamen. And
    them Russians.
The Russia wants to eat us alive. The Russia's power
    mad. She wants to take our cars from out our garages.
Her wants to grab Chicago. Her needs a Red Readers'
    Digest. Her wants our auto plants in Siberia. Him
    big bureaucracy running our fillingstations.
That no good. Ugh. Him make Indians learn read. . . .

—Allen Ginsberg, "America"

America regenerated itself in nature. Pioneers entered "the wild and picturesque haunts of the red man" in "our national infancy." The country
matured by replacing Indians, those who made the first seventy-five years
of its history believed. Historians, however, often split this maturing process into discrete compartments, and drain each of its symbolic significance.
Frontiersmen, it is said, simply took Indian land, in a process lacking moral
or psychological meaning for them. Benevolent national statesmen, limited
by their commitment to popular democracy, sought to contain the worst
frontier excesses.[1]

    Jackson's life explodes this dichotomy. Jackson began on the frontier.
Failing as speculator, frontier politician, and family man to establish his
authority securely, he returned to nature in Indian war. A deadly combat
of brothers secured Jackson's birthright, and prepared him to claim national authority. The symbolic significance to whites of "the sons of the
forest" made Jackson's history possible.

    The cultural myth about Indians performed a double task. It justified
the history of America, and it justified the histories of individual men. Its
first stage addressed the "children of nature," the Indian primitiveness
which doomed the race. This imaginative anthropology of the Indian
character will be examined in the present chapter. Its second stage cele-

brated the heroic struggle in which the white brother won the birthright of the red. This was not merely myth, but Andrew Jackson's history; it is the subject of the next chapter. The third stage portrayed the paternal responsibilities of whites toward the remaining red children. "The infant with whom [the red man] used . . . to contend," Thomas L. McKenney explained, "had become a giant of overpowering strength."[2] Acting, to recall Van Buren's words, as the Indians' "guardians" and "benefactors," white fathers redeemed the debt to the children they had replaced. Chapters 6 and 7 trace the development of Jackson's paternal Indian politics.

I

The American family began, in the ante-bellum white imagination, with the mother and child. Indians were "the children of nature," "the sons of the forest."[3] They were children because of their unrestrained impulses, and because they remained unseparated from nature. Indians, in the white view, had never severed the maternal tie. White metaphors resemble, to their details, psychoanalytic descriptions of fantasies of the oral stage of infant bliss.

Thomas McKenney, chief administrator of Indian affairs from 1816 to 1830, offered the typical picture of the aboriginal tribes in pre-Columbian times.

> Onward, and yet onward, moved the bands, clothed in winter in the skins of beasts, and in the summer free from all such encumbrances. The earth was their mother, and upon its lap they reposed. Rude wigwams sheltered them. Hunger and thirst satisfied, sleep followed—and within this circle was contained the happiness of the aboriginal man.[4]

Indians were perfectly at home in nature. They had a primitive, preconscious, pre-civilized innocence. They had not yet become separated from the earth, but enjoyed "almost without restriction or control the blessings which flowed spontaneously from the bounty of nature."[5] Savages lived in a world of plenty, protected and nurtured by mother nature. Their world was Eden, or paradise.

Their connectedness to nature in no way restricted Indian freedom, in the white view. Aborigines were free to wander from place to place without losing the tie to nature. Manly and independent, they "never submitted themselves to any laws, any coercive power, any shadow of government." Their social order seemed perfectly anarchic. They would neither take orders nor give them, British and American commanders of Indian warriors complained. Their perfect individual liberty extended, in the white view, within the Indian family. Sam Houston ran away from

home as an adolescent and lived several years among "the untutored children of the forest"; he said he liked "the wild liberty of the red man better than the tyranny of his own brothers." The eighteenth-century Scotch
trader James Adair, who lived among the Cherokees for thirty years, wrote,

> Their darling passion is liberty. To it they sacrifice everything, and in the
> most unbounded liberty they indulge themselves through life. They are
> rarely chided even in infancy, and never chastise with blows. Reason, they
> say, will guide their children when they are come to the use of it, and
> before that time they cannot commit faults.

Although Indians spoke often to whites of the land and the bones of their
fathers, the savages' connection to nature and freedom from paternal governmental authority seemed to excite white imaginations most.[6]

Some whites emphasized the original maternal comfort enjoyed by
Indians. Others, of a more independent, adventurous, or rational cast,
stressed savage liberty. Indians in both views gained strength from their
connection to nature. Savage liberty and maternal nurturing recall the
early "dual-unity" stage of the mother-child relationship, in which the
child imagines himself at once omnipotent and protected because he is not
separated from the mother.[7]

Francis Parkman reduced the metaphor to its psychological essence:

> The Indian is hewn out of rock. You can rarely change the form without
> destruction of the substance. Races of inferior energy have possessed a
> power of expansion and assimilation to which he is a stranger; and it is this
> fixed and rigid quality which has proved his ruin. He will not learn the
> arts of civilization, and he and his forest must perish together. The stern,
> unchanging features of his mind excite our admiration from their very
> immutability; and we look with deep interest on the fate of this irreclaim-
> able son of the wilderness, the child who will not be weaned from the
> breast of his rugged mother.[8]

Why the sense of doom in Parkman's passage? Why cannot the bliss
of the infant at the mother's breast be sustained? Why must the Indian
relinquish Eden or die, and why can he not give it up? The whites gave
two related answers. First, the Indians would not work; they were improvident and lacked the "principles of restraint"[9] necessary to preserve
themselves against adversity. Overlooking, for their own political and
myth-making functions, extensive Indian agriculture (which had kept the
first white settlers from starving), whites perceived Indians simply as wandering hunters.[10] They could not be made to turn to agriculture; they
would not "subdue and replenish" the earth, as the incessantly quoted
biblical injunction ordered. They would not forsake the primitive, oral,

accepting relation with nature and try to control and subdue her. They would not accumulate property, build lasting edifices, make contracts, and organize their lives around rules and restraints. They would not, so to speak, move from the oral to the anal stage.

The typical description of this unwillingness revealed the writer's own sense of loss, his own envy of the presumed Indian condition. Lewis Cass, the politician who had most dealings with northern Indians in the decades following the War of 1812, sympathized,

> It is easy, in contemplating the situation of such a people, to perceive the difficulties to be encountered in any effort to produce a radical change in their condition. The *fulcrum* is wanting, upon which the lever must be placed. They are contented as they are; not contented merely, but clinging with a death-grasp to their own institutions. . . . To roam the forests at will, to pursue their game, to attack their enemies, to spend the rest of their lives in listless indolence, to eat inordinately when they have food, to suffer patiently when they have none, and to be ready at all times to die . . . how unwilling a savage would be to exchange such a life for the stationary and laborious duties of civilized societies.

In McKenney's words,

> Who are they of all the race of Adam, that would surrender all the freedom, and the abundance, that were enjoyed by the North American Indian, when his country was first invaded by our race, and place himself, voluntarily, under the restraints which civilization imposes? It is not in the nature of man to do this. It requires, before he can bring himself to endure the labor and toil that attend upon the civilized state, the operation of that stern law—necessity.[11]

As long as the Indians held property in common, they could not break their tie to nature; they would not work and save. "Separate property in land is the basis of civilized society." "The absence of it is the cause of want and consequently of decrease of numbers." Without private property there was no individual incentive to appropriate the fruits of one's labor. Moreover, the stage before private property was, in the liberal view, the stage prior to the development of active, individuated egos. "The absence of the *meum* and *teum*, in the general community of possession . . . is a perpetual operating cause of the *vis inertiae* of savage life. . . . [Private property] may not unjustly be considered the parent of all improvements." "At the foundation of the whole social system lies individuality of property. It is, perhaps, nine times out of ten, the stimulus that manhood first feels; with it come all the delights that the word home expresses."[12]

The oral stage, in Freudian theory, precedes development of a separate, individuated ego. White Americans implicitly applied the same personality theory to the Indians. Indians, in the white view, lived in an undifferentiated relation to nature. In James Madison's words, "By not incorporating their labor, and associating fixed improvements with the soil, they have not appropriated it to themselves." Nature appropriated to oneself through work underlay ownership and control of the self.[13] Lacking private property, Indians lacked a self they could call their own. Since they remained in oral dependence on nature, Indians could not take care of themselves.

The Indian dependence on the oral stage was not metaphysical. He who does not work will one day not be able to eat. The primitive bounty of nature, Americans insisted, was not inexhaustible. As the whites invaded Indian land, killed their game, and destroyed their crops, Indians began to starve in large numbers. This was taken as a sign of their improvidence; their alleged failure to use government rations frugally was further evidence.[14] Horace Greeley, crusading anti-slavery editor and future presidential candidate, summed up the white consensus after a trip through the west in 1859:

> The Indians are children. Their arts, wars, treaties, alliances, habitations, crafts, properties, commerce, comforts, all belong to the very lowest and rudest ages of human existence. . . . Any band of schoolboys from ten to fifteen years of age, are quite as capable of ruling their appetites, devising and upholding a public policy, constituting and conducting a state or community as an average Indian tribe. . . . [The Indian is] a slave of appetite and sloth, never emancipated from the tyranny of one passion save by the ravenous demands of another. . . . As I passed over those magnificent bottoms of the Kansas . . . constituting the very best corn land on earth, and saw their men sitting round the doors of their lodges in the height of the planting season, . . . I could not help saying, "These people must die out— there is no help for them. God has given the earth to those who will subdue and cultivate it, and it is vain to struggle against his righteous decree."[15]

[margin note: women did these things typically]

Childish irresponsibility, Greeley insists, will bring deserved death upon the Indians; one need no longer pity them, or hesitate over expansion onto Indian lands. More deeply, Greeley, McKenney, and Cass could not envy unambiguously the Indian world of childhood freedom and maternal protection. Such longing violated just the liberal independence and self-reliance which called it forth. In Greeley's formulation, rage at the need to forsake one's own private Eden was directed against those who refused to forsake theirs. Having lost their own Eden, the whites could take Indian land as well.

The rage was not simply that of an anal society against its own fantasies of oral bliss. There was another argument, about another rage. The Indians, it was held, had by their own primitive violence given up their right to inhabit Eden.

II

The mythology of Indian violence turned Indians into "monsters in human shape." "Infuriated hell-hounds," they disturbed the "forest paradise" instead of inhabiting it. Remove the Indians from the southwest, said Tennessee Governor Wylie Blount, and each settler "will cultivate his own garden of Eden."[16]

In part those who emphasized Indian violence did not stress savage nobility. Many writers, however, recognized the deep intimacy between innocence and violence. Men like Francis Parkman and Lewis Cass stressed them both equally and found them inextricably related—as innocence and violent loss of self-control would be in children. Sometimes the same Indians were pictured alternately as playful and warlike. Like children, these Indians were not responsible for their violence; they lacked the intelligence and sense of responsibility of more advanced peoples. Elsewhere, in a literary cliché, Indians were split into the noble savage and the "starved wolf," "the man who would scalp an infant in his cradle."[17]

Violent Indians predominated for frontier settlers. Even they found a place for heroic warriors, but the sentimentality of McKenney, revolving around Indians nurtured by nature, was largely absent. It is well to understand, therefore, the common root of innocence and violence, bliss and rage, as these emotions were projected onto the children of nature.

Melanie Klein has suggested that the infant at the breast has primitive rages as well as fantasies of bliss and plenty. He totally devours the breast, in these "body destruction fantasies," and enters the mother and devours her imagined bodily contents. In part these fantasies of the "manic feast" are innocent in origin; in part they express the infant's primitive destructive impulses. Infant sadism is given added force from rage at the withdrawal of the breast. The infant wants to retaliate against the protective mother who has withdrawn her nurture. These vengeful fantasies are themselves intolerable, as the infant both creates from his projections a persecutory mother who must be destroyed, and blames himself and his devouring desires for the loss of the breast.

I am not sure what it means to speak of infant aggressive rages, or to allege that separation anxiety engenders in the baby elaborated fantasies of oral bliss and rage. Such language may well impose adult categories meaningless to infant experience. But the oral stage engenders both the energy for those fantasies and their content. Later childhood or adult longing to return to the imagined state of oral bliss is inseparable from vengeful rage against the mother, self-accusations, and persecutory fantasies.[18]

For our purposes two points must be stressed. First, oral bliss and primitive rage both aim to end the separation of the child from the mother; both involve "regression to the phase that preceded the evolution of the ego [and] . . . the testing of reality."[19] In fantasy the mother and the separate ego are destroyed. Since oral rage aims at total unity and destruction, Mrs. Klein labels it "schizophrenic" or "insane."

Second, longing for union carries with it desire for vengeance. Those suffering from separation anxiety experience both longing for union with the mother and primitive rage against her. Some find it more acceptable openly to indulge nostalgia for nurturing; thus in a McKenney the bliss is open, the rage present but disguised. For a man like Jackson, however, and for the movement he fathered, nurture was anathema. Here the destructive passions were more available, the others more defended against. For such men the identification with Indians was an identification with Indian violence; they longed at once to experience rage and to destroy the spontaneous natural life, embodied in Indians, which called it forth. Violence joined nurture and liberty as a defining Indian quality which liberal society found both attractive and forbidden, and with which it had to come to terms.

The identification with Indian violence was not normally straightforward. Some fabled backwoodsmen, seeking vengeance for the massacres of their families, became like the ferocious Indians they imagined. Others, like Davy Crockett, slipped unselfconsciously from killing Indians to scalping corpses and participating in Indian victory rituals.[20] Conservative easterners insisted that respectable frontiersmen like Jackson were also as violent and barbaric as Indians. Frontier leaders rejected this identification. They admitted their own violence only as a temporary response to Indian violence. The vengeful Indian served, in the east and on the frontier, as a scapegoat for violent fantasies; his punishment relieved the guilt they engendered.

For some Americans terror of Indians was not simply fantasized. Many on the frontier saw their families killed, wounded, or scalped by Indians. Many more, as young children, hid under beds while their relatives fought off Indian attacks, or participated, from adolescence on, in defending their homes. Tennessee Senator Felix Grundy asserted that the scalping of his brother was his first childhood memory. Lewis Cass remembered seeing, as a ten-year-old, his father returning home with Indian scalps. Countless other children and adults heard stories, real or exaggerated, of Indian massacres.[21]

Stereotypes of Indian violence, then, grew from an actual historical situation. Had they been manufactured from thin air, they could hardly have achieved their cultural dominance. Aided by the culture, the psyche created fantasies out of its available experience. Atrocity stories, exaggerated and universalized, provided a horrifying and tempting cultural symbol. Personal projections shared in, and powered, the cultural stereotype.

From an early and vulnerable age children learned to identify Indian "monsters" with their own private fantasies. Indians were the bogeymen who frightened children in early America. The doctor who had attended dying Seminole warrior Osceola hung the Indian's skull on his bedpost to frighten his misbehaving children.[22] In Thomas McKenney's words,

> Which of us has not listened with sensations of horror to nursery stories that are told of the Indian and his cruelties? In our infant mind he stood for the Moloch of our country. We have been made to hear his yell; and to our eyes have been presented his tall, gaunt form with the skins of beasts dangling around his limbs, and his eyes like fire, eager to find some new victim on which to fasten himself, and glut his appetite for blood. . . . We have been startled by the shriek of the dying mother; and hushed that we might hear the last sigh of the expiring infant. . . .[23]

Melanie Klein comments about nursery anxieties such as these,

> We get to look upon the child's fear of being devoured, or cut up, or torn to pieces, or its terror of being surrounded and pursued by menacing figures, as a regular component of its mental life; and we know that the man-eating wolf, the fire-spewing dragon, and all the evil monsters out of myth and fairy stories flourish and exert their unconscious influence in the phantasy of each individual child, and it feels itself persecuted and threatened by those evil shapes.[24]

Culturally shared imagery brought a violent savage to life in the inner worlds of nineteenth-century Americans. The savage evoked powerful feelings of primitive rage, structured into an elaborate set of connected images. First, Indian violence was exterminatory; it threatened ego boundaries, political boundaries, and personal dismemberment. Second, the imagery of violence, as McKenney's language suggests, was oral. Third, women and children were its targets. Finally, the violence was perceived as presexual.

Whites fought Indians in the name of self-defense. They understood by self-defense both the defense of frontier families against Indian attacks and the defense of "infant communities" against attacks which would annihilate the political body. "Guardians to this infant settlement" on the Cumberland feared in 1783 that powerful tribes threatened "ye peace and welfare of this our infant settlement."[25] Indians attacked America before the secure emergence of the country. They exemplified fears that the independent nation could not survive, fears that had led many Americans to intrigue at its dismemberment.[26] Indians were the first enemies the young country had to conquer. Expressing his gratitude for Jackson's invasion of Florida in pursuit of the Seminoles, Mississippi Senator George Poindexter proclaimed, "You have protected us in the time of our infancy against the inexorable Red Sticks and their allies; you have compelled them to relinquish possession of our land, and ere long we shall strengthen into full manhood under the smiles of a benefecient Providence."[27]

Indians attacked the young nation at its boundaries, keeping them confused and insecure. Whites' images indicate that concern over the country's boundaries aggravated, and was reinforced by, concern over the boundaries of their own egos. A securely individuated ego requires a stable sense of boundaries between self and environment, and whites insisted America too needed stable boundaries to mature. At the same time mobility and expansion aborted stable environments in America and tied national identity to individual mobility and expansion across the continent. This generated ambivalence about boundaries and limits, and Indians suffered for it.

On the one hand, Indians were a threat to stable boundaries. Mobility, many writers feared, destroyed stability and family attachments. But Indian culture embodied these qualities *in extremis*. Indians, one nineteenth-century writer explained, were peculiarly characterized by "the absence of private property," the "want of a home," the practice of "roaming from place to place," and "the habit of invading without scruple the land of others." Only private property, whose significance for liberalism I have already noted, saved mobile, expansionist Jacksonian America from fitting this description.[28]

Indians not only embodied absence of boundaries; they also invaded white boundaries. Peace talks with the Indians "infesting our frontier," wrote the young Andrew Jackson in 1794, "answer no other Purpose than opening an Easy door for the Indians to pass through to Butcher our citizens." Florida, complained a southern Senator during the Second Seminole War, was "bleeding at every pore." As long as Indians remained on Georgia land, insisted Governor G. M. Troup, Georgia's "political organization is incompetent; her civil polity is deranged; her military force cannot be reduced to systematic order and subordination; the extent of her actual resources cannot be counted; and all because Georgia is not in the possession of her vacant territory." Security was possible only once the Indian threat on the borders was finally stilled and whites did not have to coexist with independent realities unconnected to them and beyond their control.[29]

The vision of Indian violence threatening the selfhood of young

America reversed the actual situation. The expanding nation reiterated the claim of self-defense as it obliterated one tribe after another. Self-defense against the Indians, as we shall see, excused expansion into Florida, Texas, and (less successfully) Canada.[30] Indians were the bad children on whom whites projected their own aggressive expansionism.

Indians hardly endangered American existence, in spite of the language of self-defense. But this rhetoric expressed a deeper truth. American identity was based on expansion. Resisting the westward movement, Indians threatened to contain the country within a fixed space and a fixed social structure. Standing in the path of expanding, independent, young America, one tribe after another would, as Thomas Hart Benton put it, "be swallowed up" in "the wave of American population." Swallowing Indians, America would not be forced to coexist with recalcitrant realities, nor suffer from exterminatory rages provoked by its own aggression.[31]

White descriptions of Indian atrocities concretely expressed the terror of primitive rage. Lewis Cass insisted that Indians were taught from infancy to take pleasure in war and inflicting cruelty, that they indulged a "never tiring love of vengeance," and that a "man-eating Society" which devoured prisoners flourished among some tribes. A nineteenth-century history of the eastern frontier was more graphic: "The Indian kills indiscriminately. His object is the total extermination of his enemies." "Those barbarous sons of the forest exercised . . . the full indulgence of all their native thirst for human blood." Prisoners were saved "for the purposes of feasting the feelings of ferocious vengeance of himself and his comrades, by the torture of his captives."[32]

These passages and countless others like them pictured Indian violence as insane, exterminatory, and dismembering. Its method was oral; and it was protected by primitive magic. Melanie Klein and Géza Róheim describe the aggressive fantasies of adults experiencing separation anxiety in just these terms.

Indians on the warpath were "maddened"; "they fought with the raging fury of maniacs," and their aim was total extermination of the whites. "War, a war of extermination, which calls into the most excited action all the baser elements of his nature, seems the element of his keenest enjoyment and glory." Indians tortured and dismembered their enemies; scalping and other mutilations received prominent attention. Even if a scalped victim survived, it was said, "such injuries to the head often resulted in insanity." Some victims, saved by innumerable head punctures made to form a scab, were allegedly doomed to invalid status the rest of their lives. These tales powerfully linked Indians to nightmares of dismembering madness.[33]

Indian rage was oral. Stories of aboriginal cannibalism received wide prominence in early America. Literal cannibalism, reported in captivity and traveler narratives, shaded easily into the metaphors of cannibalism which dominated white descriptions of savage warfare. One Indian was said to claim, at the outbreak of the Creek War, that he "had got fat eating white people's flesh." The Indians' "thirst for the blood of their reputed enemies is not to be quenched with a few drops," wrote James Adair. "The more they drink, the more it inflames their thirst." The Seminoles, in the words of another writer, "saturated themselves with the blood of American women and children" and retired to their Florida homes; they returned "to glut their vengeance by repeated feasts of innocent blood."[34]

Indians were protected by primitive magic. Prophets convinced them they were omnipotent, beyond harm from bullets. War cries and terrifying war paint indicated to the whites that Indians sought victory through terror and awe rather than practical, adult methods of warfare. White generals and Indian agents, sometimes whistling in the dark, insisted that their soldiers were not children and would not be frightened by Indian shrieks and costumes.[35]

Indian monsters, then, carried out forbidden infantile violence. They partially embodied guilt felt over the child's own aggressive and destructive fantasies. Indian atrocities, as subsequent chapters will show, not only justified wars against Indians; in response to Indian violence whites themselves engaged in fantasies and activities expressing primitive rage. Punishing the criminals permitted them to participate in the forbidden criminal activity.[36]

Indians directed their primal rage, in the white view, against "aged matrons and helpless infants." "The savage . . . buries the tomahawk in the mother's breast, and imbrues his hands in her infant's blood." He "snatched the infant from the nipple of its mother, and bashed its brains out against a tree." "Even the foetal state is criminal . . . ," wrote the Reverend Joseph Doddridge. "It is not enough that the foetus should perish with the murdered mother; it is torn from her pregnant womb and elevated on a stick or pole, as a trophy of victory. . . ." Men could defend themselves; their killing had little symbolic significance. But "helpless women have been butchered, and the cradle stained with the blood of innocence."[37] John Vanderlyn's early-nineteenth-century American painting the *Death of Jane McCrea* shows an Indian holding his victim by the hair. One of Jane's breasts is exposed, and the arm of the Indian about to tomahawk her could equally be aimed at hair, neck, or naked breast. (See Plate 7.) [38]

Exterminatory aggression transformed Indians into bad "children of nature" who totally destroyed the mother and the "innocent babe." Purified by his elimination of these monsters, the good child could grow safely to manhood. "Are we not the true sons of our sires?" asked Maine

Congressman Jonathan Cilley during the Second Seminole War. "Our country is our common mother; and when and while blows are aimed at her, and when she is attacked and bleeding from the wounds of an enemy, who of her sons will not fly to her defence."[39]

Indians not only murdered white women; they also treated their own women badly. Savages gained innocent bliss at the expense of their women. The Indian reposed in nature on the lap of his mother, McKenney explained, but "his squaw" paid the price. "Alas! then, as now, her shoulders were made to bear the weight, and her hands to perform the drudgery of the domestic labor."[40]

Indian men made their women work; white men did not. Indian men left lazy or shrewish wives; white men were trapped. The Moravian minister John Heckewelder reported an Indian's description of the advantages of Indian marriage over white. (The squaw, Heckewelder explained, is referred to as "he" in the passage, since Indian languages contained only the masculine pronoun.)

> White man court—court—court—maybe one whole year! maybe two year before he marry! . . . Well, now suppose cross! scold so soon as get awake in the morning! scold all day! scold until sleep!—all one; he must keep him! White people have law forbidding throwing away wife, be he ever so cross! must keep him always! Well! how does Indian do? . . . no danger he be cross! no! Squaw knows too well what Indian do if *he* cross! throw *him* away and take another! Squaw love to eat meat! no husband! no meat! Squaw do everything to please husband! he do the same to please squaw! live happy![41]

Indians had to be civilized, in McKenney's view, so they would learn to respect their women. The pure, honored white female personified civilized virtues. At the same time expanding America subdued mother nature, and understood this victory in personal terms. Jacksonians' personifications of their enemies—whether effeminate aristocrats or the devouring, "monster hydra" bank—expressed fear of domination by women. The culture resolved its ambivalence over women by splitting femaleness into powerful, uncontrolled menaces, which had to be destroyed, and feminine enforcers of civilized values, who had to be served and protected. A female, robed America, telegraph wires attached to her limbs, floats above the westward movement in a popular nineteenth-century chromolithograph. She directs the disappearance of the Indians. (See Plate 6.) Because Indian men were not separated from savage, rocklike nature, they brutalized Indian women. Once again Indians resolved white ambivalences in unacceptably self-indulgent ways, and had to be punished for it. White self-indulgence came only in the punishment.[42]

The Indian threat to women was not perceived as sexual or Oedipal. Indians did not kill men to possess women. Mothers, not fathers, were the targets of Indian violence. This violence, moreover, was not sexual. Sexual assaults played almost no role in stories of Indian atrocities, in striking contrast to the mythology of blacks. Winthrop Jordan writes,

> Negroes seemed more highly sexed to the colonists than did the American Indians. . . . Far from finding Indians lusty and lascivious, they discovered them to be notably deficient in ardor and virility. (Eventually and almost inevitably a European commentator announced that the Indian's penis was smaller than the European's.) And the colonists developed no image of the Indian as a potential rapist; their descriptions of Indian attacks did not include the Indians "reserving the young women for themselves." In fact, the entire interracial complex did not pertain to the Indians.[43]

Jordan believes white mythology treated Indians more kindly than Negroes. Blacks were sexual threats who had to be repressed; Indians were the first Americans. Certainly there was greater identification with Indians. "The vices of Indians," said Henry Clay, "posed no danger to whites, or to their purity." Clay was contrasting Indians with blacks. The lust of black men and the ardor of black women corrupted white America, in the white imagination. Indian sexuality did not stimulate such fears. But that did not make the Indian danger any less threatening. Blacks represented sexual threat and temptation; the relation had reached the stage of heterosexual desire. The Indian was a fragment of the self, that primitive, oral part which was dangerously indolent and aggressive and therefore, in the name of self-defense, had to be destroyed. Indians evoked images of dismemberment, insane ferocity, and loss of individual identity. They called forth the pre-ego state of undifferentiated bliss and rage. As Leslie Fiedler puts it, if blacks were about sex, Indians were about madness.[44] Blacks were a sexual, Oedipal threat to white men; Indians were a pre-Oedipal aggressive threat to the mother-child relationship. Fathers had not yet entered the picture. They could not, until whites, returning to the bond between mother and child, had protected and purified it. By killing Indians, whites grounded their growing up in a securely achieved manhood, and securely possessed their land.

CHAPTER 5

VIOLENCE AND WAR: THE SUBLIMATION OF THE DEATH INSTINCT INTO AUTHORITY

I should rather have a dead son than a disobedient one.

—Martin Luther

I

"There can be no doubt," wrote Lewis Cass, "that the Creator intended the earth should be reclaimed from a state of nature and cultivated; that . . . a tribe of wandering hunters . . . have a very imperfect possession of the country over which they roam." "Jacob will forever obtain the inheritance of Esau," said Congressman Richard Wilde. "The earth was given for labor, and to labor it belongs."[1] The conflict between Jacob and Esau enshrined for Bible-reading Americans the right of the farming brother to claim the inheritance of the hunter. Every family in Protestant America knew this tale—"that nasty story of brotherly strife abetted by maternal self-indulgence and fraud that has, throughout history, held everyone with horrified fascination."[2] The story of Jacob and Esau prefigured the history of America, but it hardly provided secure grounding for the justice of white claims.

The Lord said to Rebekah, in the Book of Genesis,

> Two nations are in thy womb, and two manner of people shall be separated from thy bowels; . . . and the elder shall serve the younger. And when her days to be delivered were fulfilled, behold, there were twins in her womb. And the first came out red, all over like an hairy garment; and they called his name Esau.

Esau, the hunter, was loved best by his father. Rebekah loved Jacob, who tilled the soil. Esau came home from the hunt one day faint with hunger, and asked Jacob for food.

> And Jacob said, Sell me this day thy birthright. And Esau said, Behold I am at the point to die: and what profit shall this birthright do to me? And Jacob said, Swear to me this day; and he sware unto him: and he sold his birthright unto Jacob. Then Jacob gave Esau bread and pottage of lentils; and he did eat and drink, and rose up, and went his way. Thus Esau despised his birthright.

When Isaac was old and his eyes were dim, he told Esau to bring him venison, and promised to bless him before he died. Rebekah dressed Jacob in animal skins to impersonate Esau and receive his father's blessing. Isaac blessed Jacob:

> God give thee of the dew of heaven, and the fatness of the earth, and plenty of corn and wine: Let people serve thee, and nations bow down to thee: be lord over thy brethren: . . . cursed be every one that curseth thee, and blessed be he that blesseth thee.

Then Esau came to his father, and Isaac discovered the deception.

> And when Esau heard the words of his father, he cried with a great and exceeding bitter cry, and said unto his father, Bless me, even me also, O my father. And he said, Thy brother came with subtilty, and hath taken away thy blessing. . . . And Isaac his father answered and said unto him, Behold, thy dwelling shall be the fatness of the earth, and of the dew of heaven from above; And by thy sword shalt thou live, and shalt serve thy brother; and it shall come to pass when thou shalt have the dominion, that thou shalt break his yoke from off thy neck. And Esau hated Jacob because of the blessing wherewith his father blessed him; and Esau said in his heart, The days of mourning for my father are at hand; then will I slay my brother Jacob.[3]

Esau, the red brother, lived from the "fatness of the earth, . . . and the dew of heaven." The twin born first was hunter and warrior. Jacob dispossessed him, using the very techniques by which whites acquired Indian land. "It may be taken as a certainty," Jefferson had said, "that not a foot of land will ever be taken from the Indians without their own consent." Starving Indians gave their consent, as Esau had, for the promise of food. They "sold their birthright," wrote the Reverend Jeremiah Evarts, "for a *mess of pottage.*" Often when legitimate chiefs refused to consent, whites signed treaties with chiefs who falsely claimed authority, or hired Indians to impersonate those with legitimate title. Gaining title to land by contract, treaty, and consent fitted liberal doctrine. But such title was contaminated. It grounded the white birthright on "subtilty," legal tricks, and feminine wiles instead of heroic action.[4]

Herman Melville's retelling of the Jacob-and-Esau story, *Israel Potter*, portrayed a conflict between Benjamin Franklin and John Paul Jones for the soul of young Israel. "History," wrote Melville, "presents few trios more akin upon the whole, than Jacob, Hobbes, and Franklin; three labyrinth-minded, but plain-spoken Broadbrims, at once politicians and philosophers; keen observers of the main chance; prudent courtiers; practical Magicians in linsey-woolsey." John Paul Jones, with "tawny cheek," "savage, self-possessed eye," "a look of a parading Sioux," and "tattooing such as is seen only on thorough-bred savages," had "an aspect as of a disinherited Indian chief in European clothes." Franklin and John Paul Jones collaborated to fight the revolution. Thereafter their paths diverged; Israel followed "the prowling brave"; he was buried, after many misadventures, in Potter's field.[5]

Israel Potter was Esau's cry of vengeance against the triumphant Jacob. In Jefferson's words again, "After the injuries we have done them they cannot love us, which leaves no alternative but that of fear to keep them from attacking us, but justice is what we must never lose sight of and in time may recover their esteem." Jefferson hoped for justice based on Indian consent. A nation of Jacobs, inwardly identified with Esau, required something more. And there was another alternative. As Secretary of War Henry Knox wrote George Washington, "The Indians being the prior occupants, possess the right of soil. It cannot be taken from them unless by their free consent, or by the right of conquest in a just war."[6]

Andrew Jackson had been too much a Franklin in public life; he wanted to become a John Paul Jones. He had acquired land in bargains, speculations, and legal fees, and was cut off from secure possession of it. He badly needed a just war. War against the Indians would permit Jackson to reexperience his feelings of primitive violence, purify the self of them, and establish legitimate title to the land. He could destroy lingering fears of feminine domination and grow securely to manhood.

Melville would write, "Intrepid, unprincipled, reckless, predatory, with boundless ambition, civilized in externals but a savage at heart, America is, or may yet be, the Paul Jones of nations." Jackson may have been "a savage at heart," but he did not aim to restore Esau's birthright. Only as Esau could he sanctify Jacob, as Paul Jones sanctify Franklin. Jackson, to paraphrase Carl Schorske, would sublimate instinctual rage into authority.[7]

Men confidently possessed the land, frontier leaders believed, only if they had conquered it themselves. Soldiers who fought in the French and Indian, Revolutionary, and 1812 wars were paid in the land they had won. During the Second Seminole War, Thomas Hart Benton sponsored legislation to provide a land bounty to any pioneer who would settle in Florida and defend it against the Indians. "Armed occupation was the true way of settling a conquered country," said Benton. "The children of Israel entered the promised land, with the implements of husbandry in one hand, and the weapons of war in the other."[8]

"The blockade, the stockade, the rifle," said Benton, "have taken the country and have held it." "Let us go back to the ancient and wise practice of our forefathers." In the words of Missouri's other Senator, Louis Linn, "These men would fight for their land, and would love it the more because they had to fight for it. . . . They would make a most effective force to grapple with the Indian, knife in hand, and drive him from his fastnesses."[9]

Kentucky Judge James Ballard, in an 1828 campaign speech, suggested the psychology which underlay armed conquest. Judge Ballard had fought with Jackson at New Orleans; his speech for Jackson recalled the battle spirit of the Kentucky riflemen:

> Apart from the ordinary impulses of patriotism activating men who defend their country's soil against an invader, there was in the heart of hearts of these men a deeper feeling akin almost to fanaticism. Most of them had been born while yet the shadow of the Indian tomahawk hung over Kentucky. Their baby eyes had seen the glare of burning cabins, their young ears had heard the savage war-whoop, and not a few of them had gazed upon the mutilated remains of fathers, mothers, brothers or sisters slain and scalped at their own thresholds.
>
> They knew that all through the dark and bloody infancy of their beloved state British instigation had been at the back of the red demons who wrought all those horrors, and for this they held the British government responsible. . . . So here they transferred to the serried ranks before them all the deadly hate, all the pitiless revenge and all the mortal animosity which had been burned into their souls toward the Indians. . . .
>
> Consider further that men so actuated and so endowed with skill in use of deadly weapons were not merely brave, but that courage was their instinct, congenital, imbibed with mother's milk, that in their code no allowance was made for cowardice.[10]

A courage "imbibed with mother's milk" and tested against Indian attacks during Kentucky's "dark and bloody infancy" inspired the New Orleans defenders. Jackson, I have suggested, was not convinced that he had imbibed courage with his mother's milk. Nor had he fought Indians during Tennessee's infancy. He had encountered them instead in intrigue, diplomacy, and land speculation. This set Jackson apart from the original Tennessee pioneers, and set the stage for his efforts to acquire, in violence, authority.

II

The first settlers on the Cumberland won their land in combat with the Indians. The struggle, as they experienced it, was a fairly equal one, and they triumphed without outside help. The Cumberland valley was the farthest outpost of the settled frontier. The several dozen families who came there in 1780 were 100 miles overland from the nearest white settlement. The land they settled on north of the Cumberland River had been included in Richard Henderson's purchase of Kentucky from the Cherokees in 1775. But this purchase was of dubious validity; it was repudiated by Virginia and North Carolina, which both claimed the region.[11]

On the Indian side the purchase was equally dubious. Indian tribes lacked centralized political structures, and the validity of land cessions varied widely. Georgia and the temporary state of Franklin in what is now east Tennessee signed "treaties" with a few Indians or small bands, ceding lands these Indians did not live or sometimes even hunt on. Claiming with outraged innocence their right to land so ceded, Georgia and Franklin provoked several Indian wars in the late eighteenth century. Henderson himself signed with a more representative and larger collection of Cherokees, including leading men of the tribe. Nevertheless, the cession was not recognized by some Cherokee bands or, until 1783, by the Chickasaws, who also claimed part of the region. By 1780 many Indian villages near the Cumberland contained Indians from more than one tribe, and included whites who had intermarried with Indian women. The loyalties binding such villages to the Cherokee or Chickasaw nations as a whole were attenuated. As John Donelson led pioneers on the long trip down the Cumberland River, Indians called from the shore, "Brothers, how do ye do-o-o-o, come ashore"; it was impossible to know whether their intentions were peaceful. Other Indians attacked a boat which lagged behind, killing several members of the party.[12]

The Cherokees ceded only the land north of the Cumberland, but whites built fortified stations on both sides of the river. Indians made intense and frequent raids on the settlements. Some of the stations were abandoned as many settlers returned to Kentucky or east Tennessee. Once only two stations remained and it seemed the last settlers would be forced to leave. Whites who ventured outside the stations to hunt or tend the fields were always in danger.

The Creeks intermittently raided the Cumberland settlements as part of their frontier war against Georgia. That state made a practice of fabricating treaties and settling Creek land. By the middle 1780s the Creeks were concentrating their attacks solely against Georgia. In 1783 the Chickasaws accepted the white claim to the Cumberland valley. In 1785, after five years of constant warfare between settlers and Cherokees, the Cherokee treaty of Hopewell ceded a large tract of land south of the Cumberland River. Whites now had title to the land they had settled, including the present site of Nashville.

The apparent resolution of legal title provided only a temporary lull in the fighting. Nashville and the surrounding settlements remained under periodic Indian attack for ten years more. The Chickamauga branch of the Cherokees did not recognize the Hopewell treaty. From their mountain villages along the Cumberland, Chickamaugas attacked parties coming down the river, and raided Nashville itself. Settlers in east Tennessee, across the Cumberland Mountains, also violated the treaty. They continued to move onto Cherokee lands, provoking warfare in east Tennessee. Frontier raids against peaceful Cherokee villages, more easily accessible than the Chickamaugas, created further conflict.[13]

When Jackson came to the Cumberland in 1788, the frontier was in turmoil. Whites were often killed along the trail he took, and Indians and whites were killed in middle Tennessee during the first months of his residence there. Jackson's first political effort, a few months after his arrival, sought rapprochement with Spain and trade with the Indians, to end the attacks on the frontier.[14]

The effort at accommodation failed, doomed by the continual advance of the frontier into Indian territory. For the next several years Jackson, like other Tennessee leaders, advocated all-out Indian war. He attacked peace rumors in 1793, writing, "It is Two much to be dreaded, that they Indians has made use of this Finesse to Lull the people to sleep that they might save their Towns and open a more Easy Road to Comit Murder with impunity." "Peace talks" with the Indians "infesting our frontier," he wrote in 1794,

> are only Delusions; and in order to put us of[f] our Guard; why Treat with them does not Experience teach us that Treaties answer No other Purpose than opening an Easy door for the Indians to pass through to Butcher our Citizens.[15]

The federal government, however, wanted peace with the southern Indians. Its first priority was expansion in the northwest; a militant expansionist policy there provoked an Indian war which America did not win until 1794. The country lacked arms, money, and men to fight an Indian war in the south as well. Washington and Secretary of War Henry Knox blamed the southern frontiersmen for provoking Indians by moving onto treaty-guaranteed land. They refused to send soldiers or authorize military expeditions. They signed the treaty of Holston with the Cherokees in 1791, over strong frontier objections. By this treaty the tribe ceded considerable land in east Tennessee on which whites had already settled, and permitted a road to be run through Cherokee country connecting east and middle Tennessee. Many whites violated the treaty as soon as it was signed, moving onto Indian land. Others, like Jackson, continued to buy land claims in Indian territory. Indians, given the right by the treaty to punish intruders, attacked the Tennessee frontier as it expanded onto Cherokee land; they also attacked a stockade just outside of Nashville, and attacked the territorial capital at Knoxville. Some villages thought continued white expansion violated the treaty and justified retaliation; many raids were adventures by independent villages that never accepted the treaty in the first place.

Militia expeditions attacked peaceful Indian villages as well as hostile ones. John Sevier, lacking authorization from the federal administration, invaded the Cherokee nation in 1793 after the Knoxville raid. The next year the Tennessee territorial assembly called for a congressional declaration of war against the Creeks and Cherokees, claiming that Indians had killed 200 settlers since the Holston treaty. Jackson feared the dissolution of the Cumberland settlements. "The frontier Discouraged and breaking and numbers leaving," he wrote. "The Territory . . . is Declining fast, and unless Congress lends us a more ample protection this country will have at length to break or seek a protection from some other Source than the present." Jackson insisted "the whole Cherokee Nation ought to be scurged" for refusing to turn over alleged murderers demanded by whites. Finally in the fall of 1794 James Robertson led a successful but unauthorized expedition against the Chickamauga towns and destroyed them. That same year a federal army defeated the northwestern Indians in the battle of Fallen Timbers. From then on relative peace reigned on the Cumberland frontier. Tennessee was admitted to statehood in 1796; Indian relations had been the most important problem of the territorial period.[16]

Jackson feared invasion of frontier boundaries and the breakup of frontier settlements during his first years in Tennessee. His metaphors suggest early disintegrating threats to the ego; given the vulnerable state of the nascent frontier settlements, they make a certain sense. In part, however, Jackson's alarmist language served other functions than simple self-defense. There was no actual danger, by the time Jackson came to the Cumberland, that Indians could destroy the frontier settlements. The first settlers experienced such genuine fears; by 1794, with 15,000 inhabitants in middle Tennessee, more than survival was at stake.

The elite which followed the original pioneers sought not merely survival but growth; the language of self-defense obscured aggressive intentions. William Blount advocated violating the Hopewell treaty. He opposed the Holston treaty because the Cherokees retained Muscle Shoals, which he coveted, and because he desired an Indian war. Blount and other speculators did not seek simply to defend existing settlements. They wanted to open new territory and increase the value of land they owned in and near Indian country. Jackson himself was a large speculator by 1794, with extensive holdings in Indian territory. Expansionist, speculative aims fed his belligerence.[17]

Disguising his motives, Jackson accused the Indians of designs actually his own. He first sought to "lull" the Indians "to sleep" with the 1789 "Finesse" of Indian trade, to "open a more Easy Road" to expansion. He then favored war. The expanding frontier invaded Indian boundaries, and whites wanted war as much as or more than Indians. Whites signed treaties only to move onto lands retained by Indians, and bought and sold land in Indian country. Was the "Savage Tribe that will neither adhere to Treaties, nor the Law of Nations" the Cherokees or the American Scotch-Irish? Jackson's language suggests a primitive identification with the Indians in which he ascribed to them characteristics of his own people. He was talking about himself.[18]

Whites insisted upon a significant difference between their tribe and the Indians. Just as Jackson grounded his land speculations on law, so he demanded treaty sanction for his own aggression. He obtained federal payment for Robertson's unauthorized invasion, in his only significant congressional activity. He cited Indian butchery to justify the invasion; he also insisted, however flimsy his case, that Robertson's attack was justified under law.[19] Frontier passions required legal sanction. They required, in the psychoanalytic phrase, permission from the superego. They were righteously punitive, not simply libidinal. Want was legitimized in the language of law.

Excessive legalism had, however, its dangers. Jackson followed a legal calling in his first decade and a half in Nashville. He was lawyer, Congressman, Senator, and then Judge of the Tennessee Superior Court from 1798 to 1804. Unlike the first frontier leaders, he did not fight Indians.[20]

General James Robertson and Governor John Sevier, the first pioneer Tennessee leaders, led countless expeditions against the Indians. Robertson defended his own home against Indian attack as well. He and Jackson's father-in-law, John Donelson, founded Nashville. But Donelson was a planter and land speculator, not an Indian fighter, and Jackson followed in his footsteps. He came to the Cumberland after the first settlers, when the land was already won. Indian campaigns remained a prominent feature of frontier life for half a dozen years after Jackson came to Tennessee. Jackson, like most other wealthy frontier gentry, did not join them. He often traveled the dangerous road from Nashville to east Tennessee, but he never defended his home against Indian attack, and he participated only once in pursuit of raiding Indians. When an Indian ambush killed a companion outside of Knoxville, Jackson fled the scene. One biographer surmises that he alarmed the frontier, but he did not participate in the Sevier expedition which followed. Jackson was not a quixotic Indian fighter, but an aspiring young lawyer and land speculator. In the county militia he held the position of judge advocate. Jackson dealt with Indians as land speculator and political intriguer. He had done nothing heroic to establish his own right to the land, to gain authority through its conquest.[21]

Jackson entered maturity, the evidence suggests, deeply divided within himself. He was a successful lawyer and land speculator in public life, and participated in intrigues to win territory. Split from this external "false self system" (R. D. Laing)[22] was a violent inner core. Its only outlet lay in duels and private quarrels, and it threatened always to turn against the outer self. Just too young to fight in the Revolutionary War, Jackson had come just too late to the frontier. Both latecomings left a weight of unearned substance on him. He needed instinctual sanctification for his public success, and he needed to legitimize, control, and bring into his public personality his powerful internal rage. Jackson lacked, in his own estimation, the authority of the revolutionary fathers and of his own predecessors on the frontier. He called Robertson "the *father* of our infant State";[23] there was envy underneath the admiration. Jackson needed a just war, and he sought a military career.

Jackson ran unsuccessfully in 1796 for major general of the Tennessee militia. Governor John Sevier supported his opponent. Military leadership, like politics, was a career favored by southern planters. Jackson sought the position partly to strengthen his credentials as a member of the slaveholding gentry. Military leadership also had a personal meaning in the south, of particular significance to Jackson. He ran for general at the moment when David Allison's failure jeopardized his material prosperity, and after attacks on Rachel had cast doubts on the virtue of his private life. The failure to achieve military leadership, combined with his financial difficulties, may well have seemed to Jackson a judgment on his legal, land-speculating, self-indulgent existence. He accepted appointment as Judge of the Tennessee Superior Court and insisted on the majesty of the law. But his legal authority was claimed, not personally earned in battle. He continued buying and selling land and slaves, supervising his plantation, and running his store. He sought to save himself from disaster as Allison's notes came due. In 1802 he ran again for the highest office in the state militia.[24]

This time Sevier himself was Jackson's opponent. Sevier, barred by the Tennessee constitution from a fourth consecutive gubernatorial term, was enormously popular in Tennessee. He had led thirty-five Indian attacks, and had introduced the Indian war shout as a battle cry for his soldiers. He had won a decisive victory in his last campaign, which had followed the Cherokee attack on Knoxville and the ambush of Jackson and his companion. Fifteen years earlier Sevier had led the revolutionary troops in the British defeat at Kings Mountain, the decisive revolutionary battle in the country of Jackson's boyhood. Sevier's victories protected Jackson without the younger man's participation. Jackson had no achievements comparable to those of the revolutionary father.[25]

Sevier had joined the Blount faction during Tennessee's territorial days. The popular hero from east Tennessee was now at odds with middle Tennessee's wealthy planters like Jackson who succeeded to factional leadership. The militia field officers, members of the frontier gentry, split their votes between Sevier and Jackson. Governor Spencer Roane cast the deciding vote for Jackson.

Jackson and Sevier had feuded after the 1796 election, and they reopened their quarrel now. Sevier was reelected governor in 1803, in spite of Jackson's charges of land fraud against him. Bitterness between the two men intensified. Insisting Sevier had insulted Rachel's honor, Jackson issued a duel challenge from the Sign of the Indian Head Tavern. Twice the two men met and almost came to blows, but Sevier avoided an actual duel. Frustrated, Jackson brawled instead with Secretary of State William Maclin, a Sevier supporter.

Jackson's quarrel with Sevier hurt his popularity. He had replaced Sevier as frontier general formally but not actually, and his new position failed to gain him Sevier's authority. A succession of Tennessee governors in the next decade assigned him no battles to fight. Sevier, reelected to the statehouse, divided the Tennessee militia in two. He demoted Jackson to brigadier general of the West Tennessee Division.[26]

Jackson wanted to become a leader of men in war. He had to demonstrate his control over both the violent emotions called forth by war and the troops who went forth into battle. He wanted to control aggression and use it, not be the slave of undisciplined violence. The militia, Jackson insisted as soon as he became major general, required "subordination and discipline." This was his major theme in the next decade. The militia was indeed an anarchic, individualistic fighting force. Desertion was common and easy, officers' orders were often disobeyed, men fought when it suited them and returned home when it did not. The future leader of Jacksonian Democracy sought to institute control. He opposed the practice by which soldiers elected their field officers. "We want men capable of command," he explained, "who will fight and reduce their soldiers to strict subordination." He favored compulsory military service and drill for all young men, to diffuse military discipline and ardor throughout the population.[27]

Leading a disciplined force in battle, Jackson would demonstrate his authority. Our soldiers need only be told of the invasion of our rights, an abortive 1809 divisional order ran, "to see them like a band of brothers pressing forward into the ranks to Defend the rights liberties and independence, so dearly Bot. and Bequeathed to us by our fore-fathers." Jackson had written a year earlier,

> My pride is that my soldiers has confidence in me, and on the event of a war I will lead them on, to victory and conquest. Should we be blest with peace, I will resign, my military office, and spend my days, in the sweet calm of rural retirement.[28]

Peace was not a genuine blessing, however. Jackson required an actual campaign before he could claim the mantle of "our forefathers" over his "band of brothers." In the absence of war, private quarrels took the place of thwarted public military ambition. There is a repetitive, un-satisfied quality to these quarrels, as Jackson sought and failed to connect them to a heroic public task.

Jackson fought with Sevier in 1803. He began that same year a pro-tracted, vituperative quarrel with General James Wilkinson, commanding the federal army at New Orleans. A revolutionary soldier, Colonel Thomas Butler, had refused Wilkinson's order to cut his hair; Jackson rushed to his defense. Wilkinson, he wrote, was persecuting the "upright . . . col-onel." Hair was one of the "gifts of nature," not subject to capricious military orders from "a base and vindictive mind." Butler was cashiered from the service and died shortly thereafter; his sons became Jackson's wards.[29]

Another quarrel led, in 1806, to Jackson's first consummated duel. Jackson had issued many duel challenges in the preceding twenty years, often on the smallest provocation. In the only duel he had actually fought, however, both contestants had fired in the air. The 1806 duel originated from barroom gossip over a forfeited horse race. It reflected personal and political enmity between the Erwins and the Donelsons, two leading middle Tennessee clans. Rachel's name entered the exchange of letters, and Jackson challenged Charles Dickinson, son-in-law of Joseph Erwin. Dickinson, the younger man, was much the better shot. Jackson decided to let him fire first and not to rush his own reply. Seriously wounded, he gave no sign, took careful aim, waited while the seconds determined that his misfire did not count as a shot, and killed his man. Dickinson died, to Jackson's special satisfaction, believing he had missed his opponent. When friends remarked on Jackson's fortitude, the General replied that he would have killed Dickinson had Dickinson shot him through the brain.[30]

"My dear sir," Jackson's New Orleans factor Washington Jackson wrote after the duel, "its now well known to the world that you are a man of true courage and honor, and therefore hope you'll not endanger yourself in affairs of this nature, particularly with young men." The advice came too late; Jackson was gaining, even in Tennessee, an unsavory reputation for violence. He longed to demonstrate his "courage and honor" in the service of the country, but here too his efforts rebounded against him.[31]

Aaron Burr first visited the Hermitage in 1805, and remained in close contact with Jackson for more than a year thereafter. Burr had embarked on a visionary, expansionist scheme. He dreamed of secession, and of ruling a southwestern empire—Texas, Florida, and the American southwest. Jackson had toyed with secession a decade earlier; now, with middle Tennessee pacified and the Mississippi securely American, he sought only to expand American territory, not to dismember the nation. Burr easily convinced him this was his own desire, and Jackson deeply implicated himself in Burr's schemes. He ordered troops raised on his authority as militia general, his mercantile firm built the boats Burr needed for his expedition, Jackson personally endorsed Burr's notes, and his nephew Stockley Hays traveled with Burr to the south.

The southwestern frontier had long desired war with Spain and the conquest of Texas and Florida for the United States. Jefferson and much of his Cabinet expected war with Spain during the 1804–07 period; Jefferson was demanding cession of west Florida from Spain under a wholly unjustified interpretation of the Louisiana Purchase boundary.

There was all the difference, however, between government-sanctioned expansionist schemes and independent filibusters. After Burr was exposed, Jackson first wrote that he had raised the Tennessee militia under Burr's secret War Department orders. Burr claimed, according to Jackson, that he was authorized to lead an invasion of Florida and Texas in the event of the "inevitable" war with Spain. Burr may have told

Jackson this story, among others, but it is doubtful that Jackson believed it. He later wrote he knew Burr was acting independently of the War Department. According to Jackson's new version, Burr planned merely to settle with his men on the Washita River. If the "inevitable" war with Spain broke out, Burr would gain a commission thanks to his friendship with Secretary of War Henry Dearborn.[32]

Jackson was, as his later unauthorized Florida invasions suggest, willing to provoke a war with Spain for southwestern expansion. Sadly for Jackson, however, the Burr conspiracy resulted only in public discredit and more private strife. Receiving evidence of Burr's secessionist aims, Jackson sent cryptic letters to Jefferson and to Mississippi Governor W. C. C. Claiborne. "The Ides of March, remember," wrote Jackson, as if Burr were a conspirator aiming to kill a king. He thanked the revolutionary soldiers who offered their services against Burr. "Should the disorganizing *traitor* attempt the *dismemberment of our country*," he told them, the example of the troops, "commanded, too, by the *father* of our infant State, General James Robertson," would deter him.[33]

Then Jackson reverted to his earlier trust of Burr and blamed the conspiracy on General Wilkinson (who was indeed implicated) and Secretary of War Dearborn (who was not). When Dearborn questioned Jackson's involvement with Burr, Jackson replied with a duel challenge. He laid the entire conspiracy at Dearborn's door. "You stand, convicted at the bar of justice," he wrote, "of the most notorious and criminal acts, of dishonor, dishonesty, want of candour and justice. . . . You are . . . more unprincipled and worthy of punishment, than the nine tenths of those who have suffered under Robesphere, Marat and Wilkinsons despotism." He accused Dearborn of hounding Colonel Butler from the army and causing his death to prevent Butler from resisting his machinations.[34]

Subpoenaed to testify at Burr's Richmond trial, Jackson publicly proclaimed his sympathy for Burr and his hostility to the administration. He attacked Jefferson for failing to defend the republic against its foreign enemies. Secretary Dearborn, he wrote, could only send him "the merest old woman letter." "I fear we want nerve to purge the body politick of Treason and conspiracy," he told Governor Claiborne. Jackson rightly suspected that General Wilkinson was on the Spanish payroll. Thwarted in his efforts to produce evidence, he asked,

> My god is it possible, that the influence of a great and Publick villain and his friends in this infant republick are such as to overawe the poor but virtuous from disclosing evidence. . . . the virtuious patriot who had courage anough to step forward to warn the country to unmask

Treason and Treachery fell a ruthless victam before the impious and thundering accusations of Wilkison untill *virtue itself* stood *appalled* and *amased* at the sight of the hardy villain Who spurns the power of truth and enquiry and riding triumphant over virtue and his accusers.[35]

Wilkinson was guilty of intrigue, but so was Jackson. Did the force of Jackson's rage derive in part from his projection onto Wilkinson of his own involvement in Burr's conspiracy and earlier frontier intrigues? Guilt and innocence aside, Jackson expressed his feelings in significant language. He turned the metaphors of the revolutionary pamphleteers against the American government itself. "Virtue," intended by the "God of nature" to defend the "infant republick," found itself too weak to do so. "A great and publick villain," "riding triumphant over virtue," threatened the country. Jackson longed to come to the defense of America. But the Burr conspiracy further isolated him. His Tennessee popularity, undermined by the Sevier quarrel and the Dickinson duel, declined further. He had developed a reputation for rash judgment and quick temper, and had turned the Washington administration against him.

Seeking to reverse his declining political fortunes, Jackson tried to foment an Indian war. He seized on rumors of Indian atrocities in 1808, and stories that secret foreign agents were circulating among the tribes. He wrote Jefferson, "These scenes bring fresh to our recollection the influence during the revolutionary War, that raised the scalping knife and tomhalk against our defenceless women and Children." The militia "will pant for the orders of our government to punish a ruthless foe." But Jefferson refused to issue orders for a frontier war, and Jackson's several mobilizations of the militia had to be canceled.[36]

Jackson supported Monroe against Madison for President in 1808, believing Monroe would take a more aggressive course against Indians and English. His efforts found little support even in Tennessee. Jackson had been forced, in addition, to liquidate his store and sell more land to meet his debts. Friends and relatives were moving south to a colony of flourishing planters near Spanish-held Baton Rouge. Jackson decided in 1810 to move once again to the frontier. He sought an appointment as Judge for Madison County in southern Mississippi territory. Frustrated in his hopes for military leadership in a southwestern campaign, Jackson would move there himself.[37]

American planters were settling and speculating in Spanish territory as well as their own. Shortly, with President Madison's connivance, they would "revolutionize" the Baton Rouge portion of west Florida. Jackson was informed of these developments, and watched them benignly, but he did not participate.[38] His letter indicating interest in the Mississippi judgeship was melancholy:

From my persuits for several years past, from many unpleasant occurrencies that took place during that time it has given to my mind such a turn of thought, that I have laboured to get clear off [of]. I have found this impossible, and unless some new persuit to employ my mind and thoughts, I find it impossible to divest myself of those habits of gloomy and pevish reflections that the wanton and flagitous conduct, and unmeritted refle[c]tions of base calumny, heaped upon me has given rise to. in order to try the experiment how far new scenes might relieve me from this unpleasant tone of thought, I did conclude to accept that appointment.

"Base calumny, heaped upon me," wrote Jackson, filled him with "gloomy and pevish reflections." War alone could reinvigorate his spirits, but war did not seem likely.

. . . from the Temporizing disposition displayed by congress, I am well aware that no act of insult, degredation or contumely offerred to our goverement will arouse them from their present lethergy and temporiseing conduct, untill my name sake [British envoy F. J. Jackson] sets fire to some of our seaport Towns and puts his foot aboard a British man of war. Then perhaps, the Spirit of 76. may again arise. . . . some of our old republican friends, have either lost their usual good judgt. or their Political principle. from all which I conclude that as a military man I shall have no amusement or business, and indolence and inaction would shortly destroy me.[39]

III

His "name sake" must initiate war, Jackson had written, else "indolence and inaction would shortly destroy me." The War of 1812 rescued Jackson from these "gloomy and pevish reflections." Impatient for the actual declaration of war, he issued an elaborate call to arms early in 1812. "We are going to fight," Jackson told his troops, "for the reestablishment of our national charector."

We are the free born sons of america; the citizens of the only republick now existing in the world; and the only people on earth who possess rights, liberties, and property which the[y] dare call their own. . . . [We will] vindicate our right to a free trade, and open a market for the productions of our soil, now perishing on our hands because the *mistress of the ocean* has forbid us to carry them to any foreign nation. . . . The advocates of Kingly power shall not enjoy the triumph of seeing a free people desert themselves, and crouch before the slaves of a foreign tyrant. . . . The free sons of the west will never submit to such degradation. . . .[40]

"*The mistress of the ocean*" and her "*infatuated king*," in Jackson's language, threatened the independence of America's sons. As Congressman John Rhea, a Tennessee war hawk, put it, "Nothing but the reduction of this nation to a servile state of colonial existence can satiate the appetite of voracious England."[41]

"The young men of America," Jackson's call to arms continued, "unencumbered with families and free from the embarrassment of domestic concerns," will enlist in the army. "They will never prefer an inglorious sloth, a supine inactivity to the honorable toil of carrying the republican standard to the heights of Abraham." As Jackson described his soldiers to Madison, "It was columbia's true sons who had walked forth, awaked by the infringement of there independance, bequeathed to them by there Revolutionary parents, Sunk to the Grave in procuring this precious patrimony who were assembling under their Eagles."[42]

America's sons, in the second war of American independence, would vindicate the birthright of their revolutionary fathers. The sons had merely inherited their patrimony; acquiring wealth, they had acquired "voluptuousness and effeminacy" too. An 1820 biography of Jackson began,

> From the conclusion of the war for American independence, to the commencement of that which secured it, the Americans were almost wholly diverted from the study of military tactics. . . . The mild arts of peace were substituted for the ruthless carnage of war; and a rising people, who had severed the ligament that bound them to a European monarch, commenced the enjoyment of self-government. . . .
>
> Sudden wealth was the result of the exertions of the different classes of Americans. The voluptuousness and effeminacy usually attendants upon the possession of it, were rapidly diminishing that exalted sense of national glory.[43]

Jackson would urge the city of New Orleans to battle in similar phrases:

> Inhabitants of an opulent and commercial town, you have by a spontaneous effort shaken off the habits, which are created by wealth, and shewn that you are resolved to deserve the blessings of fortune by bravely defending them. . . . Natives of the United States! they are the oppressors of your infant political existence, with whom you are to contend—they are the men your fathers conquered whom you are to oppose.[44]

Comparison with the revolutionary fathers had burdened the sons. Now, battling constricting parental presences, they could establish their independence. Defeating the oppressors of the "infant republick," its leaders would acquire manly authority.[45]

This widely shared symbolism had specific personal significance for Jackson. Father to his troops, he would inherit the mantle of the revolutionary fathers. Lecturing his soldiers on the importance of discipline, Jackson announced,

> The relative situation of your General to you, is, that of a father to his family, and as such he pledges himself to do *his* duty. Your *moral duty* then, is obedience—your duty as *Soldiers* is subordination; this yielded without coercion—united as a band of brothers, we will overthrow all opposition.[46]

Jackson scolded his troops when they became mutinous before their first march because they had not been paid. "Let it be remembered," he told them, "that the duty of a parent is to chastise and bring to obedience an undutiful child. The Major General has pledged himself to act towards you as a father, and now exhorts you to obedience." Jackson appointed John Reid one of his aides, and "felt truly gratified, on the information, that you would become one of my family during the present Campaign."[47]

Wrote Freud, "The Commander-in-Chief is a father who loves his soldiers equally, and for that reason they are comrades among themselves."[48] Seven nephews served with Jackson during the War of 1812,[49] making the transition from family to army seem a natural one. Its implications were radical, however. The shift in Europe from a medieval, communal, clan existence to the child-centered, conjugal family had increased the role of the army both in child-rearing and in nation-building. Adolescents in the late eighteenth and the nineteenth centuries were meant to acquire discipline in the army. The army substituted shared ego ideal (the leader) and shared desire (for conquest) for actual family blood ties. In the symbolism of seventeenth-century Puritan militants, men left the profane family world to do battle against the devil. They fought under a paternal God; Puritan theology shifted God the father and the family father from loving, organic presences to military enforcers of command and obedience. Jackson was heir to these traditions, and they played a powerful role in his personal history.[50]

Jackson wanted revenge against the British, he wrote Tennessee Governor Wylie Blount, because of his memories of the Revolution. He had been brought up under British tyranny, and "altho young embarked in the struggle for our liberties, in which I lost every thing that was dear to me, *my brothers and my fortune*."[51] Jackson was an adolescent during the Revolution, only slightly younger than the "band of brothers" he would now lead against the British. Turning the army into a family would help avenge the loss of his own family.

Neither the family Jackson remembered nor the one he sought to create had any women. Jackson did not list his mother among his revolutionary losses. Families with women had betrayed Jackson, first with his mother's desertion and death, then with the charges against him and Rachel. The army was a family without women. "Young men" would enlist "unencumbered with families and free from the embarrassment of domestic concerns." They would sacrifice their actual families to preserve their honor. The General Orders Jackson sent to Governor Blount proclaimed, "Perish our friends, perish our wives, perish our children, the dearest pledges of heaven—nay, perish *all* terrestial considerations, but, let the honor and fame of a volunteer—soldier be untarnished and immaculate."[52]

Jackson, in the absence of women and "terrestial considerations," would exercise total control over his sons. The father in Freud's primal horde monopolized the women and dominated the sons. But the father's authority could not sustain itself against the sons' desires. The sons rose and slew the father, and fought for the women among themselves.[53] Freud imposed his psychological insight on human prehistory; Jackson sensed its lessons in his actual history. His mother died at the onset of his puberty, and his desire for Rachel implicated him in the charges which caused her such grief. A family without women, as source of either desire or sustenance, contained nothing to turn brothers against the father or against one another. The sons would not divide in contention for women; they would "unite as a band of brothers" in pursuit of land.

"Turn your eyes to the south!" Jackson told his Tennessee volunteers.

> Behold in the province of West Florida, a territory whose rivers and harbors are indispensable to the prosperity of the western, and still more so of the eastern Division of the State. . . . It is here that an employment adapted to your situation awaits your courage and your zeal; and while extending in the quarter the boundaries of the Republic to the Gulf of Mexico.[54]

Florida, the war hawks proclaimed, was "indispensable to complete the figure of the American republic." Jackson and the other war hawks planned to annex Canada as well. They also wanted to end British harassment of American shipping and safeguard a commercial route to the Gulf of Mexico. Farmers could then market their products, ending the agricultural depression brought by the British embargo to the south and west. Such commercial aims were stated in personal metaphors suggesting that war would unblock the course of triumphant American expansion. As Jackson described the tasks he set his troops,

> In placing before the volunteers the illustrious actions of their fathers in the war of the revolution, he presumes to hope that they will not prove themselves a degenerate race. . . . The Theatre on which they are required

to act is interesting to them in every point of view. Every Man of the western Country turns his eyes intuitively upon the mouth of the Mississippi. He there beholds the only outlet by which his produce can reach the markets of foreign nations or the atlantic States: Blocked up, all the fruits of his industry rots upon his hand—open and he carries on a trade with all the nations of the earth. To the people of the western Country is then peculiarly committed by nature herself the defence of the lower Mississippi and the city of New—Orleans.[55]

It was one thing to state war aims, another to realize them. Jackson longed to invade Canada or Florida, but his reputation was that of a hot-tempered, unreliable man; he and the Tennessee militia were ignored. Finally late in 1812 Madison asked Governor Blount to raise volunteers. They would serve under General Wilkinson in an invasion of west Florida. Madison did not call out the Tennessee militia; perhaps he hoped to avoid Jackson. Blount, however, sent Jackson to command the troops. To serve under Wilkinson was a "bitter pill" for Jackson, "but for my country's good I will swallow [it]." No sooner had he arrived in Natchez than he received an order canceling the mission. Madison had failed to obtain congressional support for the invasion of west Florida, and Jackson was ordered to discharge his troops.[56]

The new Secretary of War, John Armstrong, explained that he intended his order to reach Jackson while the volunteers were still in Nashville. Jackson thought Armstrong had different intentions. Armstrong, he believed, had plotted to obtain additional troops for Wilkinson. Released without food, separated from their homes by "the vultures of the savage wilderness," the volunteers would have no choice but to enlist in the regular army. He wrote his friend, militia quartermaster W. B. Lewis,

Is this the reward of a virtuous administration, to its patriotic sons, or is it done by a wicked *monster*, to satiate the vengeance, of a combination of hypocritical Political Villains, who would sacrifice the best blood of our Country, to satiate the spleen of a villain who their connection with in acts of wickedness they are afraid to offend?[57]

Jackson disobeyed orders and marched his soldiers home. He wrote Rachel, "although their Patriotism has been but illy rewarded by an ungrateful officer, (not Country) it is therefore my duty to act as a father to the sick and to the well and stay with them until I march them into Nashville." John Reid, who served with Jackson during the march home, wrote,

Many of the troops under his command were young men, the children of his neighbors and acquaintances, who had delivered them into his hands, as a guardian, who, with parental solicitude, would watch over and protect their welfare. . . . Add to this, those young men who were confused by sickness, learning the nature of the order he had received, implored him, with tears in their eyes, not to abandon them in so great an extremity, reminding him, at the same time, of his assurances, that he would be to them as a father.[58]

The march home was grueling. Food was scarce, and many of the volunteers were ill. Jackson shared the hardships of his men. Troops who had been frightened of him before the campaign now looked upon him with affection. Admiring his toughness, they gave him the name "Old Hickory."[59]

The march was a triumph for Jackson, but it seemed to place him further than ever from leadership in war. Denied war, Jackson participated in a private quarrel once again. He acted as second in a duel between one of his militia officers, William Carroll, and Jesse Benton, brother of another. An exchange of provocative letters between Jackson and the Benton brothers followed the duel. When Jesse and Thomas Hart Benton came to Nashville, Jackson and two of his nephews sought them out. Jackson attacked Thomas Hart Benton with a riding whip. He was severely wounded in the left shoulder in the ensuing gun fight.[60] Two weeks later, as Jackson lay weak and haggard in bed, news of the Creek massacre at Fort Mims arrived in Nashville. This signaled the outbreak of the Creek War and the most decisive eighteen months of Jackson's life.

IV

America sought to conquer not only Florida and Canada in the War of 1812, but Indian territory as well. Southern Indians at the outbreak of war inhabited two-thirds of Georgia, most of Alabama and Mississippi, the western third of Tennessee, and a western strip of Kentucky. Northwestern Ohio and most of the rest of the northwest territory remained Indian land. The war hawks wanted to end Indian harassment on the frontiers and safeguard westward expansion. They believed that northern and southern Indians, armed and instigated by the Spanish and British, and inspired by the Shawnee warrior Tecumseh, would unite against America. The massacre at Fort Mims confirmed them in this view.

The actual origins of the Creek War were more complex. The Creek War began as a civil war. The Creek nation was originally a large confederation of villages which generally acted together in war but lacked central state authority. In response to white contact, tribal authority centralized. The partly white chief Alexander McGillivray, who sought to resist American penetration in the late eighteenth century, furthered tribal centralization. So did Creek agent Benjamin Hawkins, who succeeded Mc-Gillivray as a major presence in the tribe. Hawkins was offended by tribal anarchy and economic communism when he went to live with the Creeks in 1797. He strengthened the authority of the town chiefs and elevated a single chief to "Speaker" for the nation.

Unlike McGillivray, Hawkins aimed to make the Creeks more dependent on America. He insisted, in violation of Creek traditions, that an old chief be publicly whipped; the chief had obstructed U.S. surveyors running the boundary line with Spain. The government also required Creek chiefs to discipline tribal members for robbery and murder along the frontier. By 1800 the United States had established its sovereignty over the tribe.

Hawkins convinced some Creek women to spin and weave, and promoted staple-crop agriculture. Plantation agriculture, intermarriage, trade, and treaty annuities increased social differentiation within the nation, creating a small wealthy class of mixed ancestry. The same process was occurring in the other southern tribes. Young warriors and Creek prophets rebelled against these innovations. They felt separated from their historic tribal past by the impact of white contact. Like Tecumseh in the north, they wanted to return to the ways of their fathers. They opposed cash-crop agriculture and centralized tribal authority. They embraced a messianic faith, in a pattern recurrent among Indian tribes, to revitalize their traditions. Older "progressive" chiefs who had adopted white ways—plantation agriculture, cattle-raising, and the beginnings of Christianity and mission education—opposed the young "red sticks." Most partly acculturated Indians favored accommodation with the whites; but young Red Eagle, nephew of McGillivray, was a red-stick leader.[61]

The red sticks chafed at tribal discipline and sought heroic exploits. Early in 1813 older chiefs, under Hawkins' urging, executed several young warriors who had killed whites on the frontier. The red sticks retaliated, and the two sides engaged in occasional intratribal raids. Their conflict had a geographic basis. The red sticks were strong in the upper towns of northern Alabama; most of the lower towns in Georgia were hostile to them. These lower towns would support Jackson in the Creek War.[62]

Like Tecumseh, the red sticks opposed white expansion. It is uncertain, however, whether substantial numbers of Indians intended to make war on the United States. William Henry Harrison initiated the northern Indian war in 1811, in a campaign to drive the Indians farther west and regain lost personal popularity.[63] Jackson and other Tennesseeans sought to extend the Indian war to the south. Early in 1812, before the congressional declaration of war against England, Jackson called out the Tennessee militia at an unfounded rumor of Creek attacks. There was sporadic violence in the following months, some initiated by Indians, some by whites. In May several Creeks killed and scalped two families on the Duck River, taking one woman prisoner.

The Creeks, wrote the *Nashville Clarion*, "have supplied us with a pretext for a dismemberment of their country." The Tennessee legislature called for troops sufficient "to exterminate the Creek nation." Governor Blount sent Tennessee rangers in pursuit of the Creeks; they encountered a small band and wounded several Indians. The rangers have "got some blood; it will keep the war alive," Thomas Hart Benton wrote Jackson. But "some blood" failed to initiate a full-scale war; warning his "friend and brother" Chickasaw Chief George Colbert not to aid the Creeks, Jackson threatened, "the whole Creek nation shall be covered with blood." He met with his officers and planned an invasion of Creek country. He hoped the state legislature would authorize and finance the invasion; if not, he would act on his own.[64]

The wretch who could view the massacre, wrote the *Clarion*, "and feel not his spirit kindle within him and burn for revenge, deserves not the name of a man; and the mother who bore him should point the finger of scorn and say, 'He is not my son.'" Elizabeth Jackson could not point a finger at her son. We are determined, wrote Jackson,

> to avenge the death of our butchered wives and infants. When we make the case of Mrs. Manly and her family and Mrs. Crawly our own—when we figure to ourselves our beloved wives and little prattling infants, butchered, mangled, murdered, and torn to pieces, by savage bloodhounds, and wallowing in their gore, you can judge of our feelings. . . . we are ready and pant for vengeance. . . . Is a citizen of the united States, to remain under the barbarous lash of cruel and unrelenting Savages; confined to a mortar, naked, lacerated and compelled, thus to prepare food for her tormenters for six months without any other notice of the general government, than mere direction for a demand to be made by the agent. . . . the brave sons of Tennessee, may under the authority of the state by their prowess and heroism wipe from the national charector, this blushing shame.[65]

To make the "butchered, mangled" infants and naked, brutalized mothers "our own," wrote Jackson, would rouse the "brave sons of Tennessee" to "pant for vengeance." Jackson threatened to "penetrate the creek Towns" on his own authority "and think myself Justifiable, in laying waste their villages, burning their houses, killing their warriors and leading into Captivity their wives and children, untill I do obtain a surrender of the Captive, and the Captors."[66]

Jackson's threats failed to bring about war with the Creeks.[67] American provocations against the Seminoles, an offshoot of the Creek tribe living in Florida and southern Georgia, also did not ignite an Indian war. Filibusterers and Georgia and east Tennessee militia, encouraged by President Madison, invaded east Florida in the early months of the war. They used the excuse of Seminole border atrocities in an effort to gain the territory for the United States. Madison withdrew his support at the last moment, and the expedition failed. In the spring of 1813 General Wilkinson occupied Spanish-held Mobile, claimed by America under the Louisiana Purchase.[68]

That same spring a party of red sticks journeyed to Pensacola, in east Florida, to receive weapons, ammunition, and supplies. Creek trade had gone to Spanish Florida for decades, but now there was fear the red sticks were preparing for war. On their way home, in July, they were attacked at Burnt Corn by lower Creeks and Mississippi territorial militia. The battle of Burnt Corn was the first of the Creek War. Initially the red sticks were defeated; when their attackers fell on the abandoned Spanish supplies, the red sticks returned and routed them.[69]

Leaders of the lower Creeks feared red-stick retaliation. With neighboring whites, they had fortified the plantation of Samuel Mims, a wealthy, partly white Creek, at the outset of the civil war. Many Creek and white frontier families now took refuge there. The commander at Fort Mims, discounting the possibility of an Indian attack, left the stockade open and unguarded. The red-stick attack on August 30, 1813, killed almost all the 250 inhabitants. Many women and children died in fires set to the blockhouse during the fighting. Red sticks killed others, mutilating live, wounded, and dead bodies after the victory. One scalped woman nursed her still warm infant back to life and set off for help.[70]

The Fort Mims attack, in frontier eyes, was an unprovoked Indian massacre of whites. On September 18, after news of the massacre reached Nashville, leading citizens called for a war to "exterminate the Creek Nation and Abettors." Governor Blount told the legislature that "the employment of a competent force at once would teach those barbarous sons of the woods their inferiority." Jackson, weak and bed-ridden from his wounds in the Benton brawl, had apparently missed his chance. A bullet had fractured his left shoulder. His arm, which the doctors wanted to amputate, was useless. He was weak with fever and loss of weight. Nevertheless, he insisted upon leading the troops. If the federal government would leave him alone, he wrote Mississippi Governor David Holmes, "we will give peace in Israel."[71]

Jackson issued his call to arms without waiting for Madison to act. Under the law, the federal government called for volunteers. The enrolled soldiers then elected their officers. Jackson himself, however, issued the call for volunteers. The officers who had marched with him to Natchez and back several months earlier recruited their former soldiers. Jackson wanted to act quickly, before the federal government shunted him aside again. In two weeks his troops were ready to march. The mounted cavalry left first. It was commanded by John Coffee, Jackson's close friend, business partner, and nephew, who had joined Jackson in the fight with the Benton brothers. Jackson, still too weak to ride, followed with the bulk of the volunteers a few days later.[72]

Jackson was forty-six years old in 1813. The smallpox he had survived during the Revolutionary War left him with lasting fevers, and he had recurrent malaria as well. He was plagued by chronic constipation and dysentery, and had been suffering from rheumatism for a decade or more. These diseases left him thin and almost emaciated, and gave his skin a permanent yellowish character. The Dickinson wound had left him with lung trouble and recurrent breast pains. At the same time he carried himself with enormous dignity. Even in relatively good health, standing six feet one inch and weighing 145 pounds, he had a stern, skeletal appearance. Now, sitting stooped in the saddle, his left arm in a sling, this tall, cadaverous figure must have looked like the horseman of death.[73]

Jackson warred against and triumphed over his own body during the Creek campaign. His left arm was useless. He suffered from fever, nausea, and pain in the unhealed shoulder during the entire campaign. The dysentery was worst of all. Jackson marched to war during an attack, and sometimes had to remain in the same position for hours, standing stooped, his shoulders over a rail, to relieve the spasms. Rage and bad temper marked Jackson during the war; his bodily difficulties merged with those he faced from Indians and from his own troops.[74]

A letter to Coffee suggests how Jackson identified the body as one of his enemies. While Coffee was wounded and out of action, his cavalry broke under a Creek charge. Jackson reassured Coffee that a man could not control his health, but his letter suggested the opposite. In Jackson's words,

> Indisposition and health are not within our control, and ought not be subjects of inquietude, altho your present indisposition fills me with regret, when I find your Brigades patriotism is as much indisposed, as you are in body, which, in all probability would have been prevented had your health been such as you could have been at their head—their disgrace prevented, and also examplanary punishment to many.[75]

The conflict between body and will raised the severest challenges to Jackson's authority; he established his authority by triumphing over the body. Jackson's troops, to begin with, had to distinguish themselves from Indians by controlling their passions. Such control permitted primitive identification with savages to eventuate not in chaotic violence but in victorious authority. Jackson's talks to his troops followed a consistent pattern. He first described the atrocities of the "inhuman butcherers" against women and children. His images, as he put it in describing the Duck River massacre, made the Indians' victims "our own." They roused his men to "pant with vengeance." They aroused primitive identification with Indian violence. Jackson then insisted that his troops must not fight like "barbarians." "We must conquer as men who owe nothing to chance; and who in the midst of victory can still preserve order. We must commence the campaign by an unviolable attention to discipline and subordination."[76]

Discipline distinguished white volunteers from Indian warriors. Indians refused to submit themselves to discipline; therefore they were not an efficient fighting force, and they engaged in the barbarities of savage warfare. "Deluded victims," they were "doomed to destruction by their own restless and savage conduct." Jackson sought to weld his own troops into "engines of destruction."[77] But the militia too was undisciplined, as the events of the campaign would show. "The cowardly dogs cannot stand a charge," Jackson wrote of the Indians after his own troops had broken under an Indian assault and been saved by Jackson's Cherokee allies. As Amos Kendall described the Kentucky militia which fought with Jackson, "The soldiers are under no more restraint than a herd of swine. Reasoning, remonstrating, threatening, and ridiculing their officers, they show their sense of equality, and their total want of subordination."[78] During his defense of New Orleans, Jackson complained to Secretary of War Monroe in similar terms about his Indian and white troops. The Indian warriors, he wrote, were unreliable because after every battle they wanted to return home for a dance. The militia, he complained in another letter, were unreliable because they were "strongly recalled to their families and home" by their "habits of life" after a single battle.[79]

The Indians believed in primitive, magical methods of warfare, and there was danger they would convince their white enemies. The red sticks, Jackson told his troops, "rely, more, for victory, upon their grim visages, and hideous yells than upon their bravery, or their weapons." "Boasting" was no substitute for soldiers who were "silent, firm, obedient, and attentive . . . and perform your duties." Indian tricks could not scare such soldiers, insisted Jackson; "brave men will laugh at the subterfuge which they hoped to alarm them."[80]

Further to confuse white troops with Indian, Jackson himself recruited Indian warriors. He insisted that all Creeks not willing to fight the red sticks be treated as enemies, and obtained the aid of many Creeks and of several hundred Cherokees. "We are all brothers, fighting in one cause," Jackson wrote a Cherokee chief concerned about the division of the spoils of war.

The Path killer your chief and my brother, Col Brown . . . the cherokees—
the Friendly creeks and the united States, . . . we are all fighting in one
cause, we are all brothers—then if one brother, finds his brothers horse, in
the possession of the Red Sticks, it is agreed by the chiefs, on all sides that
it is to be delivered up, to the brothers to whom it belongs. But if either
party, cherokees, friendly creeks or whites, takes property of the Red
Sticks, the property belongs to those who take it—this is acting like friends
and brothers.[81]

Jackson called them brothers, but he underestimated the importance of
his Indian allies. A week before the climactic battle, in which they played
a crucial role, he complained that he had to feed the Indians from his own
provisions. He wrote General Thomas Pinckney, "The very moment I can
rid myself of them with a good grace, and without leaving improper im-
pressions on their minds, I shall certainly do so. At Emuckfaw [where
Cherokees had just helped avert a rout of the white troops] I must find or
make a pretext for discharging the greater part of them; and perhaps the
whole except my guides."[82]

On October 13 Jackson arrived at the Coosa River, deep in Creek
country, and built Fort Strother there. Early in November the cavalry,
under Coffee, fought the first battle and won the first victory of the Creek
War. They attacked and burned the Creek village of Tallushatchee, killing warriors, women, and children alike. Six days later Jackson himself led
his troops in a victory. The Indians attacked "like a cloud of Egyptian
locusts, and screaming like devils," wrote volunteer Davy Crockett. They
were quickly surrounded by Jackson's troops; at the end of the encounter
there were 300 dead Indians, 15 dead whites.

The Creeks were greatly outnumbered in both battles, and escaped in
the second through a hole opened in Jackson's lines. Nevertheless, these
were the first victories for the United States in the War of 1812, and they
brought Jackson great praise. In the words of a typical correspondent,
"The victories gained by you against the Indians will hand your name
down, to posterity, as the first of patriots." Jackson sent cloth worn by
the slain Indians to the ladies of Tennessee. His troops cut strips of Indian
skin for bridle reins and souvenirs.[83]

The worst period of the war now began. The heart of Creek country lay far from white settlement, and Jackson's battle plans required long
supply lines. Problems of supply prevented the commanders of the Georgia, Mississippi, and east Tennessee militias from rendering significant aid
during the war. The contractors on whom Jackson's army depended for
food failed to provide it. Before the first battle Jackson wrote, "There
is an enemy whom I dread, much more than I do the hostile Creeks—
you know I mean the meagre monster 'famine.'" Lack of supplies had

hindered the march to Fort Strother; now hunger forced the army to return there instead of pursuing the Creeks. Jackson raged at the contractors. At the same time, hunger provided him with a test of his ability to control his body. He would live, he said, on acorns. To be well-fed smacked of self-indulgence. He insisted to Governor Blount that he needed supplies so his troops could advance: "I cannot lie still and eat publick Beef, in idleness."[84]

Neither Jackson nor his troops were eating beef, however. Controlling one's own body was one thing, controlling hungry troops another. A contemporary chronicler of the Creek campaign observed, "Men who will face death in its most horrible forms, will turn to children at the approach of famine." Retreating toward Nashville for food, the troops refused to march back. Jackson's failure to supply food had created a challenge to his authority. At first he stopped the retreating militia by placing the volunteers in their path. Then he reversed the process. After finally feasting on a drove of cattle, one company began to march for home. Jackson and a few of his staff rushed to the head of the troops and turned them back. Then, in the face of more discontent, Jackson stood alone in front of his men, left hand disabled, musket in his right, and threatened to fire on the first man who started for home. Joined by Coffee and John Reid, he held the troops, and they returned to Fort Strother.[85]

The triumph was temporary, however. Soon Jackson was involved with his officers and men in disputes over the length of their service. The volunteers believed their term was up December 10, one year, as the law provided, after they had been called to duty for the march to Natchez. Jackson insisted the one year had to be served entirely in the field. His own irregular recruiting methods—calling the same men back to service after the lapse of months—had returned to haunt him. To permit his troops to keep their government-issue muskets after the Natchez march, Jackson had formally discharged them. When they asked for their discharges now, he insisted, to their bewilderment, that he lacked the authority. On one occasion Jackson ranged his artillery against the volunteers to prevent them from marching back to Tennessee. Colonel William Martin appealed to Jackson that the men had loved and obeyed him like "an affectionate father"; now their term of enlistment had expired and they needed to return to their crops. A petition of soldiers appealed to Jackson's "warm and parental feeling toward us." But Jackson was unbending. He insisted he had no power to discharge the men. To Martin he replied, "I have pledged myself to act as a father to them. I know I have performed the task faithfully. It is not the duty of a father to deceive." To Rachel he wrote, "Pressed with mutiny and sedition of the volunteer infantry—To surpress it, having been compelled to arrange my artillery, against them, whom I once loved like a father loves his children." Jackson was still not ready to blame the ordinary soldiers. "One thing is certain," he wrote. "The officers, and not the soldiers were at the root of the discontent." Officers had come between the General and his men; it was the first appearance of a major theme of Jacksonian Democracy.[86]

Finally Jackson had to give in. He had tried in vain "to save men . . . whom I love as a fond father loves his children from that eternal disgrace that will await them if they attempt to leave their standard." Not only was he forced to let the volunteers go; in succeeding weeks other troops also insisted on returning home. Some had enlisted in the state militia for three months; later received into the regular army for terms of six months, many were not aware of the change. Others simply left. Jackson got no help from Governor Blount, who sensed that Tennessee public opinion was against Jackson and sided with the soldiers. Alone Jackson could not hold his men; he sent each one home, as he put it, "with a smok-tail in his teeth, with a petticoat as a coat of mail to hand down to posterity." Fort Strother remained almost undefended, but Jackson rejected Blount's advice to return to Tennessee for more troops and supplies. Blount had "bawled aloud for permission to exterminate the Creeks," and should now be willing to back Jackson up. Bawling politicians and men running home with mothers' apron strings in their mouths were hardly redeeming the "national charector." At the outset of the war Jackson had prophesied that "the free sons of the west," "unencumbered with families and free from the embarrassment of domestic concerns," would enlist in the army. "They will never prefer an inglorious sloth, a supine inactivity to the honorable toil of carrying the republican standard to the heights of Abraham." That prophecy was turning to ashes in the mouth of this Abraham. Hunger, sustenance, and families at home were proving stronger than paternal authority. "Since the battle of Talluhatchee and Talledega," wrote one observer from the edge of Indian country, "the army of General Jackson has crumbled to pieces." It was, a biographer asserts, "probably the supreme crisis of his career."[87]

Jackson struggled to raise more troops. He wrote to Rachel's minister requesting aid in recruiting soldiers:

> While we fight the savage who makes war only to gather scalps and who feels malignity only because he delights in blood we are, through him, contending against an enemy of more inveterate character and deeper designs, who would demolish a fabrick cemented by the blood of our fathers!

Urging the east Tennessee volunteers to reenlist, he reminded them of "the cannibals who revelled in the carnage of our inoffensive citizens at Fort Mims." If only supplies would come, he wrote Coffee, "we would soon reach the promised land that flows with milk and honey."[88]

In January 1814, temporarily reinforced by troops and supplies, Jackson advanced again. He aimed for the Creek stronghold at the Horseshoe Bend of the Tallapoosa River, seventy-five miles south of Fort Strother. The Creeks attacked at Emuckfau Creek, three miles from the Horseshoe Bend. Fighting the first battle in which they were not heavily outnumbered, they inflicted heavy casualties on Jackson's troops. Troop and supply problems forced Jackson to retreat after the battle; the Indians followed, attacking as the whites crossed Enotachopco Creek. Part of Jackson's line broke, and only the action of a detachment under General Carroll averted a rout. Finally, with the help of Jackson's Cherokee and Creek allies, the red sticks were driven back. Sandy Donelson, one of Jackson's nephews, was killed in this battle.[89]

Returning to Fort Strother, Jackson raged at the "little yelping *currs*" in Tennessee criticizing his conduct, at the militia which had retreated, and at the soldiers returning to Tennessee "leaving our country a prey to the enemy or to be protected by the cherokees." "I feel for their disgrace, I feel for their fallen character—but I feel happy, that none of their disgrace can or will attach to me—I have done my duty I know and I have the flatering approbation not only of the president but by the secretary of war in his late letter to me."[90]

Jackson feared in fact that the "disgrace" of his troops *would* "attach" to him. As new, untried volunteers arrived at camp, he complained, "I will have to risque my charector and the publick service upon raw and inexperienced troops again." Rachel reassured him:

> Those wretches that tryed to . . . injer you & Genl Coffee has . . . Disgraced themselves Etarnaly. Theay ar Dead no theay dont raise ther Eyes or heads in the world. . . . Let me assure you no man is or can be more praised and applauded than you are. . . . Some writer Saide while Genl Harrison was makeing his appearance in the Drawing room and ball rooms Gel Jackson was makeing conquests through [manner?] and Every disadvantage possible.[91]

The arrival of fresh troops permitted Jackson to reassert his authority over his men. He had long blamed his old enemy General William Cocke for failures in the campaign. Cocke commanded the east Tennessee militia; his authority was independent of Jackson's, and he had not followed Jackson's directives. Jackson sent him back to Tennessee under arrest. He wanted Cocke tried for treason.[92]

Jackson's battle to establish paternal authority now reached its climax. John Woods, a seventeen-year-old recruit, refused to clean up his food and threatened his officer with a gun. Jackson, as a slightly younger boy, had refused a British officer's order, but this was the American army and Jackson was in command. He mistakenly believed Woods had participated in his company's earlier mutiny; in fact the soldier had just taken his brother's place in the ranks. Suffering from "a severe attacke of the Bowell complaint," Jackson was particularly short-tempered. He ordered Woods executed, "in presence of all the troops." A court-martial confirmed the judgment.[93]

Jackson had failed to instill "discipline and subordination" in his ranks and weld his troops into "engines of destruction" under his paternal control. The sacrifice of Woods would demonstrate his authority. The proceedings of an earlier court-martial suggest the significance of the execution for Jackson. A captain had fired his gun in camp, hoping to kill a wild hog and supplement the scarce provisions. Such lack of discipline set a bad example for the men, said Jackson; a court-martial ordered him to administer a reprimand.

The reprimand, Jackson told the captain,

> imposed a very painful duty upon your Genl. While he views as his children those men who have so willingly united their destinies with his . . . to mark a soldier with disgrace is to attack him at a point where all his sensibilities are most alive. . . . How then shall a Genl who stands in the relation of a father to his children be made the instrument of inflicting this wound without himself feeling a portion of its pain? But it may become his duty and from that duty he must not shrink whatever sacrifice of feeling the performance of it may occasion him.[94]

Jackson merely administered a reprimand to the court-martialed captain. But in December, after he had threatened to fire on the volunteers to stop their "shamefull desertion," Jackson actually imagined killing "his child" to save him from disgrace. He complained to Rachel about

> the once brave and patriotic volunteers—who a few privations, sunk from the highest devotion of patriots—to mere, wining, complaining, seditioners and mutineers—to keep whom from open acts of mutiny I have been compelled to point my cannon against, with a lighted match to destroy them— that was a grating moment of my life—I felt the pangs of an affectionate parent compelled from duty to chastise his child—to prevent him from destruction and disgrace and it being his only duty he shrunk not from it—even when he knew death might ensue.[95]

Jackson did not shrink, later that winter, from the execution of young Woods. He had the power to reduce Woods' sentence. He spent two sleepless nights before deciding not to do so. Then he walked out of earshot of the firing squad, and the soldier was killed. Thirty years later a eulogist praised Jackson's mother for sacrificing his brothers to the Revolution. "Like Abraham, she would have sacrificed him too, had not her hand been stayed by an invisible power."[96] No power stayed Jackson's hand. "Perish our children," he had written, "but let the honor and fame of a volunteer soldier be untarnished and immaculate." Jackson had promised to bring "the Republican standard to the heights of Abraham" and secure "peace in Israel." Did he now think of Isaac?

Immediately after the execution, Jackson marched his troops to the Horseshoe Bend. On March 27, 1814, he fought the climactic battle of the Creek War there. One thousand Creeks faced 1,400 whites, 500 Cherokees, and 100 Creek allies. More Indians fought and were killed in this battle than in any other in the history of American-Indian warfare. The Creeks erected breastworks and stood Jackson's charge. His Cherokee allies swam the Tallapoosa River, released the boats upon which the Creeks had depended for escape, and attacked them from the rear. Aided by this maneuver, Jackson's troops stormed the Creek positions. The Creeks fought almost to the last man and lost 800 warriors. There were few white casualties. One of the prophets, blamed by Jackson for maddening the Indians and causing the war, "was shot in the mouth by grape shot; as if Heaven designed to chastise his impostures by an appropriate punishment." Jackson sent "a warrior bow and quiver" to "my little Andrew." He wrote, "Having destroyed three of their principl[e] prophets . . . having tread their holy ground as the[y] termed it, and destroyed all their chiefs and warriors on the Tallapoosee river above the big bend, it is probable they may now sue for peace."[97]

Jackson had carried out the plan he had made at the beginning of the Creek War. He had marched "to the heart of their own country." There the Creeks had been forced to fight. "It is not to be expected," Jackson had earlier written, "that they will abandon the soil that embosoms the bones of their forefathers." Now he marched to the Hickory Ground, most sacred spot in the Creek nation. Old Hickory now named the fort on the Hickory Ground Fort Jackson and dictated peace to the tribe. He had incorporated in combat the Indians' magic—their heroism, their violence, their land.[98]

Jackson's victory over the Creeks was the turning point of his life. He achieved the American army's first dramatic military triumph. In a war largely devoid of American victories, he became a national hero. "You have saved this country," Judge Harry Toulmin wrote from Alabama. General Pinckney appointed Jackson commander of the southern division of the regular army. He was deluged by requests from men wanting to become "members of your family," or recommending others for posts in the army. He encouraged one of his officers, in the first flush of victory, to marry against the opposition of the girl's father. Jackson himself participated in the ceremony. He wrote to the father, a wealthy Nashville merchant and friend, that the bridegroom was admittedly without property. But "he possesses enterprise and will make a *fortune, whilst many who possess fortune by descent will spend it, and make their family wretched.*" He defended the children's disobedience, urged parental forgiveness, and wrote that Mrs. Jackson and he would be mother and father to the couple in the meanwhile.[99]

Jackson's victory emancipated him from parental domination and established him in the ranks of the revolutionary fathers. He was patriarch over his own military family. Controlling his body, conquering Indians, and executing one of his soldiers, he had sublimated instinct into authority. But the instincts from which his authority derived were both primitive and partial. Death, aggression, and violence had, for Jackson, unbounded destructive power; he had transformed them, in that form, into sources of paternal authority. Libido, nurture, physicality—the tender, feminine qualities—were equally overwhelming in Jackson's imagination, and he had defeated them. These emotions had threatened all through the campaign to undermine his authority, destroy his character, and cause his disgrace. Libido, a threat to authority, was excluded from the public world. It found distorted expression instead where it could be controlled, as the private end of public action, the prize of possession, the spoil of war.

V

Indians had been "lords of the soil"; they were no longer. Jackson had won the land, and it was his to dispose of. He was furious that Indian agent Benjamin Hawkins had permitted some of the friendly Creeks to return to their homes. "I did tell him the Territory I had assigned them," he wrote.[100]

The government, however, did not recognize Jackson's right to distribute Creek land. It did not appoint him to the treaty commission, and sought a moderate treaty in which the Creeks would renounce their connection to Spain, surrender the prophets responsible for the fighting, and compensate the United States in Creek territory for the cost of the war. The friendly portion of the tribe, General Pinckney wrote Jackson, should be guaranteed their land.[101]

Jackson and his officers were furious. They demanded a "voice from Tennessee" to protect the "vital interest of our state." Jackson's officers and leading Nashville citizens successfully petitioned to have Jackson appointed to the treaty commission. Pinckney instructed Jackson to treat on the administration's terms, but Jackson enforced his own objectives. He dictated a treaty, over the bitter protests of the friendly Creeks, ceding half the land of the nation. It was the largest single Indian cession of southern American land.[102]

Jackson had demonstrated his power over the Creeks, and won the right to their birthright. He favored giving his soldiers preferential rights to purchase the land they had conquered, so "it would be settled by a hearty race that would defend it." He told Secretary of War Monroe the government could defeat the northwestern Indians if it gave large land bounties to soldiers who would "make themselves masters of the soil." The Creeks recognized this principle. They donated Jackson a three-mile-square tract of land on which he and his descendants should live, so "it may always be known what the nation gave it to him for." Jackson accepted the donation on condition the value of the land were used "to aid in clothing their naked women and children." Such a use insulted the gift, replied the chiefs, and Jackson accepted it outright.[103]

The tract was valuable, and Jackson did not want to relinquish it. He feared, however, that Congress would believe fraud, not heroism, had gained him the land. A friend who acted for Jackson in land matters lobbied Congress to let the donation stand. "Your case," he wrote Jackson in a letter the General marked "private" three times, should be distinguished from ordinary Indian gifts to private individuals. When Congress removed the donation from the Creek treaty, an officer who had served with Jackson wrote him, "After this patriotism must expect to be impoverished—and the Bold Defenders of their country rely on their approving conscience for a reward of their labors." Jackson and his soldiers would have to purchase land in the conquered territory.[104]

The Fort Jackson treaty took land from Jackson's Creek allies as well as from those who had fought against him. Big Warrior, chief of the friendly Creeks, protested; Jackson replied,

> Brother, listen . . . The United States would have been justified by the Great Spirit, had they taken all the land of the nation merely for keeping it a secret, that her enemies were in the nation. Listen—the truth is, the great body of the creek chiefs and warriors did not respect the power of the United States—They thought we were an insignificant nation—that we would be overpowered by the British.

As Jackson catalogued Creek presumptions, he worked himself into a rage.

> They were fat with eating beef—they wanted flogging—they had no idea they could so easily be destroyed. They were mad—they had a fever— we bleed our enemies in such cases to give them their senses.[105]

Boastful Indians had dreamed, as they feasted, that they could destroy the United States. Their dreams were mad fantasies, said Jackson; he had flogged the Creeks and brought them to their senses. Jackson's vindictive rhetoric overrode opposition to his treaty. A chief who had fought with Jackson reported, "He threatened us and made us comply with his talk. . . . I found the General had great power to destroy me."[106]

Jackson claimed power to destroy the Indians but not to protect them. He told the friendly chiefs he was powerless to guarantee their lands or attend to their other claims, as Pinckney's letter had promised. "My powers do not extend to embrace, by treaty or capitulation, the promises contained therein," he insisted. In fact Jackson used his power to override the guarantees Pinckney had ordered him to make.[107] He claimed powerlessness while experiencing the first full flush of mature political power. Jackson's triumphant will did not enhance his sense of personal responsibility; it rather swept him into the service of larger forces. Jackson emphasized discipline and law. But his was not a law which limited and structured desire, providing ideals to hold the self responsible. Rather his ego merged with a primitive law, sanctifying primitive aggression.

Jackson's will was the servant of social forces as well as instinctual ones. His victory, he insisted, must guarantee American military and economic interests. He took a wide strip of Creek territory adjoining Florida; this would separate the Creeks from Spanish territory, arms, and influence, and deny them a sanctuary after frontier raids. Friendly Creeks inhabited this Georgia land, but Jackson gave more weight to military considerations than to Pinckney's promises. He also acquired the western portion of the Creek nation, to connect the Tennessee settlements with those in lower Alabama. He wanted to bring the Creek land to market quickly, to provide settlers to defend the country against future Indian, Spanish, or British attacks.[108]

The quick sale of Creek lands served another purpose. Jackson had conquered "the cream of the Creek country," and it would guarantee southwestern prosperity. He had supplied the expanding cotton kingdom with a vast and valuable acreage.[109]

VI

Others gave immediate attention to cotton land; Jackson did not. As soon as he signed the Fort Jackson treaty, he began an invasion of Florida. Citing the danger from British and Indian attacks, he acted without authorization from Washington. Jackson claimed the British would strike the south through Florida. He attributed to them plans for servile insurrection and massacre. As Jackson's friend and biographer John H. Eaton explained, the British hated the Americans because of their defeat in the Revolutionary War and "visit the sins of the father upon the child."[110]

Jackson's two months in west Florida had no effect on the British, and delayed the defense of New Orleans. His aim was conquest. Jackson had longed since the beginning of the war to acquire Spanish Florida for the United States. Further to justify his invasion, he exaggerated the threat from Florida Indians. Jackson had told the Creeks who rejected the Fort Jackson treaty that they were free to go to Florida. He now cited the danger of Indian attack from the Spanish province. There had been border conflicts between Americans and Florida Indians for several years, and Jackson provided no convincing evidence these had increased in tempo. His target, however, was no longer Indians. He had defeated Indians in the Creek War, and turned now to those who manipulated and controlled them.[111]

The movements of Florida Indians, said Governor Blount, "have, for a long time, been secretly planned and directed by our enemies," the Spanish and British. One British officer did boast he would arm the Florida Indians and use them against the United States. The British-Indian alliance during the 1812 War was no figment of frontier imaginations. As for the Spanish, their authority in Florida was weak. They traded with the Seminoles, and may knowingly have provisioned them for raids, but they could control Indian activity in Florida no better than they could British.[112]

Jackson insisted, nevertheless, that González Manrique, Pensacola Governor, secretly instigated and controlled Indian border raids. He accused Manrique of receiving "the matricidal band" of Indians "for whom your Christian bowels seem to sympathize and bleed so freely," "as the father his prodigal son." Such accusations permitted Jackson to indulge his own ferocity. He wrote the Governor,

> It is not on the heads of helpless women and children that retaliation will be made, but on the head which countenanced and excited the barbarity. He is the responsible person, and not the poor savage whom he makes his instrument of execution. An Eye for an Eye, Toothe for Toothe and Scalp for Scalp.

Repeating the "Scalp for Scalp" threat, Jackson wrote Manrique that his men would execute three Spanish sailors if "your Indians" were responsible for the murder of an overseer and the escape of several slaves.[113]

If the Spanish were mobilizing their Indians, Jackson would mobilize his. "I shall arm my Indians," he wrote Manrique. "You have thrown the gantlet and I will take it up." In fact Jackson had planned to enlist

Indian troops to fight the Spanish and British well before his accusations against Manrique. He was, Cherokee agent R. J. Meigs wrote, simply following the practice of the European powers. They had instigated the Creeks, "whose ferocity has been let loose by the English and Spanish against their greatest benefactors." Jackson now ordered Cherokee and Choctaw warriors enrolled in his army. Choctaw agent John McKee responded, "we may count pretty well on our Choctaws." But perhaps it would be best, he continued, to tell them they were fighting Indians, not whites. "When they have joined the army they will fight alongside of your soldiers against white or red foes—of this I have no doubt." Benjamin Hawkins told the Creeks the British were stealing slaves. He promised them $50 for every black returned to his master; the Creeks themselves could enslave those without owners.[114]

Jackson was later criticized for raising Indian troops in his 1818 Florida invasion. He replied by defending it as common practice during every Indian war. "During the late war with Great Britain," he said, "I was directed to compel (by coercive measures if it became necessary) all the warriors of the four Southern Tribes to enroll themselves in our defense." Jackson had received no such order from Washington; he acted solely on permission from his own superego.[115]

Having enrolled his Indian troops, Jackson prepared to invade Pensacola. He urged Manrique to surrender the Spanish fortification, and threatened, "I will not hold myself responsible for the conduct of my enraged soldiers and Indian warriors."[116] Jackson's preparations for the Florida campaign suggest the intensity of his identification with Indian violence. An evil "father" had instigated "the matricidal band" of brothers. Jackson would use his Indians for revenge.

Jackson easily conquered west Florida; to the dismay of the southwest, it was returned to Spain after the war. He turned next to the defense of New Orleans. Finally Jackson could challenge the British directly instead of striking at them through their instruments and inferiors. America had won few victories against the British as Jackson prepared to defend New Orleans. With Napoleon defeated, the country's situation looked particularly bleak. "English coming to swallow U.S.," one New Englander wrote. Jackson himself feared that America would be dismembered by a "combined coalition" and "apportioned amongst the powers of urope."[117]

Jackson's victory at New Orleans electrified the country. First he advanced at night against the more numerous British forces. Then his line withstood the British charge, killing the commanding general and many of his immediate subordinates. The British suffered 2,037 casualties, the Americans 71. Jackson "restored and inflamed the national self-love." New Orleans established him as the preeminent American hero.[118]

Americans overlooked the prosaic military causes of the British defeat. They credited Jackson's energy, perhaps correctly, with a central role in the drama. He unified New Orleans, it was said, and roused the lethargic city to action. He triumphed, as in the Creek War, over his own infirm body. In the words of one observer,

> During all the exciting events of this campaign Jackson had barely the strength to stand erect without support; his body was sustained alone by the spirit within. Ordinary men would have shrunk into feeble imbeciles or useless invalids under such a pressure. The disease contracted in the swamps of Alabama still clung to him. Reduced to a mere skeleton, unable to digest his food, and unrefreshed by sleep, his life seemed to be preserved by some miraculous agency.

A nephew expected "Uncle Jackson" to collapse at any moment. But he did not. "Although . . . ready to sink under the weight of sickness [and] fatigue," wrote his chief of engineers,

> his mind never lost for a moment that energy which [caused] insurmountable obstacles [to melt before him. This] energy . . . spread . . . to the whole army, . . . composed of heterogeneous elements . . . speaking different languages, and brought up in different habits. . . . There was nothing . . . it did not feel capable of doing if he ordered it to be done.[119]

Jackson defeated first the "barbarous sons of the forest," then the decadent and bloodthirsty Spanish, and finally the root "oppressors" of America's "infant political existence." He gained, in his ultimate victory, providential support. "I command you to God," Rachel wrote her husband after the death of Sandy Donelson in the Creek War. "His Providential Eye is on you his parental tender Care is garding you." Rachel helplessly resigned herself, in adversity, to God's power. Jackson experienced Providence as an access of personal omnipotence. The country agreed. "Praise ye the Lord for the avenging of Israel," proclaimed one newspaper headline. Many spoke of providential intercession. Jackson wrote Mississippi Governor Holmes, "If ever there was an occasion on which Providence interfered, immediately, in the affairs of men it seems to have been on this. What but such an interposition could have saved this Country?" The tiny number of American casualties and the huge British losses provided evidence for Divine intervention. "The unerring hand of providence shielded my men," wrote Jackson.[120]

New Orleans climaxed Jackson's rise to national heroic stature. His biblical journey, as we have imagined it, began with Jacob and Esau struggling for the birthright of Isaac. It progressed, with the execution of John Woods, to Abraham's sacrifice of Isaac. Jackson defeated the Creeks after this execution; he acquired Isaac's birthright as Abraham, not as Jacob or Esau. Now, at New Orleans, Jackson engineered a triumph of death for the British troops. As living British soldiers rose from the field of battle strewn with dead bodies, he was reminded of the resurrection.[121]

Battle-induced unity disintegrated after the climactic engagement, and Jackson increased his vigilance. Six soldiers left the Mobile garrison in 1814, claiming they had agreed to serve for three months and not six. A court-martial ordered them executed; after the battle of New Orleans Jackson approved the order. He feared that the atmosphere in New Orleans, fed by peace rumors, would turn his troops into a mob. "I cannot permit the Laurels of Louisiana to be Tarnished by the Lurking Demon of discord, that attempts to insinuate itself into her ranks," he insisted. He promised to "crush this monster in the Bud" and punish all who aided "this hidra." Martial law had not been declared in America since the ratification of the Constitution; Jackson, acting without authority, had imposed it on New Orleans before the battle. Now he used the power he had granted himself. Many French citizens resided in the city. Some members of the militia registered as French aliens so they could leave the army. To end this practice, Jackson ordered all French citizens to remove 120 miles from the city. Louis Louaillier, a member of the territorial assembly who had heretofore supported Jackson, objected; Jackson ordered him jailed. When Federal Judge Dominick Hall granted *habeas corpus* to Louaillier, Jackson had him arrested too. His order read,

> Having received proof that Dominick A. Hall has been aiding and abetting and exciting mutiny within my camp, you will forthwith order a detachment to arrest and confine him, and report to me as soon as arrested. You will be vigilant. The agents of the enemy are more numerous than was expected.

Jackson's own military court acquitted Louaillier of Jackson's charge of spying, but Jackson returned him to jail anyway.[122]

As soon as official word of peace arrived, Jackson ended martial law and released all prisoners. He submitted himself to trial under a contempt citation issued by Judge Hall. It was one of his finest moments. He stood as the defender of the court, restraining a crowd of his partisans from disrupting the trial. He announced, "The same arm that protected from outrage this city, against the invaders of the country, will shield and protect this court, or perish in the effort." The civil law was once again paramount, Jackson told the crowd, and he was obligated to obey it. "I risked all the consequences; and you have seen me meet the penalty

of my aggression, and bow with submission to the sentence of the law."
The town raised $1,000 to pay his fine, but Jackson ordered the money
used to provide for the women and children of the soldiers slain in battle. He paid his fine himself.[123]

Jackson had gloried for the moment in the exercise of illegal authority. Now, paying for his "aggression," he stood as the defender of the
country and the embodiment of its laws. As a young land lawyer and
judge, Jackson had represented the law; now, as military hero, he embodied it. His primitive violence no longer stood outside the law, at
war with his legal position. Jackson had sublimated rage into authority.
In the words of an admirer, "He stood amidst the citizens of New Orleans, like a father in the midst of a family, who owed their temporal
felicity to his assiduous labours." As Jackson imagined the future, "Years
will continue to develop our inherent qualities, until, from being the
youngest and weakest, we shall become the most powerful nation in the
universe."[124]

"Services Genl, are soon forgotten," a friend wrote Jackson in 1816.
"But yrs never can for you must ever be looked upon as only next to
Washington." Jackson had paid his first visit to Mount Vernon a few
months earlier. He gave no hint there of his early opposition to the man
he now called "the patriarch of our liberties." Instead he was furious
that "the bones of the father of his country" were "Permitted to moulder"
in their original "dark, narrow cell" at the foot of an overgrown hill.
"Must the charge of ingratitude," asked Jackson, "forever rest upon re-
publicks?"[125]

CHAPTER 6

PRIMITIVE ACCUMULATION AND PATERNAL AUTHORITY

The Indian, in the dreary solitudes of his woods, cherishes the same ideas, the same opinions, as the noble of the Middle Ages in his castle; and he only needs to become a conqueror to complete the resemblance. Thus, however strange it may seem, it is in the forest of the New World, and not among the Europeans who people its coasts, that the ancient prejudices of Europe still exist.

—Alexis de Tocqueville, Democracy in America, *Vol. I, chapter 18*

I

From 1814 to 1824, Jackson was the moving force behind southern Indian removal. Including the treaty of Fort Jackson, eleven treaties of cession were held with the southern Indians in this period. Jackson was responsible for all but two with the Georgia Creeks, and was himself present at six. His treaties acquired three-quarters of Alabama and Florida, one-third of Tennessee, one-fifth of Georgia and Mississippi, and smaller portions of Kentucky and North Carolina. His friends and relatives received many of the patronage appointments—as Indian agents, traders, treaty commissaries, surveyors, and land agents—created by his treaties. Jackson's ideas exercised powerful influence on the administration's Indian policy; he wrote often to Monroe while the Virginian was first Secretary of War and then President, and exchanged letters with Secretary of War Calhoun as well. During this period Jackson developed the approach which culminated in his presidential Indian-removal program. His active agency in clearing the southern states of Indians, and the certainty that he would finish the job, helped make him the southern candidate for President. When Jackson turned in the 1820s from Indian removal to presidential politics, other negotiators could acquire—in a fraudulent treaty which created a political crisis—only the Creek land in Georgia. It seemed that only Jackson's techniques and the force of his personality could obtain the southern Indians' remaining land.[1]

Jackson first developed, in Indian relations, the major formulas of Jacksonian Democracy.[2] This was not fortuitous. Indian removal laid the foundations for both the triumphs and the anxieties of Jacksonian culture. Comparison with Europe makes clear the importance of the Indians in America. The early liberal state grew in feudal Europe by destroying local centers of tradition and self-governance and clearing the obstacles to market capitalism. Nationalism and the expanding market also undermined local autonomy and self-sufficiency in America, but there was no feudalism standing in the way. Indian tribes offered the most significant symbolic resistance to liberal uniformity.

In Europe capitalism struggled with feudalism; the contrast between "savagery" and "civilization" dominated the ante-bellum American imagination. Just as Sir Walter Scott offered feudal romances to industrializing England, so Fenimore Cooper, following Scott's example in the new world, turned to the wilderness. His Indian tales and those of others provided America with its national literature in the Jacksonian period, while Indian removal configured Jacksonian politics.[3]

The Indian may have been a "monarch of the wilds," but he was not a European king. Southern Indians may have been "lords paramount," but they were not feudal lords.[4] They lacked the power of the European aristocracy, and did not embody the traditions of the men who overthrew them. European liberalism, rebelling against power, tradition, and mature authority—the fathers—produced a powerful political thought. Indians, I have suggested, were children, not fathers, in the American imagination. Like the young King Alfred, they "swayed the sceptre of [their] infant realms."[5] The resistance they offered was the resistance of primitiveness and fantasy. The qualities of mind accompanying primitive accumulation in America are not compelling for their theoretical power and logical sophistication. What rather demands attention is the half-conscious, regressive journey into the interior of the American psyche that accompanied Indian removal and westward expansion.

Indian removal influenced not simply American politics and culture. It defined for America the economic stage of primitive accumulation. In Rosa Luxemburg's words,

> Capital is . . . faced with difficulties because vast tracts of the globe's surface are in the possession of social organizations that have no desire for commodity exchange or cannot, because of the entire social structure and the forms of ownership, offer for sale the productive forces in which

capital is primarily interested. The most important of these productive forces is of course the land. . . . Since the primitive associations of the natives are the strongest protection for their social organizations and for their material bases of existence, capital must begin by planning for the systematic destruction and annihilation of all the non-capitalist social units which obstruct its development. With that we have passed beyond the stage of primitive accumulation.[6]

Jackson acted, like the early European nation-state, as the agent for primitive accumulation. Primitive accumulation in early modern Europe assaulted domestic feudal classes. European imperialism carried out primitive accumulation against the colored peoples of the world. The expansion of European settler societies—Australia, South Africa, the United States—was characterized by internal imperialism.[7] Jackson assaulted the "primitive associations of the natives." He liberated land from communal use and thrust it into the market. There it was the major stimulus to capitalist development. Jackson cleared the obstacles to market capitalism, politically and by force, before the market could act on its own.

Jackson forged American national identity in westward expansion and Indian removal. The struggle with the Indians produced a powerful nationalism, a militant liberal egalitarianism, and a charismatic national political figure. Indian removal also generated, although to a lesser extent than the European struggle against feudalism, a strong national state. Jackson began, through Indian relations, to understand himself as the tribune of the people against selfish and entrenched leaders. He relied on personal leadership to overcome the obstacles to his will. He fought conspiratorial enemies who were seeking to overwhelm republican virtue. He emphasized agrarian values against the Indian way of life. He built the patronage political machine that would carry him to power against entrenched traditional leaders. And he developed the mixture of primitive rage, agrarian nostalgia, and acquisitive capitalism which formed the core of Jacksonian Democracy.

Northern presidential aspirants—William Henry Harrison and Lewis Cass most importantly—also built careers around Indian removal. But northern Indians, after the War of 1812, offered less resistance to removal. Northern tribes were smaller and more numerous than the five southern Indian confederations. They were less settled than the southern tribes, and never developed so large-scale an agriculture or so complexly stratified a social structure. Most northern Indian tribes were heavily dependent on white traders, exchanging furs, for example, for tribal necessities. Large tribal debts, often hugely inflated, gave traders a powerful influence over the Indians.

Liberal contractual market mechanisms—treaties, bribes, the repayment of debts—were sufficient to dispossess most northern tribes. Some bands, dependent on disappearing game, were willing to move. The leaders of others were induced by drink, debts, or presents to cede their land. Typically a tribe was concentrated on smaller and smaller reservations before the remnant moved west, or disappeared. Northern removal did not proceed entirely without Indian opposition. Tribes resisting American expansion fought with the British in the War of 1812. But only brief or isolated resistance survived the end of British support in the northwest. The Six Nations in New York, who resisted removal most successfully, retained small reserves in the east. Tribes in Illinois and Wisconsin fought brief, unsuccessful wars against advancing miners and settlers and government removal efforts. Tribes south and west of Lake Superior retained eastern land until the 1840s or later, thanks less to successful Indian resistance than to the delay in pressure from white expansion.[8]

From 1815 to 1844, Indian resistance centered in the south. The confederations of Choctaws in southern Mississippi, Creeks in Alabama and Georgia, and Cherokees in Alabama, Georgia, North Carolina, and Tennessee each contained approximately 20,000 members. The Chickasaws in northern Mississippi and the Seminoles in Florida were about one-quarter the size, but they benefited from the presence of the larger tribes. An independent village life characterized all five confederations, as was the case with the northern tribes. But the southern Indians were more settled and agricultural, and had begun to develop centralized resistance to pressures for land cessions. Thanks largely to the presence of wealthy Indians of mixed ancestry, there was significant plantation agriculture in the southern tribes, and Christianity had influence in some of them. A more assimilated leadership—backed by the overwhelming sentiment of ordinary Indians—was better able to resist white demands. The degree of adaptation to American culture varied among the tribes. The Cherokees, considered the most civilized by white observers, developed a written alphabet and widespread literacy in the aboriginal language.[9]

Market and contract failed to dispossess the southern tribes; more thoroughgoing state intervention was required. In the south, therefore, the premises underlying Indian removal were pushed furthest, most developed, and most exposed. Liberalism did not generally meet in America obstacles that forced it to articulate its underlying premises. Southern Indians opened fissures exposing the core assumptions of expansionist liberalism.

The south was already vulnerable to such exposure. Liberalism attacked paternal political power in theory; capitalism weakened it in practice. But market liberalism also engendered longings for paternal authority, and Indian removal gave these longings their historic task. Primitive accumulation rested upon the paternal political claim. Paternalism over Indians, unmediated by complex white social structures and devoted to atomizing the tribes, was the mirror image of liberalism. It set a single power over the mass of theoretically equal children. Statesmen from all sections of America asserted paternal authority over Indians. Southern-planter paternalism, however, offered primitive accumulation its most important indigenous model. Slavery helped Jackson define the paternal state in whose name he removed Indians. Marrying paternalism to liberal egalitarian assumptions, he provided a structure for American expansion. But the slave model of paternalism, appropriate enough to Indian removal, contained force and violence at its core. Indian removal exposed the sadistic underside of American expansion and the difficulties of building from liberal assumptions a structure of legitimate public authority.

Thanks to southern slavery and southern Indian resistance, the logic of Indian removal was carried furthest in the south. But the dispossession of the Indians was nationwide. Indian removal had the support of southwesterners like Jackson and Thomas Hart Benton; of northwesterners like William Henry Harrison, Lewis Cass, and John Tipton of Indiana; of seaboard southerners like Jefferson, William Crawford, John C. Calhoun, and the first Superintendent of Indian Affairs, Thomas L. McKenney; and of northeasterners like John Quincy Adams, Martin Van Buren, and the Dutch Reformed minister J. F. Schermerhorn.

Jackson's version of Indian removal was in part shared across America. In part it was southern, in part western, in part tied to rapid westward expansion and the market revolution of the early nineteenth century, and in part uniquely his. Let us now trace its development.

II

The treaty of Fort Jackson had not defined the northern and western limits of the Creek cession. This was common practice in Indian treaties; it gave white surveyors opportunity to engross more land. But the area left unbounded by the Creek treaty was unprecedented in size. Where the Creek lands bordered on the Cherokee, Choctaw, and Chickasaw nations, commissioners appointed by the President were left to determine the extent of Creek territory. These commissioners had the power enormously to aggrandize Creek claims, and therefore the extent of land ceded to the United States. Their leeway was particularly great because the borders of Indian nations were shifting and in dispute, because much of this land was hunting range with only a scattering of villages, and because in practice tribes shared hunting lands. The existence of hunting range was essential for the subsistence and cultural and social autonomy of the tribes; the absence of settled villages gave the commissioners great room for maneuver.

Jackson feared, however, that the commissioners appointed by Madison would not take advantage of their situation. Congress had provided for three boundary commissioners, but Jackson pressed for the appointment of John Coffee in addition. Secretary of War Crawford authorized General E. P. Gaines, one of the commissioners, to add Coffee if Benjamin Hawkins, the old, sick Creek agent, died or resigned. Jackson wrote Coffee he had been given a provisional appointment. Coffee proceeded to Fort Strother, in the northern portion of the disputed land, and waited a short time for the other commissioners to arrive. Then, although he had no authority to proceed on his own, he began to run the treaty line along the northern and western boundaries of the cession. He told Jackson his intentions, Jackson heartily approved them, and the two may have agreed verbally on this procedure before Coffee left for Fort Strother.[10]

There was good reason for Coffee's haste, and for his acting on his own. Creek claims to the land he was surveying were dubious indeed. Cherokees actually resided on much of it. Coffee collected affidavits from Creeks and from local whites that the land in question—a fifty-mile-wide strip across northern Alabama south of the Big Bend of the Tennessee River—belonged to the Creeks and had only been loaned to the Cherokees. But Cherokee title had been recognized in the United States–Cherokee treaty of 1806. The Creek claim seems to have surfaced only at the Fort Jackson treaty, where it was seized upon, if not originated, by Jackson. The Cherokees present at Fort Jackson objected vehemently, and the boundary was left for the boundary commissioners to determine.[11]

The actual basis of the white claim did not lie in Creek title. This was land through which Jackson's troops had marched on their way to conquer the Creeks; they claimed it as a spoil of war. Conquering land from an allied tribe which had helped win the Creek War was not the best claim to title. But the southwest had long coveted this valuable strip of land, longed to possess it, and would not relinquish it now. It was south of Muscle Shoals, in which Jackson had a historical interest. Speculators had wanted this land since the 1780s. (At that time, lacking prevision, they had approached the Cherokees about it.)[12] The land south of the Shoals contained some of the best cotton acreage in the south. Coffee denied gossip that he and Jackson planned to purchase there; the gossip, as we shall see, was perfectly accurate.[13]

The administration did not authorize the original commissioners to survey the northern and western boundaries of the Creek cession, pending a resolution of the conflicting claims. But, as Jackson and Coffee knew, an Indian line, however arrived at, drew settlers to its borders like a magnet. The legalities could catch up with the settlers. Jackson, in Washington during the winter of 1816, knew the Cherokees had come there to protest

Coffee's plans. For that reason he encouraged his friend to proceed with dispatch. He told Coffee to continue running the line over Cherokee and Chickasaw opposition. He approved of Coffee's plan to buy the acquiescence of Cherokee Chief Richard Brown, who had fought with Jackson, by running the line around Brown's village. Jackson told Coffee to raise troops on Jackson's authority to overcome Indian resistance and protect his surveyors, although he was not "legally authorized" to do so. Coffee should raise troops without requesting permission from the War Department, wrote Jackson, since Acting Secretary of War John Armstrong could not be trusted. Jackson ordered a Chickasaw chief not to interfere with Coffee's line, once it reached land claimed by that tribe.[14]

The original three commissioners wrote Coffee to meet them at the southern boundary of the cession, described in the treaty, so they could complete the southern line. They told him he was not authorized to run the northern and western boundaries. Coffee received some of this correspondence while he was surveying, but he ignored it. By March he had run a line around the entire northern and western portion of the cession, at the expense of Cherokee land in the north and Chickasaw and Choctaw claims in the northwest and west. Secretary Crawford had no knowledge of Coffee's activities, or even that he was acting as a commissioner. He wrote the original three commissioners in March to delay surveying the northern boundary until a treaty was concluded with the Cherokees. But he was too late. Jackson and Coffee had accomplished a giant land grab.[15]

How, one wonders, could these two men not have been aware of the illicit character of their activities? Yet neither consciousness of culpability nor pride in successful chicanery enters their extensive correspondence on the Creek line. The entire matter is conducted, to read their letters, on the highest moral plane. Those who see Jackson merely as an acquisitive swindler—a confidence man—badly miss the point. He needed to ground acquisitiveness on moral bedrock. The more egregious the activity, the more he engaged in falsification of memory, denial, militant self-righteousness, and projection of his own motivations onto others. Jackson's relations with the victimized Cherokees illustrate this proposition.

Secretary of War Crawford signed an agreement with the Cherokees in March 1816. It recognized their right to the land in question, and compensated them for damage to livestock and crops inflicted by Jackson's troops and those of the east Tennessee volunteers on the march through Cherokee country during the Creek campaign.[16] Jackson was legally subordinate to Crawford, and it might seem he had been outmaneuvered. This reckoned without the force of Jackson's personality and the power of Coffee's line.

Crawford's Cherokee convention enraged Jackson. Informed of his soldiers' depredations during the Creek campaign, Jackson had been sternly angry at the perpetrators and had promised reparation. Now, just two years later, he insisted strongly and at great length that the Tennessee troops were not guilty. The charges proved, he wrote, "that no confidence is to be placed in the honesty, or justice of an Indian." As for the whites supporting these false charges, their motives were deeply corrupt. Jackson gathered affidavits from his officers. He insisted the charges were meant to bring disgrace on him and his army. The evidence of depredations— partly by deserters, partly by hungry troops, partly for sport—was over- whelming. But Jackson could not entertain this evidence for a moment. His punitive conscience, fed by the recent land grab, could not be directed against himself. In addition, to admit the Cherokee claims was to admit that the territory marched through by his troops, claimed as Creek by him and Coffee, actually belonged to the Cherokees.[17]

Jackson was equally furious at Crawford's territorial agreement with the Cherokees. "An Indian . . . will claim everything and anything," he wrote in response to the Cherokee, Chickasaw, and Choctaw claims. Give in to them on this land and they will begin to claim the neighboring, wrote Jackson, substituting an imaginary process of Indian expansion for the actual history of white expansion.[18] It was pure projection. All Jackson's affidavits and legal claims simply papered over an unlimited white appetite for land, grounded in no legitimate title. Such unlimited hunger generated the fantasies of unlimited Indian claims in which Jackson indulged.

Jackson's bitter enmity with Crawford, which significantly affected the 1824 presidential campaign, dates from these events. The government had given the Cherokees, Jackson complained to Coffee, the most valuable part of the Creek cession. But Jackson was hardly defeated. He and Coffee encouraged squatters to move onto the disputed land, and to refuse to obey presidential orders to remove. Jackson himself, as general in charge of re- moving intruders on Indian lands, refused to obey presidential orders to do so. He predicted that the militia would refuse to carry out such orders, that bloodshed and "civil war" would result, and that Tennessee would never permit the disputed land to return to Indian hands. He reminded the Secretary of War that Tennessee citizens had driven the Cherokees from their villages in the unauthorized expedition of 1793. They would not permit "the prowling lion of the forest" who had murdered their women and children, and whose land they had conquered in the late war, to remain. Threatening a renewed Indian war, he wrote that Tennessee citizens would "wreak their vengeance on this tribe."[19]

Crawford finally backed down. He agreed to hold treaties with the Cherokees, Choctaws, and Chickasaws. The treaties would determine the limits and validity of tribal claims and get the tribes to relinquish them.

Jackson had finally begun removing intruders; Crawford now suspended the order. He sent Coffee to deal with the Choctaws in the southwest. Jackson met with the Chickasaws and Cherokees in the north. All three tribes acquiesced in the Jackson-Coffee demands, ceding land equivalent to perhaps one-quarter of the total Indian losses from the Creek War. To some extent the government paid for dubious tribal claims, but it also coerced the cession of legitimate Indian title, including valuable cotton acreage.[20]

The tribes did not submit readily, however, and Jackson employed the two weapons which dominated all his later Indian treaties. The treaties would not have succeeded, he wrote, "unless we addressed ourselves feelingly to the predominant and governing passion of all Indian tribes, *i.e.,* their avarice or fear." Jackson played on both passions. He told the tribes the government could not remove whites from the land they claimed; if the Indians insisted on their claims, they would be annihilated. The Cherokees, he wrote Secretary of State Monroe, must be made to see "what is really to be feared, that is, there own destruction by an irratated people." Only the treaty "prevented the destruction of many of our red brethren."[21]

Jackson's use of "fear" had developed in sophistication since Fort Jackson. There he had threatened the Indians himself. Now he no longer took responsibility for the contemplated violence; he split it from himself, attributed it to others, and posed as the Indians' protector. One would never have guessed he was the leader of the "irratated people" seeking vengeance against "our red brethren." Thanks to his triumphs in the Creek War, he now had violence under control and at his service.

Jackson's use of the second passion, "avarice," remained more primitive. In the first place he told the Cherokees that their claims for depredations during the Creek War would be investigated and found fraudulent, and their land would be taken without compensation as punishment. This was wholly fanciful, but, given Jackson's successes to this point, the Cherokees had legitimate cause for anxiety.[22]

Secondly, Jackson practiced extensive bribery. He complained that the chiefs consulted the entire Chickasaw nation and "seemed more anxious to maintain their popularity, than to promote the views of the Govt, or the best interests of the nation they ruled." But moneyed gifts or reservations of valuable land could separate the chiefs from the tribal interest. Since many of the chiefs were beginning to engage in plantation agriculture and were heavily in debt, bribery made a powerful appeal.[23] Chickasaw Chief George Colbert received a $100 lifetime annuity for "his long service and faithful adherence to the United States government." Altogether, $4,500 was spent in money presents at the Chickasaw treaty. Jackson wrote, "Secrecy was enjoined as to the names. Secrecy is necessary, or the influence of the chiefs would be destroyed, which has been, and may be useful on a future occasion."[24] This was plain talk; unlike fear, bribery was not yet clothed with benevolence. At his next treaty Jackson would pose as the defender of the "real Indians" against the chiefs he was bribing. But analysis of that development must wait upon a discussion of Jackson's and Coffee's own personal reward in the land they had acquired for America.

III

The Creek War and the treaties of 1814 and 1816 opened the heart of the cotton kingdom to white settlement. "The tract of land acquired by the contest will be extensive and valuable," John Coffee had early confirmed. We will take the best land as indemnity for the war, he wrote his father-in-law, Captain John Donelson III, and permit the Indians to settle on the rest. John Donelson IV, riding with Uncle Jackson on military business before the Fort Jackson treaty, kept his eye out for good land.[25] Behind the southwest's eagerness for Indian land lay the workings of the market. Jackson's methods of acquiring Indian land had graphically illustrated primitive capitalist accumulation; it was time now for the market itself to take over.

Jackson urged "bringing this land into markett speedily." "Bring it into markett," he explained, and the settlers who purchased would defend the western country. The driving demands for Indian land were actually economic. Cotton prices doubled from 1814 to 1816, in the boom following the War of 1812. Exhaustion of old cotton land was a further pressure for expansion. Southern planters made great efforts to bring more land into cultivation, and doubled cotton output between 1814 and 1819. Land was sought by everyone—great and small planters, speculators, yeomen farmers, squatters, petty-claim dealers. Some Tidewater planters feared the exodus to the west; they worried about the decline in seaboard power, and economic competition from new, fertile cotton lands. Crawford represented this interest, and did not share Jackson's urgency. But the pressures for immediate action were powerful within Georgia and South Carolina, as well as farther west, and many southeasterners, rich and poor, moved to the newly opened lands.[26]

Hunger for Alabama land reached an intensity never seen before in America. Land in northern Alabama near Muscle Shoals, obtained in the Coffee-Jackson swindle, was particularly coveted. "The Alabama will be the garden of America," predicted one southerner. By 1816 the squatters on the Creek cession numbered 10,000 and included wealthy planters like future Alabama Governor Thomas Bibb. He and his brother William Bibb, a Georgia Senator and the first Governor of Alabama, made big purchases at the land sales. Many of the other squatters could not afford the prices. Still, if they could raise one cotton crop on the public land, they had started on the way to wealth. Thousands who did not squat and plant immediately traveled over the country in search of good locations. One southeastern correspondent reported, "The Alabama Feaver rages here with great violence and has *carried off* vast numbers of our citizens."[27]

John Coffee was at the center of all this activity. He expected, even before the Fort Jackson treaty, to be appointed surveyor of the Alabama lands; Jackson secured the office for him late in 1816. Surveying jobs typically were given to former military officers who had conquered the land. It was a lucrative profession. Surveyors could no longer, as in the days of John and Stockley Donelson, mark out enormous wilderness tracts for themselves. The land was still wild, requiring, one Alabama surveyor complained, "men as hard as a Savage" to survey it. But it had, since the 1780s, greatly increased in value. Everyone knew the best soil would be turned to cropland immediately. Coffee's position made his fortune.[28]

The land office was the most important government office in the west. Almost all land officers were land speculators, sometimes acting legally, sometimes not. Surveyors knew the land, and bid from this intimate knowledge. But that was only part of their advantage. Requests for information on land poured in to Coffee from prospective purchasers. Land surveys were proceeding rapidly, he wrote his wife in May 1817. "I never saw such anxiety, as exhibits itself here, all trying to get rich quick by the purchase of land in this tract of country." Coffee entered detailed notes on the quality and characteristics of the land in his field notes and plat books. He made an agreement with the land-office clerks in which he received half of any land, money, or other gratuities they were paid for purchasing, locating, or giving information about land. No information was to be imparted without a fee. Jackson had suggested this procedure, and it was common. Government officials typically used the power or information gained by their positions to acquire land or money for themselves, their relatives, and their friends. Few drew sharp lines between public and private business.[29]

One customer wrote Coffee, "I shall more particularly depend on you after you have served yourself and some of your most particular friends." Coffee served his friends and relations well. His father-in-law, wealthiest member of the Donelson clan, hoped to buy two sections of land and sell one to pay for both. "This is my way of speculation," he wrote Coffee. Other members of the clan were also interested. Brother-in-law Lemuel Donelson wrote, "If you see any speculation that you may think profitable I should like to have a finger in the pie." John McLemore, married like

Coffee to a daughter of Rachel's brother, wanted Coffee to purchase a lot for him "with a view to selling out at some distant period on a speculation." Coffee also looked after Jackson's land interests. Jackson had "been making some conditional contracts for land on the coast," and was contemplating buying a sugar estate. "A great speck'l. is to be made at present in this quarter," he wrote his nephew John Hutchings.[30]

Jackson had long been interested in the Muscle Shoals region. His friend and sometime agent A. P. Hayne (brother of the South Carolina Senator) thanked Jackson for information about Muscle Shoals. He regretted he could not accept Jackson's invitation to stay at the Hermitage. Traveling through the cession, he wrote Jackson, "Such a field for the acquirement of wealth I have never before witnessed. A capital cannot be emplyed too soon in the Cntry. Speculation in *Land* is superior to Law or Physick." Jackson convinced the government to build an armory and foundry at Muscle Shoals, further increasing the value of land in the area. He planned to meet with Coffee in May 1817 "to take a small view of the country," and consulted Coffee several times on desirable sites.[31]

Coffee formed a land company to bid on lands. Shares were divided among Jackson and other Tennesseeans on the one hand, and wealthy Philadelphia speculators on the other. Jackson preferred that Coffee not involve himself in a land company, and make contracts with individuals instead; but he acquiesced in the arrangement. Coffee bought stock for himself and his friends and relations in several other land companies, formed primarily to speculate in town lots. Jackson was included, although not heavily, in these purchases.[32]

The sales were scenes of high excitement. "There appears to prevail something like a land mania," one land-office register reported. The government had provided easy credit terms for the sale of public lands; it required only a one-quarter down payment. Government land scrip awarded in the settlement of the Yazoo land frauds further increased the purchasing power of those present at the sales. Sale of the land below Muscle Shoals early in 1818 brought unprecedented prices. Some land sold for as much as $78 an acre; sales at $40 an acre were common. Jackson had hoped to be at that first sale, but was fighting Indians in Florida instead. Coffee and James Jackson took care of his interests. Coffee's land company purchased a site at the foot of the Shoals, and laid out the town of Florence there. Jackson retained several Florence town lots until 1838. At the Huntsville land sales in 1818 more than 40,000 tracts were sold, totaling 2.2 million acres.[33]

At a sale later in the year Jackson himself bought land near the Shoals; as a mark of respect, no one bid against him. Others were not so lucky. At the first sale large companies conspired in an attempt to keep the prices down and avoid competitive bidding; this would augment their profits when they resold the land. The pressure of buyers was too great, however, and fierce competition bid up the prices. This hardly benefited small farmers, who could not afford such sums. Almost all the land went into the hands of large planters, investors, and speculators. The receiver of public moneys at Huntsville used $80,000 of federal funds as the down payment to enter 50,000 acres in his own name. He later defended his action on the grounds that it had kept the land from large, conspiring speculators. At subsequent sales land companies more successfully reached agreements which kept the initial price down; in many cases resales followed immediately. When the panic of 1819 hit Alabama, it left the state with an $11 million land debt, more than half of the total for the entire country. But millions of acres had gone into cultivation.[34]

Coffee himself entered eighty-three tracts in his own name during 1818. The land comprised 16,000 acres and a stated value of $76,000. He planned to resell some immediately and hold other tracts on longer-term speculation. Fees for sharing his expert knowledge also augmented his fortune. He moved with his family from Nashville to Huntsville and began a life as wealthy land speculator, surveyor, and planter. He continued, as surveyor general of Alabama, to buy land from the government and resell it. Many others who had fought with Jackson also moved onto the lands they had conquered and began careers in politics or plantation agriculture.[35]

Jackson did not follow Coffee's road. He had, almost single-handedly, set in motion the beginnings of rapid American economic development. The cotton kingdom, including the land Jackson won from the Indians, financed the American economic expansion of the succeeding decades. For the next quarter-century Jackson continued to acquire from the Indians the cotton lands necessary for capitalist development. But while Jackson acted in the service of capitalist expansion, he did not become wealthy himself. He continued to speculate and make money from his Indian activities, but such acquisitiveness was far more characteristic of his friends and relations than it was of him. Coffee, Overton, and brother-in-law John Donelson made fortunes; Jackson did not.

He represented, rather, the earlier and more heroic stage of primitive accumulation. He embodied the primitive psychic force which cleared the way for market expansion; mundane capitalists and politicians followed. Polks and Van Burens, or their local counterparts in business and politics, could run the machine; but first Jackson had to remove the obstacles to its operation and infuse it with his personal legitimacy. Indians were the first obstacle; Jackson spent the bulk of his public time after 1816, as he had since 1812, removing them. He developed his patriarchal authority, and the Jacksonian ethos, in the process.

IV

Jackson developed the theory and methodology of primitive accumulation in several stages. He had obtained Indian land in the Creek War and the treaties which followed it by undisguised bribery and force. He also exploited "avarice" and "fear" to obtain a treaty with the Cherokees in 1817. A small Tennessee branch of the tribe had obtained permission from Jefferson in 1809 to migrate to Arkansas. The chief of this band was John Jolly, in whose home Sam Houston had lived as a child for several years. Jolly's followers included wealthy mixed-bloods who wanted to be free from tribal rule. The Arkansas Cherokees had been given land, and the government now sought territory in compensation from the eastern branch of the tribe. It also hoped that more Cherokees would emigrate west to join Jolly's band. Jackson was enlisted to make the treaty.[36]

Jackson bribed several chiefs to obtain the land cession. "By a private article," he paid money to individual chiefs who lived in the newly ceded territory. He also made gifts to other chiefs, and presented $1,000 to an agent of the Arkansas Cherokees "To stop his mouth and attain his consent."[37]

He also played upon Cherokee "fear." When the tribe refused to treat, Jackson falsely told them they were bound by an agreement between Jefferson and the Arkansas Cherokees to cede eastern land in return for the Arkansas land. He threatened to make a separate treaty with the Arkansas Cherokees to obtain eastern land. He had no power to do this, but the frightened eastern Cherokees agreed to the cession. Acting Secretary of War George Graham worried that Congress would refuse to ratify the treaty when it learned of Jackson's tactics; he knew the tribe had made no agreement with Jefferson. Jackson reassured him. He wrote that when the Cherokee council denied there had been an agreement, Jackson made each member stand and say whether he wanted to give "their father the P. [Jefferson] the lie." Each, according to Jackson, said he did not, and "we completely exposed this base attempt of fraud and deception." The treaty proceedings contradict Jackson's account. They show that while no Cherokee wanted to call Jefferson a liar, many denied any agreement had been made with him. Jackson's reassurances convinced Graham, however, and he accepted the treaty.[38]

"Fear" and "avarice" obtained the treaty. At the same time, under the pressure of Indian resistance and the demands of national political leadership, Jackson began to elaborate more sophisticated versions of fear and avarice. He took the first steps during the 1817 negotiations. "Avarice" came to mean the application of market mechanisms to Indian land. Jackson sought to break tribal connections to the land and give individual Indians the right to own and sell their own plots. He also advocated Indian removal to the west for those savages who could not participate in civilized market processes. The Indian-removal program, and the paternalism used to justify it, derived from "fear"; as the tribes failed to succumb to avarice, the need for force led Jackson to his Indian paternalism.

Jefferson first posed the alternatives of civilization and removal. He and other early American statesmen believed that Indians who remained in their savage state could not resist the white advance and would become extinct. There were only two ways to avoid Indian extinction. First Indians could turn to agriculture, Christianity, and civilization, ultimately intermarry with whites, and, as Jackson would later put it, "become merged in the mass of our population." Second, they could be transported to an area west of American settlement. Jefferson planned that the Indians east of the Mississippi should be moved to the northern portion of the Louisiana Purchase. Small groups of Indians, like John Jolly's, began moving to this territory in the early nineteenth century.[39]

Many of the Indians most willing to move west, as Jolly's migration indicated, were the more civilized, agricultural tribal members. The theoretical choice offered the tribe in 1817, however, was between remaining savage and moving to the west, or becoming civilized and remaining in the east. Government representatives told the Indians they could take individual plots of land and place themselves under state law, or move to Arkansas and retain tribal ownership of land.

These alternatives shared an underlying identity. Both required the tribe to break its communal ties to its historic tribal territory. Both were methods of obtaining Indian land. Jefferson's program began with the premise that Indians would surrender land as they were civilized. In the first stages of civilization they would trade furs, incur debts, and be willing to "lop off" excess lands to pay for them. Jefferson explained, "The wisdom of the animal which amputates and abandons to the hunter those parts for which he is pursued should be theirs, with this difference, that the former sacrifices what is useful, the latter what is not." Jefferson established trading posts in Indian territory to entice the tribes into debt; he offered to assume the debts as payment for tribal cessions of land. This process, which obtained substantial Indian land, perfectly illustrates the government's use of market mechanisms.[40]

To gain Indian land, Jefferson wrote Jackson in 1803, "we consider leading the Indians to agriculture. . . . When they shall cultivate small spots of earth, and see how useless their extensive forests are, they will sell. . . ." It was soon clear, however, that Indians did not first turn to agriculture and then cede land. The government would have to reverse the process. As the tribes surrendered land to the government, they could no longer live by hunting and foraging; they would have to turn to agriculture, work and save, and plan for the future. Joseph McMinn, administering the 1817 Cherokee treaty, explained to the tribe, "Your people, as well as all others, must become industrious from necessity, for none ever will from choice; and the greater the space they have to occupy, the greater will be their inducement to idleness." In the words of Cherokee agent R. J. Meigs,

> I would lead them to civilization without injuring an individual, until they gradually and almost imperceptibly become blended with ourselves. And to effect this, they must circumscribe their immense limits; for while they can roam through extensive forests . . . they will not make use of their physical or mental faculties to raise themselves up. Poor human nature, alone, revolts at the thought of the labor required and the sacrifices to be made to arrive at a state of civilization.[41]

Jefferson's debt policy acquired southern Indian territory, but it worked too slowly. Meigs suggested the government had a paternal duty to take Indian land. As long as Indians were "nursed and protected in the enjoyment of their vast extent of land," they did not have to "like the white people depend on their own exertions." "They actually need some stronger excitement to industry than they now have. If they were my own children I would say the same."[42]

Agriculture not only reduced tribal holdings; it also established individual private property in the land. Southern Indians had always had an extensive agriculture, but it was not based on private property. Progress, in the white view, depended upon personal ownership. Communal Indian relations, and in particular communal use of the land, had to be shattered. "No one will exert himself to procure the comforts of life," Secretary of War Crawford told the Senate, "unless his right to enjoy them is exclusive." Even Indians with plantations were theoretically growing cotton on tribal lands. When a Cherokee delegation visited Jefferson in 1809, preparatory to their Arkansas migration, he urged them to legalize individual property in improved land.[43]

Jackson's 1814 Creek treaty was the first to grant Indians individual ownership of land. Secretary Crawford, not Jackson, had originated the idea. He and General Pinckney promised friendly Creek chiefs individual reservations in the Creek lands ceded the United States. Jackson's treaty provided that any chief who had fought with the United States, and whose improvements lay in the ceded territory, could retain for himself and his descendants a section of land containing his improvements. Since the Creek treaty took land belonging to Creeks who had fought with Jackson, this was a politic provision. White soldiers were granted land bounties in Indian land; Indian warriors were granted bounties in what was left of their own land.[44]

Crawford continued to advocate individual allotments of tribal land, and Jackson and Coffee provided some in the 1816 treaties. As in 1814, however, these reservations had more the character of bribes than of sustained social policy. Jackson supported the idea of Indian agriculture in the same *pro forma* spirit. He had Coffee tell the Choctaws "to lay aside all ideas of hunting and become like us." Like his grants of individual reservations, this statement was narrowly instrumental to the central purpose of getting the tribes to reduce their holdings.[45]

Jackson had a more ambitious aim in 1817. He hoped, for the first time, entirely to eliminate tribal control of southern land. This aim required more than bribery and threats; it required a developed, theoretical rationale. Jackson's 1817 treaty was the first based centrally on the twin doctrines of agriculture and removal.

The treaty permitted individual Cherokees to migrate west and join the Arkansas branch of the tribe; tribal lands in the east would be reduced proportionately. Indians who stayed in the east could obtain individual sections of land if they became United States citizens and agreed to live under American law. If an Indian with his own allotment migrated west, the United States would take title to his land; if he remained on his land until he died, the title would descend in fee simple to his children. Jackson's Cherokee treaty was the first to employ individual allotments on a large scale, and the first which gave individual Indians the right to sell their land. Two months later a treaty Lewis Cass made with northern Indians also granted individual allotments, and vested the right to sell in the Indians themselves, not just in their children. Individual allotments freed Indians from their land and subjected them to market mechanisms. Jackson used allotments to obtain southern Indian land during his presidential Indian-removal program. From 1887 to 1934 a federal law requiring individual ownership of tribal territory was the principal method of dispossessing the Indians.[46]

Jackson crystallized the theories of allotment and removal in practice, but the ideas originated elsewhere. He himself invented another justification for breaking up the tribal structure. During the Creek War, Jackson had blamed his officers for sowing discontent among the troops and undermining his paternal military authority. He now presented himself as the protector of ordinary Indians oppressed by selfish Indian chiefs. This conception brought Jackson one step closer to his version of Indian paternalism, a version which assaulted the tribe in the name of protecting its members.

The Cherokee treaty negotiations introduced the rhetoric of Jacksonian Democracy into American politics. When the Cherokee chiefs strongly objected to the removal proposals, Jackson posed as the defender of honest, poor Indians against self-aggrandizing tribal leaders. "There cannot be (except in England) as corrupt and Despotic government as now exists in this nation," he exclaimed. "There are more virtue in the native Indian than in the white men and halfbreed."

> I believe every native of the nation left to themselves, would freely make this election [to remove]. But they appear to be overawed by the council of some white men and half breeds, who have been and are fattening upon the annuities, the labours, and folly of the native Indian, and who believe, that their income would be destroyed by the removal of the Indians. These that I have named are like some of our bawling politicians, who loudly exclaim we are the friends of the people, but who, when the[y] obtain their views care no more for the happiness or wellfare of the people than the Devil does—but each procure influence through the same channell and for the same base purpose, *self-aggrandisement*.[47]

"Bawling," self-aggrandizing politicians fattened on the labor of others instead of working hard themselves; they gained infantile oral gratification at the expense of those they were supposed to serve. Despotic governments thwarted individual freedom; in the same spirit of bourgeois individualism, Jackson denounced tribal assumption of individual Indian debts. He asked, "How can the claim of one man in Justice be converted to the payment of another debt, without his consent[?]"[48]

Thus far the doctrine was familiar, if the language was particularly graphic. Jackson had not before applied bourgeois political ideas against the tribal structure, however. Equally important, although he had often stood as the defender of women and children, or of the virtue of America as a whole, he had never specifically defended the poor against entrenched political leadership. He now asserted that the greed of the "rich" Indians interfered with the right of the "poor" to go west. Jackson told the tribe,

> Friends and Brothers Listen; Let the whole nation hear. Is there one among you that can say this is not justice to all; has not every man among you a free choice to go or stay and has not the poor indian, as well as the rich a right freely to make a choice, is the poor Indian as free as the rich and his welfare as much concerned.

Jackson played upon this theme. He demanded that the tribal annuity be paid the "poor Indian" instead of "this corrupt created tyranny of thirteen who fatten on corruption"; otherwise "justice . . . will never be done the poor." Temporarily unsuccessful with this tactic, he had to wait until his presidential election to institute it.[49]

These formulations, with their attack on selfish entrenched leaders and their radical economic edge, became familiar Jacksonian doctrine in the 1830s. They originated in Indian removal as Jackson sought to break the "poor Indians" from actual protective ties—to the land and the tribal structure—and substitute his own protection on the one hand, the freedom of the marketplace on the other.

Jackson had blamed the power of selfish Cherokee chiefs a year earlier, after Crawford temporarily frustrated the Jackson-Coffee land grab. He wrote, "In this matter the Indians—I mean the real Indians, the natives of the forest are little concerned. It is a strategem only acted on by the designing half-breeds and renegade white men who have taken refuge in their country." But Jackson did not yet pose as the defender of the "real Indians"; he was more straightforward about his own aims. "If all influence but the native Indian were out of the way," he wrote, "we would have but little trouble." The language of 1817 was an important advance in the development of the Jacksonian appeal. It dressed expansionist self-interest in the clothes of moral concern.[50]

The Cherokee treaty obtained a relatively small cession of land, and provided the Arkansas Cherokees with a portion of the tribal annuity. These, said Jackson, were not the important provisions. Every Cherokee who wanted to emigrate would be enrolled for removal and given a rifle, a blanket, and other provisions. Every Cherokee who wanted to take an individual section of land and subject himself to state law had that alternative. At the end of a year a tribal census would be taken. The tribe would lose eastern land in proportion to the population now living in the west; Indians taking individual plots would not be counted in the eastern tribal census.[51]

Nothing in the treaty required individual Indians either to remove west or to take individual plots, but Jackson confidently predicted that "the principle established by the treaty . . . will give us the whole country in less than two years." Only those Cherokees would remain who were "prepared for agricultural pursuits, civil life, and a government of laws." This was a small minority of the tribe; the rest would go west.[52]

To prod the Indians into making their individual choices, Jackson urged that state laws be extended over the Cherokee tribe. This would protect individual Indians from tribal coercion. Again this step had to await Jackson's Presidency. In its absence Tennessee Governor Joseph McMinn, a frequent visitor to the Hermitage, began to act upon Jackson's interpretation of the treaty. While still governor, McMinn obtained

the job of enrolling Cherokee emigrants, and took up residence in Cherokee country. He told the tribe that under the treaty it had entirely to
relinquish collective ownership of its land. Combining bribery with in-
timidation, he induced numbers of Cherokees to sign enrollment registers, telling them they must either go west or take individual plots and
subject themselves to state law. Many Indians who had signed the registers to obtain money or goods were rounded up to be taken west
against their wills. When the Cherokee council protested and sought to
interfere, McMinn tried "purchasing their friendship." That failing, he
called for the intervention of the Tennessee militia. He delayed the tribal
census so that more Indians, having enrolled for removal or taken individual plots, would not be counted.[53]

McMinn urged the tribe to stop resisting his efforts. "Your policy,"
he told the Cherokee council, "is in direct opposition to the very humane
course pursued and intended by your father, the President of the United
States, to be continued towards your nation until the final accomplish-
ment of the great design of your becoming a part of the American
family."[54]

McMinn acted in the service not merely of the presidential father
but of the Divine father as well. The Governor wrote that he longed
to remove the entire tribe:

> Until that is done my mind will never rest in Peace in worldly matters,
> nor can any Human power stop its progress, though it may not be the
> will of the all wise disposer to permit me to see it otherwise than he
> did the Beloved father in relation to the Land of promise, and with his
> will I hope I shall be able to give a Christian assent. . . . Thousands un-
> born are to reap a rich reward from the acquisition of the Cherokee
> claim.[55]

In addition to his public service for "thousands unborn," McMinn
hoped to reap an immediate "rich reward" from the promised Cherokee
land. He had a speculative interest in Cherokee territory, which led him
humorously to call himself one of the "Land senators." McMinn assured
the government during his administration of the treaty, "I have not and
expect to make not one cent from this land." This was not true. Contrary to government orders, he leased improved land vacated by Cherokee migrants to white farmers and pocketed the rents himself. Cherokee
outcries ultimately forced McMinn to stop this practice, and to stop the
coercive enrollments as well. But McMinn's efforts had not been fruit-
less. To end his operations in their country, the Cherokees agreed to a
treaty early in 1819 ceding substantial lands in Tennessee, Georgia, and
Alabama.[56]

Like the other efforts at Indian removal in this period, Jackson's theory and McMinn's practice were only partially successful. But they laid the basis, in every detail, for the policy of Indian removal Jackson successfully implemented as President.

V

Jackson attended two more successful Indian treaties in this period, the Chickasaw treaty of 1818 and the Choctaw treaty of 1820. The first of these carried market mechanisms—avarice—to the extreme they seemed capable of sustaining, and provoked charges of corruption against the General. In the second Jackson spoke of himself for the first time as the paternal protector of red children. There was a relationship between these two developments.

Jackson had long urged Monroe to obtain the Chickasaw land in western Tennessee; in 1818 he received permission to make a treaty. The western third of Tennessee, still in Chickasaw hands, contained many of North Carolina's warrants to her revolutionary soldiers, located in the 1783–84 speculation. It was, one petition of Tennesseans insisted, "their patrimony purchased by the blood of their fathers." In fact most of the warrants had long since been bought up by speculators, claim dealers, and land lawyers, including prominent signers of the petition. The area contained some of the best virgin cotton land in the south. A trail of speculators with claims or aspirations in the western land followed Jackson to the Chickasaw treaty ground.[57]

The Chickasaw chiefs, some of them wealthy planters, knew the value of their land. Jackson was furious that they sought to take advantage of their knowledge. "They Colberts say," he wrote, "they will part with their land for the price the u. States gets for theirs. These are high toned sentiments for an Indian." Jackson had a formula to deal with such recalcitrance. He wrote Secretary of War Calhoun, "We must address ourselves to their fears and indulge their avarice." To play upon their avarice, Jackson arranged to have the annuity payment due for two years under the 1816 treaty delayed until the 1818 meeting. Many in the tribe had grown dependent on the annuity, either for subsistence or to pay individual and tribal debts. Delaying annuity payments to stimulate new treaties was common practice. Jackson's other appeal to tribal "avarice" had more originality.[58]

The government had not supplied sufficient money to purchase the Chickasaw land. "Moneyed presents" were distributed to individual chiefs, but the Colberts wanted more. Jackson arranged for speculators present with an interest in the western lands to put up $20,000 to purchase Colbert's ferry, a reserve at Muscle Shoals ceded the family in the 1816 treaty. On the open market it was worth many times what the speculators paid for it.[59]

Jackson arranged for himself and W. B. Lewis, future member of the Kitchen Cabinet, to sign a bond for the money. The title would be in the name of James Jackson, Jackson's friend and business agent. If the government wanted the reserve, it would pay $20,000 to the speculators and assume the title. Otherwise the reserve would fall immediately into private hands. It might be "high toned" for Indians to speculate on tribal land, but not for whites.[60]

Private individuals typically made money from government connections, but the procedure Jackson employed violated the minimal standards of public ethics accepted during this period. Direct private purchase of Indian land had been frowned on since the early days of the republic, and was prohibited by law. Congress insisted that the United States pay the additional $20,000 and take title to the reserve.

Jackson denied he had put up any of the $20,000 or expected to profit personally from the deal. His aims went beyond personal speculation. Jackson acted in the service of market expansion, but he was not narrowly dominated by market values. His acquisitive friends were, however. W. B. Lewis sought to profit from the treaty not merely by his interest in Colbert's ferry but by another speculation as well. The ceded Chickasaw land contained a large salt lick. Salt was essential on the frontier for feeding stock and storing food; towns and farms required an adequate supply. Ownership of salt licks made many frontier fortunes. Jackson and Coffee had tried to purchase one in Indian territory in 1802, but could not raise the money. Tennessee friends of Jackson asked permission of the government in 1812 to work the lick in Chickasaw country, "if by any means it can be extended consistently with a sense of propriety." These schemes were typical of unending white efforts to profit from mineral resources in Indian lands. But state and federal law prohibited citizens from leasing land from Indian tribes; the Chickasaw treaty would have to grant the lick to an individual Indian first, before whites could exploit it.[61]

Lewis went to the treaty with Jackson. Jackson had provided him with the lucrative post of commissary of treaty provisions, and he also acted as a "confidential agent" for the commissioners. Lewis attended the treaty because he held claims on the Indians lands. He also had his eye on the salt lick. Most observers expected the lick to be ceded with the rest of the Chickasaw Tennessee lands, but the Colbert family, in a special treaty article, obtained personal possession. After the treaty Lewis emerged with a 199-year lease on the salt lick; in return he was to supply the tribe annually with salt.[62]

Those who had hoped to obtain the lick themselves, and others who believed the state should mine it, objected to Lewis' deal. He had secretly obtained a "monopoly," it was charged, with Jackson's connivance. Jackson's friends assumed Lewis had acted with the General's knowledge, in spite of Lewis' and Jackson's denials. Knowledgeable or not, Jackson was not implicated in the affair, and did not profit personally from it. Lewis' role, however, was suspicious in the extreme.[63]

Lewis had contributed $3,000 to the $20,000 used to purchase Colbert's ferry. He later denied obtaining anything for this money; he claimed he simply wanted to insure the success of the treaty because of his interest in the western lands. This is most unlikely. It is equally unlikely the Colberts would have relinquished the lick simply in return for salt. Lewis' $3,000 was probably a bribe to the Colberts to obtain the lick.[64]

There is further evidence of this. When the treaty was ratified, the United States assumed title to Colbert's ferry. Lewis, later claiming the timing was coincidental, rushed to have his lease to the lick confirmed by the tribe. The government was returning him the $3,000 he had paid the Colberts; did he want to insure he would still keep the lease?[65]

The story has a final twist. Exploration and drilling revealed that the lick had no salt. Lewis proposed that the tribe buy the lease back from him and sell it to the United States, "as the Gover. is so liberally disposed toward its Red children." When that plan failed, he rented the land to settlers, violating the terms of the lease. At the 1826 and 1830 Chickasaw treaties, Lewis and his partner Robert Currin sought to purchase the land outright from the tribe. They could then sell it on the market, recoup their losses in drilling for salt, and make a handsome profit besides. At the 1830 treaty, which Jackson attended, Currin's purchase of the land was inserted as a supplemental article in the treaty. Commissary to the treaty, Currin may have bribed the tribe with presents, in addition to the money he agreed to pay the Colberts. The sale violated the federal prohibition against private purchase of Indian land. In any case, the Senate did not ratify the 1830 treaty. Altogether, Lewis complained, it was a most "unprofitable speculation."[66]

Jackson himself was more fortunate. Accused of interests in Colbert's ferry and the salt lick, he indignantly insisted he had not profited personally from the treaty. In fact he had. Jackson owned Chickasaw land in western Tennessee. He had bought a half-interest in 5,000 acres on the Chickasaw bluffs for $100 in 1796, and still retained a quarter-interest. The treaty greatly appreciated the value of the land; Jackson sold half his remaining interest for $5,000. The original tract was now owned jointly by Jackson, John Overton, and General James Winchester. They hoped to promote the bluffs as a town site. Calling their town

Memphis, they laid out plots and arranged for a land sale. Jackson, how-ever, did not benefit as much as he might have from the birth of Mem-phis. He sold his final share of the bluffs to a nephew in 1823. Jackson was now a presidential contender, and he wanted to quiet concern over his interest in land which his treaty had increased in value.[67]

Jackson's friends had sought to profit from the Chickasaw treaty, and he had made money as well. He had gone further there than ever before in marrying private speculative interests to Indian land cessions. The growing resistance of the Indians required this step. But simple re-liance on "avarice" was troubling Jackson. He was turning, in private life and public philosophy, away from material interests. He was begin-ning, in the context of Indian "fear," to develop a conception of paternal authority. The 1818 Chickasaw treaty and the 1820 Choctaw treaty were the first in which Jackson made major assertions of paternal authority over the Indians. We trace now the development of Jackson's paternal-ism.

VI

If Indians were "red children," whites thought of themselves as parents. Policy-makers had insisted since colonial days on their parental obliga-tions to the Indian tribes. A colonial Massachusetts law, for example, classified Indians with children and the insane. Leaders of the new nation sought from the outset to subject Indians to a paternal presidential au-thority. In legal relations, too, Indians were the "wards" of the state. If one takes seriously the evidence of speeches and documents, whites could not imagine Indians outside the parent-child context.[68]

"What then," asked Alabama Governor John Murphy, "is to be done for this people, who had priority of us in the occupation of this favored land? . . . The United States should assume a parental guardianship over them" and extend the benefits of education and religion. P. B. Porter, John Quincy Adams' Secretary of War, explained, "In their present desti-tute and deplorable condition and which is constantly growing more helpless, it would seem to be not only the right but the duty of the govern-ment to take them under its paternal care, and to exercise over their persons and property the salutory rights and duties of guardianship."[69]

Presidents called Indians their children. So did frontier governors, Indian agents, treaty commissioners, generals, Secretaries of War, and Superintendents of Indian Affairs. Jackson, however, almost never used the parent-child metaphor before 1814.[70]

It may seem that Jackson's animosity toward Indians provides the explanation. Indians were "ferocious bloodhounds," not young members of the American family. Others hostile to Indians used parental language, however, and Jackson's policy was no kinder to the tribes after the Creek War than it had been before. Others were content to use a vocabulary without establishing their right to do so; Jackson was not. He had defeated Indians in the Creek War; no longer the fraternal rival of "our red brethren," he had gained paternal authority.

As if to symbolize the new relationship, Jackson adopted a three-year-old Indian boy during the Creek War; his troops had killed the boy's parents in the first battle of the war. "At the battle of Tohopeka," explained Jackson's close friend John H. Eaton, "an infant was found, pressed to the bosom of its lifeless mother." Hearing that the Indian women planned to kill the baby, Jackson "became himself the protector and guardian of the child." Lincoyer's plight reminded Jackson of his own youth. He wrote Rachel,

> Keep Lincoya in the house—he is a savage [illegible] that fortune has thrown in my [illegible] his own female matrons wanted to [illegible] because the whole race and family of his [illegible] was destroyed—I therefore want him well taken care of, he may have been given to me for some valuable purpose—in fact when I reflect that he as to his relations—is so much like myself I feel an unusual sympathy for him . . . [71]

Jackson identified himself with the "orphan" Lincoyer, endangered by "female matrons," in the same letter that contemplated killing his own soldier children.[72] He sent Lincoyer to "my little andrew" to replace a slave child who had recently died. "—to amuse him, and to make him forget the loss, I have asked Colo. Hays to carry Lyncoya to him—he is about the size of Theodore and much like him." Jackson wanted to "adopt him as one of our family."[73]

Lincoyer lived for several years in Jackson's household, attending a nearby country day school. "I have my little sons, including Lyncoya at school," Jackson wrote in 1822. Then he apprenticed the boy to a harness-maker, the same trade the youthful Jackson had briefly followed. Lincoyer died at sixteen of tuberculosis.[74]

Jackson had adopted Lincoyer in 1813, but he was not yet ready to adopt paternal language for Indians as a whole. He did not do so until after his victories at Horseshoe Bend and New Orleans. Some lower Creeks threatened late in 1815 to resist the running of the Fort Jackson treaty line. Jackson reminded them, "By the order of your father the President of the united states I marched an army into your nation to protect those who remembered his talk, and held him fast by the hand in friendship." He asserted presidential paternalism to remind the Creeks of his power. For the next two years he used the paternal metaphor infrequently, and tied it always to the threat of punishment. His use of paternal language signified no evolution from rage to benevolence, but a gained confidence in the ability to threaten.[75]

The paternalism of Jackson's predecessors appeared more benevolent, but it too required the obliteration of Indian cultural and political autonomy. It offered the Indians only permanent childhood—savagery—or evolution in the image of white civilization. The high Federalist minister Jedidiah Morse, proposing to plant "Education families" among the tribes, retained a household image of the civilizing process. But if his "parental or guardian authority" was more corporate than that envisioned by most Indian policy-makers, he shared both their coercive intent and their vision of the Indian future.[76] Jackson's predecessors, however, imagined a slow process of expansion; they gave the Indians more time. The tribes, under the pressure of debts, education, and an advancing settler population, would voluntarily cede their lands. Washington, Jefferson, and Calhoun gained Indian land through treaties, fraudulent or otherwise, and relied on the spontaneous workings of society—speculators, intruders, traders, debt, whiskey, disease, and bribery—to make the Indians consent to leave. In the early nineteenth century, however, the southern Indians developed sustained resistance to ceding their land. At the same time, as chapter 8 will suggest, the westward expansion of market and population dramatically increased the pressure on Indian land. Jackson developed his Indian paternalism to resolve this conflict. He sought to overcome Indian resistance and legitimize white pressure. He insisted on the government's parental responsibilities to abort the process by which Indians were, in white language, growing up and acting independently of white wishes.

Treaties pretended that tribes were formally equal to the government and free to refuse to treat. As the southern tribes began to act on the basis of this fiction, Jackson, using parental language, urged the government to end it. From 1817 through 1821, Jackson pushed hard and unsuccessfully to substitute unilateral government action for Indian treaties. Indians, he claimed, were subjects of the United States, not independent nations, and had no right to refuse to cede their land. Congress, as "the proper Guardian," "should extend to the Indians its protection and fostering care." It should take Indian land as whites required it, at the same time providing for Indian needs. Treaties were necessary when the government was weak; it now had strength "sufficient to affect any object which its wisdome, humanity and justice may please to adopt with regard to these unfortunate people."[77]

Jackson's language was benevolent, but his aim was control. He wrote fellow Chickasaw commissioner Isaac Shelby, urging an end to Indian treaties: "If the present spirit of the Indians are not checked, by some act of the government showing them their real state of dependence, in a short time no cession of land will be obtained from them." To make matters worse, Indian chiefs grew more sophisticated in evaluating their lands. Some made exorbitant demands for personal or tribal money, which angered Jackson at the Chickasaw treaty. Others simply refused to be bribed. Before the attempted Choctaw treaty of 1819, Jackson wrote the agent, "You may say to the chiefs that we are instructed not only to be liberal to the nation but to them individually." The government had a secret agent of mixed parentage among the tribe; you may tell him, Jackson wrote, he "will be amply rewarded" "if a treaty is made." But bribery failed to gain Choctaw land, and Jackson offered government legislation as an alternative. He wrote Calhoun,

> It is now discovered that nothing can be done with the Indians without corrupting their Chiefs—this is inconsistent with the virtue, and principles of our Government. It is high time the Legislature should interpose its authority and enact laws for the regulation and control of the Indian Tribes. If they have too much Territory circumscribe them, furnish them with instruments of agriculture and you will thereby lay the foundation of their civilization. this means will be more [illegible] and just than by corrupting their chiefs to acquire their country which is the only means by which it can be affected.[78]

Jackson led the opposition to the traditional treaty policy. Others joined him. Spokesmen for the state of Georgia, for example, cited the Fort Jackson treaty as precedent to prove that consent was not required for whites to take Indian land. It had long been frontier doctrine that the Indians had no title to their soil. Tennessee leaders had argued in the 1790s that the United States had the right to take Indian land at its convenience. Such a naked assertion had never won widespread acceptance. In an 1816 letter to Jackson, Cherokee agent Meigs rephrased the doctrine in terms of Indian needs instead of white desires. Meigs developed the paternal rationale in several letters. He explained, "By the nature of the compact between the United States and the Cherokee, they were considered as in a state of minority."

> From the bottom of my heart I wish them well. If I was their natural father I would say to them, My children, let us never break the bond of union; while united we are respectable; let *us all* go to the west. . . . If every tribe of Indians be permitted to put their veto on the measures advised by the government, it will be impossible to save them from extinction. . . . Their safety depends on their dependence; but it is difficult to make them comprehend this.[79]

Monroe supported the Jackson-Meigs proposals in messages to Congress, but Congress did not respond. Jackson unsuccessfully urged the

President to take Chickasaw lands on his own without a treaty; Jackson was sent to treat instead. He presented his thwarted plans to the Chickasaws as if they had won acceptance. He told the tribe that if it refused to cede its Tennessee land, Congress would pass a law taking it. He wrote, "This plain language of truth has brought them to their senses." Jackson had transformed his own wishes into objective fact, removed himself from responsibility for them, and used his objectified desires to club the tribe into submission. In the context of this pathology, he resorted to the familial metaphor. "Your white brothers" want the Chickasaw land, Jackson told the tribe, and if you refuse to treat, "your father the President" will give it to them. He will not, said Jackson, protect you from their desires.[80]

At the Choctaw treaty of Doaks Stand two years later Jackson went further. In the face of stiffened Indian resistance, he made his most sustained use of Indians' "fear." For the first time, and in the context of child murder, he imagined himself as their father.

Jackson began with a conciliatory speech. He told the tribe, "As children of the same family, we entreat you to do justice to one another." But the Choctaws were not persuaded, and Jackson began to threaten. If you refuse to treat, he warned the tribe, the government will treat solely with "your brothers"—the few dozen Choctaws across the Mississippi. Such a treaty, "cutting up your country," would destroy the tribe. He told the Choctaws that their father, the President, would withdraw his fatherly protection. They would have no more chances to treat, and Congress would pass a law taking their land. He began to use paternal language promiscuously. Still calling the Indians "friends and brothers," he referred again and again to "your father the President." He mixed threats with concern. If the Choctaws did not cede their land, he told the tribe, whites would move onto it anyway. The tribe would be scattered and destroyed, as had happened to so many other "red children." Some would join the enemies of the United States. "We may then," said Jackson, "be under the necessity of raising the hatchet against our own friends and brothers. Your father the President wishes to avoid this unnatural state of things."[81]

The next day, for the first time, Jackson spoke of himself as the Indians' father. He reminded the tribe he had fought to protect them from the British. Many of them had followed him to battle, and he felt like a "friend and father" to them. As if to save them from his own "unnatural" infanticidal fantasies, he urged them to follow his advice. They did. They ceded one-third of their eastern land, in return for land across the Mississippi. Many Choctaws were granted individual allotments; the remainder were free to enroll for emigration. Jackson was confident emigrating agents would quickly clear Mississippi of most of the tribe.[82]

Jackson had sworn, after the government refused to abolish treaties, that he would attend no more. He made an exception for the Choctaws, but that treaty was his last. The tribe failed to emigrate in any numbers at all. Whites were living on the land supposedly provided the Indians in the west, the same problem which had plagued Cherokee removal.[83] Jackson had called Indians his children, but he lacked the power to compel them to act as he wanted. He turned away from Indian affairs, sought the Presidency, and did not return to Indian removal until after his election.

Jackson had first imagined Indians as "savage bloodhounds"; he needed to fight a war of brother against brother to possess the land and establish his authority. Winning that war, Jackson began to speak of Indians as children of a paternal President. He used paternal language sparingly, however, and solely to threaten the tribes and deny their autonomy. At the same time, in the face of tribal resistance, he imagined himself the defender of the "poor Indians" against self-aggrandizing tribal leaders. Further tribal resistance pushed him to more extended use of the paternal metaphor. He supported R. J. Meigs' proposals that the paternal government should take Indian land and turn the tribes to agriculture. He opposed the treaty fiction of Indian autonomy, and urged Congress to become the tribal "guardian." In his last two treaties Jackson constantly reminded the Indians of their presidential father. Finally, in the context of infanticide, he called himself the Indians' father for the first time. This was not simply fantasy. Before the last treaties Jackson had fought and killed Indians again, in the Seminole War. Just as the Creek War had established his right to call the Indians children, so the Seminole War established his own personal (and murderous) paternity. We now examine Jackson's Florida campaign.

VII

Jackson had gained one of his territorial objectives from the Creek War, but not both. He had acquired "the cream of the Creek country," but he had failed to obtain Florida. Jackson's presence, the terms of the Fort Jackson treaty, and the nature of the southern Indian frontier made another war over the Spanish province very likely. Florida was the major political issue during President Monroe's first term.[84]

The treaty of Fort Jackson acquired Creek land along the Georgia-Florida border. Most of the bands living there, however, were not at war with the United States, were not at Fort Jackson, and had not agreed to leave their land. Many of these villages had only a tenuous relation to the Creek federation. Villages on the Florida border and in the Spanish province formed the Seminole nation, a mixture of indigenous Florida Indians and Creeks who had migrated south during the eighteenth century. The Seminoles did not consider themselves bound by the Fort Jackson treaty, and had not ceded their land.[85]

The Seminoles were joined, after the Creek defeat, by a number of red sticks who refused to acknowledge Jackson's treaty. They fled south, either to continue the war or to escape from American jurisdiction into Florida. Some southern Creeks had resisted the running of the Fort Jackson treaty line, but acquiesced under the threat of force. The Seminoles —living mostly in Florida but with villages also above the border—had not yet felt the effects of the treaty.

British traders and adventurers in Florida encouraged the Seminole belief in the illegality of the Fort Jackson line. During and shortly after the war two officers, Captain George Woodbine and Colonel Edward Nicholls, worked for the British government. Nicholls trained Seminole and red-stick warriors in 1814; when he left Florida after the treaty of Ghent, he urged them to resist the American advance. Woodbine and Nicholls had British authority, although they exceeded their instructions. It was perhaps natural for Americans to see the Scottish trader Alexander Arbuthnot as their replacement. Arbuthnot defended Seminole interests in Florida in 1817–18, corresponding with British officials but acting entirely on his own. He was joined in Florida by Robert Ambrister, a British adventurer with dreams of leading an Indian war.[86]

Whites on the American side of the border played as provocative a role as Ambrister and Arbuthnot. Settlers were moving illegally onto land in southern Georgia obtained by the Fort Jackson treaty. Indians still inhabited this land, and a series of border attacks and counterattacks followed. White intruders apparently initiated the fighting, but neither Indians defending their land nor the invading whites distinguished fighting residents from peaceful ones. Women and children were killed on both sides. In response to white charges of Indian atrocities, Jackson ordered the destruction of Indian villages that refused to surrender the murderers of whites. Military threats against Indian towns became frequent during 1817.[87]

Further inflaming the whites, escaped slaves had long been taking refuge in Creek and Seminole villages. Members of these tribes had also begun to acquire slaves through either purchase or capture. But slavery under the aborigines had little in common with plantation slavery. Indian Negro slaves generally lived in their own villages and cultivated their own corn. They existed in relative independence of their Indian masters. They or their children easily slipped into free status, augmenting the significant number of free Negro tribal members. Extensive intermarriage further blurred the lines between Indian and black, slave and free. These mixed villages of Indians and blacks, particularly outside American jurisdiction in Florida, enraged southern slave-owners. They feared the Seminoles would raid plantations, or act as a stimulus to slave escapes.[88]

In 1816 Jackson destroyed a fort in Spanish Florida, on the Apalachicola River, manned by blacks. He claimed that the fort threatened stability on the frontier and in the plantations; in fact it had merely refused to permit Jackson to provision an American wilderness fort via the Apalachicola River in Spanish territory. Jackson's Indian allies were promised loot from the fort, including slaves or a bounty for them. After the destruction of the Negro fort, Jackson's officers threatened Seminole villages with attack if they did not return escaped slaves. Jackson and other southerners wanted to eliminate Florida as a sanctuary for escaped slaves and for Indians raiding the frontier. Jackson also insisted that Florida was essential to the defense of the United States. He urged that it be densely settled as a barrier to foreign attacks through the peninsula (hardly a likely enemy strategy).[89]

Many of Jackson's friends knew the value of the good Florida cotton land. James Jackson, John H. Eaton, and Jackson's nephew John Donelson IV undertook a speculation in Pensacola lands in 1817. They counted on the quick acquisition of Florida by sale or conquest. Armed with a letter of introduction from Jackson to the Pensacola governor, Donelson made extensive purchases in the city of Pensacola and acquired 12,000 acres on the bay. Just before leaving Florida early in 1818, he learned of the outbreak of the Seminole War.[90]

There were two immediate causes of this war, and General Edmund P. Gaines was the instrument of them both. Commanding the American troops along the Florida border, under Jackson's authority, Gaines had threatened Seminole villages in southern Georgia since late in 1816. He planned expeditions to recapture escaped slaves, and in concert with Jackson threatened to destroy Seminole villages refusing to turn over alleged murderers of white intruders. Giving Jackson advance notice, Gaines planned late in 1817 to attack the village of Fowltown.[91]

Fowltown lay within land ceded to the United States under the treaty of Fort Jackson. The village had not fought in the Creek War, however, had not been present at Fort Jackson, and refused to abandon its home. Acting Secretary of War George Graham warned Gaines not to attack Fowltown in pursuit of murderers, but he did authorize removal of Indians on land ceded the United States by the Fort Jackson treaty. Either just before or just after receiving Graham's letter, Gaines sent a detachment of troops to bring him the Fowltown chief and village headmen. The villagers fired on and beat back the white troops. In retaliation for the attack, Seminoles ambushed a boatload of American soldiers and their families coming up the Apalachicola. The Indians killed virtually the entire party, and the Seminole War had begun.[92]

Gaines was an ardent expansionist. He had earlier reported to Jackson frontier plans to attack Pensacola, saying the army would maintain benevolent neutrality. Gaines, however, lacked Jackson's vision; it is doubtful if he intended the Fowltown attack to set off an invasion of Florida. Using regular army troops, Georgia militia, and Tennessee veterans he raised on his own authority, Jackson planned and executed the conquest of Florida. He crossed the border, burning Seminole villages as he came to them. He attacked St. Marks, east of the Apalachicola River, which divided east from west Florida, and seized the Spanish fort. "The modern Sodom and Gomorrow are destroyed," he wrote Rachel. He then marched west and seized Pensacola, threatening to "put to death every man found in arms" if the Spanish resisted. Jackson justified the Pensacola capture with rumors of Indian concentrations there; in fact the rumors were false and the Alabama-Florida frontier remained relatively peaceful.[93]

Jackson set up an American military government in Pensacola, abolished the Spanish tariff on American shipping, and confidently expected Florida would not return to Spanish hands. Back in Nashville in August, he ordered Gaines to seize St. Augustine, deep in the interior of Florida, on rumors that Indians were concentrating there. Jackson hoped thereby to convince Monroe of continued Spanish hostility. But Monroe learned of Jackson's orders before Gaines acted, and countermanded them. He intended, to Jackson's dismay, to return St. Marks and Pensacola to Spanish hands. Monroe argued that the invasion of Florida had been necessary to punish the Indians, but was not an aggressive war of conquest against Spain. Nevertheless, Jackson's invasion helped convince Spain to sell Florida before it lost it. The United States took possession in 1821, and Monroe sent Jackson to Pensacola as governor.[94]

Jackson invaded Florida, he said, to put an end to Indian attacks. He pointed to the murder of frontier families and the slaughter of the boatload of soldiers, women, and children. In the familiar language, "Helpless women have been butchered, and the cradle stained with the blood of innocence." Jackson had used Indian atrocities during his first Florida invasion to permit him to contemplate his own. Once again the Indian murder of women and children freed Jackson to urge American attacks on Indian women and children. He wrote Graham, "The protection of our citizens will require that the wolf be struck in his den."[95]

Florida could not remain, in Jackson's words, a "sanctuary" for murder. As one of his defenders explained,

Knowing that geographical boundaries were not the boundaries of right and wrong, and determining to penetrate the darkest recesses of guilt, and punish its instigators, he entered the Spanish province of Florida with his forces. . . .

It would have been but a pastime for these blood-seeking, desperate Seminoles, to have saturated themselves with the blood of American women and children, and merely to be driven to their homes in the forests of Florida, only to prepare to glut their vengeance by repeated feasts of innocent blood. Are the swamps and ravines of Florida, like the horns of ancient alterns, a protection for murderers?[96]

Jackson did not act, he swore, "from a wish to extend the Territorial limits of the United States." "The immutable laws of self-defense," "bottomed on the broad basis of the law of nature and of nations," required him to defend the frontier against Indian attack. There is obvious deception here, given Jackson's expressed territorial interest in Florida, but the deception reached into Jackson himself. "Self-defense justified me in every act I did," he wrote when his invasion came under attack, and he believed his own words. Defense of America, thought Jackson, required constant expansion. Areas contiguous to the United States but out of its control were vulnerable to European penetration.[97]

An independent Florida was particularly dangerous. It contained a tribe of mixed Indians and Negroes which, in the whites' cultural nightmare, joined liberated black physical passion to Indian violence. The tropical Florida landscape seemed physically to embody these "darkest recesses of guilt." White language describing the Seminoles acquired exterminatory fury. In the words of one writer,

The Seminole Indians are not a *"legitimate"* tribe of *native* Americans. They are an association of desperados, who have been banished from other tribes, and who have drawn into their confederacy, many runaway negroes, whose African sullenness, has been aroused to indiscriminate vengeance, by the more frantic fury of the American natives.[98]

These were the "monsters" under British and Spanish control. Jackson believed "that the Indian war had been excited by some unprincipled foreign or private agents." He accused the Pensacola Governor, as he had in 1814, of sending out Indian raiding parties which slaughtered frontier families; he regretted he had not "hung him for the Deed." Such a view treated Indians as centrally and conspiratorially directed, without wills of their own. It denied them legitimate grievances, such as frontier provocations or desire to keep their land. It turned them into helpless children, manipulated either by the British and Spanish or by the Americans. Jackson imagined the Seminoles in that relation of total subordination that he himself hoped to establish. "The savages," he wrote, "must be made dependent on us." It was as if the Seminole War were a desperate conflict between the good father and the bad, for control of the Indian children.[99]

Bad fathers were physically present at St. Marks. Jackson captured Ambrister and Arbuthnot, the British adventurer and Scottish trader residing with the Indians. Here were the "unprincipled . . . agents" who had driven the Indians to war. Ambrister had indeed led the Indians in one battle. Arbuthnot had taken no active part in the fighting. He had supplied the Seminoles with provisions, warned them of Jackson's invasion, and generally sought to defend their interests against American "aggressions." In a letter which fell into Jackson's hands he wrote, "I am in hopes that those aggressions of the Americans on the Indian territory are not countenanced by the American Government, but originate with men devoid of principle, who set laws & instructions at defiance, & stick at no cruelty & oppression to obtain their ends."[100]

Jackson summarily court-martialed and executed Arbuthnot and Ambrister. He also hanged the Indian prophets blamed for inciting the war. Jackson justified the executions on the wholly fanciful ground that men from a neutral country aiding one nation at war with another were pirates in international law and could be killed upon capture. He would not, his critics pointed out, have applied this doctrine to Lafayette. Forced to abandon the ground of piracy, Jackson and his defenders argued that the laws of war did not apply to conflicts with savages. In Jackson's words,

> Acting as chiefs of the negroes and Indians, Arbuthnot and Ambrister, by numerous acts of atrocity, had become identified with those monsters— associates in the war! They were the principal authors of the hostilities of the ferocious savages, who observed none of the rules of civilized warfare, who never gave quarter, and only took prisoners for the purpose of torturing! . . . Both acted as chiefs of the motley banditti, giving them counsel and exciting them to war; and one of them actually led those black and red combatants to battle. . . .
>
> Their criminality was of a deeper dye than that of the Indian chiefs. They were the paymasters for human scalps; and to discharge that high trust, had exiled themselves from their native land, and plunged into the recesses of the wilderness, and groped their way to the Indian camp, for the express purpose of working upon the feelings of the ignorant and untutored savages, to instigate them to lay waste the abodes of industry and innocence, and obtain our Soil with the blood of slaughtered women and children! . . . Such wretches are more criminal than any painted red-sticks.[101]

Jackson had killed Indians and the "paymasters for human scalps" who instigated them; he had earned, finally, the right to call Indians his children.

It was only after the Seminole campaign, as we have seen, that he did so. Reporting to Rachel his hanging of the Indian prophets, he asked her to kiss "my Two sons," Andrew Jackson, Jr., and Lincoyer. This is his first recorded reference to Lincoyer as his son.[102]

Jackson now talked paternally to the Seminoles for the first time. One of his principal aims, when he returned to Florida as governor in 1821, was the removal of the Seminoles. If westward removal was not possible, the tribe should be concentrated together in an inland area, deprived of outlets to the sea, and denied Cuban trade and influence. Jackson told three Florida Indian chiefs that the bad counsel they had listened to

> compelled your Father the President to send his white children to chastise and subdue you, and thereby give peace to his children both red and white. . . . I give to you a plain, straight talk, and do not speak with a forked tongue. It is necessary that you be brought together, either within the bounds of your old Nation, or at some other point, where your Father the President may be enabled to extend to you his fatherly care and assistance.[103]

Congress had appropriated no money for removal and all that was possible for the moment was the concentration of the bands. Jackson resigned the Florida governorship before a treaty was held. His friend and former military subordinate James Gadsden negotiated the resettlement.[104]

Seminole villages, scattered over a large portion of Florida, were independent of one another. Gadsden told as many chiefs as he could contact that all who did not appear at the treaty would be forced to comply with its provisions. At the treaty itself, Gadsden postulated a split between predatory whites and a benevolent, paternal President. The President would protect the Indians against the greed and violence of less enlightened whites. In Gadsden's words,

> Like a kind father, the President says to you, there are lands enough for both his white and his red children. His white are strong, and might exterminate his red, but he will not permit them. He will preserve his red children.

He would, that is, if they ceded the bulk of their Florida lands. The split between benevolent, paternal whites and predatory ones permitted the former to use the latter to club the Indians, without taking responsibility for the contemplated extermination.

A few of the wealthier chiefs received reservations for themselves and their entourages along the Apalachicola River in north Florida, in return for signing the treaty. The remainder of the tribe was moved to a barren and swampy waste in south central Florida. Gadsden was given authority to survey the boundary line as far northward as was necessary to include sufficient arable land to keep the Seminoles from starving.[105]

VIII

The invasion of Florida demonstrated authority over Indians, but it raised other doubts about Jackson's authority. He conquered Florida without presidential authorization. Secretary of War Calhoun instructed Gaines to pursue the Seminoles into Florida and destroy their villages, but not to attack the Spanish towns and forts. Monroe made these orders public after Jackson entered Florida. The Cabinet was surprised at the capture of St. Marks and Pensacola; at first only Secretary of State John Quincy Adams defended the General, and Calhoun and Crawford favored a public censure. Monroe opposed censure, but wanted Jackson to take responsibility for the seizures. He wrote outlining Jackson's defense. Jackson could provide evidence that the Indians had been directed by Spanish officers and provisioned in Spanish forts. He could show he had chased Indians to the forts, and attacked them only after they had taken refuge there. This was a manufactured series of events; Jackson could not demonstrate it. He argued instead from the general grounds of self-defense, pointing to alleged Indian concentrations around St. Marks and Pensacola. Orders to end Seminole attacks, he insisted, gave him responsibility to choose the appropriate means.[106]

Jackson added another justification in 1831. Calhoun had ordered Gaines at the outbreak of the war not to attack Spanish forts. Jackson objected. Urging Monroe to conquer Florida, he wrote, "Let it be signified to me through any channel (say Mr. J. Rhea) that the possession of the Floridas would be desirable to the United States, and in sixty days it will be accomplished." In 1831 Jackson claimed he had received the requested letter from Tennessee Congressman John Rhea. He had burned it at Monroe's request, he said, during the 1819 congressional investigation of the Seminole invasion.[107]

Monroe denied this story from his deathbed, and all the available evidence refutes it. A letter from Rhea in December 1818 supports Jackson's invasion, "believing as far as I have read that you have acted for public good"; there is no consciousness here of secret knowledge. Jackson himself, in private letters to Monroe justifying his conduct, never referred to any secret authorization. One letter urged Monroe not to relinquish Florida, hardly indicating Jackson thought he had permission to conquer it.[108]

Jackson applied to the aged Rhea in 1831 for confirmation of his story. Rhea, in his dotage, could remember no such letter. He agreed to testify to any story of which Jackson "reminded" him. Jackson also convinced a reluctant Overton to testify he had seen the Rhea letter. Overton was vague on details; again it was a matter of friendship. Jackson's final witness, Henry Lee, was an unreliable member of Jackson's entourage. He had once denied seeing the Rhea letter, was now out of favor, and saw an opportunity to return to the President's good graces. Martin Van Buren, whose autobiography contains not a single word critical of Jackson, simply assumed Monroe had not written a Rhea letter.[109]

In spite of these facts, only one historian has charged Jackson with deliberate falsification. Richard Stenberg argued that Jackson consciously fabricated the Rhea story sometime after the Seminole War, to support himself against expected political attacks on his Florida campaign. John Bassett, Jackson's biographer and editor of his correspondence, offered a different interpretation. Rhea was mediating between Jackson and Monroe on another matter, and Bassett surmised that Jackson misinterpreted one of Rhea's letters as authorizing him to take Florida. Bassett could cite no existing letter in his biography, but subsequently discovered one subject to such a misinterpretation.[110]

Bassett's hypothesis, however, hardly solves all the problems. There is still no evidence Monroe ordered a letter-burning, and since Bassett's Rhea letter is still extant, what letter did Jackson burn? Moreover, Jackson claimed to have burned the letter in 1819, but the date of the burning entered on the margin of the original letter to Monroe in Jackson's letter book is "this April 12, 1818." The marginal notation is entered as if it were made the day the letter was burned. If in fact the notation was entered after a lapse of years, it may reveal a faulty memory about the dates of the Seminole controversy.[111]

Historians anxious to establish objective truth have, as in the case of Jackson's marriage, overlooked the thin line separating conscious from unconscious deception. Jackson received no answer at all to his original letter. W. B. Lewis asserted Jackson could infer his authority from Monroe's silence, and Jackson may well have believed this.[112] Perhaps after a lapse of years Jackson "remembered" that he had had permission for the invasion and felt justified in fabricating details (the letter-burning at Monroe's request) to support what was for him an essential truth. Perhaps Jackson, rereading Rhea's letter when he had forgotten the episode to which it actually referred, bolstered his assurance that he had received permission from the superego.

Jackson may have confused his request for a letter from Rhea with the letter Rhea actually sent because both Rhea episodes involved challenges to his personal authority. The actual Rhea letter concerned a bitter fight between Jackson and the War Department; the department had issued an order to an officer temporarily in Washington but under Jackson's command. Jackson strongly objected to the circumvention of his authority. Rhea reported Monroe's conciliatory attitude just as Jackson was preparing to invade Florida.[113]

The Rhea episode must not be dismissed, however, as an unimportant example of Jackson's faulty memory. It is one more piece of evidence that Jackson built his authority on the unconscious falsification of memory and experience. Jackson denied depredations by Tennessee troops against the Cherokees, although he had admitted them two years earlier; he invented a Cherokee agreement with Jefferson and reported Cherokee acknowledgments of that agreement contradicted by the written record; and he called "the plain language of truth" his unsupported wish, conveyed as fact to the Chickasaws, that Congress planned to take their Tennessee land if they did not cede it.

These incidents in the dispossession of the Indians reflect a larger pattern. Jackson began his career as a land-speculating member of the frontier elite; hostile to the founding fathers, he engaged in regional filibusters and contemplated secession and civil war. The Seminole War was his most successful regional filibuster. At the same time, as we shall see in a moment, the war capped a process by which Jackson was transforming himself into his opposite—a nationalist leader hostile to speculation and sectional selfishness, who proclaimed his indebtedness to the founding fathers, and paternally defended the people against entrenched elites.

Accurate memory would undermine this transformation and shatter the authority Jackson was building. Jackson was more preoccupied with the past than the ordinary politicians of the day; and, unlike them, he sought to base his authority upon instinctual power. He journeyed more deeply into himself than others, but the journey was neither conscious nor based upon the truth about his instincts and his past. Often, as with the Rhea letter and the depredations by his Tennessee troops, Jackson collected affidavits to support his memory. He followed this procedure in duel challenges and land-title disputes too. The piles of paper, however, failed to obscure the actual past. Jackson projected onto others the history and desire he hid from himself. He raged at those who threatened validly to connect his past and present, memory and desire, primitive violence and paternal authority. Truth itself, as Simone Weil has said, endangers such a character structure. Lacking fidelity to the created world, it is the sort which builds empires.[114]

IX

Jackson required the Rhea letter for the intrigues of presidential politics. He did not require it, in 1819, to legitimize his invasion of Florida. Con-

1. *Andrew Jackson*, Asher B. Durand, 1835

4. (opposite, above) *The able Doctor, or America Swallowing the Bitter Draught,* Paul Revere cartoon, 1774

5. (opposite, below) *The Downfall of Mother Bank,* lithograph, 1833

6. (above) *American Progress,* chromolithograph, after a John Gast painting, 1872

7. (above) *Death of Jane McCrea*, John Vanderlyn, 1804

8. (opposite) *Andrew Jackson*, John Vanderlyn, 1819

9. *Andrew Jackson*, 1856 Lafosse lithograph, after a Mathew Brady daguerreotype

gressional committees investigated the invasion, and objected to Jackson's behavior. Henry Clay, sensing a western rival for the Presidency, warned of the danger to the republic posed by military chieftains. The administration defended Jackson, although not with the enthusiasm he desired. But Jackson's military prowess had made him a hero, and he toured the east in triumph. He began to be spoken of for the Presidency, and made his first response early in 1821. He had just agreed to return to Florida as its first American governor.[115]

It is not clear why Jackson went back to Florida. He had long expressed the wish to retire from public life. His health was particularly bad after the Seminole campaign, and he longed for the calm of rural retirement. When a congressional reduction in the strength of the army forced one of the two major generals out of the army, Jackson resigned. Rachel urged him to turn down the proffered Florida governorship, and at first he did so. Friends who wanted patronage jobs in Florida helped convince him to change his mind. Jackson also desired public evidence that Monroe approved of his Florida invasion. Perhaps he saw this vindication and the civil post as steps toward the Presidency.[116]

Jackson and his friends discovered to their dismay that Secretary of the Treasury Crawford had preempted most of the Florida patronage positions for his own supporters. Still, Jackson gained some jobs for his allies. He also gave business advice. He urged nephew John Donelson to retain his property in Pensacola, as it would soon become valuable. To his close friend Dr. James Bronaugh, surgeon general of the southern division of the army, he wrote, "A great spec might be made at Pensacola and Ft St Augustine, by the purchase of negroes from subjects who will leave the Territory." Once in American hands Florida would be closed to the slave trade; it would be more difficult to smuggle slaves from Cuba to the United States via Florida, and their price would rise.[117] Jackson himself, however, speculated neither in Negroes nor in Florida land. The governorship did not benefit him financially; rather it raised and resolved challenges to his authority.

Jackson's valedictory to the army after accepting the Florida post emphasized discipline, subordination, and paternal authority once again. General Jacob Brown, army commander-in-chief, had issued an order blaming the high rate of desertion upon the undue severity of officers toward their men. Officers, Brown's order read, were in a position of trust toward their soldiers and should protect them. Jackson attacked Brown's effort to tarnish his officers' reputation. He blamed desertion instead on the want of "adequate punishment." Opposing mere imprisonment for desertion, Jackson advocated "Stripes and Lashes" for the first two offenses and execution for the third. His address concluded,

To you my Brother officers who remain in the service of your country, permit me to recommend to you, to harmonize with each other like a band of brothers—in fact you are brothers in arms, and it is your duty to conduct *yourselves*, so that your enemies in private life shall [not] have just cause to censure. each captain is the father of his company, it is his family.[118] continue then, as you have heretofore done under my command, to watch over it with a fathers tenderness and care, treat your companies like children, admonish them; if that will not prevent disobedience *coertion must.* . . . The want of discipline, the want of order promises a total disregard to obedience and will produce a spirit of insubordination as destructive to an army as cowardice itself, and will lead to disaster and disgrace in any army. . . .[119]

Jackson sought as Governor of Florida to infuse civil life with paternal military discipline. The Spanish transfer of authority proceeded slowly; Jackson thought this a calculated insult to his office. The chronic diarrhea from which he suffered in Pensacola contributed to his suspiciousness, irritability, and insistence on control. Lawyer friends told him that Colonel José Callava, the Spanish Governor, retained possession of papers containing evidence for a suit they were prosecuting against the large trading firm of Innerarity. This firm dominated Seminole Indian trade, and Jackson had long feuded with it. Now he leaped to the defense of the mulatto widow plaintiff. He jailed Callava when the Colonel did not relinquish papers in his possession. The intervention of Federal Judge Eligius Fromentin against Jackson, like Judge Hall's intervention in New Orleans, made him even angrier. He jailed Callava, he wrote Secretary of State Adams, "dictated by the imperious rules of justice, to save the unprotected orphan from being ruined by the most cruel oppression, by the most corrupt, and wicked combination, I ever investigated." He explained,

I was determined to administer the Govrt. for the happiness of all, and prevent the poor and humble from the Tyranny of wealth and power. . . .
Refer to the marcial law upon which our republican constitution is founded. Deut. Chapter 1st ver. 17 ye shall not respect persons in Judgment; *but* ye shall hear the small as well as the great; ye shall not be afraid of the face of man; for the Judgment is gods. . . .[120]

The republic, wrote Jackson, was founded on "marcial law." Jackson proclaimed that law, in Florida as with Indians, to defend the poor against the rich. Judge Fromentin, he wrote, believes "the laws of the United States are only made for the punishment of the humble and penniless; but whenever opposed to wealth and power they must remain inoperative." This may be Spanish practice, said Jackson, but it was not American. "In general the great can protect themselves, but the poor and humble require the arm and shield of the law."[121]

Fathers, for Jackson, controlled inner impulses and children in the world. Jackson had successfully asserted paternity first over soldiers and then over Indians. Might not fatherhood now also extend its protecting arm to the generality of poor, weak, and virtuous? Might it not reform the civilian world? Watching as Jackson presided over the ceremonial transfer of Florida from Spanish to American rule, one of his former officers observed,

> Pensacola is destined eventually to become the great emporium of the Gulf of Mexico, and to enjoy a large share of the trade of the west. Under the paternal government of Jackson, we hope soon to emerge from the weakness of infancy, and to escape from the restrictions of nonage. . . . To him who so gallantly stood forth the champion of his country is now confided the nurture and guardianship of the last offspring of freedom, the youngest child of the family of free and federated America.[122]

CHAPTER 7

INDIAN REMOVAL

A "long journey" usually means death in the symbolic language of the dream.

—*Géza Róheim*, The Panic of the Gods

Indian removal, Andrew Jackson wrote after he left the Presidency, was the "most arduous part of my duty, and I watched over it with great vigilance." The Indian-removal bill, Alabama Congressman Dixon Lewis maintained, was "known as the leading measure" of the Jackson administration. Massachusetts Congressman Edward Everett called it "the greatest question that ever came before Congress, short of the question of peace and war."[1]

Indian removal involved the massive population transfer of eastern Indians to land west of the Mississippi River. By the end of Jackson's administration, every tribe east of the Mississippi and south of Lake Michigan, save for two tiny bands in Ohio and Indiana, had come under government removal programs. Jackson and Van Buren largely completed the elimination of Indians from the northeast, but northeastern removal involved only a few thousand Indians. The major northeastern Indians, the Iroquois confederation in New York, ultimately resisted removal. The Six Nations maintained their numbers and tribal integrity better than any removed tribe. Indian removal had a significant and disastrous impact on the several thousand Sac and Fox Indians of Illinois. It made inroads among the tribes of the northwestern Great Lakes region. The bulk of eastern Indians lived in the south, however, and they were the major target of removal demands. Removal uprooted 70,000 southern Indians from their homes. By 1844 only a few thousand, scattered in swamps and mountains, were left.[2]

Jackson's pre-presidential efforts failed to drive the southern tribes across the Mississippi, and his Indian policy failed on other counts as well. His paternalism remained too directly rooted in primitive rage for its benevolent claims to carry conviction. He asserted too great a responsibility for the fate of the tribes, in the face of their imminent destruction. Jackson's mature Indian policy not only gained Indian land. It also distanced itself from intimate involvement with the savages, expressed a grander concern for their condition, and protected the President from responsibility for the consequences of his acts. Jackson, in the service of these ends, successfully synthesized the two governing ideologies of his pre-presidential Indian policy—paternalism and the treatment of Indians as individual freely contracting men.

President Jackson modified and extended the paternalism which had structured Indian policy for his predecessors. He promised to rescue his "red children" from the advancing tide of white settlement in the east, protect them in the west, and help them advance to civilization. His paternal language was largely free of the exterminatory rhetoric which had marked his earlier career. It more closely resembled the rhetoric used in the Washington, Jefferson, and Monroe administrations.

This classic paternalism recognized that Indians, left to themselves, would not internalize the motivating principles of market civilization. Liberal society, as Adam Smith and John Adams had described it, progressed by emulation. Always unsatisfied with their present condition, men copied the successes of others and sought to improve themselves. They internalized personal ambition and the desire for the good opinion of others. Since the external and internalized eyes of society provided order, men could enjoy individual freedom.[3]

Indians refused to participate in this process. The techniques of market individualism, therefore, were failing to acquire Indian land. In Lewis Cass' words,

A principle of progressive improvement seems almost inherent in human nature. Communities of men, as well as individuals, are stimulated by a desire to meliorate their condition. There is nothing stationary around us. We are all striving in the career of life to acquire riches, or honor, or power, or some other object, whose possession is to realize the day dreams of our imaginations; and the aggregate of these efforts constitutes the advance of society.

But there is little of this in the constitution of our savages. Like the bear, and deer, and buffalo of his own forests, an Indian lives as his father lived, and dies as his father died. . . . He never looks around him, with a spirit of emulation, to compare his situation with that of others, and to resolve on improving it. . . . Want never teaches him to be provident, nor misery to be industrious.[4]

Indians maintained an animal identity, impervious to civilized "day dreams." The market alone could not control them, for they could ignore, as self-improving whites could not, its imperatives. They would not, to improve their position, sell their land and move west. As Cass put it, "The *fulcrum* is wanting, upon which the lever must be placed."[5] The free market liberated whites from the condition of their fathers, Cass suggested, but Indians remained "contented as they are." If they were not to "disappear with the forests," they required the intervention of a white father. He would break the Indians' dependence on nature, and supply civilized identities. Once Indians were, like whites, dissatisfied with their present condition, their self-esteem would require civilized, progressive improvement. They would then be vulnerable to market temptations, social opinion, and presidential suggestion. Ultimately, when there was "nothing stationary around them" and they had wholly internalized "the desire to meliorate their condition," the presidential father could withdraw.

This civilizing process was not explicitly infanticidal, but there was violence in it nonetheless. It offered Indians not simply help, but a redefinition of their identity. It defined them as children, which in fact they were not. It forced the tribes into childish dependence upon a white father. This was particularly devastating in a liberal culture which had eliminated legitimate hierarchal authority and believed that "manly independence" offered the only proper basis for relations among men. When such a society imported the father into politics, it was likely to impose an insecure and overbearing paternal domination. To insist that Indians be shown "their real state of dependence" upon the government was, I will argue, to infantilize them. Infantilization provides the major significance of the call for paternal authority.

The process of infantilization has been studied in many contexts—concentration camps; slave societies; total institutions such as insane asylums, old people's homes, and prisons; environments of isolation and sensory deprivation; schizophrenic families; housewives in suburban homes; and efforts to manipulate mass publics for political purposes (such as to win support for the war in Vietnam). These environments, it is argued, break the social relations, cultural norms, and normal expectations of those subjected to them. "Ceremonies of degradation" destroy the victim's connection to his previously validated social self. Individuals lose social support for their own personal experience of reality. The infantilization process, calling into question one's basic security in and trust of the environment, undermines the independent ego. Elimination of ties to objects in the environment produces an extreme sense of object loss, and consequent regression to infantile longings for protection, connection, and loss of self. Infantilization creates acute separation anxiety, and calls into question individuation beyond the dual unity of mother and baby.

The victim's blank and bare environment offers him only one remaining source of gratification, the authority who manipulates rewards and punishments. Thus the very oppressor becomes the source of values and sustenance. The infantilized victim, in the extreme case, identifies with his oppressor and seeks total dependence upon him.[6]

It could be argued that Indian removal did infantilize Indians, destroying tribal cultures and undermining, for large numbers, the simple will to live. But infantilization has often been studied from the child's perspective. The infantilization imposed on victims may well serve needs for the self-appointed parent figures. My concern is with infantilization from the parental point of view.

Tribal cultures depended upon clan and communal relationships. Among southern Indians these manifested themselves in communal agriculture, an active village life, deep ties to historic tribal territories, and a social order enforced by clan loyalties and by respect for demonstrated performance in hunting and war. Whites who lived on isolated farms mistrusted the intense life of Indian villages, and interpreted the absence of formal government institutions as invitation to chaos. They objected to tribal life not simply because it was different from their own, but also because it provided a source of resistance to their aims. The primitive Indian character resisted imposition of an externalized "false-self system" which would make Indians malleable. White policy-makers sought to break apart the Indians' extended family and ecological ties, and substitute a hierarchal, non-kinship-based paternal authority.[7]

A council of Creeks opposed a land cession with the words, "We would not receive money for land in which our fathers and friends are buried. . . . We love our land; it is our mother; and we do not think anyone would take it from us if we did not wish to part with it." An old Choctaw chief responded to Monroe with the words:

> Children, even after they have grown to be men, ought to regard the advice of their father, as when they were small. I am sorry I cannot comply with the request of my father. . . . We wish to remain here, where we have grown up as the herbs of the woods; and do not wish to be transplanted into another soil.

A Seminole chief explained to John Quincy Adams, "Here our navel strings were first cut and the blood from them sunk into the earth, and made the country dear to us."[8]

To break the strength tribes derived from their historic territory, and to demonstrate the subordinate Indian position, white authorities had insisted since colonial days that Indians address them as "father." This was not an Indian conceit, but a white one. In negotiations between William Henry Harrison and the Shawnee Chief Tecumseh, according to one report, the interpreter said to Tecumseh, "Your father requests you to take a chair." "My father!" replied the Chief. "The sun is my father, and the earth is my mother; I will repose upon her bosom." Creek Chief William McIntosh, who had bowed to white pressure and illegally signed away tribal lands in Georgia, expressed the substitution whites desired. Throwing himself on the mercy of the state, he wrote, "You have torn us up by the roots, but still you are our brothers and friends. You have promised to replant us in a better soil, and to watch over us and nurse us."[9]

Whites perceived Indians, I have suggested, as children in a nurturing, self-sustaining relationship to nature. Since that relationship expressed forbidden white longings, it could not be permitted to remain a cultural alternative. But the forbidden longings did not disappear. The parental metaphor substituted paternal domination over infantilized Indians for the dependence on nature and tribal brothers. Now the white father and his instruments were the only source of gratification. As parents, white policymakers could participate in the dual-unity situation from the position of domination instead of dependence.

The model for the white father and his red children was not a family relation permitting growth, but a family with schizophrenegenic elements. Of the parents in such families Searles writes, "In essence, the parent's need for security cannot allow him or her to feel the child as a separate identity, and the parent cannot give indication to the child that the child is capable of emotionally affecting the parent." The child must be "denied the experience of feeling himself to be an individual human entity, distinct from but capable of emotional contact with the parent."[10]

The theory of paternal assistance offered Indians aid in growing up. But the very notion of growth was infantilizing. Indians were offered only the alternatives of civilization or death. The House Committee on Indian Affairs forecast in 1818, "In the present state of our country one of two things seems to be necessary, either that those sons of the forest should be moralized or exterminated." Senator Thomas Hart Benton explained that the disappearance of the Indians should not be mourned. "Civilization or extinction has been the fate of all people who have found themselves in the track of advancing whites; civilization, always the preference of the advancing whites, has been pressed as an object, while extinction has followed as a consequence of its resistance."[11]

In the white scheme civilization meant, no less than death, the disappearance of the Indians. Only a single path to what would later be called modernization was open. Indians could not remain Indians and grow up. The only hope for civilized Indians, as Jackson put it, was to "become merged in the mass of our population." In Jefferson's words, "The ultimate point of rest and happiness for them is to let our settlements and theirs meet and blend together, to intermingle, and to become one people incorporating themselves with us as citizens of the United States." "We should take direct control of Indian land," said Georgia Congressman Richard Wilde. "We should become their real benefactors; and we should perform the office of the great father." Attacking those who mourned the eventual extinction of the tribes, he tellingly exploited the logic of the sentimental friends of the Indians.

> But the race of Indians will perish! Yes sir! The Indians of this continent, like all other men, savage or civilized, must perish. . . . What is history but the obituary of nations? . . . Whose fate do we lament? The present generation of Indians? They will perish like the present generation of white men . . .
>
> When gentlemen talk of preserving the Indians, what is it that they mean to preserve? Is it their mode of life? No. You intend to convert them from hunters to agriculturalists or herdsmen. Is it their barbarous laws and customs? No. You promise to furnish them with a code, and prevail upon them to adopt habits like your own. Their language? No. You intend to supersede their imperfect jargon by teaching them your own rich, copious, energetic tongue. Their religion? No. You intend to convert them from their miserable and horrible superstitions to the mild and cheering doctrines of Christianity.
>
> What is it, then, that constitutes Indian individuality—the identity of that race which gentlemen are so anxious to preserve? Is it the mere copper color of the skin, which marks them—according to your prejudices at least—an inferior—a conquered and degraded race?[12]

Civilization was the professed paternal aim. It required as a first step that the President break the tribal tie to the land. In part, as we saw in the previous chapter, this meant that Indians should farm individual freeholds. "A father ought to give good advice to his children," President Madison told the Cherokees, urging them to plant crops.[13] The location of Indians on individual freeholds would release substantial excess tribal land for sale. But the southern Indians resisted this policy, and it was clear to policymakers by the 1820s that wholesale Indian removal afforded the most promising method of acquiring eastern Indian land. Monroe, Calhoun, Adams, and Jackson all supported removal. They believed it would protect Indians from advancing white settlers until they were better able to protect themselves, initiate steps toward civilization as tribes relinquished their historic territory, and make available eastern land for whites.

Jefferson first advocated Indian removal. Monroe's special message of January 1825 was the first proposal to move all eastern Indians across the Mississippi, and Adams supported removal legislation too. But Monroe and Adams, in the face of stiffening tribal resistance, insisted that the tribes voluntarily consent to remove.[14]

The southern tribes, following the white example, developed both a significant staple-crop agriculture and a more centralized, articulated tribal government. The presence of wealthy chiefs of mixed ancestry, missionaries, and whites connected to tribal members undermined tribal traditions and increased stratification within the tribes. Debts to traders plagued the Indians, and the Creeks and Seminoles never recovered their prosperity after their wars against the United States. Nevertheless, the tribes retained much of their historic integrity; the bulk of southern Indians in the 1820s enjoyed a comfortable existence still meaningful in traditional terms. Their centralized government institutions departed from tribal tradition, but increased the effective resistance to tribal cessions of land.[15]

Indian resistance placed Monroe and Adams in a dilemma. They could follow Jackson's advice and unilaterally take Indian land. Jackson developed his brand of paternalism precisely for this purpose. But Monroe and Adams lacked Jackson's driving interest in removal. Unwilling to abandon the vestiges of Indian autonomy, they were unwilling to take responsibility for a unilateral, paternal seizure of Indian land. Their removal policy foundered on the contradiction between paternalism and contractual treaty freedom. Once Jackson became President, he too wished to avoid responsibility for forced removal. He could not, even had he wished to implement it, obtain congressional assent for such a policy. Unlike his predecessors, however, Jackson successfully combined paternalism with the doctrines of market freedom. His removal policy sought to force the Indians to choose to move west.

Interaction among free, independent, and equal men had one crucial advantage over the theory of paternal authority. Liberal contractual relations diffused guilt; no one could be held responsible for the condition of anyone else. Since the Indians were to be forced from their homes, it was particularly important to avoid the burden of guilt. The language of the marketplace accomplished this purpose. It pictured Indians as at once the victims of mechanized and fragmented social processes for which no one was to blame, and at the same time free to choose their own fate. This ultimate in the rhetoric of disorienting infantilization broke even the connection to a personified central authority, and left individual Indians to contend with an irresponsible social pluralism, allegedly driven by inevitable historical laws. Indians were infantilized and destroyed, but white leaders were not to blame.

Jefferson's debt policy, Crawford and Jackson's individual allotments, and Jackson's verbal assaults on the tribal structure had already used the techniques of market individualism against the tribes. But these measures worked too slowly. The first major innovation after Jackson's election was the extension of state laws over the southern Indians.

As soon as the results of the 1828 election were known, Georgia extended its laws over the Indians within the state. Alabama and Mississippi shortly followed suit. State laws abolished the tribal unit, making it illegal for tribes to punish lawbreakers or regulate the behavior of their members. The states forbade public tribal assemblies, and stripped the chiefs of their powers. Georgia subjected Indians to militia duty, state taxes, and suits for debt, though it canceled some white debts to Indians. The state denied Indians the right to vote, to bring suits, and to testify in court. It divided up Indian territory for auction in a state land lottery. Mississippi law permitted whites to settle on Indian land. Alabama set up counties in Creek and Cherokee country, and encouraged intruders to settle there. An 1832 law that forced a Creek treaty two months later gave intruders the right to purchase Indian improvements. In theory Indians were protected in the enjoyment of their farms. In practice Indians were placed under the jurisdiction of frontier counties of white speculators and intruders, and denied the right to testify in court. The states did not prosecute intrusions and depredations on Indian land.[16]

Jackson fully supported the extension of state authority. He and his fellow treaty commissioners had often threatened tribes with unilateral state or federal action if they refused to cede their lands. President Jackson told Congress, "Years since I stated to them my belief that if the states chose to extend their laws over them it would not be in the power of the federal government to prevent it." This formulation made Jackson the passive spectator of a policy he had actively advocated. As soon as he took office, he informed Congress and the tribes that the states were legally entitled to act as they had. The states, in turn, waited for Jackson's public support before passing their most egregious ordinances. The southern tribes, Jackson wrote Eaton, "are a conquered and dependant people," subject to state sovereignty the moment a state determines to exercise it. The states could take Indian land on which there were no farms or villages, Jackson told Congress. The Cherokees had set up a national tribal government in 1827; Jackson insisted, on the grounds of the murder of women and children, "that the first original inhabitants of our forests are incapable of self government by any of those rules of right which civilization teaches."[17]

American law had long held that Indian nations were not sovereign, but treaties and federal statutes clearly gave Congress and not the states authority over the tribes. There was no legal precedent for the Jackson-Georgia view. Jackson, with a backward glance at his own speculations in Indian land, cited the assignment by Virginia and North Carolina of Revolutionary War warrants in Indian land. Land claims in Indian territory, he asserted, gave states sovereignty over Indian land. This argument contradicted the plain words of the 1802 Indian Trade and Intercourse Act; it had failed to convince Monroe when Jackson first advanced it, in 1817. The Intercourse Act provided for no land cessions except by treaty or convention with a tribe, and it provided that federal law would operate in Indian territory. In 1832 the Supreme Court ruled against the extension of state law. Jackson ignored the court decision.[18]

The extension of state law was premised, in the paternal tradition, on the denial of Indian sovereignty. But it had a crucial advantage over the extension of federal authority. As Coffee wrote the President,

> . . . deprive the chiefs of the power they now possess, take from them their own code of laws, and reduce them to plain citizenship . . . and they will soon determine to move, and then there will be no difficulty in getting the poor Indians to give their consent. All this will be done by the State of Georgia if the U. States do not interfere with her law. . . . This will of course silence those in our own country who constantly seek for causes to complain—It may indeed turn them loose upon Georgia, but that matters not, it is Georgia who clamors for the Indians lands, and she alone is entitled to the blame if any there be.[19]

State action removed responsibility for the Indian plight from the shoulders of the President. Alabama was an independent state, Secretary of War Eaton explained to the Creeks, and could extend its laws over the tribe. "It is not your Great Father who does this; but the laws of the Country, which he and every one of his people is bound to regard. Every thing he has said to you on this subject has been in a spirit of kindness and friendship towards you."[20]

The extension of state law permitted Jackson to offer the tribes the freedom to stay in the east or move to the west under circumstances which made it more than likely they would choose as Jackson wanted them to. Jackson explained, "This emigration should be voluntary, for it would be as cruel as unjust to compel the aborigines to abandon the graves of their fathers and seek a home in a distant land. But they shall be directly informed that if they remain within the limits of the States they must be subject to their laws." "God forbid," said future President James Buchanan in support of the Indian-removal bill,

> that I, or that any other gentlemen upon this floor, should entertain the purpose of using the power of this Government to drive that unfortunate race of men by violence across the Mississippi. Where they are let them remain, unless they should freely consent to depart. The State of Georgia, so far as we can judge from her public acts, entertains no other intention.

"What has a Cherokee to fear from the operation of the laws of Georgia?" asked Lewis Cass. If the Indians were civilized, as their adherents claimed, they were better off under state than under barbarous rule. If they were "too ignorant and barbarous to submit to the state laws," they were "too ignorant and barbarous to establish and maintain a government of their own."[21]

Everyone understood, however, that the states intended to force the Indians from their land. "By refusing" to remove, said Secretary of War Eaton, the Indians "must, necessarily, entail destruction on their race." Cass himself, becoming Secretary of War a year after his defense of Georgia law, warned that Indians who did not remove would "sit still and perish." As Jackson put it in his first annual message, "The fate of the Mohegan, the Narragansett, and the Delaware is fast overtaking the Choctaw, the Cherokee, and the Creek. That this fate surely awaits them if they remain within the limits of the States does not admit of a doubt." But the Indians were free to make this choice. Indian removal represented an early application of what Margaret Mead would later call "democratic control" as opposed to totalitarian coercion. Liberal planning structured the environment to load the dice strongly in favor of a single alternative, and then gave the target of social planning the onus of the choice. If Indians were coerced by their situation to choose to sell their land, they were not coerced at all. If each Indian internalized the impossible situation he faced, then he, not the President or white society, would be responsible for the choices he made.[22]

Indians were offered the defining freedom of Jacksonian America, the freedom to go west. Indian removal sought to impose the white experience of mobility upon the tribes. In Jackson's words,

> Doubtless it will be painful to leave the graves of their fathers, but what do they more than our ancestors did nor than our children are doing? To better their condition in an unknown land our forefathers left all that was dear in earthly objects. Our children by thousands yearly leave the land of their birth to seek new homes in distant regions. Does humanity weep at these painful separations from everything animate and inanimate, with which the young heart has become entwined? Far from it. It is rather a source of joy that our country affords scope where our young population may range unconstrained in body or mind, developing the power and faculties of man in their highest perfection. These remove hundreds and almost thousands of miles at their own expense, purchase the lands they occupy, and support themselves at their new homes from the moment of their arrival. Can it be cruel in the Government, when, by events which it cannot control, the Indian is made discontent in his ancient home to purchase his lands, to give him a new and extensive territory, to pay the expense of his removal, and support him a year in his new abode. How many thousands of our own people would gladly embrace the opportunity of removing to the West on such conditions?[23]

How, then, come to terms with the resistance of the natives, their attachment to their historic tribal territory? "Real Indians," the whites insisted, would offer no resistance to removal, since they led a wandering life anyway. Denying Indian attachment to the land, whites called natural the wandering their policies imposed upon Indians. Whites turned Indians into wanderers by killing their game; by destroying their crops and burning their villages; and by moving a tribe from one location after another as whites wanted the land. Jackson, who had engaged in these activities, innocently asked, "And is it to be supposed that the wandering savage has a stronger attachment to his home than the settled, civilized Christian? Is it more afflicting to him to leave the graves of his fathers than it is to our brothers and children?"[24]

We have seen, however, that the perspective of civilization acknowledged Indian ties to the land, and obliged the paternal President to break them. Removal took the final step in this direction. Paternal guidance would rescue Indians from predatory whites, and overcome their resistance to moving west. In McKenney's words,

> Seeing as I do the condition of these people, and that they are bordering on destruction, I would, were I empowered, take them firmly but kindly by the hand, and tell them they must go; and I would do this, on the same principle I would take my own children by the hand, firmly but kindly and lead them from a district of the country in which the plague was raging.[25]

McKenney's language gave insufficient weight to the freedom of Indian choice. A Georgia Congressman explained that Jackson, "with a special regard for the welfare of the Indians," gave them a choice of land in the west or of remaining under state law. "And this, sir, is [supposed to be] the language of a despot! . . . It is merely a little friendly and parental advice from the President to the children of the forest."[26]

Jackson blamed his "white children" for the extension of state law, and offered his own paternal protection. He sent a talk to the Creeks two days after his inauguration:

> My children, listen:—my white children in Alabama have extended their law over your country. If you remain in it, you must be subject to that law. If you remove across the Mississippi, you will be subject to your own laws, and the care of your father, the President.

A few months later he sent Major David Haley to the Choctaws and Chickasaws with instructions for a talk:

> Say to them as friends and brothers to listen to the voice of their father, and their friend. Where they now are they and my white children are too near to each other to live in harmony and peace. . . .

Say to my red Choctaw children, and my Chickasaw children to listen—
my white children of Mississippi have extended their law over their country. . . . Where they now are, say to them, their father cannot prevent
them from being subject to the laws of the state of Mississippi . . . The
general government will be obliged to sustain the States in the exercise of
their right. Say to the chiefs and warriors that I am their friend, that I
wish to act as their friend but they must, by removing from the limits of
the States of Mississippi and Alabama and by being settled on the lands I
offer them, put it in my power to be such—There, beyond the limits of any
State, in possession of land of their own, which they shall possess as long
as Grass grows or water runs, I am and will protect them and be their
friend and father.[27]

Jackson insisted on the paternal benevolence of his removal policy
to whites as well as Indians. He attended the 1830 Chickasaw treaty
himself, and wrote W. B. Lewis after a treaty was signed, "We have
preserved my Chickisaw friends and red brethren." In his 1830 Annual
Message he explained, "Toward the aborigines of the country no one
can indulge a more friendly feeling than myself, or would go further
in attempting to reclaim them from their wandering habits." He hoped
all true friends of the Indians would "unite in attempting to open the
eyes of those children of the forest to their true condition," so they
would abandon their historic homes and cross the Mississippi.[28]

Such benevolence threatened to smother the Indians. Denying that
the father participated in the predatory desires of ordinary whites, it
deprived the Indians of the right to their anger. Paternal benevolence was
useful, moreover, even if it failed to overwhelm the tribes. If the Indians,
failing to take the President's advice, remained and were destroyed, the
President was not to blame. When the Creeks and Cherokees refused to
treat, Jackson wrote, "I feel conscious of having done my duty to my
red children and if any failure of my good intention arises, it will be
attributable to their want of duty to themselves, not to me." "I have
exonerated the national character from all imputation, and now leave
the poor deluded Creeks and Cherokees to their fate, and their annihilation, which their wicked advisers has induced."[29]

To free the government from responsibility for the Indian plight,
however, was also to assert paternal helplessness. "Your great father has
not the power to prevent" whites from moving onto Chickasaw land
and Mississippi from extending its jurisdiction, Jackson told the tribe.
Eaton wrote Choctaw agent William Ward, "It is desired and directed
that you constantly in all your intercourse, with the Indians, urge upon
them the utter inability of their Great Father to prevent the State of
Mississippi from extending their laws over their Cntry." Refusing to

enforce the Supreme Court decision against the extension of state law, Jackson wrote Coffee, "The decision of the supreme court has fell still born. . . . The arm of the government is not sufficiently strong to preserve [the Indians] from destruction." Jackson penned on Cherokee Chief John Ross' passionate plea that he protect the tribe against white intruders the notation, "We have no power over the subject matter asked for—they must apply to the state of Georgia and the other states to whom the power belongs—we are bound to extinguish for Georgia the Indian title, and we cannot interfere with the sovereign powers of a state." The workings of society were not the responsibility of the federal government, and Jackson was powerless to control them.[30]

Assertions of powerlessness may seem at odds with claims of protection; in fact, as Jackson's policy toward white intruders reveals, the two reinforced each other. Jackson had originally promised that the federal government would continue to protect Indian property after the tribes were subject to state law. Secretary of War Eaton, citing the 1802 Intercourse Act which forbade white settlement on Indian lands, promised that the federal government would remove intruders.[31] The first test of administration intentions came in Georgia. A tiny fraction of the Creek tribe signed the fraudulent treaty of Indian Springs in 1825, ceding the remainder of Creek lands in Georgia. Congress ratified the treaty, but John Quincy Adams suspended its operations when he discovered that the treaty commissioners had misrepresented tribal support for the agreement. Georgia had inspired the fraud, and Governor George M. Troup furiously insisted on the state's right to the land. Over federal protests, the state began surveying Creek country, and threatened to oppose federal interference by force. Bowing to state pressure, Adams signed two treaties in which the Creeks ceded the land Georgia had acquired illegally.[32]

Jackson had attacked Troup's "fictitious treaty." Troup was a member of the Crawford faction, with which Jackson was in bitter conflict, and Jackson had always subordinated Indian removal in Georgia to removal in the southwest. By 1828, however, Crawford support had switched to Jackson, and the faction in control of Georgia state politics strongly supported the General.[33] Shortly after the election, Georgia began surveying a large swath of Cherokee country, claiming it was actually owned by the Creeks and had been ceded in the Indian Springs treaty. This claim was pure fabrication, violating Crawford's 1816 Cherokee treaty, an 1821 Cherokee-Creek convention, and the treaty of Indian Springs as well. Georgia cited as precedent the Jackson-Coffee claim after the Fort Jackson treaty that Creeks owned north Alabama land on which Cherokees lived.

Swarms of whites, encouraged by the state, occupied the disputed lands. Jackson suspended his order removing these intruders, and sent Coffee to investigate Georgia's claim. Coffee exposed its fraudulent character, but decided on a boundary compromise between Georgia and the Cherokees. More important, by the time of his report the territory theoretically returned to the tribe had passed into actual white possession. Some white intruders were removed once; within a few months Jackson decided he would no longer remove whites from Indian land. Georgia had successfully repeated the Jackson-Coffee maneuver of 1815.[34]

Gold was discovered in another portion of Georgia Cherokee country about the time Jackson took office. Several thousand whites descended on the area, forced the Indians to cease mining, destroyed their property, and staked out claims for themselves. Jackson ordered federal troops to remove these intruders, and to stop Indians as well as whites from mining. The troops were shortly removed at Georgia's request, the whites returned, and federal authorities told the tribe it could not interfere with Georgia's authority. A year later Jackson wrote a prospective prospector that only Georgia could grant the authority to dig for gold.[35]

These encounters with Georgia set the pattern Jackson followed. Violating his original promises, he refused to remove intruders on land over which the states had extended their laws. Tens of thousands of intruders devastated the southern tribes after the extension of state law.[36] Indian removal had been justified because Indians were hunters rather than farmers; whites had the right to make productive use of the soil. Jackson had said Indians would be protected in their improvements, but could not expect to keep lands "merely because they have seen them from the mountain, or passed them in the chase."[37] In fact the southern tribes, like most eastern Indians, had always had an extensive subsistence agriculture, and they had cleared and planted additional acreage for cash-crop production. Many chiefs and partly acculturated Indians had substantial plantations. Intruders protected by Georgia law seized the farms of wealthy Cherokees like Chief John Ross, as well as those of ordinary Indians. They took possession of Indian land, stock, and improvements, forced the Indians to sign leases, drove them into the woods, and acquired a bonanza in cleared land. Protesting Indians were threatened or flogged. "Hosts of traders, who like locusts have devoured their substance" preyed on the Indians. They initiated credit purchases, claimed land as security, threatened legal action, and took possession of Indian farms. Traders, often with state encouragement, introduced whiskey on a large scale for the first time. Alcohol created chaos within the tribes, and provided another method of dispossessing Indians. Whites killed the game on which Indians subsisted, and state militia periodically attacked Indians for hunting within state lines.[38]

To attribute intruders merely to popular frontier pressure would be greatly in error. Intruders entered Indian country only with government encouragement, after the extension of state law. Leading southern planters, speculators, and their representatives were among those pushing with greatest militance for Indian removal; the Indians were not simply victimized by democratic masses. Soil exhaustion in the southeast, for example, caused large planters to press for removal. Jackson and other spokesmen for Indian removal insisted on the spontaneous, popular character of white expansion, obscuring the essential roles played by planter interests and government policy decisions.[39]

White intruders demoralized the southern tribes. The Indians were reduced, one government agent wrote, from comparative plenty to unqualified wretchedness. "They are brow beat, and cowed, and imposed upon, and depressed with the feeling that they have no adequate protection in the U.S. and no capacity of self protection in themselves." Deprived of their crops and game, large numbers of Indians faced starvation. Uncertain of their future, many stopped planting. Indians turned to alcohol as their societies collapsed; so long as tribal integrity lasted they were not so vulnerable to it. Murders among Indians and depredations against whites increased drastically as (an outlawed) tribal law lost its hold over demoralized, starving, and drunken Indians. The white man benefited from Indian violence, one observer believed, "for he like Iago, no matter which he kills, sees in it his gain."[40]

By late 1830 only one southern tribe had agreed to remove, and the administration reneged on its promise to remove intruders. Jackson decided that the extension of state law voided the Intercourse Act, and he refused to carry out its provisions. The federal government told the tribes it was powerless to remove intruders, and their only recourse was to cede their lands. In the words of Indian Affairs administrator Elbert Herring, "Safety from persecution is to be found only in emigration. The remedy is in their own hands." The War Department continued for some months to urge its agents to stop whiskey from entering Indian country, as provided in the Intercourse Act. By February 1832 it had reversed itself on whiskey too.[41]

In withdrawing the promised federal protection of Indians, Jackson was not simply bowing to state pressure. The extension of state law alone did not convince the tribes to move west; Jackson was using intruders, as he had a decade and a half earlier, to force the tribes to cede their land. His 1830 Chickasaw treaty was not ratified by the Senate, but hordes of intruders entered Chickasaw country anyway, pressuring the tribe to sign another treaty two years later. Tennessee offered not to extend its laws over the Cherokees residing within the state. It did not want to embarrass Jackson and side with the nullifiers against federal authority. But the nullification crisis passed, and Jackson wanted to be relieved of the obligation of removing intruders on Tennessee Cherokee lands. In 1834 the state extended its jurisdiction. Tennessee could request federal troops, Jackson announced, to prevent the tribal government from coercing Indians who had agreed to emigrate. Pressure from white intruders was another matter. By the end of the year intruders had occupied nearly every cultivable Cherokee plot in Tennessee.[42]

Withdrawal of government authority over intruders was not, moreover, the whole story. An 1807 law gave the federal government the right to remove intruders from the public lands before they were surveyed and sold. Indian territory became public land once it was ceded, and Jackson promised the tribes that after they sold their land he would remove intruders from it. This promise, contained in the Chickasaw, Choctaw, Creek, and Cherokee treaties, was a major tribal incentive for signing them. These treaties offered gradual rather than immediate removal, and promised the tribes a respite from white pressure in the meantime. The Choctaw and Creek treaties held out the hope that many Indians could retain their land permanently as individual allotments. These treaties promised to remove intruders until surveys had located plots of land claimed by Indian families, and released the remaining tribal holdings for sale.[43]

Jackson may have intended to remove intruders, but he did not carry out the treaty provisions.[44] His promises had helped obtain the treaties, and he was far more concerned with removing Indians than removing intruders. The Choctaws, for example, suffered from factional conflict. Greenwood Leflore, the chief who had negotiated the treaty, joined forces with Jackson; he encouraged intruders, over the protests of other chiefs, to pressure recalcitrant members of the tribe to move west. Other chiefs demanded the removal of intruders, as the treaty provided. The federal government, pleased with Leflore's hospitality, permitted them to remain.[45]

The Creeks unanimously demanded the removal of the thousands of intruders on their land. Secretary of War Cass first ignored these pleas. He changed his mind after the federal deputy marshal in Alabama sent reports of intruder violence and fraud. Under pressure from Alabama intruders, speculators, and public officials, Cass backed down once again. The outcry from Alabama grew particularly intense after one intruder fired on federal troops and was killed. The government suspended the removal order, and sent Washington, D.C., District Attorney Francis Scott Key to Alabama. Key quickly reached an agreement with the state. Agents would speed up the location of individual Creek allotments; once that process was completed, the federal government was no longer bound by the Creek treaty to remove intruders. The government set deadlines after which intruders would be removed, hoping the deadlines would fall after the location process was finished. When they did not, they were ignored. Early in 1834 the agents finished assigning allotments to the Creeks, and the government declared its responsibility toward the tribe at an end. The intruders remained.⁴⁶

Jackson and Cass wanted to avoid a collision between state and federal authority in Alabama. Alabama nullifiers supported the speculators and intruders on Creek land; Jackson's Indian policy retained his southern support against South Carolina. But Cass had refused to remove intruders almost as soon as the Creek treaty promising to do so was signed, and this encouraged state resistance later on. Bowing to the states on intruders was more than good politics. Jackson was not merely compromising; he was carrying out his own policy.⁴⁷

The difficulties of protecting Indians against southern expropriators were real, but the federal government was not merely the passive spectator of social and market events it could not control. The assertions of helplessness were policy, aimed at pressuring the Indians to move west; Jackson manipulated claims of helplessness and promises of protection in the service of Indian removal. The federal government did not merely stand by, moreover; it intervened actively to break down tribal autonomy and to load the environment with pressures which Indians liberated from tribal protection could not resist.

The use of intruders was part of this intervention. Agents of the federal government did not simply observe intruders; they actively encouraged them. Cherokee agents Hugh Montgomery and Benjamin F. Currey welcomed intruders into Cherokee country and made Cherokee improvements available to them. (Currey, like his predecessor Joseph McMinn, may have profited personally from these arrangements.) Currey argued that intruders would help convince the Cherokees to emigrate. Choctaw agent William Ward pursued a similar course. The War Department mildly chastised Currey for leasing Cherokee improvements, but refused to remove the intruders he had invited in.⁴⁸

The federal government itself made more imaginative use of the intruder issue. Jackson interpreted the Intercourse Act as giving him not the power to remove settlers and speculators from Indian territory, but the power to "order all white men" out of Indian country who were "taking measures to counteract the views of the Government in regard to the Indians." Some of these whites were missionaries with buildings and tribal connections in the eastern Indian lands, and often with genuine concern for tribal welfare as well. Others were Indian countrymen—traders or longtime residents in Indian country, usually married to Indian women. Indian countrymen often had a substantial interest in Indian land. Jackson had long believed that without the influence of missionaries and Indian countrymen, "real Indians" would not resist removal. As President he ordered that whites opposing government policy be removed from tribal lands.[49]

Commissioners Eaton and Coffee permitted white speculators, traders, whiskey sellers, and gamblers onto Choctaw treaty grounds in 1830; they ordered missionaries resident among the nation to leave. This removed the major white counterweight to government pressure, and smoothed the way for the treaty of Dancing Rabbit Creek.[50] Benjamin Currey collaborated with Georgia authorities in the arrest and detention of John Howard Payne, citing the presidential removal order as his justification. Payne, the author of "Home, Sweet Home," was visiting Cherokee country and was in sympathy with the tribe. He subsequently wrote a series of newspaper articles describing his experiences; Currey cited these *ex post facto* to justify the arrest. Francis Scott Key's "Star Spangled Banner" better expressed the intentions of federal Indian policy than "Home, Sweet Home." After the 1835 Cherokee treaty was signed by a small minority of the tribe, Jackson ordered out of the nation whites who sought to expose the fraud.[51]

Georgia jailed missionaries who opposed removal. Eaton had promised Governor George Gilmer that the federal government would remove those opposing "the kind wishes and charitable designs entertained by the Government towards our Red Brothers." But Jackson decided it was best if Georgia acted for itself. He facilitated the arrest of the missionaries by removing their authority to distribute federal mail (which placed them outside state jurisdiction). The Supreme Court held that the federal government, not the states, had authority over whites in Indian country, but Georgia ignored the court order to free the jailed ministers.[52]

In other ways as well the federal government hid behind the fiction of autonomous state and market processes while it actively intervened against the tribes. Indian agents often defrauded their charges, contributing to the disorienting market pressures that undermined tribal integrity. Chickasaw agent Benjamin Smith, an old Jackson crony, appropriated tribal perquisites for his own personal use, stole tens of thousands of dollars in tribal annuities, swindled Indians with depreciated bank notes, and paid Indians bounties for stolen horses which he resold. He was finally dismissed from government service, but never was prosecuted. Other agents also committed frauds against the tribes. Dishonest graft aside, agents typically used their positions to speculate in Indian land, deal in Indian trading goods, benefit relatives with farms or trading posts in Indian country, and advance their own political careers.[53]

The Indian Bureau acted as more than a servant of market forces. It employed a number of "confidential agents" in Indian country. They were hired to urge removal, keeping secret the government employment which might prejudice the tribes against them. Shortly after his first inauguration, Jackson sent Tennessee Governor William Carroll to visit the tribes. Eaton wrote Creek agent John Crowell, "Our desire is, that his approach to the nation and passage through it, may be secret and private, and that together you and he, may succeed in inducing the Indians to remove." Eaton explained to Carroll:

> The President has this matter much at heart and the Country at large are deeply interested. . . . Your silent approaches to the Chiefs may secure for you an influence and power which might be lost, were they beforehand to know you were approaching them in an official character. After you have felt them, and prepared them, and wiped away all prejudice, a treaty might be stipulated to be held.[54]

Carroll's mission was quickly exposed, but the government did not change its policy. It paid Indian countrymen and part-white secret agents to provide it with information and push government policy while ostensibly speaking in the tribal interest. The secret-agent policy was applied most vigorously against the Cherokees, the tribe which resisted removal most persistently. Jackson had proposed the employment of a "confidential agent" in 1820 to enroll Cherokees for emigration. Currey now hired several, including a confidant of John Ross.[55]

The employment of secret agents shaded into bribery of influential, partly acculturated Indians. Treaties contained land reservations for cooperating chiefs; in addition the administration supplied moneyed presents, often ostensibly for the performance of some service.[56] Elaborating his instructions to Governor Carroll, Eaton explained that the President opposed holding open treaties; the Indians had learned they lost their lands in treaties, and would not agree to meet.

> There is no doubt however, but that the mass of people would be glad to emigrate; and there is little doubt that they are kept from this exercise of their choice, by their Chiefs, and other interested and influential men among them, who, tenacious of their authority, and their power, and unwilling to forego their gainful positions, keep them under the ban of their dictation.
>
> Nothing is more certain that if the Chiefs or influential men could be brought to endorse the measure, the rest would implicitly follow. It becomes, therefore, a matter of necessity . . . to move upon them in the line of their own prejudices; and by the adoption of any proper means, break the power that is warring with their best interests. . . . The best

resort is believed to be that which is embraced in an appeal to the chiefs and influential men—not together, but apart, at their own houses; and by a proper exposition of their real condition rouse them to think of that; whilst offers to them of extensive reservations in fee simple and other rewards would, it is hoped, result in obtaining their acquiescence. This had—their people, as a body, it is believed, would gladly go.

The President views the Indians as the children of the Government. He sees what is best for them and that the perseverance in their refusal to fly the danger that surrounds them, must result in their misery and final destruction. He would, if appeals to reason fail, induce them, by rewards to avoid the threatened calamity.[57]

The Indians were children who did not know their own best interests; bribes from a paternal President would free tribal members to act "not together, but apart." At the same time, the government indignantly denied stories it had attempted to bribe Chief Ross as "too incredible to do much injury." In adjoining paragraphs of a letter to Currey, Herring first denounced "the charge of bribery against the President and Secretary of War," and then continued, "In the policy of removing the Cherokees to the west, it is desired to bring to the aid of the Government the cooperation of honorable and influential men; and your arrangement on that subject with Judge Underwood is approved and, will be fulfilled by the Department." Underwood was the Ross confidant Currey had secretly placed on the government payroll. Ross, to be sure, was incorruptible. But Herring's moral outrage against charges of government bribery suggests a disassociated consciousness, driven completely out of touch with itself by the character of the actions it countenanced.[58]

The extension of state law, the encouragement of intruders, and the employment of bribery and secret agents all undermined tribal integrity. Jackson also intervened directly against the tribal structure. The Choctaw tribe was badly divided by rivalries between pagans and Christians and between part and full Indians. Missionary influence, white settlement, and individual opportunities for self-aggrandizement fragmented a historically decentralized tribal structure. The tribe had three self-governing districts, and each had replaced older full-Indian chiefs in the 1820s with part-white leaders pledged to resist removal pressures. But the new leaders signed the treaty of Dancing Rabbit Creek in 1830, after much of the tribe had left the treaty ground. The three districts thereupon elected new chiefs opposed to removal. Jackson refused to recognize the new chiefs, and rewarded those who had signed the treaty and their supporters. Eaton wrote the tribe, "Stop quarrelling and falling out among yourselves. It is childish for you to do so."[59]

To overcome the resistance of Cherokee, Chickasaw, and Creek chiefs to removal, Jackson ordered that annuities no longer be paid collectively to the tribes. The chiefs used the annuities to support the expenses of tribal government, and to pay their own personal debts and those of other members of the tribe. They viewed debts as a collective tribal responsibility, and wanted to avoid debt-induced pressure for land cessions. Jackson had long opposed the collective assumption of debts. He insisted that tribal annuities be divided into equal sums for payment to individual Indians. But he promised the return of collective annuities if the tribes signed removal treaties.[60]

The Cherokee annuity, for example, was divided into equal amounts of 44 cents and promised to individual Indians who made the long trip to agent headquarters. Tribal members, united behind Chief John Ross, refused to accept this money. The annuity payment accumulated for several years, and Jackson offered individual Cherokees their share of the accumulated sum if they enrolled for removal. Despairing of a tribal removal treaty, Jackson resorted to the methods of individual emigration practiced after his 1817 treaty. Removal would occur, in Cass' words, "by the free choice of every individual, looking to his own circumstances, and to those of the tribe." Benjamin F. Currey, Superintendent of Cherokee Emigration, enrolled Indians, paid them for their improvements, and turned their farms over to white settlers. He gave the Indians money to sign emigration rolls. Cass explained to Jackson, "The Indians are easily swayed by others, and, like children, if immediate possession of a favorite object is not attained, it loses much of its value."[61]

The government finally advised Currey to hold back money due the Indians until they had reached the west. Commissioner Herring explained, "It is a parental care watching over and providing for improvident children," who would spend their allowances as soon as they received them. Were the money held until the Indians reached the west, Cass pointed out, they would be more likely actually to emigrate. Currey ignored these instructions for several months. The money he paid the Indians passed quickly into the hands of traders, many especially appointed to induce the Indians to contract debts. Then Currey used troops to force reluctant Indians to remove. The administration was not yet ready for this step, however, and the efforts at individual emigration removed mainly the small number of educated Cherokees who actually had made "the free choice" to move west.[62]

Cass threatened Ross, after the failure of individual emigration, that the government would treat "with the whole or any portion of your people." He sent the Reverend J. F. Schermerhorn to acquire part of Cherokee country from the small educated tribal faction that had come to favor removal. This effort failed too, and Jackson and Cass determined they would obtain a treaty for the whole country or none of it. Schermerhorn, meeting the expected opposition from the bulk of the tribe, evolved a "confidential" plan. He arranged a meeting at New Echota with the pro-removal faction, and wrote, "We shall make a treaty with those who attend, and rely upon it." Currey arranged with the Georgia militia to arrest Ross in his Tennessee home and prevent him from coming to Washington to protest Schermerhorn's plan. Ross was held in a Georgia jail for twelve days. The militia also, with Schermerhorn's and Currey's collaboration, seized the Cherokee newspaper printing press to prevent the paper from opposing Schermerhorn's treaty.[63]

Virtually the entire Cherokee tribe stayed away from New Echota; Schermerhorn made his treaty with the few who were there. Major W. M. Davis, appointed before the ratification of the treaty to enroll the tribe for removal, wrote the Secretary of War:

> Sir, that paper . . . called a treaty, is no treaty at all, because not sanctioned by the great body of the Cherokee and made without their participation or assent. I solemnly declare to you that upon its reference to the Cherokee people it would be instantly rejected by nine-tenths of them, and I believe by nineteen-twentieths of them. There were not present at the conclusion of the treaty more than one hundred Cherokee voters, and not more than three hundred, including women and children. . . . Mr. Schermerhorn's apparent design was to conceal the real number present and to impose on the public and the government upon this point. The delegation taken to Washington by Mr. Schermerhorn had no more authority to make a treaty than any other dozen Cherokee accidentally picked up for the purpose.[64]

Jackson closed his eyes to Schermerhorn's methods, and recommended that the Senate ratify the treaty; it did so by one vote. Jackson rejected petitions signed by thousands of Cherokees opposing the treaty, ordered Ross not to come to Washington to oppose the treaty, and refused to recognize the existing Cherokee government. He stated that a meeting of thousands of tribal members in council to oppose the treaty was "in direct contradiction to the plighted faith of their people." He had ordered General Wool, stationed in Cherokee country, to break up such councils, and raged when the General failed to do so. He called Ross' subsequent visit to Washington to protest the treaty "impertinence in the extreme."[65]

To obtain Cherokee land, Jackson sanctioned a prolonged, direct government assault on the tribe. The method of acquiring Creek, Choctaw, and Chickasaw land was rather different. These treaties gave individual plots of land to thousands of Indians. Each was then free to sell his plot and cross the Mississippi or remain under state law. In Mary Young's words, "Once the contract was signed, and the Indian became a freeholder and a free agent, what he chose to do, in the grip of intolerable confusion and under the spur of 'legitimate' coercion, was his own business and need not trouble the conscience."[66] Since the government had left each Indian free to make his own decision, it was not implicated in the extraordinary fraud, thievery, and violence which followed.

Jackson early tried to use individual allotments to obtain tribal land, but his pre-presidential efforts met with limited success. Three days after his inauguration he told the Creeks that those who wished to remain in Alabama could have "land laid off for them and their families, in fee." Taking individual allotments, Jackson indicated, was the only way in which Indians could remain in the east under state law. In addition, some chiefs wanted substantial individual allotments for themselves, or were influenced by white speculators who saw an opportunity to acquire Indian land.[67]

Jackson intended that only a few leading men should accept allotments, but the Creeks, Choctaws, and Chickasaws insisted on the right of ordinary Indians to claim them. Their treaties were the first to provide allotments for the mass of tribal members, and set the precedent for the allotments policy of the post-Civil War period. The Chickasaws viewed allotments merely as a method enabling the tribe rather than the government to benefit from the high market price of Indian land in the middle 1830s. Individual Indians, aided sometimes by a tribal committee, realized an excellent price for their land. The tribe went west with relatively little suffering.

Allotments, Jackson believed, would initiate a market-induced removal. Once Indians had claimed individual reserves, the remainder of Indian land would be freed for sale. "When the reserves are surveyed," he wrote, "it will require but a short time to compleat the ballance and have it into markett." As for the Indians taking individual freeholds, "they will sell and move to the west."[68]

The Creeks and many Choctaws, however, wanted to remain on their freeholds. The Choctaws were the first to learn that the government intention conflicted with their own. Choctaw agent William Ward refused to register the names of hundreds of Indians who applied for allotments. He destroyed records, erased names, hid from delegations, rejected representations by village headmen, closed tribal registers for days at a time, was often drunk, and finally submitted the names of only sixty-nine applicants. Jackson first insisted, in answer to tribal complaints, that only Congress could provide more allotments. But his friend Samuel Gwin, Mississippi registrar of public lands and a leader of the state Jacksonians, belatedly convinced Jackson to change his mind. Jackson held out substantial Choctaw lands from the second public sale, in October 1834, while the additional Choctaw claims were investigated. Gwin was not acting to benefit the Indians. He and his lawyer and speculator associates hoped to profit by permitting individual Choctaws to locate "floating" claims in any unsold tribal land. Lawyers representing these claimants, or speculators purchasing the claims, would then make a substantial profit. The battle over Choctaw floating claims between Gwin and a rival group of speculators lasted for years, and played a significant role in Mississippi party politics. Its outcome made little difference to the tribe. Like most who had gotten their names on the original register, the latecomers had long since lost their claims to legal fees, debts, intruders, and land companies.[69]

The disposal of Creek territory illustrated how the market operated to deprive Indians of their freeholds. The Creek treaty promised allotments to every head of household. There were few safeguards, however, in the procedures by which Indians could register for their holdings and sell them. Jackson and Cass permitted the certifying agents to interpret the regulations flexibly. It was not necessary, for example, that the agent actually witness the sale of land, or see the Indian seller at all.[70]

With the active collaboration of the certifying agents, Indians were defrauded of their lands on a massive scale. Individual intruders and speculators did their part, but land companies were the greatest culprits. The most important, the Columbus Land Company, included bank presidents and other wealthy speculators among its leading members. A Georgia Congressman and the nephew of Secretary of State John Forsyth belonged to the company. C. A. Harris, appointed Commissioner of Indian Affairs in 1836, was heavily in debt to members of the Columbus Land Company. He was dismissed two years later for speculating in Indian land.

Land-company agents and individual purchasers hired Indians to impersonate actual freehold owners. The Columbus Land Company took a group of Indians from one agent to another to sign contracts for claimed land. Eli Shorter, president of a Georgia bank and a leading company stockholder, insisted he had to match the techniques of other purchasers. "Stealing is the order of the day," he wrote, "and out of the host of Indians at the agency, I don't think there are ten *true* holders of land." Speculators obtained contracts with actual owners at a fraction of the value of the land by employing threats, whiskey, and inflated claims of debt. They set up stores in Creek country, permitted the Indians to buy on credit, and obtained title to land as security. Indians were whipped, were paid in depreciated bank notes, and were forced to return money as soon as a contract was signed. In the words of one speculator, "Hurrah, boys—here goes it—let's steal all we can."

Government certifying agents accepted bribes to approve fraudulent contracts. They were among the biggest speculators themselves, and often had an interest in the contracts they approved. They rushed to provide speculators with choice plots, and sanctioned purchases before Indian land locations had even been made. Often they refused to show Indians where their locations were. They accepted contracts without observing cash payments, and forwarded erased and badly blotted deeds of sale.[71]

Reports of the massive frauds soon reached Washington, and an investigator recommended a general review of the certified contracts. Jackson and Cass insisted such action was beyond the authority of the executive. Commissioner Herring wrote one certifying agent, "All that could be done for them by a faithful and vigilant guardian has been done by the department." In Cass' words,

> Our citizens were disposed to buy and the Indians to sell. . . . The subsequent disposition which shall be made of these payments seems to be utterly beyond the reach of the Government. . . . The improvident habits of the Indians can not be controlled by regulations. . . . If they waste it, as waste it they too often will, it is deeply to be regretted yet still it is only exercising a right conferred upon them by the treaty.[72]

Jackson also defended the Indians' right to sell. He had rejected suggestions a year after the Creek treaty was signed that the government reacquire Creek lands to protect the tribe from fraud in the sale of allotments. Such action interfered with the rights of buyers and sellers, said Cass. It also required settlements with speculators who had already acquired formal title to the land. These speculators strongly opposed government intervention, but Jackson convinced himself his refusal to intervene rescued the government from their contamination. "No concession will ever be made by me in favor of *such* men," he insisted. "A pure government cannot, nay ought not to be influenced by such corruption." The government, Jackson and Cass believed, need take no responsibility for the market it had unleashed on the tribe. Speculators would defraud Indians, while the government remained "pure." Cass admonished his agents for dubious practices, but he continued to approve the vast majority of their contracts.[73]

The government could not rest with this position, however. Defrauded and starving Creeks refused to leave for the west until their grievances were satisfied. Some resolution of the fraud charges seemed necessary before the tribe would leave Alabama, and Cass sent John B. Hogan to investigate the frauds. Cass wanted a quick disposal of the charges, and ordered Hogan to confine himself to cases where Indians came forward unbidden, produced witnesses, and were confronted by white purchasers. But Hogan initiated a full-scale, independent examination of the Creek contracts. He wrote, "A greater mass of corruption, perhaps, has never been congregated in any part of the world, than has been engendered by the Creek treaty in the grant of reservations of land to those people." Most contracts, he pointed out, were so fraudulent that white purchasers refused to appear. The mass of Indians were in no position to act as individual plaintiffs and initiate legalistic proceedings. Hogan recommended the reversal of hundreds of contracts, the bulk of those negotiated, in the first land district he examined.[74]

Cass and Jackson disapproved most of these recommendations. They ordered Hogan to speed up the review of contracts, and to observe legal formalities in every case. These instructions were intended decisively to limit the number of cases reviewed. Creeks were refusing to emigrate, pending the outcome of the fraud investigations. Certifying agent J. W. A. Sanford, a substantial speculator in Creek lands and a participant in the frauds, had been given a government contract to emigrate the Creeks. Resigning his position in the emigration company, Sanford complained, "The suspension of the sales and certification of Indian lands has, in itself alone, presented an insuperable obstacle to the undertaking; and so long as that measure is persisted in, all future efforts at emigration, whether on the part of the government or the company, must prove futile and abortive." Hogan's investigation had turned to Sanford's district. When a small war broke out there in May 1836, Cass ordered the end of the fraud investigation and the military transport of thousands of Creeks across the Mississippi.[75]

Indians were offered the opportunity to compete as free men, living under state law and selling their land; they failed. This was the lesson officials drew from the results of the allotment policy. McKenney had insisted from the beginning that Indians were too immature to compete in the marketplace. We cannot stop them, he wrote, from immediately wasting money for their improvements. "All we can do is advise these people, who at best as a people, are nothing but children, and ought to be treated as such." Indians were victimized under the allotment policy, said Jackson, because of their "improvident" character. Jacksonian policy stripped Indians of tribal protection and placed them at the mercy of marauding whites, government officials, and their own debased desires. Indians were rendered helpless and placed in situations where they behaved, from the white point of view, irrationally. Their actions were then attributed to their "inveterate," "improvident," childlike character. Indians were not forced to act in regressed and childlike ways; they were children. They were not placed in double-bind situations and driven crazy; they were "maddened." In John Ross' words, "I knew that the perpetrator of a wrong never forgives his victims."[76]

Market and paternalistic perspectives on the Indians successfully reinforced each other. Indians were victimized by the market, policy-makers insisted, because they were children. The government explained the failure of market and civilization to benefit the tribes not by white actions but by Indian character. Countless efforts to civilize Indians, Cass explained, had foundered on Indian improvidence. In spite of efforts to civilize the Creeks and Cherokees, "the great body of the people are in a state of helpless and hopeless poverty. . . . The same improvidence and habitual indolence . . . mark the northern tribes." Removal was offering the Indians one more chance to become civilized, and any "failure must be attributed to the inveterate habits of this people and not to the policy of the government."[77]

The promise of civilization placed Indians in a double bind. It offered them a civilized identity while white policy deprived them of the tribal resources which could sustain any identity at all. Indians were deprived not merely of emotional sustenance but of actual food. Their crops destroyed, their game killed, and their future bleak, large numbers of southern Indians faced starvation. Cass had previously attributed the scarcity of game in Indian country to the "improvident" methods of the Indian hunt. This fantasy blamed white threats to tribal game supplies on the Indian character. Ignoring the extensive Indian agriculture destroyed by intruding whites, Cass now asserted that Indians starved because they would not turn to agriculture. Here was the physical double bind that intermeshed with the psychic one: Indians were told to plant as their crops were destroyed; their failure to heed white advice demonstrated their improvidence.[78]

To illustrate his assertions of Indian improvidence, Cass pointed out that Congress had appropriated money to feed the starving Seminoles. The Seminoles were starving, however, not because of the "inveterate habits" of the Indians, but because the government had moved them once to land which did not easily support agriculture, and was planning to move them again to the west. Invasions of Florida by Jackson and others had burned their crops, killed their cattle, and destroyed Seminole prosperity. The demoralized Indians could hardly be expected to plant once again simply to leave their crops behind or have them devastated. Assertions about Indian character involved the refusal of the government to take responsibility for its acts.[79]

Rendering the Indians children did not simply free the government from responsibility, but also freed it to act as it wished. If Indians were driven by white pressure to "childish" squabbling among themselves, Jackson could recognize some chiefs rather than others. If a tribe was disorganized by state policies and white intruders, Jackson could treat its members as "children," ignore tribal preferences, and act in the Indians' "best interests." Georgia Governor Wilson Lumpkin, urging forcible Cherokee removal without benefit of treaty, wrote Jackson, "Have not these Indians lost all claim to national character? Ought not these Indians to be considered and treated as the helpless wards of the federal government?"[80]

Georgia and Alabama speculators and state officials, anxious to halt the Creek fraud investigation, also urged the forcible removal of that tribe. But it required a war before Jackson and Cass, confirmed in their estimate of the primitive Indian character, would take this step. Cass wrote the governors of Georgia and Alabama that so long as the tribe remained peaceful, the President would honor its treaty. Forced removal would be justified, he wrote, only if the tribe continued to refuse removal, and to "disturb the tranquility of the country." Should a war break out, the "law of necessity will certainly justify their transfer to the country provided for them west of the Mississippi."[81]

Within two months the Second Creek War had begun. Georgia Governor William Schley immediately urged the policy of military removal adopted by Jackson: "These Indians must no longer be permitted to remain where they now are, to murder our people and destroy their property *ad libitum*. It is idle to talk of treaties and national faith with such savages. The proper course to adopt with them is to treat them as wards or children, and make them do that which is to their benefit and our safety."[82]

Speculators and southern politicians had been exaggerating reports of Creek depredations for months, and holding meetings to rouse the countryside against the tribe. Starving Indians were raiding white farms, and Georgia militia and settlers were attacking peaceful Indians. The Second Creek War itself was not a coordinated conflict, but rather the intensification of raids by desperate and starving Creeks. It is even possible that speculators directly instigated the war to end the fraud investigations. The *Montgomery Advertiser* charged, "The war with the Creeks is all a humbug. It is a base and diabolical scheme, devised by interested men, to keep an ignorant race of people from maintaining their just rights, and to deprive them of the small remaining pittance placed under their control." Hogan, in spite of Cass' restraining efforts, had just begun his investigation of the land district bordering Columbus, Georgia. Certifying agent J. W. A. Sanford was a leading Columbus speculator, and there was evidence of wholesale fraud in his district. Cass had offered the speculators a way to get rid of Hogan, and perhaps they took it.[83]

Even if speculators did not inspire the hostilities, their frauds had provoked the tribe. Commissioner Herring denied the connection between frauds and violence, however. Echoing southern arguments, he insisted that since the outbreak of hostilities had not occurred in Robert McHenry's district, where Hogan had already exposed the frauds, frauds could not have caused the war.[84]

Herring would not admit that Indians responded to real grievances. He and Cass blamed the war neither on frauds nor on white seizure of Indian lands and violence against Indian families. They recognized that Indian starvation had played a role, but only in order to blame the Indian character. Improvident Indians had immediately spent the money they received for their allotments, wrote Herring. Faced with starvation, they committed depredations. Improvidence, combined with "those sudden impulses to which the Indians are liable," led them to violence. Other Creeks might join the hostiles, in Cass' words, because "of the predisposition of the Indian to war."[85]

Such explanations for Indian wars illustrate the functions of infantilizing language once again. Jacksonians used this rhetoric to explain not only the minor Second Creek War but the two protracted Indian wars which broke out during Jackson's Presidency—Black Hawk's War in the northwest and the Second Seminole War in Florida.

Jackson and Cass had both attributed Indian wars to the childish Indian character for years before they held national office. Indians were children; lacking consciousness of grievances, they fought because of their predisposition to war, and because of the influence of British and Spanish bad parents. Indians had not fought in the War of 1812 to defend their land, Cass insisted in 1827.

> It would disclose, not a mere trait of character, but a new feature of human nature, if these improvident beings with whom the past is forgotten and the future contemned, and whose whole existence is absorbed in the present, should encounter the United States in war, lest their country might be sold after the lapse of centuries.[86]

Cass wrote those words well after whites had settled land taken from hostile (and friendly) Indians in the War of 1812, and while he himself, as Governor of Michigan Territory, was clearing the northwest of formerly hostile tribes. The Sac and Fox Indians, who had fought to protect their land in 1812, fought another war with the United States shortly after Cass became Secretary of War. Cass attributed Black Hawk's War to Indian "impulse." In fact, like the Second Creek War, it derived from land conflict.[87]

Squatters had seized Sac and Fox land along the Mississippi in 1828 when the tribe was away on its winter hunt. They fenced Indian corn fields, destroyed lodges, and beat returning Indians who protested. Illinois had demanded the removal of the tribe, and an old treaty of dubious validity, confirmed after Sac and Fox hostility in the War of 1812, committed the tribe to move west once its land was sold. The federal government now advertised the land for sale. Black Hawk's faction of Sacs protested, and continued to return home after its hunts. The Sacs and

Foxes had engaged for years in intermittent tribal warfare with the Sioux and the Menominee. In the midst of the land conflict a band of Foxes killed twenty-five Menominee, retaliating for an earlier raid. Jackson sent troops to obtain the "murderers," and this initiated Black Hawk's War. Black Hawk had the support of 2,000 Indians, including bands of Foxes and Winnebagos, but the bulk of northwestern Indians refused to join him. He prepared to surrender without fighting, but a contingent of Illinois militia thwarted his efforts, and was ambushed during its pursuit of the Indians. This was the first battle of the war. Indians raided frontier settlements, and successfully evaded white troops. Frontier leaders had threatened to "exterminate all Indians, who will not let us alone." They now demanded the killing of "this bandit collection of Indians"; several took scalps themselves. Black Hawk's starving band sought peace, but his efforts were misunderstood and rejected. Discovered crossing the Mississippi, he raised a white flag. The American commander explained, "As we neared them they raised a white flag and endeavored to decoy us, but we were a little too old for them." Whites fired on the band and killed women and children.[88]

Jackson also enlisted Sioux aid in the war. Indian agent Joseph Street explained to the tribe,

> Our Great Father has forborne to use force, until the Sacs and Foxes have dared to kill some of his white children. He will forbear no longer. He has tried to reclaim them, and they grow worse. He is resolved to sweep them from the face of the earth. They shall no longer trouble his children. If they cannot be made good they must be killed. . . . Your father has penned these Indians up, and he means to kill them all.[89]

The Sioux took this infanticidal rhetoric literally. They pursued Black Hawk's fleeing, decimated band west of the Mississippi, killed much of the remnant, and received bounties for their work. The tribe had received, reported Cass, a "severe lesson" which would insure tranquility on the western frontier. Black Hawk's followers were sent to join the friendly Sac and Foxes, who had already removed to Iowa. The tribe was moved to Kansas a decade later, and to Indian territory after the Civil War. It suffered an even greater population attrition in the Iowa and Kansas years, from removal, resettlement, and white encroachments, than it had in Black Hawk's War.[90]

Jackson sent the captured Black Hawk on a tour of the east, visited and addressed the chief, and kept one of his headdresses.[91] But Black Hawk's war was a brief, successful one, and did not deeply involve the President. He played a greater role in the Second Seminole War, the longest and costliest Indian war in American history and, for those Indians who remained in Florida at its close, the most successful.

Of the five southern Indian tribes, only the Seminoles made a determined physical resistance to removal. In part, these several thousand Florida Indians shared grievances with other tribes that did not go to war. Their removal treaties, for example, were probably fraudulent. The first, signed in 1832 under dubious conditions, provided that several Seminole chiefs examine the proposed western country before removal was confirmed. It was not clear whether the chiefs alone or the tribe as a whole had the power to agree to removal. J. F. Schermerhorn, shortly to negotiate the Cherokee treaty of New Echota, accompanied the chiefs west; there they signed a removal treaty. Seminole bands in Florida protested against this treaty; Jackson and other government officials in Florida threatened to remove them forcibly if they did not abide by it. Florida Indian agent Wiley Thompson "rebuke[d] the Indian chiefs as if they were wrong-headed schoolboys" and stripped those who opposed removal of their titles. He placed the influential warrior Osceola in irons for opposing removal, and released him only after Osceola and his followers signed an agreement to move west. "These children of the forest," General Clinch explained to Cass, "are from peculiar circumstances and long habits suspicious of the white man." But, continued Clinch, "the manly and straightforward course pursued toward them by Genl. Thompson appears to have gained their confidence." Thompson's intimate relationship with Osceola, alternating between protectiveness and punitiveness, typified relations which often developed between Indians and government agents. Osceola killed Thompson at the outbreak of the war.[92]

Like members of the other southern tribes, hungry Seminoles committed depredations in the 1830s. There was factional conflict among bands opposing and favoring removal, as well as conflict between Indians and whites. Late in 1835, after Osceola's band killed a chief who favored removal, federal troops marched against the tribe. The Seminoles ambushed a boat coming up the Apalachicola River, killing soldiers and their families, and the Second Seminole War had begun.[93]

Fraudulent treaties, government attacks on the tribal structure, and interracial and intratribal conflict were not peculiar to the Seminoles, and cannot by themselves account for the war. Two factors were unique to the tribe. The first was a history of hostility to and independence of American authority. Tribal villages had long enjoyed freedom under weak Spanish rule. Jackson invaded Seminole country in 1814 and 1818, and the tribe was augmented by the migrations of hostile Creeks to Florida at the end of the First Creek War. The Seminoles were moved to south central Florida in the 1820s. Then Jackson insisted, over the bitter protests of the tribe, that it would have to live under the authority of the Creeks in the west. Seminole independence always angered Jackson. He justified his Florida invasions in part on the grounds that the Seminoles were merely a division of the Creeks. He urged in 1821 that the Seminoles be sent back to the Creeks. They ought now to join, in Benton's words, "the mother tribe, in the west."

Actually there was severe conflict between the two tribes, particularly once the Seminoles were joined by red sticks who had fought on the losing side of the Creek civil war. Creeks fought with Jackson against the Seminoles in 1818. Jackson's removal plan was thus part of his continuing vendetta against the tribe. By August 1835 the Seminoles were reconciled to removal if they could retain tribal independence in the west; the administration refused.[94]

The Seminoles had an additional reason to resist amalgamation with the Creeks. They feared the Creeks would appropriate the escaped slaves, free blacks, and Indian slaves who lived freely as part of the Seminole tribe. The Creeks demanded Seminole Negroes to obtain their share of $250,000 appropriated by Congress under an 1821 Creek treaty. This sum was to pay Georgia's claim for slaves stolen by the Creeks prior to 1802 and taken to Florida, and whatever offspring such slaves had produced. The War Department was sympathetic to the Creek claim, which was being pushed by the small group of western Creeks friendly to Georgia who had illegally ceded tribal land in Georgia and moved west. The removed Seminoles were to be placed under the authority of this Creek faction. The western Creeks sent a white lawyer into Seminole country to appropriate Negroes. He was to receive a share of the profits from his undertaking and sell slaves to white claimants and traders.[95]

The presence of these Seminole Negroes was the most important distinguishing feature of the tribe. Seminole Negroes had the greatest reason to fear removal. They were not only in danger from the Creeks; they also made the tribe a target of white slaveholders. The blacks feared, with good reason, that they would be seized by slave-catchers when the Seminoles gathered for removal. Southern speculators and Florida planters wanted to appropriate the Negroes before the tribe went west. Raiders had already attacked Indian reserves along the Apalachicola River and stolen Negroes belonging to Indian planters. Apalachicola Indians attempting to move west with their slaves were pursued by white claimants and stripped of property and Negroes.[96]

Jackson's protégé Richard Keith Call, a leading Florida politician and speculator, urged Jackson to grant permission to a group of speculators to purchase Negroes in Seminole country. Call explained, "If the Indians are permitted to convert them into specie, one great obstacle in the way of removal may be overcome." Jackson agreed, "directing the agent to see they obtain a fair price for them." Commissioner Harris explained to objecting Florida Indian agent Wiley Thompson that "their resources will be augmented, and they will not, upon their arrival west, have in their possession a species of property which . . . would excite the cupidity of the Creeks, and be wrested from them by their superior numbers and strength." True, the Negroes would be enslaved, wrote Harris, but "it is not to be presumed the condition of these slaves will be worse than that of others in the same section of the country." Thompson, however, objected that the change in the Negroes' condition would be "oppressively great," that no Indians wanted to sell Negroes, that speculators would use improper means to obtain them, and that the entrance of white slave-dealers would retard rather than further removal. Jackson retracted his permission, but it was too late to reassure the blacks.[97]

Seminole Negroes, their freedom endangered, prepared to resist removal. They received covert support from Florida free blacks and slaves, who helped supply ammunition for the tribe. Seminoles attacked Florida plantations at the outset of the war, and threatened St. Augustine in south central Florida. Some field slaves joined the uprising. General Philip Jesup, assuming command of the American troops, wrote the Secretary of War, "This, you may be assured, is a negro, not an Indian war; and if it be not speedily put down, the south will feel the effects of it on their slave population." Benton, obliquely recognizing the importance of slavery, blamed the war on the abolitionists.[98]

The administration, meeting the wishes of Florida planters, insisted it would not end the war on terms permitting Seminole Negroes to go west. Cass ordered General Winfield Scott at the outbreak of the war to "allow no terms to the Indians until every living slave in their possession, belonging to a white man, is given up." Decades-old white claims were recognized, including title to the then unborn children of escaped or captured slaves. Indians, moreover, rarely had proof they owned slaves they had actually purchased. Cass' order thus endangered the freedom of most Seminole Negroes, not merely of slaves who had escaped once the war began. To underline its interest in the Negroes, the War Department enlisted Creek warriors against the Seminoles, promising them that a bounty for captured Negroes would be paid from the Seminole annuity.[99]

General Jesup negotiated an end to the war in March 1837 which permitted Seminole Negroes to go west. Under Florida pressure, he reneged. He signed a secret agreement with some Seminole chiefs in which they agreed to turn Negroes over to white claimants. He reversed an order prohibiting slave-catchers from entering Seminole country and appropriating blacks who had gathered in camps to await removal. Negroes and Indians fled these camps, and the war continued.[100]

Many Seminole Negroes and slaves who had joined the war were dead or captured by 1837. Most of the rest responded to Jesup's renewed promise they could go west in safety. But the lawyer for the Creeks and other slave-traders tried, with administration support, to capture and sell these Negroes. Secretary of War Joel Poinsett and Commissioner of Indian Affairs C. A. Harris sought to obtain the Negroes for speculators in Creek lands. James C. Watson, a leading participant in the Creek land frauds, took Poinsett's advice and made large purchases of claims on the Seminole Negroes. Watson's brother-in-law followed the Negroes west, but the army, to Harris' dismay, thwarted his efforts to appropriate them. Finally, in 1841, the new administration determined that the 1832 Seminole treaty settled all white claims on Seminole Negroes originating prior to 1832.[101]

The august *Niles' Register* hoped, at the outbreak of the Second Seminole War, "that the miserable creatures will be speedily swept from the face of the earth." But the tribe scored early victories over American troops and forced whites to abandon most of the territory south of St. Augustine. The American army was plagued throughout 1836 by disease, insufficient numbers, rivalry among its commanders, difficulties in supplying troops in the Florida interior, and a tropical terrain uniquely suited to Indian guerrilla warfare. Jackson had faced all these problems but the last in the Creek War and overcome them. Now he gave Call, whom he looked upon as a son, an opportunity to do the same. Call had no more luck than his predecessors. He ran out of supplies, was forced to retreat, and was then incapacitated by ill health. Jackson had triumphed over these adversities; Call was dismissed in an angry letter.[102]

There were enough troops in Florida, Jackson insisted, "as might eat Powell [Osceola] and his few." Army failures made the conflict "a disgraceful war to the american character," Jackson wrote after he left office. As the war dragged on, he resorted to the language and proposals of his own earlier Florida campaigns. He complained that General Scott's "combined operations, without knowing where the Indian women were, was like a combined operation to encompass a wolf in the hamocks without knowing first where her den and whelps were." To the Secretary of War he suggested search-and-destroy missions against hidden Indian villages. American commanders should have found "where their women are" and "captured or destroyed them."[103]

Seminole resistance did not merely provoke such proposals from Jackson. It led General Jesup and his successors to violate flags of truce, capture Indians invited to negotiate, hold them as hostages, threaten them with execution if they did not bring in their followers, employ bloodhounds against the tribe, and kill cattle that American troops did not need in order to deprive the Indians of food. The barbarous treachery of the Seminoles justified these measures, Jackson and Benton insisted. In Benton's words, "A bit of white linen, stripped, perhaps, from the body of a murdered child, or its murdered mother, was no longer to cover the insidious visits of spies and enemies. A firm and manly course was taken."[104]

Jesup captured the majority of the tribe by 1838; the remaining Indians fought bitterly for four more years. They raided white settlements for food and supplies, but promised to stop fighting if they could stay in Florida. In 1842, their ranks further reduced by death and capture, the few hundred remaining Seminoles were permitted to do so.

Violent rage marked Jackson's pre-presidential Indian relations; it surfaced again among Jacksonians during the Indian wars of the 1830s. War and primitive verbal violence were not typical, however, of Jackson's presidential Indian policy. The vast majority of Indians were removed without war. The administration met their intensified, prolonged suffering with a steady impoverishment of affect.

The southern tribes experienced intense hardships in their original homes after 1828, but the long journeys west were worst of all. Tens of thousands were clothed inadequately and marched through freezing southwestern winters. Those who made the trip in the summer suffered from extreme heat and drought. Indians were fed inadequate and contaminated rations, including rancid meat, spoiled flour, and bad drinking water. In some cases food offered them was years old and had already been declared unfit to eat. They were crowded together on old, unseaworthy boats—the worst single accident killed 311 Creeks—and separated from their remaining possessions by emigrating agents, local citizens, and sheriffs prosecuting alleged debt claims. They traveled through areas in which cholera was raging. Weakened by the exhausting journey and bad food, tens of thousands caught fevers, measles, and cholera; thousands died from disease and exposure on the removal journeys alone. War, disease, accident, starvation, depredations, murder, whiskey, and other causes of death from the extension of state laws through removal and resettlement had killed by 1844 one-quarter to one-third of the southern Indians.[105]

The insistence on removal and the deadlines enforced on the tribes insured much of this suffering. Government methods also made matters worse. Contractors hired to provision Indians made money at their expense. They increased their profits by supplying bad food and unsafe boats. Jackson assigned the entire responsibility for Creek removal to contractors. In Cass' words, "The President, on full consideration, has determined to make an experiment to remove the Creek Indians by contract." The contractors would be paid $20 per head for the number of

Indians they emigrated. Cass hired the very speculators who had defrauded the Creeks, and who now saw an opportunity to make more money off the tribe. These men desired removal, Cass apparently reasoned, and they would have the incentive to accomplish it.

The Creeks objected from the outset to removal by the speculators. Cass told Hogan not to "yield to the idle whims of the Indians, and indulge them in unnecessary preferences, which amount in fact merely to a wish that certain individuals, rather than others, should be concerned in their removal." Jackson had once sworn that "a pure government" would "make no concession" to "such men," but a contractual relationship was not a concession. Contracts, in a liberal society, created reciprocal obligations. Contractors had been paid to take responsibility for removal off the shoulders of the government.[106]

The army also played a role in removal. The contractors were retained after the Second Creek War broke out, but they were joined by the army. It identified 2,500 Creeks as hostile, and removed the warriors among them in chains. Soldiers scouted Cherokee country to round up Creeks who had fled there during the war; they also collected longtime Creek residents among the Cherokees, married or otherwise connected to that tribe.[107]

Two years later, in the spring of 1838, the army rounded up 15,000 Cherokees who had refused to remove in the time allotted under the New Echota treaty. They were seized as they worked in their farms and fields, separated from their possessions, and taken to military detention camps. They remained in captivity for months while hundreds died from inadequate and unaccustomed rations. The debilitation of others contributed to deaths during the removal march.

Eaton had promised during the debates on the Indian-removal bill, "Nothing of a compulsory nature to effect the removal of this unfortunate race of people has ever been thought of by the President, although it has been so asserted." The treaty of New Echota, the government now claimed, had committed the tribe; if Indians were not mature enough to fulfill their promises, the government would have to force them.[108]

Creek removal combined military with market pressures. Emigration was stalled after the Creek War; county officials arrested many principal men of the tribe for alleged debts, in an effort to strip the Creeks of their remaining possessions. The Creeks asked the government for an advance payment of their 1837 annuity to pay these debts. General Jesup, who had put down the Creek uprising and was on his way to Florida, insisted that to obtain the annuity several hundred Creek warriors would have to fight the Seminoles. Their families, sent west without them, were deprived of their help during removal and resettlement.[109]

Another group of several hundred Creek warriors was recruited to fight voluntarily in Florida. The government wished to avoid "sacrificing our own troops to the unhealthful climate in the sickly season of the year." It detained the warriors' families in Alabama camps and promised to feed and protect them. General Jesup kept these Creek warriors, over their objections, several months past the expiration of their terms of enlistment. He explained that he would otherwise have incurred the expense of hiring militia. But Georgia and Alabama wanted the Indians out of the south. Companies of county militia invaded the Indian camps, stole stock and possessions, raped women, manhandled and mistreated the Indians in other ways, and insisted they be removed from Alabama. Commissioner Harris responded to reports of these events by initiating the removal of the Indians. The government, "guardian and protector" of the Indians, was required by "the change in the state of things" to transport them west immediately. The Creek warriors were finally permitted to leave Florida, discharged, as Secretary of War Poinsett explained to Congress, because of the expense of maintaining their families.[110]

The War Department, violating its original agreement with the Creeks, did not wait for the warriors' return before removing their families. It gathered them at Pass Christian, near Mobile, where disease, exposure, and starvation claimed 177 deaths in the party of 3,500 between March 7 and July 31, 1837. Harris regretted this suffering "as sincerely as any man can," but doubted that "anything further can be done by this office." In fact that same day he did do something further. He was concerned that the contractors would demand more money to transport Creek possessions. Creeks "had collected a much larger amount of baggage than the company, by their contract, are bound to transport," he wrote, and "the Indians are unwilling to dispose of any part of it, or to leave any part behind." He ordered the emigrating officer not to transport any "evidentally superfluous" possessions purchased from "whim or caprice," and to prevent any such purchases in the future.[111]

The worse the Indian suffering and death, as Creek removal suggests, the more disassociated the reaction of Washington officials. Indian Office records reveal monumental concern for the details of organizing removal, and monumental indifference to the suffering and death it caused. Overriding all other matters was concern for the costs of removal. Reports of suffering and death were met with demands for economy.

The Choctaws were the first tribe to be removed; the disorganized, disease-ridden removal of the first group of Choctaws, with its share of deaths, foreshadowed the fate of the other southern Indians. The War Department, however, was most concerned because the costs of removal far exceeded government expectations. The government reorganized removal, fed the Indians more cheaply and with spoiled food, forced them to walk rather than ride, reduced its costs, and increased the number of Indian dead.[112]

Creek removal caused the deaths of thousands of Indians, but that was not the government's concern. One of the Columbus speculators who had emigrated the Creeks wanted the contract to emigrate the Cherokees. Commissioner Harris listed the considerations which should govern the award, "1st, economy—2nd, the comfort, safety, and accommodation of the Emigrants, and 3rd the moral influence which the measure will probably have upon the Cherokees." Van Buren finally permitted "Ross and the others," "viewed in the light of contracters," to organize their own removal, although Jackson protested from the Hermitage that the "contract" was much too "extravagant." By the time the superintendent of Creek removal was ordered to close up Cherokee emigration, thousands of Creeks and Cherokees had died on the journey west. Commissioner Crawford's instructions made no references to these deaths. He insisted instead that the emigrating agent "avoid the loose and irregular manner of transacting business which occurred in the Creek removal." He sought to stop General Nathaniel Smith from feeding and clothing Cherokees who had escaped the military roundup and remained in the North Carolina mountains.[113]

As Indians died, the government demanded "economy" and sought to correct "the loose and irregular manner of transacting business." It sought, in Call's words, "to convert them into specie." It offered money for homes, money for land, and money incentives for removal. When Hogan exposed the Creek frauds, speculators were sure it was only because they had not found his price. Georgia insisted that Ross refused to sign a removal treaty because the government would not bribe him. Whites consistently converted what Van Buren called the "debt we owe to this unhappy race" into money.[114]

Dying Indians betrayed whites. They threatened to force them to encounter the consequences of their own policies and desires. To quote John Ross again, "the perpetrator of a wrong never forgives his victims." Whites responded to Indian deaths by deadening their own experience. Indians were turned into things—a small reserve remaining in Ohio after removal was a "blank spot," "a mote in the eye of the state"—and could be manipulated and rearranged at will. Money was the perfect representation of dead, interchangeable matter. It could not symbolize human suffering and human reproach. A money equivalent could be found for Indian attachments; they had no intrinsic, unexchangeable value. Indian love would give way to money; it could be bought. The "debt we owe to this unhappy race," converted into specie, could be paid.[115]

Indians, children of nature, had an uncontrolled instinctual life. It caused them, in the white view, first to kill and then to die. Indians lived in a relationship of basic trust with nature, but that relationship did not help them survive. Indians dead and suffering were out of control; demands for economy expressed anxiety about the loss of control in an area in which administrators could more safely experience it. Money, the solid product of self-reliance, replaced unreliable nature. Bureaucratic removal offered an enclosed realm, divorced from the human, natural world. Interchangeable entries on bureaucratic ledgers, Indians were not particular, specific, humans whose suffering could be pitied. The government would not save Indians; it would try to save money.[116]

Money, debt, and control were pervasive themes in Jacksonian democracy, and the next chapters will explore their significance. We turn now from defenses against death within the bureaucratic structure to the return of death in the world. Death cast its shadow over the entire removal experience; it deeply affected white perceptions of the westward journey itself.

Savagery, proponents of Indian removal claimed, could maintain itself only by fleeing westward. Providence decreed that "the hunting tribes must retreat before the advance of civilization, or perish under the shade of the white man's settlements." "Mature consideration," said Jackson in his Seventh Annual Message, revealed that Indians "can not live in contact with a civilized community and prosper." White settlers would be excluded from the western lands; if the tribes chose to remain uncivilized, "they are upon the skirts of the great prairies" and could hunt the buffalo which roamed there. Entirely extruded from civilization, primitive experience could maintain itself. Alleged tribal willingness to go west had indicated to some writers that childhood would not resist maturity. "They are on the outside of us, and in a place which will ever remain on the outside," the Senate Committee on Indian Affairs declared as Indian removal came to an end.[117]

But politicians who argued that isolating the savages would protect them also called for the march of civilization across the continent. Jefferson proposed the northern Louisiana territory as a home for the eastern tribes; at the same time he foresaw Indians retreating westward to the Pacific as the tide of white civilization advanced. "When we shall be full on this side [of the Mississippi]," he wrote, "we may lay off a range of States on the western bank from the head to the mouth and so, range after range, advancing compactly as we multiply." Cherokee agent R. J. Meigs, an early advocate of removal, explained,

> A disposition to migrate seems to pervade the whole eastern part of the United States; we invite that emigration here; obstacles ought to be removed. The tendency is as uniform as the law of gravitation. It can no

more be restrained *until the shores of the Pacific Ocean make it impossible to go further.*

One Cherokee, said Meigs, suggested that land given the Indians not be bounded on the west. The Indians could then continue westward; they could flee, as the post Civil War chromolithograph *American Progress* (Plate 6) would picture it, before the advancing whites.[118] Temporarily the west would place Indians "far beyond the reach of the oppression—and, I was about to say, the example of the white man."[119] Permanently, only death would. Savage integrity could ultimately maintain itself only in death.

Childhood experience could not be integrated into adult life; living it served as a reminder of what had been lost and rejected in the process of growing up. American nostalgia for childhood and the past reflected the failure of revered ideals actually to guide behavior, and the longing for what one's desires had killed. Like the dead twins in the frontier Tennessee poem, only dead Indians could safely be mourned.[120] The white father was not merely helpless to prevent death; he identified with it, longed for it, and carried it out.

Indian removal carried out violence against symbolic childhood. The fantasies of its perpetrators also expressed longings for death itself. Americans wedded to competitive advancement in the world shared an arcadian dream life. The rural home would release them from worldly cares and return them to a state of primitive security. Such longings, however, did not protect whites from mobility "to better their condition," as Jackson put it,[121] any more than they protected Indians. Jackson had longed to retire to his Hermitage refuge for thirty-five years. The heavenly father's eternal home offered the only permanent rest.

Removal promised the Indians, in Cass' words, "the probability of an adequate and final reward." It would transport them—the words are Jackson's on the death of John Coffee's mother—to "happier climes than these." Death was the western tribal utopia. Géza Róheim writes,

> [I]n the other world we have the land of wish fulfillment, the place where our infantile omnipotence of thoughts reigns supreme, and where we can be rid of all the pain and trouble that is inherent in the environment[.] The paradise once familiar to us all in our infancy, we have learned through bitter experience cannot exist in this world. Hence we use its shattered material to rebuild it at the very moment when we stand in greatest need of consolation, at the moment of death.[122]

Indians, the removal ideology asserted, were plagued by competitive forces which they and the government were powerless to resist. Removed Indians would benefit from "paternal care and guardianship." Their land would be "forever secured and guaranteed to them." "If a paternal authority is exercised over the aboriginal colonies" west of the Mississippi, wrote Cass, "we may hope to see that improvement in their conditions for which we have so long and vainly labored."[123]

A benevolent father would have total power in the west; he could free Indians from violent and competitive relations with their white brothers, and protect his red children. Jackson tried to convince the Creeks of this in the message he sent them three days after his inauguration. He told the tribe, "Your bad men have made my heart sicken, and bleed by the murder of one of my white children in Georgia. Our peaceful mother earth has been stained by the blood of the white man, and calls for the punishment of his murderers." In the west such conflicts would not arise. "Where you are now your white brothers have always claimed the land. The land beyond the Mississippi belongs to the President, and to none else; and he will give it to you forever. . . . You will be subject to your own laws, and the care of your father, the President." Jackson returned to the theme of refuge in his Farewell Address. "The philanthropist will rejoice," he said, "that the remnant of that ill fated race has at length been placed beyond the reach of injury and oppression, and that the paternal care of the General Government will hereafter watch over them and protect them."[124]

The Creeks recognized the utopian character of these promises. As early as the 1820s whites west of the Mississippi had successfully demanded land promised the southern Indians. One Creek delegation pointed out to Jackson that Alabama had recently been a remote frontier territory inhabited, like the western land offered the tribe, by Indians protected by the United States. Now whites were not only crowding Alabama Indians; they were also moving into the western territory. Their great father Jackson, they said, might protect them for a time, but he was old and a successor might not be bound by his promises.[125]

Jackson was old indeed. He suffered, as he said in his Farewell Address just before turning to the Indian question, from "advanced age and a broken frame." His promises of western utopia resembled his thoughts of death. Overton had gone beyond the reach of injury and oppression too, where his enemies could no longer hurt him. Emily Donelson also had an adequate and final reward; "she has changed a world of woe, for a world of eternal happiness." Elisabeth Coffee "has gone to the realms of bliss free from all the troubles of this wicked world." The old man, benignly surveying the destruction of the children of nature, was reconciling himself to death.[126]

Indian deaths transcended individual will and merged with the providential movement of history. America had begun with a radical assertion of the power of men to control their fate. But the country progressed through the destruction of another set of men, and responsibility for that destruction could not be faced. "The extinction of the Indians," wrote Cass, "has taken place by the unavoidable operation of natural causes, and as the natural consequences of the vicinity of white settlements." White men were placed by "Providence" on the "skirts of a boundless forest." Subduing it by industry, they advanced and multiplied by providential decree. They had superiority in arts, arms, and intelligence. How, then, could whites be blamed for the Indian plight? "Their misfortunes have been the consequence of a state of things which could not be controlled by them or us." Cass drew practical lessons from his theory of history. If the Creeks chose to stay in Alabama and "finally melt away before our people and institutions, the result must be attributed to causes, which we can neither stay nor control."[127]

As southern Indians actually began to die in large numbers, policy-makers denied not simply responsibility but reality itself. The worse the events, the less they could be admitted into consciousness. During the last large-scale Indian removal, 4,500 Cherokees died. President Van Buren and Secretary of War Poinsett ignored the deaths. They congratulated themselves instead that removal was at an end, and that they had finally permitted Chief Ross to lead the bulk of his tribe west. As Poinsett described the process,

> The generous and enlightened policy . . . was ably and judiciously carried into effect by the General appointed. . . . The reluctance of the Indians to relinquish the land of their birth . . . was entirely overcome. . . . Humanity, no less than sound policy, dictated this course toward these children of the forest.

The Commissioner of Indian Affairs amplified:

> A retrospect of the last eight months, in reference to this numerous and more than ordinarily enlightened tribe, cannot fail to be refreshing to well-constituted minds. . . . A large mass of men have been conciliated, the hazard of an effusion of blood has been put by, good feeling has been preserved, and we have quietly and gently transported 18,000 friends to the west bank of the Mississippi.

In Van Buren's words, "The wise, humane, and undeviating policy of the government in this the most difficult of all our relations foreign or domestic, has at length been justified to the world in its near approach to a happy and certain consummation."[128]

Instead of facing actual deaths, white policy-makers imagined Indian destruction as an abstracted and generalized process removed from human control and human reality. To face responsibility for specific killing might have led to efforts to stop it; avoiding individual deaths turned Indian removal into a theory of genocide. In Jackson's words,

> Humanity has often wept over the fate of the aborigines of this country, and Philanthropy has been busily engaged in devising means to avert it, but its progress has never for a moment been arrested, and one by one have many powerful tribes disappeared from the earth. To follow to the land the last of his race and to tread on the graves of extinct nations excites melancholy reflections. But true philanthropy reconciles the mind to these vicissitudes, as it does to the extinction of one generation to make room for another.[129]

Weeping over Indian deaths was immature. History rescued a man from melancholy; he could tread on Indian graves in peace. "Independance of mind and action," to recall Jackson's advice to his nephew, could not be borne. Instead a man like Jackson had to justify himself as a "real tool in the hands of" "his creator," "wielded, like a mere attamaton, sometimes, without knowing it, to the worst of purposes."[130] To be a man meant to participate, separated from the actual experience, in a genocide.

PART III

JACKSONIAN DEMOCRACY

CHAPTER 8

THE MARKET
REVOLUTION
AND THE
RECONSTRUCTION
OF PATERNAL
AUTHORITY

John Ross is now, as he always has been from the first, in the market.
Give him one or two millions, and the entire control of the five
millions embraced in the treaty, with the power of conducting the
emigration of the Indians, and all his attachment to the land of his
fathers, the soil of his birth, will die in that false and treacherous
bosom, unlamenting the necessity that compels the separation.

—*Congressman George Towns of Georgia, May 28, 1838*

I

The primitive accumulation of Indian land initiated a market revolution
in America. From 1815 to 1845, the years in which Jacksonian Democracy
emerged and flourished, America transformed itself from a household to a
market society. The extension of the market broke down family-based
household structures—subsistence agriculture, household manufacture, the
master-apprentice system, family welfare. The market undermined or transformed the stable old families which had dominated American society. It
undermined the chartered monopolies, traditional churches, and other deferential corporate forms of eighteenth-century life. It set men, goods, and
money in motion. The tensions of the Jacksonian period, writes Fred Somkin, were "largely due to an agonizing and finally unsuccessful attempt
to retain the esprit of a sacred society, a family brotherhood, within a

framework of conceptual and institutional constructs based upon freedom of contract."[1]

Westward expansion underlay the market revolution. In Douglass North's words,

It was the natural resource wealth of the American West that served as the fundamental determinant of our extensive growth in attracting capital and labor to America; it was the rich quality of the land that gave America such a substantial share of this vast international movement of people and capital during the nineteenth century.[2]

The burgeoning English textile industry and the European demand for American breadstuffs stimulated western expansion. Cotton and staple-grain exports fueled American economic growth from 1815 to 1845. Agricultural demand attracted capital to the west. It drew eastern American migrants during the first decades of the nineteenth century, and substantial European immigration by the 1840s. Commodity price rises produced booms in land prices and sales, spurring the westward movement of men and capital. Crop-marketing facilities—warehouses, banks, insurance companies, and factors—promoted the growth of northeastern ports. Profits from the export trade were plowed back into economic development. Subsistence farmers produced most of what they consumed, and lacked the surplus to purchase additional goods; farmers producing commodity crops entered the market as buyers.[3]

The cotton kingdom, expanding to the southwest, provided the key impetus to the market revolution. Cotton was the largest single American export in the decades after the 1812 War. Cotton plantation agriculture required capital investment in land and slaves. The cotton kingdom provided a market for northwestern foods; much northwestern development depended on southern expansion.[4]

Prohibitive transportation costs before 1815 inhibited the development of cash-crop agriculture. The Appalachian barrier and the cost of upriver transportation limited western opportunities; most westerners lived in a subsistence economy. The transportation revolution, as George Taylor has called it, insured the triumph of the market. Steamboats, canals, bridges, roads, dredged harbors, and finally railroads spectacularly lowered transportation costs after 1815. The transportation revolution created a national market in America by 1840. The capital and labor which built, maintained, and used the transportation infrastructure stimulated regional development. Market towns grew rapidly, and a specialized, non-food-producing urban population augmented the demand for market products.[5]

By 1860 the United States was second among the leading manufacturing nations in the world. Manufacturing and the urban industrial transformation of America marked the culmination of the market revolution. The extension of the market undermined household manufacture and the master-apprentice relationship, which together before 1815 produced most American finished products. Reduced transportation costs, expanding the market, permitted economies of scale. Specialization of production, a characteristic of market society, increased the demand for finished goods. The rise of factories and the destruction of insulated local markets doomed the master-apprentice system. Merchant capitalists invaded the mechanical trades and established small factories. Capitalists had easier access to credit than master craftsmen. They paid attention to marketing possibilities rather than product quality. They hired unskilled workers at wages lower than those paid journeymen. Journeymen owned their own tools; unskilled laborers did not. The new structure of production made it more difficult for apprentices and journeymen to become masters of their own shops. Where home manufacture persisted, families often worked on material owned by the merchant capitalist; the finished products were sold, not consumed in the home.[6]

Manufacturing gained importance in the 1820s and 1830s, but banks were still the most important corporations during those decades. Banks created capital by providing loan credit and issuing notes. Bank notes were the major circulating medium during the market revolution. Bank credit financed American economic development.

There were only twenty banks in the United States in 1798; mainly they provided short-term credit to finance the re-export trade. Shipment of Caribbean staples to Europe was the most important American commercial activity in the early years. Banks expanded rapidly in the first decades of the nineteenth century, spurred particularly by the boom in land and commodity prices at the end of the 1812 War. There were 89 banks in 1811, 246 in 1816. Bank credit financed the first surge of westward expansion, capitalizing plantations and financing land sales. Many banks failed in the 1819 panic, but the number of banks grew to 330 in the next decade. At the peak of the 1830s boom, in 1837, there were 788 chartered state banks.[7]

The market revolution brought substantial material benefits to the bulk of white Americans. *Per capita* income had remained relatively stable throughout the eighteenth century. It began to rise about 1815, and continued rising until the Civil War. The market revolution also disrupted lives, however. It fostered growing classes of rich and poor at the economic extremes, and ushered in greater class differentiation during the Jacksonian period than had heretofore existed in America. The market introduced an economic cycle, marked by severe nationwide depressions in 1819 and 1837. The mass of people, no longer primarily supporting themselves, suffered as they had not under subsistence conditions. Even in good times, large external economic institutions—bank, factory, and market itself—gained increasing control over the conditions of existence. Competing class and sectional interests developed within the market system, fragmenting political and social cohesion, and replacing a social upper class with one more directly, economically exploitative in character. Mobility and social dislocation fed personal anxieties over moral worth and social place. The panic of 1819, the first modern American depression, brought these problems of class, status, and power to a head.[8]

The 1819 panic heralded the widespread entrance of Americans into a market economy, and their dependence on staple-crop prices, credit, and international trade. The panic, it was everywhere said, confirmed the warnings of the revolutionary fathers: hunger for worldly goods profaned America, stimulated dependence, exacerbated factional conflict, and undermined control of the self. What principles of virtue would reunite the nation and dedicate it to a common purpose? The 1812 War raised these questions in the context of foreign struggle. The panic of 1819 turned America inward, and placed before Jackson the dialectical consequences of his expansionist Indian policy.[9]

Jackson had, by 1819, promoted market expansion for thirty years. As a young land speculator and cotton planter, he brought vast tracts into the commodity economy. He fought to open the Mississippi to American commerce, and to transform the southwest into a populated, commodity-producing region. Jackson typified an important class, as land speculator, planter, and expansionist politician, but had himself only small, local importance. Primitive accumulation offered him his large role. Jackson had opened large portions of Indian land to cotton cultivation by 1819. He would as President remove the southern Indians from the remainder of their territory and, raising the specter of Indian atrocities, help bring Texas into the American orbit. Jackson's expansionism created the southwestern cotton kingdom around which the market revolution took place.

Jackson fought Indians to strengthen the American character as well as to expand the national empire. War and freehold agriculture, he thought, would restore republican virtue. Jackson achieved personal authority for himself, but he helped impose a system of materialism, dependence, and impersonal authority on others. Like the revolutionary fathers, he proclaimed the virtues of republican order and extended market society.

Spiraling land and cotton prices stimulated expansion onto Indian lands after 1815; they would do so again in the 1830s. Speculative orgies, abhorred by President Jackson, followed in both periods. Cotton prices dropped precipitously in 1819 and again in 1836, as the new land was brought into production. Falling agricultural prices deflated land prices and sales, and initiated severe depressions. Jackson had made himself the instrument of a boom-and-bust economic cycle.[10]

Westward expansion against English, Spanish, and Indians at first obscured the contradictions of Indian dispossession. The market had only begun to penetrate the west before 1815. Jackson believed that expansion onto Indian land would populate the region with planters and yeomen farmers; it was not yet clear that market capitalism rather than independent agriculture would benefit. Indians still occupied vast tracts of southern and western land in the 1820s; demands for their removal spurred Jackson's presidential campaigns. Nevertheless, the 1819 panic and the struggle over presidential succession highlighted problems internal to white society. Jackson turned to these problems in the 1820s as he entered presidential politics. He did not abandon his Indian policy. He rather fled its consequences on the one hand, and applied its lessons on the other.

I I

Jackson's presidential campaigns in 1824 and 1828 subordinated the issues dividing America—tariff, internal improvements, strict construction, and federal power—to two overriding concerns: national defense and "reform." Foreign affairs dominated America in the early national period. As the attention of the nation shifted to domestic matters, General Jackson placed himself above internal political conflict. He tried to unify the country around its past.

This project required him, first of all, to shed his reputation for personal violence. Elected to the Senate in 1823, Jackson reestablished cordial relations with Senator Thomas Hart Benton, General Winfield Scott, and other old antagonists. He wrote a Nashville friend, "This has destroyed the stronghold of my enemies who denounced me as a man of revengefull Temper and of great rashness. I am told the opinion of those whose minds were prepared to see me with a Tomahawk in one hand, and a scalping knife in the other has greatly changed."[11]

Jackson's successes in Horseshoe Bend, New Orleans, and Florida elevated him above identification with Indian violence; they also freed him from doctrinaire commitments on divisive political issues. Although Jackson called himself an Old Republican, he had little loyalty to strict construction or states rights in the abstract. Jackson had opposed federal power in the cause of expansion; now he identified expansion with American nationalism. He feared that if "the despotism of urope" gained "a foothold upon the Terra firma of the American continent . . . , their foreign bayonets might make an attempt to pierce us in the south and west." Urging the importance of "national independence and national defense," Jackson supported federally financed internal improvements and a moderate tariff. The tariff would protect domestic armaments and other "articles so essential to war." Wrote Jackson, "If our liberty and republican form of government, procured for us by our Revolutionary fathers, are worth the blood and treasure at which they were obtained, it surely is our duty to protect and defend them."[12]

Jackson's Indian policy, however, had double-edged consequences. The American farmer, complained Jackson, had no "market for his surplus products." "Take from agriculture in the United States six hundred thousand men, women, and children, and you at once give a home market for more bread stuffs than all Europe now furnishes us." The tariff would protect employment in "mechanism and manufactures" for displaced farmers. Indian removal created not arcadia but a farm surplus, and farmers must follow Indians in removing from the land.[13]

This proposal violated Jackson's own values. Two months earlier he wrote Andrew Jackson Donelson, "I find mankind Treacherous, and corrupt, and virtue to be found amongst the farmers of the country alone, not about courts, where courtiers dwell." Longings for rural serenity fill Jackson's letters in the 1820s. These longings underlay the rhetoric of Jackson's presidential years. "The best part" of a country's population, he declared in 1832, "are the cultivators of the soil. Independent farmers are everywhere the basis of society, the true friends of liberty." Dispossessing Indians, Jackson had set in motion an acquisitive capitalism which undermined agrarian dreams. He was still groping, in the 1820s, for a way to overcome the contradictions of his life.[14]

Indian dispossession fully involved Jackson, but it took him only to the threshold of national power. As Jackson sought the Presidency, he was a political man estranged from the "labour and bustle" of "public life." His emphasis on national defense reflected his difficulties uniting public with private concerns. National defense sacrificed internal political regeneration to mere defensive strength. It failed to stimulate Jackson's deepest energies, or to address widespread fears of American decline. But Jackson neither retired to his farm nor acted in politics while his deepest loyalties lay elsewhere. The "domestic life" sacrificed in Jackson's quest for office returned as the model for republican restoration. Jackson's calls for "reform" brought private nostalgia into the public realm. "Reform" provided a political vision of "pure . . . friendship" and family serenity. Jackson had sought to purify America in war. He now believed the people had brought him forward to regenerate the internal institutional fabric.[15]

Jacksonian reform in the 1820s contrasted country and court. Jackson located republican simplicity in the countryside; pomp, intrigue, hidden motives, and conspiracy dominated Washington. His first concrete target, early in the 1820s, was an imagined secret coalition between the apparent presidential rivals William Crawford and Henry Clay. Jackson wrote John Coffee, "It is a child of Colo Benton and Colo Williams begot in the city last year. . . . The people begin to see this deep intrigue, and when fairly discovered they will leave all concerned on their native Dung Hills." He wrote his ally John Calhoun, "Coalition and intrigue is sta[l]king abroad through our land, with manly strides and the whole exertions of the virtuous portion of the people will be required to put it down."[16]

Jackson placed the congressional caucus, sure to nominate Crawford, at the center of Washington intrigue. If the people did not "put this unconstitutional proceeding to sleep," Jackson wrote,

> it will introduce into our Government, a sistematic system of intrigue and corruption, first secrete and last, open and undisguised; that will ultimately destroy the liberty of our country, a central power will arise here; who under patronage of a corrupt, and venal administration, will deprive the people of their liberties; and place into the executive chair whom they may will.[17]

Jackson rejoiced, after Crawford's defeat, "*The great whore of Babylon being prostrated by the* fall of the caucus, the liberty of our country is safe." The inconclusive 1824 election results, however, exacerbated Washington intrigue. No candidate received an electoral majority, and Jackson feared that "aristocratical influence" in the House of Representatives would steal the election from him. His worst fears were confirmed when Clay supported Adams for President and the victorious Adams nominated Clay for Secretary of State. This "corrupt bargain" dominated Jackson's campaign for the next four years.[18]

Jackson's other major issue, after 1824, was Adams' use of executive patronage. Patronage centralized the sources of intrigue, Jackson believed, and threatened to reestablish monarchy. A pro-Jackson House committee reported,

> The King of England is the "fountain of honor": the President of the United States is the source of patronage. He presides over the entire system of Federal appointments, jobs, and contracts. He has "power" over the "support" of the individuals who administer the system. He makes and unmakes them. . . . His spirit will animate their actions in all the elections to State and Federal office.[19]

American revolutionaries, attacking the British court, connected patronage to sexual license. Jacksonians made the same charge, with spectacular inappropriateness, against Adams. They contrasted Jackson's "republican sternness of integrity in manners" with the "dissolute barbarous prostitution of the midnight orgies of the Court of St. Petersburg" when Adams was minister to Russia. He had, it was alleged, pimped for the Czar.[20]

Jackson believed that secret powerful forces corrupting the morals of the country had to be "unmasked." He attacked "that vile hypocrisy, and deceipt, that often lurks beneath a fair exterior which is cloathed with power." He contrasted his own willingness to stand public scrutiny with his opponents' efforts at deception. Jackson regretted being taken from "peaceful retirement," but rejoiced at the opportunity to demonstrate "that my charector will stand the test of the most exact scrutiny, both public and private, and I court it from the nation." Hearing rumors that ex-President Monroe had criticized his Florida invasion, Jackson threatened to "unrobe his hypocricy and strip him, of much of his borrowed plumage." Charges against Rachel, prominent in the 1828 campaign, particularly incensed Jackson. Neither Adams nor Clay repudiated these slanders, and Jackson was convinced they secretly instigated them. Reluctantly remaining silent while his friends defended his marriage, Jackson wrote, "The *blood* of this secrete mover [behind] the curtain must *attone* for this wicked attempt."[21]

Jackson borrowed his rhetoric from revolutionary political symbolism. Jacksonian reform modeled itself on revolutionary exposés of secret British plots; reform reaffirmed kinship with the fathers.[22] But what malignant American power compared to the British king? The fear of domestic conspiracy was widespread in ante-bellum America. What explains it?

Pervasive role-playing, David Brion Davis argues, accompanied the struggle for individual success in Jacksonian America. Widespread mobility denied men stable expectations about the positions and motives of their fellows. The self-made man, writes Davis, found "that he had naïvely believed in the performances put on by his elders of the prestigious ranks, and that now he must stage a similar show." Were those who presented smiling faces secretly using others for their own advancement? Did the public face hide a contaminated inner core? These, the themes of ante-bellum literature, derived from Jacksonian life. Uncertain of the motives of others and worried about their own, Americans were preoccupied with internal states. They glorified the authentic, spontaneous, natural man who wore no masks, played no roles, and never dissembled. The natural man's appearance was at one with his inner self. Playwrights presented Andrew Jackson as the natural man on stage; Jackson so presented himself in politics.[23]

The search for conspiracies was the search in the outer world for negative feelings hidden within the self. Perhaps politicians, who strongly denied their intense ambitions, were particularly prone to conspiratorial thinking.[24] Conspiracies like "the child of Colo Benton and Colo Williams," "sta[l]king abroad our land, with manly strides," represented both unadmitted desires for "*money, office*," and power and feared parental retaliation. The reformer exposed himself to "the most exact scrutiny," as he "unmasked" and "unrobe[d]" intriguers. Contrasting his inner purity to their corruption he left "all concerned on their native Dung Hills." We have encountered themes of exposure and conspiracy before, over land title, and we will return to their climactic Jacksonian expression, the Bank War.

Psychodynamic explanations, it has been charged, divert attention from actual consolidations of power in ante-bellum America. Jackson's specific 1820s targets, however, were badly misplaced. His version of the "corrupt bargain" between Adams and Clay and his attacks on Adams' patronage had no basis in fact.

James Buchanan warned Jackson of an imminent Adams-Clay alliance early in 1825. Buchanan, a Jackson partisan, suggested that Jackson offer the Department of State to Clay. Jackson's memory converted Buchanan's temptation into an approach from Clay. He repeatedly accused Clay of proposing to him the arrangement Clay then made with Adams. Buchanan could not sustain this charge, and it embarrassed Jackson's managers. But Jackson convinced himself that he, unlike Adams, spurned the Presidency to preserve his virtue.[25]

Jackson's charges to the contrary notwithstanding, Adams did not use presidential patronage as an instrument of executive power. He refused to fire officials who opposed his election, and he maintained a separation between politics and the federal civil service. The charges against Adams actually reflected the desires of Jackson supporters for office. Jackson himself would use patronage precisely as he falsely accused Adams of doing.[26]

Jacksonian intrigue did not simply lie in the future. Jackson's managers used the "borrowed plumage" of innocuous figures to make their charges, while remaining "the secret mover[s behind] the curtain." Most important of all, Jackson had already used bribery, secrecy, intrigue, and corruption against the Indian tribes. He was discharging against conspiratorial opponents the crimes of his own past. He was experiencing himself as the victim of his own techniques.

It would be wrong, however, to dismiss Jacksonian reform simply as the rhetoric by which ambitious men disguised their own desires for "*money, office*," and power.[27] Reform rhetoric, unreliable about specific intrigues, offers insight into the qualities of Jacksonian society. The classic liberal thinkers understood that liberating people from traditional bonds did not simply set them free; rather it subjected them to the opinion of society. Men needed the good opinions of others to buy, sell, and advance in the world. Society itself was a tyrant. Seeking advancement, men hid their true motives and manipulated their fellows. They intrigued together in politics to advance factional and personal interests. The Jacksonian picture of secrecy, corruption, and intrigue was not fanciful. Jacksonian innocence was.

Fanciful innocence had real consequences. Jacksonian reform did more than simply replace one set of officeholders by another. It sought a more permanent solution to the anxieties generated by market revolution. Jacksonians sought to replace the old household political order with functionally specific political organizations, and to sanctify the new organizations with the language of family authority.

III

James Monroe was the last President who reached maturity before the Revolution. He was reelected virtually unopposed in 1820; this apparent political harmony obscured the atrophy of national political institutions and the rise of factional strife. The structure of rule at the national level, losing deep roots in the nation, was losing the power to govern. The Virginia dynasty ended with Monroe. Adams, Crawford, and Calhoun, all members of Monroe's Cabinet, squabbled over the presidential succession. John Eaton wrote Jackson, "While he who now fills the halls of the White House is slowly closing his eyes upon the *rich* trifles of the world, like an old father he stands surrounded by three full grown sons, each seeking the inheritance on his departure."[28]

Fears of irreparable factional division dominated the 1824 campaign. A Harrisburg convention supported Jackson with the words, "The union is no longer actuated by one soul, and bound together by one entirety of interest. Local and sectional prejudices are enlisted, and the hostile parties are arraying their forces with increasing animosity." The election ended as it began, in bitterness and recrimination. When the revolutionary hero Lafayette toured the country for thirteen months during and after the campaign, he received an astounding reception everywhere. Lafayette mobilized the nostalgia of a people fearful that factional bitterness and material self-aggrandizement were breaking its ties to the generation of the fathers. Lafayette was Washington's adopted son. He bridged the gap between American generations. He looked, in Jackson's words, "with a parents eye upon the private as well as the public concerns of the people of the United States."[29]

The conflict between family tradition and market society permeated politics and social life in early-nineteenth-century America. New special-purpose organizations undermined the power of traditional local elites or organized outside of them. Leonard Richards has shown, for example, that local elites opposed anti-slavery societies because these appealed over their heads to the mass of citizens, and over the heads of family fathers to women and children. The city fathers feared submergence in a centralized, impersonal, mass society, argues Richards, and they organized anti-abolitionist riots in the 1830s.[30]

School reformers, prison administrators, and defenders of the new insane asylums all believed that a disintegrating family order failed to protect children from worldly temptations. Prison administrators blamed criminal propensities on homes which lacked a father. School reformers believed that "free institutions" "multipl[ied] temptations," unleashing "terrible propensities" which the unaided family could not withstand. Without schooling "in the docile and teachable years of childhood," "insanity" would increase and society would become "suicidal."[31]

Social breakdown, it was widely feared, would come home to roost in insanity. Insanity was a disease specific to progress, thought Americans, and on the increase in the new world. "In America," reported Tocqueville, "suicide is rare but insanity is said to be more common than anywhere else." Writers attributed increasing insanity to the breakdown of paternal authority under marketplace pressures. "In this country," wrote Edward Jarvis, "no son is necessarily confined to the work or employment of his father, but all the fields of labor, of profit, or of honor are open to whomsoever will put on the harness." "All are invited to join the strife. . . . The ambition of some leads them to aim at that which they cannot reach, to strive for more than they can grasp. . . . Their mental powers are strained to their utmost tension; they labor in agitation. . . . Their minds stagger under the disproportionate burden." In stable or despotic societies, "where the child is content with the pursuit and the fortune of his father . . . these undue mental excitements and struggles do not happen. . . . These causes of insanity do not operate." Stable savage societies such as the Indian tribes had, it was said, little insanity.[32]

In a society lacking traditional, hereditary barriers, wrote Tocqueville, men had no one to blame for failure but themselves. Like Jarvis, Tocqueville found insanity to be the price of failure. But Americans also expressed the fear that worldly success, betraying the virtues of the fathers, induced inner breakdown. In the social disorder, political tension, and personal anxiety which initiated the Age of Jackson, were the fathers taking revenge? Jacksonian reform, promising to return America to the ways of the fathers, addressed itself to this anxiety.[33]

Jacksonian reform judged Washington intrigue by the standards of the fathers, and of private family virtue. The family ideal Jackson brought to politics, however, bore a weight of personal grievance and rage. It represented an idealized family, not an actual one, and it directed its destructive impulse against the family order as well as the state. The intermingling of politics and the family corrupted both realms, Jackson believed, and he sought to separate and purify them. Illegitimate family favoritism, such as England had practiced against the revolutionary fathers, was the source of republican decline.

Other reformers in the Jacksonian period also combined nostalgia for the family with analysis of its failures. School reformers, prison administrators, and defenders of the insane asylums usually blamed family weakness under market pressure, rather than old-family resistance to equal rights, for the dangers facing the republic. But, like Jacksonian politicians, social reformers constructed new institutions to carry out functions performed in the eighteenth century by the family. Frances Wright, for example, favored compulsory state schooling in the 1820s. Children should be separated from their parents, lodged in state boardinghouses, and dressed, fed, and treated uniformly. Wright was an open critic of the family; school reform in subsequent decades, under more conservative auspices, drew on her vision. If "parental ability" failed, wrote Horace Mann, it was the duty of "the government to step in and fill the parents' place." Those who constructed and administered other institutions to house dependents—orphanages, insane asylums, prisons—also insisted upon isolating the inmates from family ties. Family visits were prohibited or carefully regulated; inmates were often isolated from each other as well. These institutions housed dependents heretofore cared for within the family; they aimed to protect inmates from the corrupting influence of their natural society.[34]

Jacksonians also created functionally specific institutions—party, executive, and state—to replace the family. Aspects of the new political order, antedating Jacksonian Democracy, were developed by the Albany Regency, the Kentucky Relief Party, and the New York Anti-Masons. Jackson himself, leading the new order, had successfully assaulted the most visible and distinctive family-based social structure in America, that of the Indian tribes. He brought his principles of tribal reform to the Presidency.

Jackson's first target was the federal executive. The officeholding class grew substantially in the first quarter of the nineteenth century; Jackson removed unprecedented numbers. Earlier Presidents also replaced officeholding incumbents, but the Jacksonian call for "rotation in office" expressed new principles of social organization. Family connection, prescriptive right to a job, and the merging of civil-service status with private social status had characterized the federal executive. Jackson proposed, in Lynn Marshall's words, "a rationalized complex of offices ordered by function, and defined by rules and regulations, so as to be free in so far as possible from irregular custom and individual personalities. In this system individuals could be placed or replaced without upsetting the integrity of the whole. Men were fitted to this system, not it to men."[35]

Jackson wanted to "cleans the augean stables" of the corruption left by previous officeholders. Office, he wrote, was not "a species of property" to support "the few at the expense of the many." Joseph Nourse and his family had run the Treasury since Washington's day; Jackson promised to "clear out the Noursery." Family connections bred corruption, Jackson believed.

> Now, every man who has been in office a few years, believes he has a life estate in it, a vested right, and if it has been held twenty years or upwards, not only a vested right, but that it ought to descend to his children, and if no children then next of kin. This is not the principles of our government. It is rotation in office that will perpetuate our liberty.

When a registrar of the Treasury, employed since the Revolution and a defaulter for $10,000, pleaded for his job, Jackson wrote, "I would turn out my own father under the same circumstances."[36]

Rotation in office prevented men from abandoning "self-exertion" for dependence on government. Jackson was distressed at the number of "hungry expectants" who sought office. Disappointed office-seekers, he complained shortly after his inauguration, "are the men who cry out principle, but who are on the scent of Treasury pap. And if I had a *tit* for every one of these *pigs* to suck at, they would still be my friends." Free men should not expect sustenance from a maternal state.[37]

The Jacksonians favored an efficient administration run by "plain, industrious men." Frank Blair's *Washington Globe*, the official administration paper, announced, "Government *is a business*. It should be managed by *men of business*. . . . It is not for *show;* but for *use*." Government should rely on simple rules and regulations, not on human discretion. The first report of Fourth Treasury Auditor Amos Kendall announced, "I want no discretion. I wish to be able to turn to some law or lawful regulation for every allowance I am called upon to make."[38]

The new Jacksonian party organization also split politics from family social status and populated it with anonymous men. A new type of party organization rode to victory with Jackson in 1828. The new organizations, which had flourished for years in New York, burgeoned in several other northern states after 1824 and spread to the west and to portions of the south in the 1830s. These specialized party apparatuses neither derived authority from nor reinforced the preexisting status system. They were run by new political men, typically lawyers, whose power derived from the organization itself rather than from national office or local social standing.

The old national politicians lost control of the presidential nominating process in 1824 and never recovered it. The new party organizations, centralized at the state level, substituted state nominating conventions for congressional and local caucuses.[39]

The new organizations made direct appeals to the electorate; they did not rely simply on the status and local influence of notables. Jackson was the first presidential candidate actually to campaign for office, although his denials that he was doing so reflected the moral hold of the older, genteel pattern. A coordinated national press system published letters from Jackson and his supporters, and continued to circulate campaign literature between elections. Jackson's party managers also coordinated campaign-fund collection. After Jackson's victory, the reorganized federal executive dispensed patronage, strengthening the party organizations. The postal service was the largest single source of jobs, but other departments, like the Indian Bureau and the Land Office, also rewarded supporters and built local parties.[40]

Anonymous men inhabited the seats of power in Washington itself. Jackson relied for advice on a "Kitchen Cabinet" of his friends. These men held no elective and usually no important appointive office, often came from obscure social backgrounds, and were hidden from public view. They owed their positions to their personal ties to the President rather than to their own independent authority. Most were not Cabinet members. The Kitchen Cabinet merged the new party structure at the center with the reorganized executive branch. Amos Kendall, called by the opposition "chief cook and scullion" of the Kitchen Cabinet, organized the new national party. He was also—like the party manager, Van Buren—one of Jackson's chief policy advisers.[41]

Party organization and executive reform did not make so thoroughgoing a sweep of family influence as Jacksonian rhetoric claimed. Family relationships were as common at the top of the executive branch as they had been in Jefferson's administration. In parts of the west and south, older factional politics, often centering on frontier nabobs and family connections, persisted through the 1830s. Jackson's friends the Gwin brothers, who had moved south from Tennessee, dominated Mississippi Democratic patronage politics. "The nucleus," a tight-knit group of Jackson cronies like Richard Call, ran Florida territorial politics in the beginning; Call controlled "the land office tit." Arkansas party patronage rewarded "Sevier's hungry kinfolk."[42]

Personal ambition and desires for family preferment also permeated the new political structures. Personal ambition acted, however, in the changed political context of specialized political structures, increased power for men lacking old-family social credentials, and allegiance to durable party organizations rather than shifting personal factions.

Party allegiance also reached more deeply than before into the mass electorate. The new electoral machinery was designed to mobilize this electorate. Few Americans voted in 1824, and there was a dramatic increase in participation in 1828. Turnout continued to rise in the 1830s as a competitive two-party politics spread to most states. Durable mass allegiance to one of the two major parties characterized the Jacksonian party system through the 1840s. Jacksonian Whig rivalry created a mass, competitive, stable, two-party politics.[43]

Jacksonianism was not democratic in any simple sense. Jacksonians and their opponents insisted that the common man had triumphed in 1828, in "the great contest between the *aristocracy* and democracy of America." Kentucky politician William T. Barry, Postmaster General in the new Cabinet, explained, "Contending as we are against wealth and power, we look for success in numbers." Adams' supporters bewailed "the howl of raving Democracy" and "the infuriate mob." Voting studies fail to confirm this picture. Turnout was low in 1824, in spite of Jackson's candidacy. The increase in 1828 did not reach the heights in most states of votes for governor a generation earlier; and it did not benefit Jackson at the expense of Adams. Instead voters for both candidates turned out in states where the outcome was in doubt. The division of the vote for and against Jackson in his three presidential races was sectional rather than class. Jackson was strong in the south, and gained increasing strength in the west. He received frontier support in some areas, but elsewhere his opponents the Anti-Masons flourished on the frontier. There were issue differences between Jacksonians and their opponents in the 1820s and early 1830s, but these were more the product of narrow ethnic and economic loyalties than of mass popular uprising.[44]

Jacksonianism was initially democratic only in a special sense. "Aristocracy" meant in American political parlance a governing elite sustained by social position, old-family connection, and political privilege. When the Albany Regency insisted, "The Aristocracy and Democracy of the Country are arrayed against each other," it was making a claim not for popular rule, but for a new kind of political leadership, "democratic" in its absence of pre-political family status. The very wealthiest old northern mercantile families opposed Jackson, and even in the south he may have received his smallest percentage of support among old-family coastal planters; certainly he was not their first choice. Those holding top administrative positions under Jackson were not common men. But they were less likely than Adams and Jefferson administrators to come from families at the very top of the social order. They had improved their own status over their fathers', and now sought political power. Even Jackson's frontier strength initially derived from the ambition for power of frontier elites, and not from a mass democratic uprising against local leaders. State factional politics, western-elite support for Indian removal, and the high status of Jackson's territorial appointees all suggest that Jackson's support came from frontier leaders like himself, hungry for national power and able to organize the mass of frontier voters.[45]

Jacksonian party organizations did receive a distinctively popular vote in some areas. New York's Tammany was opposed in the wealthiest wards and supported in the poorest ones, so long as no Workingmen's ticket ran against it. But if Tammany mobilized the support of the common man, it did not relinquish control to him. The masses also failed to control the new, local party conventions. These well-organized arrangements to generate party loyalty were, as one Jacksonian put it, "bouts to show in what channel the [public] feeling . . . [should] be steered." State conventions of the people, Jackson explained, would select candidates committed to administration principles. They would prevent "coalitions between distinguished individuals" from dividing "the party which has sustained the administration."[46]

Perhaps some Jacksonian party organizations distinctively mobilized the common man; we lack the comprehensive voting studies with which to make a definitive judgment. But, whatever the electoral realities, popular appeals performed crucial ideological functions in the Jacksonian system. They supplied Jacksonians both with organizational devices for political control and with the self-confidence to govern. The breakdown of eighteenth-century order created a malaise in Washington, and cut national representatives off from sources of local legitimacy. New political organizations lacked legitimacy in a pre-existing social order. Given the suspicion with which power and ambition were viewed in republican America, the new organizations could not simply proclaim their desire for power. Instead they legitimized themselves as expressions of the popular will. They diverted attention from their own organizations, brought new energy to politics, and supplied a new governing class.[47] The "hard cider" Whig campaign of 1840 is commonly said to have perverted an authentically democratic Jacksonian impulse. But democratic Jacksonian rhetoric also disguised the realities of power. Jackson gave that rhetoric its most significant formulation.

Jackson identified himself in 1816 with the poor Indians against their existing tribal structures. He aimed to break down the authority of the tribal chiefs so that the Indians would cede their land. Three years later Jackson brought that political understanding back home. Denouncing efforts by the Tennessee legislature to provide debtor relief from the 1819 panic, he insisted, "The people are unanimous I am told . . . and are all alive upon the subject." Jackson denounced the doctrine that the legislature embodied the people. The legislature could be defeated, he wrote, if "the voice of the people . . . could be obtained."[48] Jackson's visions of popular support against the legislature were imaginary, but they took a form significant for the development of Jacksonian Democracy and the future of American politics.

Local notables and existing officeholders, Jackson insisted, did not represent the people; the hero opposing the existing structure did. Jackson had no power in Tennessee to implement this claim. Against Indians and as President he did. His internal-improvements and Bank vetoes, his nullification proclamation, and his removal of government deposits from the U.S. Bank all asserted unprecedented executive prerogatives and a new theory of political representation. The legislature represented elite interests; the executive embodied the popular will. This doctrine infused life into the nascently bureaucratic federal executive, the informal group of presidential advisers, and the specialized party apparatus. Jackson was the first modern President.[49]

Jackson's glorification of executive power underlines the distance he had traveled, in the name of the revolutionary fathers, from their vision. Blaming corruption on traditional family-political ties, Jacksonian reform favored impersonal bureaucratic institutions presided over by a strong executive. The revolutionaries opposed executive usurpation. After the Bank veto the factions opposed to Jackson united in a new Whig Party against executive tyranny. The Whigs feared that Jackson endangered a locally based, socially secure political leadership. They feared a democratic despotism based on newly created dependencies, not on traditional ones. The Whigs defended the interests of men of character, breeding, and position against domination by the new political machine. They attacked Jackson's circumvention of the legislature, and his doctrine that the executive uniquely represented the people. "The Presidential power swallows up all power," Virginia Senator John Tyler, an early Jackson supporter, complained. Mississippi Senator George Poindexter, refusing to become "a mere machine to be worked by the impetus of Executive power," also broke with Jackson. The *National Intelligencer* accused Jackson of "downright Tory doctrines" soon after the Bank veto, and the first cartoon of King Andrew appeared.[50]

Jackson did privately imagine himself in an imperial role. He scrawled "Et tu Brute" on the margin of a letter exposing Calhoun's secret opposition to his Florida invasion. "Let the Tennessee Brutus come," he wrote when his old friend Hugh Lawson White ran against Van Buren for President. American republicans normally compared themselves to Brutus, not Caesar.[51] Jackson did not answer charges of executive usurpation by proclaiming himself emperor, however. He combined his popular rhetoric with a paternal, presidential stance. He infused the new political institutions with republican, household symbolism.

I V

Jackson came to Washington old, sick, and melancholic in 1829. Few expected him to survive his first term, much less seek a second. His "separation" from Rachel in the quest for office, Jackson had written in 1823, "oppressed my mind very much." Now Rachel's death, immediately after his own victory, drove Jackson to despair. "My time cannot be long upon earth," he wrote one of Rachel's brothers. He yearned to "withdraw from the scenes that surround me to the private walks of the Hermitage, . . . there to spend my [last] days . . . at the tomb of my Dr wife." Rachel's death reinforced Jackson's nostalgia. He lived with his memories in the early White House years, and had little taste for public business.[52]

Jackson immersed himself, instead, in the personal affairs of his Secretary of War. John Eaton was one of Jackson's oldest friends; Jackson once called him "more than a son." Eaton was co-author of Jackson's first biography, and fought a duel with a member of the Erwin clan in defense of Rachel's honor. Jackson wanted Eaton in his Cabinet partly to superintend Indian removal and partly to have, in alien Washington, an old confidant close to him.[53]

Eaton's first wife, the daughter of a wealthy Cumberland planter, was the sister-in-law of W. B. Lewis. After his wife died, Eaton began a long alliance with Margaret O'Neale Timberlake. Her father owned a Washington inn where Eaton and other politicians regularly boarded; Jackson himself had stayed there in 1823. Mrs. Timberlake was married to a navy purser, for whom Eaton secured a commission. Thanks to his first marriage, Eaton had the means to befriend husband and father financially. Timberlake spent most of his time at sea.[54]

When Timberlake died in 1828, Eaton showed some reluctance to marry the widow. Jackson insisted on a quick wedding, naïvely believing it would save Mrs. Timberlake's reputation. As one Washington society lady described the scene, "Tonight the bosom friend and almost adopted son of Genl. Jackson is to be married to a lady whose reputation, her previous connection with him both before and after her husband's death, has totally destroyed."[55]

The President, the Vice President, and the members of the Cabinet traditionally gave large formal dinners; social life in Washington revolved around them. But Vice President Calhoun's wife and the wives of three Cabinet members refused social intercourse with Mrs. Eaton. This feud soon infected the struggle between Calhoun and Secretary of State Van

Buren for the presidential succession. The widower Van Buren befriended Margaret Eaton, and won Jackson's friendship. But the members of Jackson's own household resented her. Jackson had brought his nephew and ward Andrew Jackson Donelson to Washington. Donelson's wife (first cousin to her husband) and Mary Eastin, another of Rachel's nieces, also lived at the White House. Donelson was Jackson's private secretary; his wife acted as official hostess. The Donelsons and Mary Eastin sided against the Eatons.[56]

Rachel Jackson, like Margaret Eaton, had been twice married, and had also suffered attacks on her virtue. These attacks sent her to her grave just days before the Eaton wedding; no wonder Jackson identified Margaret Eaton with his own dead wife. He reproached Mary Eastin for her part in "this unholy and wicked and unjust conspiracy against female character, by which I was to be reached, and the memory of my D'r wife, who ought to have been dear to all her connections, indirectly or directly assailed." As charges against Margaret Eaton grew, Jackson collected affidavits to prove her innocence. "She is chaste as a virgin," he insisted at the Cabinet meeting he called to vindicate her reputation.[57]

The Eaton affair obsessed Jackson for most of his first presidential term. Jacksonian reform pitted family virtue against political intrigue, and the attacks on Rachel brought political intrigue murderously home. Margaret Eaton's enemies contaminated Rachel's memory, endangered Jackson's authority over his family, and tried to make him "abandon all my old friends." Jackson came to Washington, he explained, "surrounded . . . with deception, and treachery, with the exception of my old friends." Now Calhoun's partisans attacked the old man's friendship with Eaton and Lewis. They won his own ward away from him. Jackson complained, "My domestic concerns have harried my feelings more than any other event of my life. My family were overreached by the hidden intrigues of the great magician [Calhoun]. . . ."[58]

Jackson stood by "my best friend," Eaton. "I would sooner *abandon life*," he said. When Emily Donelson and Mary Eastin refused to return Mrs. Eaton's visits, Jackson sent them back to Nashville. Andrew Jackson Donelson followed. Lewis moved his family into the White House so his daughter could act as official hostess; actually Margaret Eaton played that role.[59]

Jackson insisted, in long, plaintive letters to Donelson and other members of his clan, that he could not give up "the controle of my household." "A house divided cannot stand," he wrote. He accused Donelson of betraying the filial relationship. Jackson could not imagine himself, he wrote his ward, deserting "the willing father and protector of me, and my family, in my riper years, under the falacies practised by that deceiptful intriguer, surrounded by his judases—such as Daniel of K.y. and Co., working their female Gossips by the wires of intrigue to the destruction of my father." (The reference to Daniel, often repeated, was to a brother of Donelson's, son-in-law of a Calhoun partisan in Jackson's Cabinet.)[60]

Richard Call was another young man toward whom Jackson and Rachel had acted as parents. Jackson had encouraged Call to marry against the wishes of the bride's family—"savages" Jackson called them—who were old enemies of his. When Call's father-in-law died, Jackson had told Call to file suit against his mother-in-law for a share of the inheritance. Now the Eaton affair badly damaged his own paternal relationship to Call. Call had boarded at O'Neale's in 1823 with Jackson and Eaton. Margaret's reputation for "easy virtue" had encouraged him to embrace her, but she had immediately rebuffed him. Now Call sided against the Eatons. His charges provoked Jackson's wrath.[61]

The Eaton affair threatened Jackson's paternal authority not only over his family but over his Cabinet as well. He wrote Donelson that "unity of feeling, action and harmony should exist between my family, and real friends, as well, as with my Cabinet, to enable me to counteract the deep laid plans in congress by the combination to destroy the usefullness, and credit of my administrations." He told his ward, as Donelson recorded it, "that forty members of Congress during the past winter, understanding that the female part of his family and the ladies of the cabinet officers did not associate with Mrs. Eaton, had asked him if Genl Jackson was at the head of the Government. . . . he would shew the world that Genl Jackson was at the head of Government." A plot was afoot, Jackson said he had been told, to defeat the administration in the next presidential election. "Pennsylvania '*who calls mr Calhoun* her favorite son' this son is to bring her over, and another of her sons, in my cabinet (says the conversation) is to aid in this holy work." Jackson demanded that the wives of his Cabinet officials return Mrs. Eaton's visits, and that the Cabinet officers take an oath of loyalty to her virtue. He wrote Coffee, "My cabinet must become a unit again." "All the influence of Calhoun and his secrete workers, that has defeated all my recommendations to congress (except the Indian bill), will be destroyed by union in my family, and Cabinet."[62]

Controversy over Jackson's 1818 Florida invasion deepened the split with Calhoun. Calhoun, Monroe's Secretary of War at the time, privately condemned the invasion. He permitted Jackson to believe otherwise, however; even when rumors of Calhoun's actual position reached Jackson in 1827, neither man wanted to disturb their useful political alliance. During the Eaton affair Jackson obtained definite evidence of Calhoun's original position. He added this perfidy to the Cabinet conspiracy. Jackson saw Calhoun's hand in every administration setback. He imagined Calhoun's Cabinet partisans were using their departments against him. "Calhoun and his puppits, male and female, have been secretly at work to destroy me," he wrote a cousin.[63]

In the spring of 1831, amid duel challenges and brawl threats, Van Buren engineered the resignation of five of the six members of Jackson's Cabinet. Since Cabinet members had heretofore enjoyed independent bases of authority, Jackson's ability to fire them demonstrated unprecedented presidential power. The new Cabinet members had greater status independent of politics than the old ones; they temporarily reduced Jackson's ability to act independently, particularly in the developing Bank War. Moreover, Jackson's mournfully intense family involvement continued for some months after the Cabinet resignations. Nevertheless, the Cabinet reorganization ultimately reinvigorated Jackson and strengthened his power. Harmony reestablished, the Donelsons returned to Washington. The Eatons went back to Tennessee, where Eaton failed to unseat Jacksonian loyalist Felix Grundy in a Senate battle. Jackson mildly supported Eaton, but their intense involvement had ended. Eaton secretly opposed Van Buren in 1836; when he supported Harrison in 1840, Jackson called him "the most degraded of all apostates fed, clothed, and cherished by the administration." Lewis went to live elsewhere after the Donelsons returned to the White House, and his influence over Jackson decreased. In self-pitying letters after Jackson's retirement, Lewis accused him of abandoning old friends for new, "though no son was ever more ardently attached to his father than I was to you." Hugh Lawson White refused Jackson's plea that he needed an old friend as Secretary of War to replace Eaton; White entered the presidential race against Van Buren a few years later.[64]

Two of Jackson's oldest Tennessee friends, John Coffee and John Overton, died within a few months of each other in 1833. Jackson mourned for Overton "with the feelings of David for Absalam," and for Coffee "with the feelings of David for his son Jonathan." He had in memory converted old friends from the extended family network into his children. (Overton, H. L. White's brother-in-law, was just Jackson's age.) The claimed paternity was peculiar besides; Absalom, not Jonathan, was David's son, and David had him murdered. Jackson was, in spite of his protestations, abandoning the old Tennessee clan world.[65]

New political associates, not old friends, replaced Eaton, Lewis, and Overton. Amos Kendall, Frank Blair, and Roger Taney gained importance during and after the Eaton affair. All became Jackson intimates, and Blair developed an explicitly filial relationship with the old man. By the end of 1831 Jackson's spirits had risen. Early in 1832 a doctor extracted the bullet lodged in Jackson's shoulder since the Benton brawl, and his health markedly improved. Jackson emerged from the Eaton affair less buried in mournful personal history than at any time since Rachel's death.[66]

The Eaton affair challenged Jackson's personal and political fatherhood. Victorious, Jackson did not simply demonstrate paternal authority; he established it on a new basis. Jackson purged himself of extended family loyalties, tied to the memory of his dead wife, during the Eaton affair. He was moving from traditional family ties to principle. He identified himself, in the nullification crisis and the Bank War, with the revolutionary fathers. Like Washington, said John Van Buren, "Providence denied him children, that he might be the father of his country." Jackson's only blood relatives, said Martin Van Buren, were the people, and Jackson was now to claim paternity over them all.[67]

V

The nullification crisis, totally intermingled with the Eaton affair, turned Jackson from private grievance to public order. Jackson identified the personal assaults on his authority with Calhoun's "nullification doctrine."[68] This reflected the political substance of nullification, as well as Calhoun's support among Margaret Eaton's enemies. Jackson's new nationalism received its first formulation in the struggle with South Carolina.

Eaton and Van Buren managed Jackson's 1828 campaign from their positions in the Senate. Maneuvering to gain northern support for Jackson, they provided the margin of victory for the 1828 tariff. South Carolina still hoped for Jackson's sympathy, however, not only in its efforts to repeal the tariff, but also in its claim that it could overrule federal law. Jackson had premised his Indian-removal bill on unprecedented assertions of state sovereignty over the Indian tribes. He rejected the Supreme Court decision denying Georgia authority over the Cherokee nation. If Georgia could "nullify" a Supreme Court decision with Jackson's support, thought South Carolina, it could nullify the tariff.[69]

South Carolina badly misunderstood Jackson's development, however. Jackson asserted states-rights doctrine for forty years in the service of an aggressive Indian policy. But the 1812 War transformed him from a parochial to a national expansionist. He used states rights thereafter as a weapon against the tribes, not against federal power. Just as he supported states rights against local tribes, so he supported federal rights against local states. "Indisposed by cold," complained the President, he was "surrounded with the nullifiers of the south, and the Indians in the south, and west."[70] Jackson stood for centralization and control against local, parochial loyalties.

South Carolina, in language reminiscent of the young Jackson, called nullification a second American revolution. Jackson's nullification proclamation responded,

They are not champions of liberty, emulating the fame of our revolutionary fathers, nor are you an oppressed people, contending, as they repeat to you, against worse than colonial vassalage. You are free members of a flourishing and happy Union. There is no settled design to oppress you.[71]

"Perpetuity is stamped upon the constitution by the blood of our fathers," Jackson told South Carolina; the fathers bequeathed union, not rebellion, to the sons. South Carolina raised soldiers to defy federal authority; this, wrote Jackson, "is such a crisis as the Sages who formed the constitution anticipated and intended to prohibit." He promised "to renew the pledge our heroic fathers made." "Nullification, rebellion, and secession, twinn brothers of eachother," said Jackson, threatened "civil war." "We must be prepared to act with promptness, and crush the monster in its cradle before it matures to manhood." "If, in madness or delusion, any one shall lift his paracidal hand against this blessed union," wrote Jackson in his draft of the second inaugural, "the curse of millions will fall upon their head."[72]

Jackson asserted paternal authority in the nullification crises against the "paracidal" "madness" of "civil war." His was no purely private dream. Massachusetts conservative Rufus Choate, fearing that nullification threatened disunion, urged attention to revolutionary and pre-revolutionary American history.

Reminded of our fathers, we should remember that we are brethren. The exclusiveness of State pride, the narrow selfishness of a mere local policy, and the small jealousies of vulgar minds, would be merged in an expanded, comprehensive, constitutional sentiment of old, family, fraternal regard.[73]

Choate called upon organic ties connecting actual fathers and sons; Jackson could not do so. He offered instead the new nationalism of a personal, paternal President. In his draft for the nullification proclamation he told the South Carolinians, "Seduced as you have been my fellow Countrymen by the delusive theories and misrepresentation of ambitious, deluded and designing men, I call upon you, in the language of truth and with the feelings of a father to retrace your steps."[74] South Carolina did retrace its steps. Jackson compromised on the tariff, but he insisted on the national sovereignty of the Union. Nullification established Jackson's right to the mantle of the fathers.[75]

Jackson's great presidential triumphs, over South Carolina and over the U.S. Bank, revenged him against the cities which humiliated him in his youth. Charleston and Philadelphia (home of the Bank) were the first cities young Jackson visited. He lost his inheritance in Charleston in 1781, after his mother died. He lost his fortune in Philadelphia, fourteen years later, on the Allison speculation.

Jackson threatened "Civil warr" against Washington in his youth, raged at Jefferson's timidity, and flirted with Aaron Burr. In the closing years of his Presidency, he symbolically reversed all these identifications. He supported "the Republican land marks, set up by Mr. Jefferson." Jefferson, he wrote, never sacrificed "principle and the republican fold, for the sake of office. I would abandon my only adopted son if he would permit himself to be placed in this attitude." Hugh L. White, opposing Van Buren "for the sake of office," "must fall as Burr did." Leaving the Presidency, Jackson recalled "the paternal counsels" of "the Father of his country in his Farewell Address." He warned his countrymen, in his own Farewell Address, against sectional jealousy, speculative enterprise, and factional strife. He urged them to remember the "fraternal attachment which the citizens of the several States bear to one another as members of one political family."[76]

VI

Jackson called upon the fathers to sanctify a political family far from the eighteenth-century household order. Social functions and extended family ties integrated the actual family into colonial society. Birth and breeding, convention, economic role, political action, and cultural ties connected the family to the political order; political power derived from family power. Jackson purified family influence of contaminated actual-kinship bonds; he substituted a constructed family. He took as his model the new "natural ties" (Tocqueville) of the conjugal family. The natural family, denied supporting "social ties," bound its members together by feeling instead of function.[77] Jackson infused politics with a family symbolism which derived from a patriarchal version of the conjugal family rather than from the extended household.

Social reformers in the Age of Jackson constructed new impersonal institutions, legitimized by the family, to replace the household order. An advocate of the new mental hospitals wrote, "The internal arrangements of the Asylum are nearly the same as those of a well-regulated family." The New York Juvenile Asylum claimed, "The government of the Institution has been strictly parental. The prominent object has been to give a home feeling and home interest to the children—to create and cultivate a family feeling . . . to clothe the Institution as far as possible with those hallowed associations which usually cluster about home." But the asylums, David Rothman has shown, were more like armies than families. They classified their inmates, dressed them in uniforms, drilled them, regimented their behavior, and strictly arranged and regulated their time.[78]

The asylums, suggests Rothman, resembled the new factories. And the factories also claimed to act as family surrogates. Textile-mill owners promised the benefits of paternal supervision to the young girls who left their farm families to live and work under closely regimented supervision in the New England mill towns. Like those who promoted asylums, mill-owners appealed to family to legitimize new bureaucratic forms of control.[79]

The Jacksonian era also witnessed the first extended efforts to defend slavery on paternal grounds. Southerners stressed the master's concern for his slave "family." The colonists distinguished children from slaves, and attacked English efforts to reduce them from one to the other. Now slave-owners proclaimed their concern for their slave "children." In the words of one southerner, "Ours is a patriarchal institution now, founded on pity and protection on the one side, and dependence and gratitude on the other." "I have lost three of my family," Jackson wrote his son, fearing bad treatment of his slaves by his white overseer. Market pressures and cotton production were transforming the more lax eighteenth-century tobacco plantation. The new patriarchal ideology, paralleling growth of the factory system, disguised intensification of coercive plantation social control.[80]

The family image in asylum, factory, and plantation suggested patriarchy; it did not describe a complexly related, fraternal extended family. The new paternalism disguised exploitation; it did not grow from actual family relations. The plantations were a military form of agriculture,[81] and the regimented asylums also resembled armies. Indeed, Jackson, anticipating the spokesmen for plantation, asylum, and factory, offered the army itself as the model for the new family. Actual families, Jackson's Creek War rhetoric indicated, created problems of dependence, temptation, and feminine power. The army separated sons from their natural families and subjected them to military paternal discipline. Assaulting Indian clan ties, Jackson also turned Indians into children, dependent on an omnipotent father. Jackson faced problems of personal temptation and social control at the beginning of the nineteenth century; his solutions set precedents for the institution-builders and apologists of his age.

The later reformers, although surely familiar with Indian paternalism, may have known little of Jackson's army experience. But they shared his fear of disorder, his nostalgia for the fathers, and his search for new forms of social control. Jackson's Indian relations initiated the terms in which Jacksonian society faced the decline of the family.

It was one thing to enforce patriarchy on Indians, soldiers, criminals, delinquents, and the insane. What would paternal authority mean among free white men? Like the conjugal family, the paternal Jacksonian state existed in an ideal realm. Insulated from social corruption, it unified society and symbolized virtue. This posture required that it play no positive role in social development. Free men had to care for themselves, or else they were nothing but children. "A pure government" (Jackson) had to let society be.

Whigs favored "paternal" government programs. Such "partial legislation," the Jacksonians responded, benefited "*spoiled children* in the republican family." William Leggett explained,

> Our own government, most especially, has assumed and exercised an authority over the people not unlike that of weak and vacillating parents over their children with about the same degree of impartiality. One child becomes a favorite because he has made a fortune and another because he has failed in pursuit of that object; one because of its beauty and another because of its deformity.[82]

"The world is too much governed," was the motto of Blair's *Washington Globe*. "Myriads of lilliputian fetters of artificial government and prescription," declared the *Democratic Review*'s statement of principles, "chained [human society] down to the ground." "Understood as a central consolidated power, managing and directing the various interests of society, all government is evil and the parent of evil. . . . The best government is that which governs least." Government, said Jackson, should neither abolish "natural" social inequalities "of talents, of education, or of wealth," nor add "artificial distinctions" to them. "If it would confine itself to equal protection, and as Heaven does its rains, shower its favors alike on the high and the low, the rich and the poor, it would be an unqualified blessing."[83]

Jackson took the contrast between natural and artificial distinctions from revolutionary thought. But the fathers had a less limited view of state functions. They did not condemn every positive intervention as corrupt and capricious. They imagined a community, united under the leading families, acting for the common good. Transformation of the household order undermined that vision. The fragmentation of interests as the market extended its sway made it difficult to formulate comprehensive policy that did not favor one group at the expense of others. The classic nationalists— Adams, Calhoun, Webster—either lost power or became narrow spokesmen for sectional interest. Positive state action set factions against each other; abstract nationalism, the Jacksonians believed, could unite them. Acquisitive market society, moreover, seemed more corrupt than the eighteenth-century order. Unless totally separated, state and society would contaminate each other. Only a pure state, far from the real social world, could act as unifying symbol. The Jacksonian state raised itself above private interests—the activities of Jackson's youth—to avoid contamination by them.[84]

Such a state was a dream; it bore little resemblance to the actual states in Jacksonian society. The pure state did not stop society from carrying out its business; it did not restrain speculation, control inequality, or regulate growth. The pure state lived in symbiosis with acquisitive social realities.

Government in the Age of Jackson was a battleground for private interests. Jackson early favored distribution of excess federal revenues to the states, for example. Presumably, state governments would use the money for internal improvements. But the national state would not sponsor, as John Quincy Adams had hoped, an integrated program of local improvements. Conflicting interests—including Van Buren's New York, which had completed the Erie Canal at its own expense and did not want federal money spent on competing projects—prohibited a comprehensive program. Instead states and townships fought for federal money and raised their own. Jackson attacked the "log rolling system of Internal Improvements." But federal internal-improvement expenditures doubled in Jackson's first term over what Congress appropriated under Adams. State and local governments, Whig and Jacksonian alike, spent immense sums on canals, roads, bridges, harbors, and railroads. They issued charters, conferred "artificial distinctions," and aided some men in the struggle for wealth. Jacksonian nationalism provided an umbrella under which local interests—partly bargaining at the national level, more importantly acting at the local level—used politics to advance their interests. The virtuous President presided over an acquisitive, competitive society.[85]

The *laissez-faire* Jacksonian state denied directing power to itself; it also denied self-generated, active, collective power to the people. Army, factory, plantation, and asylum subjected their inmates to patriarchal despotism; the Jacksonian state left free white men alone. It represented autocratic tendencies nonetheless, against local, participatory, "free institutions."

An egalitarian society, Tocqueville believed, destroyed the links which bound citizens together. Men lacked the traditional social supports to stand against public opinion. Each man, the equal of any other, was dwarfed by the mass. Alone in the crowd, men turned for support to a central, directing power. Political passivity, wrote Tocqueville, was a real danger in such a society. Americans combated the dangers of despotism with "free institutions"—press, civic and political associations, juries, town meetings. But Tocqueville, sharing the founders' identification of majority tyranny with legislative power, failed to see that a strong executive could also undermine free institutions.[86] Jackson's political vision illustrated that possibility.

Jackson insisted that men act alone for themselves in the private realm; he minimized their power to act together in public. His Farewell Address criticized a strong national government and urged Americans to "steady and perservering exertions" to protect their "free institutions"; superficially, Jackson's warnings resembled Tocqueville's. But the paternal address had another current as well. Jackson identified group privilege and partial association as the dangers to freedom. Speculators and stock jobbers formed factions, he warned. But "the agricultural, the mechanical, and the laboring classes . . . are incapable of forming extensive combinations to act together with united force." They lacked the means of communication, the "patronage," and the "crowds of dependents." Their influence on government was never secure. "The selfish, interested classes," Jackson wrote in an earlier letter, always threatened to "act together against the unsuspecting undisciplined classes of the community."[87]

Karl Marx would shortly make the same analysis. Farmers, he wrote in *The Eighteenth Brumaire*, were too isolated by their conditions of work to act collectively. They had

> no community, no national bond, and no political organization. . . . They are consequently incapable of enforcing their class interests in their own name. . . . They cannot represent themselves, they must be represented. Their representative must at the same time appear as their master, as an authority over them, as an unlimited governmental power that protects them against the other classes and sends them rain and sunshine from above.[88]

Marx described Louis Napoleon. Jackson, admirer of the first Napoleon, and head of a government which, "as Heaven does its rain, shower[ed] its favors alike on the high and the low," offered himself. Jackson defended the "undisciplined classes of the community," he wrote, and they favored him with "their affectionate and grateful enthusiasm." Farmers and mechanics formed "the great body of the people of the United States; they are the bone and sinew of the country." Jackson was the animating will.[89]

Marx may have been right about European farmers. Jackson, however, counterposed himself not only to Tocqueville's free institutions, but also to a tradition of independent agrarian protest. He stood, symbolically, against the Shays and Whiskey rebellions. His Napoleonic agrarianism contrasts with the Granger, Greenback, and Populist movements which succeeded him. Jackson was suspicious of the artificial links which brought men together. Invalidating the capacities of the popular ego, he perceived a barren landscape where repressive superego warred with chaotic id.

The atrophy of free institutions, Tocqueville feared, would generate "an immense and tutelary power." "It would be like the authority of a parent if, like that authority, its object were to prepare men for manhood; but it seeks on the contrary to keep them in perpetual childhood." The "fraternal attachment" on which Jackson called was passive; fearing the politics of brothers acting together, he insisted on paternal authority. Jackson praised the people while creating a surrogate to act in their name. He developed from discipline of his body, his feelings, his youthful soldiers, and his Indian enemies in the Creek War the claim to represent the "undisciplined classes of the community."[90]

Jackson acquired authority for himself. He helped build and sanctify the national political institutions which carried the north through Civil War. He introduced into American politics the symbiosis between mass-based presidential state power and a mass of politically inert citizens. He set precedents for assertions of strong, paternal presidential power in the twentieth century.[91] Jackson's negative, *laissez-faire*, paternal state made the logical marriage of paternal authority to liberal egalitarianism. But egalitarian social relations, while they could produce passivity before large institutions, undermined thoroughgoing filial loyalty. Jacksonian paternalism failed to attach men to new institutions with powerful emotional bonds. It failed to relieve them of the punitive feelings engendered by competitive individualism. Liberalism most successfully infused the state with the authority to destroy. Obstacles to market freedom, at home and in the west, placed the Bank War, Texas, and Manifest Destiny at the center of the Jacksonian agenda.

CHAPTER 9

THE MOTHER BANK

Surprise is confessed at every hand at the duration of the war in Florida. . . . The unsuspicious settlers are broken in upon—the cradled infant is torn from its repose—its little neck is writhed by savage hands, or its brain scattered abroad in fragments. . . .

Has the bird of heaven lost the lighting of his eye, or the strength of his talons, that a loathsome reptile should creep to his nest and devour his offspring, even beneath the shadow of his broad wing? . . .

It was not always thus; some sad change has come over us—the atmosphere is infected—it is unfit for respiration—and patriotism gasps for existence. What is this pestilence—this malaria? It is luxury and the love of gain. . . .

The paper system, paralyzing the heart and limbs of the body-politic, has given rise to . . . the sad effects we have so long deplored. But a glorious light is breaking in upon us. . . . The Government will have soon disengaged itself from the paper system; the political atmosphere is returning to its native purity, and patriotism will once more breathe freely. Gulliver has nearly succeeded in breaking the threads by which the Lilliputians have bound him to the earth. Samson is disengaging himself from the embraces of Delilah, and rising in his strength.

—*Senator Robert Strange of North Carolina, January 10, 1840*

Jackson achieved paternal authority in the Creek War. In the Eaton affair and the nullification crisis he successfully claimed it on a national basis. But his authority failed to inhibit the speculative, acquisitive tendencies in American society. Jackson imagined himself, in the Bank War, reaching the source of American corruption. Jacksonian Democracy began with soldier and Indian children; it culminated in the war on "the mother bank." The Bank War dominated Jackson's second term, climaxed his administration, and set the course of American party politics for a decade.

A logic of the psyche led from children to mothers, from debt to the Bank, from Indian removal to removal of the federal deposits. The very power of the Bank made it a fearsome target, however. It was one thing to assault Indians; no powerful links integrated them into the dominant social structure. The Bank stood at the apex of that structure. The U.S. Bank was the most powerful institution in America. Chartered by the federal government but privately controlled, the Bank acted as depository for federal funds. The government was the largest receiver and disperser of money; the Bank gained from federal specie a central, directing financial power. It controlled branch banks throughout the country. It influenced the behavior of state-chartered banks by the conditions it set for the reception of their notes.[1]

Nicholas Biddle, president of the Bank, scoffed at Jackson's evolution. "The worthy President," said Biddle, "thinks because he has scalped Indians and imprisoned Judges he is to have his way with the Bank." Jackson himself once put on Black Hawk's headdress before meeting a pro-Bank delegation. "I don't think those fellows would like to see me in this," he joked. Frank Blair reminded readers of the *Washington Globe*,

> When the Creek Indians, in the late war, began to murder the women and children on our frontiers, Genl. Jackson said VETO! *and the murders ceased*. . . . When the company of British Lords and government gentlemen [and American aristocrats] . . . asked the government to make them a present of some ten millions of dollars . . . Genl. Jackson said VETO!—and our liberties and institutions are still safe.[2]

Blair was right about Jackson's power, Biddle was wrong, but the destruction of the Bank could not reverse the process begun with the destruction of the Indians. The market revolution depended upon westward expansion. A different Indian policy might have altered or restrained American development; control over money and credit could not. Jackson had destroyed Indians and he could, Biddle notwithstanding, "have his way with the Bank." He could not end "the credit system" and the transformation of American society.

I

Congress chartered the Second Bank of the United States in 1816, to meet the financial problems exposed by the 1812 War. The Bank, however, intensified economic instability in its first years. Speculation in Bank stock, an easy-credit policy, and management incompetence and dishonesty contributed to the post-war speculative boom. The Bank's belated demand for specie triggered the panic of 1819. But the Bank did not cause the panic by itself. American commodity agriculture prices fell precipitously after the return of peace to Europe. The speculative land boom, strongest in the southwestern territory Jackson had conquered, also collapsed. Many state-chartered banks, unable to meet the demand for specie from the U.S. Bank or to collect land and agricultural debts, folded. The paper of others deteriorated badly. Creditors refused devalued paper, and debtors could not pay their debts.[3]

The panic hit western areas just entering the market—Ohio, Kentucky, Tennessee, and the new southwest—with particular severity. Here the debt structure financed the expansion of frontier cash-crop agriculture. Frontier farmers mortgaged their property to establish their farms; they lived by borrowing on the forthcoming crop. Countless farms now passed into the hands of merchants and bankers. Banks which suspended specie payments insisted on the payments of debts due them. "Horse leeches," as the *Nashville Clarion* called the banks, "drained every drop of blood they could suck from a suffering community." In the words of a Kentuckian, "They are the vultures that prey upon the vitals of the constitution and rob the body politic of its life blood."[4]

Demands for relief swept the west. Conflict between the Kentucky Relief Party and traditional political forces dominated that state's politics for a decade. Leaders of the Relief Party—Amos Kendall, Frank Blair, William Barry—brought settled hostility toward banks to the Jackson administration. Kendall wrote the Bank veto message, and Blair was chief propagandist of the war. Jackson himself recalled during the Bank War that he had always opposed banks. In fact his memory played him false. He had opposed demands for debtor relief after 1819 in Kentucky and Tennessee, and blamed the debtors themselves for their plight.[5]

Debts, not banks, engaged Jackson's deepest feelings in the pre-presidential years. He first established himself by prosecuting suits for debt. He prospered, like other land speculators, by borrowing large sums, and David Allison's failure almost ruined him. Jackson paid Allison's notes as they matured, but his financial situation was never thereafter secure. Jackson did not conclude from his own experience, however, that debtors were trapped in an irresponsible financial network. He paid his debts; others could pay theirs. Prudent men, Jackson warned his son and wards, only incurred debts they could pay.[6]

Jackson's oldest ward, Andrew Jackson Donelson, was admitted to West Point in 1817. "You are now entered on the theatre of the world amonghst Stranger[s]," Jackson warned him, "where it behoves you to be guarded at all points." Donelson's requests for money and Jackson's strictures against debt fill their early correspondence. Donelson served two years on Jackson's staff after graduation. He entered law school in Kentucky in 1822, in the midst of the Kentucky relief agitation. William Barry, a leader of the Relief Party, was one of his teachers; young Donelson was attracted to Barry's schemes. Jackson warned his ward against "the new fangled projects of wild speculators and unsound politicians." He feared that debt relief would tempt the youth. He worried, he wrote Donelson, that "wild, speculative notions . . . might lead you into political error, before your mind was properly prepared to form a judgment for yourself with which you would be pleased with, on mature reflection."[7]

Tennessee also experimented with debtor relief. It chartered a state-owned bank to act as a loan office and issue paper money with which debts could be paid. Jackson condemned "the desperate and wicked project," impugned the integrity of the legislature which supported it, and antagonized everyone with the fierceness of his opposition to the widely popular measure. The new state-bank notes, he wrote, would "destroy all credit abroad and all confidence at home." Debtors deserved no special consideration, said Jackson; "the modern doctrine is, because I steal my neighbor's horse, it justifies my neighbor to steal yours." Jackson supported his wealthy planter friend Edward Ward for governor in 1821. Ward opposed debtor relief; his opponent, William Carroll, also opposed the state loan office, but Carroll had the greater popular following. Jackson attributed Ward's defeat to "the new raggs of the state." "The paper system has and will ruin the state," he wrote John Donelson. Jackson preferred private-bank notes to "that trash."[8]

Jackson spoke in the name of the people, and condemned speculator influence in the new paper system. His position had support in east Tennessee, a largely subsistence region of small farms, relatively unaffected by the panic. It had no support among the farmers of middle Tennessee. Jackson's own region suffered from problems of market over-expansion which his rhetoric ignored. Jackson's condemnation of debt called upon the traditional virtues of household frugality; it offered no relief to cash-crop farmers. Jackson attacked the "Bank-mania" of state loan-office supporters. His position allied him with the private banks.[9]

Jackson's wealthy friends did not welcome his stance, however. They feared that Jackson's intransigence, as in the land-title controversies of the period, would make their own positions vulnerable. Men like W. B. Lewis reluctantly supported the state loan office to blunt popular anti-bank feeling. Jackson insisted that the loan office violated the Constitution. The Constitution forbade a state to coin money, he wrote. "Hence her attempt to make paper, money, is void." But private note-issuing banks also required state charters. Jackson's position, Lewis wrote him, threatened the constitutionality of all banks. Jackson replied that if the banks' friends did not stop the state loan office, then all banks deserved to die.[10]

Just as Jackson challenged land titles indiscriminately, so he questioned the existence of banks. Rage at debtors drove him to the foundations of the commodity economy. Jackson isolated himself from everyone in the process, and he did not pursue his anti-bank logic during the 1820s. He blamed "the Bank influence" in 1823 for Felix Grundy's reelection; Grundy had sponsored the state loan office. That same year Jackson attacked "the money power" which Treasury Secretary Crawford used to advance his presidential ambitions. These protests were isolated. Jackson and his supporters did not mention banks during the 1824 and 1828 campaigns. Jackson later remembered opposing efforts by the "mother bank" in 1817 and 1827 to establish a Nashville branch; his correspondence during those years contains no mention of the branch-bank proposal.[11] Jackson urged the Bank, after his 1828 victory, to make different appointments to the Nashville board of directors. He wrote Bank director Thomas Cadwalader,

> If it is any part of the policy of the mother Bank to conciliate the states and make their Branches acceptable to the people, then I think a portion of their board, at least, should have been composed of men better known, and possessing more extensive influence than the most of those in the directory of the Bank at Nashville do.

Biddle asked Lewis for recommendations to the board after Jackson's election, Lewis suggested Overton, and Biddle appointed him.[12]

Jackson remembered criticizing the Bank in his draft of the first inaugural, and removing the reference at the request of friends. His surviving draft, however, contains no mention of the Bank. Indian removal and the Eaton affair preoccupied Jackson during the first years of his Presidency. He paid little attention to the Bank. But in June 1829 he came out against rechartering it.[13] What made him take this step?

There is no convincing answer. Historians have exaggerated the social groups actively opposed to the Bank. Some commentators believe Jackson's anti-Bank rhetoric merely disguised the interests of state bankers and speculators chafing under Biddle's control. It is true that the Bank acted, after its initial misadventures, as a brake on inflationary pressures. Some speculators and wildcat state bankers no doubt resented its restrictiveness; the vast majority of state bankers and men of substance, however, supported the Bank. Political entrepreneurs have also been blamed for the Bank War. The Albany Regency was, as Lee Benson suggests, happy to divert Anti-Mason attacks away from its own state-bank "monopoly" to the U.S. Bank. But Van Buren did not initiate the Bank veto, and he acted as a restraining force during the war.[14]

Deepest hostility to banks existed along the frontier. The frontier suffered most seriously from money and credit problems, frontier banks were the most irresponsible, and the frontier was closest to memories of household arcadia. Anti-bank elements in Kentucky, New Hampshire, and Alabama joined Jackson's ranks in 1826 and 1827. Some of his newer Tennessee allies also objected to the recently established Nashville branch of the U.S. Bank. Jackson gave particular attention to charges that the branch banks interfered with the 1828 election.[15]

Charges that the Bank corrupted the suffrage may well have triggered the war; they spoke to Jackson's early fears of the "money power" in politics. Jackson and the new politicians he represented wanted authority independent of the traditional stratification system. But to blame the Bank War on political entrepreneurs, rising capitalists, and frontier anti-bank feeling fails to give Jackson his due. Jackson's Bank War reawakened frontier anti-bank hostility; it was not caused by it. The Bank War also liberated political and economic entrepreneurs. Interest conflicts contributed to the war, as they did to Indian relations and land-title disputes. But it was a logic of the psyche that led Jackson to the U.S. Bank after he achieved the Presidency. Against the Bank, as against Indians, Jackson's interior journey reached the source of widely shared social anxieties. Jackson's Bank War, aided by the depression that came in its wake, brought a dormant anti-bank sentiment to the center of American politics.

Jackson ignored the Bank in the 1820s; he gave his attention to the federal debt. Jackson's hostility to debt provides the best avenue for understanding his ultimate attack on the Bank. The national debt, he wrote in 1824, "is calculated to raise around the administration a moneyed aristocracy dangerous to the liberties of the country." Jackson stressed repayment of the debt in his first inaugural, placing it above tariff reduction and internal improvements in importance. He waited to pay Indians for their territory until the public-land sales; he wanted to save government money to retire the federal debt. The government paid its entire debt during Jackson's first term; he considered this one of his major achievements.[16]

Jackson often warned his son and wards against borrowing money. He worried particularly about the debts accumulated by Andrew Jackson, Jr. Jackson wanted to leave his adopted son, he wrote him, free of debt when he died. But the younger Jackson increased his father's indebtedness. He gave personal notes for land, slaves, and horses which the family could not afford. Jackson's "fatherly advice" failed to stop this practice. Reproaching his son for failing to meet a note of purchase for a Negro girl, Jackson reminded him that he had always paid his own debts punctually.[17]

Fear of debt was widespread in Jacksonian America. Tied for Jackson to loss of control over his children, this fear may also have had roots in anxieties over bodily control. There is inevitable sense of loss in the infant's separation from the mother. In part the child's body products take the mother's place; he keeps them as he could not keep her. The child takes pleasure first from the body products themselves, then from learning to control them. Holding on and letting go, says Erikson, define the issues of the anal stage. There is danger, however, that the child will try to keep food, his original link to the mother, inside him. As an ironic celebration of the debtor in McGuffey's *Reader* has it,

> There is no certainty but in instant enjoyment. Look at schoolboys sharing a plum-cake. The knowing ones eat, as for a race; but a *stupid* fellow *saves his* portion; just nibbles a bit, and keeps the rest for another time. Most provident blockhead! The others, when they have gobbled up *their* shares, set upon *him*, plunder him, and thrash him for crying out.[18]

The child wants to eat everything. He learns from his parents and his body that if he is too greedy and does not let go, he will be filled with bad inner objects. Learning self-control, the child makes valuable gains in autonomy. But he also learns—particularly in early America— to mistrust his inner body contents. He discovers a force within himself demanding purity and control. He purifies himself by expelling the bad objects within.[19]

Feces within the body or uncontrolled without serve the bad parents. They permit alien forces to expose and gain control of the self. Reformers, to recall Jackson's metaphor, "cleans the augean stables." Revealing the conspiracy-bred "child of Colo Benton and Colo Williams, . . . , [they] leave all concerned on their native Dung Hills." The anal stage, writes Erikson, lays the basis for fear of exposure, concern for reputation, a strict punitive morality, and anxiety over what is left behind. Jackson's warnings against debt raise just these issues.[20]

Debt, Jackson wrote his son, placed a man under the control of others and subjected him to ridicule.

> Be always certain, if you wish to die independent, to keep your wants within your means, always when you have the money, paying for them when bought. I have said before and now repeat—the world is not to be trusted. Many think you rich, and many you will find under false pretentions of friendship would involve you, if they can, strip you of your last shilling, and afterwards laugh at your folly, and distress.[21]

A child's feces, writes Abraham, are his first private property. Money and adult property, stripped of illicit sensual qualities, replace these body products. Property promises to win back what has been lost in separation from the mother. Money offers possibilities for possession and control that unique, variegated, sensual objects undermine. A man gains control over objects, to recall Richard Call's advice on the Seminole Negroes, if he can "turn them into specie." Bourgeois accumulation has roots in the anal stage.[22]

Accumulation offers danger as well as promise, however, and that is McGuffey's moral. One is tempted to forgo hard work and self-control for easy, speculative paths to wealth. One forgets that pleasure undermines control; one gives in to forbidden infant longings. "Gobbling" promises a timeless state in which the child will not have to pay. "The *debtor* is safe," pretends McGuffey. "The substance he has eaten up, is irreversible. The future cannot trouble his past. He has nothing to apprehend."[23] Debt actually did raise apprehensions about future and past, to which McGuffey intended to appeal. His story begins, "the first debt in the history of man is the debt of nature, and the first instinct is to put off payment of it to the last moment." Man pays "the debt of nature" when he dies. Even after death, Jackson warned his son, debt contaminated a man's reputation and burdened his children. And it reduced grown men to root as in infancy for a "tit . . . to suck the treasury pap."[24] Jackson had "gobbled" the Indians, and America could not consume the overproduction from Indian lands. Was the national debt Jackson wanted so badly to pay the debt to the children of nature?

Men lived in household society on the products of their own labor and on what they bartered with their fellows. The primitive credit relations of early market expansion depended on a network of personal trust. Market vicissitudes, as Allison's failure showed, betrayed that trust; Jackson transferred his mistrust of personal notes to bank notes and credit. Paper money, he feared, tempted men to borrow and undermined their self-control. It fed "this eager desire to amass wealth without labor." Paper money and credit turned men from "the sober pursuits of honest industry." "Excessive issues of paper," Jackson believed, caused "those fluctuations in the standard of value which render uncertain the rewards of labor."[25]

Specie provided a tangible, apparently timeless standard of value. Paper money, complained Jackson, was "trash." Its worthlessness prevented him from traveling north, as did "my old bowell complaint, which has weakened me very much, having a constant flow, in the last twelve hours, upwards of Twenty passages." Banks and speculators, in William Freehling's summary of Jacksonian hard-money doctrine, "made profits by spewing forth paper money instead of producing a material product."[26]

There was traditional hostility to paper money in America, but it was not traditionally directed against banks. Madison condemned the "rage for paper money"; he blamed this "wicked project" on debtor farmers.[27] Jackson's 1819 position had the same thrust, and McGuffey's *Reader*s also espoused conservative values. Social developments and a logic of the psyche led Jackson from debt and paper money to the Bank War.

American commerce before the market revolution primarily utilized short-term commercial notes. The expanding market depended on long-term credit. Paper and credit financed market expansion after 1815; the proliferating banks played a major, often speculative role. Suspicion of these banks and their notes was not mere fantasy. Banks issued paper and extended credit with widely varying ratios of note issue to specie reserves. State-bank notes fluctuated in value, differed from their face value, and were often heavily discounted outside the state of issue. Bank notes had no solid value independent of their maker. Easy credit and inflated paper ensnared farmers in boom times; banks exacted retribution, so it seemed, during panics.[28]

"The Borrower is a Slave to the Lender," said Frankin's Poor Richard. "Disdain the Chain, preserve your Freedom; and maintain your Independency: Be *Industrious* and *free*." But men warned against dependence by the self-improvement ethic were actually required to borrow to improve themselves. This placed Americans in a double bind. A few, like Thoreau, understood that people were trapped by their own reified material desires. "And when the farmer has got his house," said Thoreau, "he may not be the richer but the poorer for it, and it be the house that has got him."[29] But Thoreau's celibate frugality was a large price to pay for this insight. Most of those who condemned the material desires of ordinary Americans lived all too well themselves; their appeals to republican simplicity were self-serving.

Market society shattered old social bonds, and made individualism, opportunity, and self-help the cardinal values. Dissolving social boundaries promised independence; men blamed the proliferating organizations of market society for the failures of that promise. Masons, Mormons, Catholics, anti-slavery societies, state-chartered "monopolies," and banks all exercised, it was charged, conspiratorial power. Anxiety over organizational power floated through American politics; Jackson focused it on the Bank. This reflected the real power of banks, and the centrality of economics to the social transformation of America. It also reflected the symbolic centrality of money and debt in the American character.[30]

The Bank became, in the social psychology of market revolution, the locus of Jacksonian anxiety. Unhinged by market relations, the Protestant conscience turned against "the mother bank." The Bank symbolized the bad mother returning to dominate her children. Insistent self-reliance contains elements of rage against the lost mother; controlling "the paper system," she took her revenge. The bank was the central, consolidated power which overwhelmed republican autonomy. "Old mother bank" appears in Jacksonian political caricature vomiting gold coins, holding a bot-tle for the pugilist Biddle (who boxes in a ring with Jackson), and sheltering hordes of little Whig and banker devils. "Kill the great monster," wrote a Jacksonian labor leader, "and the whole brood which are hatched and nourished over the land will fall an easy prey."[31]

Jackson first attacked the Bank six months after Rachel died; perhaps her death helped turn him against the Bank. Mourning activates early grief over separation from the mother; it stimulates regressive, melancholic identification with her. Jackson lived with Rachel's melancholy during her life; in death it threatened to overwhelm him. The mourner introjects unacceptable reproaches against the dead person, and turns them against the self. Then, writes Sándor Radó, he splits the dead person in two; he retains the idealized portion within the self, and expels as feces those parts toward which he has unacceptable feelings. Perhaps Jackson purified himself, in the Bank War, of reproaches against Rachel. Did he load money with special significance after her death, as he had after his mother's, now symbolizing a longing to hold and control rather than to gamble and forget?[32]

Death filled Jackson when he came to Washington—Rachel's death, Indian death, and the multiple illnesses of his own body. He triumphed over death in the Bank War. "Scenes of corruption," wrote Jackson, made him "long for retirement, and repose in the Hermitage. But until I can strangle this hydra of corruption, the Bank, I will not shrink from my duty, or my part." Although his health was bad in 1833, as it had been at the outbreak of the Creek War, Jackson insisted that the "excitement of the Bank War" was "far better for my recovery, than all the stimulating medicine of the faculty." When Van Buren returned from England after the veto message, he found Jackson ill in bed. As Van Buren remembered it,

> He exhibited when stretched on a sick-bed a spectre in physical appearance but as always a hero in spirit. . . . Holding my hand in one of his own and passing the other through his long white locks he said, with the clearest indications of a mind composed, and in a tone entirely devoid of passion or bluster—"the bank, Mr. Van Buren, is trying to kill me, *but I will kill it.*"[33]

Jackson called, in his struggle against the Bank, on the republican virtue of the fathers. He promised to "restore to our institutions the primitive simplicity and purity" they had once enjoyed. "It is the natural instinct of wealth and power to reach after new acquisitions," Jackson reminded his Cabinet. "It was to arrest them that our Fathers perilled their lives." The charter of the First Bank, in the "infancy" of the country, violated "the system of Govt which they devised for their posterity." To destroy the Second Bank, said Jackson, was to "carry their intents into full effect." Jackson led, in his words, a "glorious revolution" against the Bank.[34]

Biddle himself made the struggle a personal one. He asked Congress to recharter the Bank four years before the original charter expired. Biddle and Clay believed that if Jackson vetoed the recharter he would lose the coming election. Their strategy not only generated the veto; it also forced the Bank on Jackson's attention. He interpreted his triumphant reelection as a mandate against the Bank. Jackson did not turn singlemindedly to the Bank until after his reelection and his nullification triumph. Then, over the opposition of two successive Treasury Secretaries, he removed the federal deposits from the Bank. Removal intensified the struggle between Jackson and Biddle; the Bank War dominated America during Jackson's second term.[35]

The Downfall of Mother Bank, a pro-Jackson cartoon, captures the symbolism of removal. The pillars of the Bank collapse around fleeing little devil children, who plead in vain with "old Nick" Biddle for help. Jackson stands to one side, as large as the Bank itself. One arm, thrust forward, holds a scroll ordering removal of the deposits. (See Plate 5.)

More than two-thirds of the federal revenues lay, a Jackson supporter explained, "under the absolute control of the mother bank at Philadelphia." Jacksonians charged—with accuracy once the Bank War started—that the Bank used its funds to finance anti-Jackson electoral campaigns and to support the life-styles of pro-Bank politicians. "We must cut the cord of corruption by removing the deposits," wrote Jackson.[36]

Biddle responded with a sharp note contraction. He hoped his manufactured panic would force Jackson to restore the deposits. A stream of pro-Bank delegations visited the White House, pleading with the President to do so. Jackson chided the delegations for their worship of material goods. He reminded one group, "The Israelites during the absence of Moses to the mount made a golden calf and fell down and worshipped it; and they sorely suffered for their idolatry. The people of this country may yet be punished for their idolatry." "Providence has power over me," he told another delegation, "but frail mortals who worship Bale and the golden calf can have none." "I would cut my right hand from my body before restoring the deposits," wrote Jackson, as if to supply the text for the mother-bank cartoon.[37]

Van Buren summed up, with his typical facility, one set of charges against the Bank. Banks sought, he wrote, "to produce throughout society a chain of dependence,

> to nourish in preference to the manly virtues that give dignity to human nature, a craving desire for luxurious enjoyment and sudden wealth, which renders those who seek them dependent on those who supply them; to substitute for republican simplicity and economical habits a sickly appetite for effeminate indulgence . . . and at last to fix upon us, instead

of those equal political rights the acquisition of which was alike the object and supposed reward of our Revolutionary struggle, a system of exclusive privileges conferred by partial legislation.[38]

The "monster hydra" not only trapped men in a "chain of dependence"; it also took other forms, "branching out annually into new heads of different shape, each devouring the substance and destroying the rights of the people." Fears of the devouring face of the "many-headed hydra" went back to the 1819 panic. As Benton exclaimed,

> All the flourishing cities of the west are mortgaged to this money power. They may be devoured by it at any moment. They are in the jaws of the monster! A lump of butter in the mouth of a dog! One gulp, one swallow, and all is gone.[39]

Banks had to be stopped from "devouring the coin of a community." Had Biddle retained the government deposits, wrote Frank Blair, "he would have blown up and swallowed all the millions that the states have divided among them." "I am ready with the screws," said Jackson as he withdrew the deposits, "to draw every tooth and then the stumps."[40]

The Bank devoured the products of men's labor. Entering her vaults in retaliation, Jackson drained her of her inner body contents. "It is useless to buffet the bank with our left hand," wrote Kendall, "as long as we feed it with our right." Jackson urged his son not to send his debts for collection to a U.S. Bank branch, else it would seem that "I was lending my means to drain the deposit Bank of its specie to aid the monster that was trying to destroy me." The Bank drained and bled its victims ("The mammoth, sir, has bled you," Jackson told a delegation), and deposit removal responded in kind. Like Indian removal and removal of federal officeholders, deposit removal purified the body politic.[41]

Others expressed fear of "the monster"; Jackson did not. He told some visitors, "I've got my foot upon it and I'll crush it." First reproaching his son for an unwise debt, Jackson then turned to the dying struggles of the Bank. "Clay reckless and as full of fury as a drunken man in a brothel," he wrote. "This mamoth of power and corruption must die, the power it possesses would destroy our government in a few years. . . . I have it chained, the *monster must perish*."[42] Ahab died, strangled by the cord of the harpoon he plunged into the whale. But Jackson "cut the cord of corruption," broke "the chain of dependence," himself "chained the *monster*," "strangle[d] this hydra," and killed it.

The defeat of "the credit system" would restore men's power over the products of their labor. Jackson favored substituting a hard metallic currency for paper. He explained, "I am for a stable metalic currency, and against *the bank* and a bank; for if we burn the old Phenix, and foster a young one from its ashes, the young will grow as hateful and injurious as the old one."[43]

Gold and silver were "full-bodied money," and they would not be subject to the power of banks. Benton proposed to replace small notes with gold coins—"Benton's mint drops" they were called. The government still required a depository for its funds, however, and at first distributed government revenue among note-issuing state banks. This was a disastrous experience, and Jackson and Van Buren came to favor a non-note-issuing federal depository. An independent treasury promised to end once and for all the association of government with banks. Van Buren's measure was known as the divorce bill, and Jackson enthusiastically supported it. "The divorce bill," he wrote,

> contains the great principle of a seperation of the government from the corrupting influence of all Banks and their paper system, when not based on a real metalic basis. The divorce is the great principle, which will lead to happy results both to the purity of the government, hapiness of the people, and a great blessing to all, by perpetuating our happy republican system from the corrupting influence of the mony power.[44]

II

Jackson killed the Bank; he did not restore republican virtue. Jacksonians defined monopoly as state-granted privilege rather than market-generated power. They promised "equal rights to all and special privileges for none" in a marketplace freed from political privilege. Until the general incorporation laws at the end of the Age of Jackson, every corporation required an individual government charter. States and the federal government did create special privilege. But the focus on government averted attention from market inequalities, acquisitive impulses, and exploitative conditions of work for which the state could not be blamed. Jacksonian anti-monopoly rhetoric attacked privilege, speculation, and easy wealth. Often it spoke in the name of enterprise; often, as in the Bank War, it confused impulses toward speculative enterprise with nostalgia for an idealized, frugal, paternal world.

Jackson's first target, from an anti-monopoly perspective, was the "corrupt and Despotic" government of the Indian tribes. He liberated the "poor Indian" from tribal government to subject him to market freedom. Thomas Hart Benton, lawyer for the American Fur Company, also used anti-monopoly rhetoric in the service of the market. Benton spurred Congress to abolish government-run trading posts in Indian territory. This government "monopoly" was no monopoly at all. It competed with the much larger American Fur Company, whose president, John J. Astor, was the richest man in America. The fur company thanked Benton for destroying the "pious monster." Benton led congressional opposition to the Bank a decade later.[45]

Secretary of the Treasury Roger Taney engineered deposit withdrawal. He continued to use anti-monopoly logic as Chief Justice of the Supreme Court. Taney rejected the claims of a state-chartered bridge company that its charter gave it exclusive rights to all transportation across the Charles River. He cited the "modern" forces of improvement and enterprise against the bridge monopoly.[46]

Taney was a state-bank director himself. He chose the Baltimore bank for which he had been counsel to receive federal deposits. If the Bank had its "brood," Jackson had his "pet banks." ("Petts" was also his term for his grandchildren.) Party patronage considerations heavily influenced the choice of deposit banks. "Those which are in hands politically friendly will be preferred," wrote Amos Kendall. In cities without Democratic banks, Jackson would choose "opposition men whose feelings are liberal." Samuel Swartwout, a Jackson crony since the days of Burr, set up a New York bank which received government deposits. He wrote Jackson:

> While millions lay in the vaults of those institutions, many of which are opposed to us in politiks, this little patriotic institution is working its way among our friends, loaning all it can to our friends, and sustaining the administration by all the means in its power.[47]

The Bank War took place during a rising business cycle. State banks used the specie reserves withdrawn from the U.S. Bank to finance a credit expansion which Biddle's more conservative practice had inhibited. Speculators and aspiring politicians took advantage of the Bank War for just the inflationary purposes Jackson's rhetoric condemned. Jackson acted, in the name of the fathers, as the servant of free market expansion. He had initiated this dynamic with his Indian policy; far from redressing the failures of that policy, the Bank War simply confirmed them. Jackson condemned the speculative ways of his youth and returned to the principles of the fathers. These principles, for him as for the fathers, helped conquer the obstacles to capitalism.

One must distinguish the effects of Jackson's policies from the conscious intentions of the major actors in his dramas. The Bank embodied the eighteenth-century alliance of state and old-family power. Most men of wealth were too tied to the old status system to oppose the Bank. Many members of the business and commercial classes, including Jackson's old Tennessee friends, left the Democratic Party over the Bank War. The war, culminating in Jackson's hard-money specie circular and the panic of 1837, reoriented Democratic support away from wealthy, enterprising, pro-Bank commercial classes who had provided factional support for Jackson in the early years. It shifted party competition from a sectional to a modified class basis. The Jacksonian mass base shifted to poorer, more isolated frontier areas, and struggles between pro-Bank Whigs and hard-money Democrats dominated party competition in many states.[48] Nevertheless, the destruction of the Bank benefited wealth over old social status; it did not benefit the common man *en masse*. Anti-Bank Democrats often attacked genuine banking abuses, but there was large disproportion between their reforms and the evils Jackson attributed to "the moneyed power."[49]

A power distant from men's lives was growing in mobile capitalist America, and men encountered it as they sold crops, bought land, and joined promotional schemes. That power was the power of the market. Identifying it instead as the U.S. Bank, Jackson helped reconcile his constituency to the market. Free market relations rarely sum up capitalism. Industrialization brought corporate control over conditions of work and exchange to the center of post-bellum America. Giant corporations and a militarized corporate state dominate America today. Corporations were beginning to emerge in Jacksonian America, but the free market system of decentralized power and minimal state direction held greater sway then than at any time in our history. This is the historical moment when free-market psychology, beginning to generate structures of power but not yet overwhelmed by them, stands most clearly revealed.

Jackson distinguished himself from ordinary politicians by the ferocity of his inner struggle. Locating the danger to self-control on a central devouring power, Jackson went to the root of market psychology. But, far from transvaluing that psychology, he sanctified it instead. There were cooperative experiments in Jacksonian America, among urban workers and in utopian communities. But Jackson himself offered neither human cooperation nor social control of wealth as alternatives to market competition. He exemplified instead the power of the individual will to slay the demons which confronted it.

The Jacksonians counterposed hard work and self-control to the credit system. These virtues actually fueled the developing market. Self-improving Americans trapped themselves in market relations. Self-reliance required them constantly to expand their control, to own objects before they could trust them. Once social conditions of household frugality were exploded, the impulse to accumulate and dominate took over. The drive for control did not achieve the promised autonomy. It threatened instead the return of a dominating power. Hatred of dependence helped generate that power, not merely as a fantasized return of the repressed, but in the actual world.

Jackson imagined a politics purified of personal family ties. His struggle substituted instead subjection to impersonal forces. The market set men free, but imprisoned them in a network of contractual obligations. Men were forced in their freedom to extend the sway of the market. Jackson directed market freedom against the tribes when he forced individual Indians to sell their land. Now, as the Bank War symbolized, he faced the market as its victim. The market's power was impersonal, but it developed from men's reified and abstracted personal desires. Men subjected themselves to the market just as, in the service of autonomy, they imprisoned inner instincts of love, spontaneity, and personal trust. The Protestant ethic, in Weber's formulation, built its own iron cage. Eighteenth-century lines of will, said Henry Adams, became nineteenth-century lines of force. "Seeking to control a larger liberty," wrote Melville in a parable of slaves and machines, "man but extends the empire of necessity."[50]

Networks of personal obligation and trust proved, in a mobile, acquisitive society, too unreliable to support political authority. Warring on personal dependence, Jackson helped establish not genuine independence but mechanized forces of self- and social control. He staged a heroic struggle against malevolent forces at the moment of the triumph not of a malevolent universe but of one created by men and indifferent to their fate.

The universe in which southern Indians lived was also undergoing this transformation. Jackson began with an active malevolence toward Indians. As his administration, united to market forces, gradually assumed destructive omnipotence over the fate of whole tribes, Jackson rose above rage to indifference. Whites prospered on the whole in Jacksonian America, and it is foolish to equate their growing subjection to impersonal, mechanized forces with the destruction of Indians. Yet in the Jacksonian period whites were beginning to become the victims of the forces they embodied.

"You have no longer any cause to fear danger from abroad," Jackson told Americans in his Farewell Address. "It is from within, among yourselves—from cupidity, from corruption, from disappointed ambition and inordinate thirst for power—that factions will be formed and liberty endangered." Jackson had slain the mother bank, but he had not laid these demons to rest. In the depression years which succeeded his Presidency, controversies over state banks loomed large in party politics. These conflicts disappointed Jacksonian expectations. Anti-Bank forces were almost never strong enough to win decisive victories, and moral crusades degenerated into factional manipulation. Instead of controlling or destroying banks, reformers watched rising manufacturing corporations take center stage. The anti-Bank impulse exhausted itself by the mid-1840s; its effort at internal political regeneration had failed. Expansion encountered less formidable obstacles; in Jackson's last years Jacksonians turned outward again.[51]

CHAPTER 10

MANIFEST DESTINY

His body has its fit resting place in the great Valley of the Mississippi;
his spirit rests upon our whole territory; it hovers over the vales of
Oregon, and guards in advance the frontiers of the Del Norte.

—*George Bancroft, eulogy of Andrew Jackson*

"The *untransacted* destiny of the American people," wrote William Gilpin
in 1846,

> is to subdue the continent—to rush over this vast field to the Pacific Ocean—
> to animate the many hundred millions of its people, and to cheer them up-
> ward . . . to regenerate superannuated nations— . . . to cause a stagnant
> people to be reborn— . . . to shed a new and resplendent glory upon man-
> kind—to unite the world in one social family—to dissolve the spell of ty-
> ranny and exalt charity—to absolve the curse that weighs down humanity,
> and to shed blessings around the world![1]

These sentiments of Jackson's young friend, written the year following the old Hero's death, expanded the Jacksonian promise for a new generation. Indian dispossession underlay Gilpin's vision of American destiny.
The regeneration begun with children of nature would "cause a stagnant
people to be reborn" and "unite the world in one social family." A country
which had solved its eastern Indian problem was now, as Jackson put it
shortly before he died, "extending the area for freedom" to the Pacific.[2]

The Indian was one symbol of divided America. He may have posed
a danger to inner harmony and economic growth; he posed no danger to
the Union. Guilt and aggression generated American fears of Indian war
and slave insurrection; the imagined "internecine" military threats were
largely fantastic. America, however, was divided along sectional lines as
well as racial ones. The conflict between slave and free states intensified
fears of inner division in Jacksonian America, and gave them political substance. When a paternal Jackson called for amnesty between red and white
brothers, he rationalized expropriation—of symbolic childhood and Indian
land. When he urged "fraternal attachment" on the states, he genuinely intended familial reconciliation. Jacksonian nationalism sacrificed Indians to

unite white brothers. It succeeded against Indians, and it joined north and south for a time. Expansion finally turned white brothers against each other, however, and led them to fratricidal war.

I

A resolution to condemn Jackson's Florida invasion and a proposal to prohibit slavery in Missouri opened the year 1819 in Congress. The Missouri debates drove southerners to their first positive defenses of slavery since the Revolution. It led northerners to hope for an anti-slavery alliance of north and west against southern political domination. Moderation prevailed on both sides, however. The Missouri Compromise kept slavery from the center of American politics for another quarter-century. This reflected sectional and economic realities. Cotton was crucial to American development, and it tied the sections together. New York merchants handled the cotton export crop, and the port city flourished. Southern cotton supplied New England textile mills, and underlay defenses of slavery by members of the New England political elite. The south also faced westward during the Age of Jackson. It expanded onto Indian lands; and early migration patterns and trade routes ran predominantly from south to west.[3]

The slave issue would have isolated the south; it did not enter politics. Westward expansion, which worked for the south, did. The Missouri Compromise is well remembered in American history; Jackson's Seminole campaign is not. But Jackson's war and the subsequent congressional investigation received more contemporary attention than the Missouri question. Jackson wrote in 1819 that his Seminole campaign would elect the next President. This was not wild megalomania; it was merely a little premature. Jackson, Indians, and westward expansion, not slavery and Negroes, structured American politics for the next generation.[4]

This choice worked to the south's advantage. The south could choose, William Freehling has shown, between minority and majority strategies for safeguarding its basic interests. South Carolina, particularly sensitive to slavery, fought for a minority veto. Slavery divided the south from the rest of the country, and South Carolina did not win wide southern support for its choice. Outside of South Carolina, states-rights sentiment was strongest in Georgia. The two states shared economic problems, and Cherokee resistance also intensified Georgia's states-rights claims. But Georgia cooperated with Jackson to remove the Cherokees, and her politicians stood high in administration councils. Jacksonian nationalism, realized in the nullification proclamation, was not directed against the south. Far from representing the south in 1832, South Carolina stood alone.[5]

The Jacksonian system defended southern interests on a national basis;

the majority southern strategy triumphed in the Age of Jackson. Jackson deemphasized slavery in favor of interests the south shared with other segments of the country. Pressures for westward expansion, intensified by the slave economy, produced southern support for Indian removal.[6] Jacksonian nationalism required minimal positive federal action; this appealed to a region hostile to the tariff and internal improvements, and fearful that an active federal government would interfere with slavery. The south was the most purely rural region in the country, and Jacksonian agrarianism had powerful southern roots. Finally, loyalty first to Jackson as the regional candidate and then to the Democratic Party influenced southern behavior.

Jackson was elected President as the southern candidate. He received the highest popular vote in the region in 1824, and swept all southern states but Kentucky in the elections of 1828 and 1832. No other region of the country supported him so disproportionately. South Carolina aside, nullification did not cost him significant southern support. For the rest of the south, compromise on the tariff was sufficient. Jackson supported downward revision in the tariff from early in the nullification crisis, and the bill that was finally passed gradually reduced the tariff to its lowest pre-Civil War levels. (There was still widespread northern support for a low tariff, since far more people produced staples for the international market than manufactured goods for domestic consumption.)[7]

The majority southern strategy did not sacrifice slavery to national cohesion. Jackson opposed every action that challenged slavery. He acquiesced in South Carolina's nullification of a Supreme Court decision defending the rights of free Negro seamen in Charleston. He supported the censorship of abolitionist literature by southern federal postmasters, and ordered his Attorney General not to enforce the constitutionally guaranteed free interstate flow of mail. He praised anti-abolitionist mobs which rioted against northern anti-slavery societies. He supported the congressional gag rule against anti-slavery petitions. Jackson's majority southern strategy defended the peculiar institution by keeping it out of national politics rather than by focusing national political attention on it.[8]

A two-party south developed for the first time after Jackson's retirement. The southern Whigs benefited more from regional antipathy to Van Buren and support for the Bank than from states-rights hostility to Jackson. For the next two decades the majority southern strategy, seeking party influence rather than sectional veto, continued to work for the slave states in both major parties.[9]

The majority southern strategy maintained southern party power during the Age of Jackson; it also supplied the ideological perspective from which Jackson approached American society. Jackson's nostalgic vision of arcadia, wedded to paternal authority and at war with the money power, was distinctively southern.

Slavery dominated southern society. It provided a basis for Jackson's paternalism, I argued above, a paternalism contaminated by the master-slave relationship and forced to operate in liberal society. Southern paternalism required absolute power and personal domination, broke up actual (black) families, and sexually debased slave and free families alike. Far from teaching the value of hierarchy, slavery made white southerners long to be free. Only George Fitzhugh, of the major southern figures, extended a thoroughgoing patriarchalism to white relationships. Calhoun and John Rives, the southern thinkers with political power, insisted they did not support Filmer against Locke. Calhoun elaborated an epicyclic contractualism. Wholly intended to defend slavery, his system of concurrent majorities derived from universal formal logic; it ignored the specific qualities of the peculiar institution. Jackson's paternalism had slaveholding roots, but he used it in the service of nationalism, market expansion, and equal rights. This was the political symbolism of the southern majority strategy.[10]

Jackson's Bank War, like his paternalism, transformed southern weaknesses into national virtues. Slavery generated intensified but impotent southern opposition to market society. Hostility to the market revolution ran deeper in the south than elsewhere in America. The south provided an agrarian focus for anti-Bank feeling.

Compared to other regions, a far higher percentage of the southern population—subsistence farmers in the backcountry and plantation slaves—lived outside the money economy. Plantations, although they were not self-sufficient, provided an extended-household ideal. Family, clan, and personal relationships continued to dominate southern society, unmediated by wider commitments or modern, impersonal institutions. Indeed, southern loyalties rarely transcended personal relations and attached themselves to towns, communities, or work. Party organizations—so important to Jacksonianism elsewhere—were slow to develop in the south; family relations configured politics.[11]

Plantation slavery retarded commerce and manufacture. Banks, towns, and commercial ventures languished. Southerners made a virtue of the region's economic backwardness. They held mercantile activities, acquisitive behavior, Yankee shrewdness, and money itself in contempt. Commercial activities, southern spokesmen asserted, contaminated the quality of life and the structure of republican liberty. Plantations offered instead a leisurely pace, a tangible, physical mode of existence, and a life lived close to the soil. John Taylor of Caroline early suggested that the cheap public domain prevented the rise of a landed aristocracy; America had rather to fear a paper aristocracy, nourished on speculation in bank stock. Calhoun and Fitzhugh also feared the rise of a moneyed aristocracy hostile to agrarian virtue. Jackson's Bank veto received its heaviest congressional support in the south.[12]

The south was the locus, during the Age of Jackson, for widely shared agrarian sentiments. Van Buren, for example, thought that republican principles were least corrupted by the money power in the agrarian south. He early favored an alliance between "the planters of the south and the plain Republicans of the north. The country has once flourished under a party thus constituted," he wrote, "and may again." The Albany Regency had roots in the manorial estates of the Hudson River Valley; this strengthened its southern orientation. Agrarianism was western too, of course; this provided the basis for the political alliance of south and west. Northerner Gilpin, for example, gave the south credit for westward expansion. Jackson drew in the north on new political institutions; the south provided agrarian roots to legitimize them. The south seemed distinctively committed, in the years of the market revolution, to eighteenth-century household ideals.[13]

The south offered more than the basis for agrarian nostalgia; it also provided the cotton exports which fueled the market revolution. The plantation lived off, and was trapped in, the market it hated. "The old style plantation" had, in Eric Wolfe's words, "a split personality."[14] The tensions between household and market, experienced throughout America, were intensified in the south.

Southern agrarianism evoked longings undermined by the actual relationships it expressed. The independent southern planter—whether a liberal like Jackson and Calhoun or a thoroughgoing Fitzhughian patriarchalist—faced impotence against the very market forces to which he offered an alternative. Plantations were more heavily involved in the market economy than other agrarian units. Their prosperity depended on production of a single crop for sale on the international market. Slaves were bought and sold, and often bred for the market too. Plantation investment in slaves required high capitalization and led most planters into debt. Planters also required credit to buy, clear, and cultivate their land, and to market their crops. Southern agrarianism put the south at the mercy of the market.

Market pressure was not simply external, impinging on a stable, coherent, seigneurial world. Potential cotton profits transformed many plantations from self-supporting, food-growing household-manufacture units into single-commodity producers. Soil depletion and the pull of virgin land spurred westward migration and disturbed stable agrarian relations. Land speculation, fraud, acquisitiveness, and upward mobility all characterized the southwest. The thirst for credit to purchase land and slaves promoted wildcat banking schemes. Market domination intensified agrarian longings; agrarianism offered no escape from the market.[15]

By the 1850s slavery openly played the central role in American political life; this development was disastrous for the south. Slavery and the slave-power conspiracy symbolized for northerners all that was wrong with American life. The evils of southern slavery were very real, but developing capitalism also generated anxieties about enslavement to market and machines. Coalescing with fears of slave society, these anxieties found a safer target in the south than at home.[16]

Southerners, for their part, insisted that slavery gave the region its distinctive virtues. For the "Herrenvolk democrats," as Pierre van den Bergh calls them, slavery protected a master race against bestial inferiors. Other southern defenders of slavery sought refuge in aristocracy. The 1850s produced, in Fitzhugh's writings, the single full-blown attack on Lockean liberalism in American thought. The cavalier ideal also embodied southern hostility to commercial, democratic values. This ideal, developed politically in South Carolina, spread throughout the south. It defended aristocratic rule against political managers, patronage, a powerful executive, and the "hungry multitude." The cavalier appealed outside the south, but he manifested the southern minority consciousness. His internal world, as revealed in political rhetoric as well as fiction, was shattered, apocalyptic, and preoccupied with decline. The slave-owner merged with the natural man in the 1820s and early 1830s to glorify a democratic arcadia. Jackson, pioneer and planter, was its symbol.[17]

Jackson emphasized order and independence; he combined equality with paternity; he supported an agrarian ideal which fed market expansion. Perhaps only a southerner could have given such dramatic form to these shared national contradictions. Jacksonian Democracy held the Union together. It offered hope for a distinctively southern solution to common American problems. That hope, promised in Indian removal, climaxed in the Bank War. But the inner tensions of southern slavery, and southern weakness against market expansion, defeated the majority southern strategy. And westward expansion, the lynchpin of the Jacksonian system, shattered the politics which produced it.[18]

II

Governor Sam Houston of Tennessee resigned his office in 1829, fled his eighteen-year-old bride, and went to live among the Arkansas Cherokee Indians. Houston kept his reasons for the failed marriage secret. Perhaps his wife remained attached to a girlhood love. Perhaps she was repelled by an ugly groin wound which Houston received while leading a charge in the Creek War. Whatever his reasons, Houston returned to the Indians with whom he had lived as a boy. He took an Indian name and an Indian wife, dropped the English tongue, and was adopted into the tribe.[19]

Houston acted in desperation, but he had dreams of glory too. He imagined leading western Indians and Texas settlers in a war of southwestern expansion. He promised a friend he would "conquer Mexico or Texas, and be worth two millions in two years."[20]

Houston was Jackson's protégé, and the two were close friends. Jackson wrote the younger man that he had heard rumors "that you had declared that you would, in less than two years, be *emperor* of that country by conquest." Jackson warned Houston against this *"illegal enterprise,"* but said he did not take the rumors seriously. "I must have really thought you deranged to have believed you had such a wild scheme in contemplation; and particularly when it was communicated that the physical force to be employed was the Cherokee Indians."[21]

Jackson may well have thought Houston mad. Mexico had put down the quixotic Fredonia uprising of Texas settlers and Indians just two years earlier, and Houston's behavior among the Cherokees did not inspire confidence in his mental balance. Houston "gave himself up to the fatal enchantress alcohol," he later wrote. He attacked the southwestern Indian agents in his sober moments for their treatment of the demoralized tribes; his own decline mirrored his description of theirs.[22]

Jackson had his own interest in Texas, nevertheless, and he never abandoned his old friend. Early in 1830 Houston arrived in Washington. He wanted a contract to remove the southern Indians; the profits would finance his revolutionary schemes. Jackson and Secretary of War Eaton encouraged Houston's efforts. They planned to award him the contract, although he did not submit the lowest bid. But the threat of political scandal intervened. Jackson decided to delay awarding removal contracts until Indian treaties were signed; Houston returned home empty-handed.[23]

He went back to Washington in December of the year following. Houston still wanted money for his Texas adventures, and he wanted to regularize his purchase of an Indian salt lick. But the old removal contract returned to plague him. Congress was investigating the Jackson-Eaton-Houston deal, and Congressman William Stanberry publicly accused Houston of fraud. Houston encountered Stanberry on the street; he knocked him down with a cane cut from a hickory sapling at the Hermitage.[24]

Congress tried Houston for contempt, and Jackson strongly defended him. When Houston returned to the southwest that summer, he carried a government commission to report on the Texas Indians. Houston visited the Hermitage on his way south. "The people" in Texas, he wrote the New York speculator financing his trip, "look to the Indians in Arkansas as auxiliaries in the event of a change. So I will pass that way and see my *old friends*."[25]

Houston left Arkansas and his Indian wife for good in December.

Texas was determined on independence, he wrote Jackson, and he planned to join the Americans who lived there. Houston did not abandon his dreams of Indian alliance, and he encouraged some Arkansas bands to migrate to Texas. But his Indian life was behind him. The road to southwestern expansion did not lie through positive Indian identification; that, as Jackson wrote, was "deranged." Indians functioned better as negative projections; America expanded not with them, but against their boundary invasions. Texas would demonstrate this lesson once again.[26]

Jackson later insisted he never countenanced Houston's filibustering schemes. He claimed to have written cautionary notes to Arkansas officials in 1829 and 1830. Mysteriously, however, neither Governor Pope nor Secretary William Fulton received these letters. Fulton was Jackson's private secretary during the Seminole campaign, and Jackson mistakenly addressed his letter to the Secretary of the Florida Territory. This slip of the pen anticipated Jackson's later confusions of Texas with Florida.[27]

Jackson may not have encouraged Houston; he did use threats of Texas revolution and Indian war to pressure Mexico to sell the province. Jackson sent his ward Anthony Wayne Butler to Mexico early in 1829. Butler was a speculator in Texas lands and had his own material interest in American annexation. He and Jackson hoped to use the techniques of Jackson's Indian treaties, fear and avarice, to acquire Texas.[28]

Mexico lacked the power to discipline its Indians, Jackson wrote Butler. Butler should tell the government that Indian violence would force America to seize the territory in self-defense. Houston led Jackson to expect a settler uprising in 1832, and Jackson used this information as a bargaining tool. If Mexico did not sell Texas, Jackson instructed Butler to warn her officials, she would lose it to revolution.[29]

Spaniards were the "slave[s] of avarice," wrote Jackson. He suggested unofficial personal approaches to important Mexican officials, and then warned Butler to "Burn this" letter. Jackson and Butler pursued their bribery schemes for five years. The President encouraged Butler to act privately, and warned him that the American government could not let itself be accused of bribery.[30]

Butler's promises of success through bribery were illusory, Jackson finally realized. He recalled his emissary after the Texas revolution began. Butler later broke with Jackson and made public the bribery attempts. Jackson furiously maintained his innocence; he insisted that Butler had acted on his own. This was indeed Jackson's paternal intention. He told Butler to approach the Mexican official "as a mere voluntary act of your own." Butler was Jackson's instrument, but Jackson did not want to be responsible for his actions. When Butler exposed Jackson's directing hand in the bribe attempts, Jackson accused him of personal betrayal. "I have never abandoned a friend," he wrote his ward, "and although I have hugged to my bosoom some vipers who after being cherished and fostered by me have attempted to sting me, but whose poison recoiled upon them and fell harmless at my feet."[31]

Fear and avarice alone failed to acquire Texas, as they had failed with the southern Indians. Jackson manufactured boundary disputes after the Creek War, and now he did so again. First he claimed that the territory ceded under the Louisiana Purchase included Texas; this claim helped precipitate the Mexican War, and we shall return to it. Second, he suggested that the western boundary of the Louisiana Purchase extended to the Nueces River, not to the Sabine. Speculators in Texas land originated this claim, and Butler brought it to Jackson. It had no support at all on ancient maps, or in American, French, and Spanish diplomatic history. But the area between the Sabine and the Nueces included most of the Mexican province of Texas, and most of the American settlements there.[32]

Jackson instructed Butler to insist on the Nueces in negotiating a boundary with Mexico. Congress ratified a commercial treaty in 1832 which recognized the Sabine boundary, but Jackson continued to advance the Nueces claim. If Mexico refused to accept the Nueces, he wrote Butler, America would take possession to the "west fork of the Sabine." (This was the President's new euphemism for the Nueces; as Jackson recognized in earlier instructions, the two rivers flowed independently into Sabine Bay.)[33]

The Texas revolution broke out in the fall of 1835; Jackson ordered General Edmund Gaines to the southwestern border to guard against Indian attack. America could not use the hostilities to acquire Mexican territory, Secretary of War Cass wrote Gaines. But

> In that portion of the country there are many Indian tribes, whose habitual predisposition to engage in war is well known, as is also their reckless disregard of the claims of humanity. . . . It may, therefore, well be, as you anticipate, that these various contending parties may approach the frontiers, and that the lives and property of our citizens may be placed in jeopardy. Should this be the case, the President approves the suggestion you make, and you are authorized to take such position on either side of the imaginary boundary line, as may be best for defensive operations. You will, however, under no circumstances, advance further than old Fort Nacogdoches, which is within the limits of the United States, as claimed by this government.[34]

Since the land to the Nueces was "claimed" by the United States, Gaines was authorized to cross the "imaginary boundary line" and penetrate deep into Mexican Texas.

There was no Indian danger on the southwestern border. Gaines and other expansionists fabricated rumors, as Jackson had in 1818. Florida at least had had a real Indian war before Jackson took Pensacola; Texas had none. Gaines' attack on Fowltown had started the Seminole War. Now he wanted to play in Texas the role Jackson had played in Florida. He spread reports of Indian danger. He recruited militia for his army, and individuals and whole companies crossed the border to aid Texas.[35]

Houston himself, commander-in-chief of the Texas army, wanted American aid. Houston had settled in Nacogdoches in 1833. He returned to the practice of law, representing large Texas and American land specu-lators, and he acquired military leadership of the Texas Americans. The revolution was premature, Houston thought. After Santa Ana defeated the other Texas armies, Houston retreated before him. "Don't get scared," he reassured a Nacogdoches friend about the advancing Mexican army. Jackson, wrote Houston, viewed Nacogdoches as neutral territory and he would not permit an unchallenged Mexican advance. There is evidence that Houston planned to retreat east of the Nueces and provoke an en-counter between Texas and American forces. In the event, however, he defeated Santa Ana at the battle of San Jacinto. The captured general signed a treaty granting Texas independence.[36]

Gaines hesitated to cross the Sabine before the battle of San Jacinto. He was no Jackson; he wanted more explicit permission from Washing-ton. Gaines grew bolder after Houston's victory. Houston and Stephen F. Austin, fearing a new Mexican attack, wrote Gaines that his advance into Texas would save the new republic. Gaines raised more American troops without authorization; he cited renewed rumors of Indian war-fare. He asked for permission to march, "like Wayne, Harrison, and Jackson," "direct to the point at which the families of the warriors are placed." Many in the "disputed territory" were American citizens, he wrote, and "we must protect them from Savage massacre." In July, with-out further orders from Washington, he sent troops to Nacogdoches.[37]

Jackson was furious. Gaines had publicly involved America after Houston won the war. If Gaines had failed to play Jackson successfully in Texas, he gave Jackson his chance to play Monroe. Jackson condemned Gaines for violating Mexican neutrality. Gaines had no authority to raise troops, wrote Jackson, and he doubted the government would pay for them. (This doctrine was familiar to General Jackson; he had heard it from Washington when he raised troops on his own authority to invade Florida.) Both Houston and Santa Ana wanted Jackson to arbitrate between Mexico and Texas; perhaps Jackson feared that Gaines' invasion compromised the appearance of American neutrality. Nevertheless, citing the American

Nueces boundary claim and the danger of Indian war, Jackson approved Gaines' advance to Nacogdoches.[38]

Jackson appeared neutral in public; he was not so in private. Santa Ana had captured Colonel Fanning's Texas army and slaughtered the prisoners of war. If Mexico now renewed the war, wrote Jackson, "I would retaliate" and "put to death" the Mexican prisoners "one for one. If Mexico made it a war of extermination, I would meet her by eye, for eye, tooth for a tooth." This was the language of the First Seminole War. Mexico did repudiate Santa Ana's treaty, signed without authority while the General was a captive, and determined to continue the war. Jackson again warned Gaines to protect the frontier against Indian attacks. He offered Gaines his own Florida logic. If Mexico could not stop her Indians from waging war on our citizens, wrote Jackson, "the law of nations and of self defense" permitted America to do it for her. If Mexico "offers succour or shelter" to marauding Indians, Gaines should pursue them into Mexico. American troops remained in Nacogdoches until December, preventing a Mexican attack.[39]

Jackson wanted Gaines and Butler to carry out his covert desires without forcing him to take public responsibility for them. This stance of public neutrality was not mere window dressing. Jackson was no longer a regional filibusterer acting outside the law. He had responsibility to preserve the Union. The south supported the Texas revolution and favored immediate annexation. But slavery was entering national politics; fearing an increase in slave-state power, the north opposed annexation.

Jackson wanted Texas for national, not sectional, reasons. Texas remained in a formal state of war with Mexico. Jackson was leaving office with the Seminole War unresolved; he may have feared a more serious war against Mexico, one that would divide the country. He surely did not want to inflame the slave issue further. And he feared jeopardizing Van Buren's election. Jackson turned down Texas requests for annexation in the fall of 1836. He delayed recognizing Texas independence until just before he left office. He warned extensively, in his Farewell Address, against the dangers sectional conflict posed to the Union. But Jackson proposed a method to the Texas envoy by which the new republic could join America. Texas should claim California northward to the San Francisco Bay, said Jackson. Such a claim would make Texas attractive to northeastern commercial interests and disarm northern opposition to annexation. Texas must turn expansion from a southern into a national issue.[40]

M. B. Lamar, second president of the Lone Star republic, tried to follow Jackson's advice. He sent an army west to New Mexico; the Mexicans overwhelmed it easily. Texas alone could not nationalize American expansion; America, thanks to Jackson's last political intervention, could.[41]

Jackson retired to the Hermitage in 1837. The old man took an active interest in politics, but played no serious role for several years. Then, in 1843, President Tyler and Secretary of State Calhoun revived the issue of Texas annexation. They pursued, in the interests of slave expansion, the southern minority strategy. They fabricated a British plot to abolish slavery in Texas. America must annex Texas, they warned, or Britain would threaten the peculiar institution throughout the south. This sectional appeal failed; the Senate rejected Tyler's annexation treaty in the spring of 1844.[42]

Calhoun and Tyler brought Texas back into American politics, however, and provided Jackson with his final political role. Tennessee Congressman Aaron Brown asked Jackson's opinion of annexation early in 1843. He made Jackson's reply public the following year, in the midst of the treaty controversy. In that letter, and in the many others Jackson wrote on Texas before he died, the old Hero provided strong support for annexation. He believed the stories of a British anti-slavery plot, in spite of letters from his anti-Calhoun friends. An independent Texas would fall into the British orbit, wrote Jackson, and Britain would encourage slave insurrections.[43]

Jackson had southern sympathies, like Cass, John L. O'Sullivan, and other spokesmen for Manifest Destiny. Unlike Calhoun, however, these men nationalized Texas. Calhoun wanted to expand slavery, Jackson to expand the Union. America, he wrote Brown in a widely quoted phrase, was "extending the area of freedom" in annexing Texas. Manifest Destiny cemented the identification of universal freedom with American expansion.[44]

The 1840s expansionists hoped to rescue America from growing tensions over slavery, and to provide the Union with regenerating national purpose. Offering dreams of unlimited land and nightmares of foreign influence, they promised "young America" a glorious future.[45] Jackson did not originate the specific expansionist arguments. But he did originate, in Indian territory, the historical experience on which they drew. Traditionally the 1840s is pictured as the great decade of westward expansion. But Manifest Destiny began west of the Appalachians in the 1812 War, not west of the Mississippi thirty years later. It began in Indian land. Jackson was a powerful force, as precedent and as ancient living authority, for 1840s expansionism.

Florida, wrote Jackson, had once exposed America to invasion. Now the southern Indians had removed west, and the new border threat lay through Texas. Jackson himself had removed the Indians west; he was pursuing his own demons, manufacturing the boundary threats which only expansion could end. "Texas has offered us the key to our safety," he wrote. "I am for receiving it, locking the door at once."[46]

Unlike the parochial southern expansionists, Jackson favored the largest claims to Oregon. "Dash from your lips the counsel of the timid," he urged newly elected President Polk. England and France wanted to "destroy this union, and prevent the spread of republican principles." America should unilaterally extend its laws over Oregon—the technique of Indian removal again—"to shut out foreign influence from our people, and thereby place our glorious union on as sure a basis as the Rocky Mountains."⁴⁷

An organic natural right, dressed in legal clothes, sustained Manifest Destiny. Those favoring the "re-annexation" of Texas argued the territory had been American until Secretary of State John Quincy Adams returned it to Spain in the 1819 Florida treaty. Jackson had advanced this argument as President. Now he denounced "the dismemberment of our territory in 1819." He remembered, in the final falsification of his own history, opposing the Florida treaty because it relinquished Texas. He cited an affidavit from George Erving, American minister to Spain, that Erving won Spain's consent to America's Texas claims and that Adams signed them away. Erving denied making any such statement. In fact it was Adams, not Jackson, who had hoped to obtain Texas in 1819. Florida alone concerned Jackson; once the Florida treaty was signed, he had sided with Adams against its Texas-oriented critics. Foreign countries posed no danger to America through Texas, Jackson wrote Adams. Now he suppressed his own earlier stance. He accused Adams and others who disputed his memory of lying.⁴⁸

The Louisiana Purchase gave America only the flimsiest claim to Texas; after 1819 she had no claim at all. But the re-annexationists, fabricating evidence and misquoting documents, convinced themselves America was regaining what was rightfully hers. The west belonged, they insisted, to "young America." Most 1840s expansionists were young men, and the old Hero gave them his parental support. We should, he wrote, "restore Texas to her vested rights under the Treaty of 1803, by which she had been deprived of for years, cast off and neglected like an orphaned child."⁴⁹

Jackson took well-publicized part in the annexation debates. He also played a decisive role in the politics of Manifest Destiny. President Tyler, seeking symbolic connection to Jackson, appointed Andrew Jackson Donelson envoy to Mexico. The old man involved himself in his ward's diplomatic efforts. Donelson was too cautious, however, and Jackson acted, most significantly, on his own.⁵⁰

Tyler's Texas treaty forced the Democrats to take a stand on annexation. Van Buren, costing himself an apparently certain presidential nomination, opposed it. Jackson broke with Van Buren for the first time. He condemned the New Yorker's Texas stand, and put pressure on him to withdraw from the race. Jackson supported James K. Polk, a Tennessee protégé, for the Democratic nomination. Polk was a colorless party stalwart; he could not have gained the nomination without Jackson's sponsorship. The Democrats tried to envelop Polk in Jackson's mantle; Herman Melville's brother, active in New York politics, dubbed him "young Hickory." Polk's nomination, wrote Jackson, would strengthen the Democracy and the cause of annexation. Stressing expansion in the contest with Clay, Polk won a narrow victory.[51]

Polk wanted Oregon and California, he told George Bancroft shortly after inauguration. Like Jackson, he believed that Texas opened the road to California. The new republic could make, Jackson's hopes notwithstanding, no claim to the Pacific. Polk tried in vain, as Jackson had, to purchase California in return for inflated private Texas-American financial claims against Mexico. Finally the President resorted to a manufactured boundary dispute. Texas controlled the territory to the Nueces, but it sometimes claimed sovereignty over the Río Bravo del Norte (Rio Grande) 1,000 miles away. This claim covered a far greater area than the Mexican province of Texas. Most of the land was unsettled by Americans or Mexicans; the few existing communities were Mexican, however, and Mexico easily defeated the Texas expedition against Santa Fe. Mexico had legal and positive sovereignty over the Río del Norte lands.[52]

Polk nevertheless urged Texas to press its boundary claim. Jackson also endorsed it. The new annexation treaty left the Texas boundary to be determined in American-Mexican negotiations. Polk knew Mexico would not accept the Río del Norte line. Making no serious negotiating efforts, he dispatched American troops to the river. This advance was part of Polk's plan for the war he had resolved upon to gain California. While preparing his war message, Polk learned that a Mexican army had attacked American soldiers on the Río del Norte. Mexico, wrote the President in his war message, "has passed the boundary of the United States, has invaded our territory, and shed American blood upon American soil." On May 11, 1846, Congress declared war on Mexico.[53]

From the Sabine to the Nueces to the Rio Grande, persistent confusion about what was inside America and what outside propelled American expansion. Incorporation and removal were the twin tactics of Jacksonian expansion, and the spokesmen for Manifest Destiny applied the lessons of Indian dispossession to justify their territorial designs on Mexico. John L. O'Sullivan wrote,

> The Mexican race now see, in the fate of the aborigines of the north, their own inevitable destiny. They must amalgamate and be lost, in the superior vigor of the Anglo-Saxon race, or they must inevitably perish.[54]

Jackson died on June 8, 1845, several months before the American march to the Rio Grande. Despite continuing money worries and a steadily worsening physical condition, his last years were peaceful. Jackson showed no agitation over his approaching death; he had achieved mythic stature in the eyes of his countrymen. Dropsy moved from his swollen limbs to his whole body, and his eyesight often failed. His mind remained active, nevertheless, and he rejoiced before he died in Texas annexation.

Friends, relatives, and the Hermitage slaves gathered around Jackson as he neared the end. "Oh, do not cry," he told his slaves. "Be good children, and we shall all meet in heaven." Sam Houston, now with his own white wife and son, arrived at the Hermitage half an hour too late. They were "denied the satisfaction of seeing him in his last moments."[55]

Two days before Jackson died, he wrote to President Polk about the Choctaw land frauds. "A parent writing to his beloved son," explained Andrew Jackson, Jr., "could not have written a more kind and affectionate letter." This letter was Jackson's last—"the last ever written," Polk called it, "by the greatest man of the age in which he lived."[56]

Jackson's death had profound impact on America. Eulogies were heard from platforms around the country. Jackson was remembered for his Indian victories, for New Orleans, and for national unification. His controversial actions, particularly the Bank War, received little notice. "His body has its fit resting place in the great Valley of the Mississippi," proclaimed George Bancroft; "his spirit rests upon our whole territory; it hovers over the vales of Oregon, and guards in advance the frontiers of the Del Norte."[57]

Jackson died at the apex of national expansion. The system he fathered survived him by less than a decade, and the Union disintegrated in its wake. The locus of power inside the Democratic Party shifted to the south after Jackson's death. The Jacksonians had proposed party government as an alternative to sectional conflict, but southern party power no longer reflected the realities of economic and social life. Burgeoning northern manufactures and the growing importance of wheat and other northwestern staples decreased cotton's central role in economic development. Internal improvements and northern and western growth moved trade from a north-south to an east-west axis. The minority southern strategy gained strength in the south, stressing southern distinctiveness and isolating the region from the rest of the country.[58]

Efforts to perpetuate Jacksonian politics in this context only exacerbated the crisis. Jacksonian expansion generated the Mexican War, but the issue of slavery in the territories won from Mexico reopened the sectional conflict the Missouri Compromise had closed. The Compromise of 1850 briefly papered over sectional divisions, but territorial expansion opened them once again. Jacksonians Thomas Hart Benton and Stephen Douglas tried in the 1850s to sacrifice Indians to preserve the union of slave and free states. Douglas and Benton promoted westward expansion, a trans-continental railroad, and the destruction of the Indian territory guaranteed the tribes under Jackson's removal bill. Expansion successfully displaced Indians. Instead of superseding sectional differences, however, it magnified them. Douglas' Kansas-Nebraska policy precipitated the Civil War. Jackson's Chief Justice, Roger Taney, also tried to take slavery out of American politics, and the other Jacksonian Supreme Court Justices supported his Dred Scott decision. But Jacksonianism could no longer suppress the slave issue; Dred Scott, like bleeding Kansas, brought Civil War. Southerners close to Jackson—Benton, Donelson, Houston, and Call—sympathized with the Constitutional Union ticket in 1860 and opposed secession.[59] They were powerless against the disintegration of the Union.

III

Jacksonian regeneration was politically exhausted by the 1850s. "Bartleby," Melville's melancholy tale of that decade, portrays the resulting split between inner and public life. For Bartleby, thrown from one patronage clerkship to another "by a change in the political administration," the democratic promise was a failure. Retreating to "his hermitage" within the office, Bartleby "prefers not to" carry out his new tasks. But this "passive resistance," as Melville labels it, produces no natural renewal. A solitary, "motionless," "cadaverous" figure, Bartleby progressively withdraws from life into death.

Bartleby's employer tries to arrest this process, and it is soon apparent that this "elderly," "safe" lawyer has more at stake than mere disinterested philanthropy. He invites Bartleby to inhabit his own private space, separated by folding doors from the rest of the office. He experiences Bartleby as an "incubus" "clinging" to him, but he cannot let him go. The lawyer treats Bartleby as the withered remains of an internal self, impoverished by a lifetime in contracts and deeds. To redeem Bartleby for legal work would justify the lawyer's life. Melancholy Bartleby, refusing the lawyer his blessing, starves himself to death instead.[60]

Billy Budd, "Isaac" to Captain Vere's "Abraham" in Melville's post-Civil War story, did forgive his executioner. Billy's benediction "God bless Captain Vere!" signified the divided American soul healed in defense of the Union. Its "republican robe" washed white (Lincoln) in the blood of a war against slavery, America experienced a new birth of freedom. But the return to revolutionary principles actually legitimized hierarchy. Billy Budd, natural innocent from the *Rights-of-Man*, was a type from Jacksonian Democracy. His sacrifice, in Melville's iconography, sanctified the nation-state and other "lasting institutions" emerging from Jacksonian society and triumphant in Civil War.[61]

The Jacksonian system had inheritors more resilient than Bartleby and Billy Budd. It left behind not only an inner world emptied by capitalist and organizational expansion, but also a model for spiritual rebirth. Since the Puritan founding, American history has proceeded by consciousness of decline from the faith of the fathers and efforts at heroic renewal. Made in the name of the fathers to revitalize the sons, these efforts regenerate a world grown dead in sin. But the paternal inheritance is double-edged; it points to material acquisition as well as ideals, to contract as well as community. To act as the fathers acted, therefore, betrays their ideals, advances the triumph of capitalism, and moves the nation ever further from the paternal world.

Successive efforts to refound America, successively disappointed, each leaves its residue. The Age of Jackson definitively located American regeneration in western violence. When the gothic novel shifts in America, writes Leslie Fiedler, from "the ruined castle of the European prototypes to the . . . heathen, unredeemed wilderness," "nature and not society becomes the symbol of evil." This shift from society to nature is as important in politics as in art. Fiedler writes,

> The European gothic identified blackness with the super-ego and was therefore revolutionary in its implications; the American gothic . . . identified evil with the id and was therefore conservative at its deepest level of implication, whatever the intent of its authors.[62]

Jacksonian idealization of nature may seem to reject American gothic; it incorporates it instead. Jacksonian symbolism found monsters in society, and made a refuge of the land. It promised western regeneration, as American gothic did not. But monsters also inhabited the Jacksonian wilderness. The triumphant American symbols of nature, synthesizing unredeemed wilderness with virgin land, retained a conservative, gothic thrust. The Jacksonian landscape, as the images of Indian policy proclaim, directed attention westward to empire; it did not redirect attention to self or society. The west thus provided not merely an actual space for capitalist expansion, but also a mythic flight from its significance. Max Weber's demystified acquisitive and bureaucratic spirit was remystified on the frontier.

This mystification carried forward into the industrial age. The post-Civil War generation, trapped not only by bureaucratic capitalism but by the limits of continental expansion as well, rediscovered the frontier promise of American life. The resistance of western Indians to white expansion ended in 1890 at Wounded Knee. "For nearly three centuries," Frederick Jackson Turner wrote later that decade, "the dominant fact in American life has been expansion." "And now . . . the frontier is gone, and with its going has closed the first period of American history."[63]

Turner's elegy was more than nostalgic. His history of "the rebirth of American society" shortly reentered politics, in overseas expansion and domestic reform.[64] Woodrow Wilson, Theodore Roosevelt, and their contemporaries discovered a mission in the Caribbean and the Philippines linking industrial America to the frontier society of the fathers. There, on the new frontier, they fought regenerating wars. ("Every argument that can be made for the Filipinos could be made for the Apaches," said Roosevelt.) There they ruled, in Wilson's words, "children . . . in these great matters of government and justice." There they substituted state and Presidential action for unregulated frontier individualism, and brought that lesson back to government at home. Turner, Roosevelt, and Wilson, imperialists like Jackson before they were reformers, renewed the frontier vision for our time. Corporate power, worldly acquisitiveness, and bureaucratic order did not crush the American spirit. Rather that "spirit" (John Quincy Adams), going "abroad in search of monsters to destroy," breathed life into the Leviathan growing at home.

NOTES

A NOTE ON SOURCES

Abbreviations in the notes refer to the following sources:

AJC: John Spencer Bassett, ed., *Correspondence of Andrew Jackson*, 6 vols. (Washington, D.C., 1926–33).

AJD: Andrew Jackson Donelson Papers, on microfilm at the Library of Congress, Washington, D.C.

AJP: Andrew Jackson Papers, Library of Congress, on microfilm at the University of California, Berkeley, Calif.

ASPIA: U.S. Congress, *American State Papers, Indian Affairs*, 2 vols. (Washington, D.C., 1834).

ASPMA: U.S. Congress, *American State Papers, Military Affairs*, 7 vols. (Washington, D.C., 1832–61).

CC: The Claybrooke Collection of the Tennessee Historical Society, Tennessee State Library and Archives, Nashville, Tenn.

C/D: The John Coffee Papers and miscellaneous papers in the Dyas Collection of the Tennessee Historical Society, Tennessee State Library and Archives, Nashville, Tenn.

LP: The W. B. Lewis Papers, New York Public Library, New York, N.Y.

OIA: Office of Indian Affairs, on microfilm at the National Archives, Washington, D.C. Files cited are Cherokee, Chickasaw, Choctaw, Creek, and Treaty.

OIALR: Office of Indian Affairs, Letters Received, on microfilm at the National Archives, Washington, D.C.

OIALS: Office of Indian Affairs, Letters Sent, on microfilm at the National Archives, Washington, D.C., and the University of California, Berkeley, Calif.

O/M: The John Overton Papers in the Murdock Collection, Tennessee Historical Society, Tennessee State Library and Archives, Nashville, Tenn.

Quotations from Jackson use published sources wherever possible. Quotations from unpublished papers follow the example of the editor of Jackson's correspondence. I have made no changes in Jackson's erratic spelling; substituted "and" for Jackson's "&"; avoided the censorious *sic;* eliminated most of Jackson's ubiquitous dashes; and otherwise altered punctuation only where necessary to make the sense clear.

INTRODUCTION

1. John Locke, *Of Civil Government* (London, 1924), *Second Treatise*, p. 140. For Hobbes and Rousseau also, American Indian societies demonstrated the historical existence of the state of nature. Cf. Hoxie N. Fairchild, *The Noble Savage* (N.Y., 1961 [first published 1928]), pp. 23–24.

2. Alexander Hamilton, James Madison, John Jay, *The Federalist Papers* (N.Y., 1961), No. 1, p. 33.

3. John Quincy Adams, *An Oration Delivered at Plymouth, December 22, 1802* (Boston, 1802), p. 8.

4. Malcolm J. Rohrbough, *The Land Office Business* (N.Y., 1968), pp. xii, 295; Stuart Bruchey, *The Roots of American Economic Growth 1607–1861* (London, 1965),

p. 82; Douglass C. North, *The Economic Growth of the United States 1790–1860* (Englewood Cliffs, N.J., 1961), p. 17; Francis S. Philbrick, *The Rise of the West 1754–1830* (N.Y., 1965), p. 319.

5. Gary B. Nash, "The Image of the Indian in the Southern Colonial Mind," *William and Mary Quarterly*, 3rd. ser., XXIX (April 1972), 197–230; Martin Van Buren, *Autobiography*, *American Historical Association Annual Report, 1918, Vol. 2* (Washington, 1920), p. 275. Cf. Mary E. Young, *Redskins, Ruffleshirts, and Rednecks* (Norman, Okla., 1961), pp. 3–5, *passim;* Annie Heloise Abel, "The History of Events Resulting in Indian Consolidation West of the Mississippi," *American Historical Association, Report of Proceedings, 1906.* Indians are simply not mentioned at all in perhaps the two major contenders for synthetic interpretations of the Jacksonian period. Cf. Arthur Schlesinger, Jr., *The Age of Jackson* (Boston, 1945); Marvin Meyers, *The Jacksonian Persuasion* (New York, 1960). Thomas H. Benton's biographer largely ignores his important role in Indian affairs; Lewis Cass' biographer offers enormous, elementary, factual errors in his abbreviated account of the Secretary of War and Indian removal. Cf. William N. Chambers, *Old Bullion Benton* (Boston, 1956); Frank B. Woodford, *Lewis Cass* (New Brunswick, N.J., 1950), pp. 180–83.

6. I am indebted to Mark Morris for help in arriving at these estimates. We used Indian Office census figures, but these are often unreliable. Often, for example, the Indian bureau took no post-removal census, and simply listed the identical number of Indians living in a tribe before and after removal. We supplemented official figures with other estimates of tribal populations and of deaths during removal. Cf. "Report of the Superintendent of Indian Affairs," March 26, 1828, U.S. Serial Set, CLXXIV, Doc. 233, pp. 5–6. "Report of the House Committee on Indian Affairs," March 3, 1836, ASPMA, VI, 154–59. "Annual Report of the Commissioner of Indian Affairs," 1837, ASPMA, VII, 785–86. "Annual Report of the Commissioner of Indian Affairs," 1843, U.S. Serial Set, CDXXXI, Doc. 1, p. 277. "Annual Report of the Commissioner of Indian Affairs," 1844, U.S. Serial Set, Vol. CDXLIX, Doc. 1, p. 34. E. A. Hayt, *Annual Report of the Commissioner of Indian Affairs, 1876–77* (Washington, 1877), pp. 489–90. Grant Foreman, *Indian Removal* (Norman, Okla., 1932), pp. 47, 111, 250, 312. Grant Foreman, *The Five Civilized Tribes* (Norman, Okla., 1934), pp. 21, 107. Grant Foreman, *The Last Trek of the Indians* (Chicago, 1946), pp. 141–43, 153. Angie Debo, *The Rise and Fall of the Choctaw Republic* (Norman, Okla., 1934), pp. 69–70. Angie Debo, *The Road to Disappearance* (Norman, Okla., 1941), p. 103. Marion L. Starkey, *The Cherokee Nation* (N.Y., 1946), p. 300. Morris L. Wardell, *A Political History of the Cherokee Nation, 1838–1907* (Norman, Okla., 1938), p. 242. William T. Hagan, *The Sac and Fox Indians* (Norman, Okla., 1958), pp. 7, 205–06. William T. Hagan, *American Indians* (Chicago, 1961), p. 85.

7. "Annual Report of the Secretary of War," 1831, ASPMA, IV, 714; Senator John Tipton, U.S. Congress, *The Congressional Globe*, VI (1837–38), Appendix, 269; Van Buren, p. 295.

8. Martin Van Buren, "Second Annual Message," Dec. 3, 1838, in James D. Richardson, ed., *Messages and Papers of the Presidents* (N.Y., 1917), III, 500.

9. William Crawford to Cherokee delegation, May 13, 1816, ASPIA, II, 109; Andrew Jackson, D. Meriwether, and J. Franklin to William Crawford, Sept. 20, 1816, ASPIA, II, 105; "Defense of Brigadier General Wool," Sept. 4, 1837, ASPMA, VII, 571; "Report of the House Committee on Indian Affairs," Feb. 21, 1823, ASPIA, II, 408; John C. Calhoun to Cherokee delegation, Feb. 11, 1819, ASPIA, II, 190; Andrew Jackson, "Farewell Address," March 4, 1837, Richardson, III, 294. Many statesmen, scientists, ministers, and travelers believed Indians were descended from one of the ten lost tribes of Israel. Cf. Nash, pp. 224–25; George W. Manypenny, *Our Indian Wards* (N.Y., 1972 [first published 1880]), p. 66; Wilbur R. Jacobs, *Dispossessing the American Indian* (N.Y., 1972), p. 65n; Charles L. Sanford, *The Quest for Paradise* (Urbana, Ill., 1961), p. 66. White language often had roots in tribal rhetoric, but whites used

familial language among themselves as well as in addressing the tribes. Familial symbols expressed powerful white conceptions; they were not merely an instrumental adaptation to Indian usage.

10. U.S. Congress, *Register of Debates,* XII (1835–36), 4551.

11. Norman O. Brown, *Love's Body* (N.Y., 1966), p. 30.

12. D. H. Lawrence, *Studies in Classic American Literature* (Garden City, N.Y., 1953 [first published 1923]), pp. 44–45.

13. I am indebted to William Roth for calling *The Death Struggle* to my attention.

14. Here and throughout I have relied heavily on Roy Harvey Pearce's seminal *Savagism and Civilization* (Baltimore, Md., 1965; first published as *The Savages of America* [Baltimore, Md., 1953]). Cf. also Winthrop D. Jordan, *White over Black* (Baltimore, Md., 1969), pp. 89–91, 247–48, 477–81; George W. Stocking, Jr., *Race, Culture, and Evolution* (N.Y., 1968), pp. 26–27, 75–100; Arthur A. Ekirch, *The Idea of Progress in America, 1815–1860* (N.Y., 1944), pp. 15–46.

15. Adams, pp. 23–25. Adams' oration was often cited in congressional debates on Indian removal. Cf. Representative Charles Haynes of Georgia, *Register of Debates,* XII, 4505.

16. Virgil J. Vogel, ed., *This Country Was Ours: A Documentary History of the American Indian* (N.Y., 1972), p. 104; Senator John Tipton, *Congressional Globe,* VI, Appendix, 270; Albert K. Weinberg, *Manifest Destiny* (Chicago, 1963 [first published 1935]), pp. 72–89; Mary E. Young, "Indian Removal and Land Allotment: The Civilized Tribes and Jacksonian Justice," *American Historical Review,* LXIV (Oct. 1958), 37–38.

17. Francis Parkman, *The Conspiracy of Pontiac* (N.Y., 1962 [first published 1851]), pp. 182–83; General Edmund P. Gaines to the inhabitants of Murder Creek, Alabama, ASPMA, I, 684; Pearce, pp. 82–118, 161–63; Ekirch, pp. 15–17.

18. Jordan, pp. 90–91.

19. Andrew Jackson, "First Annual Message," Dec. 8, 1829, Richardson, II, 458.

20. Cf. Alexis de Tocqueville, *Democracy in America,* 2 vols. (N.Y., 1945), II, 108; Louis Hartz, *The Liberal Tradition in America* (N.Y., 1955); James Madison, quoted in Abel, p. 222. "Next to the case of the black race within our bosom," Madison wrote after he left the Presidency, "that of the red on our borders is the problem most baffling to the policy of our country."

21. Henry Baudet, *Paradise on Earth* (New Haven, Conn., 1965), p. 8. Cf. Jordan, pp. 32–43; Sheldon S. Wolin, *Politics and Vision* (Boston, 1960), pp. 286–351.

22. Cf. Richard Slotkin, *Regeneration through Violence: The Mythology of the American Frontier, 1600–1860* (Middletown, Conn., 1973). I read this magnificent book after completing my own manuscript, but did incorporate some of Slotkin's insights into the introduction. We share a similar perspective on American development.

23. Weinberg, p. 195; Thomas Hart Benton in ASPIA, II, 512.

24. Jackson to Andrew Jackson Donelson, Nov. 21, 1819, AJC, II, 441.

25. The analysis summarized here joins the psychoanalytic theories of Melanie Klein and Géza Róheim to the interpretation of America as a liberal society. Cf. Géza Róheim, *The Origins and Functions of Culture* (N.Y., 1943), *Magic and Schizophrenia* (N.Y., 1955), *The Panic of the Gods* (N.Y., 1972); Melanie Klein, *Contributions to Psychoanalysis* (London, 1948), and Melanie Klein et al., eds., *New Directions in Psychoanalysis* (London, 1955).

26. Lawrence, p. 93.

27. A. Alvarez, *The Savage God: A Study of Suicide* (London, 1972), pp. 104–08, contains the best brief understanding of the death instinct I have seen. Cf. Sigmund Freud, *Beyond the Pleasure Principle,* in James Strachey, ed., *The Standard Edition of the Complete Psychological Works of Sigmund Freud,* XVIII (London, 1955), 9–64,

the writings of Melanie Klein cited in note 25 above, and Norman O. Brown, *Life against Death* (N.Y., 1959).

28. Hannah Arendt, *The Origins of Totalitarianism,* 2nd ed. (N.Y., 1958), pp. 192–97. See also her discussion of imperialism, pp. 124–47.

29. "Our Indian Policy," *The United States Magazine and Democratic Review,* XIV (Feb. 1844), 169. John L. O'Sullivan is probably the author.

30. Cf. Bernard W. Sheehan, "Indian-White Relations in Early America: A Review Essay," *William and Mary Quarterly,* 3rd. ser., XXVI (April 1969), 267–86, and "Paradise and the Noble Savage in Jeffersonian Thought," *William and Mary Quarterly,* 3rd ser. XXVI (July 1969), 327–59, especially pp. 358–59. Sheehan rejects moralistic condemnations of American Indian policy from the culture-conflict perspective. He also argues that the noble-savage myth led whites harshly to judge their displacement of Indians. But this myth was integral to American culture. Sheehan seems to wish that American culture could purge itself of the myth; then it could adopt a culture-conflict perspective on its own behavior, and not judge itself so harshly. For Sheehan's own interpretation of white-Indian relations, cf. his *Seeds of Extinction: Jeffersonian Philanthropy and the American Indian* (Chapel Hill, N.C., 1973). My criticism is developed in "Indian Extinction, American Regeneration," *Journal of Ethnic Studies,* II (Spring 1974), 93–104.

31. My understanding of ideology and its relation to human action has benefited from Hanna Fenichel Pitkin, *Wittgenstein and Justice* (Berkeley, Calif., 1972), pp. 241–80; and Clifford Geertz, "Ideology as a Cultural System," in David E. Apter, *Ideology and Discontent* (N.Y., 1964). Cf. also Peter Winch, *The Idea of a Social Science and Its Relation to Philosophy* (N.Y., 1965); Alisdair MacIntyre, "A Mistake About Causality in Social Science," in Peter Laslett and W. G. Runciman, eds., *Philosophy, Politics, and Society* (Second Series), (N.Y., 1962); Michael Paul Rogin and John L. Shover, *Political Change in California* (Westport, Conn., 1970), pp. 178–82; Murray B. Edelman, *The Symbolic Uses of Politics* (Urbana, Ill., 1964).

32. On the law of combined and uneven development, cf. Hartz, pp. 3, 236–37; Leon Trotsky, *Permanent Revolution* (Calcutta, 1947). On primitive capitalist accumulation, see chapter 6, below.

33. Cf. Erik H. Erikson, *Childhood and Society,* 2nd ed. (Middlesex, Eng., 1963), p. 327, and *Young Man Luther* (N.Y., 1962); Joseph Campbell, *The Hero with a Thousand Faces* (N.Y., 1956); Erich Fromm, *The Dogma of Christ and Other Essays* (N.Y., 1963), pp. 3–11.

34. John William Ward, *Andrew Jackson—Symbol for an Age* (N.Y., 1955); Meyers, pp. 3–5.

35. Cf. Fred Weinstein and Gerald M. Platt, *The Wish to Be Free* (Berkeley, Calif., 1969), pp. 26–28.

36. Jackson, "Announcement to His Soldiers," Nov. 14, 1812, AJC, I, 241.

CHAPTER ONE

1. Edwin G. Burrows and Michael Wallace, "The American Revolution: The Ideology and Psychology of National Liberation," *Perspectives in American History,* VI (1972), 168. This chapter relies heavily on the analysis and evidence Burrows and Wallace provide.

2. Cf. David J. Rothman, *The Discovery of the Asylum* (Boston, 1971), pp. 4–53; Terence Martin, "Social Institutions in the Early American Novel," *American Quarterly,* IX (Spring 1957), 75–79; Michael Walzer, *The Revolution of the Saints* (Cambridge, Mass., 1965), pp. 199–231; Bernard Bailyn, *Education in the Forming of American Society* (Chapel Hill, N.C., 1960), pp. 15–21; John Demos, *A Little Common-*

wealth (N.Y., 1970), pp. 183–88; Arthur W. Calhoun, *A Social History of the American Family,* 3 vols. (N.Y., 1917–19), II, 11.

3. Stuart Bruchey, *The Roots of American Economic Growth 1607–1861* (London, 1965), pp. 29–70, 188–203; Jackson T. Main, *The Social Structure of Revolutionary America* (Princeton, N.J., 1965), pp. 10–113; Curtis P. Nettels, *The Emergence of a National Economy 1775–1815* (N.Y., 1962), p. 281. On commodity and exchange relationships, cf. Karl Marx, *Capital,* 3 vols. (Chicago, 1906–09), I, 41–106; C. Patrick O'Donnell, "What is Property?", unpublished seminar paper, University of California at Berkeley, 1972.

4. Bruchey, pp. 38, 49, 57–61; Main, pp. 100–13, 161–62; Sidney H. Aronson, *Status and Kinship in the Higher Civil Service* (Cambridge, Mass., 1964), pp. 37–45; Calhoun, I, 229, 242; Gerald W. Mullin, *Flight and Rebellion: Slave Resistance in Eighteenth-Century Virginia* (N.Y., 1972), pp. vii, 3–12, 19–24.

5. Burrows and Wallace, p. 255; Rothman, pp. 16, 30–53. (The quote is on p. 43.)

6. Bailyn, pp. 16–17; Demos, pp. 62–69; Main, p. 280; Rothman, p. 13; Philip J. Greven, Jr., "Family Structure in Seventeenth-Century Andover, Mass.," *William and Mary Quarterly,* 3rd ser., XXIII (April 1966), 255–56; Robert W. Ramsey, *Carolina Cradle* (Chapel Hill, N.C., 1964), pp. 27–129.

7. Burrows and Wallace, pp. 255–67; Greven, pp. 234–56; Philip J. Greven, Jr., "Historical Demography and Colonial America," *William and Mary Quarterly,* 3rd ser., XXIV (July 1967), 447; Gerda Lerner, "The Lady and the Mill Girl: Changes in the Status of Women in the Age of Jackson," *American Studies,* X (Spring 1969), 5–9.

8. Burrows and Wallace, pp. 260–62, 264–67. For references to "reason and experience," cf. Thomas Jefferson to John Adams, Nov. 13, 1787, to James Madison, Dec. 20, 1787, in Adrienne Koch and William Peden, eds., *The Life and Selected Writings of Thomas Jefferson* (N.Y., 1944), pp. 435, 438.

9. J. R. Pole, "Historians and the Problem of Early American Democracy," *American Historical Review,* LXVII (April 1962), 626–46; John Adams, *A Defense of the Constitutions of the Government of the United States of America . . . ,* in *The Works of John Adams,* Charles F. Adams, ed., 6 vols. (Boston, 1851–65), IV, 392–97, and "Letters to John Taylor," in *Works,* VI, 451–52; Thomas Jefferson, "Notes on Virginia," in Koch and Peden, p. 263; Jefferson to John Adams, Oct. 28, 1813, Koch and Peden, pp. 632–33; Aronson, pp. 1–12; Gordon S. Wood, *The Creation of the American Republic 1776–1787* (Chapel Hill, N.C., 1969), pp. 46–124, 213, 237.

10. Wood, pp. 319–89; Pauline Maier, "Popular Uprisings and Civil Authority in Eighteenth Century America," in Stanley N. Katz, ed., *Colonial America: Essays in Politics and Social Development* (Boston, 1971), pp. 308–38; Thomas Paine, *Common Sense,* in Moncure Conway, ed., *The Writings of Thomas Paine,* 4 vols. (N.Y., 1892–1908), I, 82. The Shippen quote is from Wood, p. 47.

11. Burrows and Wallace, pp. 169–74; Walzer, pp. 149–96.

12. Burrows and Wallace, pp. 182–90.

13. Bernard Bailyn, *The Origins of American Politics* (N.Y., 1970), and "Politics and Social Structure in Virginia," in James M. Smith, ed., *Seventeenth Century America: Essays in Colonial History* (Chapel Hill, N.C., 1959), p. 114. My analysis of colonial political structure and revolutionary ideology is heavily indebted to Bailyn's work.

14. Burrows and Wallace, pp. 196–206, 215–34; Bernard Bailyn, *The Ideological Origins of the American Revolution* (Cambridge, Mass., 1967), pp. 25, 46–52, *passim;* Paine, I, 83, 93, 99; "Jonathan Mayhew on the Right of Revolution," in Edmund S. Morgan, ed., *Puritan Political Ideas* (Indianapolis, Ind., 1965), pp. 314, 317. Bailyn quotes Patrick Henry on p. 253. Cf. Winthrop Jordan, "Familial Politics: Thomas Paine and the Killing of the King, 1776," *Journal of American History,* LX (Sept. 1973), 294–308.

15. Burrows and Wallace, pp. 193–203, 203n.

16. Bailyn, *Ideological Origins*, pp. 56–62; Wood, pp. 18–28, 40.

17. Charles G. Keshian, "The Political Character of the Novels of Charles Brockden Brown," unpublished Ph.D. dissertation, University of California at Berkeley, 1972, contains Revere's engraving on p. 284, and many examples of personifications of England and America in republican literature.

18. Norman Jacobson, "Political Science and Political Education," *American Political Science Review*, LVII (Sept. 1963), 565, suggests the political significance of Paine's fable. Cf. Thomas Paine, "Cupid and Hymen" and "Common Sense," in *Writings*, I, 36–40, 100.

19. Bailyn, *Ideological Origins*, pp. 135–36; Wood, pp. 52–53; Burrows and Wallace, p. 192.

20. Wood, pp. 52–53; John Adams, "Thoughts on Government," *Works*, IV, 199. Cf. Bailyn, *Ideological Origins*, pp. 94–125.

21. John Adams, *A Dissertation on the Canon and Feudal Law*, *Works*, III, 460–61. Cf. Paine, *Common Sense*, *Writings*, I, 85–86.

22. Bailyn, *Ideological Origins*, pp. 94–160 (the quotes are on pp. 126, 120, 119); Adams, *Canon and Feudal Law*, *Works*, III, 445, 457.

Charles Brockden Brown's political allegory, *Arthur Mervyn*, places the innocent republican youth at an imagined primal scene. Arthur finds himself in the locked bedroom of his benefactor, in the company of a sleeping baby. He hides in a closet to escape detection, and learns that the baby is the illegitimate son of his benefactor; the duplicitous man wishes his wife to accept the baby in place of one she has lost. Husband and wife retire to bed. Fearing detection, and twice waking the couple, Mervyn finally escapes from the room. Cf. *Arthur Mervyn* (N.Y., 1962 [first published 1799 and 1800]), pp. 32–34.

23. Adams, *Canon and Feudal Law*, *Works*, III, 448, 454.

24. Wood, pp. 46–74, 99; Bailyn, *Ideological Origins*, pp. 138–43; Paine, *The Rights of Man*, *Writings*, II, 422. The quote in the text is from Wood, p. 60.

25. Herbert Marcuse, *One-Dimensional Man* (Boston, 1964), pp. 56–83.

26. Bailyn, *Origins of American Politics*, pp. 66–98, 124, 136–38.

27. Sam Adams, *Writings*, Harry Alonyo Cushing, ed., 4 vols. (N.Y., 1904–08), II, 206. I am indebted to Marvin Cohen's work on Sam Adams for this quote.

28. Quoted by Burrows and Wallace, p. 203.

29. Paine, *Common Sense*, *Writings*, I, 86–87, 100. Thomas Jefferson, "Autobiography," in Koch and Peden, p. 25.

30. Jefferson, "Autobiography," in Koch and Peden, pp. 25–26.

31. Wood, pp. 100, 79, 197–222, 246–51; Bailyn, "Politics and Social Structure," pp. 107–12; Bailyn, *Origins of American Politics*, pp. 131–32; Main, p. 283.

32. Bailyn, "Politics and Social Structure," pp. 107–11; Alexis de Tocqueville, *Democracy in America*, 2 vols. (N.Y., 1945), I, 30, 50–53.

33. Thomas P. Abernethy, *From Frontier to Plantation in Tennessee* (Chapel Hill, N.C., 1932), pp. 59–60. See below, chapter 3.

34. Bailyn, *Origins of American Politics*, pp. 96–124; Wood, pp. 73–77.

35. Wood, p. 40.

36. Max Weber, *The Protestant Ethic and the Spirit of Capitalism* (N.Y., 1958), pp. 104–05, 115, *passim*; Perry Miller, *The New England Mind: The Seventeenth Century* (N.Y., 1939); Erik H. Erikson, *Young Man Luther* (N.Y., 1962); Henry Adams, *Mont-Saint-Michel and Chartres* (Garden City, N.Y., 1959 [first published 1905]), pp. 307–08; Thomas More Brown, "The Image of the Beast: Anti-Papal Rhetoric in Colonial America," in Richard O. Curry and Thomas M. Brown, eds., *Conspiracy: The Fear of Subversion in American History* (N.Y., 1972), pp. 1–20.

For discussions of the Anne Hutchinson persecution from the perspective of Puritan antagonism to feminine power (a perspective badly neglected by historians), cf. Paula Rabinowitz, "Anne Hutchinson: Revolutionary," unpublished undergraduate paper, University of California at Berkeley, 1971, and Jeannette Gustafson, "Anne Hutchinson and the Antinomian Controversy," unpublished senior thesis, University of California at Berkeley, 1972.

37. Edmund S. Morgan, "The Puritan Ethic and the American Revolution," *William and Mary Quarterly*, 3rd ser., XXIV (Jan. 1967), 3–43; Jordan, pp. 304–06; Burrows and Wallace, p. 229.

38. Cf. Walzer, pp. 190–96; Burrows and Wallace, pp. 255–67.

39. Burrows and Wallace, pp. 242–50; Daniel H. Calhoun, *Professional Lives in America* (Cambridge, Mass., 1965), p. 12.

40. Kenneth Lockridge, "Land, Population, and the Evolution of New England Society, 1630–1790," in Katz, pp. 488–90; Wood, pp. 76–77.

41. Wilbur R. Jacobs, *Dispossessing the American Indian* (N.Y., 1972), pp. 37–38, 109–10; Francis S. Philbrick, *The Rise of the West, 1754–1830* (N.Y., 1965), pp. 1–52; Marc Egnal and Joseph A. Ernst, "An Economic Interpretation of the American Revolution," *William and Mary Quarterly*, 3rd ser., XXIX (Jan. 1972), 4–9; George Washington to William Crawford, Sept. 21, 1767, in Virgil J. Vogel, ed., *This Country Was Ours: A Documentary History of the American Indian* (N.Y., 1972), pp. 56–57.

42. Egnal and Ernst, pp. 3–38; cf. Bruchey, pp. 43–47.

43. Egnal and Ernst, p. 16; Charles G. Sellers, Jr., "Private Profits and British Colonial Policy: The Speculations of Henry McCulloh," *William and Mary Quarterly*, 3rd ser., VIII (Oct. 1951), 535–51.

44. Bailyn, *Origins of American Politics*, pp. 102–04; Wood, pp. 146, 47.

45. Wood, pp. 75–90; Lockridge, pp. 467–91; Main, pp. 183–92, 286–87; Bruchey, pp. 67–70; Rothman, pp. 5, 57; James A. Henretta, "Economic Development and Social Structure in Colonial Boston," in Katz, pp. 450–65.

46. Burrows and Wallace, pp. 211–15.

47. John Adams, *Defense, Works*, IV, 401; Wood, pp. 363–499. The quotes are on pp. 482, 418.

48. *Ibid.*, pp. 506–21, 562 64. The quotes are on pp. 475, 521.

49. *Ibid.*, pp. 342–43, 446–49, 506 47; Maier, pp. 336–38.

50. Wood, pp. 499–506, 547–62; Alexander Hamilton, James Madison, John Jay, *The Federalist Papers* (N.Y., 1961), Nos. 10, 51, pp. 77–84, 320–25; William Appleman Williams, *The Contours of American History* (Chicago, 1966), pp. 145–46, 158–62.

51. Wood, p. 467; Jackson T. Main, *The Antifederalists* (Chapel Hill, N.C., 1961), pp. 187–281; Bruchey, pp. 95–115; Douglass C. North, *The Economic Growth of the United States 1790–1860* (Englewood Cliffs, N.J., 1961), p. 46; Joseph Dorfman and R. G. Tugwell, *Early American Policy: Six Columbia Contributors* (N.Y., 1960), p. 33; Staughton Lynd, *Class Conflict, Slavery and the United States Constitution* (Indianapolis, Ind., 1967). The quotes are from Wood, and Dorfman and Tugwell.

52. Jefferson to Phillip Mazzei, April 24, 1796, in Koch and Peden, pp. 537–38; Bruchey, pp. 117–21.

53. Hannah Arendt, "What Is Authority," in *Between Past and Future* (N.Y., 1968), pp. 92–93, 120–24. Cf. Hannah Arendt, *On Revolution* (N.Y., 1963).

54. Quoted in Dwight Anderson, "The Quest for Immortality: Abraham Lincoln and the Founding of Political Authority in America," unpublished Ph.D. dissertation, University of California at Berkeley, 1972, pp. 1–2; cf. pp. 50-56.

55. Burrows and Wallace, pp. 224–25, 296. The young Abraham Lincoln explicitly raised this question; like Jackson, he worked out its consequences in his career. Cf. Abraham Lincoln, "Address to the Young Men's Lyceum of Springfield," Jan. 27, 1838, in T. Harry Williams, ed., *Selected Speeches, Messages, Letters* (N.Y.,

1957), pp. 5–14; Norman Jacobson, "Lincoln's Abraham," *The Helderberg Review*, I (Spring 1971), 15–17; Edmund Wilson, *Patriotic Gore* (N.Y., 1966), pp. 106–08; Anderson. Norman Jacobson first suggested to me the importance in American history of sons' efforts to liberate themselves from the constraining institutions of the fathers. On anxiety over American identity in the post-revolutionary years, cf. Lawrence J. Friedman, *Inventors of the Promised Land* (N.Y., 1975), especially chapters 1 and 2.

56. Ralph Waldo Emerson, "Nature," in Brooks Atkinson, ed., *The Selected Writings of Ralph Waldo Emerson* (N.Y., 1950), p. 3. I use the literature of the American Renaissance in this book for insight into the Jacksonian consciousness, not as quantitative evidence for the existence of that consciousness. Jacksonian politics and westward expansion made accessible the experience from which the American romantics made art. Transcendentalism derived, however, not simply from the power of Jackson and the forces he symbolized, but from the failed and ambiguous Jacksonian promise. Cf. Alan Heimert, "Moby Dick and American Political Symbolism," *American Quarterly*, XV (April 1963), 498–534.

57. Emerson, p. 6.

58. Henry David Thoreau, *Walden*, Sherman Paul, ed. (N.Y., 1957), pp. 46–47; Arthur Schlesinger, Jr., *The Age of Jackson* (Boston, 1945), p. 448.

CHAPTER TWO

1. Marquis, James, *Andrew Jackson: The Border Captain* (Indianapolis, Ind., 1933), pp. 1–11, 18–31; Augustus C. Buell, *History of Andrew Jackson*, 2 vols. (N.Y., 1904), I, 16–19, 57–58; S. Putnam Waldo, *Memoirs of Andrew Jackson* (Hartford, Conn., 1820), pp. 25–26; Richard B. Morris, "Class Struggle and the American Revolution," *William and Mary Quarterly*, 3rd ser., XIX (Jan. 1969), 20.

2. Waldo, p. 35; John William Ward, *Andrew Jackson—Symbol for an Age* (N.Y., 1955), p. 71. For the symbol of Jackson as a self-made man, cf. pp. 166–80.

3. Marvin Meyers, *The Jacksonian Persuasion* (N.Y., 1960), pp. 121, 127–28; Richard L. Rapson, "The American Child as Seen by British Travellers, 1845–1935," *American Quarterly*, XVII (Fall 1965), 526; Arthur E. Bestor, "Patent-Office Models of the Good Society: Some Relationships Between Social Reform and Westward Expansion," *American Historical Review*, XLVIII (April 1953), 506–16; Alexis de Tocqueville, *Democracy in America*, 2 vols. (N.Y., 1945), II, 202–08.

4. Andrew Jackson to William Williams, Sept. 25, 1819, AJC, II, 431; Buell, I, 25; James Parton, *Life of Andrew Jackson*, 3 vols. (Boston, 1866), I, 97; Herbert J. Doherty, *Richard Keith Call: Southern Unionist* (Gainesville, Fla., 1961), pp. 14, 27–28; Richard K. Call to Jackson, Oct. 14, 1821, AJC, III, 129n; Jackson to Call, March 9, 1826, *American Historical Magazine and Tennessee Historical Society Quarterly*, IV (April 1899), 104; Jackson to Call, Nov. 15, 1821, AJC, III, 130.

5. James, pp. 3–6; Robert W. Ramsey, *Carolina Cradle* (Chapel Hill, N.C., 1964), pp. 176–77, 191–92; George P. Germany, "The South Carolina Governing Elite, 1820–1860," unpublished Ph.D. dissertation, University of California at Berkeley, 1972, pp. 11–13, 20.

6. Ramsey, pp. 21, 152–85, 191–92; W. J. Cash, *The Mind of the South* (N.Y, 1954), pp. 18–110; Kenneth S. Lynn, *Mark Twain and Southwestern Humor* (Boston, 1959), pp. 25–30; Arthur K. Moore, *The Frontier Mind* (Lexington, Ky., 1957).

7. *Sketches of Eccentricities of Col. David Crockett*, quoted in Vernon L. Parrington, *Main Currents in American Thought*, 2 vols. (N.Y., 1954 [first published 1927]), II, 168. Here the horse-alligator serves genteel Whig purposes, but Jacksonians also identified themselves by that symbol. Cf. Parrington, II, 165–72; Lynn, pp. 52–61;

William Murrell, *A History of American Graphic Humor*, 2 vols. (N.Y., 1933), I, 110, 113, 141.

8. Jackson to George W. Campbell, Oct. 15, 1812, AJC, I, 236–38; Parton, I, 349–60. Twenty years earlier Mrs. Caffery and her small son had been captured by Indians. When she was released two years later, Mrs. Caffery was forced to leave her son with the Indians. This experience must have fueled Jackson's anger at the Indian agent, but his letter mentions not a word of it. Cf. A. W. Putnam, *History of Middle Tennessee* (Nashville, Tenn., 1859), pp. 375, 491.

9. Herman Melville, *Billy Budd, Sailor and Other Stories* (Baltimore, Md., 1967), p. 331.

10. Parton, I, 156–57; John Spencer Bassett, *The Life of Andrew Jackson*, 2 vols. (N.Y., 1925), I, 329. Daniel Webster attributed these words to Jefferson, and their authenticity is debatable.

11. Parton, I, 64.

12. Hannah Arendt, *On Revolution* (N.Y., 1963), pp. 78–83.

13. Parton, I, 58–69; Melville, p. 376.

14. Buell, II, 410–11.

15. W. H. Sparks, *The Memories of Fifty Years* (Philadelphia, 1882), pp. 147–48. Sparks badly garbled the circumstances in which Jackson took leave of his mother; still, the colloquial language of his version is plausible. Buell reports substantially the same message: "Avoid quarrels as long as you can without yielding to imposition. But sustain your manhood always. Never bring a suit at law for assault and battery or for defamation. The law affords no remedy for such outrages that can satisfy the feelings of a true man." Cf. Buell, I, 56; James, p. 30.

16. John Henry Eaton, *The Life of Andrew Jackson* (Philadelphia, 1824), p. 434. The only version Jackson wrote down himself is in a late letter to Van Buren: "I have to this old age, complied with my mother's advice 'to indict no man for assault and battery or sue him for slander.' " Jackson to Martin Van Buren, Dec. 4, 1838, AJC, V, 573. According to Mrs. Polk, James Crawford once wanted to arrest an eighteen-year-old who had beaten the twelve-year-old Andrew. " 'No sir!' exclaimed Aunt Betty. 'No son of mine shall ever appear as a complaining witness in a case of assault and battery. If he gets hold of a fellow too big for him, let him wait till he grows some and then try it again!' " Buell, II, 411.

17. On separation anxiety and oral rage, cf. Melanie Klein, "The Early Development of Conscience in the Child," "A Contribution to the Psychogenesis of Manic-Depressive States," and "Mourning and Its Relation to Manic-Depressive States," in *Contributions to Psychoanalysis* (London, 1948), pp. 267–77, 282–338; Géza Róheim, *Magic and Schizophrenia* (N.Y., 1955), pp. 119–227, "Primitive High Gods," in *The Panic of the Gods* (N.Y., 1972), pp. 57, 87–90; Erik H. Erikson, *Childhood and Society*, 2nd ed. (Middlesex, Eng., 1963), pp. 53–74, 239–43; John Bowlby, "Separation Anxiety," *International Journal of Psychoanalysis*, XLI (1960), 89–113, "Processes of Mourning," *International Journal of Psychoanalysis*, XLII (1961), 317–40, "The Nature of the Child's Tie to His Mother," *International Journal of Psychoanalysis*, XXXIX (Sept.–Oct. 1958), 350–73; Sándor Radó, "The Problem of Melancholia," *International Journal of Psychoanalysis*, IX (Oct. 1928), 420–38; Annie Reich, "Early Identifications as Archaic Elements in the Superego," *Journal of the American Psychoanalytic Association*, II (March 1954), 218–38; Harold F. Searles, "Data Concerning Certain Manifestations of Incorporation," in *Collected Papers on Schizophrenia and Related Subjects* (London, 1965), pp. 39–69. The Erikson quote in the text is from *Young Man Luther* (N.Y., 1962), p. 103.

18. Robert Jay Lifton, "Woman as Knower: Some Psychohistorical Perspectives," in Lifton, ed., *The Woman in America* (Boston, 1965), p. 34.

19. Francis Tomlinson Gardner, "The Gentleman from Tennessee," *Surgery, Gynecology, and Obstetrics*, LXXXVIII (March 1948), 404–11; Louis S. Goodman

and Alfred Gilman, *The Pharmacological Basis of Therapeutics,* 2nd ed. (N.Y., 1958), pp. 394–96. I am grateful to my brother-in-law, Dr. Robert Stanger, for explaining the functions of the parasympathetic nervous system to me.

20. And which could not tolerate criticism of the national identity. Americans are not merely thin-skinned, wrote Mrs. Trollope; they "have, apparently, no skins at all." Quoted in Edward Pessen, *Jacksonian America* (Homewood, Ill., 1969), p. 15. Cf. Quentin Anderson, *The Imperial Self* (N.Y., 1971).

21. Richard Hofstadter, *The Paranoid Style in American Politics* (N.Y., 1965), p. 132.

22. The John Henry legend, Erikson suggests, embodies American assertions of self-reliant independence. John Henry is born with a gigantic appetite, but his parents have not fed him. He says, "Don't get me mad on de day I'm bawn, because I'm skeered of my own se'f when I gits mad." John Henry boasts of how much he can eat; then, since he cannot rely on his parents and does not need to, he leaves home forever. Underlying the proclaimed independence are a sense of disappointment in his parents, a gigantic appetite, and a threat of violence. Cf. Erikson, *Childhood and Society,* pp. 288–90.

23. Jackson, "Proclamation on Taking Possession of Pensacola," May 29, 1818, AJC, II, 375; Tennessee Governor Wylie Blount, quoted in William A. Walker, Jr., "Tennessee, 1796–1821," unpublished Ph.D. dissertation, University of Texas, 1959, p. 290; Jackson to Blount, July 10, 1812, "General Order," Dec. 15, 1813, AJC, I, 231, VI, 429.

24. Erikson, *Childhood and Society,* pp. 239–40.

25. *Ibid.,* p. 241. For the best extended discussion of themes of basic trust in the oral stage, cf. the articles by John Bowlby cited at note 17 above.

26. Jackson to Call, Nov. 15, 1821, AJC, III, 130.

27. Jackson to John Coffee, June 20, 1828, AJC, III, 409, to Andrew Jackson Donelson, Feb. 24, 1817, March 21, 1822, AJC, II, 275, III, 156.

28. Jackson to A. J. Donelson, Nov. 21, 1819, AJC, II, 441.

29. Bernard Wishy, *The Child and the Republic* (Philadelphia, 1968), pp. 3–56; Robert Sunley, "Early Nineteenth-Century American Literature on Child Rearing," in Margaret Mead and Martha Wolfenstein, eds., *Childhood in Contemporary Cultures* (Chicago, 1955), pp. 151–54; William E. Bridges, "Family Patterns and Social Values in America, 1825–1875," *American Quarterly,* XVII (Spring 1965), 4–8. On the rise of the conjugal family in Europe, cf. Philippe Ariès, *Centuries of Childhood* (N.Y., 1962).

30. Sunley, pp. 153, 159, 162; David J. Rothman, *The Discovery of the Asylum* (Boston, 1971), p. 218.

31. Bray Hammond, *Banks and Politics in America from the Revolution to the Civil War* (Princeton, N.J., 1957), p. 331; Ward, pp. 164–65. Whigs adopted the same rhetoric. Massachusetts Senator John Davis, the *Boston Courier* claimed, "was not cradled in wealth; he was not nursed and dandled into a politician." Cf. Norman Jacobson, "The Concept of Equality in the Assumptions and Propaganda of Massachusetts Conservatives, 1790–1840," unpublished Ph.D. dissertation, University of Wisconsin, 1951, p. 302n.

32. Barbara Welter, "The Cult of True Womanhood: 1820–1860," *American Quarterly,* XVIII (Summer 1966), 150–52, 162–73; Wishy, pp. 3–79; Sunley, pp. 159–60.

33. Marquis James, *The Raven* (N.Y., 1962 [first published 1929]), pp. 29–30. The implicit sexual invitation distinguishes Mrs. Houston's injunction from Mrs. Jackson's.

34. Joseph F. Kett, "Adolescence and Youth in Nineteenth Century America," *Journal of Interdisciplinary History,* II (Autumn 1971), 186–89; William R. Taylor, *Cavalier and Yankee* (N.Y., 1961), pp. 82–93; Waldo; John Reid and John H. Eaton,

The Life of Andrew Jackson (Philadelphia, 1817). Eaton subsequently republished this biography, with some additional material, under his own name. Citations in the text are to the 1824 edition.

35. Cf. Erikson, *Young Man Luther*, pp. 98–125.

36. Sigmund Freud, "Mourning and Melancholia," in James Strachey, ed., *The Standard Edition of the Complete Psychological Works of Sigmund Freud*, XIV, (London, 1957), 243–58.

37. James, *Jackson*, pp. 33–36.

38. Jackson to Blount, Jan. 4, 1813, AJC, I, 254–55. (Underlining in original.)

39. Waldo, p. 35; James, *Jackson*, pp. 36–37.

40. Parton, I, 104–09; James, *Jackson*, p. 39.

41. James, *Jackson*, pp. 39–41.

42. Cf. R. W. B. Lewis, *The American Adam* (Chicago, 1955), pp. 1–7, 49–50, 127–29. Several leading Jacksonian expansionists—Thomas Hart Benton, Richard K. Call, and John L. O'Sullivan—had lost their fathers in childhood. Cf. William N. Chambers, *Old Benton Bullion* (Boston, 1956), p. 11; Julius W. Pratt, "John L. O'Sullivan and Manifest Destiny," *New York History*, XIV (July 1933), 217; Doherty, p. 3.

43. Reich, p. 236; Otto Rank, *The Myth of the Birth of the Hero*, discussed in Nathan G. Hale, *Freud and the Americans* (N.Y., 1971), p. 344; Erikson, *Young Man Luther*, pp. 123–25; George Bach, "Father-Fantasies and Father-Typing in Father-Separated Children," *Child Development*, XVII (Mar. 1946), 63–80.

44. These themes are developed in chapters 1, 5, and 8. Cf. Fred Somkin, *Unquiet Eagle: Memory and Desire in the Idea of American Freedom, 1815–1860* (Ithaca, N.Y., 1967), pp. 3–7, 148–57, 176–92.

45. James, *Jackson*, pp. 71–73; Buell, I, 91–94; Walker, p. 168; A. P. Whitaker, "Spanish Intrigue in the Old Southwest," *Mississippi Valley Historical Review*, XII (Sept. 1925), 170n.

46. Richard Hofstadter, *The American Political Tradition* (N.Y., 1948), pp. 46–47; Harriette S. Arnow, *Seedtime on the Cumberland* (N.Y., 1960), 275–76, 370, 381, 424n; Chase Mooney, *Slavery in Tennessee* (Bloomington, Ind., 1957), pp. 113, 184.

47. The family relationships identified in this paragraph come from Donelson family trees in the Coffee-Dyas papers and in W. W. Clayton, *History of Davidson County, Tennessee* (Philadelphia, 1880), p. 137; and from Clayton, pp. 134–37, 198, 479; James, *Jackson*, p. 66; Arnow, pp. 216, 234, 276; Thomas P. Abernethy, *From Frontier to Plantation in Tennessee* (Chapel Hill, N.C., 1932), pp. 54, 59.

48. Walker, pp. 18–23, 126; Clayton, p. 73; Abernethy, p. 241.

49. Cf. the excellent analysis in Daniel H. Calhoun, *Professional Lives in America* (Cambridge, Mass., 1965), pp. 62–85.

50. George Dangerfield, *The Era of Good Feelings* (N.Y., 1952), p. 220; Walker, p. 168; Gerald W. Mullin, *Flight and Rebellion: Slave Resistance in Eighteenth-Century Virginia* (N.Y., 1972), pp. vii, 3–12, 19–24; Eugene D. Genovese, *The World the Slaveholders Made* (N.Y., 1969), pp. 96, 122–238. Meminger is quoted on p. 195.

51. Genovese, pp. 122–238; Ronald T. Takaki, *A Pro-Slavery Crusade* (N.Y., 1971), pp. 84–102; Mooney, pp. 52, 91.

52. Bassett, I, 66; James, *Jackson*, pp. 101–12.

53. Tocqueville, I, 375–81, II, 99–128; Jackson to Edward Livingston, Jan. 7, 1820, AJC, III, 1; Stanley Elkins and Eric McKitrick, "A Meaning for Turner's Frontier," *Political Science Quarterly*, LXIX (Dec. 1954), 566–82.

54. Buell, I, 155; James, *Jackson*, p. 47; Putnam, p. 618.

55. Jackson to Waightstill Avery, Aug. 12, 1788, AJC, I, 5.

56. Jackson to John McNairy, May 9, 1797, to William Cocke, June 24, June 25, 1798, AJC, I, 34–35, 48–49; Jackson to McNairy, March 27, 1799, AJP; Walker, pp. 18, 97–101. The Dickinson duel and the quarrel with Sevier are discussed in chapter 5.

57. Calhoun, pp. 7, 17–18; Cash, pp. 82–93; John Hope Franklin, *The Militant South* (Cambridge, Mass., 1956), pp. 15–18, 44–50; Jackson T. Main, *The Social Structure of Revolutionary America* (Princeton, N.J., 1965), pp. 107, 204–11; Jackson to Cocke, June 25, 1798, AJC, I, 49.

58. Jackson to Call, Nov. 15, 1821, AJC, III, 130.

59. Bassett, II, 729–30.

60. James, *Jackson*, p. 56; Buell, I, 94–98.

61. On Jackson's marriage, cf. James, *Jackson*, pp. 64–78; Parton, I, 147–52. Samuel G. Heiskell, *Andrew Jackson and Early Tennessee History*, 3 vols. (Nashville, Tenn., 1920), I, 443–49 reprints Overton's complete statement.

62. Marquis James, *Andrew Jackson: Portrait of a President* (Indianapolis, Ind., 1937), p. 156.

63. James, *Jackson: Border Captain*, p. 67, *Portrait of a President*, pp. 207–13, 269–76; Arthur W. Calhoun, *A Social History of the American Family*, 3 vols. (N.Y., 1917–19), II, 33. The Eaton affair is discussed below, chapter 8.

64. Arnow, pp. 373n, 424n; James, *Jackson: Border Captain*, pp. 68–71, 382. James also reports testimony, from an apparently reliable source, that Rachel "eloped" from Kentucky with Jackson (p. 76), further suggesting the two planned to marry when he went to Kentucky to get her. Arnow discovered the crucial evidence from the estate settlement, but failed to relate it to the controversy over Jackson's marriage.

65. Edmund S. Morgan, *Virginians at Home* (N.Y., 1952), p. 79; A. W. Calhoun, I, 36–38; Heiskell, I, 443–44. Colonel James Robertson, one of Nashville's founders, performed marriage ceremonies on the Cumberland until 1783, when North Carolina formally extended its laws. Cf. Putnam, p. 116.

66. Cf. Róheim, *Panic of the Gods*, p. 192; Joel Kovel, *White Racism: A Psychohistory* (N.Y., 1970), pp. 48–50.

67. On the relationship between money, debt, and women, cf. chapters 3 and 9 below.

68. For the Nashville serial, cf. Anne K. Nelson and Hart M. Nelson, "Family Articles in Frontier Newspapers: An Examination of One Aspect of Turner's Frontier Thesis," *Journal of Marriage and the Family*, XXXI (Nov. 1969), 647–48. For discussions of the political and psychological significance of sentimental and gothic fiction, and the literary implications of political symbolism, cf. Leslie A. Fiedler, *Love and Death in the American Novel* (N.Y., 1960), pp. 3–212; Masao Miyoshi, *The Divided Self* (N.Y., 1969), pp. 3–103; Leo Lowenthal, *Literature and the Image of Man* (Boston, 1957), pp. 140–49; Charles G. Keshian, "The Political Character of the Novels of Charles Brockden Brown," unpublished Ph.D. dissertation, University of California at Berkeley, 1972.

69. Terence Martin, "Social Institutions in the Early American Novel," *American Quarterly*, IX (Spring 1957), 74–80; Keshian, pp. 29–33, 47–51.

70. Martin, *loc. cit.*

71. Taylor, pp. 83–96; Ward, pp. 11–90.

72. J. R. Pole, "Historians and the Problem of Early American Democracy," *American Historical Review*, LXVII (April 1962), 645. The best single treatment of the loss of family functions to other institutions is Rothman, *Discovery of the Asylum;* cf. also William R. Taylor and Christopher Lasch, "Two 'Kindred Spirits': Society and Family in New England, 1839–1846," *New England Quarterly*, XXXVI (March 1963), 33. The economic underpinnings are provided in Stuart Bruchey, *The Roots of American Economic Growth 1607–1861* (London, 1965); George R. Taylor, *The Transportation Revolution* (N.Y., 1951). Dubious about this line of thought is Edward N. Saveth, "The Problem of American Family History," *American Quarterly*, XXI (Summer 1969), 311–29.

73. D. H. Calhoun, p. 12; Tocqueville, II, 202–25; Welter, pp. 150–51; James S. Young, *The Washington Community, 1800–1828* (N.Y., 1966), pp. 49–64; Ward, p.

192; W. R. Taylor, pp. 17, 96–98; John Demos, *A Little Commonwealth* (N.Y., 1970), pp. 187–88.

74. Jackson to Robert Hays, Aug. 24, 1801, AJC, VI, 424–25; Thomas Hart Benton, quoted in Parton, I, 346; Jackson to George Rutledge, Oct. 7, 1803, AJP; Jackson to John Coffee, Dec. 27, 1824, AJC, III, 270. Cf. Jackson to Rachel Jackson, Dec. 28, 1823, in Avery O. Craven, ed., "Letters of Andrew Jackson," *Huntington Library Bulletin*, No. 3 (Feb. 1933), p. 119.

75. Michel Chevalier, *Society, Manners, and Politics in the United States,* John W. Ward, ed. (Garden City, N.Y., 1961), pp. 299–300.

76. Welter, pp. 150–74; W. R. Taylor, pp. 169–74; Gerda Lerner, "The Lady and the Mill Girl: Changes in the Status of Women in the Age of Jackson," *American Studies*, X (Spring 1969), 5–15.

77. Cf. Tocqueville, II, 209–17; William Wasserstrom, *Heiress of All the Ages* (Minneapolis, Minn., 1959).

78. Welter, pp. 154–56, 162.

79. Parton, I, 138–39.

80. Jackson to Robert Hays, Nov. 2, 1797, AJC, I, 39; Jackson to Hays, Dec. 6, 1796, AJP; Jackson to Rachel Jackson, Sept. 17, 1799, AJC, VI, 423–24; John Coffee to Jackson, April 23, 1804, AJP; Rachel Jackson to Jackson, Feb. 10, 1814, AJC, I, 459.

81. Jackson to John Overton, Nov. 18, 1823, CC; John Donelson to Coffee, Jan. 12, 1824, C/D. In 1825 Rachel was again, in Jackson's words, "much debillitated, her mind much affected, and spirits remarkable depressed, with want of appetite and cannot sleep." Jackson to Coffee, Dec. 1, 1825, March 2, 1826, May 2, 1826, C/D.

82. Welter, pp. 171–73; James, *Jackson: Border Captain*, pp. 91, 139, 329, *Portrait of a President*, p. 24.

83. Buell, I, 152–53.

84. James, *Portrait of a President*, pp. 169–70; Welter, p. 162.

85. Coffee to Mary Coffee, Jan. 20, 1814, C/D; Jackson to Overton, Nov. 8, 1823, CC; Rachel Jackson to Jackson, Feb. 18, 1813, AJP.

86. Nelson and Nelson, pp. 647–48.

87. *Ibid.*, p. 649.

88. Lynn, pp. 25–26; Curtis Dahl, "The American School of Catastrophe," *American Quarterly*, XI (Fall 1959), 380–90.

89. Tocqueville, II, 147.

90. *Ibid.*, I, 264–80, II, 306–12, 334–39. Cf. Michael Paul Rogin and John L. Shover, *Political Change in California* (Westport, Conn., 1970), pp. 187–90.

91. Meyers, p. 121; Lilian B. Miller, "Painting, Sculpture, and the National Character 1815–1860," *Journal of American History*, LIII (March 1967), 696–706.

92. Welter, pp. 163–64.

93. *Ibid.*, pp. 158–59.

94. Cf. Joseph Campbell, "Bios and Mythos: Prologemena to a Science of Mythology," in George B. Wilbur and Warner Muensterberger, eds., *Psychoanalysis and Culture* (N.Y., 1951), pp. 329–43; Erikson, *Young Man Luther*, pp. 115–19; Róheim, *Panic of the Gods*, p. 197.

95. Alexis de Tocqueville, "A Fortnight in the Wilds," in *Journey to America,* J. P. Mayer, ed. (London, 1959), p. 339; Chevalier, p. 300; Pessen, p. 86; Lerner, pp. 5–10; Welter, pp. 166–67, 173.

96. Welter, pp. 154–55, 171; Floyd Bryan Strong, "Sex, Character, and Reform in America, 1830–1920," unpublished Ph.D. dissertation, Stanford University, 1972, chapter 3; Róheim, *Panic of the Gods*, p. 197 (italics in original); Patricia Cline Cohen, "Attitudes Toward the Body and Their Social Implications in Nineteenth Century America," unpublished paper, 1970, p. 24.

97. Leslie A. Fiedler, *The Return of the Vanishing American* (N.Y., 1968), pp. 50–136; James, *Raven*, pp. 22–23, 68–80.

98. Walker, pp. 22–23; James, *Jackson: Border Captain*, pp. 80–90; William H. Masterson, *William Blount* (Baton Rouge, La., 1954), pp. 138–53.

99. Putnam, p. 529; W. C. C. Claiborne, circular, Jan. 9, 1797, AJP; Jackson to ?, Feb. 10, 1810, to William Dickson, Sept. 1, 1801, to Overton, Jan. 22, 1798, AJC, I, 198, 58, 43; Jackson to John Donelson, Jan. 18, 1797, AJP.

100. Jackson to George W. Campbell, April 28, 1804, AJC, I, 90–91.

101. "Remonstrance of Citizens west of the Alleghanies," 1793, AJP; Walker, p. 34; James, *Jackson: Border Captain*, p. 80; Jackson to Nathaniel Macon, Oct. 4, 1795, AJC, I, 17–18.

102. Whitaker, pp. 163–76; James, *Jackson: Border Captain*, pp. 58–62, 84.

103. Jackson to Patten Anderson, Jan. 4, 1807, AJC, I, 161; Ward, pp. 182–85; Parton, I, 218–19; Henry Tazewell to Jackson, July 20, 1798, AJC, I, 50–54; W. C. C. Claiborne to Jackson, March 22, 1800, AJP. For Jackson's references to Caesar, see p. 72, and below, chapter 5, p. 138, and chapter 8, p. 267.

104. Andrew Jackson, "Farewell Address," March 4, 1837, in James D. Richardson, ed., *Messages and Papers of the Presidents* (N.Y., 1917), III, 293–97; Jackson to Chief Justice Roger Taney, Oct. 13, 1836, AJC, V, 429–30.

CHAPTER THREE

1. Cf. John William Ward, *Andrew Jackson—Symbol for an Age* (N.Y., 1955), pp. 13–78. The quotes are from pp. 30, 238n.

2. Henry Nash Smith, *Virgin Land* (N.Y., 1950); Perry Miller, "Nature and the National Ego," in *Errand into the Wilderness* (N.Y., 1964), pp. 204–16, and "The Location of American Religious Freedom," "The Romantic Dilemma in American Nationalism and the Concept of Nature," in *Nature's Nation* (Cambridge, Mass., 1967), pp. 150–62, 197–207. Adams is quoted in Albert K. Weinberg, *Manifest Destiny* (Chicago, 1963 [first published 1935]), pp. 60–61. Emerson is quoted in Neil Harris, *The Artist in American Society: The Formative Years 1790–1860* (N.Y., 1966), pp. 178–79.

3. Sidney H. Aronson, *Status and Kinship in the Higher Civil Service* (Cambridge, Mass., 1964), p. 45.

4. Francis S. Philbrick, *The Rise of the West 1754–1830* (N.Y., 1965), p. 92; Hector St. John Crèvecoeur, *Letters from an American Farmer* (N.Y., 1963), pp. 36–37.

5. Frederick Jackson Turner, *The Frontier in American History* (N.Y., 1962 [first published 1920]), p. 214; Curtis P. Nettels, *The Emergence of a National Economy 1775–1815* (N.Y., 1962), p. 59; Arthur P. Whitaker, *The Mississippi Question 1795–1803* (N.Y., 1934), p. 9; A. W. Putnam, *History of Middle Tennessee* (Nashville, Tenn., 1859), pp. 147, 185; Andrew Jackson to John Coffee, Dec. 22, 1813, AJC, I, 405.

6. Smith, p. 135; Arthur K. Moore, *The Frontier Mind* (Lexington, Ky., 1957), pp. 13–15, 203, 31. Cf. Smith, pp. 54–63. For a more complex interpretation of the Boone myth, stressing themes of violent wilderness regeneration central to ante-bellum American culture, cf. Richard Slotkin, *Regeneration through Violence: The Mythology of the American Frontier, 1600–1860* (Middletown, Conn., 1973), pp. 268–465, 507–14.

7. Loren Baritz, "The Idea of the West," *American Historical Review*, LXVI (April 1961), 629n.

8. Turner, p. 4. Turner shared the imaginative world of the westward movement; his work is not reliable history, but it does make myth accessible. Cf. Smith, pp. 291–305.

9. Erikson writes of Luther, "He always objected to the Madonna's mediation in the then popular scheme of religion. He wanted *God's* recognition. . . . he could say

that Christ was defined by two images: one of an infant lying in a manger, 'hanging on a virgin's tits,' . . . *and* one of a man sitting at his Father's right hand." Erik H. Erikson, *Young Man Luther* (N.Y., 1962), p. 119. Cf. Henry Adams, *Mont-Saint-Michel and Chartres* (Garden City, N.Y., 1959 [first published 1905]), pp. 307–12.

10. R. W. B. Lewis, *The American Adam* (Chicago, 1955), pp. 5–7.

11. Turner, p. 261.

12. *Ibid.*, pp. 261, 268; Alexis de Tocqueville, *Democracy in America*, 2 vols. (N.Y., 1959), II, 166. For Jackson's appeals to nature, cf. Jackson to President Thomas Jefferson, Aug. 7, 1803, to ?, Feb. 10, 1810, and to George W. Campbell, Oct. 15, 1812, AJC, I, 67–68, 198–99, 236–38; discussed respectively in chapter 5, pp. 136 and 139, and chapter 2, p. 42.

13. John Locke, *Of Civil Government* (London, 1924), pp. 129–38. Thomas Jefferson, "Notes on Virginia," in Adrienne Koch and William Peden, eds., *The Life and Selected Writings of Thomas Jefferson* (N.Y., 1944), pp. 277–81.

14. Aubrey C. Land, "Economic Behavior in a Planting Society: The Eighteenth Century Chesapeake," *Journal of Southern History*, XXXIII (Nov. 1967), 480; Malcolm J. Rohrbough, *The Land Office Business* (N.Y., 1968), p. xii.

15. Benjamin H. Hibbard, *A History of the Public Land Policies* (N.Y., 1939 [first published 1924]), pp. 1–5, 490; Paul Wallace Gates, *The Farmer's Age: Agriculture 1815–1860* (N.Y., 1960), p. 51.

16. Cf. Douglass C. North, *The Economic Growth of the United States 1790–1860* (Englewood Cliffs, N.J., 1961), and chapter 8 below.

17. Aronson, pp. 35–42; Jackson T. Main, *The Social Structure of Revolutionary America* (Princeton, N.J., 1965), pp. 10–18, 50–66, 139, 183–92; Philbrick, pp. 91–93.

18. Nettels, p. 150.

19. James E. Young, *The Washington Community, 1800–1828* (N.Y., 1966), pp. 1–28.

20. Land, pp. 471–82; Aronson, p. 37; Paul Wallace Gates, "The Role of the Land Speculator in Western Development," in Vernon Carstensen, ed., *The Public Lands* (Madison, Wis., 1968), p. 349; Hibbard, pp. 209–11.

21. Gates, "Role of Land Speculator," pp. 351–52; Thomas P. Abernethy, *Western Lands and the American Revolution* (N.Y., 1937); Ray Allen Billington, *Westward Expansion* (N.Y., 1960), pp. 93–94, 133–34, 146–49, 165–67, 250–51; J. R. Pole, "Historians and the Problem of Early American Democracy," *American Historical Review*, LXVII (April 1962), 636.

22. Paul Wallace Gates, "Tenants of the Log Cabin," *Journal of American History*, XLIX (June 1962), 4, 6.

23. Thomas P. Abernethy, *From Frontier to Plantation in Tennessee* (Chapel Hill, N.C., 1932), pp. 42–60; Putnam, p. 89; Harriette S. Arnow, *Seedtime on the Cumberland* (N.Y., 1960), pp. 200–01, 310; William H. Masterson, *William Blount* (Baton Rouge, La., 1954), pp. 68–89.

24. Angie Debo, *The Road to Disappearance* (Norman, Okla., 1941), p. 54; Abernethy, *Frontier to Plantation*, pp. 42–60; Arnow, pp. 310–14; Samuel C. Williams, *Beginnings of West Tennessee in the Land of the Chickasaws* (Johnson City, Tenn., 1930), pp. 41–45.

25. Arnow, pp. 216–17, 318–34; Williams, pp. 41–48; Abernethy, *Frontier to Plantation*, pp. 50–63; Marquis James, *Andrew Jackson: The Border Captain* (Indianapolis, Ind., 1933), pp. 51–55.

26. Abernethy, *Frontier to Plantation*, pp. 87–90, 98, 133; Merritt P. Pound, *Benjamin Hawkins: Indian Agent* (Athens, Ga., 1951), p. 49; Masterson, pp. 177–78.

27. Putnam, pp. 62, 77–79; A. P. Whitaker, "The Muscle Shoals Speculation, 1783–1789," *Mississippi Valley Historical Review*, XIII (Dec. 1926), 365–69.

28. Masterson, p. 100; Whitaker, *Mississippi Question*, pp. 106–08; Thomas P.

Abernethy, *The South in the New Nation, 1789–1819* (Baton Rouge, La., 1961), pp. 136–68.

29. Annie Heloise Abel, "The History of Events Resulting in Indian Consolidation West of the Mississippi," *American Historical Association, Report of Proceedings, 1906*, p. 245; U.S. Congress, *American State Papers, Public Lands*, 8 vols. (Washington, D.C., 1832–61), I, 125–26; U.S. Serial Set, XVIII, Doc. 31 (Dec. 14, 1818), pp. 1–5; Payson Jackson Treat, *The National Land System 1785–1820* (N.Y., 1910), p. 366.

30. James, pp. 71–73; Augustus C. Buell, *History of Andrew Jackson*, 2 vols. (N.Y., 1904), I, 93; Arnow, p. 330.

31. Abernethy, *Frontier to Plantation*, p. 269; Williams, pp. 124–25n; Arnow, p. 339.

32. Jackson to Robert Hays, Jan. 25, 1798, to John Jackson, June 18, 1805, AJC, I, 45, 114–16; James Jackson to Jackson, Sept. 21, 1805, Joseph Anderson to Jackson, Jan. 5, 1806, AJP.

33. AJC, I, 70n; Buell, I, 114–19. For examples of Jackson's land dealings, cf. AJP for the dates of April 2, 1800, May 10, Oct. 1, 1801, July 13, 1802, Sept. 12, 1803, July 28, July 30, Aug. 23, 1804, Dec. 14, 1806, May 10, 1811.

34. Perry Miller, "Errand into the Wilderness," in *Errand*, pp. 1–15, "The Location of American Religious Freedom," in *Nature's Nation*, p. 156.

35. James Madison, "Property and Liberty," in *The Complete Madison*, Saul K. Padover, ed. (N.Y., 1953), pp. 267–69. Madison probably borrowed his definition of property from Blackstone. Cf. Carstensen, "Introduction," p. xiii, and p. 101 below.

36. Norman O. Brown, *Love's Body* (N.Y., 1966), p. 3.

37. Locke, p. 40; Brown, p. 4.

38. Locke, pp. 140, 158–60, 164–66, 180; Perry Miller and Thomas H. Johnson, eds., *The Puritans*, 2 vols. (N.Y., 1963), I, 101–02; John Quincy Adams, *An Oration Delivered at Plymouth, December 22, 1802* (Boston, 1802), p. 17.

39. Frederick Merk, *Manifest Destiny and Mission in American History* (N.Y., 1966), p. 9; Billington, pp. 157–58; Arnow, pp. 172–73; Samuel G. Heiskell, *Andrew Jackson and Early Tennessee History*, 3 vols. (Nashville, Tenn., 1920), I, 179–88. The document was written by Richard Henderson (Arnow, p. 243). For compacts on the New England frontier in the 1770s, cf. Gordon S. Wood, *The Creation of the American Republic 1776–1787* (Chapel Hill, N.C., 1969), pp. 284–89.

40. Locke, pp. 134, 164–66, 178; Heiskell, I, 180–85.

41. Heiskell, I, 180–82, 183–84. The quote is from p. 180. Bracketed words were reconstructed by Heiskell from the torn and defaced original.

42. Locke, pp. 122–23, 130, 159–61; Heiskell, I, 184–85.

43. Heiskell, I, 180. Captain John Donelson's first son, born the year of the Nashborough Covenant, was the first white male child born in the Cumberland valley. Donelson named him Chesed, which means "covenant love." The baby died in infancy. Twenty-two years later Donelson named another son Chesed; that baby also died in infancy. Cf. W. W. Clayton, *History of Davidson County, Tennessee* (Philadelphia, 1880), pp. 135, 137; Putnam, p. 622. These sources claim that Chesed is the Hebrew name for "destroyer." For the proper translation I am indebted to Rabbi Gordon Freeman. Cf. F. H. W. Gesenius, *Hebrew and English Dictionary of the Old Testament*, rev. ed. (N.Y., 1959), pp. 338–39.

44. Arthur W. Calhoun, *A Social History of the American Family*, 3 vols. (N.Y., 1917–19), I, 75.

45. Thomas Jefferson to James Madison, Sept. 6, 1789, to Samuel Kercheval, July 12, 1816, Koch and Peden, pp. 488–93, 673–76; Calhoun, pp. 278–79. James I based royal absolutism on a father's power to "dispose of his Inheritance" as he pleased: "Now a Father may dispose of his Inheritance to his children, at his pleasure: yea, even disinherite the eldest upon just occasions, and preferre the youngest, according to his liking; make them beggers, or rich at his pleasure; restrain, or banish them out of his presence, as hee findes them give cause of offence, or restore them in favour againe with

the penitent sinner: So may the King deale with his Subjects." Cf. Edwin G. Burrows and Michael Wallace, "The American Revolution: The Ideology and Psychology of National Liberation," *Perspectives in American History*, VI (1972), 170.

46. Cf. Staughton Lynd, *Intellectual Origins of American Radicalism* (N.Y., 1969), pp. 77–84; Joseph L. Blau, ed., *Social Theories of Jacksonian Democracy* (N.Y., 1947), pp. 318, 355–64; Jefferson to Madison, Sept. 6, 1789, Koch and Peden, p. 488; Jackson to Andrew Jackson, Jr., Nov. 19, 1834, AJC, V, 311; cf. chapter 9 below.

Inheritance symbolized the sins as well as the accomplishments of the fathers. For Jefferson, as Winthrop Jordan has brilliantly shown, the issue was slavery. Jefferson sought to escape the inheritance of slavery on his own plantation, where his father-in-law had fathered some slaves and Jefferson himself or a favorite nephew had fathered others. Cf. Winthrop D. Jordan, *White over Black* (Baltimore, Md., 1969), pp. 430–75.

47. Cf. William Appleman Williams, *The Contours of American History* (Chicago, 1966), pp. 182–83; Philip J. Greven, Jr., "Family Structure in Seventeenth-Century Andover, Mass.," *William and Mary Quarterly*, 3rd ser., XXIII (April 1966), 242–56, "Historical Demography and Colonial America," *William and Mary Quarterly*, 3rd. ser., XXIV (July 1967), 152–53; Robert W. Ramsey, *Carolina Cradle* (Chapel Hill, N.C., 1964), pp. 21–22, 201n; Carl Schurz, quoted in Turner, p. 337.

48. James, pp. 11–13.

49. For the picture of uncertain land title in this paragraph and the ones following, I have relied on Treat, pp. 24–25, 198–229; Hibbard, pp. 12, 36–43; Gates, *Farmer's Age*, pp. 11, 54–55; Arnow, pp. 213, 317; and especially the remarkable Gates essay "Tenants of the Log Cabin," pp. 3–8, 28–29.

50. Paul Wallace Gates, "Private Land Claims in the South," *Journal of Southern History*, XXII (May 1956), 183–204; R. S. Cotterill, "The National Land System in the South: 1803–1812," *Mississippi Valley Historical Review*, XVI (March 1930), 496–99.

51. Gates, "Tenants," pp. 4–5.

52. Tocqueville, II, 109–28; Stanley Elkins and Eric McKitrick, "A Meaning for Turner's Frontier," *Political Science Quarterly*, LXIX (Sept. and Dec. 1954), 321–53, 565–602.

53. AJC, I, 48n; "Early Connection with Masonry," "September 5th A.L. 5801 A.D. 1801," AJC, I, 59; Richard P. McCormick, *The Second American Party System* (Chapel Hill, N.C., 1966), pp. 92–96, 141–44, 337; Clayton, p. 364.

54. Jackson, "Address to the Freemasons of Shelbyville, Kentucky," 1816, AJP; Jackson to Chief George Colbert, June 5, 1812, AJC, I, 226–27; Governor W. C. C. Claiborne to Jackson, Feb. 4, 1802, AJP; Jackson to William Cocke, June 24, 1798, AJC, I, 48–49; James Parton, *Life of Andrew Jackson*, 3 vols. (Boston, 1866), III, 187; Jackson to W. B. Lewis, Aug. 13, 1823, Nov. 30, 1827, LP.

55. John H. De Witt, "Andrew Jackson and His Ward, Andrew Jackson Hutchings," *Tennessee Historical Magazine*, 2nd ser., I (Jan. 1931), 102.

56. Abernethy, *Frontier to Plantation*, p. 133; Stockley Donelson to Jackson, March 2, 1794, James Grant to Donelson, March 14, 1795, to Jackson, Nov. 16, 1795, Donelson to Jackson, June 16, 1796, AJP.

57. Abernethy, *Frontier to Plantation*, pp. 164–66, 172–76; Donelson to James Glasgow, June 12, 1794, C/D; Jackson to John Overton, Jan. 22, 1798, AJC, I, 42.

58. Abernethy, *Frontier to Plantation*, pp. 171–78; Jackson to Overton, Jan. 22, 1798, AJC, I, 42; Donelson to Jackson, Oct. 20, 1800, Andrew Jackson Papers of the Tennessee State Library; Donelson to Jackson, March 10, 1801, June 14, 1802, deeds of conveyance John Love to Jackson, June 12, 1802, AJP.

59. William A. Walker, Jr., "Tennessee, 1796–1821," unpublished Ph.D. dissertation, University of Texas, 1959, pp. 136–42; Masterson, p. 333.

60. Grant to Donelson, March 14, 1795, AJP; Grant to Overton, Jan. 9, 1795, CC; Jackson to Overton, June 9, 1795, AJC, I, 13–15, 13n.

61. Jackson to Overton, June 9, 1795, AJC, I, 13–15; Overton to Jackson, March 8, 1795, AJP; James, pp. 78–79.

62. Jackson to Overton, June 10, 1795, CC; Jackson to Overton, June 9, 1795, AJC, I, 13–15; James, pp. 78–79; Whitaker, *Mississippi Question*, pp. 13–14; Masterson, pp. 212–13, 235, 260.

63. James, p. 79; John Spencer Bassett, *The Life of Andrew Jackson*, 2 vols. (N.Y., 1925), I, 37; Jackson, "The Allison Transaction," undated, AJC, I, 22. Charles G. Sellers, Jr., "Banking and Politics in Jackson's Tennessee, 1817–1827," *Mississippi Valley Historical Review*, XLI (June 1954), 76.

64. Whitaker, *Mississippi Question*, pp. 13–14; Philbrick, p. 340; Robert V. Remini, *Andrew Jackson and the Bank War* (N.Y., 1967), pp. 18–25. Cf. below, chapter 9, pp. 282–83.

65. Abernethy, *Frontier to Plantation*, pp. 262–64; James, pp. 141–42; Parton, I, 251–53.

66. Abernethy, *Frontier to Plantation*, pp. 263–64, 268–69, 293; Herbert J. Doherty, *Richard Keith Call: Southern Unionist* (Gainesville, Fla., 1961), p. 14; James, p. 407n.

67. Gates, "Tenants," pp. 3–6, 27; Putnam, p. 185; Walker, pp. 325–34. (The Sevier quote is on p. 332.) Overton's compromise did not end the conflict between Tennessee and North Carolina. Cf. Treat, pp. 347–50.

68. Gates, "Tenants," pp. 12–17; Abernethy, *Frontier to Plantation*, pp. 262–68.

69. Gates, "Tenants," pp. 15–17, 24–27.

70. *Ibid.*, pp. 21, 26.

71. *Ibid.*, p. 27; Abernethy, *Frontier to Plantation*, pp. 265–67; Clayton, pp. 98–99; Daniel H. Calhoun, *Professional Lives in America* (Cambridge, Mass., 1965), pp. 84–85.

72. Abernethy, *Frontier to Plantation*, p. 264.

73. *Ibid.*, pp. 265–67; James, p. 142; Sellers, pp. 79–82. Sellers was the first to understand the significance of Jackson's break with Overton, but wrongly attributes it to a Jackson-Darby defense of popular interests.

74. Overton to Jackson, April 3, 1822, O/M; Jackson to Lewis, April 29, 1833, LP.

75. Jackson to Overton, Dec. 9, 1821, Overton to Jackson, April 3, 1822, O/M; Jackson to John Coffee, April 15, 1823, AJC, III, 194–95; Abernethy, *Frontier to Plantation*, pp. 265–68; Sellers, pp. 80–81.

76. Jackson to Coffee, Aug. 15, 1823, C/D.

77. Overton to Jackson, March 29, 1822, O/M. Cf. the Duke of York's speech quoted as the epigraph to this chapter. Title conflict, usurpation, and civil war were the subjects of Shakespeare's Wars of the Roses tetralogy, and *Richard III* was the most popular play on the American frontier. Cf. Louis B. Wright, quoted in American Conservatory Theatre program, "Shakespeare's Consummate Villain," *Performing Arts* (Fall 1974), p. 25.

78. Jackson to Overton, Nov. 8, 1823, P. M. Miller to Overton, April 18, 1823, CC; Jackson to Coffee, Sept. 23, 1824, C/D; Jackson to Coffee, June 20, 1828, AJC, III, 409–10; Charles G. Sellers, Jr. "Jackson Men with Feet of Clay," *American Historical Review*, LXII (April 1957), 541–49.

79. Turner, p. 205; John Demos, "Developmental Perspectives on the History of Childhood," *Journal of Interdisciplinary History*, II (Autumn 1971), 325n. The following discussion is heavily indebted to Demos' analysis of the Puritan family. I lack the data, however, to compare Puritan child-rearing patterns with those in the old southwest, or to base the analysis on specific child-rearing practices. Cf. John Demos, *A Little Commonwealth* (N.Y., 1970), pp. 134–39, and "Developmental Perspectives," pp. 319–25.

80. Cf. Joel Kovel, *White Racism: A Psychohistory* (N.Y., 1970), pp. 48–49, 264–71; Erik H. Erikson, *Childhood and Society*, rev. ed. (Middlesex, Eng., 1965), pp. 74–77, 243–46; Carstensen, p. xiii. Quotes are from pp. 89, 97, above.

81. Erikson, *Young Man Luther*, p. 122; cf. above, chapter 2, p. 58.

82. Jacksonian child-rearing literature provides some evidence of indulgence in infancy, followed by early, insistent toilet training, and ambivalence toward childhood independence. Demos believes that Puritan children were indulged in infancy and weaned abruptly in the second year, and that the Puritan parent disciplined his "wilfull" child at the very stage when a baby begins to establish his own autonomy. He associates this child-rearing pattern with land-title disputes and suits for trespass and slander in Puritan New England. Puritans, he suggests, dreamed of communal harmony while they fought among themselves. Cf. Demos, *Little Commonwealth*, pp. 134–39, "Developmental Perspectives," pp. 319–25; Bernard Wishy, *The Child and the Republic* (Philadelphia, 1968), pp. 36–40, 77–79; Robert Sunley, "Early Nineteenth-Century American Literature on Child Rearing," in Margaret Mead and Martha Wolfenstein, eds., *Childhood in Contemporary Cultures* (Chicago, 1955), pp. 153–57, 159–60.

83. Alexis de Tocqueville, "A Fortnight in the Wilds," in *Journey to America*, J. P. Mayer, ed. (London, 1959), p. 372.

84. American eating habits, claimed European observers, belied the bounty offered at American social banquets. Americans devoured their enormous meals as if the food would not last, rapidly, competitively, and silently. Cf. Edward Pessen, *Jacksonian America* (Homewood, Ill., 1969), pp. 19–26.

85. Hibbard, pp. 209–12; Gates, *Farmer's Age*, pp. 2–8, 142–44, 163–64; Tocqueville, *Democracy in America*, II, 166.

86. Rohrbough, pp. 90–91; Gates, *Farmer's Age*, p. 400.

87. Jackson, "Proclamation," April 2, 1814, AJC, I, 494; Gates, *Farmer's Age*, plates facing p. 140; Miller, "Nature and National Ego," pp. 213–14; Charles L. Sanford, *The Quest for Paradise* (Urbana, Ill., 1961), pp. 146–52.

88. North, pp. 61–76, 156–68, 189–206, "International Capital Flows and the Development of the American West," *Journal of Economic History*, XVI (Dec. 1956), 493–505; Aronson, pp. 58–59, 86–87, 92, 96.

89. Miller, "Nature and National Ego," pp. 205–06.

90. J. W. Schulte Nordholt, *The People That Walk in Darkness* (N.Y., 1960), pp. 43–44; Gates, *Farmer's Age*, p. 2; Moore, pp. 42, 56; Miller, "Nature and National Ego," p. 212.

91. George D. Harmon, *Sixty Years of Indian Affairs* (Chapel Hill, N.C., 1941), p. 239; Rohrbough, p. 211; George Dangerfield, *The Era of Good Feelings* (N.Y., 1952), p. 351; Treat, p. 16.

92. D. W. Winnicott, "Psychoanalysis and the Sense of Guilt," in John D. Sutherland, ed., *Psychoanalysis and Contemporary Thought* (London, 1958), pp. 23–24.

93. Harris, pp. 199–207. The quote is on p. 207.

94. Putnam, p. 148.

95. Charles G. Sellers, Jr., *James K. Polk Jacksonian, 1793–1843* (Princeton, N.J., 1957), p. 3.

96. Part III will develop some of the themes abbreviated here. For sympathetic interpretations of the pastoral ideal in Jacksonian America, cf. Ward, pp. 32–41; Leo Marx, *The Machine in the Garden* (N.Y., 1964).

97. Marvin Meyers, *The Jacksonian Persuasion* (N.Y., 1960), p. 15.

98. Miller, "Nature and the National Ego," pp. 205–07; Weinberg, p. 119.

99. Weinberg, pp. 60–61; Smith, p. 297.

100. Alexander Hamilton, James Madison, John Jay, *The Federalist Papers* (N.Y., 1961), pp. 79–84; Jefferson to Madison, Dec. 20, 1787, in Koch and Peden, pp. 440–41.

101. Cf. Arthur P. Whitaker, *The Spanish-American Frontier 1783–1795* (Boston, 1927), pp. 7–9, 19–50, 68–76, 94–101, 185, *Mississippi Question*, pp. 24–101; Philbrick, p. 174.

102. Walker, p. 34; "Remonstrance of citizens west of the Alleghany Mountains . . . ," 1793, AJP.

103. Whitaker, *Mississippi Question*, pp. 101, 190–204; Thomas P. Abernethy, *The South in the New Nation 1789–1819* (Baton Rouge, La., 1961), pp. 247–48.

104. Whitaker, *Spanish-American Frontier*, pp. 10–11, 53–54, 69, *passim*.

105. "Remonstrance of citizens west of the Alleghany Mountains . . . ," 1793, AJP; Abernethy, *South in New Nation*, pp. 46–60, 192–206; Whitaker, *Spanish-American Frontier*, pp. 111–20, "Spanish Intrigue in the Old Southwest," *Mississippi Valley Historical Review*, XII (Sept. 1925), 154–76; James, pp. 58–66; Jackson to Daniel Smith, Feb. 13, 1789, AJC, I, 7–8.

106. Jackson to John McKee, May 16, 1794, AJC, I, 12–13.

107. Billington, p. 238; Abernethy, *South in New Nation*, pp. 106–28; Whitaker, *Spanish-American Frontier*, pp. 185–90.

108. Billington, pp. 240–41; Whitaker, *Mississippi Question*, pp. 102–13, 291–92; Abernethy, *South in New Nation*, pp. 172–75, 188–91; Isabel Thompson, "The Blount Conspiracy," *East Tennessee Historical Society Publications*, II (1930), 3–21; Walker, pp. 97–101; Masterson, pp. 298–327.

109. Cf. below, chapter 5.

CHAPTER FOUR

1. F. P. Prucha, *American Indian Policy in the Formative Years* (Cambridge, Mass., 1962) is the major statement of this position. Fr. Prucha has recently modified his dichotomy. He now finds Jackson benevolent toward the Indians not only as President but from his early frontier days. Cf. F. P. Prucha, "Andrew Jackson's Indian Policy: A Reassessment," *Journal of American History*, LVI (Dec. 1969), 527–39. On "our national infancy," cf. chapter 3, p. 104.

2. Thomas L. McKenney, *Memoirs, Official and Personal*, 2 vols. (N.Y., 1846), II, 124.

3. These phrases enter virtually every discussion of the Indian question. Cf. "Report of the House Committee on Indian Affairs," Feb. 21, 1823, ASPIA, II, 408; George J. F. Clark to Captain John Bell, Aug. 15, 1821, ASPIA, II, 415; and references below in the text. On the general identification of savages with children, cf. Hoxie N. Fairchild, *The Noble Savage* (N.Y., 1961 [first published 1928]), pp. 190, 230, 366–90.

4. McKenney, II, 33. These stock descriptions of the noble savage endured in America after they died out in Europe, and were used not simply by literary men but by the makers of Indian policy. Cf. Fairchild, pp. 20, 79, 298–99, 363–64.

5. William Robertson, quoted in Bernard W. Sheehan, "Paradise and the Noble Savage in Jeffersonian Thought," *William and Mary Quarterly*, 3rd ser., XXVI (July 1969), 337. Robertson, the eighteenth-century Scotch common-sense philosopher, deeply influenced American perceptions of Indians. Lewis Cass, for example, cited Robertson as the foremost authority on the Indian and incorporated his views wholesale in his own essays and reports. Cf. Richard Drinnon, "Violence in the American Experience: Winning the West," *The Radical Teacher* (Chicago), Dec. 30, 1969, p. 41.

6. Thomas Jefferson, "Notes on Virginia," in Adrienne Koch and William Peden, eds., *The Life and Selected Writings of Thomas Jefferson* (N.Y., 1944), pp. 210–13, 221; Harriette S. Arnow, *Seedtime on the Cumberland* (N.Y., 1960), p. 176; Marquis James, *The Raven* (N.Y., 1962 [first published 1929]), pp. 22, 25. Cf. also Roy Harvey Pearce, *Savagism and Civilization* (Baltimore, Md., 1965; first published as *The Savages of America* [Baltimore, Md., 1953]), pp. 152–53; Sheehan, "Paradise," pp. 352–55; Staughton Lynd, *Intellectual Origins of American Radicalism* (N.Y., 1969), p. 85.

7. On dual-unity, cf. Géza Róheim, *Magic and Schizophrenia* (N.Y., 1955), pp. 93–118, 194–200, 221–27. See p. 181 for a garden of Eden fantasy. Cf. also Harold E. Searles, *Collected Papers on Schizophrenia and Related Subjects* (London, 1965), pp. 39–69, 177–91.

8. Francis Parkman, *The Conspiracy of Pontiac* (N.Y., 1962 [first published 1851]), p. 63. According to a 1794 school text, savage freedom kept the Indian "in a state of infancy, weakness, and the greatest imperfection." Quoted in Pearce, p. 161.

9. Lewis Cass, "Annual Report of the Secretary of War for 1831," ASPMA, IV, 714.

10. Pearce, pp. 68–70; Angie Debo, *The Road to Disappearance* (Norman, Okla., 1941), pp. 19–21, 369; R. S. Cotterill, *The Southern Indians: The Story of the Civilized Tribes Before Removal* (Norman, Okla., 1954), pp. 9–11; Wilcomb E. Washburn, "The Moral and Legal Justification for Dispossessing the Indians," in James Morton Smith, ed., *Seventeenth Century America: Essays in Colonial History* (Chapel Hill, N.C., 1959), pp. 19–23.

11. [Lewis Cass], "Removal of the Indians," *North American Review*, XXXI (Jan. 1830), 75; McKenney, I, 123–24.

12. Representative Richard Wilde, *Register of Debates*, VI, 1093; J. B. Kinney, *A Continent Lost—A Civilization Won* (Baltimore, Md., 1937), pp. 102, 109, quoting from reports of the Commissioners of Indian Affairs for 1832 and 1838.

13. Albert K. Weinberg, *Manifest Destiny* (Chicago, 1963 [first published 1935]), p. 86. Cf. C. B. McPherson, *The Political Theory of Possessive Individualism* (N.Y., 1964), pp. 53–70, 137–142, *passim*.

14. Cf. Captain Eugene F. Ware, "The Indian War of 1864," in Wilcomb E. Washburn, ed., *The Indian and the White Man* (N.Y., 1964), pp. 284–88; and chapter 7 below, p. 232.

15. Quoted in James Parton, *Life of Andrew Jackson*, 3 vols. (Boston, 1866), I, 401. Few ante-bellum government officials would have agreed with Parkman and Greeley that Indian primitivism entirely foreclosed the possibility of civilizing Indians. However, as chapter 7 will suggest, civilization required, in the white view, the sacrifice of all Indian qualities. Civilization, like death, meant the destruction of Indians. For this reason, and because whites sensed the difficulties of turning Indians into replicas of themselves, a sense of doom permeated discussions of the Indian future. This, the interpretation of Roy Harvey Pearce (in *Savagism and Civilization*), is challenged by Bernard W. Sheehan, *Seeds of Extinction: Jeffersonian Philanthropy and the American Indian* (Chapel Hill, N.C., 1973). For my critique of Sheehan, cf. "Indian Extinction, American Regeneration," *Journal of Ethnic Studies*, II (Spring 1974), 93–104.

16. Malcolm J. Rohrbough, *The Land Office Business* (N.Y., 1968), p. 59; Parkman, pp. 323n, 463; Governor Wylie Blount to General Thomas Flournoy, Oct. 15, 1813, ASPIA, I, 856.

17. Cf. McKenney, I, 112–13; Fairchild, pp. 90–91.

18. Cf. Melanie Klein, "The Early Development of Conscience in the Child," "A Contribution to the Psychogenesis of Manic-Depressive States," and "Mourning and Its Relation to Manic-Depressive States," in *Contributions to Psychoanalysis* (London, 1948), pp. 267–77, 282–338; Sándor Radó, "The Problem of Melancholia," *International Journal of Psychoanalysis*, IX (Oct. 1928), 420–38; George Géro, "The Construction of Depression," *International Journal of Psychoanalysis*, XVII (Oct. 1936), 423–61; Annie Reich, "Early Identifications as Archaic Elements in the Superego," *Journal of the American Psychoanalytic Association*, II (March 1954), 218–38.

19. Róheim, *Magic and Schizophrenia*, p. 224.

20. Cf. Robert Montgomery Bird, *Nick of the Woods* (N.Y., 1928 [first published 1837]); James Hall, "The Pioneer," in *Tales of the Border* (Philadelphia, 1835); Herman Melville, *The Confidence Man* (N.Y., 1954), pp. 151–64; Pearce, pp. 214–50; Randy Byrne, "Literature and Aggression—A Study of the American Indian in Nineteenth-Century American Fiction Prior to the Civil War" (dissertation prospectus, Department of English, University of California at Berkeley, Oct. 1972); David Crockett, *Life of David Crockett* (Philadelphia, 1865), p. 92.

21. Arnow, p. 290; S. Putnam Waldo, *Memoirs of Andrew Jackson* (Hartford,

Conn., 1820), p. 128; Parton, I, 140; Frank B. Woodford, *Lewis Cass* (New Brunswick, N.J., 1950), pp. 8–10.

22. John K. Mahon, *History of the Second Seminole War, 1835–1842* (Gainesville, Fla., 1967), p. 218.

23. McKenney, I, 230.

24. Klein, "Early Development of Conscience," p. 268.

25. Cass, "Removal," p. 108. A. W. Putnam, *History of Middle Tennessee* (Nashville, Tenn., 1859), p. 185.

26. For Jackson's early intrigues, cf. above, chapter 3, pp. 108–09, and below, chapter 5, pp. 137–38.

27. Parton, II, 547.

28. James Hall, quoted in Pearce, p. 120; cf. Arthur A. Ekirch, *The Idea of Progress in America, 1815–1860* (N.Y., 1944), p. 183. I am indebted to William Roth for his insights on self, boundaries, and mobility in America.

29. Jackson to John McKee, May 16, 1794, AJC, I, 12–13; *Register of Debates*, XIV (1837), 554; G. M. Troup to John C. Calhoun, Feb. 28, 1824, ASPIA, II, 735.

30. Cf. below, chapters 5, 6, and 10.

31. Thomas Hart Benton, "Report of the Senate Committee on Indian Affairs," May 14, 1824, ASPIA, II, 512. That expansion is the key to American history is suggested in William Appleman Williams' seminal *The Contours of American History* (Chicago, 1966).

32. [Lewis Cass], "Policy and Practice of the United States and Great Britain in Their Treatment of Indians," *North American Review*, XXIV (April 1827), 372–76; Reverend Dr. Joseph Doddridge, "Notes on the Settlements and Indian Wars . . . ," in Washburn, pp. 271–73.

33. Waldo, p. 86; *Congressional Globe*, VI, Appendix, 79; Bird, pp. 252–53; Arnow, p. 288; General Edmund P. Gaines to Jackson, May 18, 1816, AJP. Stories of Indian atrocities were embellished and exaggerated out of proportion to their actual occurrence. Cf. Nathaniel Knowles, "The Torture of Captives by the Indians of Eastern North America," *American Philosophical Society, Proceedings*, LXXXII (1940), 151–225; Sheehan, *Seeds of Extinction*, pp. 196–98.

34. Richard Slotkin, *Regeneration through Violence: The Mythology of the American Frontier, 1600–1860* (Middletown, Conn., 1973), pp. 90–91, 124–26, 244, 249–50, 328–29; Nimrod Doyell to Benjamin Hawkins, May 13, 1813, ASPIA, I, 843; Parton, II, 431; Sheehan, *Seeds of Extinction*, pp. 194–95, 200–01; Waldo, p. 299. Jackson's use of this rhetoric is cited in succeeding chapters. For a fictional account of frontier warfare in which Indians "eat him up" whites and whites "eat" Indians, cf. Bird, pp. 33, 180, 183, 203, 244, 331.

35. Benjamin Hawkins to Hoboheilthle Micco, Peter McQueen, and other Creek chiefs, July 6, 1813, ASPIA, I, 848; Parton, I, 524; Jackson "To the Troops," Oct. 24, 1813, AJC, I, 337–38; Jackson, "General Orders," March 24, 1814, AJC, I, 488; William T. Hagan, *The Sac and Fox Indians* (Norman, Okla., 1958), pp. 158–61.

36. The classic statement is Sigmund Freud, *Totem and Taboo*, in James Strachey, ed., *The Standard Edition of the Complete Psychological Works of Sigmund Freud*, XIII (London, 1953), 72: "If one person succeeds in gratifying a repressed desire, the same desire is bound to be kindled in all the other members of the community. In order to keep the temptation down, the envied transgressor must be deprived of the fruit of his enterprise, and the punishment will not infrequently give those who carry it out an opportunity of committing the same outrage under cover of an act of expiation. This is indeed one of the foundations of the human penal system."

37. Jackson to James Monroe, Aug. 10, 1818, AJC, II, 386; Representative Hopkins Holsey, *Register of Debates*, XIII (1836–37), 1542; Representative Alexander Buckner, *Register of Debates*, VIII (1831–32), 791; Sheehan, *Seeds of Extinction*, p. 195; Jackson, "Proclamation on Taking Possession of Pensacola," May 29, 1818, AJC, II,

375. Cf. Parton, I, 546; Mahon, pp. 247–48; Doddridge in Washburn, p. 273. Nick of the woods, the Quaker turned Indian-scalper and "truculent madman" by the slaughter of his wife and children, had, as a gesture of friendship, given the Indians the weapons with which they murdered his family. Cf. Bird, pp. 251–52, 386.

38. The painting depicts a famous Revolutionary War atrocity. Cf. Cass, "Policy and Practice," p. 376. For a Vanderlyn portrait of Jackson, see Plate 8.

39. *Congressional Globe*, VI (1837–38), Appendix, 78–79. Cilley died by this credo shortly after he expressed it. He was killed in a duel with Kentucky Representative William Graves. Cf. *Congressional Globe*, VI, 200–02.

Nathaniel Hawthorne's work, preoccupied with Oedipal guilt and the "sins of the fathers," contains an example of Indians as surrogate father-killers. The protagonist of "Alice Doan's Confession" kills his double. The murder revives his infant memory of his father, identifying the killer with Indians, the murdered man with the father. Cf. Frederick C. Crews, *The Sins of the Fathers* (N.Y., 1966), pp. 44–55. On Indians and American women and children, cf. Leslie A. Fiedler, *The Return of the Vanishing American* (N.Y., 1968), pp. 50–134.

40. McKenney, II, 33–34. Cf. Parton, I, 401–02; Arthur C. Calhoun, *A Social History of the American Family*, 3 vols. (N.Y., 1960 [first published 1917–19]), I, 283. Women in the southern tribes actually had more significant public power than their white counterparts. Cf. Cotterill, p. 14; Arnow, p. 185.

41. Sheehan, "Paradise," p. 357n.

42. Cf. Fiedler, *Vanishing American;* Leslie A. Fiedler, *Love and Death in the American Novel* (N.Y., 1960); chapter 9 below. McKenney once made "a woman" of a warrior to punish him. Cf. Michael Paul Rogin, "Liberal Society and the Indian Question," *Politics and Society*, I (May 1971), 304.

43. Winthrop D. Jordan, *White over Black* (Baltimore, Md., 1969), pp. 162–63. Cf. Mahon, p. 125.

44. Cf. Lawrence J. Friedman, *Inventors of the Promised Land* (N.Y., 1975), chapter 6; Jefferson, "Notes," pp. 210–13, 221, 255–62; Jordan, pp. 136–78, 457–81; Fiedler, *Vanishing American*, pp. 178–89.

There was, to be sure, an occasional sexually threatening Indian in ante-bellum writing. But Indian violence clearly dominated white images. Sexually menacing Indians appear in only one of the Leatherstocking tales, and they covet not the light but the part-Negro sister. Indians in *Nick of the Woods* have "drunk the blood of women and children"; the white villain is the "ravisher." (Cf. Bird, pp. 244, 367.) Vanderlyn's painting *Death of Jane McCrea* (plate 7) presents the implicit possibility of sexual violence. But compare that painting to Revere's Revolutionary War engraving (Plate 4), where the threat is clearly rape, not murder. Jefferson did defend Indians against European charges of sterility, but the dangerous passions he attributed to blacks are entirely absent from his Indians.

CHAPTER FIVE

1. [Lewis Cass], "Removal of the Indians," *North American Review*, XXXI (Jan. 1830), 77; U.S. Congress, *Register of Debates*, VI (1829–30), 1103. Cf. William T. Hagan, *American Indians* (Chicago, 1961), p. 68.

2. Millard Meiss, *Giotto and Assisi* (N.Y., 1960), p. 11.

3. Book of Genesis, 25: 20–34, 27: 1–46 (King James version). Norman Jacobson first called my attention to the significance of this tale for white-Indian history.

4. Reginald Horsman, *Expansion and American Indian Policy, 1783–1812* (East Lansing, Mich., 1967), p. 106. Jedidiah Morse, *A Report to the Secretary of War of*

the United States on Indian Affairs (St. Clair Shores, Mich., 1972 [first published 1822]), Appendix, p. 181.

5. Herman Melville, *Israel Potter* (N.Y., 1924), pp. 73, 88, 98, 153. Cf. Perry Miller, *Nature's Nation* (Cambridge, Mass., 1967), pp. 223–24.

6. Merritt P. Pound, *Benjamin Hawkins: Indian Agent* (Athens, Ga., 1951), p. 52; Albert K. Weinberg, *Manifest Destiny* (Chicago, 1963 [first published 1935]), p. 81. The just-war language is also found in the Northwest Ordinance. Cf. H. S. Commager, *Documents of American History* (N.Y., 1963), "Northwest Ordinance," p. 131.

7. Melville, p. 192; Carl Schorske, "Politics and the Psyche in fin de siècle Vienna: Schnitzler and Hofmannsthal," *American Historical Review*, LXVI (July 1961), 946.

8. U.S. Congress, *The Congressional Globe*, VIII (1839–40), Appendix, 71.

9. U.S. Congress, *The Congressional Globe*, VII (1838–39), Appendix, 162–63, XI (1841–42), 818. "The true fathers of the state," in Robert M. Bird's novel of the Kentucky frontier, were not educated and refined men, but those who "wrested from the savage the garden of his domain." Cf. *Nick of the Woods* (N.Y., 1928 [first published 1837]), p. 8.

10. Augustus C. Buell, *History of Andrew Jackson*, 2 vols. (N.Y., 1904), II, 43–44.

11. Harriette S. Arnow, *Seedtime on the Cumberland* (N.Y., 1960), pp. 200–01, 283–310; Ray Allen Billington, *Westward Expansion* (N.Y., 1960), pp. 171–73; Marquis James, *Andrew Jackson: The Border Captain* (Indianapolis, Ind., 1933), pp. 72–74.

12. Arnow, p. 236; James, pp. 52–54; A. W. Putnam, *History of Middle Tennessee* (Nashville, Tenn., 1859), pp. 62–75.

13. The preceding four paragraphs are based on Arnow, pp. 289–314; Horsman, pp. 24–31; R. S. Cotterill, *The Southern Indians: The Story of the Civilized Tribes Before Removal* (Norman, Okla., 1954), pp. 35–74; James Mooney, "Myths of the Cherokees," *Bureau of American Ethnology, Annual Report*, XIX (1897–98), Part 1, 61–66; Helen Hunt Jackson, *A Century of Dishonor* (Boston, 1889), pp. 264–67.

14. James, pp. 58–61; A. P. Whitaker, "Spanish Intrigue in the Old Southwest," *Mississippi Valley Historical Review*, XII (Sept. 1925), 154–76; Jackson to General Daniel Smith, Feb. 17, 1789, AJC, I, 7–8.

15. Jackson to John McKee, Jan. 30, 1793, May 16, 1794, AJC, I, 12, 12–13.

16. The preceding two paragraphs are based on William A. Walker, Jr., "Tennessee, 1796–1821" (unpublished Ph.D. dissertation, University of Texas, 1959), pp. 21–22; Mooney, pp. 62–78; Horsman, pp. 50, 73–78; Cotterill, pp. 97–111; James, pp. 73–74; George D. Harmon, *Sixty Years of Indian Affairs* (Chapel Hill, N.C., 1941), p. 46; Jackson to John McKee, May 16, 1794, AJC, I, 13.

17. The preceding two paragraphs are based on Arnow, pp. 290–302, 318–30, 340–42; Walker, p. 21; Cotterill, pp. 58–64; James, pp. 72–79.

18. Jackson to John McKee, Jan. 30, 1793, AJC, I, 12.

19. James, p. 85; Jackson, "Draft of Report of Committee of Congress" [Jan. 17, 1797], AJC, I, 25–26.

20. Arnow, pp. 334–35.

21. *Ibid.*, pp. 248, 301–03, 334–35; James, pp. 43–44, 62, 74; Putnam, pp. 54–61, 257–64, 287–88, 316–18, 367–431, 466–69, 476–90; Arthur P. Whitaker, *The Mississippi Question 1795–1803* (N.Y., 1934), p. 20.

22. R. D. Laing, *The Divided Self* (Middlesex, Eng., 1965), pp. 65–105.

23. Putnam, pp. 580–81.

24. Walker, pp. 126–35; John Spencer Bassett, *The Life of Andrew Jackson*, 2 vols. (N.Y., 1925), I, 34–35, 75–76; James, pp. 81–90.

25. Arnow, pp. 194–95; James, p. 74.

26. On the Jackson-Sevier quarrel, cf. James, pp. 91–100; Walker, pp. 135–43, 149–59.

27. Jackson to Colonel McKinney, May 10, 1802, to George Duffield, June 25,

1802, to Governor Wylie Blount, Feb. 15, 1810, to John Coffee, Sept. 15, 1812, AJC, I, 62–63, 201–03, VI, 427.

28. Jackson, "Division Order," Feb. 20, 1809, Jackson to Daniel Smith, November 28, 1807, AJC, I, 195, 184.

29. James, pp. 101–02, 139; Jackson to President Thomas Jefferson, Aug. 7, 1803, AJC, I, 67–68; Jackson to Colonel Thomas Butler, Aug. 25, 1804, AJP.

30. James, pp. 112–25.

31. Washington Jackson to Jackson, June 19, 1806, AJC, I, 146; Walker, pp. 100–01; James Parton, *Life of Andrew Jackson*, 3 vols. (Boston, 1866), I, 305.

32. On Jackson and the Burr conspiracy, cf. James, pp. 110–11, 127–30; Buell, I, 192–98; Thomas P. Abernethy, *The South in the New Nation 1789–1819* (Baton Rouge, La., 1961), pp. 261–71, 279–82; Francis S. Philbrick, *The Rise of the West 1754–1830* (N.Y., 1965), pp. 228–29, 247; Curtis P. Nettels, *The Emergence of a National Economy 1775–1815* (N.Y., 1962), p. 323; Jackson to Daniel Smith, Nov. 12, 1806, to George Campbell, Jan. 15, 1807, AJC, I, 153–55, 167–69; notice to Jackson to pay Burr's note for $500 endorsed by Jackson, Jan. 29, 1807, AJP.

33. Jackson to Governor W. C. C. Claiborne, Nov. 12, 1806, AJC, I, 153; Putnam, pp. 580–81.

34. James, pp. 130–36; Jackson to Claiborne, Nov. 12, 1806, to Jefferson, Nov. 12, 1806, to Secretary of War Henry Dearborn, March 17, 1807, AJC, I, 152–53, 156, 172–74.

35. James, pp. 137–39; Buell, I, 204–05; Abernethy, pp. 146–69, 192–206, 261–71, 290–94; Jackson to Patton Anderson, Jan. 4, 1807, to Governor W. C. C. Claiborne, Jan. 8, 1807, to [unknown], Feb. 10, 1810, AJC, I, 160–61, 163–65, 198–99.

36. Jackson to Jefferson, April 20, 1808, Jackson, "Division Order," April 20, 1808, AJC, I, 186–87, 188. "In the publick streets of Knoxville you appeared to pant for combat," Jackson had written Sevier in his duel challenge. Cf. James, p. 98.

37. James, pp. 145–46; Bassett, I, 34–35; S. Williams to Jackson, April 25, 1808, AJP.

38. Philbrick, pp. 214–20, 231. The Jackson Papers reveal Jackson's continued interest in moving to Mississippi territory. See letters to and from Jackson for the dates of May 20, June 10, Oct. 24, and Dec. 5, 1810; Oct. 9 and Oct. 23, 1811, AJP.

39. Jackson to Jenkins Whiteside, Feb. 10, 1810, AJC, I, 200.

40. Jackson, "Division Orders," March 7, 1812, AJC, I, 221–22.

41. Walker, p. 249. Language similar to Jackson's is quoted on pp. 244–60.

42. Jackson, "Division Orders," March 7, 1812, Jackson to President James Madison, March 15, 1813, AJC, I, 222, 292–93.

43. S. Putnam Waldo, *Memoirs of Andrew Jackson* (Hartford, Conn., 1820), pp. 11–12.

44. "Jackson's Address to the Troops in New Orleans," Dec. 18, 1814, AJC, II, 118. This address was probably drafted by Edward Livingston.

45. Several writers have suggested that the post-revolutionary generation contrasted its own materialism unfavorably with the heroism of the revolutionary fathers. Cf. Marvin Meyers, *The Jackson Persuasion* (N.Y., 1960); Fred Somkin, *Unquiet Eagle: Memory and Desire in the Idea of American Freedom, 1815–1860* (Ithaca, N.Y., 1967).

46. Jackson, "General Orders," Dec. 13, 1812, AJC, I, 249.

47. Jackson, "General Orders on Martial Law," Dec. 31, 1812, Jackson to John Reid, Dec. 30, 1812, AJC, I, 253–54, 252.

48. Sigmund Freud, *Group Psychology and the Analysis of the Ego*, in James Strachey, ed., *The Standard Edition of the Complete Psychological Works of Sigmund Freud*, XVIII (London, 1955), 94.

49. Arnow, p. 327n; James, p. 248; W. W. Clayton, *History of Davidson County, Tennessee* (Philadelphia, 1880), p. 479; John Coffee to Mary Coffee, Jan. 30, 1814, C/D.

50. Cf. Philippe Ariès, *Centuries of Childhood* (N.Y., 1962), pp. 241–68, 315–36,

353–64; Michael Walzer, *The Revolution of the Saints* (Cambridge, Mass., 1965), pp. 268–95; Freud, pp. 93–100, 111–16.

51. Jackson to Blount, Jan. 4, 1813, AJC, I, 254–55. Cf. above, chapter 2, p. 52.

52. Jackson to Blount, Dec. 21, 1812, AJC, I, 251.

53. Sigmund Freud, *Totem and Taboo, Standard Edition*, XIII (London, 1953), 125–61, *Group Psychology*, pp. 122–28.

54. Jackson, address to troops, July 31, 1812, AJP.

55. Walker, p. 254; Nettels, pp. 321–23; Julius W. Pratt, "Western Aims in the War of 1812," *Mississippi Valley Historical Review*, XII (June 1925), 37–50; Malcolm W. McMillan, "Jeffersonian Democracy and the Origins of Sectionalism," in Arthur S. Link and Rembert W. Patrick, eds., *Writing Southern History* (Baton Rouge, La., 1965), pp. 115–16; Jackson, "Announcement to His Soldiers," Nov. 14, 1812, AJC, I, 241–42.

56. Walker, p. 279; Bassett, I, 79–85; Jackson to Blount, Nov. 11, 1812, to George Campbell, Nov. 29, 1812, to Secretary of War John Armstrong, March 15, 1813, Armstrong to Jackson, Feb. 5, 1813, AJC, I, 238–39, 244, 275, 291–92.

57. James, pp. 156–58; Armstrong to Jackson, April 10, 1813; Jackson to Armstrong, March 15, 1813, to W. B. Lewis, April 9, 1813, AJC, I, 291–92, 304, 305.

58. Jackson to Rachel Jackson, March 15, 1813, AJC, I, 296; John Henry Eaton, *The Life of Andrew Jackson* (Philadelphia, 1824), p. 23. Reid wrote the first four chapters of this biography before he died, and is listed as co-author on the first edition (1817).

59. Parton, I, 380; James, pp. 158–59.

60. James, pp. 160–63. Jackson's wound was dressed with poultices of wood cuttings, in the manner prescribed by Indians. Cf. Robert V. Remini, *The Election of Andrew Jackson* (Philadelphia, 1963), p. 158.

61. Benjamin Hawkins to Judge Harry Toulmin, Oct. 28, 1813, AJP; Cotterill, pp. 124–29; Pound, pp. 161–63, 218–28; Angie Debo, *The Road to Disappearance* (Norman, Okla., 1941), pp. 4–71.

62. Debo, pp. 78–80; Edwin C. McReynolds, *The Seminoles* (Norman, Okla., 1957), pp. 58–59; documents reprinted in ASPIA, I, 839–56.

63. George Dangerfield, *The Era of Good Feelings* (N.Y., 1952), pp. 25–33. Jackson, offering Harrison the aid of the Tennessee militia, wrote that the Indians had been "excited by some secrete influence." Jackson to Brigadier General James Winchester, Nov. 28, 1811, AJC, I, 209.

64. Walker, pp. 257, 267–76; Debo, p. 78; Samuel C. Williams, *Beginnings of West Tennessee in the Land of the Chickasaws* (Johnson City, Tenn., 1930), p. 81; Jackson to Blount, June 4, 1812, July 3, 1812, July 10, 1812, to George Colbert, June 5, 1812, AJC, I, 225–27, 230; Jackson to Blount, July 8, 1812, AJP.

65. Walker, p. 268; Jackson to Blount, July 10, 1812, AJC, I, 231–32. Jackson's lurid description of Mrs. Crowley's captivity was fanciful. Cf. AJC, I, 225–26n, for Mrs. Crowley's version.

66. Jackson to Blount, July 3, 1812, AJC, I, 230.

67. His vituperative quarrel with Indian agent Silas Dinsmore followed. Cf. above, chapter 2, pp. 41–42.

68. McReynolds, pp. 44–50; Walker, pp. 280–83.

69. McReynolds, pp. 58–59; H. S. Halbert and T. H. Ball, *The Creek War of 1813 and 1814* (Chicago, 1895), pp. 115–42; Pound, p. 228.

70. Halbert and Ball, pp. 78–80; Robert B. McAffee, *History of the Late War in the Western Country* (Lexington, Ky., 1816), pp. 462–63; Alabama Creeks to Secretary of War, May 29, 1815, OIALR.

71. Walker, pp. 288–90; Jackson to Governor David Holmes, Sept. 26, 1813, AJC, I, 322. Jackson, urging an invasion of the Creek nation before Fort Mims, had discounted the significance of civil war. Reports that the Creek War originated in internal

conflict, Governor Blount agreed, were merely "a blind to the credulous." Cf. Jackson to Blount, July 13, 1813, Blount to General Thomas Flournoy, Oct. 15, 1813, ASPIA, I, 850, 855.

72. Bassett, I, 92–93.

73. Francis Tomlinson Gardner, "The Gentlemen from Tennessee," *Surgery, Gynecology and Obstetrics*, LXXXVIII (March 1948), 404–08; John William Ward, *Andrew Jackson—Symbol for an Age* (N.Y., 1955), p. 164; James, pp. 168–69; Eaton, p. 431.

74. Gardner, *loc. cit.* Parton, I, 547–48.

75. Jackson to John Coffee, Dec. 22, 1813, AJC, I, 404.

76. Jackson, draft of speech to the troops, 1813, AJP, 2nd ser.; Jackson, "General Orders," Sept. 18, 1813, "To the Troops," Oct. 24, 1813, "General Orders," March 24, 1814, AJC, I, 315–16, 337–38, 486–88; Parton, I, 426, 433.

77. Jackson to General Thomas Pinckney, Feb. 16, 1814, AJC, I, 462–63; Jackson to his troops, Nov. 6, 1813, AJP.

78. Jackson to Pinckney, Feb. 17, 1814, AJC, I, 465; Philbrick, pp. 268–69n. Indian troops, complained an eighteenth-century British officer, "are like the Devil's Pigg; they will neither lead nor drive." Cf. Arnow, p. 176.

79. Jackson to Pinckney, Feb. 17, 1814, to Secretary of War James Monroe, Nov. 16, 1814, Jan. 25, 1815, AJC, I, 465, II, 101–02, 151–52.

80. Jackson, "To the Troops," Oct. 24, 1813, "General Orders," March 24, 1814, AJC, I, 337–38, 488.

81. Jackson to Pinckney, Feb. 16, 1814, AJC, I, 462; Jackson to Colonel John Lowry, March 15, 1814, AJP.

82. Jackson to Pinckney, March 23, 1814, AJP.

83. James, pp. 168–70; Herbert J. Doherty, *Richard Keith Call: Southern Unionist* (Gainesville, Fla., 1961), p. 6; John Coffee to Mary Coffee, Oct. 24, 1813, Nov. 4, 1813, C/D; Halbert and Ball, p. 276; Parton, I, 437–48; Joseph K. Green to Jackson, Nov. 28, 1813, AJP.

84. Francis Paul Prucha, *The Sword of the Republic: The United States Army on the Frontier 1783–1846* (Toronto, 1969), p. 115; Bassett, I, 95; James, p. 168; Jackson to the wealthy citizens of Madison County, Mississippi, Oct. 23, 1813, to Blount, Nov. 29, 1813, AJC, I, 335, 362.

85. Waldo, p. 69; Bassett, I, 100–03; Parton, I, 452–63.

86. Colonel William Martin to Jackson, Dec. 4, 1813, AJC, I, 369–70; artillery company petition to Jackson, Dec. 15, 1813, AJP; Jackson to Martin, Dec. 4, 1813, to Coffee, Dec. 11, 1813, to Rachel Jackson, Dec. 14, 1813, AJC, I, 371, 382, 391.

87. Jackson to Martin, Dec. 4, 1813, AJC, I, 372; "Proceedings of a Court Martial in the Creek War," Oct. 15, 1813, *American Historical Magazine and Tennessee Historical Society Quarterly*, VI (July 1901), 253–55; Bassett, I, 104–08; James, pp. 175–76; Waldo, p. 98; Bassett, I, 112.

88. Jackson to Reverend Gideon Blackburn, Dec. 3, 1813, "General Order," Dec. 15, 1813, to Coffee, Dec. 22, 1813, AJC, I, 365, VI, 429, I, 405.

89. Halbert and Ball, pp. 269–75; Mooney, pp. 90–92; McAffee, pp. 462–87; John Coffee to Mary Coffee, Jan. 30, 1814, C/D; James, pp. 177–79.

90. Jackson to W. B. Lewis, Feb. 13, 1814, LP.

91. Jackson to John Reid, Feb. 8, 1814, Rachel Jackson to Jackson, March 11, 1814, AJC, VI, 431, I, 476–77.

92. Jackson to Rachel Jackson, March 12, 1814, Reid to Jackson, April 9, 1814, AJP; Bassett, I, 109–14.

93. Parton, I, 506–11; Jackson to Rachel Jackson, March 12, 1814, AJP; "General Orders, Case of John Woods," March 12, 1814, "To John Woods, General Orders," March 14, 1814, AJC, I, 479, 480–81. Mad Anthony Wayne, preparing for his northern Indian campaign in the 1790s, had executed soldiers. He cited the language

of the war regulations issued at the outbreak of the Revolution. Men under Wayne's command were court-martialed for many offenses, but executed only for desertion or equally serious charges. Cf. Parton, I, 508; Richard C. Knopf, "Crime and Punishment in the Legion, 1792–1793," *Bulletin of the Historical and Philosophical Society of Ohio,* XIV (July 1956), 232–37.

94. "Proceedings of a Court Martial," pp. 354–55.

95. Jackson to Rachel Jackson, December 29, 1813, Avery O. Craven, ed., "Letters of Andrew Jackson," *Huntington Library Bulletin,* No. 3 (Feb. 1933), p. 114.

96. James, pp. 180–91; Ward, p. 112.

97. James, pp. 181–82; Mooney, pp. 94–96; Jackson to Blount, March 31, 1814, to Rachel Jackson, April 1, 1814, AJC, I, 92–94.

98. Jackson, draft of speech to the troops, 1813, AJP, 2nd ser.; Parton, I, 333; Bassett, I, 90–95; James, p. 182.

99. Secretary of War John Armstrong to Jackson, May 22, 1814, Judge Harry Toulmin to Jackson, June 22, 1814, AJC, II, 4, 9; Colonel W. P. Anderson to Jackson, Aug. 22, 1814, AJP; Jackson to Josiah Nichols, June 9, 1814, AJC, II, 5–6.

100. "On the State of the Indians," *North American Review,* XVI (Jan. 1823), 34; Jackson to Pinckney, May 18, 1814, AJC, II, 1–2.

101. Armstrong to Pinckney, March 17, 1814, ASPIA, I, 836–37; Pinckney to Jackson, April 7, 1814, AJC, I, 496–97, 497–98n; Pinckney to Benjamin Hawkins, April 23, 1814, AJP.

102. Coffee to Lewis, April 18, 1814, LP; Charles C. Royce, "Indian Land Cessions in the United States," *Bureau of American Ethnology, Annual Report,* XVIII, Part 2 (1896–97), see maps.

103. Jackson to Pinckney, May 18, 1814, to Monroe, Nov. 16, 1814, AJC, II, 3, 103; James, pp. 189–90; statement of Charles Cassedy, Aug. 8, 1814, statement of Benjamin Hawkins, Aug. 8, 1814, ASPIA, I, 837.

104. Colonel Arthur P. Hayne to Jackson, March 27, 1816, AJC, II, 237–38; Hayne to Jackson, May 31, 1816, July 11, 1816, Colonel James Gadsden to Jackson, July 1, 1816, AJP.

105. Jackson to Big Warrior, record of proceedings in Fort Jackson treaty, August 1814, AJP.

106. Chief Tustunnugga to Creek Council, Sept. 18, 1815, OIA Treaty File, Fort Jackson Treaty.

107. Jackson to Armstrong, undated, Pinckney to Hawkins, April 23, 1814, ASPIA, I, 857–58. After forcing the Creeks to sign his treaty, Jackson arranged to feed and clothe their starving women and children. "I know your humanity would bleed for them," he wrote his wife. F. P. Prucha does not describe this series of events, but he finds others like it evidence of Jackson's "justice and fairness" toward the tribes. I do not. Cf. James, p. 190; F. P. Prucha, "Andrew Jackson's Indian Policy: A Reassessment," *Journal of American History,* LVI (Dec. 1969), 529–31.

108. Jackson to Armstrong, Dec. 16, 1813, Jackson to Pinckney, May 18, 1814, Jackson to Armstrong, Aug. 10, 1814, AJC, I, 396–97, II, 2–3, 24–26; Jackson response to testimonial dinner, May 14, 1814, AJP.

109. Jackson to John Overton, Aug. 10, 1814, CC. Cf. below, chapter 6.

110. James, pp. 190–91; Eaton, pp. 241–42.

111. Halbert and Ball, pp. 270–72; Jackson to Governor Peter Early, Oct. 10, 1813, to Monroe, Oct. 26, 1814, AJC, I, 331, II, 83; Judge Harry Toulmin to Jackson, June 22, 1814, AJC, II, 9–11; Toulmin to Colonel Milton, May 4, 1814, T. U. Wilson to Pinckney, May 20, 1814, AJP; Bassett, I, 127, 132.

112. Blount to General Thomas Flournoy, Oct. 15, 1813, ASPIA, I, 855; Bassett, I, 132.

113. Jackson to Governor González Manrique, Aug. 24, 1814, Sept. 9, 1814, AJC, II, 28–29, 44.

114. Jackson to Manrique, Sept. 9, 1814, AJC, II, 45; Bassett, I, 132; Cotterill, p. 189; R. J. Meigs to Jackson, Feb. 11, 1814, John McKee to Jackson, Aug. 27, 1814, AJP; Jackson to Colonel Robert Butler, Aug. 27, 1814, to Monroe, Oct. 26, 1814, Nov. 20, 1814, AJC, II, 31–33, 82–83, 101–02; Benjamin Hawkins to Creeks, Aug. 30, 1814, AJP.

115. Annie Heloise Abel, "The History of Events Resulting in Indian Consolidation West of the Mississippi," *American Historical Association, Report of Proceedings, 1906*, pp. 263–64.

116. Jackson to Manrique, Nov. 6, 1814, AJC, II, 92.

117. James, p. 192; Jackson to Colonel Robert Butler, Aug. 27, 1814, Aug. 28, 1814, AJC, II, 32, 34.

118. Bassett, I, 200; Parton, II, 241–42. Jackson's biographers all discuss the Battle of New Orleans in great detail. The best interpretive treatment is Ward, pp. 3–29. Géza Róheim, *The Panic of the Gods* (N.Y., 1972), pp. 206–20, analyzes myths in which heroes rescue panicking gods. A phallic hero, in Róheim's interpretation, rescues men from fears of oral annihilation. Such myths help establish the possibility of secure separation from the parents. The American imagination, I am suggesting, gave the Battle of New Orleans this significance.

119. Ward, pp. 17–22; Parton, II, 71, 102; James, p. 256.

120. Rachel Jackson to Jackson, Feb. 10, 1814, AJC, I, 459–60. Cf. Rachel Jackson to Jackson, Mar. 21, 1814, AJC, I, 483. Ward, pp. 107–08; Jackson to Governor David Holmes, Jan. 18, 1815, AJC, II, 145; James, p. 267.

121. James, p. 267.

122. Jackson to Governor W. C. C. Claiborne, Feb. 3, 1815, AJC, II, 156; Parton, II, 277–97, 312–13; Bassett, I, 224–26; James, pp. 271–82; Waldo, pp. 180–81. Abraham Lincoln cited Jackson's suspension of *habeas corpus* in New Orleans as precedent for his own suspension of the writ without congressional authorization during the Civil War. Cf. Abraham Lincoln to "Hon. Erastus Corning & Others [June 12] Washington 1863," in *Selected Speeches, Messages and Letters*, T. Harry Williams, ed. (N.Y., 1957), p. 228.

123. Eaton, pp. 417–23.

124. Waldo, p. 272; Parton, III, 330.

125. Hayne to Jackson, March 27, 1816, "Jackson's Visit to Mount Vernon," Nov. 1815, AJC, II, 237–38, 219–20. Jackson followed Washington's example in the year of his death. He refused a Roman sarcophagus offered as his tomb on the grounds that such pomp violated republican simplicity. Cf. Ward, pp. 115–16.

CHAPTER SIX

1. Charles C. Royce, "Indian Land Cessions in the United States," *Bureau of American Ethnology, Annual Report*, XVIII, Part 2 (1896–97), see maps and list of treaties. Annie Heloise Abel, "The History of Events Resulting in Indian Consolidation West of the Mississippi," *American Historical Association, Report of Proceedings, 1906*, p. 276, stresses Jackson's role in Indian policy during this period.

2. Mary E. Young is the first modern scholar to place Indian relations at the center of Jacksonian Democracy. Cf. *Redskins, Ruffleshirts, and Rednecks* (Norman, Okla., 1961), pp. 3–4, 10, 189–93.

3. On savagery, civilization, and Indians in literature, cf. Roy Harvey Pearce, *The Savages of America* (Baltimore, Md., 1965); Henry Nash Smith, *Virgin Land*, (N.Y., 1950); John William Ward, *Andrew Jackson—Symbol for an Age* (N.Y., 1955), pp. 30–45; Perry Miller, "Nature and the National Ego," in *Errand into the Wilderness* (N.Y., 1964), pp. 204–16; Paul A. W. Wallace, "Cooper's Indians," *New York History*, XXXV (Oct. 1954), 55–78. Kentucky's early history of Indian war-

fare, according to one writer, was comparable to the "tales of knight-errantry" and the "Waverley novels." (Cf. "Western History," *North American Review*, XLIII [July 1836], 10.) Marvin Meyers' discussion of Cooper as a Jacksonian (*The Jacksonian Persuasion* [N.Y., 1960], pp. 57–100) misses the significance of his Leatherstocking tales.

4. Jack Gregory and Rennard Strickland, *Sam Houston with the Cherokees, 1829–1833* (Austin, Tex., 1967), p. 58; Governor George M. Troup to Secretary of War Barbour, Aug. 26, 1826, ASPIA, II, 739.

5. This conceit is Thomas McKenney's. Cf. *Memoirs, Official and Personal,* 2 vols. (N.Y., 1846), I, 82.

6. Rosa Luxemburg, *Accumulation of Capital* (N.Y., 1964), p. 370. On primitive accumulation generally, cf. pp. 368–418; and Karl Marx, *Capital,* 3 vols. (Chicago, 1906–09), I, 784–848; Barrington Moore, *Social Origins of Dictatorship and Democracy* (Boston, 1966), pp. 3–29.

7. On Australia, cf. C. D. Rowley, *The Destruction of Aboriginal Society* (Canberra, Aust., 1970).

8. On the northern Indian situation, cf. Abel, pp. 250–59, 266–68, 276–77, 383–85, 388–91, 405–12; Grant Foreman, *The Last Trek of the Indians* (Chicago, 1946); William T. Hagan, *The Sac and Fox Indians* (Norman, Okla., 1958); Paul W. Gates, "Introduction," *The John Tipton Papers*, Nellie A. Robertson and Dorothy Riker, eds. (Indianapolis, Ind., 1942), I, 3–52. Gates' essay is a neglected masterpiece.

9. On the southern tribes, cf. Abel; Young; Grant Foreman, *Indian Removal* (Norman, Okla., 1932); Angie Debo, *The Road to Disappearance* (Norman, Okla., 1941); John K. Mahon, *History of the Second Seminole War, 1835–1842* (Gainesville, Fla., 1967), pp. 1–17; Arthur H. DeRosier, Jr., *The Removal of the Choctaw Indians* (Knoxville, Tenn., 1970), pp. 3–13; Marion L. Starkey, *The Cherokee Nation* (N.Y., 1946); R. S. Cotterill, *The Southern Indians: The Story of the Civilized Tribes Before Removal* (Norman, Okla., 1954) pp. 9–15; Robert F. Berkhofer, *Salvation and the Savage* (Lexington, Ky.), 1965; and other sources cited in chapters 5–7.

10. Abel, pp. 278–79; Cotterill, p. 195; Jackson to John Coffee, Dec. 4, 1815, Feb. 2, 1816, C/D; Coffee to Jackson, Dec. 27, 1815, AJP; Coffee to Jackson, Jan. 21, 1816, Jackson to Coffee, Feb. 13, 1816 (private), Feb. 13, 1816 (public), AJC, II, 225, 230–33. Coffee was also armed with authority from Jackson's subordinate General Edmund P. Gaines to act as a fourth commissioner. Gaines had no power to add to the commission, however, and even he had not authorized Coffee to act alone. Cf. Gaines to Coffee, Nov. 28, 1815, OIALR.

11. Robert Searcy to Coffee, Dec. 28, 1815, William Dawson and Robert Mayo to Coffee, Dec. 29, 1815, Alexander Ewing to Coffee, Dec. 30, 1815, AJP; Colonel Robert Butler to Jackson, Dec. 31, 1815, "Statement of Creek Chiefs and Head Men," Jan. 22, 1816, Jackson to Secretary of War William Crawford, June [13?], 1816, AJC, II, 223, 226, 246–47. Searcy and Butler belonged to the Donelson clan.

12. Cf. above, chapter 3, p. 83.

13. Coffee to Jackson, Dec. 27, 1815, AJP.

14. Abel, p. 279; Cotterill, p. 194; Coffee to Jackson, Feb. 8, 1816, AJP; Jackson to Coffee, Feb. 13, 1816, to George Colbert, Feb. 13, 1816, AJC, II, 231–33; Coffee to Crawford, March 15, 1816, OIALR; W. B. Lewis to *Columbus Observer* (draft), Sept. 20, 1824, LP.

15. Gaines to Coffee, Nov. 28, 1815, Feb. 10, 1816, Coffee to Commissioners, Feb. 17, 1816, March 13, 1816, to Crawford, March 15, 1816, April 15, 1816, OIALR; Crawford to Commissioners, March 14, 1816, AJP.

16. Abel, p. 279; Crawford to Jackson, March 8, 1816, Jackson to Crawford, June 10, 1816, AJC, II, 235–36, 243–45.

17. Jackson to General William Cocke, Dec. 28, 1813, to Captain Rufus Morgan, Feb. 1, 1814, to Crawford, June 16, 1815, to Coffee, July 21, 1816, AJC, I, 414,

442n, II, 249, 254–55; R. J. Meigs to Jackson, Aug. 7, 1816, Isaac Thomas to Jackson, Aug. 12, 1816, Colonel William Martin to Jackson, Oct. 31, 1816, AJP.

18. Jackson to Coffee, Feb. 13, 1816, to Crawford, June 10, 1816, AJC, II, 231–32, 244–45.

19. Abel, pp. 279–80; Jackson to Coffee, April 13, 1816, Coffee to Major William Russell, June 15, 1816, C/D; Jackson to Crawford, June 10, 1816, June [13?], 1816, AJC, II, 245–46, 248–49; Jackson, D. Meriwether and J. Franklin to Crawford, Sept. 20, 1816, ASPIA, II, 105.

20. Cotterill, pp. 196–201; Royce, *loc. cit.* Jackson's nephew and former business partner John Hutchings supplied provisions for the Chickasaw treaty. Cf. Jackson to Crawford, Aug. 18, 1816, ASPIA, II, 120–21.

21. Cotterill, pp. 198–201; Jackson to Secretary of State James Monroe, July 8, 1816, to Coffee, July 19, 1816, Sept. 19, 1816, AJC, II, 252–53, 260; Jackson, Meriwether and Franklin to Crawford, Sept. 20, 1816, ASPIA, II, 120–21.

22. Jackson to Coffee, July 26, 1816, AJC, II, 256.

23. Bribery of Indian chiefs did not begin with Jackson. It originated in colonial presents to gain Indian allies. These presents made the tribes dependent on Europeans and European goods, but the practice of gift-giving assimilated easily to Indian gift-giving customs, and was not consciously aimed at splitting chiefs from the tribal interests. Colonial gift-giving was rarely used to purchase Indian land; Indians considered this a misuse of gifts, and it made them hostile. By Jefferson's administration, gift-giving had changed its meaning. Now the primary purpose of gifts was to overcome tribal resistance to land cessions. Jackson, as the text suggests, consciously used bribes for this purpose. Although it is important to understand the roots of presents to Indians in Indian customs, it is wrong to overlook the shift in their character, and to explain the extensive bribery at early-nineteenth-century treaties as accommodation to Indian culture. Cf. Wilbur R. Jacobs, *Wilderness Politics and Indian Gifts* (Lincoln, Neb., 1966 [first published 1950]); Cotterill, pp. 151–53; Reginald Horsman, *Expansion and American Indian Policy, 1783–1812* (East Lansing, Mich., 1967), pp. 125–26, 136–40; Bernard W. Sheehan, "Indian-White Relations in Early America: A Review Essay," *William and Mary Quarterly*, 3rd ser., XXVI (April 1969), 277.

24. "Treaty with the Cherokees," "Treaty with the Chickasaws," Jackson, Meriwether, and Franklin to Crawford, Sept. 20, 1816, ASPIA, II, 92–93, 104–05.

25. Gordon T. Chappell, "John Coffee: Surveyor and Land Agent," *The Alabama Review*, XIV (in two parts, July and Oct. 1961), 188; Coffee to John Donelson III, April 25, 1814, "Letters from General John Coffee," *American Historical Magazine and Tennessee Historical Society Quarterly*, VI (April 1901), 188–89; John Donelson IV to Coffee, July 5, 1814, C/D.

26. Paul Wallace Gates, *The Farmer's Age: Agriculture 1815–1860* (N.Y., 1960), p. 59; Malcolm J. Rohrbough, *The Land Office Business* (N.Y., 1968), pp. 96–99; Gordon T. Chappell, "Some Patterns of Land Speculation in the Old Southwest," *Journal of Southern History*, XV (Nov. 1949), 464–65; Thomas P. Abernethy, *The Formative Period in Alabama, 1815–1828* (University, Ala., 1965), pp. 25–26; Jackson to Monroe, Nov. 12, 1816, to Coffee, Dec. 20, 1816, to President James Monroe, March 4, 1817, AJC, II, 263–64, 270–71, 277–78; Jackson to Acting Secretary of War George P. Graham, June 11, 1817, ASPIA, II, 142.

27. Abernethy, pp. 49–50, 64–65; Gates, *Farmer's Age*, p. 62; Rohrbough, pp. 90–91, 115; Thomas Bibb to Jackson, Dec. 20, 1816, AJP.

28. Chappell, "John Coffee," pp. 184–91; Rohrbough, p. 101; Jackson to Monroe, Nov. 12, 1816, AJC, II, 264; John Donelson IV to Coffee, July 5, 1814, C/D.

29. Rohrbough, pp. 21, 32; Gates, *Farmer's Age*, p. 62; Gates, *Tipton Papers*, pp. 6–7; Chappell, "Some Patterns," p. 48; John Coffee to Mary Coffee, May 21, 1817, C/D; Jackson to Coffee, June 21, 1817, AJC, II, 298.

30. Chappell, "John Coffee," pp. 194, 243–46; John McLemore to Coffee, July 18, 1818, Lemuel Donelson to Coffee, Sept. 5, 1818, C/D; Jackson to John Hutchings, April 22, 1816, AJC, II, 241.

31. A. P. Hayne to Jackson, Nov. 27, 1816, Jan. 10, 1817, AJP; Jackson to Coffee, Dec. 26, 1816, to Monroe, March 4, 1817, to Secretary of War John C. Calhoun, Jan. 27, 1818, AJC, II, 270–71, 278, 350–51.

32. Chappell, "Some Patterns," p. 472, "John Coffee," p. 246.

33. Rohrbough, pp. 115–24; Abernethy, pp. 64–65; John Coffee to Mary Coffee, Feb. 16, 1818, C/D; Jackson to Coffee, Jan. 27, 1818, to Andrew Jackson Hutchings, Aug. 2, 1838, AJC, II, 352, V, 562.

34. Coffee to Jackson, Feb. 12, 1818, Jackson to Isaac Shelby, Nov. 24, 1818, AJC, II, 353–54, 401; Rohrbough, pp. 115–30; Gates, *Farmer's Age*, pp. 58–63; Abernethy, p. 69; Chappell, "Some Patterns," p. 473.

35. John Coffee to Mary Coffee, Feb. 10, 1818, Feb. 14, 1818, C/D; Chappell, "John Coffee," pp. 246–50.

36. Abel, p. 282; Cotterill, p. 203.

37. U.S. Commissioners to Graham, July 9, 1817, AJC, II, 305.

38. Cotterill, p. 203; President Thomas Jefferson to Cherokees, Jan. 9, 1809, Cherokee chiefs and headmen to Commissioners, July 2, 1817, ASPIA, II, 125, 143; U.S. Commissioners to Graham, July 8, 1817, AJC, II, 302–04; "Minutes of the Proceedings of the Cherokee Treaty," July 4, 1817, AJP.

39. Abel, pp. 241–49; Tennessee Governor Joseph McMinn to Crawford, Oct. 25, 1816, Graham to Jackson, June 11, 1817, ASPIA, II, 115, 142; Andrew Jackson, "First Annual Message," James D. Richardson, ed., *Messages and Papers of the Presidents* (N.Y., 1917), II, 458.

40. George Dangerfield, *The Era of Good Feelings* (N.Y., 1952), p. 27; DeRosier, pp. 27–32; Samuel C. Williams, *Beginnings of West Tennessee in the Land of the Chickasaws* (Johnson City, Tenn., 1930), p. 62; Cotterill, pp. 139–49; Hagan, pp. 9–14; Seymour Dunbar, *A History of Travel in America*, 3 vols. (Indianapolis, Ind., 1915), II, 419, 470–82.

41. DeRosier, p. 26; Crawford to Jackson, Meriwether, and Franklin, July 3, 1816, McMinn to Cherokees, Nov. 23, 1818, R. J. Meigs to Crawford, Aug. 19, 1816, ASPIA, II, 101, 487, 114.

42. Meigs to Calhoun, May 20, 1820, OIALR.

43. Crawford to Senate, March 13, 1816, Jefferson to Cherokees, Jan. 9, 1809, ASPIA, II, 26–27, 125; Jefferson to the chiefs of the Cherokee Nation, Jan. 10, 1806, in Adrienne Koch and William Peden, eds., *The Life and Selected Writings of Thomas Jefferson* (N.Y., 1944), p. 578.

44. "Treaty with the Creeks, 1814," Article 1, Charles J. Kappler, ed., *Indian Treaties, 1778–1883* (N.Y., 1972 [first published 1904]), p. 108; Pinckney to Hawkins, April 23, 1814, ASPIA, I, 858; J. B. Kinney, *A Continent Lost—A Civilization Won* (Baltimore, Md., 1937), pp. 81–88.

45. Young, p. 11; Jackson to Coffee, Sept. 19, 1816, AJC, I, 260.

46. "Treaty with the Cherokee, 1817," Kappler, pp. 140–44; Kinney, pp. 81–88; William T. Hagan, *American Indians* (Chicago, 1961), pp. 139–48.

47. U.S. Commissioners to Graham, July 8, 1817, Jackson to Colonel Robert Butler, June 21, 1817, AJC, II, 300–04, 299.

48. Commissioners to Graham, July 8, 1817, AJC, II, 304.

49. Jackson talk to Cherokees, June 28, 1817, AJP; Commissioners to Graham, July 8, 1817, AJC, II, 303–04.

50. Jackson to Crawford, June 10, 1816, to Butler, Sept. 5, 1816, AJC, II, 243–44, 259.

51. Jackson to Coffee, July 13, 1817, AJC, II, 307; "Treaty with the Cherokee, 1817," Kappler, pp. 140–44.

52. Commissioners talk to Cherokees, July 4, 1817, AJP; Commissioners to Graham, July 8, 1817, Jackson to Coffee, July 13, 1817, AJC, II, 304, 307.

53. Commissioners to Graham, July 4, 1817, AJC, II, 304; Marquis James, *The Raven* (N.Y., 1962 [first published 1929]), p. 44; Abel, pp. 282-84; McMinn to Calhoun, July 7, 1818, ASPIA, II, 528-29; McMinn to Calhoun, Calhoun to McMinn, McMinn to Cherokees, letters between July 29, 1818, and Nov. 25, 1818, ASPIA, II, 479-90; McMinn to Calhoun, letters between Nov. 29, 1818, and Oct. 20, 1819, OIALR.

54. McMinn to Cherokees, Nov. 23, 1818, ASPIA, II, 487.

55. McMinn to Daniel Graham, Nov. 12, 1818, "Correspondence of Joseph P. McMinn," *American Historical Magazine and Tennessee Historical Society Quarterly*, IV (Oct. 1899), 328.

56. McMinn to Daniel Graham, June 1, 1819, Jan. 16, 1820, "Correspondence of Joseph P. McMinn," *American Historical Magazine and Tennessee Historical Society Quarterly*, V (Jan. 1900), 48, 58; McMinn to Crawford, Oct. 25, 1816, Calhoun to Cherokee delegation, Feb. 11, 1819, Calhoun to McMinn, March 6, 1819, ASPIA, II, 115, 190; McMinn to Calhoun, March 20, 1819, March 30, 1819, Calhoun to McMinn, May 6, 1819, OIALR; "Treaty with the Cherokee, 1819," Kappler, pp. 177-80.

57. Jackson to Monroe, March 4, 1817, AJC, II, 278; Jenkins Whiteside and others to the President, undated, ASPIA, II, 90; Williams, p. 87; Thomas P. Abernethy, *From Frontier to Plantation in Tennessee* (Chapel Hill, N.C., 1932), p. 273.

58. Jackson to Isaac Shelby, Aug. 11, 1818, Oct. 30, 1818, AJC, II, 388, 399-400; Jackson to Calhoun, July 13, 1818, Calhoun to Jackson, July 30, 1818, Jackson to Calhoun, Aug. 18, 1818, ASPIA, II, 178-79.

59. Calhoun to Shelby and Jackson, May 12, 1818, ASPIA, II, 173-74. W. B. Lewis to *Columbus Observer*, draft, Sept. 20, 1824, LP; Abernethy, pp. 273-74; Williams, p. 295. Williams reprints the secret journal of the Chickasaw treaty, pp. 282-302; references to those pages are to the treaty proceedings.

60. Jackson and Shelby to Calhoun, Oct. 30, 1818, AJC, II, 399-400; Lewis to Coffee, Sept. 27, 1828, C/D. In one of Jackson's versions of the story, the extra $20,000 was intended to provide an extra year of annuities for the tribe, rather than to bribe the Colberts. This seems not to have been the case. Cf. Williams, pp. 88-91; James Parton, *Life of Andrew Jackson*, 3 vols. (Boston, 1866), II, 528-32.

61. Harriette S. Arnow, *Seedtime on the Cumberland* (N.Y., 1960), pp. 285-86; Gregory and Strickland, p. 127; Gordon T. Chappell, "The Life and Activities of General John Coffee," *Tennessee Historical Quarterly*, I (March 1942), 128; George Deaderick to Jackson, Sept. 14, 1802, AJP; John Strother, John Reid, and Jonathan Robertson to Secretary of War William Eustis, Aug. 31, 1818, Cass to Calhoun, March 10, 1820, OIALR; Senator John Williams to John Overton, Jan. 15, 1819, CC.

62. Abernethy, *Frontier to Plantation*, pp. 273-75. "Report of the House Committee on Public Lands," 22nd Congress, 1st sess., Jan. 6, 1832, Doc. No. 488, pp. 2-43; Lewis statement, Aug. 20, 1819, AJC, II, 443-44n.

63. Williams to Overton, Jan. 15, 1819, CC; Lewis statement, Aug. 20, 1819, AJC, II, 443-44n; Lewis to *Columbus Observer*, draft, Sept. 20, 1824, LP; John H. Eaton to Coffee, March 30, 1832, C/D; Abernethy, *Frontier to Plantation*, p. 276.

64. Lewis later claimed the lick had cost him and his partner $3,000 to drill for salt. This sum was far in excess of the apparent cost of drilling; perhaps the $3,000 was actually the cost of the bribe. To further suggest a connection between Colbert's reserve and the lick, James Jackson had, like Lewis, an interest in both. Cf. Lewis to *Columbus Observer*, draft, Sept. 20, 1824, LP; Lewis to Coffee, April 13, 1832, C/D; "Report of the House Committee on Public Lands," p. 7.

65. Lewis to *Columbus Observer*, draft, Sept. 20, 1824, LP; Eaton to Coffee, March 30, 1832, C/D.

66. "Report of House Committee on Public Lands," pp. 2-43; Eaton to Coffee,

July 22, 1826, Aug. 12, 1826, Lewis to Coffee, Sept. 12, 1826, Nov. 25, 1826, April 13, 1832, Coffee to Robert Currin, Oct. 23, 1831, C/D.

67. Jackson to McMinn, Aug. 25, 1819, AJC, II, 426; Abernethy, *Frontier to Plantation*, pp. 269–70, 273–74; Williams, pp. 124–30.

68. *Worcester v. Georgia*, VI Peters (1832), 512–59; Kinney, pp. 9–10.

69. Governor John Murphy to the House of Representatives, Jan. 16, 1826, ASPIA, II, 646; P. B. Porter, "Annual Report of the Secretary of War," Dec. 2, 1828, ASPMA, IV, 4.

70. The single reference, and I am grateful to Professor James C. Curtis for pointing it out, is in a letter to Chickasaw Chief George Colbert before the outbreak of the Creek War. Jackson warned Colbert that "your Father the President" would treat him as an enemy if he did not stop Creeks from bringing scalps, captives, and stolen horses through Chickasaw country. The fraternal metaphor dominates that letter, however. Jackson used the "Friend and Brother" form of address five times, and twice more referred to Colbert as his "Brother." Cf. Jackson to George Colbert, June 5, 1812, AJC, I, 226–27.

71. John Henry Eaton, *The Life of Andrew Jackson* (Philadelphia, 1824), pp. 436–37; Jackson to Rachel Jackson, Dec. 29, 1813, Avery O. Craven, ed., "Letters of Andrew Jackson," *Huntington Library Bulletin*, No. 3 (Feb. 1933), p. 115.

72. See above, chapter 5, p. 155.

73. Jackson to Rachel Jackson, Dec. 20, 1814, in Samuel G. Heiskell, *Andrew Jackson and Early Tennessee History*, 3 vols. (Nashville, Tenn., 1920), III, 288; Jackson to Rachel Jackson, Dec. 19, 1813, AJC, I, 400–01; Jackson to Rachel Jackson, March 4, 1814, Craven, p. 115.

74. Eaton, pp. 436–37; Jackson to James Gadsden, May 2, 1822, AJC, III, 161; Marquis James, *Andrew Jackson: The Border Captain* (Indianapolis, Ind., 1933), p. 357, and *Andrew Jackson: Portrait of a President* (Indianapolis, Ind., 1937), pp. 24, 60; Parton, I, 439–40.

It was common for men involved in Indian relations to adopt Indian children. Eaton did so. (Cf. Peggy Eaton, *Autobiography* [N.Y., 1932], pp. 162–68.) Thomas McKenney adopted a Cherokee boy the same age as his son. McKenney educated him, he explained, so he could freely enter white society. The Cherokee became a frontier lawyer, and killed himself when a white woman refused his offer of marriage. Two other Indian boys lived in the McKenney household while McKenney was Superintendent of Indian Affairs. When the Jackson administration fired McKenney, it took them from him, over his frantic protests. Cf. his *Memoirs, Official and Personal*, II, 109–17, I, 188–89; Acting Secretary of War P. G. Randolph to McKenney, Oct. 5, 1830; Samuel Hamilton to McKenney, Oct. 9, 1830, Randolph to John Crowell, Oct. 11, 1830, OIALS.

75. Jackson to Creeks, Sept. 4, 1815, AJC, II, 216–17.

76. Early in 1816, for example, when the Chickasaws resisted Coffee's Creek line, Jackson wrote them, "The President of the U States loves his red children, and will do justice to them; but he will punish his red children when they attempt by force to do wrong. I write this as your friend and brother and as a friend of your nation to save you from involving yourself in trouble." Jackson to George Colbert, Feb. 13, 1816, AJC, II, 233. Cf. Jackson to Coffee, Sept. 19, 1816, AJC, II, 260.

77. Jackson to Monroe, March 4, 1817, to Calhoun, Sept. 2, 1820, Jan. 18, 1821, AJC, II, 278–81, III, 32, 36–38; Abel, p. 285.

78. Jackson to Shelby, Aug. 11, 1818, AJC, II, 387; Jackson to John McKee, April 22, 1819, to Calhoun, Aug. 24, 1819, OIALR.

79. McMinn to Cherokees, Nov. 18, 1818, "Report of a Select Committee of the House of Representatives" (by Georgia Congressman John Forsyth), March 15, 1824, ASPIA, II, 485–86, 503; A. W. Putnam, *History of Middle Tennessee* (Nashville,

Tenn., 1859), pp. 550–60; Meigs to Jackson, Aug. 16, 1816, AJP; Meigs to Crawford, Aug. 19, 1816, ASPIA, II, 114; Meigs to Calhoun, Feb. 10, 1819, OIALR.

80. James Monroe, "Second Annual Message," and "Second Inaugural Address," Richardson, II, 46, 92; Jackson to Monroe, March 4, 1817, AJC, II, 278; Williams, pp. 292–93.

81. DeRosier, p. 64; Jackson to Calhoun, Dec. 30, 1818, AJC, II, 405–06; Samuel Overton, "Journal of the Treaty of Doak's Stand," Oct. 3–21, 1820, ASPIA, II, 229–31, 234–37, 239–40.

82. Overton, "Journal," Choctaw Commissioners to Calhoun, Oct. 21, 1820, ASPIA, II, 237, 242–43; "Treaty with the Choctaw, 1820," Kappler, pp. 191–95.

83. Jackson to Calhoun, June 19, 1820, Calhoun to House of Representatives, Feb. 4, 1823, to Edmund Folsom, March 27, 1821, Folsom to Calhoun, Nov. 24, 1821, ASPIA, II, 232, 393–95; DeRosier, pp. 70–98.

84. James, *Jackson*, p. 409n.

85. J. Leitch Wright, Jr., "A Note on the First Seminole War as Seen by the Indians, Negroes, and Their British Advisers," *Journal of Southern History*, XXIV (Nov. 1968), 565–66; Mahon, pp. 3–5.

86. Wright, pp. 568–75; James, *Jackson*, pp. 309–10; Alexander Arbuthnot to Chief Officer commanding at Fort Gaines, March 3, 1817, Major James Dinkins to Gaines, June 1, 1817, AJP.

87. James W. Silver, *Edmund Pendleton Gaines: Frontier General* (Baton Rouge, La., 1949), pp. 60, 64–69; D. B. Mitchell to the Secretary of War, March 30, 1817, Gaines to Calhoun, Aug. 25, 1817, ten Indian towns to the Commanding Officer at Fort Hawkins, Sept. 11, 1817, ASPIA, II, 156, 158, 159; Gaines to Jackson, Feb. 17, 1817, AJP; Jackson to Gaines, April 8, 1816, AJC, II, 238–39; Gaines to Calhoun, Jan. 12, 1818, OIALR.

88. Foreman, *Indian Removal*, pp. 315–17; Kenneth Wiggins Porter, "Negroes and the Seminole War 1835–1842," *Journal of Southern History*, XXX (Nov. 1964), 427–30.

89. Mahon, p. 23; Duncan L. Clinch to Jackson, Oct. 28, 1816, AJP; Jackson to Gaines, April 8, 1816, to Monroe, June 20, 1820, AJC, II, 238–39, III, 28.

90. John Spencer Bassett, *The Life of Andrew Jackson*, 2 vols. (N.Y., 1925), I, 292–93; James, *Jackson*, p. 310; Jackson to William Williams, Sept. 25, 1819, John Donelson, Jr., "Affidavit," Jan. 13, 1820, AJC, II, 430–32, III, 6–7; Gaines to Seminoles, June 30, 1817, to Jackson, July 10, 1817, Oct. 1, 1817, Oct. 23, 1817, Dec. 2, 1817, AJP; Gaines to Jackson, Nov. 21, 1817, ASPIA, II, 160; testimony of Eaton and Butler before Select Committee of the Senate, reporting Feb. 24, 1819, ASPMA, I, 750–51.

91. D. E. Twiggs to Gaines, Aug. 11, 1817, Gaines to Jackson, Dec. 2, 1817, AJP; Graham to Gaines, Oct. 30, 1817, Gaines to Jackson, Nov. 21, 1817, ASPIA, II, 159, 160.

92. Gaines to Jackson, Feb. 14, 1817, AJP; Mahon, pp. 25–26; Jackson to Calhoun, March 25, 1818, April 8, 1818, April 9, 1818, May 5, 1818, to St. Marks Commanding Officer, April 6, 1818, General Robert Butler to General Daniel Parker, May 3, 1818, Jackson to Calhoun, June 2, 1818, ASPMA, I, 698, 700–04, 708, II, 99–100.

93. James, *Jackson*, pp. 306–09. Jackson to Rachel Jackson, April 8, 1818, "Proclamation on Taking Possession of Pensacola," May 29, 1818, AJC, II, 357, 374–75; Bassett, I, 271–73.

94. Jackson to Calhoun, June 2, 1818, to Gaines, Jan. 10, 1818, to Calhoun, Jan. 10, 1818, Calhoun to Gaines, Sept. 1, 1818, ASPMA, I, 708, 744–45; Monroe to Senate, March 18, 1818, ASPIA, II, 154.

95. Jackson, "Proclamation on Taking Possession of Pensacola," May 29, 1818, AJC, II, 374–75; Jackson to Graham, Dec. 16, 1817, ASPIA, II, 162.

96. Jackson to Graham, Dec. 16, 1817, ASPIA, II, 162; S. Putnam Waldo, *Memoirs of Andrew Jackson* (Hartford, Conn., 1820), pp. 297–99.

97. Jackson, "Proclamation on Taking Possession of Pensacola," May 29, 1818, to Gaines, Aug. 7, 1818, to Monroe, Aug. 10, 1818, to George Campbell, Oct. 5, 1818,

AJC, II, 374–75, 384–86, 398. The transformation of self-defense into aggression was not original with Jackson. "If the English do not give us the satisfaction we demand," threatened President Jefferson after England attacked an American ship, "we will take Canada, which wants to enter the Union; and when, together with Canada, we shall have the Floridas, we shall no longer have any difficulties with our neighbors; and it is the only way of preventing them." (Quoted by William Appleman Williams, *The Contours of American History* [Chicago, 1966], p. 192.) On the psychology of self-defense and expansion, see chapter 4 above, pp. 120–22.

98. "Report of the House Committee on Indian Affairs," Feb. 21, 1823, ASPIA, II, 408–12. See pp. 411–12 for testimony on the alleged bad character of the Seminoles, and the government of the tribe by mulatto slaves. Cf. Waldo, p. 290.

99. Jackson to Calhoun, May 5, 1818, to Campbell, Oct. 5, 1818, AJC, II, 365–68, 397.

100. Jackson to Calhoun, May 5, 1818, AJC, II, 365; Alexander Arbuthnot to Bahama Governor Charles Cameron, undated, ASPMA, I, 724; Wright, pp. 572–73.

101. "Minutes of the Proceedings of a Special Court," with accompanying documents, April 26, 1818, Jackson memorial to Senate, Feb. 23, 1820, ASPMA, I, 721–34, 757.

102. Jackson to Rachel Jackson, April 8, 1818, AJC, II, 357–58.

103. Jackson to Calhoun, Sept. 2, 1821, Sept. 17, 1821, Seminole Commissioners to Calhoun, Sept. 26, 1823, ASPIA, II, 414, 440–41; Jackson, "Talk with Indian Chieftains," Sept. 20, 1821, AJC, III, 118–121.

104. Calhoun to Jackson, Nov. 16, 1821, AJC, III, 132; Jackson to Calhoun, Sept. 2, 1821, Sept. 17, 1821, ASPIA, II, 414.

105. "Treaty with the Florida Indians," communicated to the Senate with accompanying documents, Dec. 15, 1823, ASPIA, II, 430–42.

106. Calhoun to Gaines, Dec. 16, 1817, ASPIA, II, 162; Monroe to House of Representatives, March 25, 1818, ASPMA, I, 680–81; Dangerfield, pp. 137–38; Bassett, I, 272–78.

107. Jackson to Monroe, Jan. 6, 1818, AJC, II, 345–46, 346n; Bassett, I, 246–47.

108. John Rhea to Jackson, Dec. 18, 1818, Jackson to Monroe, June 2, 1818, Aug. 19, 1818, AJC, II, 403–04, 376–78, 389–91. Cf. Rhea to John Overton, Feb. 5, 1818, CC.

109. James, *Jackson*, p. 409n; Overton to Jackson, June 2, 1831, Jackson to Rhea, June 2, 1831, AJC, IV, 287–89; Richard R. Stenberg, "Jackson's Rhea Letter Hoax," *Journal of Southern History*, II (Nov. 1936), 484–85, 493–95; Martin Van Buren, *Autobiography, American Historical Association Annual Report, 1918, Vol. 2* (Washington, 1920), p. 387.

110. Stenberg, pp. 490–93; Bassett, I, 248–49; Rhea to Jackson, Jan. 12, 1818, AJC, II, 348.

111. Stenberg believes Jackson first planned to claim burning the letter during the 1818 Seminole campaign itself. He later moved the date back a year so he could claim the burning was at Monroe's request. Cf. Stenberg, pp. 490–93; AJC, II, 346n; marginal notation on Jackson to Monroe, Jan. 16, 1818, AJP.

112. Stenberg, p. 481.

113. The dispute over Major Long had nearly led to a duel between Jackson and General Winfield Scott. Jackson learned that Scott opposed his stand. Associating him with the "intermeddling pimps and spies, and whores of the War Dept.," Jackson challenged Scott to a duel. "Is it due from a brother officer," he wrote Scott, "to assail in the dark the reputation of another, and stab him in a moment when he cannot expect it." Scott declined the duel, just as Jackson was leaving Nashville to fight the Seminoles. Perhaps Jackson, working himself up for the Seminole invasion, provoked a private conflict of "brothers" over his authority, resolved in the public war. The sequence is reminiscent of Jackson's brawl with the Benton brothers prior to the Creek War. Cf. Jackson to Brigadier General Winfield Scott, Dec. 3, 1817, AJC, II, 338–39; James, *Jackson*, pp. 302–03; chapter 5 above, p. 145.

114. Simone Weil, "The Great Beast," in Richard Rees, ed., *Selected Essays* (London, 1962), pp. 89–144. Cf. Hannah Arendt, "Truth in Politics," *Between Past and Future* (N.Y., 1963), pp. 227–64.

115. James, *Jackson*, pp. 322–26; Jackson to Monroe, Feb. 11, 1821, to Major Allan Campbell, March 31, 1821, AJC, III, 38–39, 45.

116. Jackson to Monroe, Aug. 10, 1818, Feb. 11, 1821, to Dr. James C. Bronaugh, Feb. 11, 1821, to Coffee, March 1, 1821, to Calhoun, May 22, 1821, "Memoranda," Feb. 1822, AJC, II, 387, III, 38–39, 40–41, 58–59, 148–50; Arthur W. Thompson, *Jacksonian Democracy on the Florida Frontier* (Gainesville, Fla., 1961), p. 2; Herbert J. Doherty, Jr., "Andrew Jackson's Cronies in Florida Territorial Politics," *Florida Historical Society Quarterly*, XXXIV (July 1955), 4–6.

117. Herbert J. Doherty, Jr., *Richard Keith Call: Southern Unionist* (Gainesville, Fla., 1961), pp. 16–18; Jackson to Bronaugh, Feb. 11, 1821, June 9, 1821, Jackson to Secretary of State John Quincy Adams, May 1, 1821, Jackson to Captain John Donelson, July 31, 1821, AJC, III, 39, 52, 65, 88; Silver, pp. 85–86.

118. Compare Freud on the army: "Every captain is, as it were, the Commander-in-Chief and the father of his company." *Group Psychology and the Analysis of the Ego*, in James Strachey, ed., *The Standard Edition of the Complete Psychological Works*, XVIII (London, 1955), 94.

119. Parton, II, 592–93; Jackson, "Address to His Army on Giving Up Command," May 31, 1821, AJC, III, 62–63.

120. Parton, II, 614–42; James, *Jackson*, pp. 348–55; Jackson to Adams, Aug. 26, 1821, "Memoranda," Feb. 1822, AJC, III, 112, 150.

121. Parton, II, 636, 641.

122. *Ibid.*, II, 602–03.

CHAPTER SEVEN

1. Andrew Jackson to Francis P. Blair, June 4, 1838, AJC, V, 553; U.S. House of Representatives, *Register of Debates*, VI (1829–30), 1122, VII (1830–31), 685–86.

2. Andrew Jackson, "Seventh Annual Message," Dec. 7, 1835, in James D. Richardson, ed., *Messages and Papers of the Presidents* (N.Y., 1917), III, 171; Annie Heloise Abel, "The History of Events Resulting in Indian Consolidation West of the Mississippi," *American Historical Association, Report of Proceedings, 1906*; Grant Foreman, *The Last Trek of the Indians* (Chicago, 1946); William T. Hagan, *The Sac and Fox Indians* (Norman, Okla., 1958), pp. 104–229; and the Indian census sources cited in introduction, note 6.

3. John Adams, *Discourses on Davila, The Works of John Adams*, Charles F. Adams, ed., 6 vols. (Boston, 1851–65), VI, 232–81; Sheldon S. Wolin, *Politics and Vision* (Boston, 1960), pp. 286–351.

4. [Lewis Cass], "Policy and Practice of the United States and Great Britain in Their Treatment of Indians," *North American Review*, XXIV (April 1827), 391; cf. Thomas L. McKenney, *Memoirs, Official and Personal*, 2 vols. (N.Y., 1846), II, 82–83, 120–24.

5. [Lewis Cass], "Removal of the Indians," *North American Review*, XXXI (Jan. 1830), 75, quoted above, chapter 4, p. 116.

6. Among the studies of infantilization, cf. Bruno Bettelheim, "Individual and Mass Behavior in Extreme Situations," *Journal of Abnormal Psychiatry*, XXXVIII (Oct. 1943); Bruno Bettelheim, *The Informed Heart* (Glencoe, Ill., 1960), pp. 107–263; Stanley Elkins, *Slavery* (Chicago, 1959), pp. 81–139; Erving Goffman, *Asylums* (N.Y., 1961); Harold F. Searles, *Collected Papers on Schizophrenia and Related Subjects* (London, 1965), pp. 254–83, 717–51; R. D. Laing, *The Divided Self* (Middlesex, Eng., 1965), pp. 172–205; R. D. Laing and A. Esterson, *Sanity, Madness and the Family*

(Middlesex, Eng., 1970); Jules Henry, *Culture Against Man* (N.Y., 1965), pp. 322–474; Betty Friedan, *The Feminine Mystique* (N.Y., 1963), pp. 276–98; Walter O. Weyrauch, "Law in Isolation, The Penthouse of Astronaughts," *Trans-Action* (June 1968), pp. 139–46; Isidore Ziferstein, "Psychological Habituation to War: A Sociopsychological Case Study," *American Journal of Orthopsychiatry*, XXXCIII (April 1967), 467–68. For a magnificent early formulation, cf. Victor Tausk, "On the Origins of the Influencing Machine in Schizophrenia," in Robert Fliess, ed., *The Psychoanalytic Reader* (N.Y., 1948).

7. Wilbur R. Jacobs, *Dispossessing the American Indian* (N.Y., 1972), pp. 8–30; Mary E. Young, *Redskins, Ruffleshirts, and Rednecks* (Norman, Okla., 1961), pp. 6–11; Angie Debo, *The Road to Disappearance* (Norman, Okla., 1941), pp. 4–21, 84–85; R. S. Cotterill, *The Southern Indians: The Story of the Civilized Tribes Before Removal* (Norman, Okla., 1954), pp. 9–15; John K. Mahon, *History of the Second Seminole War, 1835–1842* (Gainesville, Fla., 1967), pp. 9–31.

8. James W. Silver, *Edmund Pendleton Gaines: Frontier General* (Baton Rouge, La., 1949), p. 118n; Chief Pooshamataha in General Council of Choctaw tribe, Aug. 12, 1819, ASPIA, II, 230; Mahon, p. 2.

9. Jacobs, pp. 120–21; "Indian Biography: Collections of the Maine Historical Society," *North American Review*, XXXIV (April 1832), 460–61; Creek chief William McIntosh to Georgia legislature, April 12, 1825, ASPIA, II, 757. Cf. Paul A. W. Wallace, "Cooper's Indians," *New York History*, XXXV (Oct. 1954), 58, 68–78.

10. Searles, pp. 40–42.

11. F. P. Prucha, *American Indian Policy in the Formative Years* (Cambridge, Mass., 1962), p. 220; Thomas Hart Benton, "Speech on the Oregon Question," in C. Merton Babcock, ed., *The American Frontier* (N.Y., 1965), p. 223.

12. Andrew Jackson, "First Annual Message," Dec. 8, 1829, Richardson, II, 458; George Dangerfield, *The Era of Good Feelings* (N.Y., 1952), p. 27; *Register of Debates*, VI (1829–30), 1088, 1103. Wilde's language is taken almost verbatim from "On the State of the Indians," *North American Review*, XVI (Jan. 1823), 39–40.

13. Cass, "Policy and Practice," p. 382.

14. Abel, pp. 241–49; Foreman, p. 50; "Our Indian Policy," *The U.S. Magazine and Democratic Review*, XIV (Feb. 1844), 174–75.

15. Cf. the sources cited in note 7 above; and Marion L. Starkey, *The Cherokee Nation* (N.Y., 1946); Arthur H. DeRosier, Jr., *The Removal of the Choctaw Indians* (Knoxville, Tenn., 1970), pp. 3–22, 90–95.

16. James Mooney, "Myths of the Cherokees," *Bureau of American Ethnology, Annual Report*, XIX (1897–98), Part 1, 117–18; George D. Harmon, *Sixty Years of Indian Affairs* (Chapel Hill, N.C., 1941), p. 199; Young, pp. 15–16; DeRosier, pp. 100–05; Grant Foreman, *Indian Removal* (Norman, Okla., 1932), pp. 73, 108–09.

17. Secretary of War John H. Eaton to Tennessee Governor William Carroll, May 29, 1830, OIALS; "Journal of Proceedings," attempted Chickasaw treaty, Oct. 27, 1826, ASPIA, II, 722; Benjamin L. Smith to Chickasaws, Dec. 9, 1826, OIA Chickasaw file; Jackson, "First Annual Message," Dec. 18, 1829, "To the Senate," Feb. 22, 1831, Richardson, II, 458, 541; Jackson to the Secretary of War [1831?], AJC, IV, 219–20; Eaton to John Forsyth, Oct. 14, 1829, OIALS; chapter 6, above, pp. 183, 191–2.

18. *Johnson* v. *McIntosh*, 8 Wheaton (1823), 543–604; "An Act to regulate trade and intercourse with the Indian tribes," March 30, 1802, U.S. Congress, *Debates and Proceedings* (1801–03), Appendix, pp. 1315–22, Sections 5, 12, 21; Jackson to President Monroe, March 4, 1817, to the Secretary of War [1831?], AJC, II, 279–80, IV, 220; *Worcester* v. *Georgia*, VI Peters (1832), 512–59.

19. Young, p. 15.

20. Eaton to Creeks, May 30, 1820, OIALS.

21. Jackson, "First Annual Message," Richardson II, 548; *Register of Debates*, VI, 356; Cass, "Removal," p. 102.

22. Eaton to Carroll, May 29, 1830, OIALS; Lewis Cass, "Annual Report of the Secretary of War," Nov. 21, 1831, ASPMA, IV, 714; Jackson, "First Annual Message," Richardson, II, 458; Margaret Mead, *And Keep Your Powder Dry*, 2nd ed. (London, 1967), pp. 186–89.

23. Andrew Jackson, "Second Annual Message to Congress," Dec. 6, 1830, Richardson, II, 521. The comparison with white emigration was ubiquitous. Cf. Commissioners Duncan Campbell and James Meriwether to Cherokee council, Oct. 21, 1823, Commissioners Thomas Hinds and John Coffee to Chickasaw council, Oct. 25, 1826, ASPIA, II, 430, 720; Jackson to Chickasaws, "Journal of Proceedings, Chickasaw Treaty of Aug. 31, 1830," OIA Treaty file; DeRosier, p. 129; T. H. Crawford, "Annual Report of the Commissioner of Indian Affairs," Nov. 25, 1838, U.S. Serial Set, *Executive Documents*, Vol. 344, Document 2, 411. When the Cherokees were told to imitate the westward migration of the whites, a writer in the *Cherokee Phoenix* responded, "Our white brethren have more knowledge than we have and they are better skilled in travelling and commencing new settlements, why then do they not go and possess that good land for themselves." Starkey, p. 108.

24. Abel, pp. 244, 267; William T. Hagan, *American Indians* (Chicago, 1961), pp. 81–87; Jackson, "Second Annual Message," Richardson, II, 522.

25. Francis Paul Prucha, "Thomas L. McKenney and the New York Indian Board," *Mississippi Valley Historical Review*, XLVIII (March 1962), 653.

26. Representative Thomas Foster, *Register of Debates*, VI, 1034.

27. Jackson to Creeks, March 22, 1829, OIALS; Abel, p. 373.

28. Jackson to W. B. Lewis, Aug. 31, 1830, AJC, IV, 179; Jackson, "Second Annual Message," Richardson, II, 520, 523.

29. Jackson to John Pitchlynn, Aug. 5, 1830, to Lewis, Aug. 25, 1830, AJC, IV, 169, 177.

30. Seymour Dunbar, *A History of Travel in America*, 3 vols. (Indianapolis, Ind., 1915), II, 575–76; Eaton to William Ward, July 31, 1829, OIALS; Jackson to Coffee, April 7, 1832, AJC, IV, 430; Jackson notation on John Ross to Jackson, March 28, 1834, Hermitage papers, copy in Tennessee State Library

31. Jackson, "First Annual Message," Richardson, II, 458; Jackson notation on Creek chiefs to Secretary of War, Feb. 1, 1830, OIA Creek file; Eaton to Governors of Tennessee, Mississippi, and Alabama, April 18, 1829, to Governor George Gilmer, June 1, 1830, OIALS.

32. Abel, pp. 335–56; "Proceedings in Relation to a Creek Treaty," ASPIA, II, 727–862.

33. Jackson to Edward G. Butler, July 25, 1825, Dec. 8, 1825, AJC, III, 288–89; George Gilmer for a Select Committee of the House of Representatives, Jan. 7, 1822, ASPIA, II, 259; Ulrich Bonnell Phillips, "Georgia and States Rights," *American Historical Association Annual Report*, II (1901), 96–120.

34. George Baldwin to Eaton, July 25, 1829, Cherokee delegation to Eaton, Jan. 4, 1829, Feb. 11, 1830, Dec. 22, 1830, Coffee to Eaton, Dec. 3, 1829, Jan. 15, 1830, Jan. 21, 1830, Hugh Montgomery to I. Wales, Aug. 13, 1829, Montgomery to Eaton, April 2, 1829, May 9, 1829, March 30, 1830, June 8, 1830, Montgomery to Ross, Sept. 3, 1829, Ross to Montgomery, Oct. 28, 1829, Gilmer to Coffee, Nov. 30, 1829, OIA Cherokee file.

35. Foreman, *Indian Removal*, pp. 229–30; Starkey, pp. 110–11; Captain T. M. Brady to Eaton, June 28, 1830, Cherokee delegation to Jackson, and Jackson endorsement, March 26, 1830, Cherokee delegation to Eaton Dec. 22, 1830, Gilmer to Jackson, June 17, 1830, OIA Cherokee file; Acting Secretary of War P. G. Randolph to Montgomery, June 26, 1830, Randolph to General A. Macomb, June 26, 1830, OIALS; Jackson to Colonel Robert Love, Dec. 10, 1831, AJC, III, 382.

36. One observer estimated 40,000 intruders in Cherokee country alone by early 1835. Samuel G. Smith to Jackson, Feb. 6, 1835, AJC, V, 324–25.

37. Jackson, "First Annual Message," Richardson, II, 458. Cf. Francis Jennings, "Virgin Land and Savage People," *American Quarterly*, XXIII (Oct. 1971), 520–22, 536–40, for similar Puritan rationalizations disguising a similar process of expropriation.

38. Foreman, *Indian Removal*, pp. 151–52, 246–52, *passim;* Starkey, pp. 114–16, 156–58, 172, 207–17; Harmon, p. 212; J. J. Abert to Secretary of War Lewis Cass, June 2, 1833, Jeremy Anstill to Cass, July 13, 1833, Aug. 6, 1833, OIA Creek file; J. Allen to Eaton, Feb. 7, 1830, Oct. 23, 1830, to Cass Oct. 5, 1833, Jan. 4, 1834, OIA Chickasaw file; Major Ridge and John Ridge to Jackson, June 30, 1836, OIA Cherokee file.

39. That large southern planters and speculators provided the major impetus for southern Indian removal is suggested by Thomas P. Abernethy, *The Formative Period in Alabama, 1815–1828* (University, Ala., 1965), pp. 147–48, 176–77; Phillips, pp. 96–120, 136; Eugene D. Genovese, *The Political Economy of Slavery* (N.Y., 1965). Cf. also Paul Wallace Gates, *The Farmer's Age: Agriculture 1815–1860* (N.Y., 1960), pp. 2–8.

40. J. J. Abert to Cass, June 2, 1833, OIA Creek file.

41. John H. Eaton, "Annual Report of the Secretary of War," Dec. 1, 1830, ASPMA, IV, 586; Eaton to Gilmer, June 1, 1830, Acting Secretary of War Samuel Hamilton to Montgomery, June 7, 1831, OIALS; Jackson, "To the Senate," Feb. 22, 1831, Richardson, II, 536–41; Hamilton to William Ward, Oct. 5, 1831, Elbert Herring to Benjamin F. Currey, Feb. 10, 1832, OIALS.

42. Foreman, *Indian Removal*, 197–99; Herring to Cherokee delegation, May 1, 1833, to Currey, Feb. 10, 1834, to Montgomery, Feb. 27, 1834, to Currey, Sept. 8, 1834, to Montgomery, Nov. 25, 1834, OIALS; J. F. Campbell to Cass, Aug. 11, 1833, Montgomery to Herring, Nov. 1, 1834, OIA Cherokee file.

43. Foreman, *Indian Removal*, pp. 108–13; Cass to Samuel W. Dickson, Aug. 9, 1833, OIALS; "Treaty with the Creeks, 1832," Article 5, "Treaty with the Chickasaws, 1832," Article 15, "Treaty with the Cherokees, 1835," Article 16, Charles J Kappler, ed., *Indian Treaties, 1778–1883* (N.Y., 1972 [first published 1904]), pp. 341, 361, 446.

44. General John Wool did remove intruders in the Cherokee nation for a brief period, and restore Indian improvements to their owners. Cf. Foreman, *Indian Removal*, pp. 279–80; "Proceedings of a Court of Inquiry . . . ," Oct. 9, 1837, ASPMA, VII, 532–45, 563–71.

45. Foreman, *Indian Removal*, pp. 73–74, 116–24; Greenwood Leflore to Cass, May 28, 1831, Moshulatubbee to Cass, Oct. 22, 1831, F. E. Plummer to Cass, May 22, 1832, Ward to Cass, June 29, 1832, A. Campbell to Cass, Aug. 5, 1832, OIA Choctaw file; Cass to Plummer, May 23, 1832, OIALS.

46. Young, pp. 76–80; Foreman, *Indian Removal*, pp. 114–28. Indian Office records provide a detailed chronicle of the Creek intruder controversy. Cf. letters from Cass and Commissioner of Indian Affairs Elbert Herring for the dates of Dec. 8, 1832, May 7, 10, June 10, Aug. 10, 26, Oct. 22, 29, 31, Nov. 2, 18, 22, Dec. 27, 1833, Jan. 1, March 12, 1834, Feb. 25, 1837, OIALS; and in OIA Creek file, letters to Cass from J. Anstill, Nov. 15, 1832, July 3, 31, Aug. 5, Oct. 16, 26, 1833, R. L. Crawford, Aug. 5, Sept. 15, Dec. 6, 1832, July 18, Oct. 3, Dec. 20, 1833, Feb. 1, March 2, 25, April 22, 1834, D. H. Lewis, Dec. 15, 1832, Niah-micco and Tuskeniah, Dec. 20, 1832, Governor C. C. Clay, Oct. 8, 1833, Francis Scott Key, Dec. 4, 6, 10, 18, 1833.

47. Cf. Young, p. 30.

48. Cherokee delegation to Jackson, April 6, 1829, Montgomery to McKenney, April 6, 1830, to Herring, Nov. 1, 1834, Currey to Carroll, July 6, 1835, to Herring, Nov. 15, 1835, OIA Cherokee file; Cass to Montgomery, April 22, 1833, OIALS.

49. McKenney to Indian agents, Feb. 17, 1829, Eaton to Ward, July 31, 1829, Randolph to Ward, Oct. 29, 1830, OIALS; Ward to Eaton, Nov. 14, 1830, OIA Choctaw file.

50. DeRosier, pp. 120–21; Journal of the Choctaw Treaty of Dancing Rabbit Creek, Sept. 15, 1830, Sept. 17, 1830, OIA Treaty file.

51. Starkey, pp. 260–63; Foreman, *Indian Removal*, p. 268n; Lieutenant John

Hooper to General R. Jones, Nov. 10, 1835, Currey to Herring, April 6, 1836, Colonel William G. Hansell to Currey, March 31, 1836, M. H. Underwood to Currey, March 31, 1836, Currey to Jackson with Jackson's endorsement, March 24, 1836, OIA Cherokee file; Jackson to Wool, Sept. 7, 1836, ASPMA, VII, 554; Jackson to Coffee, April 7, 1832, AJC, IV, 430.

52. Eaton to Gilmer, May 4, 1831, OIALS; Gilmer to Eaton, April 20, 1831, OIA Cherokee file; *Worcester* v. *Georgia*, VI Peters (1832), 512–59; Starkey, pp. 131–44.

53. B. L. Smith to McKenney, Nov. 7, 1827, to Eaton, July 25, 1829, Dec. 26, 1829, Eaton to Smith, June 17, 1829, John L. Allen to Jackson, Jan. 23, 1830, to Eaton, Feb. 7, 1830, OIA Chickasaw file; McKenney to Eaton, Feb. 17, 1829, OIALS; Ross to Jackson, March 12, 1834, OIA Cherokee file; Paul W. Gates, "Introduction," *The John Tipton Papers*, Nellie A. Robertson and Dorothy Riker, eds. (Indianapolis, Ind., 1942), I, 3–52; Mahon, pp. 84–85.

54. Eaton to John Crowell, June 15, 1829, to Carroll, July 15, 1829, OIALS.

55. Starkey, pp. 196–97; Foreman, *Indian Removal*, p. 230; Eaton to Carroll, Aug. 15, 1829, Samuel McConnell to Cass, Sept. 6, 1833, William G. Hansell, Samuel Rockwell, and M. H. Underwood to C. A. Harris, March 17, 1837, Reverend J. F. Schermerhorn to Harris, March 23, 1837, OIA Cherokee file; Herring to Currey, March 21, 1833, Cass to Currey, Jan. 9, 1836, OIALS; Jackson to Secretary of War John C. Calhoun, Sept. 2, 1820, AJC, III, 31.

56. Cf., for example, Herring to Cass, Feb. 24, 1834, OIALS; Currey to A. Ross, May 20, 1836, OIA Cherokee file, "Treaty with the Chickasaws, 1834," Article 10, in Kappler, p. 421.

57. Eaton to Carroll, May 29, 1829, OIALS.

58. Herring to Montgomery, April 22, 1833, to Currey, May 3, 1833, OIALS; Currey to Herring, April 22, 1833, Aug. 26, 1833, OIA Cherokee file.

59. Foreman, *Indian Removal*, pp. 28–29; Young, pp. 22–23, 30 35; DeRosier, pp. 90–96, 112–28; Ward to Eaton, Nov. 4, 1830, Dec. 13, 1830, OIA Choctaw file; Samuel Hamilton to Ward, April 11, 1831, Eaton to Ward, Nov. 24, 1830, to Choctaw chiefs, Nov. 24, 1830, OIALS.

60. Starkey, p. 150; Hamilton to H. G. Lamar, May 21, 1831, to Ward, May 21, 1831, Cass to Cherokee delegation, March 2, 1833, OIALS; Crowell to Eaton, Aug. 8, 1830, Creeks to Cass, Feb. 8, 1830, OIA Creek file; Eaton to Benjamin Reynolds, Dec. 9, 1830, OIA Chickasaw file.

61. Starkey, p. 150; Randolph to Montgomery, June 18, 1830, OIA Cherokee file; Herring to Currey, July 10, 1833, Cass to Gilmer, Aug. 12, 1831, Herring to John Martin and William S. Goody, March 10, 1832, Cass to Jackson, Feb. 16, 1832, OIALS.

62. Herring to Currey, Nov. 26, 1831, Feb. 6, 1832, Cass to Congressman Richard Wilde, Feb. 10, 1832, OIALS; John Walker to J. A. Standifer, Feb. 13, 1834, Herring to Schermerhorn and Carroll, Feb. 2, 1835, OIA Cherokee file; Foreman, *Indian Removal*, pp. 244–45.

63. Cass to John Ross, June 12, 1834, to Governor Wilson Lumpkin, Feb. 11, 1835, to Schermerhorn, Sept. 26, 1835, to John Ross, Jan. 4, 1836, Jan. 16, 1836, to Senator Thomas Hart Benton, Feb. 13, 1836, to John Ross, March 9, 1836, OIALS; Hooper to Jones, Nov. 10, 1835, Schermerhorn to Cass, Oct. 28, 1835, Oct. 30, 1835, March 3, 1836, Ross to Cass, Feb. 29, 1836, H. McCoy to Cass, Feb. 29, 1836, Cherokee delegation to Cass, April 22, 1836, to Van Buren, March 16, 1837, OIA Cherokee file; Foreman, *Indian Removal*, pp. 264–71.

64. Foreman, *Indian Removal*, p. 270.

65. Harris to General John Wool, Oct. 12, 1836, Cass to Wool, Sept. 3, 1836, ASPMA, VI, 1050, VII, 556; Jackson endorsement on Ross to Jackson, Feb. 28, 1837, OIA Cherokee file.

66. Young, p. 45.

67. Jackson to Creeks, March 23, 1829, OIA Creek file; Cass, "Removal," pp. 85–86,

120; Harmon, p. 202; Young, pp. 35–39; above, chapter 6, pp. 180–81.

68. Young, pp. 12–13, 46; Cass to Creeks, Aug. 10, 1835, ASPMA, VI, 776; Creek delegation to Cass, March 19, 1832, Crowell to Cass, Jan. 25, 1832, OIA Creek file; Jackson to Coffee, April 7, 1832, AJC, IV, 429–30.

69. Young, pp. 51–72; Harmon, pp. 227–28, 236–44; DeRosier, pp. 135–37; Acting Secretary of War Mahlon Dickerson to George W. Martin, Oct. 13, 1834, OIALS; James Roger Sharp, *The Jacksonians Versus the Banks* (N.Y., 1970), pp. 75–83. Andrew Jackson, Jr., planned, with Gwin's help, to purchase Mississippi Indian lands; Jackson gave him extensive advice. Cf. Jackson to Andrew Jackson, Jr., March 1, 1836, AJC, V, 388–89.

70. Cass, regulations for certifying Creek contracts, with Jackson's endorsement, Nov. 28, 1833, supplementary regulations, Dec. 18, 1833, OIALS.

71. The Creek frauds can be followed in Young, pp. 74–88, 91; Harmon, pp. 205–09; Foreman, *Indian Removal*, pp. 129–34. Massive documentation is provided in "Causes of Hostilities of the Creek and Seminole Indians in Florida," ASPMA, VI, 574–783; and in letters in OIALS under the dates July 24, 1833, Jan. 11, March 18, March 19, June 25, July 28, Aug. 7, Aug. 12, 1834, Jan. 23, Feb. 15, Feb. 22, March 19, March 20, 1836.

72. Herring to R. W. McHenry, April 3, 1834, ASPMA, VI, 586; Cass to R. J. Meigs, Oct. 31, 1834, OIALS.

73. Young, pp. 80–85; Cass to Meigs, Nov. 13, 1834, to J. J. Abert, May 25, 1833, to Gabriel Moore, May 28, 1834, OIALS; Abert to Cass, May 20, 1833, July 8, 1833, Eli Shorter to Abert, June 13, 1833, Jackson notation on Enoch Parsons to Jackson, Sept. 21, 1833, OIA Creek file.

John Watson, who styled himself a "plain old farmer," wrote Jackson describing personal attacks on the President by members of the Columbus Land Company. Jackson's marginal note on Watson's letter connected the company's frauds against the Indians with its abuse of himself. Watson's letter convinced Jackson not to make a deal with the speculators. But this was just what the speculators wanted, and Watson may possibly have sought to aid them. He was probably related to James Watson, a leader of the Columbus Land Company. He was certainly no friend of the Creeks. He later organized a meeting in Columbus to stir up the country against the tribe, and then, disastrously for the Creeks, organized their warriors to fight the Seminoles. John Watson to Jackson, July 14, 1833, OIA Creek file; John B. Hogan to Cass, March 28, 1836, ASPMA, VI, 617–18, and below, pp. 241–42.

74. Foreman, *Indian Removal*, p. 133; Cass to John P. King, April 23, 1835, to Leonard Tarrant, April 28, 1835, to John B. Hogan, Sept. 9, 1835, Jan. 15, 1836, March 11, 1836, Hogan to Cass, March 30, 1836, Cass to Alabama Governor C. C. Clay, March 12, 1836, John W. A. Sanford and Co. to Cass, March 1, 1836, Cass to Sanford and Co., March 12, 1836, ASPMA, VI, 593–95, 601, 610–11, 614–15, 618–19, 627, 759, 780.

75. Cass to Hogan, March 11, 1836, May 19, 1836, to General Thomas Jesup, May 19, 1836, J. W. A. Sanford to W. Blue, Nov. 3, 1835, ASPMA, VI, 614–15, 622–23, 745. Once the Creeks were out of Alabama, the government reopened the fraud investigations.

76. McKenney to J. C. Mitchell, April 30, 1829, Cass to Abert, May 25, 1833, OIALS; Starkey, p. 283.

77. Lewis Cass, "Annual Report of the Secretary of War," Nov. 21, 1831, Nov. 30, 1835, ASPMA, IV, 714, V, 631; Cass, "Removal," p. 70.

78. Cass to Calhoun, Oct. 21, 1820, OIALR; Cass, "Policy and Practice," p. 400; Cass, "Annual Report," Nov. 21, 1831, ASPMA, VI, 715. The supply of game also suffered from Indian dependence on traders, which caused them to overhunt fur-bearing animals. Removal itself, bringing masses of Indians west of the Mississippi, upset the balance between wild life and the hunting tribes there. Cf. Jacobs, pp. 23–30; Hagan, *American Indians*, pp. 85–86.

79. Cass, "Removal," p. 70; Mahon, pp. 26–30.

80. Lumpkin to Jackson, May 20, 1835, AJC, V, 351; cf. above, pp. 224–25.

81. Cass to Governor William Schley, Feb. 23, 1836, to Clay, March 12, March 19, April 15, 1836, ASPMA, VI, 626–28; Cass to Congressman James K. Polk, Feb. 18, 1836, OIALS.

82. Schley to Cass, May 17, 1836, ASPMA, VI, 446.

83. Young, pp. 82–83; Foreman, *Indian Removal*, p. 147; Harmon, p. 212; Hogan to Cass, June 2, 1835, Oct. 24, 1835, Nov. 2, 1835, to General George Gibson, Jan. 23, 1836, Sanford and Co. to Gibson, May 14, 1835, Captain John Page to Cass, May 9, 1836, to Gibson, May 10, 12, 16, 18, 1836, Sanford to Cass, May 15, 1835, Robert McHenry to Cass, July 22, 1835, documents on the outbreak of the Creek war, ASPMA, VI, 670, 728, 748, 763, 768–71, 653, 662, 576–81, 702–05; Herring to Sanford, Feb. 25, 1834, Feb. 27, 1834, OIALS.

84. Representative Hopkins Holsey, *Register of Debates*, XIII (1836–37), 1543; Major John Howard to Cass, May 9, 1836, ASPMA, VI, 652–53; Herring to Cass, June 6, 1836, OIALS.

85. Herring to Cass, June 6, 1836, OIALS; Cass to Jesup, May 19, 1836, ASPMA, VI, 622–23.

86. Cass, "Policy and Practice," p. 420. For Jackson's belief that bad parents controlled warlike Indians, cf. above, chapter 5, pp. 153, 160–61, and chapter 6, pp. 197–98.

87. Lewis Cass, "Annual Report of the Secretary of War," Nov. 25, 1832, ASPMA, V, 23–24; Hagan, *Sac and Fox Indians*, pp. 220–24.

88. Hagan, *Sac and Fox Indians*, pp. 46–79, 104–11, 124–35, 166–86; Cass, "Annual Report," Nov. 25, 1832, ASPMA, V, 29–30; Dunbar, II, 464.

89. Hagan, *Sac and Fox Indians*, pp. 187–89; Dunbar, II, 461.

90. Hagan, *Sac and Fox Indians*, pp. 187–92, 205–06; Cass, "Annual Report," Nov. 25, 1832, ASPMA, V, 24; Foreman, *Last Trek*, pp. 141–52; *Annual Report of the Commissioner of Indian Affairs, 1860–61* (Washington, D.C., 1861), p. 215.

91. Marquis James, *Andrew Jackson: Portrait of a President* (Indianapolis, Ind., 1937), p. 366; Frank B. Woodford, *Lewis Cass* (New Brunswick, N.J., 1950), p. 176; Hagan, *Sac and Fox Indians*, pp. 198–99; *Niles' Register*, XLIV (June 15, 1833), 256.

92. Mahon, pp. 74–79, 82–85, 89–99; Edwin C. McReynolds, *The Seminoles* (Norman, Okla., 1957), pp. 140–45; Representative Horace Everett, *Register of Debates*, X (1833–34), 4144–59; Foreman, *Indian Removal*, pp. 321–23; Harris, "Abstract," Feb. 9, 1836, Thompson to Cass, Dec. 28, 1834, April 24, 1835, to General George Gibson, June 3, 1835, Harris to Thompson, May 20, 1835, Clinch to Cass, Aug. 24, 1835, Cass to Clinch, Oct. 22, 1835, to Thompson, Oct. 28, 1835, ASPMA, VI, 60, 70, 73–76, 494, 552.

93. Mahon, pp. 94–101; Everett, *Register of Debates*, X, 4154; Joseph W. Harris to Gibson, Dec. 30, 1835, ASPMA, VI, 561–63.

94. Mahon, pp. 1–70; Mark F. Boyd, "The Seminole War: Its Background and Onset," *Florida Historical Quarterly*, XXX (July 1951), 52–53; Cass to Gibson, Jan. 30, 1832, Eaton to Cass, March 8, 1835, Clinch to Cass, April 24, 1835, Seminole council to Cass, Aug. 19, 1835, Jackson to Seminoles, Feb. 16, 1835, ASPMA, VI, 472, 492–95, 524; Jackson to Calhoun, Sept. 2, 1821, Sept. 17, 1821, "Treaty with the Florida Indians," Feb. 2, 1826, ASPIA, II, 414, 614–44; Everett, *Register of Debates*, X, 4147–48; Senator Thomas Hart Benton, U.S. Congress, *The Congressional Globe*, VI (1837–38), Appendix, 353; McReynolds, pp. 83–84.

95. Everett, Register of Debates, X, 4147–48; Representative Joshua Giddings, *Congressional Globe*, IX (1840–41), Appendix, 347; "Causes of Hostilities of the Creek and Seminole Indians in Florida," ASPMA, VI, 450–71.

96. Kenneth Wiggins Porter, "Negroes and the Seminole War 1835–1842," *Journal of Southern History*, XXX (Nov. 1964), 427–31; Boyd, p. 37; McReynolds, pp. 133–34;

Giddings, *Congressional Globe,* IX (1840–41), Appendix, 348; Thompson to William P. Duval, Jan. 20, 1834, ASPMA, VI, 451–52.

97. Richard K. Call to Jackson, March 22, 1835, Thompson to Harris, April 27, 1835, June 17, 1835, Harris to Thompson, May 22, 1835, Jackson endorsement on Thompson to Harris, June 6, 1835, ASPMA, VI, 464, 480–81, 512, 533, 478; Herring to Call, March 26, 1835, Harris to Thompson, July 11, 1835, OIALS; McReynolds, pp. 150–52.

98. Porter, pp. 433–34; Mahon, pp. 101–03; Jesup to Secretary of War Benjamin F. Butler, Dec. 9, 1836, ASPMA, VII, 821; Senator Thomas Hart Benton, *Register of Debates,* XII (1835–36), 821.

99. R. Jones to Cass, Feb. 9, 1836, Cass to General Winfield Scott, Jan. 21, 1836, Jesup to Butler, Feb. 17, 1837, to Jones, March 26, 1837, to Secretary of War Joel R. Poinsett, Sept. 22, 1837, ASPMA, VI, 57–58, 62, VII, 832, 834, 882; McReynolds, pp. 185–86; Porter, pp. 438–39; Mahon, pp. 200–04.

100. Porter, pp. 438–39; Mahon, pp. 202–04.

101. Porter, pp. 445–47; Mahon, pp. 205–06, 251–52; McReynolds, pp. 211–12; Harris to Nathaniel Collins, May 9, 1938, to George C. Reynolds, July 6, 1838, OIALS.

102. Mahon, pp. 122, 135–93; Butler to Call, Nov. 4, 1836, ASPMA, VI, 992. For Jackson's relationship to Call, see below, chapter 8, p. 270.

103. Jackson to James Gadsden, Nov. 1836, to Poinsett, Dec. 13, 1837, Oct. 1, 1837, "Memorandum," April 1837, AJC, V, 434, 521–22, 512–13, 468.

104. Mahon, pp. 205–311; Jackson to Poinsett, Aug. 27, 1837, AJC, V, 506–08; Benton, *Congressional Globe,* VI, Appendix, 353–56.

105. Mooney, pp. 131–32; Foreman, *Indian Removal,* pp. 44–104, 152–90, 253–63, 273–312. For the estimate of Indian dead, see the sources cited in introduction, note 6, above.

106. Cass to Hogan, Feb. 24, 1836, Sanford to Hogan, April 3, 1835, Hogan to Gibson, Nov. 6, 1835, ASPMA, VI, 779, 738, 745–46; Harris to Page, Jan. 24, 1837, April 26, 1837, to J. C. Watson, May 8, 1837, OIALS. Sanford was subsequently appointed Indian agent for the Creeks in the west. (Cf. Harris to Sanford, March 15, 1837, OIALS.)

Indian removal by contract is reminiscent of the late-eighteenth-century vendue method of caring for dependent children. Child paupers were sold to the lowest bidders at public auctions; the townships paid the bidders to maintain the children. Cf. Susan Grinel, "The Development of Child Welfare Institutions," unpublished paper, University of California at Berkeley, 1972, pp. 27–29.

107. Foreman, *Indian Removal,* pp. 152–53; Harris to Page, Dec. 22, 1836, OIALS. This operation was suspended a year later. Harris to Lieutenant Edward Deas, Oct. 14, 1837, OIALS.

108. Foreman, *Indian Removal,* pp. 276–90; Mooney, pp. 131–32; Cass, "Removal," p. 120.

109. Foreman, *Indian Removal,* pp. 161–62; Cass to Jesup, July 11, 1836, ASPMA, VI, 1047.

110. Foreman, *Indian Removal,* pp. 180–83; Cass to Hogan, April 12, 1836, Poinsett to Jesup, March 27, 1837, Harris to Page, Feb. 17, 1837, OIALS; Jesup to Poinsett, April 11, 1837, George C. Reynolds to Major Wilson, March 31, 1837, Lieutenant T. J. Sloan to [unknown], March 31, 1837, Joel S. Poinsett, "Annual Report of the Secretary of War," Dec. 5, 1837, ASPMA, VII, 867–70, 572. The Commissioner of Indian Affairs wanted to make sure that none of the hostile Creeks still loose in Alabama would benefit from the arrangements made for the friendly Creeks. Any Creeks outside the detention camps, he instructed the army officers in Alabama, should be treated as hostiles; the government sent the friendly Creeks out to hunt them down. Cf. Harris to Page, Jan. 30, 1837, OIALS.

111. Foreman, *Indian Removal,* pp. 184–87; Harris to Hogan, Aug. 5, 1837, to Page, Aug. 5, 1837, OIALS.

112. DeRosier, pp. 148–62.

113. Harris to General Nathaniel Smith, April 26, 1838, to Deas, Sept. 21, 1837, to Smith, Sept. 5, 1838, Crawford to Page, Nov. 14, 1838, OIALS; Jackson to Felix Grundy, Aug. 23, 1838, *American Historical Magazine and Tennessee Historical Society Quarterly,* V (April 1900), 140; Crawford to Smith, Jan. 17, 1839, Feb. 11, 1839, OIALS.

114. Sanford and Co. to Gibson, May 14, 1836, ASPMA, VI, 763; Lumpkin to Jackson, May 20, 1835, AJC, V, 350; Representative George Towns, *Congressional Globe,* VI (1837–38), 366. Call and Van Buren are first quoted above, pp. 4 and 237.

115. Senator William Allen, *Congressional Globe,* XI (1841–42), Appendix, 688. Cf. Joel Kovel, *White Racism: A Psychohistory* (N.Y., 1970), pp. 110–17, 164–65.

116. On the petrification of experience, cf. Laing, *Divided Self,* pp. 46–52, 112–13.

117. Joel R. Poinsett, quoted in Arthur A. Ekirch, *The Idea of Progress in America, 1815–1860* (N.Y., 1944), pp. 43–44; Andrew Jackson, "Seventh Annual Message," Dec. 7, 1835, Richardson, III, 171–72; Young, pp. 47–51; Roy Harvey Pearce, *Savagism and Civilization* (Baltimore, Md., 1965 [first published as *The Savages of America;* Baltimore, Md., 1953]), pp. 173–74; A. Grenfell Price, *White Settlers and Native Peoples* (Melbourne, Aust., 1949), p. 16.

118. DeRosier, p. 27; A. W. Putnam, *History of Middle Tennessee* (Nashville, Tenn., 1859), pp. 589–90; R. J. Meigs to Secretary of War William Crawford, Nov. 8, 1816, ASPIA, II, 115.

119. Tennessee Representative John Bell, quoted by Representative Henry Storrs, *Register of Debates,* VI (1829–30), 994.

120. Cf. above, pp. 68–69.

121. Cf. above, p. 215.

122. Cass, "Annual Report of the Secretary of War," Nov. 21, 1831, ASPMA, IV, 714; Jackson to Coffee, Feb. 28, 1804, AJC, I, 82–83; Géza Róheim, *The Panic of the Gods* (N.Y., 1972), p. 161. For European traditions which viewed the west as a land of eternal life and happiness, of apocalypse and the end of history, and their influence in America, cf. Loren Baritz, "The Idea of the West," *American Historical Review,* LXVI (Dec. 1961), 618–41.

123. Benjamin F. Butler, "Annual Report of the Secretary of War," Dec. 3, 1836, ASPMA, VI, 814; Jackson, "Seventh Annual Message," Richardson, III, 171–72; Cass, "Removal," p. 121.

124. Jackson to Creeks, March 23, 1829, OIALS; Jackson, "Farewell Address," March 4, 1837, Richardson, III, 294.

125. Creeks to Jackson, June 13, 1835, OIA Creek file.

126. Jackson, "Farewell Address," Richardson, III, 293; Jackson to Lewis, April 29, 1833, LP; Jackson to Andrew J. Donelson, Dec. 31, 1836, to Andrew Jackson Hutchings, Jan. 26, 1838, AJC, V, 442–43, 533.

127. Cass, "On the State of the Indians," p. 34; Cass, "Removal," pp. 107, 120–21.

128. Foreman, *Indian Removal,* p. 312n; Joel R. Poinsett, "Annual Report of the Secretary of War," Nov. 28, 1838, T. H. Crawford, "Annual Report of the Commissioner of Indian Affairs," Nov. 25, 1838, U.S. Serial Set, *Executive Documents,* CCCXLIV, 101, 412; President Martin Van Buren, "Second Annual Message," Dec. 3, 1838, Richardson, III, 497.

129. Jackson, "Second Annual Message," Richardson, II, 520–21.

130. Jackson to Andrew Jackson Donelson, Nov. 21, 1819, AJC, II, 441. Cf. chapter 2, above, pp. 48–49.

CHAPTER EIGHT

1. Douglass C. North, *The Economic Growth of the United States 1790–1860* (Englewood Cliffs, N.J., 1961); Edwin C. Rozwenc, ed., *Ideology and Power in the Age of Jackson* (Garden City, N.Y., 1964), pp. ix–xiv; Stanley M. Elkins, *Slavery* (Chicago, 1959), pp. 27–37; Fred Somkin, *Unquiet Eagle: Memory and Desire in the Idea of American Freedom, 1815–1860* (Ithaca, N.Y., 1967), pp. 6–7.

2. Douglass C. North, "International Capital Flows and the Development of the American West," *Journal of Economic History*, XVI (Dec. 1956), 493–94. Cf. Ellen von Nardhoff, "The American Frontier as a Safety Valve: The Life, Death, Reincarnation, and Justification of a Theory," *Agricultural History*, XXXVI (July 1962), 123–42.

3. North, *Economic Growth*, pp. 51–154, and "International Capital Flows," pp. 493–502.

4. North, *Economic Growth*, pp. 62–75, and "International Capital Flows," pp. 495–97; Edward Pessen, *Jacksonian America* (Homewood, Ill., 1969), pp. 108–09.

5. George R. Taylor, *The Transportation Revolution* (N.Y., 1951); Stuart Bruchey, *The Roots of American Economic Growth 1607–1861* (London, 1965), p. 94.

6. North, *Economic Growth*, pp. v, 156–75; Pessen, pp. 114–21; Bruchey, pp. 86–92; Curtis P. Nettels, *The Emergence of a National Economy 1775–1815* (N.Y., 1962), pp. 281–86; Walter Hugins, *Jacksonian Democracy and the Working Class* (Stanford, Calif., 1960), pp. 51–56.

7. Nettels, pp. 292–304, 340; Pessen, p. 39; James Roger Sharp, *The Jacksonians Versus the Banks* (N.Y., 1970), pp. 25–27.

8. Bruchey, pp. 32–33; Nettels, p. 281; Paul Wallace Gates, *The Farmer's Age: Agriculture 1815–1860* (N.Y., 1960), pp. 293–94; Douglas T. Miller, *Jacksonian Aristocracy* (N.Y., 1967); Pessen, pp. 47–52, 358; Edward Pessen, "The Egalitarian Myth and American Social Reality: Wealth, Mobility, and Equality in the 'Era of the Common Man,'" *American Historical Review*, LXXVI (Oct. 1971), 989–1034; Charles G. Sellers, Jr., "Banking and Politics in Jackson's Tennessee, 1817–1827," *Mississippi Valley Historical Review*, XLI (June 1954), 61–66.

9. Sellers, *loc. cit.*; North, *Economic Growth*, pp. 178–84; Somkin, pp. 17–24.

10. North, *Economic Growth*, pp. 12–14, 178–84, 200–02.

11. Andrew Jackson to George W. Martin, Jan. 2, 1824, AJC, III, 222.

12. Jackson to W. B. Lewis, Dec. 7, 1823, LP; Jackson to Secretary of War John C. Calhoun, Aug. 1823, to L. H. Coleman, April 26, 1824, AJC, III, 202, 249–51; John Spencer Bassett, *The Life of Andrew Jackson*, 2 vols. (N.Y., 1925), I, 344–46. Jackson also supported the tariff to placate commercial-minded backers in Tennessee and the west.

13. Jackson to Coleman, April 26, 1824, AJC, III, 250.

14. Jackson to Andrew Jackson Donelson, Feb. 26, 1824, to John Coffee, Jan. 23, 1825, AJC, III, 232, 274–75; Andrew Jackson, "Fourth Annual Message," Dec. 4, 1832, in James D. Richardson, ed., *Messages and Papers of the Presidents* (N.Y., 1917), II, 600.

15. Jackson to Rachel Jackson, Dec. 3, 1823, in Avery O. Craven, ed., "Letters of Andrew Jackson," *Huntington Library Bulletin*, No. 3 (Feb. 1933), p. 121; Jackson to Coffee, Jan. 23, 1825, AJC, III, 274, Jackson to Coffee, April 10, 1830, C/D. Cf. Robert V. Remini, *The Election of Andrew Jackson* (Philadelphia, 1963), pp. 73–74.

16. Jackson to Donelson, March 21, 1822, AJC, III, 156; Jackson to Coffee, Feb. 17, 1823, C/D; Jackson to Calhoun, Aug. 1823, AJC, III, 203.

17. Jackson to Coffee, Mar. 28, 1824, AJC, III, 242.

18. Jackson to John Overton, Jan. 10, 1825, CC.

19. Bassett, II, 386–88; Remini, p. 46.

20. Remini, p. 117; Thomas G. Watkins to Overton, Dec. 31, 1826, CC.

21. Jackson to Donelson, March 21, 1822, March 6, 1824, to Hugh L. White, Feb. 7, 1827, to Richard K. Call, May 3, 1827, AJC, III, 156, 235, 335, 355.

22. David Brion Davis, *The Slave Power Conspiracy and the Paranoid Style* (Baton Rouge, La., 1969), p. 11. See chapter 1, above.

23. Davis, pp. 24–30.

24. Pessen, *Jacksonian America*, pp. 196–202.

25. Remini, pp. 28–29, 65; Bassett, II, 389–91. Congressman Sam Houston, a Jackson intimate, actually proposed the Secretary-of-State bargain to Clay after the 1824 election. Cf. Marquis James, *The Raven* (N.Y., 1962 [first published 1929]), pp. 48–49.

26. Bassett, II, 386–88.

27. Hugh L. White to Jackson, April 7, 1827, AJC, III, 353.

28. George Dangerfield, *The Era of Good Feelings* (N.Y., 1952); James S. Young, *The Washington Community, 1800–1828* (N.Y., 1966), pp. 41–64, 229–49; John Eaton to Jackson, Dec. 3, 1822, AJC, III, 179.

29. Paul C. Nagel, "The Election of 1824: A Reconsideration Based on Newspaper Opinion," *Journal of Southern History*, XXVI (Aug. 1960), 373; Somkin, pp. 131–74; Jackson to the Marquis de Lafayette, April 17, 1829, AJC, IV, 23.

30. Leonard L. Richards, *"Gentlemen of Property and Standing"* (N.Y., 1970), pp. 57–62, 81. Cf. Lynn L. Marshall, "Opposing Democratic and Whig Concepts of Party Organization," in Edward Pessen, ed., *New Perspectives on Jacksonian Parties and Politics* (Boston, 1969), pp. 38–39, 63.

31. David J. Rothman, *The Discovery of the Asylum* (Boston, 1971), pp. 64–76; Horace Mann, "The Necessity of Education in a Republican Government," in Rozwenc, pp. 144–51; Michael B. Katz, *The Irony of Early School Reform* (Cambridge, Mass., 1968), pp. 40–51, 174–76.

32. Alexis de Tocqueville, *Democracy in America*, 2 vols. (N.Y., 1945), II, 147; Rothman, pp. 110–15. Jarvis is quoted on p. 115.

33. Tocqueville, II, 144–47; Somkin, pp. 3–24; Marvin Meyers, *The Jacksonian Persuasion* (N.Y., 1960).

34. Joseph L. Blau, ed., *Social Theories of Jacksonian Democracy* (N.Y., 1947), p. xviii; Hugins, pp. 132–35, 143–45; Katz, pp. 43, 174–76, 187; Rothman, pp. 94–108, 134–51, 180–91, 221–34.

35. Bruchey, pp. 196–97; Sidney H. Aronson, *Status and Kinship in the Higher Civil Service* (Cambridge, Mass., 1964), pp. vii, 3–19; Marquis James, *Andrew Jackson: Portrait of a President* (Indianapolis, Ind., 1937), p. 214; Marshall, pp. 50–53.

36. Jackson to Coffee, May 30, 1829, AJC, IV, 39; Marshall, pp. 50–51; Aronson, p. 140; Bassett, II, 447; James, *Portrait*, p. 192.

37. Jackson to Coffee, May 30, 1829, to John C. McLemore, April 1829, AJC, IV, 39, 21; James, *Portrait*, p. 182.

38. Marshall, pp. 63–64, 51–53; Jackson to Coffee, May 30, 1829, AJC, IV, 39.

39. Remini, pp. 52–61, 87–98; Marshall, pp. 47–48, 54–59; Aronson, p. 85; Richard P. McCormick, *The Second American Party System* (Chapel Hill, N.C., 1966), and "Political Development and the Second Party System," in William N. Chambers and Walter Dean Burnham, eds., *The American Party Systems* (N.Y., 1967), pp. 90–116.

40. Remini, pp. 62–63, 76–102; Marshall; McCormick, *Second American Party System*.

41. Marshall, pp. 44–45.

42. Aronson, p. 141; McCormick, *Second American Party System*, pp. 177–321, 345–46; Herbert J. Doherty, *Richard Keith Call: Southern Unionist* (Gainesville, Fla., 1961), pp. 70–78; Edwin A. Miles, "The Jacksonian Era," in Arthur S. Link and Rembert W. Patrick, eds., *Writing Southern History* (Baton Rouge, La., 1965), p. 139.

43. McCormick, *Second American Party System*, pp. 13–15, 331–54, and "New Perspectives on Jacksonian Politics," *American Historical Review*, LXV (Jan. 1960), 288–301.

44. Remini, pp. 86, 190; Marshall, pp. 42–43; McCormick, "New Perspectives," pp. 294–97, *Second American Party System*, pp. 92–96, 140–44, 337; Lee Benson, *The*

Concept of Jacksonian Democracy (Princeton, N.J., 1961), pp. 21–32; Donald J. Ratcliffe, "The Role of Voters and Issues in Party Formation: Ohio, 1824," *Journal of American History*, LIX (March 1973), 847–70; Herbert Erschowitz and William G. Shade, "Consensus or Conflict? Political Behavior in the State Legislatures during the Jacksonian Era," *Journal of American History*, LVIII (December 1971), 591–621.

The social basis of the division between Jacksonians and Whigs is still a subject of historical debate. Sectionalism declined as the second party system established itself in the 1830s; it may have been replaced, as I suggest in chapter 9 below, by a class conflict induced by the Bank War. This development affected party divisions from the middle 1830s to the 1850s, but it postdated Jackson's own electoral campaigns. See chapter 9, below, pp. 293–94 and note 48.

45. Remini, p. 192; Frank Otto Gatell, "Money and Party in Jacksonian America: A Quantitative Look at New York City's Men of Quality," *Political Science Quarterly*, LXXXII (June 1967), 235–52; Charles S. Sydnor, *The Development of Southern Sectionalism* (Baton Rouge, La., 1948), pp. 193–97, 205, 340–45; Aronson, pp. 58–68, 167–77. (I follow Aronson's data, not always his interpretations.)

Clay and Adams supporters challenging the congressional caucus in 1824, as well as Jackson men, also claimed to represent the people. Cf. Bassett, I, 325; Thomas P. Abernethy, *The Formative Period in Alabama, 1815–1828* (University, Ala., 1965), p. 153.

46. Hugins, pp. 209–15; McCormick, *Second American Party System*, pp. 349–50; Remini, pp. 87, 92; Jackson to Tilghman A. Howard, Aug. 30, 1833, AJC, V, 166.

47. Cf. Young, p. 249; Remini, pp. 51–120; Benson, pp. 3–85.

48. Jackson to W. B. Lewis, July 15, 1820, July 26, 1820, LP. Cf. chapter 6, pp. 182–83, above, and chapter 9, pp. 282–83, below.

49. Cf. Marshall, pp. 40–42.

50. *Ibid.*, pp. 40–42, 54–60; Robert V. Remini, *Andrew Jackson and the Bank War* (N.Y., 1967), pp. 143–45, 168–69; Edwin A. Miles, "Andrew Jackson and Senator George Poindexter," *Journal of Southern History*, XXIV (Feb. 1958), 63.

51. Sydnor, p. 201; Jackson to Felix Grundy, Oct. 5, 1835, AJC, V, 372. On the republican identification with Brutus, cf. Somkin, p. ix. Thomas Hart Benton insisted, "I did not join in putting down the Bank of the United States to put up a wilderness of local banks. . . . I did not strike Caesar to make Antony master of Rome." Quoted in Sharp, p. 11.

52. Jackson to Rachel Jackson, Nov. [1823], Craven, p. 120; James, *Portrait*, pp. 196–97, 239. Cf. Jackson to Coffee, April 10, 1830, AJC, IV, 135. Jackson once during this period thanked Van Buren for stopping his horse from rearing; but he wondered if his escape from death was worth celebrating. Cf. Martin Van Buren, *Autobiography, American Historical Association Annual Report, 1918, Vol. 2* (Washington, 1920), p. 403.

53. Jackson to Rachel Jackson, Mar. 2, 1824, AJC, III, 233; Doherty, p. 14.

54. James, *Portrait*, pp. 69–71, 202–04.

55. *Ibid.*, pp. 210–18, Bassett, II, 461.

56. James, *Portrait*, pp. 202–23.

57. Jackson to Mary Eastin, Oct. 24, 1830, AJC, IV, 187; James, *Portrait*, p. 213.

58. Jackson to Coffee, May 13, 1831, to Donelson, May 5, 1831, to Coffee, Dec. 28, 1830, AJC, IV, 282, 273, 216. Cf. also Jackson to Donelson, Oct. 10, Nov. 16, 1830, AJC, III, 196, 206. In his draft of his first Annual Message, Jackson wrote, "I am not a father only by adoption to be concerned for the fate of my children. No other wish on this side of the grave remains to me, but that my country may be prosperous, and happy, and that she may have preserved to her, her liberties unimpaired forever." Compare this inappropriate personal reference, removed by Van Buren, with Jackson's successful paternal claims after the resolution of the Eaton affair. Cf. Jackson, "Draft of the First Annual Message," Dec. 8, 1829, AJC, IV, 102, 97n.

59. Jackson to Coffee, May 13, 1831, AJC, IV, 282; James, *Portrait*, pp. 243–44, 270–72.

60. Jackson to Donelson, May 5, March 24, 1831, AJC, IV, 273–78, 251–54.

61. Doherty, pp. 14, 21–25, 33, 46; Jackson to Coffee, April 13, 1827, C/D; Jackson to Call, Mar. 9, 1826, July 5, 1829, AJC, VI, 481–83, IV, 50–51.

62. Jackson to Donelson, May 5, 1831, March 24, 1831, to Coffee, Dec. 28, 1830, Statement of Andrew Jackson Donelson, Oct. 10, 1830, AJC, IV, 273, 252–53, 217, 202.

63. William H. Freehling, *Prelude to Civil War–The Nullification Controversy in South Carolina, 1816–1836* (N.Y., 1966), pp. 189, 220–25; James, *Raven*, p. 53; James, *Portrait of a President*, pp. 237–39, 535; Bassett, II, 553–56; Remini, *Bank War*, p. 68; Jackson to McLemore, June 27, 1831, AJC, IV, 304.

64. James, *Portrait*, pp. 274–78; Bassett, II, 539; Sellers, p. 83, and "Jackson Men with Feet of Clay," *American Historical Review*, LXII (April 1957), 549–50; Marshall, p. 55; Jackson to White, April 29, 1831, June 1, 1831, White to Jackson, June 15, 1831, Jackson to Amos Kendall, July 19, 1835, to President Martin Van Buren, May 12, 1837, Lewis to Jackson, Aug. 30, 1839, AJC, IV, 271, 287, 295–96, V, 356–57, 489, VI, 24; Lewis to Jackson, Sept. 17, 1835, to Allen Hall, July 12, 1837, LP.

65. Jackson to Lewis, April 29, 1833, to Van Buren, July 24, 1833, AJC, V, 66, 143.

66. James, *Portrait*, pp. 285–92; Bassett, II, 705–06; Frank P. Blair to Jackson, April 15, 1837, May 20, 1839, Jackson to Blair, Feb. 8, 1843, AJC, V, 475, VI, 15, 200.

67. B. M. Dusenbery, ed., *Monument to the Memory of General Andrew Jackson Containing Twenty-five Eulogies and Sermons Delivered on Occasion of His Death* (Philadelphia, 1846), p. 104; Arthur Schlesinger, Jr., *The Age of Jackson* (Boston, 1945), p. 39.

68. Jackson to Coffee, May 13, 1831, AJC, IV, 283.

69. Remini, *Election of Andrew Jackson*, pp. 168–79; Freehling, p. 234.

70. Jackson to Van Buren, Jan. 13, 1833, AJC, V, 3.

71. Andrew Jackson, "Proclamation," Dec. 6, 1832, in Richardson, II, 652–53. Edward Livingston, who had drafted Jackson's appeal to the citizens of New Orleans (above, chapter 5, p. 141), drafted the proclamation.

72. Jackson to Joel R. Poinsett, Dec. 2, 1832, "Note," Nov. [1832?], to Van Buren, Dec. 15, 1832, to Andrew J. Crawford, May 1, 1833, to Lewis Cass, Dec. 17, 1832, "Second Inaugural Address," March 1, 1833, AJC, IV, 494, 493, 500, V, 72, IV, 502, V, 27; James Parton, *Life of Andrew Jackson*, 3 vols. (Boston, 1866), III, 370–71.

73. Somkin, p. 191.

74. Jackson to Edward Livingston, AJC, IV, 494; compare "Proclamation," Richardson, II, 652.

75. The best history of the nullification crisis is Freehling, pp. 247–94.

76. Jackson to Joseph Conn Guild, April 24, 1835, to Maunsel White, Dec. 1, 1836, AJC, V, 338–41, 440; Jackson, "Farewell Address," in Richardson, III, 292–308. Cf. above, chapter 2, pp. 73–74, chapter 5, pp. 137–39.

77. Tocqueville, II, 202–08; William R. Taylor and Christopher Lasch, "Two 'Kindred Spirits': Sorority and Family in New England, 1839–1846," *New England Quarterly*, XXXVI (March 1963), 33.

78. Rothman, pp. 105–08, 151–52, 230–35; Katz, pp. 43–51, 187–89.

79. Rothman, pp. 152–54; Katz, pp. 94–96; Charles L. Sanford, *The Quest for Paradise* (Urbana, Ill., 1961), pp. 155–75; Norman Jacobson, "The Concept of Equality in the Assumptions and Propaganda of Massachusetts Conservatives, 1790–1840," unpublished Ph.D. dissertation, University of Wisconsin, 1951, pp. 237–38.

80. Edwin G. Burrows and Michael Wallace, "The American Revolution: The Ideology and Psychology of National Liberation," *Perspectives in American History*, VI (1972), 194–95; Ronald T. Takaki, *A Pro-Slavery Crusade* (N.Y., 1971), p. 122; Jackson to Andrew Jackson, Jr., July 4, 1829, AJC, IV, 49–50; James, *Portrait*, p. 500; Eugene D. Genovese, *The World the Slaveholders Made* (N.Y., 1969), pp. 195–200;

Gerald W. Mullin, *Fight and Rebellion: Slave Resistance in Eighteenth-Century Virginia* (N.Y., 1972), pp. viii, 161.

81. James C. Bonner, "Plantation and Farm: The Agricultural South," in Link and Patrick, p. 152.

82. William Appleman Williams, *The Contours of American History* (Chicago, 1966), pp. 265–70; Benson, pp. 86–109, 237–53; Jackson to Howard, Aug. 20, 1833, AJC, V, 165; William Leggett, "True Functions of Government," in Blau, p. 76; for Jackson's reference to "pure government," see above, chapter 7, p. 230.

83. [John L. O'Sullivan?], "The Democratic Principle," in Rozwenc, pp. 306, 309; Jackson, "Veto Message," July 10, 1832, in Richardson, II, 590.

84. The best interpretations of the *laissez-faire* Jacksonian state are Williams, pp. 227–50; Benson, pp. 86–109, 216–37.

85. McCormick, "Political Development," p. 111, and *Second American Party System*, p. 355; Freehling, pp. 191, 247; Bruckey, pp. 124–34; Louis Hartz, *Economic Policy and Democratic Thought: Pennsylvania, 1776–1860* (Cambridge, Mass., 1948); Jackson to Howard, Aug. 20, 1833, AJC, V, 165.

86. Tocqueville, focusing on Jackson's *laissez-faire* rhetoric, believed he was weakening the Presidency. Cf. I, 430–33, for Tocqueville's views of Jackson's Presidency, and I, 73, 95–98, 198–205, 251–297, II, 10–13, 99–132, 275–76, 311–12, for his discussions of majority tyranny and free institutions.

87. Jackson, "Farewell Address," in Richardson, III, 298, 299, 305, 306; Jackson to Howard, Aug. 20, 1833, V, 165–66.

88. Karl Marx, *The Eighteenth Brumaire of Louis Bonaparte*, in Karl Marx and Friedrich Engels, *Selected Works*, 2 vols. (Moscow, 1955), I, 334–35.

89. Jackson, "Veto Message," in Richardson, II, 590; Jackson to Howard, Aug. 20, 1833, AJC, V, 165–66; Jackson, "Farewell Address," in Richardson, III, 305.

90. Tocqueville, II, 336; Jackson, "Farewell Address," in Richardson, III, 297.

91. "The average American is just like the child in the family," Richard Nixon explained after his reelection. "You give him some responsibility and he is going to amount to something. If, on the other hand, you make him completely dependent and pamper him too much, you are going to make him soft, spoiled, and eventually a very weak individual." Cf. "The Talk of the Town," *New Yorker*, XLVIII (Nov. 25, 1972), 48; Michael Rogin and John Lottier, "The Inner History of Richard Milhous Nixon," *Trans-Action*, IX (Nov.-Dec. 1971), 19–28; Michael Rogin, "Max Weber and Woodrow Wilson: The Iron Cage in Germany and America," *Polity*, III (Summer 1971), 557–75.

CHAPTER NINE

1. Cf. Bray Hammond, *Banking and Politics in America from the Revolution to the Civil War* (Princeton, N.J., 1957), pp. 251–325; George R. Taylor, *The Transportation Revolution* (N.Y., 1951), pp. 301–07.

2. Marquis James, *Andrew Jackson: Portrait of a President* (Indianapolis, Ind., 1937), pp. 363, 267; Robert V. Remini, *Andrew Jackson and the Bank War* (N.Y., 1967), p. 100.

3. Hammond, p. 259; Charles G. Sellers, Jr., "Banking and Politics in Jackson's Tennessee, 1817–1827," *Mississippi Valley Historical Review*, XLI (June 1954), 61, 66–67; Joseph H. Parks, "Felix Grundy and the Depression of 1819 in Tennessee," *East Tennessee Historical Society Publications*, X (1938), 20–21; Samuel Rezn128ck, "The Depression of 1819–1822, A Social History," *American Historical Review*, XXXIX (Oct. 1933), 28–38; Charles S. Sydnor, *The Development of Southern Sectionalism* (Baton Rouge, La., 1948), pp. 104–17.

4. Parks, p. 20; Sellers, p. 69; Rezn128ck, p. 31; Sydnor, pp. 115–16; James Roger Sharp, *The Jacksonians Versus the Banks* (N.Y., 1970), pp. 176–77.

5. Lynn L. Marshall, "The Genesis of Grassroots Democracy in Kentucky," *Mid-America*, XLVII (Oct. 1965), 269–87; Andrew Jackson to Thomas H. Benton [June 1832?], AJC, IV, 445–46; Thomas P. Abernethy, *From Frontier to Plantation in Tennessee* (University, Ala., 1967 [first published 1932]), pp. 227–31, and "Andrew Jackson and the Rise of Southwestern Democracy," *American Historical Review*, XXXIII (Oct. 1927), 67–68; Sellers, pp. 76–82. My interpretation of the Bank War differs somewhat from Sellers', but I have benefited from this article and from our several conversations about Jackson.

6. Cf. Remini, pp. 18–20; chapter 3, above, pp. 94–96.

7. Jackson to Andrew Jackson Donelson, Feb. 24, 1817, AJC, II, 275, 275n; Jackson to Donelson, Feb. 18, 1823, AJD. Vol. 1 of the Andrew Jackson Donelson papers contains many Jackson letters to Donelson, and to Jackson's ward Edward Butler, also at West Point, concerning debts.

8. Jackson to W. B. Lewis, July 15, July 26, 1820, Lewis to Jackson, July 17, 1820, LP; Rezneck, pp. 44–46; Parks, pp. 24–40; Jackson to John Donelson, Sept. 3, 1821, AJC, III, 117.

9. Parks, pp. 23–31; Jackson to A. J. Donelson, July 15, Oct. 11, 1822, AJC, III, 167, 179.

10. Jackson to Lewis, July 15, July 26, 1820, Lewis to Jackson, July 17, 1820, LP; Jackson to A. J. Donelson, Feb. 18, 1823, AJD.

11. Jackson to Secretary of War John C. Calhoun, Aug. 1823, AJC, III, 202–04; Jackson to Lewis, Sept. 21, 1821, collection of the J. P. Morgan Library, photostat in LP; Thomas P. Govan, review of Marvin Meyers, *The Jacksonian Persuasion*, *Journal of Southern History*, XXIV (Feb. 1958), 116; John Spencer Bassett, *The Life of Andrew Jackson*, 2 vols. (N.Y. 1925), II, 430; Jackson to Benton [June 1832?], AJC, IV, 445–46; St. George L. Soissat, "Some Phases of Tennessee Politics in the Jackson Period," *American Historical Review*, XIV (Oct. 1908), 60–67.

12. Jackson to Thomas Cadwalader, Nov. 16, 1828, AJC, III, 445; Lewis to John Overton, June 23, Aug. 14, 1830, CC.

13. Bassett, II, 425–30, 599; Remini, pp. 39–77; Lynn L. Marshall, "Opposing Democratic and Whig Concepts of Party Organization," in Edward Pessen, ed., *New Perspectives on Jacksonian Parties and Politics* (Boston, 1969), p. 55.

14. Hammond, pp. 277–365; Jean Alexander Wilburn, *Biddle's Bank: The Crucial Years* (N.Y., 1967), pp. 31–116; Lee Benson, *The Concept of Jacksonian Democracy* (Princeton, N.J., 1961), pp. 47–65; Walter Hugins, *Jacksonian Democracy and the Working Class* (Stanford, Calif., 1960), pp. 177–96; Frank Otto Gatell, "Sober Second Thoughts on Van Buren, the Albany Regency, and the Wall Street Conspiracy," *Journal of American History*, LIII (June 1966), 19–40.

15. Sharp, pp. 25–26, 93–107, 160–73; Remini, pp. 45–51; Soissat, pp. 62–67; James, pp. 254–56; Bassett, II, 573; Marshall, "Grassroots Democracy," pp. 272–84.

16. Jackson to L. H. Coleman, April 26, 1824, AJC, III, 250; William H. Freehling, *Prelude to Civil War—The Nullification Controversy in South Carolina, 1816–1836* (N.Y., 1966), pp. 190–91, 247.

17. James, p. 369; Jackson to Andrew Jackson, Jr., Feb. 12, Feb. 16, March 9, May 4, Nov. 19, 1834, AJC, V, 247–49, 253–54, 263–64, 310–11. Cf. Jackson to Andrew Jackson Hutchings, April 18, 1833, AJC, V, 69.

18. "Envy and Debt: Two Stories," in Edwin C. Rozwenc, ed., *Ideology and Power in the Age of Jackson* (Garden City, N.Y., 1964), p. 139.

19. Cf. Joel Kovel, *White Racism: A Psychohistory* (N.Y., 1970), pp. 49, 264–68; Norman O. Brown, *Life Against Death* (N.Y., 1959), pp. 234–304; G. William Domhoff, "Historical Materialism, Cultural Determinism, and the Origin of the Ruling Classes," *Psychoanalytic Review*, LVI (1959), 278–85; Erik H. Erikson, *Childhood and Society*, 2nd ed. (Middlesex, Eng., 1963), pp. 75–79.

20. Erikson, pp. 243–46. Cf. Karl Abraham, "Contributions to the Theory of Anal Character," in *Selected Papers* (London, 1927), pp. 370–92.

21. Jackson to Andrew Jackson, Jr., Nov. 16, 1833, AJC, V, 226.

22. Karl Abraham, "A Short Study of the Development of the Libido, Viewed in the Light of Mental Disorders," *Selected Papers*, pp. 425–26; Kovel, pp. 49, 264–68.

23. Rozwenc, p. 139.

24. *Ibid.*, p. 137; Jackson to John Coffee, March 22, 1829, AJC, IV, 14.

25. Marvin Meyers, *The Jacksonian Persuasion* (N.Y., 1960), pp. 27, 28; Andrew Jackson, "Farewell Address," in James D. Richardson, ed., *Messages and Papers of the Presidents* (N.Y., 1917), III, 302.

26. Jackson to James Gadsden, May 2, 1822, AJC, III, 161; Freehling, p. 190.

27. Alexander Hamilton, James Madison, John Jay, *The Federalist Papers* (N.Y., 1961), No. 10, p. 84.

28. Remini, pp. 36–37; Sharp, pp. 17–18; Francis S. Philbrick, *The Rise of the West 1754–1830* (N.Y., 1965), pp. 340–41.

29. Benjamin Franklin, "Preface to Poor Richard Improved: 1758," in *Autobiography and Selected Writings*, Larzer Ziff, ed. (San Francisco, 1969), p. 222; Henry David Thoreau, *Walden*, Sherman Paul, ed. (N.Y., 1957), p. 22.

30. Cf. David Brion Davis, "Some Themes of Countersubversion: An Analysis of Anti-Masonic, Anti-Catholic, and Anti-Mormon Literature," *Mississippi Valley Historical Review*, XLVII (Sept. 1960), 205–24, and "Some Ideological Functions of Prejudice in Ante-Bellum America," *American Quarterly*, XV (Summer 1963), 115–25; Leonard L. Richards, *"Gentlemen of Property and Standing"* (N.Y., 1970), pp. 58–73; Fred Somkin, *Unquiet Eagle: Memory and Desire in the Idea of American Freedom, 1815–1860* (Ithaca, N.Y., 1967), pp. 34–44.

31. Kovel, pp. 49, 232; William Murrell, *A History of American Graphic Humor*, 2 vols. (N.Y., 1933), I, 127–28; Frederick Robinson, "A Program for Labor," in Joseph L. Blau, ed., *Social Theories of Jacksonian Democracy* (N.Y., 1947), p. 338.

32. Sigmund Freud, "Mourning and Melancholia," in James Strachey, ed., *The Standard Edition of the Complete Psychological Works of Sigmund Freud*, XIV (London, 1957), 243–58; Sándor Radó, "The Problem of Melancholia," *International Journal of Psychoanalysis*, IX (Oct. 1928), 435; chapter 2, above, pp. 51–52.

33. Jackson to Hardy M. Cryer, April 7, 1833, to Anthony Wayne Butler, Oct. 1, 1833, AJC, V, 53, 213; Martin Van Buren, *Autobiography, American Historical Association Annual Report, 1918, Vol. 2* (Washington, 1920), p. 625.

34. Jackson to Tilghman A. Howard, Aug. 20, 1833, "Paper Read to the Cabinet," Sept. 18, 1833, to Governor William Findlay, Aug. 20, 1834, AJC, V, 165, 195, 285. Cf. Meyers, pp. 28–30.

35. Remini, pp. 72–77; Wilburn, p. 5; Basset, II, 613–14.

36. Hammond, p. 357; Remini, pp. 91–99; Norman Jacobson, "The Concept of Equality in the Assumptions and Propaganda of Massachusetts Conservatives, 1790–1840," unpublished Ph.D. dissertation, University of Wisconsin, 1951, pp. 290–301; Edwin A. Miles, "Andrew Jackson and Senator George Poindexter," *Journal of Southern History*, XXIV (Feb. 1958), 59–60; Jackson to Vice President Martin Van Buren, Aug. 20, 1833, AJC, V, 168.

37. Hammond, p. 43; Glyndon G. Van Deusen, *The Jacksonian Era 1828–1848* (N.Y., 1959), p. 83; Jackson to Van Buren, Jan. 3, 1834, AJC, V, 238.

38. Meyers, p. 161.

39. Jackson to Cryer, April 7, 1833, AJC, V, 52; Robinson in Blau, p. 333; Sydnor, p. 113.

40. Curtis P. Nettels, *The Emergence of a National Economy 1775–1815* (N.Y., 1962), p. 299; Frank P. Blair to Jackson, Jan. 16, 1838, AJC, V, 529; Remini, p. 127.

41. Bassett, II, 634; Jackson to Andrew Jackson, Jr., Nov. 27, 1834, AJC, V, 313; Hammond, p. 430. As early as 1818, Jackson complained that a Tennessee bank "fed

by government deposits" refused to honor the personal notes he wrote to finance the Florida invasion. Jackson to President James Monroe, Jan. 21, 1818, AJC, II, 349.

42. Hammond, p. 430; Jackson to Andrew Jackson, Jr., Feb. 16, 1834, AJC, V, 248–49.

43. Jackson to Van Buren, Aug. 16, 1834, AJC, V, 282.

44. Remini, p. 25; Charles G. Sellers, Jr., *James K. Polk Continentalist 1843–1846* (Princeton, N.J., 1966), p. 19; Jackson to Van Buren, April 4, 1838, V, 547.

45. Chapter 6, above, pp. 181–83; William N. Chambers, *Old Bullion Benton* (Boston, 1956), p. 111; Hammond, pp. 340–41.

46. Hammond, pp. 335, 360; *Charles River Bridge* v. *Warren Bridge*, 11 Peters (1837), 535–53; Frank Otto Gatell, "The Baltimore Pets: A Study in Banking and Politics," *Business History Review*, XXXIX (Spring 1965), 205–27.

47. Hammond, p. 335; Frank Otto Gatell, "Spoils of the Bank War: Political Bias in the Selection of State Banks," *American Historical Review*, LXX (Oct. 1964), 35–58; Jackson to Andrew Jackson, Jr., April 29, 1835, AJC, V, 342; Remini, pp. 116–17; Bassett, II, 453–54; James, p. 444.

48. This interpretation follows Charles G. Sellers, Jr., "Who Were the Southern Whigs?" *American Historical Review*, LIV (Jan. 1954), 335–46, and Sharp, *passim*. Some evidence from other studies supports the electoral significance of the Bank War; some does not. The most important studies are Benson, pp. 123–207, 288–328; Frank Otto Gatell, "Money and Party in Jacksonian America: A Quantitative Look at New York City's Men of Quality," *Political Science Quarterly*, LXXXII (June 1967), 235–52; Herbert Erschowitz and William G. Shade, "Consensus or Conflict? Political Behavior in the State Legislatures during the Jacksonian Era," *Journal of American History*, LVIII (December 1971), 593–603, 613; Richard P. McCormick *The Second American Party System* (Chapel Hill, N.C., 1966), pp. 131, 191–95, 206, 228, *passim*. (The cited pages contain evidence of the Bank War's impact on party divisions, although McCormick believes that non-issue factors, particularly the replacement of Jackson by the northerner Van Buren, best explain shifts in the party vote.) Benson makes the best-supported case against class-based party divisions (in New York), but Gatell refutes the evidence for the New York City upper class. Cf. also Richard P. McCormick, "Suffrage Classes and Party Alignments: A Study in Voting Behavior," *Mississippi Valley Historical Review*, XLVI (Dec. 1959), 398–402; Wilburn, pp. 20–30; Edwin A. Miles, "The Jacksonian Era," in Arthur S. Link and Rembert W. Patrick, *Writing Southern History* (Baton Rouge, La., 1965), pp. 142–43; Arthur W. Thompson, *Jacksonian Democracy on the Florida Frontier* (Gainesville, Fla., 1961), pp. 2–28; Chambers, p. 187; Thomas B. Alexander et al., "Who Were the Alabama Whigs?" and "The Basis of Alabama's Ante-Bellum Two-Party System," *Alabama Review*, XVI and XIX (Jan. 1963 and July 1966), 5–19, 243–76; Grady McWhiney, "Were the Whigs a Class Party in Alabama?," *Journal of Southern History*, XXIII (Nov. 1957), 510–22.

49. Cf. Sharp, *passim;* Jackson, "Farewell Address," in Richardson, III, 301–06.

50. Max Weber, *The Protestant Ethic and the Spirit of Capitalism* (N.Y., 1958), pp. 181–82; Henry Adams, *The Education of Henry Adams* (N.Y., 1931 [first published 1907]), pp. 426–27, *passim*; Herman Melville, "The Bell-Tower," in *Great Short Works of Herman Melville* (N.Y., 1966), p. 260.

51. Jackson, "Farewell Address," in Richardson, III, 307–08; Sharp, pp. 25–28, 75–87, 126–59, 203, 304–07, 318–29.

CHAPTER TEN

1. Quoted in Henry Nash Smith, *Virgin Land* (N.Y., 1950), p. 40.
2. Andrew Jackson to Aaron V. Brown, Feb. 9, 1843, AJC, VI, 201.

3. George Dangerfield, *The Era of Good Feelings* (N.Y., 1952), pp. 199–245; Charles S. Sydnor, *The Development of Southern Sectionalism* (Baton Rouge, La., 1948), pp. 124–30; Norman Jacobson, "The Concept of Equality in the Assumptions and Propaganda of Massachusetts Conservatives, 1790–1840," unpublished Ph.D. dissertation, University of Wisconsin, 1951, pp. 255–56; Douglass C. North, *The Economic Growth of the United States 1790–1860* (Englewood Cliffs, N.J., 1961), pp. 63, 126.

4. Sydnor, p. 130; Andrew Jackson to W. B. Lewis, Jan. 30, 1819, LP.

5. William H. Freehling, *Prelude to Civil War—The Nullification Controversy in South Carolina, 1816–1836* (N.Y., 1966), pp. 7–48, 203–04, 234, 265–66, 290–92; Richard H. Brown, "The Missouri Crisis, Slavery, and the Politics of Jacksonianism," *South Atlantic Quarterly*, LXV (Winter 1966), 55–72.

6. On the expansionist pressures of the slave economy, cf. Eugene D. Genovese, *The Political Economy of Slavery* (N.Y., 1965).

7. Richard P. McCormick, "New Perspectives on Jacksonian Democracy," *American Historical Review*, LXV (Jan. 1960), 299, and *The Second American Party System* (Chapel Hill, N.C., 1966), pp. 331–35; Freehling, pp. 199, 247–48, 296.

8. Freehling, pp. 111–16, 340–53; Leonard L. Richards, *"Gentlemen of Property and Standing"* (N.Y., 1970), pp. 50–52, 63–64; Jackson to Postmaster General Amos Kendall, Aug. 9, 1835, AJC, V, 360–61.

9. McCormick, "New Perspectives," pp. 299–301, and *Second American Party System*, pp. 13–15, 335–54, *passim;* Charles G. Sellers, Jr., "Who Were the Southern Whigs?" *American Historical Review*, LIV (Jan. 1954), 335–46; Brown, pp. 70–72.

10. Cf. above, chapter 2, pp. 56–57, chapter 6, pp. 168–69, chapter 8, p. 275; Louis Hartz, *The Liberal Tradition in America* (N.Y., 1955), pp. 145–200; Eugene D. Genovese, *The World the Slaveholders Made* (N.Y., 1969), pp. 124–238; Edwin G. Burrows and Michael Wallace, "The American Revolution: The Ideology and Psychology of National Liberation," *Perspectives in American History*, VI (1972), 251–53; Paul Conner, "Patriarchy: Old World and New," *American Quarterly*, XVII (Spring 1965), 48–62; George Fitzhugh, *Sociology for the South* (Richmond, Va., 1854), and *Cannibals All! or Slaves Without Masters* (Cambridge, Mass., 1960 [first published 1857]); John C. Calhoun, *A Disquisition on Government*, C. Gordon Post, ed. (Indianapolis, Ind., 1954); Charles G. Sellers, Jr., "The Travail of Slavery," in Sellers, ed., *The Southerner as American* (Chapel Hill, N. C., 1960), p. 46.

11. David M. Potter, *The South and the Sectional Conflict* (Baton Rouge, La., 1968), pp. 5–30, 69–73; W. J. Cash, *The Mind of the South* (N.Y., 1954), pp. 18–110; C. Vann Woodward, "The Southern Ethic in a Puritan World," *William and Mary Quarterly*, 3rd ser., XXV (July 1968), 343–70; North, p. 130; McCormick, *Second American Party System*, pp. 177–320; George P. Germany, "The South Carolina Governing Elite, 1820–1860," unpublished Ph.D. dissertation, University of California at Berkeley, 1972, pp. 164–79. My view of the south has also been shaped by Eugene Genovese's *Political Economy of Slavery* and *The World the Slaveholders Made*. Genovese rightly treats the south as a planter-dominated slave society. Unlike the other writers cited here, he believes that the south was fundamentally anti-liberal and anti-capitalist. Yet he also provides valuable insight into the impact of liberal Protestant market patterns on slave society.

12. Cf. the works cited in note 11, above, and Stuart Bruchey, *The Roots of American Economic Growth 1607–1861* (London, 1965), p. 169; Thomas P. Abernethy, *The South in the New Nation 1789–1819* (Baton Rouge, La., 1961), p. 442; Glydon G. Van Deusen, *The Jacksonian Era 1828–1848* (N.Y., 1959), p. 39; North, pp. 3–7, 132; James Roger Sharp, *The Jacksonians Versus the Banks* (N.Y., 1970), pp. 260–66; Jean Alexander Wilburn, *Biddle's Bank: The Crucial Years* (N.Y., 1967), pp. 8–19. Wilburn argues that party loyalty to Jackson, not ideological opposition to the Bank, explains southern support for the veto.

13. Brown, pp. 56, 62–63, 69; William R. Taylor, *Cavalier and Yankee* (N.Y., 1961), pp. 242–54, 316.

14. Quoted in Genovese, *World the Slaveholders Made*, p. 11.

15. Cf. note 11, above, and Sydnor, pp. 252–62; Sharp, pp. 36–40; Bruchey, pp. 153–55; North, pp. 3–7, 123–32; Dangerfield, pp. 214–16.

16. Cf. Eric Foner, *Free Soil, Free Labor, Free Men* (N.Y., 1970); David Brion Davis, *The Slave Power Conspiracy and the Paranoid Style* (Baton Rouge, La., 1969).

17. Pierre L. van den Bergh, *Race and Racism: A Comparative Perspective* (N.Y., 1967), p. 88; George M. Fredrickson, *The Black Image in the White Mind* (N.Y., 1971), pp. 58–70; Freehling, pp. 327–34; Germany, pp. 222–55; Potter, pp. 69–73; Taylor, pp. 67, 90–114, 146–70, 292–97, 323, 334–40.

18. Cf. William Appleman Williams, *The Contours of American History* (Chicago, 1966), pp. 276–300.

19. Marquis James, *The Raven* (N.Y., 1962 [first published 1929]), pp. 65–68, 84, 108, 116–22, 147; Jack Gregory and Rennard Strickland, *Sam Houston with the Cherokees, 1829–1833* (Austin, Tex., 1967), p. 5.

20. James, p. 147.

21. *Ibid.*, pp. 147–48; Gregory and Strickland, p. 137; Grant Foreman, *Pioneer Days in the Old Southwest* (Cleveland, O., 1926), p. 204.

22. Richard Drinnon, *White Savage: The Case of John Dunn Hunter* (N.Y., 1972), pp. 201–29; James, pp. 125–30; Gregory and Strickland, pp. 33, 55–58, 110–16. "My God, is the man *mad*," Jackson wrote when he heard of "poor Houstons disgrace." Jackson to John C. McLemore, April, 1829, AJC, IV, 21.

23. James, pp. 111–14; Gregory and Strickland, p. 129; Foreman, pp. 184–89, 199–204.

24. James, pp. 136–40.

25. Jackson to Anthony Wayne Butler, April 19, 1832, AJC, IV, 436; Foreman, pp. 199–204; James, pp. 149–60; Gregory and Strickland, pp. 132–34; Richard R. Stenberg, "The Texas Schemes of Jackson and Houston, 1829–1836," *Southwestern Social Science Quarterly*, XV (Dec. 1934), 240.

26. James, pp. 151–52, 160. Houston never betrayed his Indian allies, however. He tried to obtain Texas lands for the tribes, and futilely opposed the exterminatory wars of other Texas leaders. Cf. James, pp. 254–55; Gregory and Strickland, pp. 152–53.

27. James, pp. 149–51; Stenberg, pp. 232–37; Jackson to William S. Fulton, Dec. 10, 1830, AJC, IV, 212–14.

28. Richard Stenberg, "Jackson, Anthony Butler, and Texas," *Southwestern Social Science Quarterly*, XIII (Dec. 1832), 264; Marquis James, *Andrew Jackson: Portrait of a President* (Indianapolis, Ind., 1937), pp. 406–07.

29. Jackson to Butler, Oct. 10, 1829, Mar. 23, 1830, Feb. 15, 1831, Feb. 25, March 6, 1832, AJC, IV, 79–81, 129–30, 243–45, 409–10, 414–15.

30. Stenberg, "Jackson, Anthony Butler, and Texas," 267–69, 274–75; John Spencer Bassett, *The Life of Andrew Jackson*, 2 vols. (N.Y., 1925), II, 675–76; Jackson to Butler, Oct. 10, 1829, Sept. 4, 1832, Oct. 30, Nov. 27, 1833, Butler to Jackson, July 18, 1832, AJC, IV, 79–81, 472, V, 221–22, 228–29, IV, 463–64.

31. Jackson to Butler, Oct. 10, 1829, Nov. 27, 1833, March 16, 1841, AJC, IV, 79–81, V, 228–29, VI, 94.

32. Richard Stenberg, "Jackson's Neches Claim, 1829–1836," *Southwestern Historical Quarterly*, XXXIX (April 1936), 255–60; Frederick Merk, *The Monroe Doctrine and American Expansionism 1843–1849* (N.Y., 1967), pp. 137–39; Jackson to Butler, March 23, Oct. 7, 1830, Feb. 25, 1832, Nov. 27, 1833, AJC, IV, 129–30, 183–84, 409–10, V, 228–29.

33. Stenberg, "Neches Claim," pp. 260–62; Butler to Jackson, Jan. 2, 1832, Jackson to Butler, Feb. 25, 1832, Nov. 27, 1833, AJC, IV, 390, 409, V, 228–29.

34. Secretary of War Lewis Cass to General Edmund P. Gaines, April 25, 1836, ASPMA, VI, 1044–45; Stenberg, "Texas Schemes," pp. 246–47, and "Neches Claim," pp. 264–70.

35. James W. Silver, *Edmund Pendleton Gaines: Frontier General* (Baton Rouge, La., 1949), pp. 192–97, 210, 213; Bassett, II, 679.

36. James, *Raven*, pp. 170–75, 185–92, 202–09; Silver, p. 215; Stenberg, "Neches Claim," pp. 264–67, and "Texas Schemes," p. 248.

37. James, *Raven*, p. 216; Silver, pp. 204–11. Bassett, in AJC, V, 415n, says Gaines entered Texas in June.

38. "Appeal by Stephen F. Austin," April 15, 1836, Jackson to Governor Newton Cannon, Aug. 3, Aug. 6, 1836, to Kendall, Aug. 12, 1836, AJC, V, 397–98, 415–18, 420–21; Stenberg, "Neches Claim," pp. 271–73; Cass to Gaines, July 11, 1836, ASPMA, VI, 1045; Bassett, II, 679.

39. Jackson to Francis P. Blair, Aug. 12, 1836, to Gaines, Sept. 4, 1836, to Houston, Sept. 4, 1836, AJC, V, 418–19, 423–25; Stenberg, "Neches Claim," p. 274; Silver, p. 212.

40. James, *Raven*, pp. 218, 227–28, and *Portrait*, pp. 412–13; Bassett, II, 678–82; Andrew Jackson, "Farewell Address," in James D. Richardson, ed., *Messages and Papers of the Presidents* (N.Y., 1917), III, 295–97; Frederick Merk, *Manifest Destiny and Mission in American History* (N.Y., 1966), p. 52, and *Monroe Doctrine*, pp. 9, 107. On the importance of commercial goals in Pacific expansion, cf. Norman A. Graebner, *Empire on the Pacific* (N.Y., 1955).

41. James, *Raven*, pp. 261–62; Merk, *Monroe Doctrine*, p. 107.

42. Merk, *Monroe Doctrine*, pp. 9–29.

43. Charles G. Sellers, Jr., *James K. Polk Continentalist, 1843–1846* (Princeton, N.J., 1966), pp. 50–51; Merk, *Monroe Doctrine*, p. 29; Jackson to Aaron V. Brown, Feb. 12, 1843, to Blair, May 11, 1844, AJC, VI, 201–02, 286.

44. Jackson to Brown, Feb. 12, 1843, AJC, VI, 201; John William Ward, *Andrew Jackson—Symbol for an Age* (N.Y., 1955), pp. 135–37, 251n; Julius W. Pratt, "John L. O'Sullivan and Manifest Destiny," *New York History*, XIV (July 1933), 221–32. Jackson's letter was rewritten before publication in the *Washington Globe*. His own words were "extending the area for freedom."

45. Merk, *Manifest Destiny*, pp. 24–60; Sellers, *Polk*, p. 214; Pratt, pp. 221–27; Ward, pp. 144–49; Albert K. Weinberg, *Manifest Destiny* (Chicago, 1963 [first published 1935]), pp. 100–58.

46. Jackson to Kendall, Jan. 15, 1845, to Lewis, May 11, 1844, AJC, VI, 364, 288. Cf. Jackson to the Editors of the Nashville *Union*, May 13, 1844, to Benton, May 14, 1844, AJC, VI, 289–93.

47. Sellers, *Polk*, pp. 235–36; Jackson to Lewis, July 12, 1844, LP.

48. Weinberg, pp. 100–58; Merk, *Monroe Doctrine*, pp. 133–38; Dangerfield, pp. 141–53; Richard Stenberg, "Andrew Jackson and the Erving Affidavit," *Southwestern Historical Quarterly*, XLI (Oct. 1937), 142–53; Bassett, I, 271–73; James Parton, *Life of Andrew Jackson*, 3 vols. (Boston, 1866), III, 657; Jackson to President James Monroe, June 20, 1820, to Brown, Feb. 12, 1843, to Lewis, Aug. 1, 1844, to Kendall, Jan. 15, 1845, AJC, III, 28, VI, 201, 306–08, 364. Early in his efforts to acquire Texas, on Aug. 12, 1829, Jackson wrote Van Buren, "The god of the universe had intended this great valley to belong to one nation." Cf. AJC, IV, 57.

49. Merk, *Monroe Doctrine*, p. 138, and *Manifest Destiny*, pp. 53–55; Jackson to Blair, July 26, 1844, AJC, VI, 304.

50. President John Tyler to Jackson, Sept. 17, 1844, Jackson to Andrew Jackson Donelson, Dec. 2, 1844, AJC, VI, 319–20, 334–36; Sellers, *Polk*, pp. 227–28.

51. Sellers, *Polk*, pp. 71–73, 140; Jackson to Blair, May 11, 1844, to Lewis, May 11, 1844, to the Editors of the Nashville *Union*, May 3, 1844, to Benton, May 14, 1844, to

Blair, May 18, 1844, June 7, 1844, AJC, VI, 285–94, 297, Jackson to Lewis, June 18, 1844, LP.

52. Sellers, *Polk*, pp. 232–34; Merk, *Monroe Doctrine*, pp. 106, 133–60; Stenberg, "Neches Claim," pp. 266–67.

53. Sellers, *Polk*, pp. 222–26; Merk, *Monroe Doctrine*, pp. 139–60.

54. Pratt, p. 235. Cf. Weinberg, pp. 89–91; Taylor, p. 216.

55. James, *Portrait*, pp. 490–500; Houston to President James K. Polk, June 8, 1845, AJC, VI, 414n–415n.

56. Jackson to Polk, June 6, 1845, Andrew Jackson, Jr., to A. O. P. Nicholson, July 12, 1845, AJC, VI, 413–14, 413n–414n.

57. B. M. Dusenbery, ed., *Monument to the Memory of General Andrew Jackson Containing Twenty-five Eulogies and Sermons Delivered on Occasion of His Death* (Philadelphia, 1846); Merk, *Monroe Doctrine*, p. 134.

58. Van Deusen, pp. 199–207; Bruchey, p. 156; North, pp. 204–06; George R. Taylor, *The Transportation Revolution* (N.Y., 1951), pp. 153–75.

59. Smith, pp. 28–44; James C. Malin, "Indian Policy and Westward Expansion," *Humanistic Studies*, II (Nov. 1921), 11–81; Virgil J. Vogel, ed., *This Country Was Ours: A Documentary History of the American Indian* (N.Y., 1972), pp. 142–44; Brown, pp. 70–72; William N. Chambers, *Old Bullion Benton* (Boston, 1956), pp. 420–33; Herbert J. Doherty, *Richard Keith Call: Southern Unionist* (Gainesville, Fla., 1961), pp. 147–61; James, *Raven*, pp. 304–28.

60. Herman Melville, "Bartleby," in *Billy Budd, Sailor and Other Stories* (Baltimore, Md., 1967), pp. 66, 67, 69, 72, 86, 59, 60, 90, 91.

61. Herman Melville, "Billy Budd, Sailor," in *ibid.*, pp. 392, 400, 341; Abraham Lincoln, "Speech at Peoria, Illinois," Oct. 16, 1854, "The Gettysburg Address," Nov. 19, 1863, in T. Harry Williams, ed., *Selected Speeches, Messages, and Letters* (N.Y., 1957), pp. 56, 246–47; Norman Jacobson, "Lincoln's Abraham," *The Helderberg Review*, I (Spring 1971), 15–17; George Frederickson, *The Inner Civil War* (N.Y., 1965).

62. Leslie A. Fiedler, *Love and Death in the American Novel* (N.Y., 1960), pp. 147–48.

63. Frederick Jackson Turner, *The Frontier in American History* (N.Y., 1962 [first published in book form 1920]), pp. 219, 38.

64. For an elaboration of this argument, with documentation and citation of further sources, see *ibid.*, pp. 205, 219; William Appleman Williams, "The Frontier Thesis and American Foreign Policy," *Pacific Historical Review*, XXIV (Nov. 1955), 379–95, and *The Contours of American History* (Chicago, 1966); Walter La Feber, *The New Empire* (Ithaca, N.Y., 1963); Michael Rogin, "Max Weber and Woodrow Wilson: The Iron Cage in Germany and America," *Polity*, III (Summer 1971), 557–75, and "Truth Is Stranger than Science Fiction," *The Listener and B.B.C. Television Review*, July 25, 1968, pp. 117–18; Jeffrey A. Messinger, "Theodore Roosevelt and the Philippines: Imperialism as a 'Field of Action,'" unpublished seminar paper, University of California at Berkeley, 1974.

INDEX

A NOTE ABOUT
THE AUTHOR

Michael Paul Rogin is associate professor of political science at the University of California, Berkeley. He was born in Mt. Kisco, New York, in 1937 and received his B.A. from Harvard, and his M.A. and Ph.D. from the University of Chicago. He was a visiting lecturer in Uganda and England and has taught at Berkeley since 1963. Mr. Rogin was awarded a Guggenheim Fellowship for 1972–73 and is the author of *The Intellectuals and McCarthy: The Radical Specter* (1967), which won the Albert J. Beveridge Award from the American Historical Association. He has contributed articles and reviews to many publications, including *The New York Times Book Review, The Progressive, The Listener,* and the *Journal of American History.* He lives in Berkeley with his wife and two children.

A NOTE ON
THE TYPE

This book was set on the Linotype in Janson, a recutting made direct from type cast from matrices long thought to have been made by the Dutchman Anton Janson, who was a practicing type founder in Leipzig during the years 1668–87. However, it has been conclusively demonstrated that these types are actually the work of Nicholas Kis (1650–1702), a Hungarian, who most probably learned his trade from the master Dutch type founder Dirk Voskens. The type is an excellent example of the influential and sturdy Dutch types that prevailed in England up to the time William Caslon developed his own incomparable designs from them.

This book was composed by American Book–Stratford Press, Inc., New York, New York, and printed and bound by The Book Press, Brattleboro, Vermont. The typography and binding design are by Cynthia Krupat.

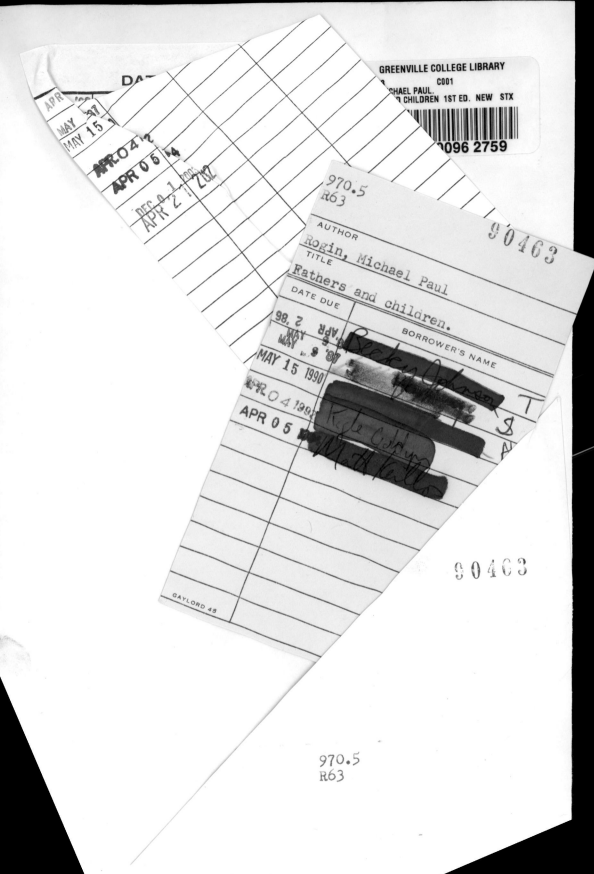